The 50th Annual
Brigham Young University
Sidney B. Sperry Symposium

Covenant of Compassion

Caring for the Marginalized and Disadvantaged in the Old Testament

Edited by Avram R. Shannon, Gaye Strathearn,
George A. Pierce, and Joshua M. Sears

Published by the Religious Studies Center, Brigham Young University, Provo, Utah, in cooperation with Deseret Book Company, Salt Lake City, Utah.

© 2021 by Brigham Young University. All rights reserved.

Printed in the United States of America by Sheridan Books, Inc.

DESERET BOOK is a registered trademark of Deseret Book Company.

Visit us at DeseretBook.com.

Any uses of this material beyond those allowed by the exemptions in US copyright law, such as section 107, "Fair Use," and section 108, "Library Copying," require the written permission of the publisher, Religious Studies Center, 185 HGB, Brigham Young University, Provo, UT 84602. The views expressed herein are the responsibility of the authors and do not necessarily represent the position of The Church of Jesus Christ of Latter-day Saints, Brigham Young University or the Religious Studies Center.

Cover and interior design by Emily V. Rogers

Cover image courtesy of ChurchofJesusChrist.org and Wikimedia Commons

ISBN 978-1-9503-0414-1

Library of Congress Cataloging-in-Publication Data

Names: Shannon, Avram R., editor. | Strathearn, Gaye, editor. | Pierce, George A., editor. | Sears, Joshua M., editor.
Title: Covenant of compassion : caring for the marginalized and disadvantaged in the Old Testament / edited by Avram R. Shannon, Gaye Strathearn, George A. Pierce, Joshua M. Sears.
Description: Provo, Utah : Religious Studies Center, Brigham Young University : Salt Lake City, Utah : Deseret Book, [2021] | Includes index. | Summary: "This book presents a series of essays discussing Latter-day Saint readings on the teachings of the Old Testament about taking care of those who are marginalized or otherwise disadvantaged"-- Provided by publisher.
Identifiers: LCCN 2021016999 | ISBN 9781950304141 (hardback)
Subjects: LCSH: Bible. Old Testament--Criticism, interpretation, etc. | Compassion--Biblical teaching. | Compassion--Religious aspects--Judaism.
Classification: LCC BS1199.C585 C68 2021 | DDC 221.6/6--dc23
LC record available at https://lccn.loc.gov/2021016999

Contents

Introduction — vii

KEYNOTE ADDRESSES

1. Sidney B. Sperry: Seeking to Know the Word — 1
   V. Wallace McCarlie Jr. and Andrew C. Skinner

2. "A Kingdom of Priests, and an Holy Nation": The Work of Covenant Women and Men Making Societal Zion — 29
   Sharon Eubank

COVENANT OF CONCERN

3. The Cry of the Widow, the Fatherless, and the Stranger: The Covenant Obligation to Help the Poor and Oppressed — 47
   David Rolph Seely and Jo Ann H. Seely

4. Covenantal Command: Love Thy Neighbor — 73
   Kerry Muhlestein

5. "Behold These Thy Brethren!": Deeply Seeing All of Our Brothers and Sisters — 101
   Joshua M. Sears

WOMEN

6. Recognizing Responsibility and Standing with Victims: 127
   Studying Women of the Old Testament
   Amy Easton-Flake

7. Models of Motherhood: Expansive Mothering 157
   in the Old Testament
   Avram R. Shannon and Thora Florence Shannon

8. Naomi, Ruth, and Boaz: Borders, Relationships, 183
   Law, and *Ḥesed*
   Gaye Strathearn and Angela Cothran

THE POOR

9. The Poor and the Needy in the Book of Isaiah 213
   Dana M. Pike

10. "The Lord Hath Founded Zion, and the Poor 237
    of His People Shall Trust in It": Covenant
    Economics, Atonement, and the Meaning of Zion
    Matthew L. Bowen

11. Remembering Redemption, Avoiding Idolatry: 265
    A Covenant Perspective on Caring for the Poor
    Jennifer C. Lane

REFUGEES

12. Their Story Is Our Story Because We Were Strangers: 293
    The Relevance of Exodus 22:21 and Leviticus 19:33–34
    in Refugee Awareness Work
    Elizabeta Jevtic-Somlai and Robin Peterson

13. The Experience of Israelite Refugees: Lessons Gleaned   323
    from the Archaeology of Eighth-Century-BC Judah
    George A. Pierce

14. The *Gēr* in the Pentateuch and the Book of Mormon: 353
    Refugee Treatment under the Mosaic Law
    Krystal V. L. Pierce

PERSONS WITH DISABILITIES

15. Disability and Social Justice in Ancient Israelite Culture   383
    David M. Calabro

16. "Open Thou Mine Eyes": Blindness and   407
    the Blind in the Old Testament
    Richard O. Cowan

PROPHETIC CRITIQUES

17. Covenants, Kinship, and Caring for   427
    the Destitute in the Book of Amos
    Joshua M. Matson

18. Justice and Righteousness: Jeremiah against   449
    King and People
    David A. LeFevre

19. "Go Ye and Learn What That Meaneth": Mercy and   469
    Law in the Old Testament's Prophetic Literature and
    in the Gospels
    Daniel O. McClellan

Index   501

Introduction

This volume marks the fiftieth anniversary of the annual Sidney B. Sperry Symposium at Brigham Young University. For half a century, Latter-day Saints have been blessed by scholars and other religious educators who have shared insightful messages from the beloved scriptures of The Church of Jesus Christ of Latter-day Saints. Their inspiring research on the texts and teachings of the Old Testament, New Testament, Book of Mormon, Doctrine and Covenants, and Pearl of Great Price have helped fulfill the Lord's injunction to "seek ye diligently and teach one another words of wisdom; yea, seek ye out of the best books words of wisdom; seek learning, even by study and also by faith" (Doctrine and Covenants 88:118).

In this year's symposium, we focus on the oldest and largest of our standard works, the Old Testament. This year's theme, caring for marginalized and disadvantaged people in the Old Testament, was prompted by repeated calls from living prophets and other Church leaders that members of the Church should "lead out"[1] in confronting modern social challenges such as poverty,[2] racism,[3] sexism,[4] nationalism,[5] religious discrimination,[6] and the world's growing refugee crisis.[7] As Elder Dale G. Renlund taught, "How we deal with advantages and disadvantages is part of life's test. We will be judged not so much by what we say but by how we treat the vulnerable and disadvantaged."[8]

In the October 2019 general conference, President Russell M. Nelson highlighted some of these humanitarian concerns, declaring, "As members of the Church, we feel a kinship to those who suffer in any way. As sons and daughters of God, we are all brothers and sisters. We heed an Old Testament admonition: 'Thou shalt open thine hand wide unto thy brother, to thy poor, and to thy needy' [Deuteronomy 15:11]."[9] It is no coincidence that President Nelson quotes from the Old Testament in his discussion, since it contains numerous passages dictating how the ancient Israelites were to treat those among and around them. Although the Old Testament is a collection of ancient texts, and while some of its social and cultural assumptions are out-of-date, the book remains strikingly relevant in many ways. Its stories, laws, and admonitions had important things to say about how covenant people should interact with others, and many of the challenges the Israelites faced are still with us today. Like President Nelson, we believe the Old Testament still has valuable teachings for us in our day.

We recognize that discussions of economic class, social responsibility, refugee assistance, gender equality, and social justice can be sensitive and that many of these issues, including even the vocabulary used to describe them, have become politically charged. This volume is not intended as policy advocacy nor is it interested in partisan politics. Rather, our sincere hope is that by better understanding what the word of the Lord has to say about these issues, readers can then continue, in whatever ways they feel are best, to do the hard work of figuring out how to translate scriptural principles to modern, real-world application. Elder Gerrit W. Gong reminds us that it is part of God's work that we "create lasting justice, equality, fairness, and peace in our homes and communities."[10] We hope that all people can find common ground in these sacred goals, even if they share honest disagreements about the best ways to reach them.

Because this book covers a wide range of topics, we have arranged the chapters thematically. In honor of the fiftieth anniversary of the Sperry Symposium, we begin with a brief historical discussion of the life and contributions of Dr. Sidney B. Sperry. The organization of the remaining papers takes broad inspiration from the Lord's words to Zechariah: "Execute true judgment, and shew mercy and compassions every man to his brother: and oppress not the widow, nor the fatherless, the stranger, nor the poor" (Zechariah 7:9–10). These categories of disadvantaged groups are frequently discussed in Old Testament law, such as in the pairing of "the poor and stranger" (Leviticus 19:10; compare 23:22) or the common triad "the stranger, the fatherless, and the widow" (Deuteronomy 26:12; compare Exodus 22:21–23; Deuteronomy 10:18; 14:29; 16:11; 24:17–21; 27:19). Following an introductory section that presents the doctrines and principles of this topic broadly, we arrange sections with articles discussing Old Testament teachings about women, people who are economically poor and needy, refugees and displaced persons, and individuals with physical disabilities. The book finishes with chapters discussing the teachings of Old Testament prophets as they critiqued the ancient Israelites' performance regarding their responsibility to care for one another.

The authors in this book explore the teachings of the Old Testament from a variety of perspectives. They employ a variety of scholarly tools, and some focus on a specific biblical book while others examine a topic across several Old Testament texts. We would like to thank each of the authors for their hard work and the expertise they bring to their contribution. We also express appreciation for the many people who worked behind the scenes to make this volume possible, including those who reviewed articles. We would like to thank the staff of Religious Education, especially Beverly Yellowhorse and her assistants. Her institutional memory and tireless efforts made the production of this volume infinitely easier. Finally we would like to thank the staff from the Religious Studies Center at Brigham Young University—Scott Esplin for his support as publications director; Shirley Ricks and Devan Jensen for their editorial supervision; Don Brugger, Meghan Rollins Wilson, and Cara Nickels for their editorial help; Brent Nordgren for his assistance with publication details; and Emily V. Rogers for the cover and interior design.

We hope that this volume will help you gain a greater appreciation for the Lord's call (which he has made through prophets both ancient and modern) that we be a people of "one heart and one mind," who "dwel[l] in righteousness" with "no poor" among us (Moses 7:18).

Avram R. Shannon
Gaye Strathearn
George A. Pierce
Joshua M. Sears
Beverly Yellowhorse
R. Devan Jensen
2021 Sperry Symposium Committee

Notes

1. Russell M. Nelson, "Let God Prevail," *Ensign*, November 2020, 94.
2. See Jeffrey R. Holland, "Are We Not All Beggars?," *Ensign*, November 2014, 40–42; Sharon Eubank, "And the Lord Called His People Zion," *Ensign*, March 2020, 26–29. In 2009 the Church announced that its threefold mission would be augmented with a fourth: caring for the poor and needy. See Scott Taylor, "LDS to Boost Emphasis on Helping the Needy; Salt Lake Temple Not Closing," *Deseret News*, December 11, 2009, www.deseret.com. The current Church Handbook instructs on the core work

of the Church: "Living the gospel of Jesus Christ, caring for those in need[,] inviting all to receive the gospel[,] and uniting families for eternity" (*General Handbook: Serving in The Church of Jesus Christ of Latter-day Saints*, 0.1, ChurchofJesusChrist.org).

3. See Gordon B. Hinckley, "The Need for Greater Kindness," *Ensign*, May 2006, 58; Nelson, "Let God Prevail," 94; Dallin H. Oaks, "Love Your Enemies," *Ensign*, November 2020, 28–29; Dallin H. Oaks, "Racism and Other Challenges" (Brigham Young University devotional, October 27, 2020), www.speeches.byu.edu.

4. See M. Russell Ballard, "The Trek Continues!," *Ensign*, November 2017, 106; Neil L. Andersen, "The Voice of the Lord," *Ensign*, November 2017, 124; Jean B. Bingham, "United in Accomplishing God's Work," *Ensign*, May 2020, 60–63.

5. See Ballard, "The Trek Continues!," 106; Andersen, "Voice of the Lord," 124; M. Russell Ballard, "Children of Heavenly Father" (Brigham Young University devotional, March 3, 2020), www.speeches.byu.edu.

6. See M. Russell Ballard, "Doctrine of Inclusion," *Ensign*, November 2001, 35–38; Ronald A. Rasband, "Faith, Fairness, and Religious Freedom," *Ensign*, September 2016, 26–33; Dale G. Renlund, "Our Good Shepherd," *Ensign*, May 2017, 31–32.

7. See Linda K. Burton, "'I Was a Stranger,'" *Ensign*, May 2016, 13–15; Patrick Kearon, "Refuge from the Storm," *Ensign*, May 2016, 111–14; "Losing Everything Twice: President Uchtdorf's Refugee Experience," Church News, May 5, 2016, www.churchofjesuschrist.org.

8. Dale G. Renlund, "Infuriating Unfairness," *Liahona*, May 2021, 43.

9. Russell M. Nelson, "The Second Great Commandment," *Ensign*, November 2019, 98.

10. Gerrit W. Gong, "All Nations, Kindreds, and Tongues," *Ensign*, November 2020, 40.

Keynote Addresses

1

Sidney B. Sperry
Seeking to Know the Word

V. Wallace McCarlie Jr. and Andrew C. Skinner

Marking the fiftieth anniversary of the annual Sidney B. Sperry Symposium, this essay describes in part the man for whom the symposium is named and whom it honors. His life story, which has remained relatively unknown, provides many lessons applicable to Latter-day Saint religious scholars today. Herein we trace some of what he did to become the first person in The Church of Jesus Christ of Latter-day Saints to receive a PhD in the field of ancient languages and civilizations of the Near East.

The adolescent Sidney B. Sperry, in a sacred moment with his grandfather, an ordained patriarch, was promised in the name of the Lord that he would "have the privilege of going forth into the world to lift up [his] voice in defense of Zion."[1] That day, young Sidney learned he had "pled with the Father" in the premortal realm to "take an active part in the great work of God in the Latter-days."[2] Patriarch

Sidney B. Sperry, courtesy of the Religious Studies Center.

Sperry also promised him that he would have the privilege of teaching the word of God to many, many people.

Before World War I, with a degree in chemistry, Sidney had dreamed of pursuing a PhD in chemistry in Berlin. After serving in the war, however, his feelings understandably changed. Upon his return, he was called as a missionary to the Southern States Mission (1919–21), where he was chosen to serve as the equivalent of district president; he served in this calling for most of his mission. Early in his mission experience, Sidney had not necessarily chosen his life's path, but he had nevertheless entered upon it. He would become an active teacher of God's word for the remainder of his life—the next six decades. He would teach in seminaries and institutes for nine years and at Brigham Young University for the next five decades. Sidney had aspired early on, probably before his mission, "to know more about the scriptures than any man living."[3]

Adam S. Bennion, superintendent of Church schools, played a key role in recruiting Sidney. Bennion "sought to employ only the very best teachers and . . . required that all instructors be morally clean, obey the Word of Wisdom, and live their religion. He particularly sought out teachers 'whose spiritual glow' would 'enkindle religious enthusiasm on the part of those instructed.'"[4] In inviting Brother Sperry to consider teaching in the Church school system, Brother Bennion did not need to twist Sidney's arm. A desire to teach God's word had grown within him. It is clear that Sidney wanted to pursue a doctorate, but he now had family responsibilities since he had married Eva L. Braithwaite on September 1, 1921. A position in the Church school system offered him a chance to formally begin his life's work as a gospel teacher. Sperry responded to the need for faithful teachers in the system. Bennion's offer apparently came in 1921, and Sperry began teaching in 1922.

One thing Brother Sperry observed upon entering the seminary system is that its three-year theology curriculum lacked a specific course on the Book of Mormon.[5] He joined in expressing the need for greater focus on the Book of Mormon, gospel scholarship, and the nurturing of faith. As principal of American Fork Seminary, he, along with his colleague at Pleasant Grove Seminary, articulated this desire in a letter to the president of Brigham Young University (BYU): "There is a great opportunity and need at the present time to vitalize and illustrate the teachings of the restored gospel."[6] The letter continued, "Many valuable faith promoting incidents and manifestations have failed to be recorded where they are available," appealing to President Franklin S. Harris's "desire to promote the faith of the youth of Zion."[7] Brother Sperry went on to say that with the approval of the Church Commissioner of Education, John A. Widtsoe, the seminary teachers were asking for written accounts of the most faith-promoting incidents in Latter-day Saints' lives in every stake and mission throughout the Church. The goal was to publish these accounts and integrate them into the curriculum.

In a 1924 Church school system conference that Sperry attended, Bennion acknowledged what Sperry had observed—teachers were generally "slighting" the Book of Mormon. The conference produced a clearer vision of what Sperry thought should happen: "I am particularly anxious that . . . we shall cultivate genuine appreciation of and a love for the Book of Mormon on the part of our young men and women," and that "no book should be better known by our students . . . than the Book of Mormon."[8] The leaders now wished the Book of Mormon to serve a more prominent role in building the faith of the rising generation. Sperry had applied these principles in his own classes and was glad to see these policies move forward.

Since the First Vision, none of those who had accepted the Prophet Joseph Smith's message had earned a PhD in the field of ancient Near Eastern studies. Before entering American Fork Seminary's doors as principal in the fall of 1922, Sperry had already begun his graduate coursework in history, political science, education, and psychology in pursuit of his advanced degree, having matriculated as a graduate student at BYU that summer. He may have received guidance that this graduate work would serve as a springboard for him. The tuition was also relatively inexpensive in comparison to more robust academic institutions. He continued with this plan during the summers of 1923 and 1924, taking further courses in history, physics, the philosophy of education, and education administration. Later, however, because of the caliber of scholarship at more established universities, he lamented his decision: "I'm almost sorry I ever went to the B.Y.U."[9] Still, by 1924, Sperry knew a little more French, thanks to his work in Provo.

Sperry was well-liked among his colleagues and regarded as one who spoke having authority. On April 23, 1923, Elder James E. Talmage ordained him a high priest, and he was called to the high council in the American Fork Stake. Elder Talmage confided in Brother Sperry that a number of the General Authorities thought the Church should have among its ranks a scriptural scholar, a theologian who could stand up to the world in defense of Zion. Elder Talmage and others trusted Sperry and thought he possessed the ability to succeed. After his summer graduate courses in 1924, Sperry was asked to establish the seminary program at Weber College, in Ogden, Utah, that fall. He would miss his associates at the American Fork Seminary and his association with the stake presidency in his ecclesiastical calling, but he would now serve as Weber's principal. The academic year of 1924–25 was a crucial time in Sperry's life, as he decided BYU would not help him in his goal of becoming a PhD-holding scriptural scholar among the Saints. His decision would significantly affect the Church school system, BYU, and the Church. It would take faith and sacrifice as Sperry left Utah and his family. As his time at Weber came to a close, the leaders and students expressed gratitude for the teacher he had been and for the truths he had taught.[10]

From the main areas settled by Latter-day Saints, especially in Utah, those Saints pursuing doctoral degrees specializing in fields *other than* Near Eastern scriptural studies tended to go either westward to the University of California at Berkeley or eastward to the University of Chicago.[11] Besides Chicago in the Midwest, graduate students tended to go to Cornell in the East, with a few attending Harvard, Columbia, or the University of Wisconsin at Madison. The most popular institutions for graduate study other than Berkeley in the West included the University of California at Riverside and, in fewer cases, Stanford.[12] But Sidney did not have prior precedent to rely on as he embarked on his novel enterprise. Thoughtfully, Sperry did his best to decide where to go, noting that the Divinity School at Chicago stood out above other options. Harvard's Divinity School was not yet in full ascent, Union Theological Seminary would have been costlier, and neither Cornell nor the University of Wisconsin had full-fledged divinity schools. None of the westward universities had full-fledged divinity schools either nor was the religious education at the level of what Sidney perceived Chicago's standard was. In the end, Sperry chose Chicago because of its standard of scholarship. In Sperry's own words, privately shared with Eva, he wrote of someone considering following his footsteps: "He will sure be foolish if he ever goes to California," signaling Sperry's preference for Chicago.[13]

Sperry knew the University of Chicago was considered a metropolis of learning during the 1920s. Besides boasting the University, the city was deemed a cultural and social mecca in which the arts and sciences flourished. Chicago's citizenry was high-minded about its city and university, and for good reason. In just 25 years, the University of Chicago had reached a scholarly pinnacle and built an infrastructure that other great universities had only attained after 250 years, and this intellectual and physical growth had "probably never been equaled in the history of learning."[14] Sidney B. Sperry entered the University of Chicago in 1925 on the heels of this growth, in a time when the future medical school's plans had been approved, a theology building was under construction, and plans for the Divinity Chapel were moving forward.[15]

That same year Chicago's president wrote of the University's Divinity School: "The list of books which have been written or edited by the members of the faculty is a very long one, possibly surpassing that of any other theological faculty in the country."[16] The president was not presumptuous in saying such things, for the Divinity School housed some of the most illustrious and able scriptural and ancient Near East scholars of the time. The distinguished Belgian scholar

Franz Cumont, for example, indicated that James Henry Breasted's 1924 published acount of a singular discovery illuminating ancient Syria "can hardly be exaggerated" and "throws vivid light upon numerous questions."[17] Indeed, among Chicago's professors with whom Sperry would study closely were some of the most erudite scholars in the United States and in the world. Martin Sprengling, for instance, had mastered "a dozen languages, eastern and western, [which] were his 'open sesame' to the storehouse of the history and culture of the Mediterranean world and particularly to the mainsprings of Near Eastern thought and patterns of life."[18]

The year Sperry arrived, one of Chicago's newspapers published a piece entitled "Chicago and Its Universities," revealing the milieu in which Sperry had entered. It exulted: "Chicago is no city which sits at the nation's gate to take toll. It buys and sells, but, more important, it creates. It is a mighty workshop. To it flock the young men and women who are to inherit leadership of the empire of which Chicago is the capital. Here they are trained in the professions, in the arts, and in the sciences. . . . The middle west knows only one aristocracy: the aristocracy of competence. No standard of scholarship which these new professional schools may maintain can be too exacting. The middle west, and Chicago in particular, needs the best youth with the best training."[19]

This move to Chicago entailed serious sacrifice on the family's part, but especially on Eva's. On June 15, 1925, Sperry boarded the train in Salt Lake City en route to Chicago after Eva and Lyman ("buddy,"[20] as Sidney called him), who was born almost two years before, moved to Manti, Utah, where Eva's widowed father, Robert Braithwaite Jr., would accommodate both his daughter and grandson. Just a month and a half removed from their separation, the reality of the moment was setting in for Eva. Without her husband, she would shoulder the weight of the family basically alone, and she was eight months pregnant with their second child.[21] To be back with her father, who was fifty-eight years old, and to know that she would not likely see or be with Sid for more than a year was almost too much to bear. Over the last four years, in support of her husband's spiritual goals, which she had adopted as her own, she felt ping-ponged, moving four times. Sidney tried to encourage her while also revealing his profound feelings about Chicago: "Be brave and use all your will power to come thru. You will be alright and after a while maybe we can settle down permanently and raise our family. I've not regretted choosing Chicago as my school. It certainly is wonderful and interesting as well. Believe me I ought to know something about the Bible if my plans go right. So cheer up dear."[22]

Sidney's goal of knowing more about the scriptures than any earthly person continued. In Chicago, he was riveted on his scriptural studies. "How the time has flown! I suppose it flies so fast because *nearly every minute of my time is taken in listening to lectures and studying.*"[23] He regretted nothing about Chicago except that Eva and Lyman were not with him. To Eva, he confided: "There is a wonderful class of men to teach here. They sure know their stuff. Glad I came."[24] Together his four professors that quarter combined for ninety-four years of teaching experience. Three were full professors, and they had all been educated at major centers of learning, including Berlin, Oxford, Yale, and Chicago. All were exacting in their specialty areas of Hebrew, Greek, New Testament and early Christian literature, the history and civilization of the Near East, and Isaiah. For Sperry, it was an exhilarating quarter of learning under these professors, including John Merlin Powis Smith, who at the time had been the editor of the *American Journal of Semitic Languages and Literatures* for seventeen years running.[25]

As his scriptural studies continued, the same theme of constant study continued: "This is Sunday and I am here in my room studying,"[26] and a few weeks later when writing Eva, he mused: "As time flies so fast when studying I thought it best to write you before it gets too late. We have so much to do that it takes about all the time we can get to get our work done."[27] Though Sperry's load was a grind, and it was a great sacrifice to be separated, he wanted Eva to feel that her sacrifice was not in vain and to feel his deep love for her: "Well I hope our plans work out alright and *I believe they will*. It will pay us to sacrifice a year or two [to start off] much as we hate to. . . . Would have a hard time telling you *how much I love you* though. Cheer up and tell me soon that there is another buddy boy or girl in the family and that you are all right."[28] As it turned out, the next day their second child and first daughter, Claire Elaine Sperry, was born in Manti, Sanpete County, Utah. Eva's Western Union Telegram to Sidney a day later read, "Nine pound baby girl nine thirty yesterday doing fine Love Eva 1225P."[29]

Though most of Sperry's intellectual experiences at Chicago were focused on scriptural studies, his scientific background as a chemist and his knowledge in mathematics led colleagues in other disciplines to bring him into their intellectual discussions. One such occasion prevented Sperry, as he penned later, from writing Eva because he was "invited to a supper by a group of men who were anxious for me to join their conversation. We were talked to after supper by a world-famous mathematician, Dr. Lunn, who talked about the theory of relativity as applied to practical affairs."[30] A member of the National Academy of Sciences and an energetic teacher, Arthur Constant Lunn was a full professor in Chicago's mathematics department, arguably one of the three most prestigious mathematics departments in the United States at the time—the other two being Harvard and Princeton. Lunn was an impressive genius who had a great impact on a number of world-renowned scientists through his teaching and work.[31] Sperry must have been invigorated with Lunn, who "integrated everything into one gorgeous whole."[32] As Sperry came to the conclusion of this intellectually demanding and enthralling summer quarter, he confided to Eva, "Have been having exams today and have three tomorrow. It is pretty late now and I ought to be in bed. . . . Tomorrow ends school and I am rather glad because it surely has been a grind."[33]

That fall, the theme of challenging intellectual work in his scriptural studies had not changed. If anything, it had become increasingly arduous. Running at full capacity, he wrote Eva, "The time goes so fast that I can't keep track of the date. There ought to be more hours in the day. It seems like there isn't time to accomplish what one would like to."[34] Later he explained one reason why: "My course is very stiff here mainly on account of Hebrew. Not a single student that started with me has continued, and consequently I had to get into a class where students have had a lot of Hebrew. There are but four in the class at that. The Egyptian is bad enough too."[35] Despite the strain, Sperry noted privately to Eva that his professors were taking note of his work ethic and especially his ability to learn ancient languages, both Hebrew and Egyptian. Noting Sperry's talent in his Egyptian course, T. George Allen, a foremost expert of Egyptian funerary literature, encouraged Sidney, telling him that the universities throughout the nation needed people like him to specialize in Egyptology.[36] This encouragement led Sidney to quip to Eva, "You may see a great deal of the U.S. yet."[37]

Meanwhile, Eva's feelings about the distance between them had deepened. Their financial ability to sustain the Chicago dream was also more uncertain. Sidney shared his thoughts with Eva: "Hold on dear the best you can. If we don't sacrifice now we'll regret it the rest of our lives. . . . [Our sacrifice will enable us to] do [our] part of the world's work. You don't want me to fail to do my part do you? It is what a man sacrifices and accomplishes in life that develops him. Well dearie bye bye. I love you and those babies with all my heart."[38] Not much later he penned, "I know you are lonely dear without me and heavens knows I am only too lonely myself. . . . So far as expenses are concerned dear it will be absolutely out of the question for us to be together in Chicago, much as I would like it. Living is awfully high here and rent is a fright. I'll have to get you settled in a home and then make it by summers back here or during any quarter of 3 months that I can. Can you hold out till next June or September at the very latest depending on the money we can borrow? . . . Write and let me know dear. I know you will be lonely but if you can stick it out that far it sure would be a big help. . . . I w[as] figuring . . . last night . . . the cheapest way for me is to do just what I'm doing."[39]

The demands of Sperry's program remained unrelenting. He apologized to Eva: "I hope you will not think I am neglecting you too much. My course this quarter is so stiff that I am kept on the go. Hope to write you tomorrow. Bye Bye. Love Sid."[40] This continued as he delved deeper into his studies: "Saturday I had to study Egyptian all day."[41] Despite the grind, Sidney received good news just before Christmas that members of his old stake presidency in American Fork would sign on a loan note he took out to continue his studies and support his family. "Received the $500 check today and a letter from Pres. Chipman saying that he and his counselors would sign for me up to $1000. Awfully good of them. . . . I'm awful glad the money arrived when it did."[42] Then on Christmas Eve he penned, "Dearest Eva: . . . Hope you got the money I sent you in time to get a little Christmas. . . . Wish it could have been all you needed or wanted. . . . Just got thru with exams. It's an awful strain. . . . Heaps of love and kisses."[43]

To conserve resources, Sidney never planned to travel to Utah for Christmas and would remain away from his family. His academically rigorous life continued in January unabated: "I'll write often as possible. Am awfully busy."[44] By the winter of 1926, the grind had taken its toll on both Eva and Sidney. For his part, he asked Eva a question: "Can you guess how much I weigh now? I weigh . . . 40 lbs less than when I last saw you. . . . Am looking forward . . . to September when I can be with you again. Life would be a dreary, dull existence without you and our kiddies."[45] It had been almost nine months since he had seen Eva and Lyman, and he had never seen his oldest daughter. In his absence, his daughter had received her name and a blessing by another priesthood bearer. Sidney was happy about this since he would be gone too long for the family to wait. It would be another eight months before he would see them again or, in his daughter's case, for the first time.

The winter quarter of 1926 would bring Sidney to his fourth course in Hebrew and another course in Egyptian, taught by the same professor in Egyptology who had encouraged him to consider it as a specialty. He would also study Greek and portions of the New Testament under a different professor of Biblical and Patristic Greek, Edgar Johnson Goodspeed. Finally, he studied what was then entitled "History of Antiquity II: The Oriental Empires, 1600 BC to Alexander the Great." This course was typically taught by James Henry Breasted, though he was not in Chicago during this quarter,[46] and examined the civilizations of Egypt, Asia Minor, Assyria, Chaldea, the Hebrews, and Persia. The course also analyzed government, art, architecture, religion, and literature. Finally, it looked at the early civilization of Europe, both before and after the Indo-European migrations into Greece and Italy.

The spring quarter would further Sperry's understanding of the history of early Christianity as he studied under his third distinct New Testament professor, Shirley Jackson Case. Sperry would also take another advanced course in Hebrew, study the history of Judaism, and learn Hieratic and Late Egyptian at the feet of James Henry Breasted, studying the main text of the course in German, and learning selected portions of Georg Möller's *Hieratische Lesestücke*. By the end of spring, Sperry had formed a strong foundation of Egyptian, including demonstrating a proficiency in its hieroglyphic, hieratic, demotic, and Coptic scripts. The summer quarter was not only a culmination of his master's work at Chicago before returning to Utah, but also a synthesis for Sperry as he strengthened his Semitic language prowess, learning from the preeminent American scholar who was also one of the most accomplished Assyriologists worldwide, D. D. Luckenbill.[47] Sperry also intensively studied the comparative grammar of the Semitic languages under Martin Sprengling, whose encyclopedic knowledge "followed the course of classical thought and its ramifications into the Judeo-Christian and Islamic worlds."[48] Sprengling was a "severe but inspiring teacher," and "his genius was at its best in the seminar room where his methods were often Socratic."[49] Sperry followed in Sprengling's footsteps in terms of the knowledge he amassed and in the fact that during the summer of 1926 he had already demonstrated high proficiency in Hebrew, Aramaic, Assyrian, and Syriac, though the mastery of this last language came later. Sprengling would later become one of Sperry's major PhD dissertation advisers. For now, Sperry would complete his master's thesis using his knowledge of Hebrew and the Book of Mormon.

In the summer of 1922, Elder Joseph Fielding Smith, Apostle and Church Historian, had written, "The study of Hebrew is the most important of all the languages for our young people at this time. . . . The day of the Gentile is drawing to its close and the day of the Jew is at hand, so far as the Gospel is concerned."[50] The president of BYU concurred: "It seems to me very desirable for us to have scholars in various languages, particularly those which have had to do with the work of the chosen people of the Lord on the earth. Among these of course Hebrew ranks first. . . . I think it would be highly desirable for the Church University to offer courses in Hebrew . . . I should certainly like to have a good man in Hebrew connected with our institution if we could afford it."[51] Elder Smith replied, "I have always regretted that we had no scholars in the Church who understand Hebrew and also Egyptian, both languages being of the greatest value to us."[52]

Just over three and a half years later, Elder Smith must have been pleased to have received Sperry's request for the First European edition of the Book of Mormon to assist in the writing of his thesis. For his thesis, Sperry planned to employ some of his now extensive Hebrew ability in producing and examining a collation of the parallel Masoretic, King James, and Book of Mormon Isaiah texts. Elder Smith was happy to loan Sperry a physical copy of the requested Book of Mormon.[53]

Under the direction of faculty members in Chicago's Old Testament department, Sperry's thesis was entitled "The Text of Isaiah in the Book of Mormon."[54] Scholars of the Old Testament, of course, study variants in different versions of the same biblical text to answer questions about their provenance and history. Sperry's thesis is one example of how he connected his study of the Book of Mormon to his Old Testament studies. As a rationale for his thesis topic, he explained,

> The Book of Mormon makes plain that the Nephites brought the Brass Plates with them from Jerusalem. These were the Hebrew Scriptures giving an account from the creation down to the beginning of the reign of Zedekiah, King of Judah. In other words, the Nephites had with them a Hebrew bible containing the scriptures known in Israel prior to 600 BC. We might, therefore, expect to find quotations from the Brass Plates in the Book of Mormon. Not only so, but what is of greater interest to biblical scholars [is that] these quotations would presumably be from an uncorrupted text.[55]

Sperry began by providing a relatively "brief statement of the origin and contents of the Book of Mormon," which, he stated, "will assist greatly in making clear the nature of the problem . . . of this thesis."[56] He then stated, "Joseph Smith Jr. . . . affirmed he translated the Book of Mormon by the gift and power of God." Before quoting from what would have been the forepart of the Book of Mormon then in circulation, Sperry referenced the First Vision as "a Divine manifestation of profound significance," which Joseph had "received."[57] He presented another rationale for the study: "There are to be found in the Book of Mormon numerous quotations from the Brass Plates including the sayings or writings of some prophets not mentioned in the Old Testament. An investigation of these quotations from the Brass Plates is important" because "there are about six hundred thousand people constituting the membership of . . . The Church of Jesus Christ of Latter-day Saints . . . who believe the Book of Mormon to be a Divine record."[58] Therefore, said Sperry, "such an investigation offers one avenue of scientific approach to the claims of the [Latter-day Saint] people."[59]

Sperry then framed a question he wanted to answer: "Critics of the [Latter-day Saints] have often charged that the text of Isaiah in the Book of Mormon has been taken bodily from the King James

Version. Such charges, if true, would manifestly tend to disprove that the Book of Mormon is an independent record because it is a well known fact that the parallel text of Isaiah in the King James Version is very corrupt in many places."[60] So Sperry's question became whether or not all the text of Isaiah (about twenty-one complete chapters) in the Book of Mormon was simply the same as the King James Version of the Bible. If there were differences, that would provide evidence for the unique characteristics of the text in the Book of Mormon.

Some of his significant findings in regard to this main question include the following: 54 percent of the verses of the text of Isaiah in the Book of Mormon "contain differences, compared with the King James' version,"[61] and "many of these differences are very great."[62] Thus the Book of Mormon text "points to very notable corruptions, where these differences occur, in our Masoretic texts."[63] Furthermore, "the collation reveals so many great differences between the two texts that one is most compelled to doubt the veracity of such writers as Linn who infer The Book of Mormon text of Isaiah to have been 'appropriated bodily' from the King James' text."[64] Sperry then explains, "Where these great differences exist between The Book of Mormon and the King James' version the modern critical Hebrew text favors in nearly every instance the reading as given by the King James' translation."[65] Again, this means that the Book of Mormon text is unique. Finally, "Critics have accused Joseph Smith of quoting verbatim from the King James' version, not even omitting the italics supplied by the translators."[66] It turns out, however, that "the Book of Mormon . . . has different translation[s] at points where italics occur in" nearly half the verses.[67] Therefore, "considering the nature of the words in italics this is quite a striking evidence of Joseph Smith's independence in translating the text of Isaiah."[68]

Sperry's thesis had thus demonstrated that the Isaiah text in the Book of Mormon was not "appropriated bodily" from the King James Bible but, rather, had its own unique fingerprint. His thesis could not have examined all the questions one might raise for inquiry regarding the text of Isaiah in the Book of Mormon, but it yielded eight summary findings, all of which either added to our knowledge of the Book of Mormon, affirmed the Book of Mormon's unique characteristics, or brought up fruitful questions for further investigation. Studying the words of Isaiah, as well as the Book of Mormon itself, became one of Sperry's lifelong lines of inquiry that permeates most of his writings.

Not including his thesis, the final examination for his master's degree (which would be accomplished by the end of the summer of 1926), or the previous twenty hours of graduate coursework Sperry had completed at BYU prior to Chicago, Sperry had now completed sixty-three hours of graduate coursework at Chicago in five terms, an arduous endeavor even for the most talented student. On August 26, 1926, Sperry passed his final examination for his master's degree and on September 3, 1926, was awarded an AM degree in the Department of Old Testament Literature and Interpretation from the University of Chicago. He now had the foundation to pursue his PhD in ancient Near Eastern languages and civilizations.

At long last, he traveled home to reunite with his beloved Eva and their children, Lyman and Claire—the daughter he had never met. After reaching the train station in Salt Lake City, Sidney traveled further to Manti, Utah, where his family was staying. The reunion was joyful. Sperry would almost immediately take the position as principal of the Moroni Seminary in Sanpete County for the academic year 1926–27. In June 1927 Sperry would take the train back to Chicago once again to continue his quest to know more about the scriptures than any living person. This time, however, he stayed for only one quarter, to his family's delight, during which he intensively studied and translated Isaiah texts, Babylonian texts, and other ancient texts.

He was asked to be principal at Pocatello Seminary in Idaho for the 1927–28 academic year, which would require the family to move from Manti, Utah, to Pocatello for one year. After that year, Sidney took his family back to Manti before returning to Chicago for another four quarters (summer, fall, winter, spring), from June 1928 to May 1929 to complete his PhD coursework. That Chicago summer continued to raise the level of Sperry's ability in and knowledge of Hebrew, its Semitic relatives, and the manners and customs of the Hebrews as he studied under Ludwig Köhler, visiting professor of Old Testament from Zurich, Switzerland. During that time Sidney's esteemed grandfather, patriarch Harrison Sperry Sr., passed away. He was believed to have been the last known Latter-day Saint to have personally known the Prophet Joseph Smith.[69] He was the very man who had spiritually predicted that Sperry would be doing what he was doing during this period. That fall Sidney continued growing in his mastery of textual analysis, translating, and interpreting, again focusing mostly on Hebrew and its Semitic relatives.

After the passing of Sperry's grandfather the previous summer, the winter of 1929 provided new life. Sidney and Eva's third child, and second son, Richard Dean Sperry, was born on January 5 in Manti. The winter also provided intensive opportunities for Sperry to further master Hebrew, Aramaic, Syriac, and other languages while at the same time to extend his knowledge and understanding of Arabic and Islamic studies. He also passed his language examinations in French and German in January and March, respectively. The spring quarter of 1929 found him deepening his knowledge of Arabic grammar, lexicography, rhetoric, and literature. During these last two quarters, Sperry worked closely with two of his dissertation advisors, William Creighton Graham and Martin Sprengling. On March 13, 1929, John Merlin Powis Smith recommended Sidney B. Sperry for a PhD from the Department of Oriental Languages and Literatures, and on April 13, 1929, the graduate faculty approved the recommendation. Since earning his master's degree, Sperry had further taken fifty-one credit hours of intensive courses in many Semitic languages and demonstrated his mastery. The spring of 1929 was the last time Sperry would ever take courses again as a PhD candidate in Chicago. The Chicago journey had essentially come to a close.

Without interruptions, Sperry would likely have completed his PhD in 1929. In fact, in letters to Sperry from Apostles such as Elder Talmage, Church leaders were already addressing him as "Dr. Sperry."

While moving forward in early 1929 with his dissertation plans, two things happened that adjusted Sperry's course. First, he received a call from Joseph F. Merrill, Church Commissioner of Education, requesting that he teach two Old Testament courses at BYU.[70] Each course would be six weeks in duration during the summer term and would be taught to seminary and institute teachers. Sperry accepted this opportunity with excitement and zeal, despite the fact that it would delay the completion of his PhD. By now Sperry was a "popular teacher in the seminary system," and during his six-week course in the summer of 1929, he "ignited a fire in the seminary system with the new, critical approaches of . . . textual analysis, archaeological investigation, and historical exegesis" of the Old Testament.[71]

T. Edgar Lyon, a future renowned teacher and author, was extraordinarily impressed with Sperry's knowledge and the way he opened up the scriptures. Never had Lyon seen the scriptures come alive quite like they did under Sperry's tutelage. Inspired by his Chicago experience, his methodology, as well as his faith, was contagious. Sperry's classes the summer of 1929 "were a revelation to Lyon and many other teachers in the [seminary] system."[72] Lyon's biographer writes of the impact of these summer sessions:

> The summers of 1929 and 1930 [both of which Sperry organized himself] were life-changing educational moments for Lyon as well as his students. . . . From Sperry, Lyon realized that there was a new and exciting realm of biblical scholarship. He began to understand that education was not just listening to professors, reading their standard texts, and then reproducing canonized information on tests as he had done as an undergraduate. Rather, education and learning could be exciting, even thrilling, involving the use of original sources and ancient languages. Lyon learned that investigation of standard texts must be creative, using modern techniques and innovative approaches.[73]

Edward H. Holt, acting president of BYU in 1929, wrote to President Franklin Harris, who was in Russia, updating him on Sperry's accomplishments in the Alpine summer school: "Sperry is pleasing the Seminary people very much. Dr. Merrill has been down four or five times and seems very much interested."[74]

The second request was that Sperry direct the Latter-day Saint institute of religion adjacent to the University of Idaho in Moscow, Idaho. Sperry accommodated this request as well and was happy to do so because it benefited the Lord's Church. He would serve as director of the institute at Moscow for two years after teaching at BYU in 1929. He would also assist Commissioner Merrill in securing world-class scholars to teach at BYU in the summers of 1930,[75] 1931, and 1932, while also organizing these courses.[76] But another event changed Sperry's course once again.

Elder David O. McKay was a moving force in having Sidney B. Sperry and Guy C. Wilson become the two inaugural faculty members of a new, full-time religious education department at BYU.[77] Indeed, Elder McKay was extremely anxious for Sperry to *simultaneously* join Wilson at BYU full-time in the fall of 1930.[78] But Commissioner Merrill had the tough task of replacing Sperry in Moscow, Idaho, when there were no plausible replacements, which is why Merrill wrote to President Harris: "We think, however, that we can get [Elder] McKay to consent to postpone a year the coming of Brother Sperry."[79] If Sperry would have come when Elder McKay intended, Sperry would have had the honor, with Wilson, of being one of the two inaugural full-time religious education faculty members at BYU. The fact that this scenario did not happen because the seminaries and institutes needed him for one more year is not a hindrance to Sperry's contribution to BYU and the Church Educational System, but rather a testament to it. Furthermore, Sperry became the pioneer Elder McKay had hoped for once Sperry joined as the second full-time faculty member in the new department. During this period, Sidney and Eva received the gift of their fourth child and second daughter, Phyllis Sperry, born June 27, 1930, in Moscow, Idaho.

Meanwhile he worked on completing his doctoral dissertation in preparation for his dissertation defense and final examination.

Sperry's dissertation, entitled "The Scholia of Bar Hebraeus to the Books of Kings," was a pioneering endeavor. Bar Hebraeus (1226–86), "one of the greatest historians of the Middle Ages," was "particularly interested in reviving Syriac language and literature and in bringing Muslim scholarship to the attention of the Christians."[80] Sperry wrote, "Bar Hebraeus made available for missionaries and laymen of the Syriac church, practically all the learning of his day. The amount of work he did was prodigious and covered the fields of grammar, history, lexicography, mathematics, astronomy, poetry, theology, philosophy and Biblical exegesis. Norman MacLean has written: 'Perhaps no more illustrious compiler of knowledge ever lived.'"[81]

Sperry's dissertation dealt with Bar Hebraeus's commentary[82] on the biblical books of Kings. Specifically, it was an original translation into English—the first in history—of Bar Hebraeus's commentary, which was originally composed in Syriac. Sperry collated eighteen different manuscripts, comparing the divergent texts so as to create the most faithful translation. Where the Syriac texts differed significantly, he noted and discussed those differences in his translation. Where they concurred, he noted those manuscripts that were in agreement. His dissertation comprised an introduction, translation, and collation of all Bar Hebraeus's commentary material on the books of Kings, which amounted to about two hundred pages. Sperry's dissertation was part of a larger work envisaged by the Oriental Institute of the University of Chicago, in which all of Hebraeus's notes on the Bible were to be "critically edited and translated" in order to issue a "critical edition of the Peshitto."[83] The Peshitto was the first major translation from the putatively original Hebrew and Aramaic sources of the Old Testament into Syriac. To this day, the Peshitto version is the authoritative translation of the Bible in all of the Syriac-speaking churches,[84] including the "Syriac Orthodox, Assyrian church of the East, Maronite, Chaldean," and Syrian Catholic.[85] Chicago scholars wanted to create the best translation possible of this Syriac translation of the Bible.

Furthering this objective, the Oriental Institute published *Barhebraeus' Scholia on the Old Testament: Part I: Genesis—II Samuel*.[86] Martin Sprengling and William Creighton Graham edited this volume. The second volume would begin with what Sperry had created and would combine the work of others for the translations through Malachi, but this dream of making the second half of Hebraeus's Old Testament commentary available in English was never realized. Sperry's work was nonetheless well received, original, and informative. It not only highlighted the extreme care he took with his research but also marked his fluency in Syriac.

In the end, Sperry would return to Chicago for a number of weeks during the summer of 1931, culminating in his dissertation defense and examination. Upon passing, he received his PhD on August 28, 1931, from the Department of Oriental Languages and Literatures. Writing to Eva, Sidney exhaled, "The hard grind is finally over, I have reached my objective"; he wished she could have been with him at the graduation exercises.[87]

True to his never-ending quest to know as much of the scriptures as any earthly person could, he now desired to avail himself of a singular opportunity to go to the Holy Land. During this period, multiple General Authorities checked in on him, encouraging him to come to BYU. They were concerned he might go elsewhere, which he had frankly thought about. He was the prototype for what Church leaders had envisioned BYU could become. Because of his exemplary record of accomplishments at Chicago, he received a fellowship from the University of Chicago to do postdoctoral research in archaeology, languages, and history in the Near East for the 1931–32 academic year.

The first doctoral scriptural scholar of the Near East from The Church of Jesus Christ of Latter-day Saints was now off to the Holy Land a century after the Church's founding. Ross T. Christensen, a member of BYU's religious education faculty, observed that Sperry "was actually the first serious student of the ancient Near East to appear among the Latter-day Saints since the days of the prophet Joseph Smith."[88] After Sperry's passing, Truman G. Madsen, himself a BYU faculty member of notoriety, perceived in 1978 that Sperry "was perhaps the Church's most knowledgeable Hebraist."[89] Madsen also indicated that Sperry "was a goldmine of knowledge and information that nobody tapped" and lamented: "I wish I could have tapped into all of his knowledge."[90] Sidney B. Sperry had aspired to know the scriptures, the word of God, and to teach and learn God's word the rest of his life. His scholarly influence and example of faithfulness to the restored gospel continues to inform Latter-day Saint religious scholarship today.

V. Wallace McCarlie Jr. is director of the Division of Orthodontics and Dentofacial Orthopedics and an associate professor at East Carolina University in Greenville, North Carolina.

Andrew C. Skinner is a professor emeritus of ancient scripture at Brigham Young University.

Notes

1. Patriarch Harrison Sperry to Sidney B. Sperry, March 24, 1912, A Patriarchal Blessing, Salt Lake City, 1.
2. Patriarch Sperry to Sidney Sperry, March 24, 1912, Patriarchal Blessing, 1.
3. Truman G. Madsen, "Joseph Smith Lecture 2: Joseph's Personality and Character" (Joseph Smith Lecture Series, Brigham Young University, August 22, 1978), www.speeches.byu.edu.
4. The Church of Jesus Christ of Latter-day Saints, "Chapter One: By Small and Simple Things: 1912–1935," in *By Study and Also by Faith: One Hundred Years of Seminaries and Institutes of Religion* (Salt Lake City: The Church of Jesus Christ of Latter-day Saints, 2015), 45.
5. Roy A. Welker to George H. Brimhall, Paris, Idaho, August 22,1922, Franklin S. Harris Presidential Papers (hereafter Harris MSS), Brigham

Young University Archives, Harold B. Lee Library, L. Tom Perry Special Collections, Provo, Utah (hereafter Perry Special Collections).

6.* Samuel D. Moore Jr. and Sidney B. Sperry to Franklin S. Harris, Pleasant Grove, Utah, October 27, 1922, Harris MSS, Perry Special Collections.

7. Moore and Sperry to Harris, October 27, 1922.

8. Adam S. Bennion to Franklin S. Harris, November 3, 1924. Harris MSS, Perry Special Collections. "We are slighting [the Book of Mormon] in our present course."

9. Sidney B. Sperry to Eva B. Sperry, Chicago, July 11, 1925, in author's possession. Sperry reflects that if he would have matriculated at Chicago in 1922 instead of enrolling at Brigham Young University, he would have completed his doctoral degree much sooner. Chicago's summer term was "an ideal summer school." He added, "It wouldn't have cost me much more to have come here." Concluding, he wrote, "We have to live and learn I guess."

10. The Relief Society Bible class of Weber Seminary to Sidney B. Sperry, Weber, Utah, March 6, 1925, in author's possession.

11. See, for example, Harris MSS, Boxes 1–22, Perry Special Collections.

12. Franklin S. Harris to C. B. Lipman, Provo, Utah, September 8, 1923, Harris MSS, Perry Special Collections.

13. S. B. Sperry to E. B. Sperry, July 11, 1925.

14. Thomas W. Goodspeed, *A History of the University of Chicago: The First Quarter-Century* (Chicago: The University of Chicago Press, 1916), 472.

15. Thomas W. Goodspeed, *The Story of The University of Chicago, 1890–1925* (Chicago: University of Chicago Press, 1925), 228.

16. William M. Murphy and D. J. R. Bruckner, eds., *The Idea of the University of Chicago: Selections from the Papers of the First Eight Chief Executives of the University of Chicago from 1891 to 1975* (Chicago: University of Chicago Press, 1976), 366.

17. James Henry Breasted, *Oriental Forerunners of Byzantine Painting: First-Century Wall Paintings from the Fortress of Dura on the Middle Euphrates* (Chicago: The University of Chicago Press, 1924), 15.

18. Nabia Abbott, "Martin Sprengling, 1877–1959," *Journal of Near Eastern Studies* 19, no. 1 (January 1960): 54–55.

19. M. W. Poulson to Franklin S. Harris, Chicago, May 26, 1925, Harris MSS, Perry Special Collections. The article is attached to this letter.
20. Sidney B. Sperry to Eva B. Sperry, Chicago, July 31, 1925, in author's possession.
21. Sidney B. Sperry to Eva B. Sperry, Chicago, July 26, 1925, in author's possession.
22. S. B. Sperry to E. B. Sperry, July 26, 1925.
23. S. B. Sperry to E. B. Sperry, July 31, 1925; emphasis added.
24. S. B. Sperry to E. B. Sperry, July 31, 1925.
25. J. M. Powis Smith Papers, Biographical Note, Special Collections Research Center, University of Chicago Library. The referenced journal later became the *Journal of Near Eastern Studies*, https://lib.uchicago.edu/e/scrc/finding aids/view.php?eadid=ICU.SPCL.SMITHJMP.
26. Sidney B. Sperry to Eva B. Sperry, Chicago, August 2, 1925, in author's possession.
27. Sidney B. Sperry to Eva B. Sperry, Chicago, August 13, 1925, in author's possession.
28. S. B. Sperry to E. B. Sperry, August 13, 1925; emphasis added.
29. Sidney B. Sperry to Eva B. Sperry, Chicago, October 1925, in author's possession.
30. Sidney B. Sperry to Eva B. Sperry, Chicago, August 21, 1925, in author's possession. Lunn's theme that evening may have come from Arthur C. Lunn, "Some Aspects of the Theory of Relativity," *Physical Review* 19, no. 3 (1922): 264–65. The "group of men" referred to by Sperry may have been part of what was called the Innominates club, of which Lunn was an organizing member. It included a cadre of faculty intellectuals from the departments or fields of anatomy, bacteriology, chemistry, botany, geology, mathematics, physics, physiology, zoology, and psychology.
31. George B. Kauffman, "Martin D. Kamen: An Interview with a Nuclear and Biochemical Pioneer," *Chemical Educator* 5 (October 2000): 252–62, https://doi.org/10.1007/s00897000402a. See also Michael B. Weissman, Valentin Vankov Iliev, and Ivan Gutmanc, "A Pioneer Remembered: Biographical Notes about Arthur Constant Lunn," *MATCH Communications in Mathematical and in Computer Chemistry* 59 (2008): 687–708.

These authors indicate that Lunn demonstrated in the early 1920s what has traditionally been credited to the French physicist Louis de Broglie and Austrian physicist Erwin Schrödinger. Thus Lunn's thought was a cornerstone to what would become quantum mechanics. One of Lunn's students got an idea in his class, which these authors suggest led to that student sharing the "Nobel Prize in Physics in 1937 with George Paget Thomson for the discovery of electron diffraction."

32. Kauffman, "Martin D. Kamen," 252–62. In 1929 Lunn, together with his colleague in chemistry, published his seminal work. See Arthur C. Lunn and James K. Senior, "Isomerism and Configuration," *Journal of Physical Chemistry* 33 (1929): 1027–79.
33. Sidney B. Sperry to Eva B. Sperry, Chicago, September 3, 1925, in author's possession.
34. S. B. Sperry to E. B. Sperry, October 1925.
35. S. B. Sperry to E. B. Sperry, October 1925.
36. Sidney B. Sperry to Eva B. Sperry, Hammond, Indiana, September 21, 1925, in author's possession.
37. S. B. Sperry to E. B. Sperry, September 21, 1925.
38. Sidney B. Sperry to Eva B. Sperry, Hammond, Indiana, September 18, 1925, in author's possession.
39. S. B. Sperry to E. B. Sperry, September 21, 1925.
40. Sidney B. Sperry to Eva B. Sperry, October 21, 1925, Chicago, in author's possession.
41. Sidney B. Sperry to Eva B. Sperry, November 1, 1925, Chicago, spelling corrected, in author's possession.
42. Sidney B. Sperry to Eva B. Sperry, December 15, 1925, Chicago, in author's possession.
43. Sidney B. Sperry to Eva B. Sperry, December 24, 1925, Chicago, in author's possession.
44. Sidney B. Sperry to Eva B. Sperry, January 15, 1926, Chicago, in author's possession.
45. Sidney B. Sperry to Eva B. Sperry, February 6, 1926, Chicago, in author's possession.

46. Charles Breasted, *Pioneer to the Past: The Story of James Henry Breasted, Archaeologist* (New York: Charles Scribner's Sons, 1943), 388–94.
47. Leroy Waterman, "Daniel David Luckenbill, 1881–1927: An Appreciation," *American Journal of Semitic Languages and Literatures* 44, no. 1 (October 1927): 1–5.
48. Abbott, "Martin Sprengling, 1877–1959," 54–55.
49. Abbott, "Martin Sprengling, 1877–1959," 54–55.
50. Joseph Fielding Smith to Franklin S. Harris, Salt Lake City, September 5, 1922, Harris MSS, Perry Special Collections. He indicates that Elder John A. Widtsoe of the Quorum of the Twelve Apostles and President Anthony W. Ivins of the First Presidency concur that Hebrew is preeminent and should be taught.
51. Franklin S. Harris to Joseph Fielding Smith, Provo, Utah, September 7, 1922, Harris MSS, Perry Special Collections.
52. Joseph Fielding Smith to Franklin S. Harris, Salt Lake City, September 11, 1922, Harris MSS, Perry Special Collections. "We stand in a peculiar position as a people, in regard to education, because of the message we have for the world. The Gospel was to be preached first to the Gentile and then to the Jew (D&C 90:9). The time has now come when the Gospel message must go to the Jew and to the Lamanite, in fulfillment of the predictions of old. The Jew is, as the Book of Mormon declares he would do, 'beginning to believe in Christ.' We are certainly in need of missionaries who are acquainted with Hebrew and Jewish customs so that they will understand how to appeal to these scattered sheep of the House of Israel."
53. Joseph Fielding Smith to Sidney B. Sperry, Salt Lake City, May 24, 1926, in author's possession.
54. Sidney B. Sperry, "The Text of Isaiah in the Book of Mormon" (master's thesis, University of Chicago, 1926), title page. Submitted to the faculty of the graduate school of arts and literature for his master of arts degree.
55. Sperry, "Text of Isaiah in the Book of Mormon," 8–9.
56. Sperry, "Text of Isaiah in the Book of Mormon," 1.
57. Sperry, "Text of Isaiah in the Book of Mormon," 1.

58. Sperry, "Text of Isaiah in the Book of Mormon," 9. Sperry makes a point to write: "The correct name is, The Church of Jesus Christ of Latter-day Saints."
59. Sperry, "Text of Isaiah in the Book of Mormon," 9.
60. Sperry, "Text of Isaiah in the Book of Mormon," 10.
61. Sperry, "Text of Isaiah in the Book of Mormon," 79.
62. Sperry, "Text of Isaiah in the Book of Mormon," 82.
63. Sperry, "Text of Isaiah in the Book of Mormon," 83.
64. Sperry, "Text of Isaiah in the Book of Mormon," 79.
65. Sperry, "Text of Isaiah in the Book of Mormon," 79.
66. Sperry, "Text of Isaiah in the Book of Mormon," 80.
67. Sperry, "Text of Isaiah in the Book of Mormon," 80.
68. Sperry, "Text of Isaiah in the Book of Mormon," 80.
69. Associated Press, July 29, 1928. "Harrison Sperry, 96, the oldest member of the Church of Jesus Christ of Latter-day Saints died at his home here yesterday. The church patriarch was believed to have been the only person living who personally remembered Joseph Smith, founder of the church."
70. Franklin S. Harris to Joseph F. Merrill, January 26, 1929, Provo, Utah, Harris MSS, Perry Special Collections.
71. Thomas Edgar Lyon Jr., *T. Edgar Lyon: A Teacher in Zion* (Provo, UT: Brigham Young University Press, 2002), 115.
72. Lyon Jr., *T. Edgar Lyon*, 115.
73. Lyon Jr., *T. Edgar Lyon*, 118.
74. Edward H. Holt to Franklin S. Harris, July 7, 1929, Provo, Utah, Harris MSS, Perry Special Collections.
75. Joseph F. Merrill to C. Y. Cannon, Sidney B. Sperry, E. H. Holt, September 26, 1929, Provo, Utah, Harris MSS, Perry Special Collections. "In order to . . . keep our seminary men well satisfied . . . I think it well to get some scholar of national standing next summer to offer two courses in the field of the New Testament. . . . I certainly hope that . . . arrangements can be made with Dr. Goodspeed." None of these men copied on the letter intimately knew Goodspeed except for Sperry. This letter is, in effect, to him in order to make the invitation and connection. Cannon is involved because he was the dean of the Alpine summer school at the time and Holt

is involved because he is the secretary to the faculty and serving as acting president while Harris was in Russia. These brethren were to make the logistics work and conduct official arrangements.

76. Lyon Jr., *T. Edgar Lyon*, 115.
77. Joseph F. Merrill to Franklin S. Harris, March 28, 1930, Provo, Utah, Harris MSS, Perry Special Collections.
78. Merrill to Harris, March 28, 1930.
79. Merrill to Harris, March 28, 1930.
80. Joseph R. Strayer, ed., *Dictionary of the Middle Ages* (New York: Charles Scribner's Sons, 1983), 2:108.
81. Sidney B. Sperry, "The Scholia of Bar Hebraeus to the Books of Kings" (PhD diss., The University of Chicago, 1931), 4.
82. Scholia is a commentary on a particular subject, usually in the Latin or Greek classics.
83. Sperry, "Scholia of Bar Hebraeus," 4.
84. See, for example, M. P. Weitzman, *The Syriac Version of the Old Testament: An Introduction* (New York: Cambridge University Press, 1999), 2. "The [Peshitta] assumes . . . importance as the basis of the rich literature of Syriac-speaking Christianity." See too http://syriacorthodoxresources.org/Bible/Peshitto.html.
85. See http://syriacorthodoxresources.org/Bible/Peshitto.html.
86. See Martin Sprengling and William Creighton Graham, eds., *Barhebraeus' Scholia on the Old Testament: Part I: Genesis—II Samuel*, ed., James Henry Breasted and Thomas George Allen (Chicago: The University of Chicago Press, 1931).
87. Sidney B. Sperry to Eva B. Sperry, Chicago, August 18, 1931, in author's possession.
88. Ross T. Christensen, "Sidney B. Sperry," *Newsletter and Proceedings of the SEHA* 143 (May 1979): 6.
89. Madsen, "Joseph's Personality and Character."
90. Truman G. Madsen, conversation with author, October 30, 2005.

2

"A Kingdom of Priests, and an Holy Nation"
The Work of Covenant Women and Men in Building Zion

Sharon Eubank

I'm so pleased to be invited to speak at this year's Sperry Symposium and especially on a theme I care deeply about: "A Covenant of Compassion: Caring for the Marginalized and Disadvantaged"—particularly examples from the Old Testament.

The scope of the topic I have chosen tonight is too big to be confined simply to Old Testament times, but that is where I am going to start. The expansive vision of a covenantal kingdom of priests as a holy nation has animated prophets since Enoch actually achieved it in his day, and the promise of it has everything to do with what President Russell M. Nelson is teaching in our day—for the benefit of all, including the poor, the disadvantaged, and those who have not. So let me start with Moses and move through other prophets before linking this covenant of compassion to the latter days and the potential for the faithful to become, by covenant, kings and queens, priests and priestesses.

Moses

I see in my mind's eye a mother's hands smoothing over the basket with slime and tar. She nursed the baby one more time so he would be full and then set the little basket adrift among the reeds along the banks of the river. Who is in the basket? Of course, it is Moses. I find this one of the greatest acts of faith ever recorded. Like Hannah, like Mary, like Elizabeth—who all would later give their sons to the Lord—this mother, Jochebed, committed her precious baby to the Lord's care.

The Lord guided the basket along the Nile currents until it was spotted by Pharaoh's daughter. She opened the lid, and the baby wept. The Egyptian royal knew immediately it was one of the Hebrew babies, and she had compassion on it. She claimed the baby to be her son. Jochebed was fetched to be a wet nurse. Now, I imagine that Moses grew up in the courts of Pharaoh learning everything a prince of Egypt should know—language for diplomacy, writing for record keeping, mathematics for city building, leadership for military campaigns, music for relaxing. All the things that would help a great man succeed on the earth. But, as yet, Moses may not have known much of faith, of revelation, of priesthood keys, or of covenants with the one true God of Abraham—all the things that would help a great man succeed beyond this life and bring others with him.

When Moses grew into his adulthood, the scriptures say "he went out unto his brethren, and looked on their burdens" (Exodus 2:11). He saw an Egyptian beating a Hebrew slave. Moses had a compassionate nature, and he defended the Hebrew, killing the Egyptian. This act meant his own death, and he fled across the desert, out of the reach of Pharaoh, to a place called Midian. He must have felt as if he had forfeited all. All his diplomatic training, city building, military campaigns, and being the right hand of Pharaoh counted for nothing now. But the Lord had something different in mind for Moses. He led him to Jethro, a priest of Midian. Moses married Jethro's daughter, and his father-in-law taught Moses many things about the true gospel. In time, Jethro, who held the Melchizedek Priesthood from Abraham's line, conferred the priesthood on Moses (see Doctrine and Covenants 84:6–16). Moses wasn't destined to be a prince of Egypt, but instead he was to be a high priest, a king of the Most High God, who is the King of Kings.

When Moses freed the children of Israel from Pharaoh and brought them through the Red Sea to Mount Sinai, the Lord commanded Moses, saying, "Thus shalt thou say to the house of Jacob, and tell the children of Israel; Ye have seen what I did unto the Egyptians, and how I bare you on eagles' wings, and brought you unto myself. Now therefore, if ye will obey my voice indeed, and keep my covenant, then ye shall be a peculiar treasure unto me above all people: for all the earth is mine: and ye shall be unto me a kingdom of priests, and an holy nation. These are the words which thou shalt speak unto the children of Israel" (Exodus 19:3–6).

And they took three days to sanctify themselves, wash their clothes, and prepare to meet the Lord in covenant (see Exodus 19:10–14).

"And the Lord came down upon mount Sinai, on the top of the mount: and the Lord called Moses up to the top of the mount; and Moses went up" (Exodus 19:20).

"And all the people saw the thunderings, and the lightnings, and the noise of the trumpet, and the mountain smoking: and when the people saw it, they removed, and stood afar off. And they said unto Moses, Speak thou with us, and we will hear: but let not God speak with us, lest we die" (Exodus 20:18–19).

"And Moses said unto the people, Fear not: for God is come to prove you, and that his fear may be before your faces, that ye sin not" (Exodus 20:20).

"And Moses came and told the people all the words of the Lord, . . . and he took the book of the covenant, and read in the audience of the people: and they said, All that the Lord hath said will we do, and be obedient" (Exodus 24:3, 7).

"And Moses took the blood, and sprinkled it on the people, and said, Behold the blood of the covenant, which the Lord hath made with you concerning all these words. Then went up Moses, and Aaron, Nadab, and Abihu, and seventy of the elders of Israel: and they saw the God of Israel: and there was under his feet as it were a paved work of a sapphire stone, and as it were the body of heaven in his clearness. . . . And the Lord said unto Moses, Come up to me into the mount, and be there: and I will give thee tables of stone, and a law, and commandments which I have written; that thou mayest teach them" (Exodus 24:8–10, 12).

Well, you know the rest of the story. The people were afraid of the Lord's voice; they did not wait on the Lord; they turned from the covenant they had made and corrupted themselves with false idols.

Moses was commanded to establish a kingdom of priests, and he brought them to the mountain, but the people didn't have the traditions of Egypt out of them yet. They were afraid of themselves and certainly afraid to get too close to God. They preferred to have Moses be their spokesman, but that isn't a kingdom of priests. They received a lesser law (see Joseph Smith Translation, Exodus 34:1–2).

I suppose that nothing scares Satan more than a kingdom of priests with a temple and a prophet, because that combination of faith in the Lord Jesus Christ and willingness to act severely curtails Satan's power on the earth. He will corrupt the kingdom if he can. He doesn't want them to be able to trust their leaders. He knows that simply sowing seeds of doubt about leaders can markedly affect the rising generation. This was the tactic with the children of Israel at Sinai, and he employs it today (see Exodus 32:1–8).

The real lesson and hope of Exodus for me is how Aaron and all the other "Aarons" gathered to Moses when he asked the nation to choose between the true God and dumb idols (see Exodus 32:26). Aaron repented of his sins. He became worthy again to be a high priest, to be washed and anointed, and clothed in the priest's robes and officiate in the tabernacle for the people (see Exodus 28:1–5; 39:1, 27–32), proving again the words Jesus spoke in a different era to the repentant Alma, "Yea, and as often as my people repent will I forgive them their trespasses against me. And ye shall also forgive one another your trespasses" (Mosiah 26:30–31).

The Old Testament has some of the most basic injunctions about showing compassion for the poor, seeking our own forgiveness and compassionately forgiving others. These continue to inspire our actions today. However, the concept of a covenant of compassion is broader than looking after disadvantaged segments of society or improving our own behavior. In its purest ideal, it is absolute fidelity to the idea that "all are alike unto God" (2 Nephi 26:33) and that He truly is "no respecter of persons" (Acts 10:34), that "he inviteth them all to come unto Him and partake of His goodness" (2 Nephi 26:33), and that we must truly treat each other as family.

The Old Testament prophets had varying success with the ideal. Enoch's city reached the pinnacle "because they were of one heart and one mind, and dwelt in righteousness; and there was no poor among them" (Moses 7:18). The semicolon in the verse suggests that it was the practical actions of becoming emotionally invested in one another, unifying themselves around collective purposes, and committing to righteousness that created the condition of "no poor among them." The covenant at its root is about unity, equity, and fidelity to God's law for givers and receivers, and it revolutionizes society. After Jesus Christ taught and blessed the Nephites, Mormon expressed the concrete results in the lives of people who live by covenant—and I am captivated by these verses. I want so badly in my own life to experience a society where there are no whoredoms: "And it came to pass that there was no contention in the land, because of the love of God which did dwell in the hearts of the people. And there were no envyings, nor strifes, nor tumults, nor whoredoms, nor lyings, nor murders, nor any manner of lasciviousness; and surely there could not be a happier people among all the people who had been created by the hand of God. There were no robbers, nor murderers, neither were there Lamanites, nor any manner of -ites; but they were in one, the children of Christ, and heirs to the kingdom of God. And how blessed were they! For the Lord did bless them in all their doings" (4 Nephi 1:15–18).

Moses's and Enoch's experiences serve as powerful archetypes for the dynamic possibility of a kingdom of priests and what we must do in the latter days to lay the foundation "upon which the Zion of God shall stand" (Doctrine and Covenants 58:7). Of course, Moses's work was not all completed at Sinai. He returned to the Mount of Transfiguration with Peter, James, and John, and again to the Kirtland Temple as part of his mission to commit the keys of the gathering of Israel in the dispensation of the fullness of times (see Doctrine and Covenants 110:11; Matthew 17).

Joseph Smith's Keys

What happened in the Kirtland Temple in 1836 is one of the most significant events in human history. The Lord Jesus Christ accepted the temple—the first temple in this dispensation dedicated to the work of the Lord in what would become hundreds of temples. And then were the successive appearances of Moses, Elias, and Elijah to commit keys to make the holy work and mission efficacious and binding. Moses committed to Joseph Smith and Oliver Cowdery the keys of the gathering of Israel. The charge for the children of Israel, whether ancient or modern, is to gather, to make and keep priesthood covenants, and to become a kingdom of priests that builds Zion.

The Relief Society was founded in Nauvoo on March 17, 1842. It was organized not simply, as some mistakenly assume, as a benevolent society for women to sew shirts for the temple workmen. When Joseph turned the key to establish the Relief Society, it was to organize them "after the pattern of the priesthood" and to make them a formal part of the Restoration.[1] The Nauvoo Relief Society Minute Book records on March 31, 1842, two weeks after its founding, that Joseph taught the sisters—and notice the themes of unity and fidelity to the commandments and the reference to Zion: "All must act in concert or nothing can be done—[he taught] that the Society should move according to the ancient Priesthood, hence there should be a select Society separate from all the evils of the world, choice, virtuou[s] and holy—[Joseph] said he was going to make of this Society a kingdom of priests a[s] in Enoch's day—as in Paul's day."[2]

Joseph Smith used similar terms earlier when speaking of the relationship of all the Saints to the temple. "This 'kingdom of priests' would comprise men and women who made temple covenants."[3] He was preparing both the sisters in Relief Society and the brethren in their quorums for the temple ordinances that would shortly be revealed in Nauvoo. But Joseph faced largely the same problem that Moses faced: how to get rid of fear and a constrained mentality and free the people to be powerful in the priesthood?

The characteristics of Enoch's Zion correspond in great harmony with the essential character of temple worship and the covenants of sacrifice, obedience, faithfulness, and consecration that would soon be administered to the Saints in Nauvoo as part of the temple endowment.

These temple covenants and the outward focus of priesthood power and service to others become the fulfillment of the Old Testament foundation of concern where covenantal priestly men and women reach out from their circles to minister to those who are spiritually and temporally without. As Joseph Smith vividly expressed it, "A man [or woman] filled with the love of God, is not content with blessing his [or her] family alone, but ranges through the world, anxious to bless the whole of the human family."[4]

Through the Prophet Joseph Smith, the priesthood keys and authority and temple ordinances necessary for the foundations of Zion were again established. Nearly two hundred years later, his successor to the keys, President Nelson, would express Jehovah's covenant of compassion in these words: "The gathering of Israel is the most important thing taking place on the earth today. Nothing else compares in magnitude, nothing else compares in importance, nothing else compares in majesty."[5]

In this dispensation, the covenant will fill the whole earth. Men and women will purify their hearts by covenant and then range through the whole world anxious to bless the whole human race and gather Israel home.

Examples

I have been referring to ancient revelations and speaking in dispensations. Let me now move to concrete examples of what this might look like in an everyday application.

There are some bedrock principles to be observed in order to lay the foundations for a unified, equitable, and peaceful society where there are no poor of any kind.

Choice

In a gospel context, we call choice agency. I have a photo of a young girl choosing a winter coat from among the bales of donated warm clothing at a distribution camp in northern Iraq. The pink fake fur isn't the most practical option, but there is a delighted expression on her face. She has made her choice, and she loves her choice. In emergencies or poverty, choices get severely restricted. People often don't get to choose what they eat, where they live, what kind of work they do, where they worship, or what they wear. Protecting the ability to choose is one of the cornerstones of the Father's plan. Any time choice and self-determination are preserved (even in small instances like with a pink coat), we protect the divine gift of agency that our Father in Heaven has given each individual. Of course, the choice to worship God or not worship, according to individual conscience, and the opportunity to freely practice faith is the most fundamental of human choices.

Dignity and Meaningful Work

Jesus told His disciples that "the labourer is worthy of his hire" (Luke 10:7). When corruption and inequality circumvent the connection between meaningful work and progress, people lose hope. A positive example of how meaningful work can give hope comes from the time when the city of Mosul was liberated from ISIS forces. Families desired to come back to the city, but it was incredibly discouraging. Militants had smashed every facility, cut every wire and pipe, booby trapped every asset. The people coming back from displacement camps had very few personal resources. A Chaldean priest whose Christian church and school had been destroyed approached Lynn and Sandy Watson, who were serving a humanitarian mission. Could they help him get school supplies to start the school again? Lynn and Sandy were long schooled in covenantal principles. They knew that families were not just facing physical poverty but a poverty of self-respect and hope that things could change. They proposed that the parents of the children build the school furniture themselves with training and support from Latter-day Saint Charities. The families were skeptical—they were middle-class accountants and dentists. What did they know about building desks? But they agreed to try. A welder worked with them to weld the metal frames together. A carpenter came to show them how to make the desktops. When the school opened, not only did the children have fine desks, but the parents stood in the back of the room absolutely beaming. They felt great pride in what they had done to provide for their children. They were not failing at their tasks—they were succeeding. If they could cooperate and learn to make furniture together, they could tackle other tasks as well. Dignity and meaningful work are great healers.

Unity

Other similar activities by their very cooperative nature create a unifying force among society. Sports and music are obvious examples. They don't function and no one can have any fun if the ground rules aren't collectively observed. I have seen men from many different regions and tribes in Africa get together on a pitch in Italy and play *futbol*. For as long as the tournament lasts, animosity and status are put aside as they cooperate as a team for a single purpose. It doesn't always happen, but when it does, it feels miraculous. It demonstrates that strife can fade and that unity can succeed. I have a friend who is a world-famous violinist, but instead of playing on every concert stage in the world, he travels to out-of-the-way places and puts musical instruments into the hands of children who have been caught in war. It helps to heal their spirits as they cooperate and build a piece of music together when there has been so much destruction in their lives. Service is another unifying activity. When Christians rebuild a destroyed mosque and Muslims refurbish the broken-down cathedral of their neighbors, it changes hearts. Doing something for the good of the community that doesn't necessarily benefit one's personal life has proven to be transformative.

Respect for the Minority

A quote from Joseph Smith sits on my desk: "If I esteem mankind to be in error, shall I bear them down? No; I will l[i]ft them up, and in their own way too if I cannot persuade them my way is better; . . . I will not seek to compel any man to believe as I do, only by the force of reasoning; for truth will cut its own way."[6]

Joseph knew that "the same principle which would trample upon the rights of the Latter day Saints would trample upon the rights of . . . any other denomination [or group] who may be unpopular and too weak to defend themselves."[7] Joseph preached civil and religious liberty for the whole human race. As untidy as it might be, the principles of unity are achieved not by fiat, but "only by persuasion, by long-suffering, by gentleness and meekness, and by love unfeigned" (Doctrine and Covenants 121:41). Minority views that respect the rights of others are not only tolerated but protected in a Zion society.

Now, let me share some stories that show the impact that can happen when covenantal men and women love God and live their lives by these principles. And note how choice, dignity and meaningful work, unity, and respect for the minority are woven through these examples.

Latter-day Saint Charities and Dr. Nemam Ghafouri

Dr. Nemam Ghafouri was born in Iraq, but her family was forced to flee Saddam Hussein's regime. She was reared in Iran and then Sweden as a refugee in the 1980s. She eventually became a cardiothoracic surgeon and, when her homeland of Kurdish Iraq fell under attack from ISIS, she returned to help her people. Right away, she came into contact with the humanitarian missionary couples from the Church of Jesus Christ of Latter-day Saints serving in northern Iraq. It was a very dynamic time with fighting erupting in many corners and displaced people streaming into safer places. Facilities often had to be set up with little warning. Dr. Nemam shuttled back and forth from her practice in Sweden to the camps in Iraq, trying to raise enough money to establish medical care for the displaced people. Much to the surprise of her colleagues and family, she could not stay away and leave the work to others. She and the Latter-day Saint Charities humanitarian couples immediately recognized in each other a selfless partner. Both knew the Yezidi people were the minority of the minority. Dr. Nemam and the humanitarian service missionaries dedicated themselves to giving critical care for displaced Yezidis, hearing their stories, and pleading their cause. Together, they organized beds and sanitation for the hospital, arranged for special clothing for the elderly of the community, and built a second bakery so children wouldn't be hit by cars trying to cross the road for bread. Those projects and many others were funded by consecrated Latter-day Saints who gave a small amount of money to the humanitarian fund. Perhaps it was included on their tithing slip, or maybe their family raised funds and made a donation. However it came, those offerings to help the poor combined with the service of dedicated missionary couples who had made sacred temple covenants became the answer to prayers.

One of my favorite statements from Dr. Nemam comes from a video where she talks about the partnership to build a bakery in the camp. You can hear her energy and commitment in the words "[Seeing the people safe and happy] is what gives me the energy and power to continue. Every day there are many, many headaches and problems, but when I see this I forget everything and I start all over again. I love people. It is my passion. To help is my passion."[8]

In March of 2021, on a trip to the Syrian border to help negotiate a reunification of children with their mothers, Dr. Nemam contracted COVID-19. She was airlifted to Sweden but did not recover.[9] This bright light—gone out at the age of fifty-two—has nevertheless lit thousands of other lights.

Provo East Stake

Many years ago in the Provo East Stake, a young woman lost her husband in an unexpected accident. She had three children and very little means to support them. The bishop offered to help her finish her education, but there were many other barriers. She was filled with grief and also despair. One day, not long after the funeral, an older woman in the stake came to her home and told her, "I don't have any money to give you, but I have time. I will come each day and watch the children while you go to school." The two women agreed on a plan, and five days a week, this good woman came each morning. She helped get the children ready for school, drove them where they needed to be, helped them with their homework, and made a hot meal for the evening—for two years. More than a babysitter, she became the wise, confident friend the family needed as they mourned the absence of their father and husband. It took enormous commitment from this sister and a suspension of her own activities, but it forever changed the lives of four other people.

Damascene Cookies

I received a letter in my office a few months ago, and it said it came with a package. I didn't see a package, so I asked the office staff. They started to laugh. The package weighed four hundred pounds. It was an entire pallet of Arabic sweets and cookies. Here is an excerpt of the letter:

> Dear Respected Latter-day Saints,
>
> We owned three sweet shops in the heart of Damascus, Syria, since 1970s. We made sweets, bread, cakes and other kinds. Our business was very successful.... We were making above average income and living very comfortably, until the civil unrest started in 2011.
>
> Like many other industries, we started losing business, and within few months we had to close all our operations, letting go all of our 50 employees, and then we shut down everything and started living on savings. As the crisis became greater, we suffered, [the] pain became worse. One of my brothers "disappeared," which we hope he's still alive. Other loved ones [were] arrested and killed.
>
> Our district was unsafe and my family had to relocate to ... Ghouta in the eastern side of Damascus. Soon ... Ghouta was under siege. Food became scarce and we were hungry during the many months.... Many children including ours became malnourished. Adults were always on the look for where the next meal is coming from. Even the richest person was not able to buy anything because there was no food.
>
> Word spread around that Rahma Relief and LDS Church [were] starting a soup kitchen nearby, and we finally were glad to be able to get real food in long time. The rations were barely enough to feed my hungry family, but that's all we had and it kept us alive. We were lucky to get daily hot food, and baby milk for the children, something many families only dream of. For more than two months in 2016, we managed to get food from Rahma—LDS kitchen. Without it we would starve to death.

We also learned the LDS Church helped many people around the country and the world with food, shelter, and medicine, and for that we are very grateful for their compassion.

After Ghouta, we were evacuated with nothing but the clothes we had. After long displacement, we managed to make our way to Turkiye, and settled in Istanbul, and decided to rebuild our lives and business from zero. In 2020, we opened [our shop] and grew rapidly. . . . Now we are operating on large scale again, serving local and international clients including [in] the USA. . . .

We wanted to thank you too for funding a project that literally saved our lives. We are sure many grateful families in many countries feel your help. Please accept this small sweet sample from my shop as a small token of thanks and appreciation. I ask God the Almighty to bless you wherever you go, and in everything you do."[10]

Sports Fans to Special Service

Twenty-five years ago, a group of young students saved their money so they could travel to watch Brigham Young University play Notre Dame in South Bend, Indiana. These young men had so much fun together that they decided to choose one BYU away game each year and travel together to watch it. The group bonded in fun and camaraderie on these yearly weekends away but, somewhere over the years as they were maturing and growing more aware of the world around them, it no longer seemed enough to simply be about sports. One of the members said, "It is sometimes hard for men to grow close as a social group in things that are holy and lasting and high minded. We were men who all held the priesthood of God and we decided we could be more outwardly focused. We were trying to be consecrated rather than indulgent. We felt an inclination to focus on others living around us rather than ourselves and we felt this was a natural outgrowth of covenant keeping."[11]

Now, they cooperate on a community service project each year. They still watch BYU football, but their focus is on higher things.

In some way, these are small examples anyone can try to follow—serving a mission, organizing a bakery, helping children, a tin of cookies, small donations, sports fans who also serve. In other ways, these are revolutionary stories about how one person or a group of people can push against negative forces and literally change society for good. The covenant of compassion is not so lofty or unattainable that it cannot be practiced every day in any situation that arises. The kingdom of priests attracts other good people, and the work expands exponentially. Small, everyday actions draw their transformative power from the grace and mercy of the great High Priest, who is Jesus Christ the Son of God. As the Apostle Paul wrote to the Hebrews, "Seeing then that we have a great high priest, that is passed into the heavens, Jesus the Son of God, let us hold fast our profession. For we have not an high priest which cannot be touched with the feeling of our infirmities; but was in all points tempted like as we are, yet without sin. Let us therefore come boldly unto the throne of grace that we may obtain mercy, and find grace to help in time of need" (Hebrews 4:14–16).

This year, as the Sperry Symposium marks fifty years of serious scholarship and insights about the gospel of Jesus Christ, I commend Brigham Young University for its vision in continuing the series. I also commend the other speakers of 2021 to you and feel confident we will each learn and grow in new personal ways as we are taught by the Spirit.

I am so personally grateful for the knowledge and understanding revealed in the modern time through the Prophet Joseph Smith that links covenants and dispensations together. This beautiful gospel helps me repent of my sins, connect with others who are also working to keep covenants, and be part of something bigger than myself. It energizes every particle in me. It bonds me more tightly to the Savior Jesus Christ because a small part of His work has become my own. Perhaps I might close with the words of John the Revelator: "And from Jesus Christ, who is the faithful witness, and the first begotten of the dead, and the prince of the kings of the earth. Unto him that loved us, and washed us from our sins in his own blood, and hath made us kings and priests unto God and his Father; to him be glory and dominion for ever and ever. Amen" (Revelation 1:5–6). In His infinite compassion, He has loved us and washed us in His own blood. May we each feel the ways in which our lives can turn outward in compassion because of Him is my heartfelt prayer.

Sharon Eubank is the first counselor in the Relief Society General Presidency and the director of Latter-day Saint Charities.

Notes

1. See Sarah Granger Kimball, "Auto-biography," *Woman's Exponent*, September 1, 1883, 51.
2. "Nauvoo Relief Society Minute Book," p. 22, March 31, 1842, The Joseph Smith Papers, https://www.josephsmithpapers.org/paper-summary/nauvoo-relief-society-minute-book/20.
3. From Joseph Smith journal, January 6, 1842, referenced in Gospel Topics Essays, "Joseph Smith's Teachings about Priesthood, Temple, and Women," ChurchofJesusChrist.org.
4. "Letter to Quorum of the Twelve, 15 December 1840," p. [2], The Joseph Smith Papers, https://www.josephsmithpapers.org/paper-summary/letter-to-quorum-of-the-twelve-15-december-1840/2.
5. Russell M. Nelson, quoted in Genelle Pugmire, "Gathering Israel: What Once Was Scattered, Must Needs Be Gathered," *Daily Herald*, March 27, 2021.
6. "History, 1838–1856, volume E-1 [1 July 1843–30 April 1844],"p. 1666, The Joseph Smith Papers, https://www.josephsmithpapers.org/paper-summary/history-1838-1856-volume-e-1-1-july-1843-30-april-1844/36.
7. "History, 1838–1856, volume E-1 [1 July 1843–30 April 1844]," The Joseph Smith Papers.
8. Nemam Ghafouri, *Serving Refugees in Kurdistan* (Latter-day Saint Charities video), https://www.facebook.com/latterdaysaintcharities/videos/703754416837307.
9. Neman Ghafouri, "Doctor Who Aided Yazidis in Iraq, Dies at 52," *New York Times*, April 4, 2021.
10. Letter to author, May 2021.
11. Gary Judd, conversation with author, May 2021.

Covenant of Concern

3

The Cry of the Widow, the Fatherless, and the Stranger
The Covenant Obligation to Help the Poor and Oppressed

David Rolph Seely and Jo Ann H. Seely

On January 14, 1847, President Brigham Young, who was at Winter Quarters organizing the Saints for the trek west, received a revelation from the Lord that would become section 136 of the Doctrine and Covenants. The revelation was entitled "The Word and Will of the Lord concerning the Camp of Israel in their journeyings to the West" and commanded the Saints to "be organized into companies, with a covenant and promise to keep all the commandments and statutes of the Lord our God." The "covenant and promise" included the commandment to care for each and every one of the Saints. In this revelation the Lord alluded to and quoted from Exodus 22, which was addressed to covenant Israel, when he commanded the Latter-day Saints to care for "the poor, the widows, the fatherless, and the families of those who have gone into the army, that the cries of the widow and the fatherless come not up into the ears of the Lord against this people" (Doctrine and Covenants 136:8). In this study we will examine the theological basis of God's concern for the poor and oppressed and the laws given for their care, and we will also examine how this concern was to be implemented by society in general and by the individual—as exemplified by Job—and how the concern for the poor expressed in the law of Moses was embodied by the Messiah.

In the Old Testament the covenant community is charged with the care of the poor and the helpless, the oppressed and the disenfranchised. When the members of the covenant community do not fulfill their obligation, the Lord hears the cry of the oppressed and responds by sending his prophets to call the people to repentance. This study will look at how this charge was central to the law of Moses and how it was an important feature of other ancient Near Eastern law codes as well.

The image of the widows and fatherless is known from the law revealed on Mount Sinai now in the book of Exodus. As part of the covenant, the Lord commanded the Israelites in no uncertain terms to care for the helpless and vulnerable among them when he declared: "Thou shalt neither vex a stranger, nor oppress him: for ye were strangers in the land of Egypt. Ye shall not afflict any widow, or fatherless child. If thou afflict them in any wise, and they cry at all unto me, I will surely hear their cry; and my wrath shall wax hot, and I will kill you with the sword; and your wives shall be widows, and your children fatherless" (Exodus 22:21–24).[1] The Lord expressed the seriousness of this covenant obligation by attaching a solemn curse to not caring for the poor, and in the law of Moses the neglect of the poor is at the level of a capital offense.

The Ideal of a Just Society in the Ancient Near East

In the ancient Near East, including in Mesopotamia, Egypt, and Israel, there was an ideal of a just society in which the rights and needs of the vulnerable and helpless were acknowledged and respected. This concept was exemplified in the various cultures by terms such as *mišarum* ("righteousness" or "justice") in Akkadian, *maʿat* ("justice") in Egyptian, and *ṣedeq* or *ṣĕdāqâ* ("righteousness" or "justice") and *mišpāṭ* ("righteousness" or "justice") in Hebrew. The ideal of a just society and the responsibility of caring for the poor and oppressed is attested in ancient Near Eastern law, royal proclamations, and other literary works.²

For example, in the third millennium BC, the Sumerian king Urukagina promises the god Ningirsu that he would not deliver the widow and orphan to the powerful (Ukg. 04 B XI 30–31)³; and Ur-Nammu (ca. 2100 BC), in the prologue of his law code, declares, "I did not deliver the orphan to the rich. I did not deliver the widow to the mighty. I did not deliver the man with but one shekel to the man with one mina (i.e. 60 shekels)" (A iv 150–161, C I 22–ii 29).⁴ Similarly, in the prologue to his famous law, the Babylonian king Hammurabi (ca. 1754 BC) proclaims his responsibility to deliver the oppressed, "to cause justice to prevail in the land, [and] to destroy the wicked and the evil, that the strong might not oppress the weak" (31–33, *ANET*³, 164).

While no ancient Egyptian law code has yet been discovered, these values are also present in various Egyptian literary texts. In the "Instruction for King Meri-ka-Re" (twenty-second century BC), a ruler instructs his successor, "Do justice whilst thou endures upon the earth. Quiet the weeper; do not oppress the widow" (*ANET*³, 415). And the Egyptian text "The Protest of the Eloquent Peasant" (twenty-first century BC) recounts the story of a peasant who was traveling on a journey to Egypt when he was beaten and robbed. In his plea for aid from the Pharaoh, the peasant addresses the royal steward as "the father of the orphan, the husband of the widow, the brother of the divorcee, and the apron to him that is motherless" (*ANET*³, 408). Likewise, while no legal code has been found at Ugarit, the values of justice are found in in the "Epic of Aqhat," in which Daniel the king is described as "judging the cause of the widow, adjudicating the case of the fatherless" (*ANET*³, 151).

In the ancient Near East and the rest of the biblical world, the ideal of a just society was based on the cosmic idea that the gods (meaning Jehovah for Israelites) embodied righteousness and justice. In the cultures that developed a state, the divine values of justice and righteousness were then given to the king, the royal court, judges, and the community. In the case of Hammurabi's law, the god Shamash is called the "judge of heaven and earth"; and by giving the divine law to Shamash, Hammurabi becomes the representative of justice to the poor. Fensham describes this model in the Babylonian law code: "The protection of the weak is regarded vertically and horizontally. The vertical protection comes from the god Shamash, which therefore falls in the religious sphere, while the horizontal protection comes from the king, the substitute of the sun-god, which thus falls in the social sphere."[5] A similar concept occurs in ancient Israel, where justice is mandated from above by Jehovah. Yet it must also be administered in large part by the covenantal society that includes the king, judges, priests, and the people themselves, all of whom are responsible to adopt and implement the Lord's values in taking care of the poor and oppressed.

The Cry of the Oppressed in the Ancient Near East and in the Bible

The image of a "cry" is a vivid and dramatic image that appeals to the senses of people who are in desperate need of help or deliverance—desperate enough to vocally cry out for aid. The image of the cry of the oppressed is also found in connection with the expressions of the ideal of a just society in the ancient Near East. For example, Ur-Nammu ends the prologue with the optimistic claim that he has "eliminated enmity, violence, and *cries for justice*. I established justice in the land" (A iv 169–70, C ii 40–51).[6] In the prologue to the laws of

Lipit-Ishtar (ca. 1930 BC), the gods An and Enlil called Lipit-Ishtar to be a "wise shepherd . . . to establish justice in the land, to eliminate *cries for justice* . . . to bring about well-being to the lands of Sumer and Akkad" (i.20–37).[7] Another interesting example is found in a letter from Mari where Nur-Sin writes to Zimri Lim (a contemporary of Hammurabi) and quotes an unnamed Mesopotamian prophet's words: "I do not demand anything from you, *when a wronged man or wo[man] cries out to you*, be there and judge their case (1.52–55)."[8] This language is similar to Psalm 72, which describes the Lord giving the king of Israel his mandate to rule in justice: "For he shall deliver the needy when he crieth; the poor also, and him that hath no helper. He shall spare the poor and needy, and shall save the souls of the needy. He shall redeem their soul from deceit and violence: and precious shall their blood be in his sight" (72:12–14).

There are many terms in the Old Testament for "crying out."[9] In fact, the phrase "to cry to the Lord" is often used to describe prayer. In terms of the cries of the poor and oppressed, there are two prominent Hebrew terms that are used interchangeably: *ṣaʿāqā* (56 uses) and *zaʿāqa* (18 uses). A few examples give us a flavor of the range of cries in the Old Testament: the blood of Abel "crieth" from the ground (Genesis 4:10); the Lord hears the "cry of Sodom and Gomorrah" (Genesis 18:20); the children of Israel "cried" in their afflictions of bondage in Egypt (Exodus 2:23; 3:7, 9; Deuteronomy 26:7; 1 Samuel 12:8); the fatherless, widows, and orphans "cry" in their afflictions (Exodus 22:23); the children of Israel "cried" to the Lord in the wilderness (Numbers 11:2); in the days of the judges, the Israelites "cried" to the Lord to deliver them from oppression (Judges 3:9); and Job 34:28 mentions the "cry" of the poor ascending to heaven.

The Poor and the Needy, the Widow, the Fatherless, and the Stranger in Ancient Israel

The disadvantaged, vulnerable, and helpless people in ancient Israel can be defined in four categories: the poor and the needy, the widows, the orphans, and the strangers. These categories serve to represent all the categories of helpless and oppressed people in society.

Throughout the Bible the "poor" and the "needy" are frequently mentioned using various terms (*'ānî*, *dal*, and *'ebyônîm*) that identify people who have little or no money, land, or possessions and thus have little power, influence, or social standing. The law of Moses defines the rights of the poor and legislates programs to help them, programs that lend money with no interest (Exodus 22:25), allow poor people to glean the fields (Leviticus 19:10; 23:22), and mandate legislation to be fair when hiring and paying the poor (Deuteronomy 24:12). The prophets viewed the neglect and oppression of the poor as a sign that Israel was not living up to the covenant. The prophets specifically accused the wealthy with taking advantage of and oppressing the poor.[10] Sometimes the poor were forced to sell themselves into bond slavery to other Israelites in order to pay off their debts (Deuteronomy 15:12–15). The laws of the Sabbatical and Jubilee[11] were designed to liberate such people from debt and oppression. Deuteronomy especially champions the cause of the poor. The Lord commands the Israelites to remember

> thy poor brother, and thou givest him nought; and he cry unto the Lord against thee, and it be a sin unto thee. Thou shalt surely give him [thy poor brother], and thine heart shall not be grieved when thou givest unto him: because that for this thing the Lord thy God shall bless thee in all thy works, and in all that thou puttest thine hand unto. For the poor shall never cease out of the land: therefore I command thee, saying, Thou shalt open thine hand wide unto thy brother, to thy poor, and to thy needy, in thy land. (Deuteronomy 15:9–11)

And Proverbs includes this sobering proverb: "Whoso stoppeth his ears at the cry of the poor, he also shall cry himself, but shall not be heard" (21:13).

A passage in Exodus 22 identifies three more categories—the widows, fatherless, and strangers—and says, "Thou shalt neither vex a stranger, nor oppress him: for ye were strangers in the land of Egypt. Ye shall not afflict any widow, or fatherless child" (22:21–22). These three groups are people who are helpless, disenfranchised, and vulnerable, and thus they have often been oppressed in societies throughout history. The pairing of the widows and the fatherless (or orphans) occurs in thirty passages in the Old Testament and is distributed throughout the Law, the Prophets, and the Writings;[12] and the trio of the widows, fatherless or orphans, and strangers occurs together in nineteen passages.[13] Let us examine each of these categories to get a sense of what each of these groups represents.

A widow (Hebrew 'almānā; 55 uses in the OT) is a woman who has lost her husband and therefore her means of economic support. Because the personal, economic, and even social well-being of women in many ancient societies was inextricably connected to their relationships with men (their husbands, brothers, or sons), this put a woman without a husband in a precarious situation. A woman's ability to own and inherit property was severely limited, so marriage and the bearing of sons was essential to her welfare and security. In terms of financial security, widowhood in the Old Testament was associated with poverty,[14] indebtedness (2 Kings 4:1), and vulnerability to exploitation.[15] In terms of her own personal life, a widow's widowhood is associated with loneliness (Lamentations 1:2), mourning (2 Samuel 14:2), and weeping (Job 27:15; Psalm 78:64). In addition, widows often suffered from social abandonment and reproach (Isaiah 54:4–5). Thus we see in this ancient culture that a negative ethical value was attributed to this category of widowhood.

The fatherless, or orphans (Hebrew, *yātôm*; 42 uses in the OT), were children who were without parents for some reason. Some scholars believe that the Hebrew term *yātôm* technically means "fatherless" and refers to children who have lost their fathers, which is the way the King James Version (KJV) translates the term.[16] Others argue that the term means "orphan"—a child who has lost both parents.[17] Regardless, the orphans are described with many of the same terms as widows are in terms of poverty, vulnerability, and helplessness.

The third category of people associated with the marginalized in ancient Israel was the *gēr*, which means "a foreigner living in Israel" (92 uses in the OT)[18] and is variously translated as "stranger," "sojourner," "resident alien," or "foreigner." A modern translation could be rendered "immigrant." Following the KJV, we will use the term *stranger* (NJPS uses *stranger*; NRSV, *resident alien*; NIV, *foreigner*). This category of people consisted of foreigners who lived in ancient Israel but did not share full membership in the covenant community. These people were also perceived as having a lower social class.[19] Because they were cut off from webs of family support, they may have had a difficult time acquiring land[20] and were thus reliant on their hosts, the Israelites, for work, sustenance, and support. However, the Lord commanded the children of Israel to give the strangers equal treatment. Deuteronomy in particular stressed the Israelite role to take care of the strangers by giving them access to gather from the fields and glean the vineyards,[21] to receive of the Israelites' tithes,[22] and to benefit from the Sabbatical year.[23] The Israelites were commanded to extend impartiality in justice to the strangers.[24] Finally, the strangers were invited to participate in the worship of the Israelites as they rested on the Sabbath.[25] The Lord impressed upon the ancient Israelites the need to find love and empathy for the strangers in their midst when he said, "You shall not oppress a stranger, for you know the feelings of the stranger, having yourselves been strangers in the land of Egypt" (Exodus 23:9 NJPS). Later, the Lord commanded children of Israel to love the strangers: "When a stranger resides with you in your land, you shall not wrong him. The stranger who resides with you shall be to you as one of your citizens; you shall love him as yourself, for you were strangers in the land of Egypt" (Leviticus 19:33–34 NJPS).

Justice and Righteousness in Caring for the Poor, the Widow, the Fatherless, and the Stranger

As noted earlier, caring for the poor and the oppressed is a central theme in the Old Testament, and there is a particular set of vocabulary the Lord uses to explain the Israelites' covenant promise to care for each other. Among the many terms that express the ideal of a just society, two of the most prominent Hebrew terms were *mišpāṭ* and *ṣedeq/ṣĕdāqâ*, "judgment" and "righteousness." The term *mišpāṭ* derives from the verb *šāpaṭ*, which means "to judge"; connotes a legal decision, judgment, or claim; and is thus translated as "judgment" in the KJV. The terms *ṣedeq* and *ṣĕdāqâ* derive from the verb *ṣĕdāqâ*, which means "to be in the right" or "to be just." These related terms can both mean "blameless," "righteous," or "justice" and are translated in the KJV as "righteousness" or "justice." The two terms *mišpāṭ* and *ṣĕdāqâ* often occur together as the hendiadys "justice and judgment" (*mišpāṭ ûṣĕdāqâ*) (Genesis 18:19; Ezekiel 45:9) or "righteousness and judgment" (*ṣĕdāqâ ûmišpāṭ*) (Psalm 33:5).

The meaning of these words can be best understood from context. Often these terms are found in contexts that denote "righteousness" or "justice" in social settings and describe caring for the poor and the vulnerable in society. For example, see Psalm 72:1–4:

> Give the king thy judgments [*mišpāṭ*], O God,
>   and thy righteousness [*ṣĕdāqâ*] unto the king's son.
> He shall judge thy people with righteousness [*ṣedek*],
>   and thy poor with judgment [*mišpāṭ*]. . . .
> He shall judge the poor of the people,
>   he shall save the children of the needy,
>   and shall break in pieces the oppressor.

The biblical teaching employing these terms in the setting of caring for the poor is often described as social justice.[26] Let us review the history of social justice in ancient Israel as recorded in the Bible.

Justice and Righteousness Are Attributes of God

Justice and righteousness are attributes of God, and the scriptures teach that the origins of these ideals are described as the foundations of creation. The Psalms describe justice and judgment as the attributes of God, attributes that prescribe the values of his creations and his children.[27] Psalm 68:5 describes God as "a father of the fatherless, and a judge of the widows." Psalm 89:11–15 says the following:

> The heavens are thine, the earth also is thine:
>> as for the world and the fulness thereof, thou hast founded them. . . .
>
> Justice [*sedeq*] and judgment [*mišpāṭ*] are the habitation of thy throne:
>> mercy and truth shall go before thy face.
>
> Blessed is the people that know the joyful sound:
>> they shall walk, O Lord, in the light of thy countenance.

The image of the Lord's children walking in his light suggests that they should adopt these divine attributes of justice and judgment. Throughout the Psalms, God promises to deliver the oppressed. For example, Psalm 103:6 says, "The Lord executeth righteousness and judgment for all that are oppressed." Psalm 146:7 says, "Which executeth judgment for the oppressed: which giveth food to the hungry. The Lord looseth the prisoners."

Justice and Judgment and the Covenant of Abraham

In conjunction with the Abrahamic covenant, Genesis recounts the story of Abraham and Sarah offering aid and hospitality to the messengers coming from the wilderness. This story of patriarchal hospitality is juxtaposed with the Lord seeking to determine the wickedness of Sodom and Gomorrah since he declared he had heard "the cry of Sodom and Gomorrah . . . because their sin is very grievous" (Genesis 18:20). From Ezekiel 16 we learn that the wickedness of Sodom and Gomorrah, in addition to their other sins, was their "pride, fulness of bread, and abundance of idleness . . . neither did she strengthen the hand of the poor and needy" (16:49).

In this story of Abraham and Sarah, the Lord commended Abraham and prescribed the patriarchal virtue of hospitality to his promised posterity in the covenant: "For I [the Lord] know him, that he will command his children and his household after him, and they shall keep the way of the Lord, to do justice [*ṣĕdāqâ*] and judgment [*mišpāṭ*]; that the Lord may bring upon Abraham that which he hath spoken of him" (Genesis 18:19). Thus Abraham and Sarah model the hospitality that is lacking in Sodom and Gomorrah when they serve the messengers who come to them. When the messengers arrive in Sodom, they find hospitality only with Abraham's nephew Lot, who offers the same hospitality to the visitors as Abraham and Sarah demonstrate (see Genesis 19:1–3).

Justice and Judgment and the Law of Moses

In the story of the Exodus, the Lord demonstrated his concern for the oppressed as he heard the Israelites' cry and delivered them from bondage: "The children of Israel sighed by reason of the bondage, and they cried, and their cry came up unto God by reason of the bondage. And God heard their groaning, and God remembered his covenant with Abraham, with Isaac, and with Jacob" (Exodus 2:23–24).[28] The Lord, through his deliverance of the Israelites from Egypt, became their king (Exodus 15:18), and at Mount Sinai he became the Lawgiver. The virtues of judgment and justice were given by commandment to the children of Israel and were to be adopted and practiced. The Lord defined himself to Israel using similar attributes: "The Lord God, merciful and gracious, longsuffering, and abundant in goodness and truth" (Exodus 34:6). Just as God is merciful, he expects his covenant people to be merciful as well.

Thus the care of the poor, vulnerable, and oppressed is at the heart of the law of Moses and was an integral part of the covenant (Exodus 22:21–14). The point of the law of Moses was to create a holy people: "Ye shall be holy: for I the LORD your God am holy" (Leviticus 19:2). Part of this holiness was to adopt the divine values of justice and righteousness. The Holiness Code in Leviticus 17–26 includes numerous injunctions to care for the poor.[29] This involves the values of justice and righteousness. For example, Leviticus 19:15 says, "Ye shall do no unrighteousness in judgment: thou shalt not respect the person of the poor, nor honour the person of the mighty: but in righteousness shalt thou judge thy neighbour."

This concern for the poor and the oppressed is an integral part of the Pentateuch and is central to all three of the law codes in the Old Testament.[30] It is also central to the message of the prophets and to the Psalms and Wisdom literature. In a legal setting the Israelites were commanded in Deuteronomy 1:17 thusly: "Ye shall not respect persons in judgment; but ye shall hear the small as well as the great; ye shall not be afraid of the face of man; for the judgment is God's: and the cause that is too hard for you, bring it unto me, and I will hear it." The children of Israel were also commanded similarly in Leviticus 19:15: "Thou shalt not respect the person of the poor, nor honour the person of the mighty." An important part of the covenant was the blessings and curses connected with the giving of the Mosaic law on Sinai.[31] As noted in Exodus 22 the curse for not taking care of the widows, orphans, and strangers was destruction. This was further emphasized by the curses in Deuteronomy 27:19: "Cursed be he that perverteth the judgment of the stranger, fatherless, and widow."

Commandments for Loving and Taking Care of the Poor in the Law of Moses

As we have noted above, the ideal of justice in caring for the poor was regularly stated in the prologues of ancient Near Eastern law codes, but there is little (if any) actual legislation that protects the poor and the oppressed in the law codes. Theologian Norbert Lohfink has observed, "There is no social legislation in the code of Hammurabi. Nor is such to be found in the laws of Ur-Nammu, nor in the laws of Lipit-Ishtar, nor in any other law collection of Mesopotamia. To be sure, some few laws in these codes make a distant approach to the topic of the problems of the poor. But they never deal directly with the poor or with their rights in society."[32]

In contrast, the legal texts in the Old Testament do provide serious and sometimes comprehensive commandments and laws to covenant Israel in order to help the poor and oppressed. From these laws we can derive spiritual and temporal principles that can help us as we seek to aid the poor in the new and everlasting covenant. Throughout the scriptures God promises to hear the cry of the oppressed and deliver them. In the case of the Exodus, God demonstrated his ability to deliver his people from bondage through the miracles of the Exodus. But most often the Lord expects his covenant people to hear the cries of the oppressed and act as instruments in his hand to deliver these people from poverty and oppression.

Here are four examples of specific laws pertaining to the poor and oppressed that the Lord revealed in the law of Moses.

1. *Sharing the harvest through gleaning.* The first example is a series of laws given in which the Israelites were taught to be generous in sharing the fruits of their crops. The law as given in Leviticus 19:9–10 says: "And when ye reap the harvest of your land, thou shalt not wholly reap the corners of thy field, neither shalt thou gather the gleanings of thy harvest. And thou shalt not glean thy vineyard, neither shalt thou gather every grape of thy vineyard; thou shalt leave them for the poor and stranger: I am the LORD your God."[33] Israelites

were commanded to leave the corners of their fields and vineyards unharvested for the gleaners. The amount of the harvest left in the fields and vineyards depended on the charity and generosity of the landowner. According to the Mishnah, at least one-sixtieth of the harvest should be left, taking into account the abundance of the harvest, the financial resources of the owner of the field, and the needs of the poor (*Pe'ah* 1.1–2). A description of this process is demonstrated in the book of Ruth, where two widows are allowed the opportunity to glean the fields for their sustenance.

The principles taught by this commandment are simple. Those who have should share with those who don't. Those who own land and plant and nurture the plants should generously share their harvest with the poor. There is a built-in requirement for the poor to take action and harvest for themselves. This is an opportunity for those who have resources to exercise their generosity. Of particular note regarding this commandment is the notice that this generosity is to be given to the poor *and* the stranger. While many ancient Near Eastern law codes express concern for the poor, which parallels Israel's concern for the poor, Israel is unique in its concern and legislation on behalf of the strangers among them.[34]

2. *Third-Year Tithe*. As part of the law of Moses the Lord commanded the ancient Israelites to give a tenth of their annual produce to the Lord.[35] Tithing was a common feature in other ancient Near Eastern cultures and was given as annual offerings to the king. In Deuteronomy, every two out of three years, the tithes were to be brought to the temple, given to the Lord, and celebrated with a feast. In the third year, the tithes were to be stored in the cities where they could be used to meet the needs of the poor and the Levites, the widows and the orphans.

In Deuteronomy 26:12–13 the Lord commanded the Israelites to give their third-year tithes to the fatherless, the widows, and the orphans: "When thou hast made an end of tithing all the tithes of thine increase the third year, which is the year of tithing, and hast given it unto the Levite, the stranger, the fatherless, and the widow, that they may eat within thy gates, and be filled; then thou shalt say before the Lord thy God, . . . I have not transgressed thy commandments."[36] The prayer prescribed in Deuteronomy 26 that accompanies the tithe beautifully illustrates the thoughtful gratitude that should accompany obedience to the commandments and sharing with the poor. In this prayer the Israelite is to say, "I have hearkened to the voice of the Lord my God, and have done according to all that thou hast commanded me. Look down from thy holy habitation, from heaven, and bless thy people Israel, and the land which thou hast given us, as thou swarest unto our fathers, a land that floweth with milk and honey" (26:14–15).

3. *Sabbatical and Jubilee.* While not specifically designated just for the poor, there is a festival in the law of Moses that delivered relief for the poor and provided liberation for those in debt. The Sabbatical—to be celebrated every seventh year—was a nationwide remission of debt, freeing of enslaved persons, and a celebration of the mercy of the Lord.[37] The Jubilee was a special Sabbatical celebrated at the end of seven times seven years—in the fiftieth year (Leviticus 25:8–13). The Israelite festival was designed to liberate enslaved Israelites from debt-servitude and liberate others from debt, and the festival was similar to a tradition well-attested in Mesopotamia where the kings, usually at the beginning of their reigns, proclaimed a remission of debt and a release of debt slaves. This ritual of remission was known as *mišarum* ("justice"), and the release of enslaved persons was known as *andurārum* ("release").[38] The purpose of this law is described as follows: "There will, however, be no one in need among you, because the Lord is sure to bless you in the land that the Lord your God is giving you as a possession to occupy, if only you will obey the Lord your God by diligently observing this entire commandment that I command you today" (Deuteronomy 15:4–5 NRSV). Israel is specifically commanded here to be generous in lending to the poor, even though the seventh year of release was approaching, lest "thy poor brother . . . cry unto the Lord against thee, and it be a sin unto thee" (15:9).

The celebration of the Jubilee was also celebrated in the times of the Restoration. In 1880, at the fiftieth year anniversary of the founding of the Church in 1830, John Taylor, as President of the Church, declared a Jubilee year in the Church. On this occasion President Taylor, in the tradition of the Israelite Jubilee year, forgave half of the outstanding debt owed by the poor to the Perpetual Emigration Fund, while those who were able to pay were still encouraged to do so. President Taylor also urged all the Saints throughout the Church to forgive the debts of those who were unable to pay, and he promised the Saints that if they would forgive the debts owed to them by others, the Lord would do the same for the Saints.[39]

Social Justice and the Monarchy

With the establishment of the monarchy in ancient Israel, the Lord gave the kings the covenantal task of caring for the poor and the oppressed. This is expressed in Psalm 72:1–2: "Give the king thy judgments, O God, and thy righteousness unto the king's son. He shall judge thy people with righteousness, and thy poor with judgment." The Old Testament describes how David's rule established "judgment [mišpāṭ] and justice [ṣĕdāqâ] unto all his people" (2 Samuel 8:15), how the Lord commissioned Solomon "to do judgment [mišpāṭ] and justice [ṣĕdāqâ]" (1 Kings 10:9), and how Ezekiel and Jeremiah called on the kings of Judah to "execute judgment [mišpāṭ] and justice [ṣĕdāqâ]" (Jeremiah 22:3; Ezekiel 45:9) and warned them of destruction if they didn't (Jeremiah 22:5). Jeremiah also saw a future Davidic king who would "execute judgment [mišpāṭ] and righteousness [ṣĕdāqâ] in the land" (Jeremiah 23:5; 33:15), similar to other Near Eastern kings.

Social Justice and the Prophets

The Bible describes how in the history of Israel, especially during the period of the monarchy, the kings and the children of Israel continually slipped into apostasy by breaking the covenant. A significant sin was the forgetting of their covenantal obligation to provide judgment and justice and to give heed to the cry of the poor. The Lord sent prophets, who based their calls to repentance on the blessings and curses of the covenant, to call the kings and the people to repentance. Prophets continually warned the ancient Israelites of impending destruction if they did not repent. Let's look at a few of their dramatic warnings.

Amos was a prophet to the northern kingdom of Israel and was a champion of justice for the poor. He described the sins of Israel, saying, "Ye who turn judgment to wormwood, and leave off righteousness in the earth" (Amos 5:7), and he prescribed that Israel should "let judgment run down as waters, and righteousness as a mighty stream" (5:24). Amos also warned of impending destruction: "For three transgressions of Israel, and for four, I will not turn away the punishment thereof; because they sold the righteous for silver, and the poor for a pair of shoes; that pant after the dust of the earth on the head of the poor, and turn aside the way of the meek" (2:6–7).

Isaiah, in his memorable allegory of the vineyard, described the Lord's condemnation of Judah with a delightful wordplay: "he looked for judgment [*mišpāṭ*], but behold oppression [*mispāḥ*]; for righteousness [*ṣĕdāqâ*], but behold a cry [*ṣəʿāqā*]" (Isaiah 5:7). In his sermon about the fast, he declared, "Is not this the fast that I have chosen? to loose the bands of wickedness, to undo the heavy burdens, and to let the oppressed go free, and that ye break every yoke? Is it not to deal thy bread to the hungry, and that thou bring the poor that are cast out to thy house?" (Isaiah 58:6–7).

Jeremiah warned the kings of his time period that "thus saith the Lord; Go down to the house of the king of Judah, and speak there this word, And say, Hear the word of the Lord, O king of Judah, that sittest upon the throne of David, thou, and thy servants, and thy people that enter in by these gates: Thus saith the Lord; Execute ye judgment and righteousness, and deliver the spoiled out of the hand of the oppressor: and do no wrong, do no violence to the stranger, the fatherless, nor the widow, neither shed innocent blood in this place" (Jeremiah 22:1–3).

Social Justice and the Individual

While the responsibility of caring for the poor was assigned to the king and his bureaucracy in the law of Moses, and while the priests and Levites were assigned to preside at the altars of sacrifice and help distribute the tithes and offerings, the responsibility of caring for the poor ultimately depends on the acts of individuals. Both the Law and the Prophets address individuals. Deuteronomy addresses the Israelites and commands them to imitate God's mercy to the poor, love the stranger, and humble themselves by circumcising their hearts: "Circumcise therefore the foreskin of your heart, and be no more stiffnecked. For the Lord your God is God of gods, and Lord of lords, a great God, a mighty, and a terrible, which regardeth not persons, nor taketh reward: He doth execute the judgment of the fatherless and widow, and loveth the stranger, in giving him food and raiment. Love ye therefore the stranger: for ye were strangers in the land of Egypt" (Deuteronomy 10:16–19).

Ezekiel 18:8 describes the "just man" as the individual who has "executed true judgment between man and man" and declares that such individuals will have life:

> But if a man be just, and do that which is lawful and right,
> And hath not eaten upon the mountains, neither hath lifted up his eyes to the idols of the house of Israel . . .
> And hath not oppressed any, but hath restored to the debtor his pledge, hath spoiled none by violence, hath given his bread to the hungry, and hath covered the naked with a garment;
> He that hath not given forth upon usury, neither hath taken any increase, that hath withdrawn his hand from iniquity, hath executed true judgment between man and man,

Hath walked in my statutes, and hath kept my judgments, to deal truly; he is just, he shall surely live, saith the Lord God." (18:5–9)

Additionally, Zechariah urges individuals to establish charity in their hearts: "Thus speaketh the Lord of hosts, saying, Execute true judgment, and shew mercy and compassions every man to his brother: And oppress not the widow, nor the fatherless, the stranger, nor the poor; and let none of you imagine evil against his brother in your hearts" (Zechariah 7:9–10). Let us now look at an individual who did adopt the divine attribute of justice in his own life in order to help the poor.

Job: A Model of Justice (*mišpāṭ*) and Righteousness (*ṣĕdāqâ*)

Job is a figure who exemplifies this call of acting with individual consciousness and goodness toward his neighbors. He is an example of compassion, mercy, and righteous living, even in the midst of great wealth and abundant blessings—sometimes a difficult feat to achieve without the refining experiences of hardships. When Job's life is thrown into chaos and he loses everything of value—including his own family and health—he is even berated by his three friends who come to call him to repentance. It is in response to their judgmental sermons that Job remained steadfast in his statement of innocence: "God forbid that I should justify you: till I die I will not remove mine integrity from me" (Job 27:5). Job then defended himself by giving a declaration that embodies the model of righteousness and justice that the law of Moses demanded:

> When the ear heard me,
>   then it blessed me;
> and when the eye saw me,
>   it gave witness to me:

> Because I delivered the poor that cried,
>> and the fatherless,
>>> and him that had none to help him.
>> The blessing of him that was ready to perish came upon me:
>>> and I caused the widow's heart to sing for joy.
>> I put on righteousness, and it clothed me:
>>> my judgment was as a robe and a diadem.
>> I was eyes to the blind,
>>> and feet was I to the lame.
>> I was a father to the poor:
>>> and the cause which I knew not I searched out.
>> And I brake the jaws of the wicked,
>>> and plucked the spoil out of his teeth.
>> Then I said, I shall die in my nest,
>>> and I shall multiply my days as the sand. (Job 29:11–18)

Job heard the "cry" of the poor and fatherless and was moved to act. He "caused the widow's heart to sing for joy" and was "a father to the poor," his actions perhaps going beyond mere relief as he made an effort to meet the desires and needs of the disenfranchised. Job even went one step further—he worked to stop some of the oppression: "The cause which I knew not I searched out" (Job 29:16). In addition to his personal acts of kindness to others, Job made an effort to effect change in his society: "I brake the jaws of the wicked, and plucked the spoil out of his teeth" (29:17). He took action on two levels: providing immediate relief to the destitute and making an effort to root out the cause of some of their hardships. Job manifests personal righteousness (ṣedek), and his judgment (mišpāṭ) was "as a robe and diadem" (29:14)—he is an exemplar in both areas.[40] Later, when Job offered a series of oaths of innocence (31:13–28), he sums up his attitude toward the less fortunate like this: "Did not he that made me in the womb make him? and did not one fashion us in the womb?" (31:15). For Job, we all come from the same place, and we are all children of one God.

The Messiah as the Embodiment of Compassion and Mercy

The law given to Moses and the words of the prophets taught the ancient Israelites that the heart of their religion was to love God and to love their neighbor (Leviticus 19:18; Deuteronomy 6:5). In practice this meant to care for those who needed it most: the weak, the poor, the oppressed, and the helpless. The children of Israel learned this through the divine compassion showed them by God's delivering them from Egyptian bondage and by his mercy that he bestowed on them to continually protect and bless them in the promised land. In addition to *righteousness* and *justice*, the Lord God of Israel is defined in the biblical record by two additional adjectives that describe his feelings toward his children: *raḥûm*, meaning "compassionate," and *ḥānnûn*, meaning "merciful" or "gracious." "The Lord! The Lord! a God *compassionate* and *gracious*, slow to anger, abounding in kindness and faithfulness" (Exodus 34:6 NJPS; emphasis added).[41] These two adjectives, *compassionate* and *gracious*, are translated almost interchangeably in the different modern translations of the Bible. God, by nature, is full of compassion and mercy and, by nature, cannot help but hear the cries of the oppressed, the needy, and the suffering. The children of Israel were commanded to behave in the same way in imitation of their God.

The great prophet Isaiah taught the Israelites that it was through these characteristics of compassion and mercy that they would recognize the Messiah: "The Spirit of the Lord God is upon me; because the Lord hath anointed me to preach good tidings unto the meek; he hath sent me to bind up the brokenhearted, to proclaim liberty to the captives, and the opening of the prison to them that are bound; to proclaim the acceptable year of the Lord" (Isaiah 61:1–2).

When Jesus read Isaiah's words to those gathered in the synagogue in Nazareth and then proclaimed, "This day is this scripture fulfilled in your ears" (Luke 4:21), the people were amazed. "And all bare him witness, and wondered at the gracious words which proceeded out of his mouth" (4:22). Although the people did not believe him, as evidenced by their desire to cast him over the brow of a hill, Jesus would demonstrate during his ministry, death, and resurrection the very fulfillment of this passage in Isaiah. Jesus preached to the meek that all may be saved through faith on his name. He bound up the brokenhearted and healed the blind, the lame, those overwhelmed by evil spirits, and those overcome by grief due to the death of a loved one. He proclaimed liberty to the captives by freeing the burdened from their sins and opening the spirit prison of those bound by lack of knowledge and ordinances. He walked among the people of Galilee, Samaria, and Judea, all the while reaching out to the poor and needy, caring for the widows and orphans, and blessing the strangers. In very deed, Jesus of Nazareth was the living embodiment of the compassion and mercy taught by the law of Moses, and he would extend this compassion and mercy to all of humankind through his Atonement.

At the end of his ministry Jesus invited us all to imitate his compassion and mercy: "For I was an hungred, and ye gave me meat: I was thirsty, and ye gave me drink: I was a stranger, and ye took me in: Naked, and ye clothed me: I was sick, and ye visited me: I was in prison, and ye came unto me. . . . Inasmuch as ye have done it unto one of the least of these my brethren, ye have done it unto me" (Matthew 25:35–36, 40). In preparation for his return we are entreated to hear the cry of the oppressed and to do as he did so that we may be ready to witness the fulfillment of the end of this passage in Isaiah: "To comfort all that mourn; to appoint unto them that mourn in Zion, to give unto them beauty for ashes, the oil of joy for mourning, the garment of praise for the spirit of heaviness; that they might be called trees of righteousness, the planting of the Lord, that he might be glorified" (Isaiah 61:2–3).

Social Justice and the Messiah

In the end time, when the Lord returns to the earth as the Messiah, he will sit on his throne founded on justice and judgment, and he will judge the world in justice and righteousness. Isaiah saw this day: "And the mean man shall be brought down, and the mighty man shall be humbled, and the eyes of the lofty shall be humbled: But the Lord of hosts shall be exalted in judgment [*bamišpāṭ*], and God that is holy shall be sanctified in righteousness [*bîṣĕdāqâ*]" (Isaiah 5:15–16). In addition, Isaiah eloquently expressed God's compassionate and merciful nature when he described what that day will be like when the Lord God "will swallow up death in victory; and the Lord God will wipe away tears from off all faces" (Isaiah 25:8) and when "the voice of weeping shall be no more heard, . . . nor the voice of crying" (Isaiah 65:19).

Until that day when Jesus Christ will establish final justice and righteousness (Ezekiel 18:5–9), we, as his covenant people, are called to become like him in compassion and mercy" (Psalm 86:15). We are entrusted to hear and respond to the cries of the poor, the widows, the orphans, and the strangers and to love them and give them succor (Deuteronomy 10:16–19). As expressed by the Lord in Doctrine and Covenants 136:8 when he commanded the Latter-day Saints to care for "the poor, the widows, the fatherless," the cause of Zion that we are building is to be "of one heart and one mind," to dwell "in righteousness," and to have "no poor among" us (Moses 7:18).

David Rolph Seely is a professor of ancient scripture at Brigham Young University.

Jo Ann H. Seely is an instructor of ancient scripture at Brigham Young University.

Notes

1. If not otherwise noted, the Old Testament scriptures are cited from the King James Version (KJV).
2. See F. Charles Fensham, "Widow, Orphan, and the Poor in Ancient Near Eastern Legal and Wisdom Literature," *Journal of Near Eastern Studies* 21, no. 2 (1962): 129–39; Philip Johannes Nel, "Social Justice as Religious Responsibility in Near Eastern Religions: Historic Ideal and Ideological Illusion," *Journal of Northwest Semitic Languages* 26, no. 2 (2000): 143–53.
3. Moshe Weinfeld, *Social Justice in Ancient Israel and in the Ancient Near East* (Jerusalem: The Magnes Press, 1995), 49.
4. Martha T. Roth, *Law Collections from Mesopotamia and Asia Minor* (Atlanta: Scholars Press, 1995), 76.
5. Fensham, "Widow, Orphan, and the Poor," 130.
6. Roth, *Law Collections*, 16.
7. Roth, *Law Collections*, 25.
8. Letter #1 in Martti Nissinen, *Prophets and Prophecy in the Ancient Near East* (Atlanta: Society of Biblical Literature, 2003), 19–20.
9. For a comprehensive study on "the cry," see Richard Nelson Boyce, *The Cry to God in the Old Testament* (Atlanta: Scholars, Press, 1988).
10. See Amos 4:1; Isaiah 3:14–15; 10:2; Ezekiel 16:49.
11. See, respectively, Exodus 23:11 and Deuteronomy 15:1–8.
12. Exodus 22:22, 24; Deuteronomy 10:18; 14:29; 16:11, 14; 24:17, 19, 20, 21; 26:12, 13; 27:19; Job 22:9; 24:3; Psalms 68:5; 94:6; 109:9; 146:9; Isaiah 1:17, 23; 9:17; 10:2; Jeremiah 7:6; 22:3; 49:11; Lamentations 5:3; Ezekiel 22:7; Zechariah 7:10; Malachi 3:5.
13. Exodus 22:21–24; Deuteronomy 10:18; 14:29; 16:11, 14; 24:17, 19, 20, 21; 26:12, 13; 27:19; Psalms 94:6; 146:9; Jeremiah 7:6; 22:3; Ezekiel 22:7; Zechariah 7:10; Malachi 3:5. All eleven occurrences in Deuteronomy include widows, orphans, and strangers; Isaiah pairs widows and orphans in Isaiah 1:17, 23; 9:17; 10:2. Jeremiah has the triad of widows, orphans, and strangers in 7:6; 22:3 and has widows and orphans in 49:11. Ezekiel 22:7, Zechariah 7:10, and Malachi 3:5 also include all three categories.
14. See Ruth 1:21; 1 Kings 17:7–12; Job 22:9.

15. See Isaiah 1:23; 10:2; Ezekiel 22:7; Malachi 3:5.
16. Lamentations 5:3 says, "We are [yǝtômîm] without a father."
17. See J. Renkema, "Does Hebrew YTWM Really Mean 'Fatherless'?," *Vetus Testamentum* 45 (1995): 119–21.
18. Several Hebrew terms have similar meanings: *gēr*, meaning "stranger" or "resident alien," probably refers to people who were living in Israel more or less permanently. The terms *zār*, *nokrî*, and *tôšāb* refer to sojourners who were foreigners living in Israel more or less temporarily.
19. See, for example, the mention of strangers in the Ten Commandments, where they are listed after the servants and cattle in Exodus 20:10, and their frequent listing together with widows and orphans.
20. See Leviticus 25:23–24.
21. See Leviticus 19:10; Deuteronomy 24:19–21.
22. See Leviticus 14:29; Deuteronomy 14:29; 26:12–13.
23. See Leviticus 25:6.
24. See Deuteronomy 1:16–17.
25. See Deuteronomy 5:14. See also Mark R. Glanville, "The *Gēr* (Stranger) in Deuteronomy: Family for the Displaced," *Journal of Biblical Literature* 137, no. 3 (2018): 599–623.
26. For a comprehensive discussion, see Weinfeld, *Social Justice in Ancient Israel*.
27. For example, see Psalms 33:5–6; 93; 96:10.
28. Compare "oppression" in Exodus 3:9; Deuteronomy 26:7.
29. Some of these injunctions are found in Leviticus 19:10, 15; 23:22; 25:25, 35.
30. The law code in Exodus 20:23–23:19 is known by scholars as the Covenant Code, the collection of laws in Leviticus is known as the Priestly or Holiness Code, and the collection of laws in Deuteronomy is known as the Deuteronomic Code.
31. See Leviticus 26 and the Plains of Moab sermon recorded in Deuteronomy 27–30.
32. Norbert Lohfink, "Poverty in the Laws of the Ancient Near East and of the Bible," *Theological Studies* 52 (1991): 34–50. See, however, Fensham, who argues that there are some laws in Mesopotamia, especially in terms

of laws of inheritance and credit-slavery that were designed to protect the vulnerable. See Fensham, "Widow, Orphan, and the Poor," 131.

33. See also Leviticus 23:22; Deuteronomy 24:19–21.
34. Jacob Milgrom, *Leviticus 17–22*, The Anchor Bible (New York: Doubleday, 2000), 1627: "Concern for the poor, the widow, and the orphan is widespread throughout the ancient Near Eastern codes and edicts. Israel, however, is unique in its solicitude for the *gēr*, the alien."
35. See Leviticus 27:30; Numbers 18:21–24; Deuteronomy 14:22–29.
36. See also Deuteronomy 14:28–29.
37. See Exodus 21:2–6; Leviticus 25:1–7; Deuteronomy 15:1–18.
38. See Weinfeld, *Social Justice*, 75–96.
39. B. H. Roberts, *Life of John Taylor* (Salt Lake City: George Q. Cannon & Sons, 1892), 333–35.
40. Timothy Keller has a wonderful discussion of Job as a model of personal *ṣĕdāqâ* ("righteousness") and suggests that if we all had this personal *ṣĕdāqâ*, it would render justice (*mišpāṭ*, which punishes offenders and cares for the victims of their unjust treatment) unnecessary. Keller, *Generous Justice* (New York: Dutton Penguin Group, 2010), 10–13.
41. See Nehemiah 9:17, 31; Psalm 86:15; Psalm 111:4; Joel 2:13.

4

Covenantal Command
Love Thy Neighbor

Kerry Muhlestein

President Russell M. Nelson taught that "the covenant that the Lord first made to Abraham and reaffirmed to Isaac and Jacob is of transcendent significance."[1] In a number of settings over a sustained period of time, President Nelson has taught that the Abrahamic covenant is particularly relevant for us in our day.[2] Yet many may be asking how they are connected to this covenant or how it is relevant to them. The Abrahamic covenant is another name for the new and everlasting covenant.[3] Members of The Church of Jesus Christ of Latter-day Saints voluntarily enter into this covenant at baptism.[4] The covenant we are part of is, in its essence, the same covenant that Abraham or Israel entered into. Yet it is important to understand that while the Abrahamic, or new and everlasting, covenant is essentially the same throughout time, the details of how it is administered and what is expected therein can and do change according to the specific circumstances and culture in which it is administered.[5] For example, the covenant as it was administered to Israel at Mount Sinai was specifically a renewal of the covenant given to Abraham, Isaac, and Jacob. Yet, as it was given there, an intricate set of laws and expectations was delineated that do not seem to have been included when God entered into the covenant with Abraham.[6] Just as policies and procedures in our day evolve, so would the laws given to the ancient Israelites likely change over time to adjust to their changing circumstances. While we could technically differentiate the details between the covenant as it was administered to Abraham and the form it took at Mount Sinai, because the covenant is essentially the same, we will refer in this paper to either of these early forms as the Abrahamic covenant for purposes of simplification.

Again, baptized members of The Church of Jesus Christ of Latter-day Saints are part of the Abrahamic covenant today. While the specific ways we fulfill our covenant obligations have changed over time, such as dietary restrictions or the kinds of sacrifices asked of us, the principles behind our covenantal obligations remain constant.[7] One of these principles is the covenantal obligation to care for those who are in need. Though the mechanisms for providing and administering care for those in need are different today than they were in the days of ancient Israel, an examination of the practices and principles behind this aspect of the Abrahamic covenant in the Old Testament can still help us understand both the covenant itself and the reasons God established such a covenant with us. Here we can do only a brief survey of the principles and practices behind caring for those in need. Each element discussed here can and should be explored in greater depth in other settings.

The Covenant Forms Relationships

Jennifer Lane writes that "making a covenant in scriptural terms can best be understood as forming a new relationship."[8] She could not be more correct. While there are many aspects to the covenant, we will find that they all hinge around forming and heightening relationships. The primary relationship at issue is our relationship with God. While the principal obligation of covenant holders is to keep the commandments, these commandments are designed to create the framework for the relationship between the parties of the covenant, or between God and his people. This arrangement is most obvious through the central and greatest commandment within the covenantal laws: "Thou shalt love the Lord thy God with all thine heart, and with all thy soul, and with all thy might" (Deuteronomy 6:5). This obligation is so critical that Moses reiterates it numerous times within his discussion of the covenant (6:10–13; 10:12; 30:6, 10, 16, 20). At the end of Moses's instructions about the covenant, he again teaches the children of Israel their primary duty. He told them that "the Lord thy God will circumcise thine heart, and the heart of thy seed, to love the Lord thy God with all thine heart, and with all thy soul, that thou mayest live" (30:6). Moses further explains that he had taught them these things about the covenant "that thou mayest love the Lord thy God, *and* that thou mayest obey his voice, and that thou mayest cleave unto him: for he is thy life, and the length of thy days: that thou mayest dwell in the land which the Lord sware unto thy fathers, to Abraham, to Isaac, and to Jacob, to give them" (30:20).

When the ancient Israelites fulfilled their part of the covenant, they naturally drew closer to God and experienced a heightened relationship with him. They also experienced a variety of other blessings and promises that were intertwined with their special relationship with Jehovah. While we cannot delve into every aspect of these promised blessings in this paper, some are particularly pertinent to our topic. For example, covenant holders who truly keep the covenant are promised that they will be a peculiar treasure, or a special people, to God (Exodus 19:5).[9] They will also be a kingdom of priests and a holy nation (19:6). While aspects of holiness vary, at its core this is a way of saying that covenant-keeping Israel will be blessed with a more godly nature, a higher state, and the heightened relationship we have been speaking of.[10] In other words, the commandments of the covenant teach God's people how to emulate him, which actions combine with

God's enabling power to make them more like God and closer to him. This is stated in the law as "ye shall be holy; for I am holy" (Leviticus 11:44).

This closer and more intimate relationship also brings about a special kind of love and mercy extended to those within that close bond. There is no good English word to capture the kind of covenantal love and mercy that the Hebrew term *ḥesed* signifies, but this concept is a key component of the covenant. Simply put, those who have bound themselves close to God will find that he will always extend to them extra opportunities to receive mercy. In other words, God will unendingly offer Israel the chance to repent and return to him.[11] Just as within a marriage, *ḥesed* is a natural outgrowth of forging a special bond with each other and then creating shared, unifying experiences while working together within that bond. God's desire to extend mercy to his people is an overarching reason for much of what he does, as well as for many of the laws discussed below in which he asks for those who receive mercy from him to extend that mercy to others.

Other pertinent covenantal blessings include the inheritance of a chosen land (Genesis 12:1, 7; 13:15; 13:17; 15:7, 16, 18; 17:8; Abraham 2:6) and the promise that God would both prosper (Leviticus 26:3–10; Deuteronomy 28:3–30; Abraham 2:9) and protect (Genesis 15:1; Leviticus 25:18; Deuteronomy 28:7–12) his people within that land. These are all expressions of how God took care of those who were in a special relationship with him. Thus they are the natural result of our loving God and serving him.

A Second Kind of Relationship

In the New Testament we read the account of Christ being asked what the greatest commandment in the law was. Since keeping the law was the primary covenantal obligation, in effect the lawyer who posed the question was asking Christ what their greatest covenantal obligation was. It should have been no surprise to his audience that Christ quoted the commandment to love God as found in Deuteronomy 6:5, as cited above. This command was regarded in Judaism as the score of the Jews' religious identity.[12] What is somewhat surprising is that Christ added the second great commandment from a passage found at the end of laws about gleaning and justice being done in Israel (Leviticus 19:18).[13] From that passage the Lord said, "The second is like unto it, Thou shalt love thy neighbor as thyself" (Matthew 22:39).[14]

This introduces a second relationship that is a focus of the covenant: our relationship with each other. The scriptures clearly teach that the Abrahamic covenant is not aimed solely at binding us to God and heightening our relationship with him but also at binding us to each other and strengthening our communal relationships.

The covenant consists partially of a distinct communal aspect. Some oft-quoted scriptures about the covenant help us to realize this on some level. For example, Alma's injunction as he baptized people at the Waters of Mormon included the obligation to mourn with those that mourn, to comfort those who stand in need of comfort, and to bear one another's burdens (Mosiah 18:8–9). Even acknowledging this element of the covenant does not fully recognize just how communal the covenant is. A careful study of the Old Testament or Book of Mormon reveals that God speaks far more about saving Israel as a whole than he does about saving Israelite individuals.[15] Moreover, a large number of the laws that were to be kept as part of the covenant had to do with governing relationships between individuals.[16] God's covenant with the Israelites contained a central focus on creating loving bonds within the covenant community. As a part of this, each person has a very clear covenant obligation to care for other covenant holders who are in need, as well as for the stranger.[17] It is this latter aspect that we will study further in this article.

Covenantal Laws for Those in Need

As was noted above, one important aspect of the covenant was that God showed *ḥesed*, or covenantal mercy, to those in a covenant relationship with him. He clearly desired that those who received *ḥesed* from him should also show it to each other.[18] The laws of the covenant provided specific ways to show this mercy. In particular, the laws involved showing compassion to those who could not fully care for themselves. This also hinged on other aspects of the covenant mentioned above—namely, the ability to own land, to prosper, and to be protected. Several categories of people were at an inherent disadvantage when it came to receiving those blessings, and these are exactly the people whom the covenant laws most fully protected. As part of keeping these covenantal promises, the law was clear—those who were able were obligated to help those in need.[19] This covenant obligation is a fitting personal expression of Jehovah's covenant with Israel. Because God was the one who blessed and delivered the children of Israel from bondage, their covenant with him demanded that they in turn bless and deliver other covenant individuals,[20] especially those who were disadvantaged in being able to partake of the covenant blessings noted above.

The protected groups mentioned most often in both the Law and the Prophets are widows and orphans. Orphans are not necessarily a child without any parents, for a child without a father was considered an orphan in terms of the law and how it affected them. Most often orphans are referred to by the term *fatherless*. These two groups needed extra protection, for they had fewer rights to land and resources and less access to other legal aspects of the society. Further, they were often less capable of using whatever resources they did have in a way that would produce prosperity. They were also less able to protect themselves.

Similarly, foreigners, or resident aliens, referred to as "strangers" in the King James Version, had no inherent rights to land. Thus they were not inherently part of the covenantal promise of land and therefore were innately at a disadvantage in terms of being able to prosper or to be protected. Such strangers, referred to as resident aliens hereafter, are mentioned almost as consistently as the widow and fatherless in the Law and Prophets. Together, these three constitute the protected groups most commonly referred to in the law.[21]

Yet another disadvantaged group is the poor. The poor are mentioned less frequently than those in other disadvantaged categories, but they are included in many passages. Not enough information is available to determine exactly what constituted someone being "poor," thus qualifying them for assistance. One group that would almost certainly have received that label would have been those who were indebted and those who had gone into servitude because they could not pay their debts. Already these individuals were not prospering, but they were also either in peril of losing their land and resources or had already lost them. Thus they were certainly at a disadvantage.

While most of Israel's neighbors also had laws regarding the care of widows and orphans, they did not have the kinds of laws that Israel had concerning the poor.[22] Other cultures certainly had various kinds of literature that spoke of the needs of the poor,[23] and the prologues of law codes might mention the poor, yet their laws were not equivalent to Israel's laws that specifically addressed caring for the poor.[24]

While a general covenantal obligation requires us to love and care for everyone, we have a very specific covenantal responsibility to care for these designated groups who were unable to care for themselves. While the mechanisms for doing so have changed over time, surely the obligation to care for those who cannot care for themselves has not changed. Studying the laws, or mechanisms, that were part of these covenantal obligations in the Old Testament era will help us not only understand the scriptures in general but also better comprehend the principles still in place today for covenant holders.

The laws of the covenant were given over several periods of time. A set of laws commonly referred to as the Covenant Code was given at Mount Sinai during the initial encounter of the ancient Israelites with God as they entered into a covenant with him there. These laws are found roughly in Exodus 20–23.[25] Leviticus contains a great many more laws that were received later—much of this is referred to as the Holiness Code.[26] Deuteronomy contains the account of Moses reviewing the covenant and reestablishing it with the next generation of Israelites. Deuteronomy also contains both clarifications of the law already given and expansions on it.[27] Thus the law of the covenant expanded over time, with later additions emended to the text. Many scholars posit great lengths of time between these periods, and there is not always agreement as to which set of laws came first.[28] Regardless of the length of time it took, clearly the law developed or was revealed in distinct stages. Still, we will examine the law as a whole, focusing on how it stands as a received text today.[29] This holistic approach will best allow us to see the perceived intent behind the covenantal obligations. As one scholar observed, "a concern for the widow, the orphan, and the poor is permanently woven into the fabric of those crucial sections dealing with the covenant," both when the law was originally given at Sinai, when it was expanded upon, and when it was reconfirmed in Deuteronomy.[30] Care for others, especially those in need, is an integral and innate part of the covenant and is reflected in many of the commandments Israel was obligated to obey within the covenant.

Laws designed to help maintain the disadvantaged

Ideally, with a few provisions being made to help and protect them, the disadvantaged would be able to maintain a sustainable and enjoyable way of living. Some laws seem to be aimed at making this possible by creating circumstances in which they or their families could care for themselves. These include the law of levirate marriage and laws related to gleaning.

Levirate marriage. In order to help those who had experienced a devastating blow that could plunge them into untenable circumstances, Israelites practiced a custom that was common throughout the Near East at the time.[31] When a woman's husband died and she did not have children to care for her, the dead husband's family took over her care (Deuteronomy 25:5–10).[32] This is commonly referred to as levirate marriage, which is based on the Latin word *levir*, or "husband's brother."[33] It receives this name because it became the obligation of the brother-in-law to become a special kind of husband for the widow. He would provide for her all that she needed and represent her in society the way her husband would have.[34] If she had no children at all, it was his responsibility to provide her with a child who could both eventually inherit her previous husband's land and take care of her.[35] If she had male children who were not yet old enough to care for her, the brother-in-law would provide for all of them until the son(s) could inherit their father's land and care for their mother. In this way all widows were, in theory, to be cared for. Of course, in practice, circumstances did not always turn out this way. Still, the idea was that land was provided or maintained for the family, as was protection and the opportunity for prosperity. Further, in this way lands did not pass out of family lines, which was important for the ability of families to maintain themselves.

Gleaning. Providing enough food for sustenance was a major concern for the disadvantaged. One of the most important ways all such people were to be cared for was by others providing them the opportunity to glean.[36] Typically, gleaning meant gathering that which had been dropped or had been overlooked in a harvest. In most societies the owner of the field could either glean it himself or hire others to do it for him. This was not the case in Israel, for the gleanings were meant to be left for those in need, especially and specifically for the resident alien, the fatherless, the widow, and the poor (Leviticus 19:10; Deuteronomy 24:19).[37] Further, the Lord commanded the Israelites to do a number of other things that would increase the gleaning opportunities for the groups God had decreed he would protect. The corners of fields were to be left unharvested so that the needy could glean them (Leviticus 19:9).[38] Any sheaves that were forgotten as they were initially gathered to threshing floors were to be left for the poor (Deuteronomy 24:19). Olive trees were not to be beaten a second time, thus leaving olives in them to be gleaned (Deuteronomy 24:20). Similarly, grape vines were not to be fully cleared of their grapes (Leviticus 19:10). The promise was that the prosperity poured out upon those who kept the covenant this way would more than make up for what they had lost in leaving these things for those in need (Deuteronomy 24:19).

Perhaps the most famous story involving gleaning is that of Ruth.[39] Ruth was not only poor but also a widow and a resident alien. Thus she fit into several protected categories. Undoubtedly there were many Israelites who did not leave gleanings as they should have, just as today there are many who do not pay tithing or a generous fast offering. Yet clearly some understood the spirit of caring for those in need, as Boaz did. He not only left the required gleanings but also invited Ruth to fall under the protection of his own servants, invited her to drink of his water and to eat with his servants, and secretly instructed his servants to drop more of the harvest than usual so that Ruth could glean all the more (Ruth 2:9–16). This is an example of how the laws were ideally kept—with full intent of heart.

Continued aid, or providing for those who had become unable to care for themselves

In many circumstances these laws would not be enough for the disadvantaged to maintain themselves. In some cases perhaps just a little more help would make the difference. In others, perhaps the disadvantaged were far from being able to care for themselves and needed significant measures to be taken in order to prevent a further slide into desperate circumstances. Other laws provided not just ways for those in need to help themselves but also opportunities to be helped regardless of what effort they put forth.

The tithe. A fundamental way to care for the needy is to provide food and goods for them.[40] Every three years all Israelites were to take a tenth of their increase and bring it to their village or city. This tithe was to be stored and administered to the stranger, the fatherless, the widow, and also the Levites, who also had no land (Deuteronomy 14:28–29).[41] This obligation was so important that all Israelites had to swear that they had fulfilled it (26:12–13). Cities typically had some storerooms near the gates where the tithes would most likely have been gathered. Presumably village elders and city governors would be those who distributed these stored goods to those in need.[42] As we will see, the Lord expresses great unhappiness when those who were charged with using these goods to care for the poor did not do so honestly and generously.

Festival offerings. The Israelites were commanded to keep a number of festivals. Three of these were fairly large and involved food or harvest in one way or another. These were the Passover, the Feast of Weeks, and the Feast of Tabernacles. Israelites were commanded both to remember that they had been in bondage in Egypt before the Lord had delivered them, and, in consequence, to also remember the Levite, the resident alien, the fatherless, and the widow during these festivals (Deuteronomy 16:1–14).[43] Those in need were to come to the festivals and were to receive the gathered food as part of the festivities.[44] The Israelites were instructed that all this was because the Lord was blessing them in their increase (16:15). For each of these festivals they should not come with empty hands; rather, "every man should give as he is able, according to the blessing of the Lord thy God which he hath given thee" (16:16–17). Yet they were not only to give, they were also to rejoice together. Festivals in general were to be a time of "rejoicing" in all that the Lord had given Israel (Leviticus 23:40; Deuteronomy 12:7). At the same time, Israelites were commanded to not rejoice just by themselves, but to "rejoice before the Lord your God, ye, and your sons, and your daughters, and your menservants, and your maidservants, and the Levite that is within your gates; forasmuch as he hath no part nor inheritance with you" (Deuteronomy 12:12, also 12:18). Regarding these three festivals, the Israelites were specifically to rejoice not only with their household, its servants and the Levites, but also with the stranger, fatherless, and widow (16:14–15). This rejoicing together as the Israelites jointly held festivals and gave to the disadvantaged brought those groups into their households and families, providing a sense of unity and belonging that was likely just as important as the food was. Thus the physical, social, and emotional needs of the disadvantaged were all addressed in these festivals. The Israelites were then told that they, and especially their leaders, should do all of this justly, "that thou mayest live, and inherit the land which the Lord thy God giveth thee" (16:20). By linking the giving of food to those in need with inheriting the land, the Lord was making it clear that this generosity was part of the covenant and that the promise of covenantal blessings hinged upon the Israelites fulfilling this covenantal obligation.[45]

Helping those who had become unsustainably indebted

Even with all these laws in place, some people reached a point, through either circumstances or poor choices, in which they not only were unable to sustain themselves, but they had also indebted themselves beyond what they could hope to repay.

Such a situation could easily occur for those in the disadvantaged groups. Of course some who were not a resident alien, fatherless, or a widow also fell upon hard times. Others regularly incurred debt that they could not pay. This situation arises easily in an agrarian-based culture, such as in ancient Israel. This is because poor farmers need a tremendous number of resources, such as seeds, in order to begin their planting cycle, and many months pass before they are able to reap their harvest and make an increase on their initial investment. Borrowing was often necessary in order to make the initial planting. Surely numerous other circumstances necessitated borrowing in order for people to get by.

Lending laws. Israelites were commanded to lend liberally and not charge interest when lending but were to lend out of a desire to help. This was in contrast to their neighboring cultures, who charged interest in the 23–50 percent range.[46] In fact, Israelites were to lend to the poor even in situations that might result in an economic loss for themselves (Deuteronomy 15:9–10).[47] The promise was that such losses would be made up for in the blessings showered out upon them for keeping their covenant (15:10).[48] This was one way in which they were to care for the poor. Further, if someone lent money to the poor and took an individual's cloak as surety of repayment, the lender had to return that cloak by nightfall lest the poor person be cold during the night. Thus the Lord made it clear that lending to the poor should not put the borrowers in dire straits, something that likely protected their dignity as much as their physical well-being. Everything was supposed to be aimed at helping the poor rather than taking advantage of their situation for profit.[49]

As nature takes its cyclical course, harvests, at times, are not as abundant as hoped. In these and various other circumstances, many Israelites found themselves unable to repay their debts. In such cases, declaring bankruptcy was not an option. Instead the indebted Israelites must do all they could to repay the debt. This repayment included selling land (which deprived them of their means for prosperity) or selling children, spouses, or themselves into something like indentured servitude.[50] These situations all created circumstances that would typically lead to a cycle of poverty. The laws of the covenant included many instructions designed to provide relief from such circumstances.

Redemption. One of the ways individuals could be saved from their indebtedness was through a redeemer (Leviticus 25:25–34). Any close kinsman could act in the role of a redeemer. The closest male relative, typically the father or oldest brother (the birthright brother) was obligated to fulfill this role if he was able to. If land had been lost from the family because of indebtedness, a family member could buy it back. If a member of the family had become a servant to meet a debt, that member could be purchased back. If a kinsman redeemer was willing to redeem that family member, the kinsman could not be refused, no matter how much the new owner desired to retain the new possession or servant. If the law of redemption were practiced perfectly, no Israelite would remain in servitude and no land and its attendant opportunity for prosperity would pass out of family hands (Leviticus 25:23, 28).

Sabbath years. Every seventh year fields were to remain fallow (Leviticus 25:1–8). No planting or harvesting was to take place. Any crops that grew spontaneously—which could happen in any field, but especially in fields with crops such as grapes or olives—could be eaten by the owners but were not to be intentionally harvested. Instead anyone was free to eat from these crops. Thus the poor were given yet another opportunity to find food.

Further, personal debt was to be forgiven during the Sabbath year. Lenders were specifically warned not to refrain from lending in the sixth year (Deuteronomy 15:9). The purpose of lending was not to make a profit but rather to help the poor. Thus lending at all times, but especially in the sixth year, was supposed to be done and was deemed an extra opportunity to help the poor.

To further the clemency, those who had become servants because of failure to pay their debts were to be set free during the Sabbath year (Deuteronomy 15:12).[51] When servants were set free, they were not just turned out of the house of their masters. If such were the case, they would still have been in a difficult economic position that may well have led to their quickly falling back into a cycle of poverty and losing their freedom once again. Instead, they were to be given food and other necessary goods in generous amounts (15:12–14).[52]

The laws of the Sabbath and Jubilee years (see below) seem to aim not only at providing relief from crushing debts, but also at creating an opportunity for those who had been in such unfortunate circumstances to start over with a chance to flourish. Indeed, it has been argued that the key principles behind the Deuteronomic laws about the poor were about restoring an opportunity to create wealth, not about redistributing it.[53]

The Lord promised great bounty to anyone who observed the Sabbath year laws (Deuteronomy 15:10, 18). Thus, when kept properly, those who forgave debt or freed servants were blessed within the covenant, and, simultaneously, servitude and debt could never be crushing in the long term, for the covenant provided relief from it.

Jubilee years. After seven sets of Sabbath years, or 49 years, the next year was a special year, called the Jubilee year. In this year, on the Day of Atonement, the trump was to be sounded and liberty to be proclaimed (Leviticus 25:9). Then all captives or servants were to be set free, including those who lived in the land but were not Israelites (25:10).[54] Further, all land that had been claimed because of failure to pay a debt was to be returned to the original owners or their descendants (25:10, 13). The exception to this rule pertained to houses within walled cities (25:30),[55] which properties were presumably not the ancestral homes of their owners.

Just as in Sabbath years, enslaved persons were to be released, apparently with generous provisions. Because the Jubilee also included the release of seized lands, if all had been done properly, these released individuals would also receive restored access to land that they could work. In other words, they were to be given a fresh start with a decent chance of setting up a life situation in which they could prosper.[56] An important parallel can be drawn here—in a way this provision was designed to allow the ancient Israelites to emulate their God, who freed them from bondage and sent them into a land flowing with milk and honey, carrying with them the treasure of their former captors.[57]

Keeping all these Jubilee laws was coupled with a specific promise. "Wherefore ye shall do my statutes, and keep my judgments, and do them; and ye shall dwell in the land in safety. And the land shall yield her fruit, and ye shall eat your fill, and dwell therein in safety" (Leviticus 25:18–19). Dwelling in the promised land (Genesis 12:1, 7; 13:15, 17; 15:7, 16, 18; 17:8; Exodus 6:8; Leviticus 18:24–30; 25:18; Deuteronomy 5:33; 6:1, 18; 30:16, 20), doing so in safety (Leviticus 26:6–8; Deuteronomy 6:19; 28:7), and having that land yield abundantly (Leviticus 25:19; 26:4–10; Deuteronomy 28:4–12; 30:9) are all specific and prominent parts of the Abrahamic covenant. Thus keeping the Jubilee laws, including those laws designed to help the disadvantaged, were highlighted as a covenantal obligation.

Failure to Keep the Law and Oppression

These measures and laws all demonstrate that God is clearly serious about fulfilling his covenant obligations to his people. In part, this is why he asks each covenant member to protect and aid other covenant members. Underlying the laws and descriptions of the covenant is the idea that God comes to the aid of those who are unable to help themselves; similar conduct is expected of those who are in a covenant relationship with him and thus have experienced or expect to experience his redeeming power in their lives (Deuteronomy 24:17).[58]

On the other hand, if covenant holders are ever guilty of oppressing those whom God has promised to protect, they will find themselves in danger of God's wrathful protective measures.[59] Within the Covenant Code, the consequences of afflicting those whom God has pledged to protect were spelled out: "Ye shall not afflict any widow, or fatherless child. If thou afflict them in any wise, and they cry at all unto me, I will surely hear their cry; and my wrath shall wax hot, and I will kill you with the sword; and your wives shall be widows, and your children fatherless" (Exodus 22:22–24). Similarly at the later ratification of the covenant recorded in Deuteronomy, the Lord said, "Cursed be he that perverteth the judgment of the stranger, fatherless, and widow" (Deuteronomy 27:19).

The laws that protect the disadvantaged presume that those responsible for upholding the laws would fulfill their obligations. For example, speaking of righteous kings acting on God's behalf, the Psalmist says, "He shall deliver the needy when he crieth; the poor also, and him that hath no helper" (Psalm 72:12). Further, the Psalmist tells us that God and the king will "judge the poor of the people, he shall save the children of the needy, and shall break in pieces the oppressor" (72:4).[60] Failure to use one's position of power to help the needy is considered oppression.

Another form of oppression occurs when those in power take advantage of those who are weak. The laws mentioned above are based on the fundamental principle that no one should exploit or take advantage of others, especially the most vulnerable members of the covenant community.[61] Using a position of power to take advantage of the poor in order to aggrandize oneself was especially egregious.

Oppression also includes the failure of any covenant member to fulfill his or her covenantal obligations to help those in need.[62] Thus failure to bring a tithe or to leave gleanings was seen as oppressing the poor. This puts such covenant breakers in great danger, for God has promised to relieve his covenant people from oppression, and this typically happens by punishing or removing the oppressor. God defends and aids his covenant keepers, and God's prophets were quick to warn those who withheld their aid that they were in danger of God's wrath.[63] The prophets consistently condemned those who oppressed the poor by any means, including by withholding their aid.[64]

For example, in Jeremiah we read that the king insisted that those in Jerusalem honor the Sabbath year and free their servants. The powerful in Jerusalem did so because they were forced to, but the next day they compelled those same individuals to return to servitude (Jeremiah 34:8–11). In response, God reminded the powerful that "setting at liberty" those captives was part of the covenant they had made with him and that they were now in breach of the covenant (34:13–16) and had put his people into subjugation. God then informed them that because they had not set his people free, he would free the sword and the famine to come upon them to scatter them (34:17). Thus God informs the people of Judah that one of the primary reasons they are to be taken captive is because they oppressed the poor by failing to help them in the way they had covenanted to.

We can see a similar sentiment when Isaiah writes about the Jubilee year, speaking of it as a time to proclaim liberty to the captive—language taken from the description of the Jubliee in Leviticus. Isaiah says this is the acceptable year of the Lord, but he says more about it than that. Isaiah says that the Lord's people should "proclaim the acceptable year of the Lord, and the day of vengeance of our God; to comfort all that mourn" (Isaiah 61:2). The juxtaposition of the

Jubilee, or acceptable, year with a day of vengeance and comforting signals that God will comfort those in need by giving them liberty, even if that liberty has to come by striking down those who should be caring for them but are not.

Principles behind the Laws

These detailed laws were all based on underlying principles, each of which is linked to the Abrahamic covenant. We must remember that the covenant is about creating relationships and that the foremost relationship is the one between God and his people. As noted, an important aspect of the relationship was that God's people must become holy just as he is holy. In other words, God wants those who are in a covenant relationship with him to become more like him.[65] As a result, we find that covenantal obligations, including our obligations to love and care for our fellow beings, are based on emulating God.[66] In particular, we are to fulfill for others the same covenantal promises God fulfills for us.

We have already noted that we are to show covenantal mercy to others, just as God shows it to us. As can be seen in the statutes cited above, under the law of Moses a covenantal obligation is the opportunity to help others maintain their ability to possess the land of their inheritance. The inheritance of the land by specific Israelite families was part of the Abrahamic covenant since it was specifically applied by Moses to the children of Israel as they entered the promised land; thus maintenance of that land within Israelite families was specifically tied up with God's desire to bless those in a covenant relationship with him.[67]

Associated with this covenantal mercy is the idea that the land has always really belonged to God and that the Israelites were merely stewards of the land (Leviticus 25:23).[68] Thus, not only were they to apportion the land as directed by God through Moses, but they were also to restore it as directed by God to those who had lost it. Furthermore, God was the bestower of life and prosperity, and thus it behooved those who were serving and emulating him to bestow opportunities for a prosperous life to others.[69] It is incumbent upon each member of the covenant community to further God's plans for saving and liberating God's people from any kind of oppressive situation they may be in, for covenant members are to be godly.[70] They are to value others in the same way that Jehovah values them.[71]

Also, because God views his people as a peculiar treasure, covenant holders should likewise regard each other in this way. Thus, all covenant holders are obliged to foster the prosperity of others. Additionally, needy groups were to be protected, along with their land and the opportunity to prosper. In each of these instances covenant holders are asked to assist God in fulfilling his promises to his people that they may become the holy nation he envisions. As covenant holders emulate God, not only do they become more holy, but that holiness deepens their relationship with him. Thus the two most important aspects of the covenant are achieved as covenant holders help one another. The reverse is also true. God continually calls covenant holders his people but also tells us that if we, as a people, are not one, we are not his (Doctrine and Covenants 38:27).

Conclusion

Loving our fellow beings and caring for them is central to God's covenant, and this centrality is expressed in Moses's summary of the covenant as found in Deuteronomy. There, Moses tells the children of Israel that by paying their tithes (and presumably also by providing opportunities for gleaning, and so forth), they had "given it unto the Levite, the stranger, the fatherless, and the widow, that they may eat within thy gates, and be filled; Then thou shalt say before the Lord thy God, I have brought away the hallowed things out of mine house, and also have given them unto the Levite, and unto the stranger, to the fatherless, and to the widow, according to all thy commandments which thou hast commanded me: I have not transgressed thy commandments, neither have I forgotten them" (Deuteronomy 26:12–13).

After this, the ancient Israelites were to note that they had not engaged in forbidden actions, such as not using for unclean purposes those things they were to dedicate to God and his people. When they could verify that they had met the requirements of the covenant law, they could request of God, "Look down from thy holy habitation, from heaven, and bless thy people Israel, and the land which thou hast given us, as thou swarest unto our fathers, a land that floweth with milk and honey" (Deuteronomy 26:12–15). The reference to God swearing to give the patriarchs a land is a clear reference to the covenant. Thus Moses was teaching the children of Israel that when they had properly cared for the needy, they could in turn claim their covenant promises from God.

As a result, Moses went on to instruct the Israelites that when they could thus "avouch," or affirm, to the Lord that they were walking in his commandments and judgments, then God would honor his part of the covenant and transform them. Moses said that God "hath avouched thee this day to be his peculiar people, as he hath promised thee, . . . to make thee high above all nations, . . . that thou mayest be an holy people unto the Lord thy God, as he hath spoken" (Deuteronomy 26:17–19). Clearly, keeping the covenantal obligation to care for others was a central component for the Israelites to be a covenant people and receive covenant blessings.

Kerry Muhlestein is a professor of ancient scripture at Brigham Young University.

Notes

1. Russell M. Nelson, "Children of the Covenant," *Ensign*, May 1995, 33.
2. See, for a few examples, Russell M. Nelson, "Remnants Gathered, Covenants Fulfilled," in *Sperry Symposium Classics: The Old Testament*, ed. Paul Y. Hoskisson (Provo, UT: Religious Studies Center, Brigham Young University; Salt Lake City: Deseret Book, 2005), 1–17; Nelson,

"The Gathering of Scattered Israel," *Ensign*, November 2006, 79–81; Nelson, "Covenants," *Ensign*, November 2011, 86–89; Nelson, "The Book of Mormon, the Gathering of Israel, and the Second Coming," *Ensign*, July 2014, 26–31; Russell M. Nelson and Wendy W. Nelson, "Hope of Israel" (Worldwide Youth Devotional, June 3, 2018); and Russell M. Nelson, "Sisters' Participation in the Gathering of Israel," *Ensign*, November 2018, 68–70.

3. See Kerry Muhlestein, Joshua M. Sears, and Avram R. Shannon, "New and Everlasting: The Relationship between Gospel Covenants in History," *Religious Educator* 21, no. 2 (2020): 21–40.
4. Muhlestein, Sears, and Shannon, "New and Everlasting," 33.
5. Muhlestein, Sears, and Shannon, "New and Everlasting," 26–27.
6. Muhlestein, Sears, and Shannon, "New and Everlasting," 24–25. See Kerry Muhlestein, *God Will Prevail. Ancient Covenants, Modern Blessings, and the Gathering of Israel* (American Fork, UT: Covenant Communications, 2021), 23, 25–29.
7. Muhlestein, Sears, and Shannon, "New and Everlasting," 25–27; Muhlestein, *God Will Prevail*, 25-28. See also Michael A. Goodman, "The Abrahamic Covenant: A Foundational Theme for the Old Testament," *Religious Educator* 4, no. 3 (2003): 43–53.
8. Jennifer C. Lane, *Finding Christ in the Covenant Path: Ancient Insights for Modern Life* (Provo, UT: Religious Studies Center, Brigham Young University; Salt Lake City: Deseret Book, 2020), 8.
9. The word *peculiar* really implies that they are precious because they belong to him and are rare. The people of Israel are a special treasure to God because they are different from all his other treasures. See Muhlestein, *God Will Prevail*, 77.
10. Muhlestein, *God Will Prevail*, 76–78.
11. Gordon R. Clark, *The Word "Hesed" in the Hebrew Bible* (Sheffield: Sheffield Academic Press, 1993); Katharine Doob Sakenfeld, *The Meaning of* Hesed *in the Hebrew Bible: A New Inquiry* (Missoula, MT: Scholars Press, 1978); and Daniel L. Belnap, "'How Excellent Is Thy Lovingkindness': The Gospel Principle of *Hesed*," in *The Gospel of Jesus Christ in the Old Testament*

(Provo, UT: Religious Studies Center, Brigham Young University; Salt Lake City: Deseret Book, 2009), 170–86.

12. Norman Lamm, *The Shema: Spirituality and Law in Judaism* (Philadelphia: The Jewish Publication Society of America, 1998), 1.

13. Christopher D. Marshall, "Christian Care for the Victims of Crime," *Stimulus* 11, no. 3 (2003): 11. Marshall characterizes this as an obscure reference; indeed it is if by that one does not expect for Christ or the lawyer to draw from laws of gleaning to find the second most important commandment in the law.

14. This is how it is reported in the Matthew account. The encounter with the lawyer who asked questions about the law is also included in Mark 12:28–31, where it is also recorded that the Savior stated what the second great commandment is. In Luke 10:25–27 the Savior has the lawyer answer his question himself, and thus in this account it is the lawyer who both states that loving God is the first commandment and adds that loving our neighbor is the second.

15. See H. G. Reventlow, *Problems of Old Testament Theology in the Twentieth Century* (Philadelphia: Fortress, 1985), 87–110; Gerald G. O'Collins, "Salvation," in *The Anchor Bible Dictionary*, ed. David Noel Freedman (New York: Doubleday, 1992), 5:907–14; and Heather Hardy, "The Double Nature of God's Saving Work: The Plan of Salvation and Salvation History," in *The Things Which My Father Saw: Approaches to Lehi's Dream and Nephi's Vision*, ed. Daniel L. Belnap, Gaye Strathearn, and Stanley A. Johnson (Provo, UT: Religious Studies Center, Brigham Young University; Salt Lake City: Deseret Book, 2011), 15–36.

16. Mary Anne Poe, "Good News for the Poor: Christian Influences on Social Welfare," in *Christianity and Social Work*, ed. Mary Anne Poe (Botsford, CT: North American Association of Christians in Social Work, 2002), 63–65.

17. This is demonstrated well by Bruce C. Birch, "Hunger, Poverty, and Biblical Religion," *Christian Century* 92 (June 1975): 593–99; it is also outlined by Bruce W. Longenecker, *Remember the Poor: Paul, Poverty, and the Greco-Roman World* (Grand Rapids, MI: Eerdmans, 2010).

18. Muhlestein, *God Will Prevail*, 66; Aaron Lockhart, "Toward a Unitive Understanding of *Hesed*" (paper available at https://www.academia.edu/40178748/Toward_a_Unitive_Understanding_of_Hesed_Mercy_Defined_and_Displayed), 9–10.
19. Poe, "Good News for the Poor," 64–66.
20. Ronald A. Simkins, "Care for the Poor and Needy: The Bible's Contribution to an Economic and Social Safety Net," *Supplement Series for the Journal of Religion and Society* 14 (2017): 10.
21. Peter J. Vogt, "Social Justice and the Vision of Deuteronomy," *Journal of the Evangelical Theological Society* 51, no. 1 (March 2008): 35–44.
22. Norbert Lohfink, "Poverty in the Laws of the Ancient Near East and of the Bible," *Theological Studies* 52, no. 1 (March 1991): 37–38. Lloyd R. Bailey, "Exodus 22:12–17 [Hebrew: 20–26]," *Union Seminary Review* 32, no. 3 (1978): 286–90, also noted this, though he urged caution since there are surely other law codes from ancient Near Eastern cultures yet to be found.
23. Richard D. Patterson, "The Widow, Orphan, and the Poor in the Old Testament and the Extra-Biblical Literature," *Biblioteca Sacra* (July 1973): 227. Patterson not only notes this but provides an example from the Ugaritic tale of Keret.
24. Simkins, "Care for the Poor and Needy," 6. See also Richard Hiers, "Biblical Social Welfare Legislation: Protected Classes and Provisions for Persons in Need," *Journal of Law and Religion* 17, nos. 1–2 (2002): 50.
25. Scholars differ slightly as to which verses are actually part of the Covenant Code, with some restricting it to Exodus 21:1–22:16.
26. Henry T. C. Sun, "Holiness Code," in Freedman, *Anchor Bible Dictionary*, 3:256.
27. Blessing O. Boloje, "Deuteronomy 15:1–11 and Its Socio-economic Blueprints for Community Living," *Harvard Theological Studies* 74, no. 1 (October 2018): 1–7, argues that Deuteronomy is the most liberal in its laws for caring for those in need.
28. See, for example, Simkins, "Care for the Poor and Needy," 7–8, who considers the Covenant Code to come first, then the Deuteronomistic reform

of the Covenant Code, and then a Priestly counterreform. See also Hiers, "Biblical Social Welfare Legislation," 58n36.

29. The issue of when various sections of the Bible were created is complicated. This includes questions about when different laws of the covenant were created, including laws having to do with caring for the poor. See, for example, Ray Brasfield Herron, "The Land, the Law, and the Poor," *Word and World* 6, no. 1 (1986): 76–84; or Robert Gnuse, "Jubilee Legislation in Leviticus: Israel's Vision of Social Reform," *Biblical Theology Bulletin* 15, no. 2 (1985): 43–44. This issue is bigger than we can examine in this context. Many would argue that key portions of the covenantal laws about the poor were created during the period of the divided kingdoms or even as late as the postexilic period. I hold to the notion that the essence of the law existed by the divided kingdom era, though some tinkering and expansion likely continued for centuries. Regardless of which portion was received at what time, it appears that at any given time the Israelites and Judahites thought of the law as a unified law and took all of it as binding (though they did not always live up to it, as no society ever does fully live up to its legal expectations).

30. Patterson, "Widow, Orphan, and the Poor," 228.

31. Millar Burrows, "The Ancient Oriental Background of Hebrew Levirate Marriage," *Bulletin of the American School of Oriental Research* 77 (February 1940): 2–3.

32. Millar Burrows, "Levirate Marriage in Israel," *Journal of Biblical Literature* 59, no. 1 (March 1940): 23–33.

33. Burrows, "Hebrew Levirate Marriage," 2–3.

34. Victor P. Hamilton, "Marriage," in Freedman, *Anchor Bible Dictionary*, 4:559–69; Michael C. Kirwen, *African Widows: An Empirical Study of the Problems of Adapting Western Christian Teachings on Marriage to the Leviratic Custom for the Care of Widows in Four Rural African Societies* (Maryknoll, NY: Orbis Books, 1979), 12.

35. G. Johannes Botterweck and Helmer Ringgren, eds., *Theological Dictionary of the Old Testament*, trans. David Green (Grand Rapids, MI: Eerdmans, 1986), s.v. "ybm; yābām; yᵉbāmâ."

36. Paula S. Hiebert, "'Whence Shall Help Come to Me?': The Biblical Widow," in *Gender and Difference in Ancient Israel*, ed. Peggy L. Day (Minneapolis: Augsburg Fortress, 1989), 134–37.
37. Herron, "Land, the Law, and the Poor," 78–80. While we cannot say for certain that other societies did not have similar laws, we have no record of such laws elsewhere, and since we have extensive lists of laws for other societies, this seems to be unique to Israel.
38. David L. Baker, "To Glean or Not to Glean . . . ," *Expository Times* 117, no. 10 (2006): 406–10.
39. Kerry Muhlestein, "Ruth, Redemption, and Covenant," in *The Gospel of Jesus Christ in the Old Testament*, ed. Jared W. Ludlow, Kerry Muhlestein, and D. Kelly Ogden (Provo, UT: Religious Studies Center, Brigham Young University; Salt Lake City: Deseret Book, 2009), 189–208.
40. Eugene Borowitz, *Exploring Jewish Ethics: Papers on Covenant Responsibility* (Detroit: Wayne State University Press, 1990), 74, notes that this is how Old Testament peoples put into practice the command to help one another.
41. Herron, "Land, the Law, and the Poor," 78–81; Hiers, "Biblical Social Welfare Legislation," 71–72.
42. This aspect of the law was clearly designed to work just as well in a small village as in a highly centralized city. See Lohfink, "Poverty in the Laws," 40.
43. See also Bailey, "Exodus 22:12–17," 286–87.
44. Hiers, "Biblical Social Welfare Legislation," 69–70.
45. On inheriting promised land as language that indicates invoking the covenant, see Kerry Muhlestein "Recognizing the Everlasting Covenant in the Scriptures," *Religious Educator* 21, no. 2 (2020): 43, 52, 54–55.
46. Bailey, "Exodus 22:12–17," 287–89.
47. See Deuteronomy 15:9, for example. See also Lohfink, "Poverty in the Laws," 45–50.
48. Joel S. Kaminsky, "'The Might of My Own Hand Has Gotten Me This Wealth': Reflections on Wealth and Poverty in the Hebrew Bible and Today," *Interpretation: A Journal of Bible and Theology* 73, no. 1 (2019): 11.
49. Boloje, "Deuteronomy 15:1–11," 3–5.

50. David L. Baker, *Tight Fists or Open Hands? Wealth and Poverty in Old Testament Law* (Grand Rapids, MI: Eerdmans, 2009), 139–40, 279–85. Also Boloje, "Deuteronomy 15:1–11," 2–4.
51. Baker, *Tight Fists or Open Hands?*, 23.
52. Gnuse, "Jubilee Legislation in Leviticus," 44. The Deuteronomic command to send them forth with liberal gifts differs from the command found in Exodus 21:7–11 to send a released bondsman or woman forth with what he had brought.
53. John Bolt, "Christian Obligations: 'The Poor You Will Always Have with You,'" *Journal of Markets and Morality* 7, no. 2 (Fall 2004): 568–69.
54. Herron, "Land, the Law, and the Poor," 83–84. It is not completely clear that this applies to "strangers," or non-Israelites. Leviticus 25:10 says that liberty is proclaimed throughout the entire country, and *every* man is returned to his family, which strongly suggests it applies to all residents regardless of whether they are Israelite or not. At the same time, Leviticus 25:35–37 speaks specifically of strangers and sojourners, but only says to lend to them and avoid charging them usury. This could be taken as the only stipulation made for foreigners, but the earlier reference of setting *every* man free seems to say that even foreigners are covered under the Jubilee.
55. Herron, "Land, the Law, and the Poor," 82–84.
56. Nolan P. Bolt, "Toward an Ethical Understanding of Amos," *Review and Expositor* 63, no. 4 (1966): 405–8.
57. Gnuse, "Jubilee Legislation in Leviticus," 43–44.
58. Patterson, "Widow, Orphan, and the Poor," 233.
59. See Birch, "Hunger, Poverty, and Biblical Religion," 595–97.
60. Walter Houston, "The King's Preferential Option for the Poor: Rhetoric, Ideology and Ethics in Psalm 72," *Biblical Interpretation* 7, no. 4 (October 1999): 341–67. See also Eben H. Scheffler, "Pleading Poverty (or Identifying with the Poor for Selfish Reasons): On the Ideology of Psalm 109," *Old Testament Essays* 24, no. 1 (2011): 192–207. The law itself does not account for the presence of a king but rather speaks of leaders and people in general. The Psalms seem to take into account the law and apply it to the king.

61. Paul B. Rasor, "Biblical Roots of Modern Consumer Credit Law," *Journal of Law and Religion* 10, no. 1 (1993–94): 157, 167.
62. Boloje, "Deuteronomy 15:1–11," 5–7.
63. Poe, "Good News for the Poor," 63–67. Moshe Weinfeld, *Social Justice in Ancient Israel and in the Ancient Near East* (Jerusalem: Magnes, 1995), 35–36, has demonstrated that the frequently employed terms *judgment* and *righteous judgment*, when used by the prophets and Psalms, refers to taking care of the needy, not to executing juridical proceedings.
64. Nolan P. Howington, "Toward an Ethical Understanding of Amos," *Review and Expositor* 63, no. 4 (1966): 405–12.
65. Muhlestein, *God Will Prevail*, 78.
66. Liz Theoharis, "The Poor We Have with Us: A Deeper Look at Jesus' Words on Poverty," *Christian Century* 134, no. 9 (April 26, 2017): 26–29, notes that such emulation of God within the covenant bridged the gap between helping the poor and worshipping God.
67. Herron, "Land, the Law, and the Poor," 79.
68. Boloje, "Deuteronomy 15:1–11," 5–7.
69. H. Eberhard von Waldow, "Social Responsibility and Social Structure in Early Israel," *Catholic Biblical Quarterly* 32, no. 2 (1970): 187–89.
70. Birch, "Hunger, Poverty, and Biblical Religion," 597–99.
71. Hiers, "Biblical Social Welfare Legislation," 60.

5

"Behold These Thy Brethren!"
Deeply Seeing All of Our Brothers and Sisters

Joshua M. Sears

In October 2019, columnist David Brooks addressed the student body at Brigham Young University and identified one of the world's great challenges:

> Somehow we have entered an age of bad generalizations. We don't see each other well. "Liberals believe *that*." "Evangelicals believe *that*." "Latter-day Saints believe *that*." All groups, all stereotypes, all bad generalizations—we do not see the heart and soul of each person, only a bunch of bad labels. To me, this is the core problem that our democratic character is faced with. Many of our society's great problems flow from people not feeling seen and known: Blacks feeling that their daily experience is not understood by whites. Rural people not feeling seen by coastal elites. Depressed young people not feeling understood by anyone. People across the political divides getting angry with one another and feeling incomprehension.

Employees feeling invisible at work. Husbands and wives living in broken marriages, realizing that the person who should know them best actually has no clue. . . .

When you think about it, there is one skill at the center of any healthy family, company, classroom, community, university, or nation: the ability to see someone else deeply, to know another person profoundly, and to make them feel heard and understood.[1]

The ability to see other people "deeply" is desperately needed in our society, and Brooks's suggestions are very helpful.[2] However, the challenge of truly understanding and appreciating others is not new, and we can find additional insights in the holy scriptures. The story of Enoch in the Pearl of Great Price offers a powerful example of a righteous individual who was tutored by God to deeply see other people and thus was able to experience God's own compassion and empathy. A careful reading of this narrative suggests that Enoch began his ministry with an inclusive mandate to reach out to all people but that over time he excluded groups of people from his ministry. Below, I will begin by recounting God's gentle rebuke of Enoch's limited perspective and then review the history that helps explain how Enoch came to that point. I will then examine God's two attempts to help Enoch more deeply see those people for whom he had stopped showing concern. Enoch's spiritual journey to recognize and correct the blind spots in his love has much to teach us as we seek to recognize and correct our own.[3]

God Gently Rebukes Enoch

Enoch's story is unfortunately limited to just four verses in the Old Testament (see Genesis 5:21–24), but a greatly expanded account was revealed to the Prophet Joseph Smith and appears in Moses 6:21–7:69.[4] By way of overview, Enoch received the Spirit of God (Moses 6:26), heard a voice command him to preach repentance to the people

(6:27–30), became a seer (6:31–36), taught the people (6:37–47), and spoke of the Fall of Adam and Eve and the redemption available through Jesus Christ (6:48–68). He saw and spoke with the Lord (7:4), prophesied (7:7), and was commanded to baptize the repentant (7:10–11). His faith was so great that when enemies came to fight against the people of God, "[Enoch] spake the word of the Lord, and the earth trembled, and the mountains fled" (7:13). Enoch "built a city that was called the City of Holiness, even Zion," a place whose inhabitants "were of one heart and one mind, and dwelt in righteousness; and there was no poor among them" (7:18–19).

At that point, Enoch has another conversation with the Lord in which Enoch declares, "Surely Zion shall dwell in safety forever!" (Moses 7:20).[5] And surely everything that has happened to the people of Zion has been wonderful, miraculous. Zion is now the jewel of the earth, the very model of an ideal society. However, the narrative clause introducing the Lord's reply begins with the word *but*, indicating that the Lord will somehow critique what Enoch just said.[6] "But the Lord said unto Enoch: Zion have I blessed, but the residue of the people have I cursed" (7:20). God agrees with Enoch's assessment of Zion. *But*, God then adds by way of "gentle rebuke"[7] that the residue of the people are not so fortunate.

Webster's 1828 Dictionary defines *residue* as "that which remains after a part is taken, separated, removed or designated."[8] What does *residue* mean in this context? In the next verse, Enoch sees "all the inhabitants of the earth" and observes that "Zion, in process of time, [would be] taken up into heaven" (Moses 7:21). Then, "the residue of the people" is specifically defined as "the sons of Adam" (7:22).[9] Given Zion's departure, the "residue" refers to all descendants of Adam and Eve who remain after the righteous city of Zion is taken up into heaven. Enoch's declaration had focused on Zion's blessed status without mentioning all the other people, an omission that the Lord draws attention to.

But why direct Enoch's attention to those outside of Zion? I believe it has to do with the way Enoch's preaching had transformed over his prophetic ministry. Over the course of Moses 6 and 7, we observe that there has been a gradual narrowing of the kinds of people that Enoch has been serving.

Enoch's Narrowing Audience

Enoch had been raised in the land of Cainan, a "land of righteousness" (Moses 6:41) named after his great-grandfather (6:17). Enoch and all his ancestors back to Seth (6:10–22) were "preachers of righteousness" and "called upon all men, everywhere, to repent; and [they taught] faith . . . unto [all] the children of men" (6:23). Enoch had been called to leave his homeland of Cainan to preach repentance to other people, who for "many generations" had "gone astray . . . and [had] not kept the commandments" (6:27–28).[10] Given the righteousness ascribed to Seth's line (6:23, 41), this people who had been living in wickedness for generations likely included the descendants of Cain.[11] Whatever the ancestry of Enoch's wicked audience, the Lord had reinforced the universal nature of the "decree" Enoch was to share by declaring that it would "be sent forth in the world, unto the ends thereof" (6:30). At that early point in his prophetic career, Enoch had drawn attention to their common ancestor, "our father Adam" (6:51), and had pointed out to his wicked audience that "ye are my brethren" (6:43).

Later, however, Enoch's preaching began to narrow in scope. First, the Lord had showed Enoch a vision and instructed him to prophesy of what would happen in coming generations (Moses 7:2–4). Enoch had seen two peoples, the people of Shum and the people of Canaan, and prophesied that the people of Canaan would completely destroy the people of Shum.[12] Their land would become "barren and unfruitful, and none other people [would] dwell there . . . ; for behold, the Lord shall curse the land with much heat" (7:7–8). Enoch then saw that "there [would be] a blackness [that would come] upon all the children of Canaan, that they were despised among all people" (7:8).[13] Following this vision and prophecy, the narrative reports that Enoch excluded the people of Canaan from his preaching, not even calling them to repent (7:12). As Jeffrey Bradshaw and David Larsen point out, "The restricted scope of Enoch's ministry outlined here is in contrast to the universal extent of the teachings of the 'preachers of righteousness' [Moses 6:23] that preceded him."[14]

Second, the Lord had then showed Enoch several lands—Sharon, Enoch, Omner, Heni, Shem, Haner, and Hanannihah—and had commanded him to preach repentance and baptize (Moses 7:9–11). Enoch called upon "all [these] people," excepting those of Canaan, as already noted (7:12). In Moses 7:13, the converts that Enoch had gained are identified as a new group known as "the people of God" (7:13, 14, 19; called "his [God's] people" in verses 16–18), and later designated "Zion" (7:18–21, 23, 27, 31, 47, 53, 68–69).[15] The narrative at this point describes a series of contrasts between the people of God and other people, particularly the "enemies" of God's people who "came to battle against them" (7:13). Among "all nations" that were not part of the people of God, there was "fear," "a curse," and "wars and bloodshed" (7:13–17). At the conclusion of its report of such sharp contrasts, the narrative then informs us that Enoch "continued his preaching in righteousness unto the people of God" and that he "built a city that was called the City of Holiness" (7:19). The implication seems to be that Enoch at some point stopped preaching to all peoples and instead focused his preaching and society-building efforts on the converts he already had.[16] This interpretation is strengthened by the parallel language at two key points in the narrative: following the report in Moses 7:12 that "Enoch *continued*" to preach to all people (except those of Canaan), Moses 7:19 reports that "Enoch *continued*" to preach to the people of God (and apparently only them).

Thus we see that over the course of Enoch's ministry, he had in stages gone from preaching to all people, to preaching to all people but the people of Canaan, to preaching to only the righteous people of God. It is difficult to determine what motivated this narrowing of his audience. While the text does not preclude the possibility that Enoch was following God's express instructions, it is worth noting that neither does the text ever credit God with these changes. Tellingly, *every* statement that is attributed to God himself regarding the scope of the gospel message stresses the universality of that message:

- "[My] decree ... shall be sent forth in the world, unto the *ends* thereof" (Moses 6:30).
- "God hath made known ... that *all men* must repent" (Moses 6:50).
- "*All men, everywhere*, must repent" (Moses 6:57).
- "I give unto you a commandment, to teach these things *freely*" (Moses 6:58).
- "This is the plan of salvation unto *all men*" (Moses 6:62).
- "And thus may *all* become my sons" (Moses 6:68).[17]

This pattern makes it all the more striking that after his vision in Moses 7:6–8, Enoch, according to the narrative, "continued to call upon *all* the people, *save* it were the people of Canaan, to repent" (Moses 7:12; emphasis added). Although the Lord had cursed the *land* of the people of Canaan—not by any means a unique action in the Book of Moses (compare 5:25, 56; 7:10, 15; 8:4)—no explicit recorded instructions deny its people the opportunity to repent. Similarly, the narrative records no instructions from the Lord that Enoch was to stop preaching widely and instead focus solely on building up Zion.

God's First Attempt to Help Enoch Deeply See the Residue

And that brings us once again to Enoch's confident words to the Lord, "Surely Zion shall dwell in safety forever!," followed by the Lord's rebuttal, "Zion have I blessed, but the residue of the people have I cursed" (Moses 7:20). In response to Enoch's narrow focus, the Lord then literally expands Enoch's vision by showing him "all the inhabitants of the earth.... And Enoch also beheld the residue of the people which were the sons of Adam; . . . and lo, all the nations of the earth were before him; and there came generation upon generation" (7:21–24).

This panoramic perspective quickly turns dark: "And behold, the power of Satan was upon all the face of the earth. And he saw angels descending out of heaven; and he heard a loud voice saying: Wo, wo be unto the inhabitants of the earth. And he beheld Satan; and he had a great chain in his hand, and it[18] veiled the whole face of the earth with darkness; and he looked up and laughed, and his angels rejoiced" (Moses 7:24–26).

What is Enoch's response to this horrific scene of evil and darkness? As far as the text records—nothing. The residue of the people are living and dying on an earth shrouded in darkness while the devil laughs over them, but Enoch has apparently not internalized whatever God has been trying to show him. God, however, does react: "And it came to pass that the God of heaven looked upon the residue of the people, and he wept" (Moses 7:28).[19]

But not Enoch. After all he's seen, the message does not seem to have sunk in. As he saw generations wasting away in iniquity and despair, did he think they deserved it? Was he resentful of their violent actions against the people of Zion? Had he decided not to concern himself with their problems, as long as his own people "dwel[t] in safety forever"? We cannot know exactly what was in his mind, but it's telling that when Enoch sees God weeping, Enoch reacts with surprise.

"How is it that the heavens weep, and shed forth their tears as the rain upon the mountains?" Enoch asks, perplexed.

> How is it that *thou* canst weep, seeing thou art holy, and from all eternity to all eternity? And were it possible that man could number the particles of the earth, yea, millions of earths like this, it would not be a beginning to the number of thy creations; and thy curtains are stretched out still; . . . and also thou art just; thou art merciful and kind forever; and thou

hast taken Zion to thine own bosom, from all thy creations, from all eternity to all eternity; and naught but peace, justice, and truth is the habitation of thy throne; and *mercy* shall go before thy face and have no end. (Moses 7:28–31; emphasis added)

Enoch seems to assume that divine beings should be immune to such sadness.[20] He points to God's eternal nature and his vast creations—shouldn't those please him? Enoch draws attention to the fact that God is the perfect embodiment of all that is merciful, kind, peaceful, just, truthful, and enduring—shouldn't he then be satisfied? He even points out that God has the righteous Saints in Zion—shouldn't the presence of these wonderful people bring God enough joy? In all his reasoning, however, Enoch fails to even mention the residue and the awful conditions in which they live. It seems not to have occurred to him that there is a connection.[21] Utterly confused, Enoch repeats his query, "How is it thou canst weep?" (Moses 7:31).

God's response begins with four words. Together they are a command, a rebuke, and a sermon: *"Behold these thy brethren!"* (Moses 7:32).[22] Webster's 1828 dictionary defines *behold* as "to fix the eyes upon; to see with attention; to observe with care."[23] God's command is to look, to *really* look—or to use David Brooks's phrase, to "deeply see." Enoch's attention had been selective, but now he is commanded to widen his perspective to include everyone else.

The Lord's identification of the residue as Enoch's "brethren"—we would say "brothers and sisters" today—is crucial. Early in his prophetic career Enoch had told the wicked that they were "[his] brethren" (Moses 6:43), and he had stressed their common link to "[their] father Adam" (6:51). Had Enoch lost sight of that? His relationship with other people had certainly become more complicated since that early preaching. The people of Canaan were guilty of great violence and had become "despised among all people" (7:8). Some among those who did not convert and join Enoch's "people of God" came out "to battle against them" as "enemies" (7:13). "There were wars and bloodshed among them" (7:16), in contrast to Zion, where there was peace (7:17). If Enoch experienced a hardening toward those people guilty of such great crimes, including attempts to destroy his beloved converts, we could hardly blame him—such a reaction is only too human.

But the Lord needed Enoch to be better than human.

"*Behold these thy brethren!*" the Lord commands (Moses 7:32). His thunderous reply sweeps aside all the other possible labels for these non-Zionists—such as "people of [X]" (7:6–7, 12), "enemies" (7:13–14), "nations" (7:13, 17, 23), "residue" (7:20, 22, 28), or "inhabitants" (7:9, 21, 25). Emphasizing the point, "brethren" is repeated twice more in the verses that follow. The Lord's use of a familial term, used long before by Enoch himself, can be read as a reminder, redirecting Enoch back to the inclusive approach that had been the hallmark of his ancestors (compare 6:23). The people out there are full of violence and wickedness, yes, and they have even come up to battle the people of God, *but* they are still Enoch's brothers and sisters and deserving of his attention, and they should still have a claim upon his heart—just as they do upon God's, as demonstrated by the divine tears that fall "as the rain upon the mountains" (7:28).

"And unto thy brethren," the Lord continues, "have I said, and also given commandment, that they should love one another, and that they should choose me, their Father." Then he explains in palpable agony, "But behold, they are without affection, and they hate their own blood" (Moses 7:33). The Lord continues to lament the "great wickedness" of Enoch's "brethren" (7:36), but in highlighting their lack of "affection" and their "hate"—the only specific crimes they are charged with—can we not also detect a subtle rebuke against Enoch? "I have commanded my children to love one another," the Lord seems to say, "so why aren't *you* loving as fully as you should? How can you complacently point to the peace, prosperity, and righteousness of your own people and not react to the violence, the poverty, and the wickedness of everyone else? *They* may be without affection, but *you* shouldn't be."

God himself abhors the great wickedness of the residue and is rightfully moved to "indignation," "hot displeasure," and "fierce anger." He must act against such depravity, so he promises to "send in the floods upon them" (Moses 7:34). And yet, despite the necessity of stopping such terrible sin and suffering, God takes no pleasure in the "misery [that] shall be their doom" (7:37).[24] "Wherefore," he concludes, responding to Enoch's earlier question, "should *not* the heavens weep, seeing these shall suffer?" (7:37; emphasis added). To underscore the point, the Lord repeats that inasmuch as Enoch's brothers and sisters must experience "torment" (7:39), the heavens will weep over them, but not just the heavens: "and [also] *all* the workmanship of mine hands" (7:40; emphasis added). That surely includes Enoch, who ought to have been weeping as well.

God's Second Attempt to Help Enoch Deeply See the Residue

With that stirring explanation, the Lord once again begins to educate Enoch, showing him a vision of "[all] the children of men" (Moses 7:41) and essentially restarting the process that Enoch had already experienced back in Moses 7:21–26. But this time, Enoch saw these things differently. This time, "Enoch *knew*" (7:41; emphasis added). This time, Enoch "looked upon their wickedness, and their misery"—that is, not *just* their wickedness, but *also* their misery, in contrast to his earlier focus.

The effect of this empathy was profound. No longer puzzled by tears, Enoch himself "wept,"[25] and he "stretched forth his arms, and his heart swelled wide as eternity; and his bowels yearned; and all eternity shook" (Moses 7:41).[26] His capacity to *feel* for others had truly become godlike.[27] It had taken the Lord two visions and a series of explanations, but Enoch now deeply saw his enemies for who they really were—his siblings, people of such worth in the eyes of God that the heavens themselves wept over them. That understanding, coupled with the divine empathy that came with it, changed Enoch forever.

A Path for Us to Follow

Enoch's journey toward divine compassion for all people is immediately relevant to us. Fiona and Terryl Givens recognize the implications of his experience:

> What transpires . . . to the prophet may be the only—it is surely the most vivid—example given in scripture of what the actual process of acquiring the divine nature requires. . . . His experience of the love that is indiscriminate in its reach and vulnerable in its consequences takes him to the heart of the divine nature. This is the mystery of godliness that Enoch does not just see, but now lives for himself.
>
> Enoch's encounter with God, his vicarious experience of infinite love, serves as a template for the path to heaven he—and all of us—hope to follow.[28]

Enoch's story has much to teach us as we follow his same path. Enoch was reminded of the inclusive mandate he had initially received to reach out to "all men, everywhere" (Moses 6:23). We have observed that over time Enoch's attention narrowed, both by excluding certain peoples and by focusing only on his fellow Saints in Zion. We cannot know for certain what motivated these shifts in his preaching, but regardless of whether the Lord directed the shifts, he still wanted Enoch to come to the point where he loved and sorrowed over even the wicked who had rejected him. The Lord's repeated affirmation to Enoch that the residue of the people were "thy brethren" was not new information, but a reminder that Enoch had once identified with them as "my brethren" (7:32–33, 36; compare 6:43).

The latter-day restoration of the gospel through the Prophet Joseph Smith similarly burst upon the world with an expansive vision of all people, everywhere, as children of God.[29] New scripture described an inclusive God that "denieth none that come unto him, black and white, bond and free, male and female . . . , both Jew and Gentile" (2 Nephi 26:33). "I the Lord am willing to make these things known unto all flesh," God declared, "for I am no respecter of persons" (Doctrine and Covenants 1:34–35). This gospel was to "be free unto all of whatsoever nation, kindred, tongue, or people they may be" (Doctrine and Covenants 10:51). Even in the next life, the opportunity for salvation was revealed to be so widely available that it scandalized many who first heard of it (see Doctrine and Covenants 76).[30] In 2020 the First Presidency and Quorum of the Twelve Apostles issued a proclamation that opened by affirming this expansive vision: "We solemnly proclaim that God loves His children in every nation of the world."[31]

Despite the inclusivity built into the DNA of the Restoration, we Latter-day Saints have not always lived up to the ideals set forth in our own scriptures.[32] Like Enoch, there have been times when, despite our inclusive mandate, our vision has been selective or obscured.[33] Some, at times, have adopted cultural perceptions of racial superiority or inferiority.[34] Some, at times, have restricted opportunities for women.[35] Some, at times, have demeaned those of other faiths or downplayed the beauty and truth in their religious experiences.[36] Some, at times, have given up on "the world" and its inexhaustible problems, preferring to concentrate exclusively on helping those inside the Church.[37] As the Restoration enters its third century, we can take stock, individually and collectively, to see if there are people the Lord would have us deeply see better than we do now. As with Enoch, this does not require radical redirection as much as a return to our roots.

Although we, like Enoch, must "behold" our brothers and sisters outside of Zion with the same love and concern we would extend to those inside, we face an additional challenge that he may not have had. In Enoch's day, the people of God filled a city, but today the people of our Zion community are spread across the globe, with different languages, cultures, political persuasions, and life experiences. While Enoch only had to learn to see and love those outside his community, we may have to work just as hard to truly see and love those inside our own wards.

As the Church's membership has become increasingly diverse, modern prophets have increasingly stressed the need for us to come together in unity. January 2021 saw the debut of a new *Liahona* magazine, redesigned specifically for all Latter-day Saints to use regardless of their country or language. Whatever our differences, the First Presidency declared that "we are united in our efforts to follow the Savior and rejoice in knowing that we are all children of God."[38] Later in that issue, the new *Liahona* affirmed:

> Creating belonging is an essential part of our journey to become like the Savior. . . . God's love for His children is not exclusive, but rather all-inclusive. . . . He knows and cherishes:
>
> - The sister, recently divorced, who hurts during discussions about marriage.
> - The young adult struggling with questions, pleading for answers.
> - The sister suffering from anxiety, feeling deep loneliness and fear.
> - The young black brother, uncomfortable as his class discusses incorrect understandings about race and priesthood.
> - The sister who has not yet married and feels it means she has no value.
> - The mother of a child with disabilities, worried that his involuntary movements are distracting to others.
> - The brother with same-sex attraction, contemplating leaving the Church as he struggles to understand his future.
> - The sister who worries how she'll be judged by others as she takes her first tentative steps back to church.
>
> No circumstance, no situation, no individual is forgotten.[39]

If the Lord "knows and cherishes" those among us who are divorced, questioning, mentally ill, Black, single, disabled, gay, less active, or in whatever other circumstances, then surely Enoch's experience suggests that we must do so also.[40] Unity is not achieved by excluding those who are different, but rather by including them.[41] "These [are] thy brethren [and sisters]," the Lord reminds us, "they are the workmanship of mine own hands. . . . Love one another" (Moses 7:32–33).

Whether we are seeking to love those outside the Church or inside, Enoch's story also demonstrates that we need God's help. Enoch could not have come to the point where he could sincerely weep for his enemies had God not granted him that capacity as a spiritual gift—and even for Enoch, it took multiple sessions of divine tutoring to get there! But all of us can "pray unto the Father with all the energy of heart, that [we] may be filled with this love" (Moroni 7:48). This is the only way to build Zion and shine its light to build a better world for all. "We need God's help," Elder Gerrit W. Gong taught, "to create lasting justice, equality, fairness, and peace in our homes and communities. Our truest, deepest, most authentic narrative, place, and belonging come when we feel God's redeeming love."[42]

Finally, Enoch's story demonstrates that seeing others deeply can be deeply painful, while also showing us how to overcome that pain. When Enoch saw the terrible fate that would fall upon the wicked, "he had bitterness of soul, and wept over his brethren" (Moses 7:44). It had been easier to ignore the residue and focus on the happiness of Zion, but once Enoch fully confronted the extent of human suffering, he declared to God in agony, "I will *refuse* to be comforted!" (7:44).[43] For how could he ever again even want to be happy when so many others must suffer so much? I know I have felt that way—and so has everyone confronted with empathetic pain. Sometimes it seems that loving deeply and loving widely comes at the price of shared sorrow without end.

But God, who himself is full of empathy, has a different perspective and a reason for hope. "But the Lord said unto Enoch: Lift up your heart, and be glad; and look. And it came to pass that Enoch looked" (Moses 7:44–45). Enoch saw what we should all fix our gaze upon with an eye of faith: "the day of the coming of the Son of Man, even in the flesh. . . . And he looked and beheld the Son of Man lifted up on the cross, after the manner of men; and he heard a loud voice; and the heavens were veiled; and all the creations of God mourned; and the earth groaned; and the rocks were rent; [but then] the saints arose, and were crowned at the right hand of the Son of Man, with crowns of glory; and as many of the spirits as were in prison came forth, and stood on the right hand of God" (7:47, 55–57).

Jesus and the cross. Atonement and Resurrection. Triumph and glory. Release and relief and reunions. And Enoch, who did not feel that he could be comforted, who did not even *want* to feel comforted, now "rejoiced," exclaiming, "The Righteous is lifted up, and the Lamb is slain from the foundation of the world; and through faith I am in the bosom of the Father, and behold, Zion is with me" (Moses 7:47). The Lord responded, "I am Messiah, the King of Zion, the Rock of Heaven, which is broad as eternity; whoso cometh in at the gate and climbeth up by me shall never fall; wherefore, blessed are they of whom I have spoken, for they shall come forth with songs of everlasting joy" (7:53).

David Brooks suggests that "we all have to get a little better at . . . seeing each other deeply and being deeply seen."[44] Ultimately, Jesus Christ helps us do both. He makes it possible for us to understand, appreciate, and love all people more deeply, and he provides comfort and hope when love leads to sorrow. In the days of Enoch, "God received [Zion] up into his own bosom" (Moses 7:69), and as we await the prophesied return of Enoch's city, we can continue to build Zion among ourselves by seeing all our brothers and sisters, all over the world, more deeply—until we are of one heart and one mind and dwell in righteousness, with no poor among us.

Joshua M. Sears is an assistant professor of ancient scripture at Brigham Young University.

Notes

1. David Brooks, "Finding the Road to Character" (Brigham Young University forum address, October 22, 2019), www.speeches.byu.edu. I have added emphases and quotation marks to help clarify Brooks's meaning.
2. A year after Brooks's address, his words were quoted in Michelle D. Craig, "Eyes to See," *Ensign*, November 2020, 16.
3. Enoch's story is most often invoked for what it tells us about the nature of God. See Eugene England, "The Weeping God of Mormonism," *Dialogue: A Journal of Mormon Thought* 35, no. 1 (2002): 63–80; Daniel C. Peterson, "On the Motif of the Weeping God in Moses 7," in *Reason, Revelation, and Faith: Essays in Honor of Truman G. Madsen*, ed. Donald W. Parry, Daniel C. Peterson, and Stephen D. Ricks (Provo, UT: Foundation for Ancient Research and Mormon Studies, 2002), 285–317; Jeffrey R. Holland, "The Grandeur of God," *Ensign*, November 2003, 70–73; and Terryl Givens and Fiona Givens, *The God Who Weeps: How Mormonism Makes Sense of Life* (Salt Lake City: Ensign Peak, 2012). I will instead take a less common approach of reading Enoch's story to track what it says about Enoch himself. For previous analyses that foreground Enoch's perspective, see Daniel Belnap, "'Ye Shall Have Joy in Me': The Olive Tree, the Lord, and His Servants," *Religious Educator* 7, no. 1 (2006): 43–44; and Jeffrey M. Bradshaw, Jacob Rennaker, and David J. Larsen, "Revisiting the Forgotten Voices of Weeping in Moses 7: A Comparison with Ancient Texts," *Interpreter: A Journal of Latter-day Saint Faith and Scholarship* 2 (2012): 41–71.
4. The Book of Moses comes from Joseph Smith's new translation of the Bible and is the equivalent of the Joseph Smith Translation (JST) of Genesis 1:1–6:13. Our earliest source for Joseph Smith's dictation of this part of the JST is a manuscript known as Old Testament Manuscript 1, abbreviated OT1. John Whitmer later copied all of OT1 onto a second manuscript, known today as Old Testament Manuscript 2, or OT2. Transcriptions of OT1 and OT2 were published in Scott H. Faulring, Kent P. Jackson, and Robert J. Matthews, eds., *Joseph Smith's New Translation of the Bible: Original Manuscripts* (Provo, UT: Religious Studies Center, Brigham Young University, 2004), 75–152 and 583–851, respectively. Images of the

manuscript pages themselves are available at https://www.josephsmith papers.org/paper-summary/old-testament-revision-1 and https://www .josephsmithpapers.org/paper-summary/old-testament-revision-2.

OT2 became the working manuscript that Joseph and his scribes worked from as they continued to make refinements to the text. However, because of a variety of historical circumstances, the version that was used for the Pearl of Great Price drew upon OT1, which means that some of the revisions intended by the Prophet and his scribes are not reflected there. See Kent P. Jackson, "How We Got the Book of Moses," in *By Study and by Faith: Selections from the* Religious Educator, ed. Richard Neitzel Holzapfel and Kent P. Jackson (Provo, UT: Religious Studies Center, Brigham Young University, 2009), 136–47. I will quote from the canonical text used in the Pearl of Great Price, but in the notes I will occasionally draw attention to important alternate readings reflected in OT2.

5. I have added an exclamation point to express the confident sentiment I read in Enoch's words.

6. OT1 reads "but," which continues through the 2013 edition of the Pearl of Great Price, but in OT2 that "but" is replaced with "and" (in Sidney Rigdon's handwriting). See Kent P. Jackson, *The Book of Moses and the Joseph Smith Translation Manuscripts* (Provo, UT: Religious Studies Center, Brigham Young University, 2005), 121, https://rsc.byu.edu/book /book-moses-joseph-smith-translation-manuscripts. The Lord's statement is still a critique without the narrator's "but," given that the Lord's statement itself contains its own "but," even in OT2.

7. Jeffrey M. Bradshaw and David J. Larsen, *In God's Image and Likeness 2: Enoch, Noah, and the Tower of Babel* (Orem, UT: The Interpreter Foundation; Salt Lake City: Eborn Books, 2014), 105, 137.

8. See http://webstersdictionary1828.com/Dictionary/residue.

9. Moses 7:22 goes on to break down "the sons of Adam" into two categories. First is "a mixture of all the seed of Adam save it was the seed of Cain," and second is "the seed of Cain" themselves, which the text reports "were black, and had not place among them," meaning the general mixture of Adam and Eve's descendants. Unfortunately, "the text does not clarify what ['black'] means." Kent P. Jackson, "Cain," in *Pearl of Great Price Reference*

Companion, ed. Dennis L. Largey (Salt Lake City: Deseret Book, 2017), 84. The description of Cain's descendants as "black" has often been understood as a physical trait (skin pigmentation), but some scholars have suggested that other meanings are possible, given that colors are often used symbolically to describe nonphysical qualities. See Bradshaw and Larsen, *In God's Image and Likeness 2*, 139.

10. That Enoch's preaching occurred at a distance from his homeland in Cainan is suggested by the fact that Mahijah is unfamiliar with Enoch and demands to know where he comes from (Moses 6:40–41). See Bradshaw and Larsen, *In God's Image and Likeness 2*, 69.

11. Bradshaw and Larsen, *In God's Image and Likeness 2*, 57. On p. 67, Bradshaw and Larsen reinforce this identification by pairing the reference to "tents" among Enoch's audience (Moses 6:38) with the reference to "tents" among Cain's descendants (Moses 5:45).

12. Neither the people of Shum nor the people of Canaan are known outside the Pearl of Great Price. The people of Canaan described in Moses 7 are not the descendants of Cain, despite the similarities of the names in English (see Bradshaw and Larsen, *In God's Image and Likeness 2*, 130). Likewise, there is no apparent link between the people of Canaan described in Moses 7 and the Old Testament Canaanites—the ones among whom Abraham sojourned and whom the children of Israel conquered; see Kent P. Jackson, "Canaan, people of," in *Pearl of Great Price Reference Companion*, 85; and Bradshaw and Larsen, *In God's Image and Likeness 2*, 130–31, 139. They do, however, appear to be the same "Canaanites" mentioned in Abraham 1:21–22.

13. As punctuated in the current (2013) edition of the Pearl of Great Price, the words "there was a blackness . . . all people" (Moses 7:8) read as a continuation of Enoch's prophecy, which begins with the words "Behold the people of Canaan" (Moses 7:7). However, because the items of the prophecy otherwise are described in the future tense, in contrast to these clauses in the past tense ("there was," "they were"), I think it is better to understand the words of the prophecy as concluding with "go forth forever" (Moses 7:8) and then the remaining words as a return to Enoch's narration of what he observed in his vision. This understanding is reflected in the revised

punctuation found in Jackson, *Book of Moses*, 164. Separating observation from prophecy affects the meaning of the text: whereas Enoch's prophecy indicates that *the Lord* will "curse the land" of the people of Canaan, the "blackness" that "came upon all the children of Canaan" is reported in the passive voice, as is the fact that "they were despised among all people." "The text does not state whether that [the Lord's cursing of the land] was the cause" of the blackness or despising (Jackson, "Canaan," 85), but it is significant that, grammatically, the Lord is not depicted as actively producing those conditions. At the same time, the idea that the Lord was the agent cannot be ruled out since scripture sometimes uses the passive voice (the "divine passive") to indicate God's influence on nature, people, or events.

14. Bradshaw and Larsen, *In God's Image and Likeness* 2, 133.
15. Earlier in the narrative, in the days of Enoch's great-great-grandfather Enos, the righteous who lived in the land of Cainan are also designated "the people of God" (Moses 6:17). The text does not make clear whether there is any connection between the groups described in Moses 6:17 and Moses 7:13.
16. See Bradshaw and Larsen, *In God's Image and Likeness* 2, 105, 137.
17. The emphasis in each of these verses has been added.
18. OT1 reads "it," suggesting the chain veiled the earth, but OT2 changes this to "he," suggesting the antecedent is Satan himself. See Jackson, *Book of Moses*, 123.
19. This is the reading from OT1 (https://www.josephsmithpapers.org/paper-summary/old-testament-revision-1/18). When OT2 was first copied it read just like OT1, but a subsequent revision in Sidney Rigdon's handwriting crossed out some of the words and inserted new ones (https://www.josephsmithpapers.org/paper-summary/old-testament-revision-2/26). The revised text reads, "Enock looked upon the residue of the people & wept." It then deletes the next line indicating that "Enoch bore record of it," since there is no need to bear record of his own weeping.

    Some scholars believe that Enoch's weeping, as described in OT2, should be considered the definitive reading. See Jackson, *Book of Moses*, 166; and Colby Townsend, "Returning to the Sources: Integrating Textual Criticism in the Study of Early Mormon Texts and History,"

Intermountain West Journal of Religious Studies 10, no. 1 (2019): 77–79. Others, however, have argued that this revision cannot be definitively traced to Joseph Smith, and that it disrupts certain literary features and narrative elements that are smoother in the original version in which God weeps. See Jeffrey M. Bradshaw and Ryan Dahle, "Textual Criticism and the Book of Moses: A Response to Colby Townsend's 'Returning to the Sources,' Part 1 of 2," *Interpreter: A Journal of Latter-day Saint Faith and Scholarship* 40 (2020): 99–162.

Given that the purpose of my study is homiletic, I will follow the canonical reading based on OT1. The question of whether Enoch wept in Moses 7:28 certainly impacts my reading, but even if one prefers OT2, it is not fatal to my presentation of Enoch's character arc. OT1 indicates that Enoch did not weep in verse 28 and does weep in verse 41. In contrast, OT2 indicates that Enoch already wept in verse 28, but we can still see a change in Enoch's weeping by the time he arrives at verse 41. There, not only does Enoch weep, but he also "stretched forth his arms. And he beheld eternity, and his bowls yearned, and all eternity shook" (as worded in OT2, and as punctuated in Jackson, *Book of Moses*, 167). This would still represent significant character development, as Enoch's capacity for compassion appears to have grown to divine capacity through the vision he has experienced.

20. "Enoch does not ask, *why* do you weep, but rather, *how are your tears even possible*, 'seeing thou art holy, and from all eternity to all eternity?'" Givens and Givens, *God Who Weeps*, 24–25.
21. "Enoch has ignored [the residue]. . . . Up to this point, Enoch's only concern has been Zion." Belnap, "'Ye Shall Have Joy in Me,'" 44.
22. I have added the exclamation point to highlight what I interpret as the imperative nature of God's statement. The italics are also added.
23. See http://webstersdictionary1828.com/Dictionary/behold.
24. "It is not their wickedness, but their 'misery,' not their disobedience, but their 'suffering,' that elicits the God of Heaven's tears. . . . In the vision of Enoch, we find ourselves drawn to a God who prevents all the pain He can, assumes all the suffering He can, and weeps over the misery He can neither prevent nor assume." Givens and Givens, *God Who Weeps*, 25.

25. As noted earlier, emendations to OT2 describe Enoch already weeping back in Moses 7:28. However, Bradshaw and Dahle, who argue that the original OT1 readings are often superior to the later emendations, observe that in OT2 "Enoch weeps prematurely, thus defusing the deliberate forestalling of the dramatic moment of Enoch's sympathetic resonance with the heavens until *after* the conclusion of God's poignant speech." Bradshaw and Dahle, "Textual Criticism," 119.
26. This follows OT1 and the reading in the current Pearl of Great Price. OT2 emends the text to say, "[he] stretched forth his arms. And he beheld eternity, and his bowels yearned, and all eternity shook." Jackson, *Book of Moses*, 128, 167.
27. Belnap observes, "By witnessing God's lament, Enoch came to understand the true nature of his stewardship, which in turn allowed him to become even more like God and progress into something greater" ("'Ye Shall Have Joy in Me,'" 44). Similarly, England writes, "Enoch here sees into God's heart, changes his concept of God, and, very significantly, is moved to new compassion himself" ("Weeping God of Mormonism," 64).
28. Givens and Givens, *God Who Weeps*, 105.
29. This is not to say, of course, that the values of inclusion and respect for all people are not part of faith traditions outside of the Restoration. "[God] has inspired not only people of the Bible and the Book of Mormon but other people as well to carry out His purposes through all cultures and parts of the world. God inspires not only Latter-day Saints but also founders, teachers, philosophers, and reformers of other Christian and non-Christian religions." Dieter F. Uchtdorf, "The Church in a Cross-Cultural World," in *Global Mormonism in the 21st Century*, ed. Reid L. Neilson (Provo, UT: Religious Studies Center, Brigham Young University, 2008), 298–99. But while Restoration scriptures did not invent these aspirations, it is striking how forcefully they declare them and how insistently they call upon people to act on them.
30. See Matthew McBride, "The Vision: D&C 76," in *Revelations in Context: The Stories behind the Sections of the Doctrine and Covenants*, ed. Matthew McBride and James Goldberg (Salt Lake City: The Church of Jesus Christ of Latter-day Saints, 2016), 148–54.

31. "The Restoration of the Fulness of the Gospel of Jesus Christ: A Bicentennial Proclamation to the World," April 5, 2020, https://www.churchofjesuschrist.org/study/scriptures/the-restoration-of-the-fulness-of-the-gospel-of-jesus-christ/a-bicentennial-proclamation-to-the-world.
32. "To be perfectly frank, there have been times when members or leaders in the Church have simply made mistakes. There may have been things said or done that were not in harmony with our values, principles, or doctrine." Dieter F. Uchtdorf, "Come, Join with Us," *Ensign*, November 2013, 22.
33. See M. Russell Ballard, "Doctrine of Inclusion," *Ensign*, November 2001, 35–38.
34. See "Race and the Priesthood," Gospel Topics Essays, https://www.churchofjesuschrist.org/study/manual/gospel-topics-essays/race-and-the-priesthood; and *Saints*, vol. 2, *No Unhallowed Hand, 1846–1893* (Salt Lake City: The Church of Jesus Christ of Latter-day Saints, 2020), 69–72, 181–82, 588–91.
35. See Neylan McBaine and Thomas A. Wayment, "Discussing Difficult Topics: The Representation of Women in Today's Church," *Religious Educator* 17, no. 2 (2016): 106–17.
36. See Mauro Properzi, "Learning about Other Religions: False Obstacles and Rich Opportunities," *Religious Educator* 16, no. 1 (2015): 129–49; and Patrick Q. Mason, *Restoration: God's Call to the 21st-Century World* (Meridian, ID: Faith Matters, 2020), 39–54.
37. See Mason, *Restoration*, 1–9, 73–90.
38. "A New Publication for a Worldwide Church," *Liahona*, January 2021, 3.
39. Tracy Browning, "Including Everyone," *Liahona*, January 2021, 32–33.
40. "Without diluting the doctrine or compromising the standards of the gospel, we must open our hearts wider, reach out farther, and love more fully. By so doing, we can create more space for love, testimony, mourning, and agency. . . . Whether [their] different realities mean [other people] look, act, feel, or experience life differently than we do, the unchanging fact is that they are children of loving Heavenly Parents and that the same Jesus suffered and died for them and for us." Eric D. Huntsman, "Hard Sayings and Safe Spaces: Making Room for Struggle as Well as Faith" (Brigham Young University devotional, August 7, 2018), www.speeches.byu.edu.

41. "The Lord expects us to teach that inclusion is a positive means toward unity and that exclusion leads to division." Gary E. Stevenson, "Hearts Knit Together," *Liahona*, May 2021.
42. Gerrit W. Gong, "All Nations, Kindreds, and Tongues," *Ensign*, November 2020, 40.
43. Emphasis and exclamation point added.
44. Brooks, "Finding the Road to Character."

Women

6

Recognizing Responsibility and Standing with Victims
Studying Women of the Old Testament

Amy Easton-Flake

Some stories in the Old Testament are difficult to read because of the violence and terrors they portray. Existing in stark contrast to the many powerful Old Testament stories of God's devotion to and saving of humankind, it is easy to understand why they have traditionally been neglected. However, as Frances Taylor Gench, professor of biblical interpretation at Union Presbyterian Seminary, reminds us, "Biblical texts . . . do not exist to make us comfortable. They exist to make us think, to be engaged by God, and to effect our transformation."[1] Many of these troublesome texts—of which a significant number involve the lives of women—are well poised to do just that. The issues they raise of power, violence, abuse, complicity, and subjugation are all too relevant in today's society, and the reflection they provoke may aid us as we work toward individual and societal change. Fortunately, for the past forty years, biblical scholars who apply a feminist hermeneutic (a method or theory of interpretation that places women at the center of the study of biblical texts) have taken a special interest in studying these traumatic stories to reveal what they say about women, their situation, and their relevancy for today's readers. And what many of these scholars have uncovered is impressive. These readings and feminist hermeneutics, however, remain outside most individuals' understanding of the scriptures. To illustrate the value of reading with the women of the Bible, I highlight three stories that, when studied through a feminist lens, reinforce the continued relevancy of the Old Testament for confronting modern challenges, particularly the challenges of violence, abuse, and the exploitation of those who are marginalized and disadvantaged. A close study of the biblical narrative makes it clear that God does not condone these actions but rather desires us to recognize our responsibility to fight injustices and to stand with victims.

Since some may be wary of the term *feminism*, I begin with a brief overview of what is meant by a feminist hermeneutic and what it has contributed to our study of the Bible. After that, I turn my attention to the story of Hagar and Sarah to illustrate how to read deliberately with the female figures in the story and to share what new lessons we may find in the text when we choose to do so. I next analyze the story of Tamar's rape to disclose the power that exists in these horrifying texts, their applicability to today, and some ways in which teaching such stories may create a needed, biblically sanctioned space to discuss abuse openly within Church settings. I end with the account of women defying the Pharaoh in the book of Exodus to provide dynamic examples of how individuals can work toward ending oppression, abuse, and other social injustices.

Feminist Hermeneutic

What is feminism? Feminism has a long history that is outside the purview of this chapter, and no single definition would satisfy all those who identify as feminist. Most, however, could support the explanation of Katharine Doob Sakenfeld, professor of Old Testament literature and exegesis emerita at Princeton Theological Seminary: "A feminist, broadly speaking, is one who seeks justice and equality for all people and who is especially concerned for the fate of women—all women—in the midst of all people. Such a definition means that issues pertinent to racism, classism, and ecology, as well as peace-making, are parts of the purview of feminism."[2]

Sakenfeld's explanation of feminism fits well within the concept of feminism recently endorsed by the Church in an official statement in the January 2020 *New Era*. "Feminism can mean different things to different people. Sometimes it refers to efforts to ensure basic human rights and basic fairness for women, as well as efforts to encourage women to obtain an education, develop their talents, and serve humankind in any field they choose. Latter-day Saints support these things." The Church does not support, however, "certain philosophies and social movements bearing the feminism label [that] advocate extreme ideas that are not in harmony with the teachings of the gospel."[3]

Feminism, as the Church's statement recognizes, is a complicated label because it has frequently been used to describe positions of many different movements and groups. Proponents of first-wave feminism, second-wave feminism, third-wave feminism, postfeminism, and fourth-wave feminism have advocated for various rights and opportunities that they believed would improve women's position in the world. As members of the Church, we may readily support many of their objectives, but some we may not. Similarly, biblical scholarship produced through a feminist hermeneutic, like all biblical scholarship, is a mixed bag. Some scholarship will help us understand the scriptures, the individuals within the scriptures, and the Lord better, while some scholarship will not. Consequently, we must be careful and discerning as we engage with biblical scholarship. This caution, however, should not prevent our engagement with scholarship, as the payoff can be immense. Well-trained biblical scholars may help us understand concepts that would otherwise be baffling. In this chapter, I seek to acquaint readers with some of the best Old Testament feminist scholars and to provide an understanding of the generally accepted philosophy that undergirds feminist hermeneutics.[4]

To study scriptures through a feminist lens or with a feminist hermeneutic is to study the Bible with a sensitivity toward issues of gender. This approach focuses on traditionally marginal characters, namely women; recognizes how women's lives have been represented and distorted; and acknowledges the polyvalency (or multiplicity of readings) inherent within the Bible. As Phyllis Trible, a foremost feminist biblical scholar and professor emerita of Old Testament at Union Theological Seminary, explains, "Despite attempts at harmonization by ancient redactors and modern critics, the Bible remains full of conflicts and contradictions. It resists the captivity of any one perspective.... Understanding that every culture contains a counterculture, feminism seeks these other voices in Scripture."[5] For Trible and many other feminist exegetes, the goal of feminist hermeneutics "is healing, wholeness, joy and well-being."[6] Feminist interpreters are not dispassionate interlocutors of the text but rather individuals who use biblical stories to raise awareness of contemporary social problems and to motivate readers toward new ways of seeing and behaving.

Alice Ogden Bellis, professor of Hebrew Bible at Howard University School of Divinity, lists the following important contributions of feminist interpreters to the field of biblical studies:

1. Beginning a systematic investigation into the status and role of women in ancient Israelite [and early Christian] culture.
2. The rediscovery and assessment of overlooked biblical traditions involving women.
3. The reassessment of famous passages and books about women, such as the book of Ruth.
4. The discovery of feminine images of God in the Bible.
5. Developments in the area of translation principles relating to women's concerns.

6. Consideration of the history or reception and appropriation of biblical texts about women in various cultural settings, especially in art (both graphic and cinematographic), literature, and more recently music.[7]

To this list, I would add the recognition of how positionality influences one's reading of the text. Before the advent of a feminist hermeneutics in the 1970s, scholars largely portrayed their readings as being objective, unmarred by personal biases. Feminist interpreters, however, have revealed "the importance of social location in the act of biblical interpretation. All of us bring our own political, gender, racial, and religious biases to a biblical text, which affect not only what we see, but even the questions we think to ask."[8] The need to read the Bible outside of one's paradigm is now largely recognized and has led to an explosion of new readings that forefront scholars' positionality in their interpretations of the text.

The stories of numerous women in the Bible have been recovered and reassessed through the efforts of feminist interpreters. The focus of this chapter will now shift to displaying how the reinterpretations of three of these stories involving women provide guidance for how individuals ought to care for those who have been victimized, marginalized, or disadvantaged. I purposely refer to these texts as stories involving women rather than as women's stories because the stories are arguably never told from a woman's perspective; instead, these stories are "all authored by men, written in androcentric (i.e., male-centered) language, and reflective of male religious experience."[9] This is to be expected given the culture and time in which the Bible was created, and mentioning this fact is not intended to be a criticism. After all, if we wish to fault texts for being androcentric, we will need to take issue with the vast majority of texts written before the twentieth century.

Recognizing the Bible as an androcentric text is an important step within the feminist hermeneutic because it enables readers to ask new questions of the text and to explicitly choose to read with the females in the story—or, in other words, to try to empathetically understand and experience the story from the perspective of the female figures—rather than with the male author or narrator, as our normal reading practices have conditioned us to do. Rereading from this perspective allows us to see other readings inherent within the text. As Trible reminds us, these are not readings that we are imposing on the text but rather are readings that we are exposing. "Tradition history teaches that the meaning and function of biblical materials is fluid. As Scripture moves through history, it is appropriated for new settings. Varied and diverse traditions appear, disappear, and reappear from occasion to occasion."[10] As members of The Church of Jesus Christ of Latter-day Saints, we believe, as President Dallin H. Oaks writes, in "the principle that scriptures can have multiple meanings," and we can feel comfortable in engaging in the type of rereading that Trible is encouraging.[11] As Trible goes on to explain, we will be "unfaithful readers" if we do not continue to recover these alternative readings inherent within the text. "Therein we shall be explorers who embrace both old and new in the pilgrimage of faith."[12] In other words, the polyvalent nature of the scriptures allows us to find universal and gynocentric perspectives and meanings within androcentric texts.

Sarah and Hagar

To show how this rereading may work, I begin with the story involving Sarah and Hagar. The author or editor of Genesis frames this portion of the text as the story of Abraham, his covenant with God, and the advent of the house of Israel beginning with Abraham and continuing through Isaac (Genesis 11–25).[13] Within this story is the fascinating depiction of two women: Sarah and Hagar. When we place these women's experiences at the center of our inquiry, the text raises questions about abuse, barrenness and surrogacy, plural marriage, degrees of power, agency, and victimization. We are also compelled to think about our treatment of those who are marginalized and disadvantaged and about our responsibility to aid and assist.

Sarai, who will eventually become known as Sarah after the Lord changes her name (Genesis 17:15), is a complicated figure: she is often praised and often maligned. If we are to read with her, we must first seek to understand her and her actions in light of the cultural expectations around her. Sarah desperately desires a child, in particular a son, likely because she wants to bring about the fulfillment of God's promise to her husband that he shall have posterity as numberless as the stars in heaven (15:4–5) and because in ancient Near Eastern society a woman's worth is invariably linked to her ability to bear children. Additionally, God was believed to control the womb, so barrenness was often viewed as a punishment from God.[14] As Sarah herself stated, "Behold now, the Lord hath restrained me from bearing" (16:2).[15] What must this have been like for Sarah to endure decades of infertility, believing that God was deliberately preventing her from having a child? How difficult was it for Sarah to admit what she perceived as her incompleteness and offer Hager to Abraham with the hope that she might "obtain children by her" (16:2)?[16] Was this her idea as indicated in Genesis 16:1, or are her words a response to a commandment from the Lord? As we learn from a revelation given to Joseph Smith, the Lord "commanded Abraham to take Hagar to wife" (Doctrine and Covenants 132:65). How must Sarah have felt when Hagar conceived, and Sarah saw her own status diminishing within the household (Genesis 16:1–6)? What was life like for Sarah during the fourteen years that Hagar had a child and she did not? What anguish did Sarah suffer? What did it feel like to believe that the Lord's promise of numberless posterity made to her husband did not include her as well (15:4–5)? To read with Sarah is to recognize that the Lord's promise to Abraham did not at first specify Sarah as coprogenitor (15:2–5, Abraham 2:9–11). What astonishment did she feel when she learned that the Lord's covenant with her husband *did* expressly include her and that she was to conceive a child at ninety years old and become "a *mother* of nations" (Genesis 17:15–21)? What remarkable joy did Sarah feel when she finally conceived and bore Isaac (21:1–8)? How protective was she of her son, and how great was her fear of a dangerous rivalry between him and Ishmael? Was this a real or unsubstantiated fear (21:9–11)? How did she feel when God sanctioned her request to banish Hagar and Ishmael from the household (12:12)?

To read with Sarah, we must remember that before Hagar entered their lives, Sarah was placed in a highly dangerous situation when Abraham, as instructed by the Lord (Abraham 2:22–25), told Pharaoh during their sojourn in Egypt that Sarah was his sister. She was subsequently taken into Pharaoh's house, ostensibly into his harem to be his wife (Genesis 12:10–20). What was this experience like for Sarah? What control over her life and body did she have during this time? Though the text is unclear on whether or not she had sexual relations with Pharaoh, she would likely have lived in fear of that happening.[17] Here, Sarah is a victim who experienced and felt who knows what terrors—even if she did (one hopes) have faith that the Lord would save her as he had saved Abraham from being sacrificed by the priest of Elkenah (Abraham 1:7–16). Consequently, her subsequent oppression of Hagar should be understood within a cycle of abuse. Sadly, we know that suffering does not necessarily lead to empathy and concern for others; we must consciously choose to experience empathy and to avoid passing on the mistreatment, offenses, and perhaps even abuse that we have suffered. Though Sarah was the chosen matriarch of the house of Israel, she was also a fallen individual—like all of us—in need of a Savior.

When we read this narrative with Hagar, we discover a story of terrible victimization as we imagine how Hagar, a slave, felt as she first becomes a surrogate womb for Sarah, is then treated harshly (or perhaps even abused) by Sarah (Genesis 16:1–6), and is eventually forced into exile in the unrelenting wilderness with her son, Ishmael, where they fear for their lives (21:14–21). Yet by reading with Hagar, we also discover a woman who courageously flees her oppression, calls down assistance from heaven, receives her own promise of never-ending descendants, dares to give the divine figure who appears to her a name, has sufficient faith in the Lord to return to Abraham and Sarah (16:7–14), and eventually becomes the free matriarch of her people (21:21). Reading with Hagar does not create a monolithic understanding of her and her story; rather, as the numerous interpretations of her by feminist scholars have shown, reading with Hagar opens up a multiplicity of ways to understand her and her story.

In general, these interpretations of Hagar may be divided into critical, closed readings or open, utopian readings. As these overarching perspectives (closed or open) strongly influence the reading one uncovers in biblical stories, it is useful to identify our own leanings and that of the scholars we read. Critical or closed feminist readings "show how women in literature reflect gender constraints ... [and] the ways in which male power is imposed on female society."[18] Women's victimization, in a closed reading, is often exposed, explored, and lamented. In contrast, utopian or open feminist readings resist seeing women as passive victims. Instead, scholars of this persuasion "describe how women find means of self-assertion, survival, promotion, creativity, and self-expression within certain circumscribed and potentially limiting gender boundaries."[19] In the nuances of the text, they search for avowals of female identity and agency. Both perspectives (closed and open) are valid and necessary because together they enable a more complex and full understanding of biblical women and the contexts in which they lived.

Immersing ourselves in a critical reading of Hagar such as that offered by Phyllis Trible in *Texts of Terror* allows us, as Walter Brueggemann writes, to "notice in the text the terror, violence, and pathos that more conventional methods have missed."[20] In explaining her own book project, Trible writes, "It recounts tales of terror *in memoriam* to offer sympathetic readings of abused women.... It interprets stories of outrage on behalf of their female victims in order to recover a neglected history, to remember a past that the present embodies, and to pray that these terrors shall not come to pass again."[21] Trible's explanation of her project captures an inherent motivation within most feminist exegesis: to use the biblical text as a catalyst to enable and promote needed changes today. Trible does this in her reading of Hagar's story by making explicit the abuse Hagar suffered at the hands of Sarah and Abraham, by pointing out how the narrator consistently undermines Hagar to promote the Isaac/Israel focus of the text, and by helping readers feel the fear and anguish Hagar felt as she is exiled to the wilderness with her son and is on the brink of death. As Hagar's story depicts oppression in the familiar forms of gender, class, and nationality, it may likewise serve as a valuable starting point for discussing needed societal changes in each of these areas. Visualizing the oppression that Hagar experienced should not be shied away from since the insights we gain from it can inspire us to personally apply the counsel from our prophet, Russell M. Nelson, "to build bridges of cooperation instead of walls of segregation" and "to lead out in abandoning attitudes and actions of prejudice . . . [and] to promote respect for all of God's children."[22]

To fully appreciate Hagar we must also view her story through an open, utopian lens. To do this we begin with the remarkable moment when Hagar takes command of her own life and flees into the wilderness. From the text, we learn that conceiving a child changes Hagar. She gains a greater sense of her own worth, and she is no longer respectful and subservient to Sarah. Rather, Hagar "despised" Sarah (Genesis 16:4 KJV) or "looked with contempt on her mistress" (16:4 NRSV). We do not know what this may have looked like in actuality, but many commentators uncomfortable with Sarah's harsh treatment of Hagar have used this description to justify Sarah's conduct toward Hagar by placing the blame on Hagar.[23] Feminist interpreters recognizing the significant power differential between the two women do not allow Hagar's contempt for Sarah to justify Sarah's actions toward Hagar, but they do acknowledge how difficult this seeming loss of power and status would have been for Sarah. From the text, we learn that Sarah responds to Hagar's contempt by dealing "hardly" with her (16:6 KJV). "In the Piel stem the verb עָנָה ('anah) means 'to afflict, to oppress, to treat harshly, to mistreat.'"[24] What this looked like in reality is open to multiple interpretations. It could mean that Sarah reverts to treating Hagar like an ordinary slave, or it could mean that Sarah harshly abuses Hagar. One simply does not know. What we do know from the text is that Hagar flees from Sarah into the wilderness (16:6–7). Explaining the context in which this decision takes place, Carol Meyers, professor emerita of religious studies at Duke University, writes, "The concept of either women or men striving for personal independence is antithetical to the dynamics and demands of premodern agrarians."[25] "A person's sense of individual agency was derived from her or his contribution to household life rather than from individual accomplishment. Household members did not act on their own wants or desires."[26] Consequently, in fleeing, Hagar demonstrates both courage and a surprising sense of self.

Hagar's brief time in the wilderness establishes her as a remarkable figure. An angel of the Lord appears to her, and she becomes the first woman in the Old Testament to hear a birth annunciation and the only woman in the Bible to receive a divine promise of numerous descendants through her own prerogative rather than a man's (Genesis 16:7–12). The text states, "The angel of the Lord said unto her, I will multiply thy seed exceedingly, that it shall not be numbered for multitude. And the angel of the Lord said unto her, Behold, thou art with child, and shalt bear a son, and shalt call his name Ishmael; because the Lord hath heard thy affliction" (16:10–11). During this encounter, Hagar also becomes the only person in the Old Testament to pronounce a name on a divine messenger or, perhaps, on the Lord. Whether she is naming an angel of the Lord or the Lord himself is unclear since the text changes midway through from referencing the divine messenger as an angel of the Lord to the Lord himself: "And she called the name of the Lord that spake unto her, Thou God seest me" (16:13). While many individuals in the Bible give a name to the place where they encounter the Lord, Hagar is the only individual who actually names the Lord or the Lord's messenger.

Clearly, Hagar is a singular individual who has an important role to play in God's plan. Her experience serves as a tangible example of

Nephi's words: "He inviteth them all to come unto him and partake of his goodness; and he denieth none that come unto him, black and white, bond and free, male and female; . . . all are alike unto God" (2 Nephi 26:33). That a divine messenger came to a female slave should alert readers to the fact that God does not support the divisions we often create to separate and subjugate one another. Tikva Frymer-Kensky, professor emerita of Hebrew Bible and the history of Judaism at the University of Chicago Divinity School, adopts an open feminist reading of Hagar and Ishmael's exile, providing further support for Nephi's message. Frymer-Kensky begins by reminding us "that in a world in which slavery is accepted, Hagar and Ishmael are not sold: they are freed. Hagar and Ishmael leave Abraham's household as emancipated slaves."[27] Once in the wilderness, God miraculously preserves them and again pronounces a great future for Ishmael. Reading into the last line of their story, "his mother took him a wife out of the land of Egypt" (Genesis 21:21), Frymer-Kensky points out how Hagar has become the head of her family and lineage. "The final note in the story reminds us that Ishmael's future is shaped by Hagar's understanding. A single mother, she is both father and mother, completing her parental duties by arranging for [Ishmael's] marriage. . . . God has given Hagar that right by treating her as the head of her own family and lineage."[28] In the honors and sympathy God bestows on Hagar at various times, we may see his great regard for all people and in turn the great regard we, too, should have for all people.

For many, however, God's concern for Hagar is complicated by his command to her to return and submit to Sarah. This command has perplexed and troubled many readers who see God as a God of liberation. Unfortunately, there is no definitive or easy way to understand this directive. Many have seen it as simply a necessary part of God's plan for Abraham's descendants. After all, Ishmael, too, undergoes the rite of circumcision and gains rights of inheritance from being born in the house of Abraham. As the Lord promises Abraham, "And as for Ishmael, I have heard thee: Behold, I have blessed him, and will make him fruitful, and will multiply him exceedingly; twelve princes shall he beget, and I will make him a great nation" (Genesis 17:20). Being born in the house of Abraham and raised under Abraham's tutelage until the age of seventeen was clearly God's plan for Ishmael.[29] Likewise, the separation of Ishmael and Isaac was also possibly a part of God's plan because he sanctioned Sarah's request to expel Hagar and Ishmael from Abraham's household (21:12). Some who are dissatisfied with this answer, for a variety of reasons, turn to context to establish the impossibility of a pregnant woman surviving in the wilderness and thereby offer an alternative explanation: Hagar must return because there is no other way for her to survive.[30] While this reading is highly plausible, it is complicated by the miracles we see God perform elsewhere to sustain the lives of the children of Israel in the wilderness during the Exodus and to provide water for Hagar during her second time in the wilderness. Clearly, God is a God of miracles who can do all things, so why does he at times liberate and at other times say "return . . . and submit" (16:9)?

Womanist[31] theologian and professor emerita of theology and culture at Union Theological Seminary Delores Williams answers this question through a compelling reading of the story that shows that "God's response to Hagar's (and her child's) situation was survival and involvement in their developments of an appropriate quality of life, that is, appropriate to their situation and their heritage."[32] Williams argues that recognizing how God is at work in the survival and quality-of-life struggles of many families is equally important to seeing God at work in liberating individuals and communities. Summarizing Williams's argument, Sakenfeld writes, "Since it is unlikely that racism, sexism, or economic exploitation will disappear in the near future, our theology needs to have room for God to be at work supporting and caring about those who are oppressed within these structures from which there is no apparent escaping. God is present and at work in the struggles for survival and some degree of quality of life within all the brokenness of this world. . . . God helps people . . . 'make a way out of no way.'"[33] The sentiments from these theologians are similar to the many expressions from General Authorities in our Church regarding our need to recognize how God strengthens us in our difficulties and trials. As Elder Jeffrey R. Holland eloquently states, "[Heavenly Father and Jesus Christ] sustain us in our hour of need—and always will, even if we cannot recognize that intervention."[34] Being able to see God at work in liberation and survival/quality-of-life struggles is key to a mature faith. However, our twenty-first-century discomfort with the command for Hager to return and submit to her oppressor will hopefully persuade us to work for the liberation of all who are oppressed.

While the relationship between Sarah and Hagar is troubled and not to be emulated, the preservation of the story of their relationship has enormous value to contemporary readers because it asks us to confront and honestly evaluate how we treat those who are in any way socially or economically less advantaged than ourselves. Relating this story to contemporary women, Lynn Japinga, professor of religion at Hope College, writes, "One of the painful realities of the feminist movement has been that while middle-class white women recognized their own oppression, they did not always recognize the ways they oppressed women of other classes or ethnic groups. . . . Middle-class [white] women hired African American or Hispanic women as domestics, at times without providing adequate pay or respect."[35] Too often we recognize our own marginalization, difficulties, sorrows, and oppression without recognizing how we directly and indirectly contribute to the marginalization, difficulties, sorrows, and oppression of others. A careful reading of Sarah and Hagar's relationship obliges us to assess the ways that our privilege shapes our relationships and actions. It requires us to grapple with how we may responsibly and equitably deal with power and privilege. It urges us to consider how we contribute to the exploitation of others, how we interact with individuals of a different ethnic group or economic class, and what we will do to ensure that as we work toward our own good we do not do so at the expense of others, especially those whose position in society is more marginal than our own. Reading with Sarah and Hagar, we cannot help but feel the relevancy of their story for today. As Renita Weems—former vice president, academic dean, and professor of biblical studies at American Baptist College—writes, "Theirs is a story of ethnic prejudice exacerbated by economic and sexual exploitation. Theirs is a story of conflict, women betraying women, mothers conspiring against mothers. Theirs is a story of social rivalry."[36] Consequently, if we are willing to read authentically and openly with Sarah and Hagar (and create a space where the Holy Spirit may teach us), then the text will call us up short; it will help us recognize the various ways in which we are complicit in oppressing others, and it will inspire us to work in solidarity with one another.

Tamar

Having looked at how feminist scholars can help us see new relevancy in the story of two well-known biblical women, we turn our attention to a woman who has been systematically neglected in Christian denominations: Tamar, a daughter of King David. Tamar's story is one of a sizable group of Old Testament stories that have traditionally been left out of the Catholic lectionary, the preaching from Protestant pulpits, and the Gospel Doctrine classes of The Church of Jesus Christ of Latter-day Saints because of the pain and horrors the stories depict. While this decision is understandable, these harrowing stories have much to teach us and should not be overlooked. Tamar's story, found in chapter 13 of 2 Samuel, is one of the most disturbing stories in the Old Testament. Tamar is raped by her half-brother Amnon. Although we may be understandably uncomfortable using disturbing terms such as *rape* and *abuse* and may prefer to use terms such as *defiled* and *mistreated*, it is important for us to accurately label these events. Failing to do so prevents us from recognizing the horrors that occurred anciently and more importantly from acknowledging the horrors that still occur today. Using more euphemistic terms is part of the culture of silence that enables atrocities to continue. Consequently, although we would prefer to look away from these terrors, for the next few pages we will carefully analyze Tamar's rape to see what it reveals about Tamar and how her story can aid us in helping victims of abuse today.

A conspiracy of men aid and abet Amnon's crime, and a male conspiracy of silence follows the act. Two years later, Absalom avenges his sister by killing Amnon, but one wonders whether Absalom murders Amnon solely to get revenge for Tamar or in part to pave the way for himself to inherit David's throne.[37] In the end, Tamar is left desolate in Absalom's house, and King David is found mourning bitterly, not for Tamar but for her rapist. A highly alarming story, it has remained largely in obscurity, most often only acknowledged in discussions about the larger story of who will take over David's kingdom.[38] Phyllis Trible was the first feminist exegete to look carefully at Tamar's story to see what it said about Tamar and her experience. Through careful analysis, Trible revealed a well-crafted story in which the narrator sides with and represents Tamar as a woman of wisdom.[39] Since then, many individuals have taken up the task to read with Tamar and to not look away from the atrocity she suffered—the results have been profound.

Tamar is an articulate, strong woman who refuses to be silent. Sent by her father, David, to prepare the *biryah* (quite possibly a medicinal concoction), for her half-brother Amnon, who feigns illness and requests to have Tamar sent to him that he "may be healed through her hand" (2 Samuel 13:6),[40] Tamar goes to Amnon without suspicion.[41] The narrator emphasizes her innocence as she prepares the cakes before him at his house and then enters his bedroom to serve them to him. Once he has her alone, he seizes her, saying, "Come lie with me, my sister" (13:11). She responds with a vigorous no, reminding him that he is her brother and that he is forcing her. To persuade him to forego his plan, she speaks of their cultural heritage and communal values that label his intentions vile and evil. She also reminds him of the devastating consequences for her and for him if he proceeds. Finally, Tamar offers an alternative to rape: Amnon may ask the king to take her as his wife (13:12–13). Amnon is unpersuaded by her wisdom and viciously takes her. A number of scholars have noted how the particular phrasing in Hebrew "stress[es] his brutality . . . [and] underscores cruelty beyond the expected."[42] "The text emphasizes her helplessness by stating, 'He lay her,' not 'He lay *with* her,' omitting the preposition in describing the rape."[43] In doing so, the editor of this story names rape for what it is: a violent assault on an individual.

Even after the rape, Tamar is not silent. When Amnon's lust turns to hate and he tells her to "arise, be gone" (2 Samuel 13:15), she pleads for him to not compound his atrocity with an act that is even worse. In explaining that "this evil in sending me away is greater than the other that thou didst unto me" (13:16), Tamar wisely captures the reality of the situation. "Rape is a horrible act, but it can be a (nasty) way of acquiring wives, as the men of Benjamin acquired the girls dancing at Shiloh."[44] However, by raping her and then casting her out, Amnon consigns her to a life of "desolation" (13:20). Even banished, though, Tamar is not silent: "And Tamar put ashes on her head, and rent her garment of divers colours that was on her, and laid her hand on her head, and went on crying" (13:19). Whether these acts were done in public or in private is not clear. Frymer-Kensky postulates that Tamar performs these actions publicly, in part, to proclaim that she is an innocent victim so that she cannot be held accountable for Absalom's actions.[45] In a situation where most rape victims retreat into silence and pain, Tamar becomes an even stronger role model if she chooses to "[create] a public spectacle," as Frymer-Kensky argues: "She draws attention to her own devastation by openly revealing her plight. Not trying to hide her shame, she performs an act of grief and lament."[46]

The individual who finally responds to Tamar's cries is her full brother Absalom. And while the text makes it clear that Absalom loves his sister, his words are not those that we as twenty-first-century readers want to hear: he charges Tamar to be silent. "And Absalom her brother said unto her, Hath Amnon thy brother been with thee? but hold now thy peace, my sister: he is thy brother; regard not this thing. So Tamar remained desolate in her brother Absalom's house" (2 Samuel 13:20). With these words, Tamar disappears from the biblical narrative.

Many readers of the Bible may justifiably wonder why such a terrifying story has been preserved and why feminist scholars would want to bring it out of obscurity. What these scholars have shown, however, is the enormous value to be found in its retelling because, unfortunately, "Tamar is not an ancient anomaly. She is all around us."[47] The preservation of Tamar's story acknowledges the horrors that at times occur in families, even in families of high estimation. Her story gives voice to many of the issues that surround sexual abuse. For instance, Amnon only gains access to Tamar through the help of his cousin Jonadab and the unwitting assistance of his father, King David. As Wilda C. Gafney, professor of Hebrew Bible at Brite Divinity School, writes, "The specter of a family member enabling the sexual abuse of a relative is unfortunately a well-known and enduring phenomenon. . . . Sexual offenders are not all lone wolves. As the biblical account of Jonadab's collaboration illustrates, there are other family members, adults, who know that a child or woman or man is being abused. They say nothing or worse, they even participate."[48] Tamar's story also acknowledges the reality that the majority of rapes are acquaintance rapes in which victims know their assailants.[49]

Absalom's charge to his sister to be silent about the life-altering crime inflicted on her is a painful reminder of the culture of silence that has long surrounded rape and abuse. Victims of rape and abuse have all too often been pressured and shamed into silence. When they have spoken out, they have all too often been disbelieved, ostracized, and blamed. King David's decision to knowingly ignore Amnon's act of violence against Tamar and to eventually mourn the loss of Amnon's life rather than acknowledge Tamar's suffering is a terrifying example of an all-too-prevalent sanction of male violence upon female bodies (2 Samuel 13:36). Summarizing Tamar's story, Bellis writes: "There is no good news here, but the text invites and encourages us to write a different ending to the story, where the parent takes action, the abuser is confronted, and the victim is heard and cared for. We can write a better ending that chooses to listen rather than ignore, to offer grace and healing rather than shame."[50] Such abuse and violence must end. God does not sanction it in the Bible or in our current society.

The great power in Tamar's story is that it "provides a framework for women to talk about sexual violence, using its inclusion in the Scriptures as authority to discuss it in their own communities."[51] A powerful example of how Tamar's story is currently being used to raise awareness of sexual abuse and to work for its elimination is the Tamar Campaign. In South Africa, a mixed-gender group of theologians and clergy created Bible studies about Tamar's rape and other texts in the Bible that feature abuse to help churches address sexual violence by creating a space in which it may be openly discussed. The Bible studies are led by facilitators from the Ujamaa Center. The campaign has been so successful that it has spread to other countries within Africa and even to other continents.[52] The Bible studies begin with the group reading the text together and then asking a series of questions such as What is this text about? Who are the male characters, and what is the role of each of them in the rape of Tamar? What is Tamar's response throughout the story? What is the attitude of the narrator? Where is God in the story? The facilitator also asks a series of consciousness-raising questions such as What effect or impact does the story of Tamar have on you? Are there women like Tamar in your church or community? Tell their story. What resources are there in your area for survivors of rape? What will you now do in response to this Bible study?[53]

Reporting on the impact of the campaign on individuals in South Africa, Gerald West and Phumzile Zondi-Mabizela write, "In our experience the effects of this Bible study are substantial. Women are amazed that such a text exists, are angry that they have never heard it read or preached, are relieved to discover they are not alone, are empowered because the silence has been broken and their stories have been told."[54] This statement encapsulates why it is important to make this text and other appalling texts such as the story of the Levite's concubine (Judges 19–21) and Jephthah's daughter (Judges 11) a part of our Sunday curriculum. These texts create a biblically sanctioned space to name and discuss abuse within a church setting, and it may give individuals the freedom and space they need to share their own stories and then to work toward recovery. Silence enables the continuation of abuse. Consequently, among the great benefits of feminist scholars' biblical interpretations is that their productive readings of dismaying texts help us to openly discuss modern challenges such as violence, abuse, and the exploitation of those who are marginalized and disadvantaged. Often their readings also reveal how God and the Bible editors are not sanctioning the violence found within the Old Testament; rather, these stories exist to be condemned and to show the need for a different way. Ideally our collective study of these stories will lead to our collective resolve to end abuse in all its varied forms.

The Women of Exodus

The women of Exodus provide intriguing examples of how individuals can work toward ending abuse and overcoming social injustices. The first deliverers to appear in the book of Exodus are Shiphrah and Puah, Hebrew midwives who may themselves be either Hebrew or Egyptian—the text is ambiguous.[55] Making an independent moral decision, the midwives defy Pharaoh's order that they kill all the male babies at their birth (Exodus 1:15–17). When questioned by Pharaoh about their failure to follow out his command, they cunningly play to his belief that the Hebrews are inherently different from the Egyptians: "the Hebrew women are not as the Egyptian women; for they are lively, and are delivered ere the midwives come in unto them" (1:19). Believing their words because they reinforce his belief that the Hebrews are less human than the Egyptians and distinctly other, Pharaoh dismisses the midwives without punishment.[56] The next deliverer in the book of Exodus is Moses's mother, Jochebed. Skirting around Pharaoh's decree that "every son that is born ye shall cast into the river" (1:22), she hides her son for three months before placing him in an ark and floating him down the river under the watchful eye of her daughter, Miriam (2:1–4). Fortuitously, the Pharaoh's daughter is the one who finds the ark and becomes the next deliverer within the story. Her initial statement, "This is one of the Hebrews' children" signals to the readers that she is aware of her father's decree and intentionally disobeys his order in favor of her emotional, ethical impulse—"she had compassion on him" (2:6). Similar to Shiphrah, Puah, and Jochebed, Pharaoh's daughter refuses to carry out (or be complicit with) violence and the abuse of power. Acting in their roles as midwives, mothers, and daughters, these women do what is possible within their sphere to stop the abuses they encounter.

Speaking of the applicability of their actions for our world today, Japinga writes, "Resistance to oppression often begins in small actions. The enslaved Israelites did not have the power to defeat Pharaoh, but the midwives could save the boys and the mothers could save Moses. It is easy to be intimidated by slavery, apartheid, and segregation because these systems are so large and tenacious. They effectively demoralize and disempower people until they believe they are powerless, but sometimes when one person challenges the system, other people also refuse to be passive in the face of evil."[57] The domino effect of deliverance and the palpable impact of just one individual within the book of Exodus should encourage each of us to work in whatever ways we can to end social injustices.

A crucial insight to come out of feminist readings of Exodus is how the women crossed gender, ethnic, and class lines to fight oppression and to save others. Moses is saved and the story of the Exodus unfolds because "Pharaoh's daughter is knowingly complicit (whether or not she knows that she is paying the child's mother to nurse him) with the Hebrew women in an act of cross-gender, cross-ethnic, cross-class deliverance."[58] The "theme of crossing ethnic boundaries to effect deliverance makes its first appearance" in the ambiguity of the ethnic identity of the midwives.[59] As Jacqueline E. Lapsley, professor of Old

Testament at Princeton Theological Seminary, notes, the "ambiguous (perhaps deliberately so?) . . . ethnic identity of these midwives . . . force[es] the reader to ponder the implications of identity: what difference does it make to the story whether the women are Hebrew or Egyptian?"[60] Whether or not the midwives crossed ethnic lines to save others is unknown, but what is known, although rarely mentioned, is that the Egyptian women crossed ethnic and class lines to aid the Israelite women as they fled into the wilderness by providing them with "jewels of silver, and jewels of gold, and raiment" (Exodus 3:22; 12:35). Women throughout the first three chapters of the book of Exodus crossed traditional division lines to defy oppression and to work for the liberation of others. They are models for us of President Nelson's call "to build bridges of cooperation instead of walls of segregation," "to lead out in abandoning attitudes and actions of prejudice, . . . [and] to promote respect for all of God's children."[61]

Challenging readers to think about how this story teaches the necessity of forming cooperative networks across traditional identity divisions, Lapsley writes,

> What change might be wrought today if women of different racial, ethnic, and class backgrounds could find ways of working together in the life of the church and for the common good? . . . The deliverances effected by women in Exodus 1–4 are part of the work of God, and foreshadow the deliverance YHWH effects for Israel a few chapters later. To read Exodus 1–4 as Scripture is to read for the values the story embodies, to rejoice in the possibility of engaging in the work of God across the boundaries that separate us, and to acknowledge the challenge of it. Women who work together to protect the vulnerable and to defy violence do the work of God, and it is our work.[62]

The book of Exodus, as Lapsley and other feminist and postcolonial scholars persuasively argue, is a clarion call for individuals to reject human prejudice centered on gender, ethnicity, and class and to work cooperatively for the liberation of all people.

Not surprisingly, many feminist scholars have also turned to the book of Exodus to illuminate how the text deconstructs a worldview where men are of greater worth than women and to show instead a world where "women become the saviors of early Israel and bring on the redemption from Egypt."[63] By having Pharaoh promote the assumption that men are of greater consequence than women, through his repeated efforts to destroy the Hebrew sons and let the daughters live (Exodus 1:15–22), the text suggests this idea will need to be ridiculed and abandoned. The text effectively does this by showing that it is the women, not the men, who repeatedly undermine his plans in the first two chapters and enable the survival of Moses. As Gafney writes, "The liberation of the Israelite people in Egypt begins with Shiphrah and Puah."[64] Through careful analysis feminist scholars help readers appreciate the courageous women of Exodus who defied overwhelming power at great risk to themselves. They also bring to light the important truth that although great achievements have often been associated with one man, such as Moses and the Exodus, such achievements have actually been made possible through the efforts of many individuals—men and women—each doing his or her part to bring about change. Their efforts may remind us of the inspiring words of our past prophet, Gordon B. Hinckley:

> This church does not belong to its President. Its head is the Lord Jesus Christ, whose name each of us has taken upon ourselves. We are all in this great endeavor together. We are here to assist our Father in His work and His glory. . . . Your obligation is as serious in your sphere of responsibility as is my obligation in my sphere. . . . All of us in the pursuit of our duty touch the lives of others. To each of us in our respective responsibilities the Lord has said: "Wherefore, be faithful; stand in the office which I have appointed unto you; succor the weak, lift up the hands which hang down, and strengthen

the feeble knees" (Doctrine and Covenants 81:5). . . . The progress of this work will be determined by our joint efforts.[65]

Conclusion

The stories of women in the Old Testament have much to teach us if we will take the time to notice them and then to read with the female figures. This is accomplished as we ask new questions about the women, the story, and the context and as we seek to understand the women's struggles, choices, and situations. Doing so will not only foster regard and empathy for these women but will also help us recognize our shortcomings in our interactions with others and perhaps even our complicity in the social injustices that abound in our world today. As we then discuss these stories openly, we will create biblically sanctioned spaces to discuss difficult topics that otherwise remain in the shadows. The women discussed in this chapter serve only as a starting point to illustrate how much we can gain as we apply a feminist hermeneutic to our scripture study and learn from the many feminist scholars who have carefully set forth a wide range of readings on these biblical women. As we immerse ourselves in these studies, we will perceive a repeated call for us to recognize our responsibility to stand with victims and to fight oppression in all its many forms.

Amy Easton-Flake is an associate professor of ancient scripture at Brigham Young University.

Notes

1. Frances Taylor Gench, *Back to the Well: Women's Encounters with Jesus in the Gospels* (Louisville: Westminster John Knox Press, 2004), 81.
2. Katharine Doob Sakenfeld, "Feminist Perspective on the Bible and Theology: An Introduction to Selected Issues and Literature," *Interpretation* 42, no. 1 (January 1988): 5–6.

3. "What Is the Church's Stance on Feminism?" *New Era*, January 2020, 43.
4. To date, Latter-day Saint scholars have rarely incorporated the work of feminist biblical scholars into their readings of Old Testament women. An example of an exception to this statement would be Gaye Strathearn and Angela Cothran's "Naomi, Ruth, and Boaz: Borders, Relationships, Law, and Ḥesed," in this volume. Currently, the best work on Old Testament women from a Latter-day Saint scholar is Camille Fronk Olson's *Women of the Old Testament* (Salt Lake City: Deseret Book, 2009). Olson's work provides useful context for understanding Old Testament women and provides many helpful insights on each of the women she discusses. Her work suggests an awareness of some of the ideas to come out of feminist biblical scholarship, but she directly cites this scholarship only occasionally. Her suggested sources indicate a preference for scholars who do not identify as feminist exegetes.
5. Phyllis Trible, "If the Bible's So Patriarchal, How Come I Love It?," *Bible Review* 8, no. 5 (October 1992): 45.
6. Trible, "If the Bible's So Patriarchal," 55.
7. Alice Ogden Bellis, *Helpmates, Harlots, and Heroes: Women's Stories in the Hebrew Bible*, 2nd ed. (Louisville: Westminster John Knox Press, 2007), 19.
8. Gench, *Back to the Well*, xii–xiii.
9. Gench, *Back to the Well*, xii.
10. Phyllis Trible, "Depatriarchalizing in Biblical Interpretation," *Journal of the American Academy of Religion* 41, no. 1 (March 1973): 48.
11. Dallin H. Oaks, "Scripture Reading and Revelation," *Ensign*, January 1995, 8.
12. Trible, "Depatriarchalizing," 48.
13. Though Abraham's name is Abram and Sarah's name is Sarai at the beginning of the narrative, I use the names Abraham and Sarah throughout my analysis. The Lord does not change their names until after Hagar bears Ishmael.
14. Katharine Doob Sakenfeld, *Just Wives? Stories of Power and Survival in the Old Testament and Today* (Louisville: Westminster John Knox Press, 2003), 14.

15. All scriptures quoted are from the King James Version of the Bible unless otherwise specified.
16. "Evidence from ancient texts show that this arrangement [surrogacy], although not common, was once a regular feature of family relations. Three ancient Near Eastern marriage contracts stipulate that should the bride be barren after a specified number of years, she will give her husband her slave. . . . The best known example of surrogacy is in the laws of Hammurabi. . . . Neither Sarai, who proposes Hagar, nor Abram, who agrees, mentions obtaining the consent of the slave girl. To contemporary readers, such consent seems necessary for the arrangement to be moral. But none of the ancient texts see any ethical problem with this arrangement." Tikva Frymer-Kensky, *Reading the Women of the Bible: A New Interpretation of Their Stories* (New York: Random House, 2002), 227.
17. The King James Version of the Bible indicates that Pharaoh had not yet taken Sarah to wife: "Why saidst thou, She is my sister? so I might have taken her to me to wife" (Genesis 12:19). The much more prevalent translation is some variant of "and I took her to me to wife," found in the NIV, NLV, ESV, ISV, ASV, and so forth. This translation indicates that the Pharaoh had already taken Sarah to wife, although whether that included sexual relations is unknown. A further indication in the text that the Pharaoh may have had sexual relations with Sarai comes from comparing this account to the other account when Sarah again poses as Abraham's sister and is taken by Abimelech king of Gerar as well as the account when Rebekah poses as Isaac's sister when they are in the land of Gerar. In both of these other accounts the author specifically makes it known that Sarah and Rebekah have not been sexually taken: "But Abimelech had not come near [Sarah]" (Genesis 20:4). And in the case of Rebekah, when the king realizes Rebekah is Isaac's wife, he proclaims, "What is this thou hast done unto us? one of the people might lightly have lien with thy wife, and thou shouldest have brought guiltiness upon us" (Genesis 26:10). That no specific denial of the Pharaoh having sexual relations with Sarah occurs in the text leaves open the possibility that he did. One must hope as Latter-day Saint scholar Hugh Nibley suggested that the Lord saved Sarah by sending an angel, as he had earlier saved Abraham from being sacrificed on

the altar by the priest of Elkenah. Hugh Nibley, *Old Testament and Related Studies* (Provo, UT: Foundation for Ancient Research and Mormon Studies; Salt Lake City: Deseret Book, 1986), 99.

18. Margaret Beissinger as cited in Susan Niditch, "Folklore, Feminism, and the Ambiguity of Power: Women's Voice in Genesis?" in *Faith and Feminism: Ecumenical Essays*, ed. B. Diane Lipsett and Phyllis Trible (Louisville: Westminster John Knox Press, 2014), 56.
19. Niditch, "Folklore," 57.
20. Walter Brueggemann, editor's foreword to *Texts of Terror: Literary-Feminist Readings of Biblical Narratives*, by Phyllis Trible (Philadelphia: Fortress Press, 1984), x.
21. Trible, *Texts of Terror*, 3.
22. Russell M. Nelson, "Building Bridges," *New Era*, August 2018, 6; Nelson "Let God Prevail," *Ensign*, November 2020, 94. See also the recent changes to the *General Handbook*, 38.6.14, "Prejudice": "The Church calls on all people to abandon attitudes and actions of prejudice toward any group or individual. . . . This includes prejudice based on race, ethnicity, nationality, tribe, gender, age, disability, socioeconomic status, religious belief or nonbelief, and sexual orientation."
23. See, for example, commentary on Genesis 16:4 by John Calvin (1578) and Peter Pett (2011). "And, doubtless, from the event, we may form a judgment that Hagar was impelled to flee, not so much by the cruelty of her mistress, as by her own contumacy. Her own conscience accused her; and it is improbable that Sarai should have been so greatly incensed, except by many, and, indeed atrocious offenses. Therefore, the woman being of servile temper, and of indomitable ferocity, chose rather to flee, than to return to favor, through the humble acknowledgment of her fault" (Calvin). "Hagar cannot accept her new lack of status or her treatment and flees in the direction of Egypt, her homeland. In many ways she had given Sarai little choice. (One of the things that is said to cause the earth to tremble is 'a handmaid who is heir to her mistress' [Proverbs 30:23]). Her attempt to supplant her had had to be treated harshly in order to re-establish Sarai's overt authority. Of course her flight exacerbates her wrongdoing. She has

no right to leave the tribe and she has not been turned out" (Pett, https://www.studylight.org/commentary/genesis/16-6.html).

24. "Net Notes" Genesis 16:6, note 24. https://netbible.org/bible/Genesis+16.
25. Carol Meyers *Rediscovering Eve: Ancient Israelite Women in Context* (New York: Oxford University Press, 2013), 200.
26. Meyers, *Rediscovering Eve*, 120–21.
27. Frymer-Kensky, *Women of the Bible*, 235.
28. Frymer-Kensky, *Women of the Bible*, 236.
29. Although Ishmael is most often depicted as a young child in paintings of Hagar and Ishmael in the wilderness, the text makes it clear that he is likely around seventeen years old. In Genesis 17:25, the text states that Ishmael is thirteen years old when the Lord tells Abraham that Sarah will have a son. That likely puts Ishmael at fourteen years old when Isaac is born. Ishmael remains in the household until Isaac was weaned—an event that likely occurred when Isaac was three, making Ishmael seventeen.
30. See, for instance, Elsa Tamez's reading of this in "The Woman Who Complicated the History of Salvation," *Cross Currents* 36, no. 2 (Summer 1986): 137.
31. A womanist is a black feminist or feminist of color. Womanism seeks to bring the history and everyday experiences of black women to bear upon theological, ethical, biblical, and other religious studies.
32. Delores S. Williams, *Sisters in the Wilderness: The Challenge of Womanist God-Talk* (1993; repr., Maryknoll, NY: Orbis, 2013), 5.
33. Sakenfeld, *Just Wives?*, 22.
34. Jeffrey R. Holland, "High Priest of Good Things to Come," *Ensign*, November 1999, 38.
35. Lynn Japinga, *Preaching the Women of the Old Testament: Who They Were and Why They Matter* (1988; repr., Louisville: Westminster John Knox Press, 2017), 16.
36. Renita J. Weems, *Just a Sister Away: A Womanist Vision of Women's Relationships in the Bible* (New York: Hachette Book Group, 2005), 2.
37. Amnon is the firstborn and heir apparent to the throne. The second-born, Kileab or Chileab, isn't mentioned. Perhaps he died young. Absalom is the third born. Tamar's story occurs in the section of the Bible generally

understood to depict the contestation over who will assume David's throne. A number of years after Tamar's rape, Absalom will seek to take over David's throne (2 Samuel 13–19).
38. Alice L. Laffey, *An Introduction to the Old Testament: A Feminist Perspective* (Philadelphia: Fortress Press, 1988), 124.
39. Phyllis Trible, "Tamar: The Royal Rape of Wisdom," in *Texts of Terror: Literary-Feminist Readings of Biblical Narratives* (Philadelphia: Fortress Press, 1984), 37–64.
40. Translation from Greek by Frymer-Kensky, *Women of the Bible*, 159.
41. Frymer-Kensky, *Women of the Bible*, 158–59.
42. Trible, "Tamar," 46; see also Frymer-Kensky, *Women of the Bible*, 162; and Wilda C. Gafney, *Womanist Midrash: A Reintroduction to the Women of the Torah and the Throne* (Louisville: Westminster John Knox Press, 2017), 229.
43. Gafney, *Womanist Midrash*, 229. As Trible further explains, "now 'he lay (skb)' not, however, with her because the Hebrew omits the preposition to stress his brutality" ("Tamar," 46). To understand the verb *shakav*, Trible refers her readers to J. P. Fokkelman, *King David*, vol. 1, Narrative Art and Poetry in the Books of Samuel (Assen, The Netherlands: Van Gorcum, 1981), 104–5.
44. Frymer-Kensky, *Women of the Bible*, 164.
45. In Deuteronomy 22:22–24 we learn that a woman who cries out when she is being violated is considered innocent. If she does not, she is considered complicit. Likewise, Frymer-Kensky quotes a Middle Assyrian law that states, "If, as soon as she leaves the house, she should declare that she has been the victim of fornication, they shall release her, she is clear" (*Women of the Bible*, 165). If she does not do this, Amnon might be able to claim that Tamar seduced him or that she was a willing partner.
46. Frymer-Kensky, *Women of the Bible*, 165.
47. Bellis, *Helpmates, Harlots, and Heroes*, 153.
48. Gafney, *Womanist Midrash*, 228, 232.
49. RAINN, "8 out of 10 rapes are committed by someone known to the victim," https://rainn.org/statistics/perpetrators-sexual-violence.
50. Japinga, *Preaching the Women of the Old Testament*, 135.

51. Gafney, *Womanist Midrash*, 232.
52. Johonna McCants, "The Tamar Campaign: Breaking the Silence on Violence against Women," *Peace Signs: The Magazine of the Peace and Justice Support Network Mennonite Church USA*, March 27, 2014, https://pjsn peacesigns.wordpress.com/2014/03/27/the-tamar-campaign-breaking-the-silence-on-violence-against-women/.
53. Fred Nyabera and Taryn Montgomery, eds., *Contextual Bible Study Manual on Gender-Based Violence* (the Fellowship of Christian Councils and Churches in the Great Lakes and The Horn of Africa: Nairobi, Kenya, 2007), http://lottcarey.org/wp-content/uploads/2013/08/Tamar_Campaign_Contextual-Bible-Study-on-Gender-Based-Violence-Final.pdf.
54. Gerald West and Phumzile Zondi-Mabizela, "The Bible Story That Became a Campaign: The Tamar Campaign in South Africa (and Beyond)," *Ministerial Formation* (July 2004): 6, http://ujamaa.ukzn.ac.za/Files/the%20bible%20story.pdf.
55. Scholars are not certain about the ethnic identity of the midwives because "the Hebrew *lmldt h 'bryt* is ambiguous: it could mean 'to the Hebrew midwives' or 'to the midwives who serve the Hebrew women.'" Frymer-Kensky, *Women of the Bible*, 25.
56. For more on the role that the assumption of difference plays in the story, see Renita Weems, "The Hebrew Women Are Not Like the Egyptian Women: The Ideology of Race, Gender and Sexual Reproduction in Exodus 1," *Semeia* 59 (1992): 25–34.
57. Japinga, *Preaching the Women of the Old Testament*, 50.
58. Jacqueline E. Lapsley, *Whispering the Word: Hearing Women's Stories in the Old Testament* (Louisville: Westminster John Knox Press, 2005), 77.
59. Lapsley, *Whispering the Word*, 72.
60. Lapsley, *Whispering the Word*, 72.
61. Nelson, "Building Bridges," 6; Nelson "Let God Prevail," 94.
62. Lapsley, *Whispering the Word*, 88.
63. Frymer-Kensky, *Reading the Women*, 24.
64. Gafney, *Womanist Midrash*, 91.
65. Gordon B. Hinckley, "This Is the Work of the Master," *Ensign*, May 1995, 71.

7

Models of Motherhood
Expansive Mothering in the Old Testament

Avram R. Shannon and Thora Florence Shannon

Motherhood, both in the scriptures and in our own experiences, is a wonderful and beautiful thing, but it can sometimes be a fraught category. Societal and religious expectations on mothers can be overwhelming and can lead to despair, difficulty, and marginalization.[1] Motherhood is often defined as a narrow range of nurturing behaviors such as bearing, nursing, feeding, and fulfilling other physical needs of children.[2] Some people have used the Old Testament to proscribe women's roles to motherhood and then to define their roles of motherhood as a limited range of these mostly physical acts of childcare.[3] While these are vitally important activities, mothering encompasses more than just this physical caretaking. This paper illustrates specific examples in the Old Testament in which the roles women play can be broadened by motherhood rather than diminished or restricted by it.

Methodological Considerations

Before examining these examples of mothering in the Old Testament, we need to discuss a few points. The first is to describe what we mean regarding our idea of expansive motherhood. Neill F. Marriott, former counselor in the Young Women's General Presidency, taught that "nurturing is not limited to bearing children. Eve was called a 'mother' before she had children. I believe that 'to mother' means 'to give life.'"[4] Fundamentally, this paper is about exploring various examples from the Old Testament that show mothers giving and preserving life. This definitely includes the physical bearing and rearing of children, but it also includes supporting and feeding families. Further, it involves creating places, including communities, where individuals can live and grow. Mothering can even involve saving lives through military or political intervention. When we refer in this paper to the expansive perspective of mothering and motherhood, we are thinking of Sister Marriott's broad definition of giving life.

Next we must recognize that the Old Testament is an ancient collection, and its books reflect the ancient culture that produced them, including ancient cultural perspectives on male–female relationships.[5] These relationships were often oppressive for the women involved, and the Old Testament has been used at times to justify the continued subjugation of women. We wish to state categorically that this is not an appropriate interpretation of the scriptures, then or now, and the oppression of women has never, is not, and will never be God's will.[6]

Additionally, in this paper we draw from both the Old Testament as it has come down to us and the inspired changes in Joseph Smith's New Translation, commonly called the Joseph Smith Translation (JST).[7] This point is especially true in our discussion of Mother Eve. Elder Franklin D. Richards included in the Pearl of Great Price the first few chapters of the JST of Genesis, and today these chapters are called the Book of Moses.[8] The Book of Moses provides important insights into the character of Eve and her role as the mother of all living. As there are no significant JST changes in the stories of Deborah or Pharaoh's daughter and Jochebed, the JST does not play a role those discussions.[9]

Eve: The Mother of All Living

Because of Eve's epochal role in moving forward humanity and the plan of salvation, much religious discourse throughout the ages has focused on her and the Fall. Much of this interpretation has been negative toward Eve and by extension toward all women.[10] The Latter-day Saint perspective distinctively presents Eve as a full agent in the garden who makes a selfless choice on behalf of humanity.[11] This understanding is based on modern revelation and a close reading of Genesis 3 and Moses 4. For Latter-day Saints, her mothering does not begin after the Fall when she first bears children but is part and parcel of her actions in the Garden of Eden. As noted above, Neill Marriott explained that "nurturing is not limited to bearing children. Eve was called a 'mother' before she had children. I believe that 'to mother' means 'to give life.'"[12] Eve's motherhood encompasses more than the bearing of children and includes her choice in the garden to "open the doorway toward eternal life."[13] This understanding of Eve makes it clear that her mothering is an expansive, rather than a restrictive, category. Eve, whose name in Hebrew means "life," is presented in Genesis and in The Church of Jesus Christ of Latter-day Saints as a paradigmatic mother-figure, suggesting that her mothering in general should be understood in the expansive sense of not only being the first to bear children but also being the one to give life to all creation through her choice to eat the fruit of the tree of knowledge of good and evil.[14]

When God placed Adam in the Garden of Eden, God said, "Of every tree of the garden thou mayest freely eat: But of the tree of the knowledge of good and evil, thou shalt not eat of it, *nevertheless, thou mayest choose for thyself, for it is given unto thee; but, remember that I forbid it,* for in the day that thou eatest thereof thou shalt surely die" (Genesis 2:16–17; Moses 3:16–17; the italicized section is from Moses and is not in Genesis). Although in the text the Lord gives this commandment before the creation of Eve, it is clear that in the beginning of the Eden narrative Eve also understands which tree is off limits. "And the woman said unto the serpent, We may eat of the fruit of the trees of the garden: but of the fruit of the tree which *thou beholdest* in the midst of the garden, God hath said, Ye shall not eat of it, neither shall ye touch it, lest ye die." (Genesis 3:2–3; Moses 4:8–9; italicized section in Moses).[15]

Although God had forbidden eating the fruit of the tree of knowledge of good and evil, he had also given Eve and Adam the commandment to "be fruitful, and multiply, and replenish the earth" (Genesis 1:28//Moses 2:28). According to the Book of Mormon, Eve and Adam could not have had children as long as they remained in the garden (see 2 Nephi 2:23). While they were innocent and immortal, Eve and Adam were unable to fulfill God's commandment to be fruitful and multiply, and the plan of salvation could not move forward until they left the garden and began their mortal experience (2 Nephi 2:21–25).

Eve is persuaded by the serpent that she should eat some of the fruit because she will not die but will be as a god, knowing good and evil. Genesis records: "And when the woman saw that the tree was good for food, and that it was pleasant to the eyes, and a tree to be desired to make one wise, she took of the fruit thereof, and did eat, and gave also unto her husband with her; and he did eat" (Genesis 3:6; Moses 4:12). Although the idea came from the serpent, Eve made a conscious choice to eat the fruit. Elder Holland reminds us that "[ours] is the grand tradition of Eve, the mother of all the human family, the one who understood that she and Adam *had* to fall in order that 'men [and women] might be' and that there would be joy."[16]

After the Lord calls Eve and Adam to account, he tells them the consequences of their actions. He tells Eve, "I will greatly multiply your toil and your conceiving. Through work you will bear children, and your sexual desire will be to your husband, and he will govern you" (Genesis 3:16; authors' translation). In Hebrew, the word translated here as "toil" (as "sorrow" in the KJV), is *'iṣābûn*, a word that appears only three times in the Hebrew Bible—all of them in Genesis and two of them in context of the consequences of Eve and Adam's Fall, discussed in Genesis 3:16–17.[17] For Adam, this word describes the process of producing food from the soil. The parallel usage in Genesis 5:29, alluding back to the passage in Genesis 3, is helpful for understanding the meaning of *'iṣābûn* in Genesis 3. There, Noah is blessed as a comfort for the "toil of our hands" (Genesis 5:29). The Hebrew word for *toil* is the same word used for *sorrow* in Genesis and represents a better reading. Bearing children and producing food are labor, but neither are inherently sorrowful acts of labor.[18]

Genesis 3:16 has had a long interpretive tradition, much of which has unfortunately justified the oppression of women because of the verse's explanation about the difficulty of pregnancy.[19] It should be noted that at no point is the Lord's statement to Eve described as a "curse," an assumption that has been the root of much of the justification of this negative deployment of pregnancy. Childbearing is not a curse that women are called to bear. It does contain distinctive dangers and difficulties, especially in the ancient world and even today in places without access to modern medicine, but that does not make it a curse. In Genesis, the only curses are on the serpent and on the land. Neither Adam nor Eve are personally cursed.[20]

This first scriptural framing of motherhood focuses on the difficulties of pregnancy and the pain of labor, which Genesis couples with a statement about the subjection of the female to the male. This has often had the unfortunate tendency of leading people to link female subservience with motherhood.[21] Mothering does not need to be an act of subservience, and Eve's choice in the garden was a courageous act of motherhood—not just for her immediate children but for all of the world.[22]

Joseph Smith's New Translation adds to our knowledge of Eve's perspective about her choice. Moses 5:11 states, "And Eve, his wife, heard all these things and was glad, saying: Were it not for our transgression we never should have had seed, and never should have known good and evil, and the joy of our redemption, and the eternal life which God giveth unto all the obedient." Eve here expresses a communal view of her and Adam's choices, rather than a view focused on individual salvation. Adam's view centers much more on salvation for his own sins, saying in verse 10, "Blessed be the name of God, for because of my transgression my eyes are opened, and in this life I shall have joy, and again in the flesh I shall see God." Adam expresses personal joy, while Eve sees the goodness of their choices for her and Adam together with their descendants and has joy in that. For Eve, the choice in the garden was a choice to bring about humanity, and her choice constitutes the first act of mothering on this earth.[23]

This insight provides an important nuance to Lehi's claim that "Adam fell that men might be" (2 Nephi 2:25). In Hebrew, the word translated as the name *Adam* (*ādām*) is a common noun that means "human" or "humanity."[24] In fact, most places in Genesis 2 through 5 where the KJV text shows *Adam*, the Hebrew text simply reads *the human*.[25] This idea has possible expression in the inspired introduction to creation in Moses 1:34, "And the first of all men have I called Adam, which is many." A similar notion is visible in Genesis 1:27, where God make[s] "man ['adam] in his own image, in the image of God created he him; male and female created he them." Humanity ['adam] encompasses both males and females, and so Lehi's statement that "Adam fell that men might be" refers to both of our first parents' falls.[26] This is especially significant because we know from the scriptures that Eve was the first to make the choice to eat of the fruit of the tree of knowledge of good and evil. This means that Adam's Fall, as discussed in the scriptures, is fundamentally derived from Eve's foundational act of motherhood in choosing to eat the fruit of the tree of knowledge of good and evil.

Thus, Restoration scripture makes it very clear that Eve, as well as Adam, fell out of the garden and innocence so that they could progress. They seem not to have been fully informed when they partook of the fruit: their "eyes" were not yet "opened" (Genesis 3:5). Even with that, they—Eve in particular—made choices according to the best of their knowledge that would provide a path for humanity to come to earth and gain bodies. President Russell M. Nelson has said, "It was our glorious Mother Eve—with her far-reaching vision of our Heavenly Father's plan—who initiated what we call 'the Fall.' Her wise and courageous choice and Adam's supporting decision moved God's plan of happiness forward. They made it possible for each of us to come to earth, receive a body, and prove that we would choose to stand up for Jesus Christ now, just as we did premortally."[27] By eating the fruit first, Eve was the first to attempt to bridge the gap between the two commandments given by the Lord and to begin the mortal stage of the plan of salvation.

Sheri Dew points out how Eve broadens our perspective of motherhood: "While we tend to equate motherhood solely with maternity, in the Lord's language, the word *mother* has layers of meaning. Of all the words they could have chosen to define her role and her essence, both God the Father and Adam called Eve 'the mother of all living'—and they did so *before* she ever bore a child. Like Eve, our motherhood began before we were born. . . . Motherhood is more than bearing children, though it is certainly that."[28] This makes it clear that Eve is the mother of all living, not *just* because she would bear children but also because her choices in the Garden of Eden led to all people living on this earth as part of the eternal plan of our heavenly parents.[29] Eve provides an expansive Old Testament example of mothering through her willingness to make hard choices on behalf of humanity. She also shows us a definition of *mother* that contains but also transcends the physical bearing of children. Eve's mothering was not passive but was the result of her "far-reaching vision" for all of humanity. A mother can be someone who is willing and able to make hard choices in order to create a place where life can thrive.

Deborah: Judge, Prophetess, and "Mother in Israel"

The next Old Testament mother we will look at is Deborah.[30] Deborah represents a perspective on mothering in the Old Testament that derives from her experiences outside the domestic sphere. Deborah is one of only a few Old Testament individuals identified as a prophetess.[31] She is the only known woman to function as a judge over Israel. And she is one of only two individuals identified by the specific phrase "mother in Israel" (Judges 5:7).[32] All of these roles express an Old Testament example of a mothering figure from which we can learn about mothering in a broader application than just one's immediate family. Deborah is a mother who is able to give life through actions outside the domestic sphere; in her case, she fulfills this through fighting in Israel's wars.

Deborah is introduced in Judges in this way: "And Deborah, a prophetess, the wife of Lapidoth, she judged Israel at that time" (Judges 4:4). *Prophetess* is a word that has sometimes presented some difficulties for Latter-day Saints as they interpret the Old Testament, since the role of prophet is largely associated with priesthood callings and keys. The Church's Guide to the Scriptures is quick to clarify: "A prophetess does not hold the priesthood or its keys."[33] It is worth noting, however, that in the Old Testament it seems that not even all the *males* described as prophets held "the priesthood or its keys."[34] Although Deborah's identification as a prophetess does not specifically mean that she was a Church leader in the way that a prophet is in the modern Church of Jesus Christ, it is notable that she is the only judge in the entire book of Judges to whom prophetic gifts are ascribed. An unnamed prophet goes before Gideon in Judges 6:7–10, but Gideon is not described as a prophet nor is Samson, Ehud, Jephthah, or any of the other judges. Deborah is distinctive among the judges in this respect. She is the only judge described in the book of Judges as any kind of religious leader.[35] Her role as prophetess may connect to her motherhood since there are scriptural examples of male prophets being addressed by their followers as *father*.[36] Deborah's broader role in the community seems to be a significant part of her mothering.

Of course, just being the only female judge in the book of Judges makes Deborah distinctive. An Israelite judge (Hebrew šōpēṭ) is different from our modern conception. Israelite judges did not simply try cases. Old Testament scholars Richard Holzapfel, Dana Pike, and David Seely observe, "The book of Judges consistently depicts the judges as military leaders, i.e. deliverers."[37] In fact, the only judge described in Judges as functioning in a juridical context is Deborah (see Judges 4:5).[38] As the only female judge, Deborah is in a distinctive position, but she is also, like all the judges, involved as a military leader. As with the role of prophetess, Deborah's military role may play into her characterization as a mother: the Aramean military captain Naaman is called "father" by his servants (2 Kings 5:13), suggesting that military relationships could be understood in terms of kinship.

The story of Deborah follows the pattern of the general narrative of the book of Judges—the Israelites are in bondage to a foreign power, and the Lord calls up a judge to free them. The people oppressing Israel in the time of Deborah are the Canaanites, led by a general named Sisera.[39] Deborah encourages a man named Barak to gather the Israelites to fight against Sisera. Barak does so, and together they defeat the Canaanites. Barak will not go to battle without Deborah, highlighting the importance of her role in the military victory of the Israelites, as we would expect from her role as a judge. The coup de grâce does not come from Barak or the male Israelite soldiers but from a Midianite woman named Jael, who puts a tent spike through Sisera's head while he was sleeping. Although Deborah works through a male war-leader to fight against the Canaanites, the final victory is facilitated by a female. Indeed, the story of Deborah is one in which women are preeminent, and their mothering roles are highlighted, including those of Deborah, Jael, and Sisera's mother.[40]

Finally, we come to "mother in Israel," a phrase that seems to relate to Deborah's position as both prophetess and judge. After the conquest over the Canaanites, Deborah sings a victory song—which is called Deborah's Song by biblical scholars—in Judges 5. This may be part of her role as a prophetess, as we see the prophetess Miriam doing something similar in Exodus 15:20.[41] At the beginning of the song, Deborah describes the difficulties under which the Israelites had suffered "until that I Deborah arose, that I arose a mother in Israel" (Judges 5:7). The interpretation of this key phrase "mother in Israel" is crucial.

We know from Judges 4:4 that Deborah is married because the name of her husband, Lapidoth, is given. Although we cannot rule out that Deborah had children, we have no evidence from the biblical text itself. This means that we must be careful not to reduce Deborah's statement that she is a mother in Israel to a declaration about her having borne biological children.[42] Thus, we will consider other meanings of how she might be considered a mother in Israel.

The theme of Deborah's Song is the deliverance of the Israelites through the divine intervention of Jehovah. The Lord calls on Deborah and Barak, saying, "Awake, awake, Deborah: awake, awake, utter a song: arise Barak, and lead thy captivity captive, thou son of Ahinoam" (Judges 5:12). The Lord also describes tribes that came to fight against these Canaanites: "And the princes of Issachar were with Deborah; even Issachar, and also Barak" (Judges 5:15). As Deborah continues to describe her role as a mother in Israel through her song, she does so in terms of her leading the children of Israel to victory alongside Barak. Therefore, within the book of Judges, it seems that Deborah's being a "mother in Israel" is not directly related to whether she has children but to her active role in leading, judging, and delivering Israel. This reminds us of Neill F. Marriott's definition of a mother as a giver of life. As a mother in Israel, Deborah has given life to all the children of Israel by saving their lives, freeing others from bondage, and leading Israel to victory over the Canaanites.

As we think about Deborah's roles, we should also note that the ancient Israelites did not experience the dichotomy of women either staying at home or working outside the home that dictates much of our discourse about motherhood in the modern world. In a society built around subsistence agriculture, *everybody* worked as a part of the economy. In this environment, the economic activity of both women and men was centered in and around the home.[43] The breakdown of the household economy after the Industrial Revolution brought new questions, new challenges, and new opportunities for women, which has conditioned how we understand motherhood and mothering today. This understanding means that our modern perspective on the household economy will be different from that of the ancient world. Thus Deborah is not choosing to "work outside the home" in the modern sense because that concept is not applicable in the ancient biblical world.

However, Deborah's example can still be a model for mothers and motherhood that is not part of the traditional perspective on stay-at-home mothers. Deborah represents a mother in Israel whose mothering is not limited to her family, the bearing and raising of children, or even contributing to the household economy. Again, this is not to say that these are not vital activities, but in Deborah's case we simply do not have the evidence to know whether she had children, so her identification as a "mother in Israel" rests on other activities, including her being a prophetess and a judge. Deborah is a mother in Israel because of her abilities to lead and save her people. She teaches us the value that mothering can bring to groups larger than immediate families, even groups as large as entire societies. A mother can be someone whose pursuits outside the home can give life—these activities can include supporting a family, serving in the military, and being a religious leader.

Pharaoh's Daughter and Jochebed: The Mothers of Moses

Our final example of motherhood is that of Pharaoh's daughter and Jochebed.[44] These two women, the two mothers of Moses, illustrate the roles that women can play when working together to accomplish the Lord's work.[45] One of the women bore Moses, and the other reared Moses, but both of them were involved in saving the Israelites.[46] In our modern society, mothering can sometimes be viewed as a very personal and idiosyncratic choice, connected to contentious arguments and differences of opinion in the hows and whys of raising children.[47] But Jochebed and Pharaoh's daughter are two women from two very different cultures and socioeconomic situations who still found common ground in the mothering of Moses.[48] By working together despite their differences, these two women demonstrated the power that can be had in creating community for mothers and mothering.[49]

The narrator in Exodus does not inform us of the name of the mother of Moses until a genealogical list is given in Exodus 6:20—here we are told that her name is Jochebed.[50] The initial introduction of Jochebed describes her marriage, and the next depicts her giving birth to a male child: "And there went a man of the house of Levi, and took to wife a daughter of Levi. And the woman conceived, and bare a son: and when she saw him that he was a goodly child, she hid him three months" (Exodus 2:1–2). From this, we learn about the lineage of Moses's biological father and mother but nothing about the rest of the family. The reader meets Moses's older sister Miriam later in this biblical story, but Moses's older brother Aaron (who is almost as important as Moses in the biblical record) is nowhere to be found until Moses's adulthood.

The opening chapters of Exodus display a large number of females taking action: the midwives Shiphrah and Puah,[51] Miriam, Jochebed, and Pharaoh's daughter. Each of these women acts in some way to rescue the Israelites.[52] Jochebed is the active force in the birth and rescue of Moses, not his father, Amram.[53] Because Pharaoh had sentenced all male Israelite infants to death, Jochebed took Moses and hid him until he was three months old. As a newborn, the baby was relatively easy to hide; however, hiding the baby became more difficult as he grew, so his mother made "an ark of bulrushes, and daubed it with slime and with pitch, and put the child therein; and she laid it in the flags by the river's brink" (Exodus 2:3). Jochebed acts here to save the baby by placing it in a little boat in the Nile. This is not simply leaving the baby's fate to the elements and God: Exodus 2:4 makes clear that "his sister stood afar off, to wit what would be done to him." Miriam followed the ark, suggesting that she and her mother expected something to happen to it rather than its being destroyed in the Nile. Finding the ark is not as coincidental as it might have seemed.[54]

Unlike the baby's mother and sister, Pharaoh's daughter remains unnamed throughout the biblical narrative, making it impossible to identify her with any specific historical figure in Egyptian history.[55] According to Exodus, she is with her attendants washing herself in the river when she discovers the little boat and finds the crying baby. According to the record in Exodus, "she had compassion on him" (Exodus 2:6). One of the features of Hebrew narrative is the relative paucity of emotional exploration—thus the "compassion" of Pharaoh's daughter is worth noting.[56] The Hebrew word translated as "had compassion" is not a very common one and appears fewer than fifty times in the Hebrew Bible, though it often carries with it the sense of "to spare," especially in a military context.[57] The compassion shown by Pharaoh's daughter is not simply a passive emotion but a life-saving action. As a male Israelite baby, Moses was under a death sentence, but in her compassion, Pharaoh's daughter chooses to pull him out of the water and save him.[58]

The Bible makes it clear that this compassion was not just the ordinary compassion one feels for a baby because the text highlights the role of Pharaoh's daughter in saving a baby who was under a decree of death from the Pharaoh. Note that Pharaoh's daughter immediately recognizes the baby as "one of the Hebrews' children" (Exodus 2:6). This may be because the baby was already circumcised or because the Israelite phenotype was sufficiently different from the Egyptian. Or, the recognition may simply have occurred because the Israelites had much more reason than Egyptians to put their babies into baskets and float them down the river. But regardless of how Pharaoh's daughter identified the baby, her compassion on Moses was an intentional choice to save a baby who was from an enslaved population. Her action is liberating to Moses and potentially puts her life on the line because of her disobedience to Pharaoh's decree.[59]

Here is where the story gets particularly intriguing. An Israelite girl suddenly appears and asks Pharaoh's daughter whether she should go and call "a nurse of the Hebrew women" to breastfeed the baby (Exodus 2:7). In the ancient world, there were almost no options for feeding babies besides nursing since formula did not exist. Pharaoh's daughter needed to find a way to feed the baby, and there likely would have been Egyptian women among the slaves and servants in the palace who were lactating and able to serve as a nurse for the new baby.[60] Pharaoh's daughter did not need an Israelite nursemaid, which highlights the unusual circumstances of Pharaoh's daughter instantly agreeing to the girl's suggestion. When Pharaoh's daughter finds an Israelite baby floating in the Nile, an Israelite girl just happens to be nearby, and the girl just happens to know an Israelite woman who is currently lactating and can nurse the baby. The coincidences abound in this story. The narrative suggests the possibility that Pharaoh's daughter is aware that this is not at all coincidental but is part of Jochebed's plan to save her son. If this is the case, then Pharaoh's daughter's agreement to raise and adopt the baby makes her a part of that plan.[61]

Pharaoh's daughter summons Jochebed and agrees to pay her to nurse the baby. Such contracts were not uncommon in the ancient world.[62] And here we see the success of Jochebed's plan. Not only does she save the life of her child, but she is able to raise him for the first few years of his life—and she is paid by Pharaoh's daughter for the privilege!⁶³ The nursing contract between Pharaoh's daughter and Jochebed protected Jochebed and the baby as she nursed and raised the child. We know from other Near Eastern parallels that these contracts lasted for up to three years.⁶⁴ Moses is then brought back to Pharaoh's daughter, where he is adopted as her son.

All of this provides very positive outcomes for Moses, Pharaoh's daughter, and Jochebed. As biblical scholar Shawn W. Flynn notes, "At first Moses is condemned to die but now through the institution of adoption and wet-nursing contracts, Moses' mother has three years or more to bond with her son, living back in his own house, while his mother is even paid by the same culture that threatened his life in the first place."⁶⁵ Moses is rescued by the plan of his mother and the willingness of Pharaoh's daughter to engage with and abet that plan.

The story of Pharaoh's daughter and Jochebed reminds us that mothering and motherhood is not a one-size-fits-all proposition. Moses does not have just one mother. He does not grow up in a nuclear family, which has sometimes been seen as the norm and ideal in the modern age.⁶⁶ Yet the mothering that both of Moses's mothers perform is critical for his growth and his ability to become the person the Lord needs him to be. Jochebed conceives, bears, rescues, and nurses Moses, providing much of the physical nurturing that we associate with motherhood. Yet all of this would have come to naught without the nurturing compassion of Pharaoh's daughter, who spared a child of enslaved Hebrews and took him as her own son. In addition, she gave the child back to his mother to be nursed and reared. These two mothers show how traditional acts of motherhood lead to outcomes of great national and spiritual significance. Although these two women, to their knowledge, save only one infant and never see beyond that, their actions move the Lord's eternal purposes forward in saving the nation of Israel.

Jochebed and Pharaoh's daughter were two women from very different cultures and very different socioeconomic statuses. Jochebed already had children (Aaron and Miriam are Moses's older siblings), but we know nothing about any other children of Pharaoh's daughter, or even whether she was married. We do know, however, that she adopted Moses as her own and that he was raised among the Egyptians.[67] Rather than letting their different cultures and religions divide them, these two mothers built bridges and mothered Moses together. Without the important work of birthing, nursing, and raising Moses, the work of the Lord would not have gone forward (at least in that way). The example of Pharaoh's daughter and Jochebed shows the ways in which these two women worked together in their mothering, in spite of their different circumstances and familial statuses. They serve as a model for modern alliances that bring diverse backgrounds, perspectives, and abilities into the important work of mothering. Their experiences also create space in modern mothering for adoption and for stepparenting. Mothering need not be limited to biological considerations alone. A mother can be someone who, without regard to social or economic class, provides a way for all of our heavenly parents' children to thrive.

Conclusion

In this paper, we have looked at four women from the Old Testament who provide intriguing models for mothering in the latter days. The Old Testament, in spite of its largely male-focused culture, provides diverse models for understanding the process of mothering. Each of these models widens the scope of what mothers do and depicts mothering as an active process performed by agents. These acts of mothering can be large or small and have both immediate and eternal consequences. Mothering, as it is realized in the stories of these Old Testament women, is not only about bearing and rearing children within the household, though it is about that in part. In this context, mothering is also about making choices that build and protect both current and future children and families. Mothering is about moving the plan of salvation forward. Mothering is about gathering armies and physically delivering Israel from its captors. Mothering is about bringing together women from disparate backgrounds and perspectives in order to accomplish the goals and means of motherhood. Far from presenting a limited view of motherhood, the Old Testament presents latter-day women and men with models for understanding motherhood that are expansive, ennobling, and beautiful.

Avram R. Shannon is an assistant professor of ancient scripture at Brigham Young University.

Thora Florence Shannon is an independent scholar living in Provo, Utah.

Notes

In memory of Torvald Alistair Shannon, February 11, 2021.

1. See Alena Prikhidko and Jacqueline M. Swank, "Motherhood Experiences and Expectations: A Qualitative Exploration of Mothers of Toddlers," *Family Journal* 26 (2018): 278–84; Miriam Liss, Holly H. Schiffrin, and Kathryn M. Rizzo, "Maternal Guilt and Shame: The Role of Self-Discrepancy and Fear of Negative Evaluation," *Journal of Children and Family Studies* (2013): 1112–19. Elder Jeffrey R. Holland of the Quorum of the Twelve Apostles speaks of the anxieties that can come from both the world and the Church. Jeffrey R. Holland, "Because She Is a Mother," *Ensign*, May 1997, 35–37.

2. For a broad overview of this concept, see Lynda R. Ross, *Interrogating Motherhood* (Edmonton, AB: AU Press, 2016), 14–23. This perspective appears across a wide variety of historical and geographical places. See the discussion on motherhood in the Mediterranean during the Hellenistic period and beyond in Alicia D. Meyers, *Blessed among Women? Mothers and Motherhood in the New Testament* (Oxford: Oxford University Press, 2017), 31–38. For a discussion of this topic in early American history, see Nora Doyle, *Maternal Bodies: Redefining Motherhood in Early America* (Chapel Hill: University of North Carolina Press, 2018). For a study exploring this concept in twentieth-century England, see Angela Davis, Pamela Sharpe, Penny Summerfield, Lynn Abrams, and Cordelia

Beattie, *Modern Motherhood: Women and Family in England 1945–2000* (Manchester: Manchester University Press, 2012), 177–95. These studies are representative rather than exhaustive, but they serve to illustrate the narrow range in which motherhood has often been defined.

3. See Mary Kelly-Zukowski, "The Subversiveness of the Marginalized Women of Scripture: Models of Faith and Action for Twenty-First Century Women," *Gender Studies* 22 (2005): 30–32. The study and history of motherhood has often been a difficult topic to study, in part because of the paucity of sources. Although focused largely on American history, an excellent survey of the question appears in Jodi Vandenberg-Daves, "Teaching Motherhood in History," *Women's Studies Quarterly* 30, no. 3/4 (2002): 234–55.

4. Neill F. Marriott, "What Shall We Do?," *Ensign*, May 2016, 11.

5. Carol Meyers, *Discovering Eve: Ancient Israelite Women in Context* (Oxford: Oxford University Press, 1988), 40–46.

6. Members of The Church of Jesus Christ of Latter-day Saints do not believe that the scriptures are without error, thus there is no need for us to be tied to ancient perspectives on matters such as the treatment of women. See the excellent discussion in Jeffrey R. Holland, "My Words . . . Never Cease," *Ensign*, April 2008, 91–94.

7. For a discussion of the variety and complexity of the various kinds of JST changes, see Scott H. Faulring, Kent P. Jackson, and Robert J. Matthews, eds., *Joseph Smith's New Translation of the Bible: Original Manuscripts* (Provo, UT: Religious Studies Center, Brigham Young University, 2004), 8–11.

8. See Kent P. Jackson, *The Book of Moses and the Joseph Smith Translation Manuscripts* (Provo, UT: Religious Studies Center, Brigham Young University, 2005), 1–52.

9. All of the women discussed in our paper have also been discussed in Camille Fronk Olson, *Women of the Old Testament* (Salt Lake City: Deseret Book, 2009). Eve is discussed on pages 7–20, Deborah on pages 107–36, and Jochebed and Pharaoh's daughter are discussed as part of her treatment of Miriam on pages 90–92.

10. See Meyers, *Discovering Eve*, 72–78; Elaine Pagels, *Adam, Eve, and the Serpent* (New York: Vintage Books, 1988), 127–29. For an example of a negative interpretation of Eve in a relatively modern commentary, see Meredith G. Kline, *Genesis: A New Commentary* (Peabody, MA: Hendrickson, 2017), 20–21. See also the citations from Reformation theologians in John L. Thompson, *Reformation Commentary on Scripture: Genesis 1–11* (Downers Grove, IL: Intervarsity Press, 2012), 213–17. Note, in particular, Martin Luther's statement on p. 215. There is a similar interpretive strand within ancient Judaism; see *Genesis Rabbah* 17:7–8.

11. Olson, *Women of the Old Testament*, 12–13. For an apostolic Latter-day Saint perspective on Eve and the Fall, see Dallin H. Oaks, "The Great Plan of Happiness," *Ensign*, November, 1993, 72–75. Related to our positive view of Eve and the Fall, but taking it in a different direction, C. S. Lewis presents an intriguing possibility in his novel *Perelandra* about the Lord providing ways to move forward if Eve and Adam had chosen differently. See Benita Huffman Muth, "Paradise Retold: Lewis's Reimagining of Milton, Eden, and Eve," *Mythlore* 37 (2018): 23–44.

12. Marriott, "What Shall We Do?," 11.

13. Oaks, "Great Plan," 73.

14. The life-giving roles of Eve in Latter-day Saint thought are explored in Donald W. Parry's recent study, "Eve as a Help ('*Ezer*) Revisited," in *Seek Ye Words of Wisdom: Studies in the Book of Mormon, Bible, and Temple in Honor of Stephen D. Ricks* (Orem, UT: Interpreter Foundation, 2020), 199–232.

15. There has been much discussion of what is going on here, but it is sufficient for our purposes to note that the story makes it clear that Eve is aware of the commandment and is an agent. Biblical scholars have suggested that there are actually two accounts of the creation underlying Genesis 1 and 2. These seem to have been put together by an inspired redactor, much like the Book of Mormon. For a discussion of the sources and redaction in the creation of Genesis and the entire first five books of the Bible, see Daniel L. Belnap, "The Law of Moses: An Overview," in *New Testament History, Culture, and Society*, ed. Lincoln H. Blumell (Provo, UT: Religious Studies Center, Brigham Young University; Salt Lake City: Deseret Book,

2019), 19–34. There is an even greater in-depth discussion of this branch of scholarship in David Rolph Seely, "We Believe the Bible as Far as It Is Translated Correctly: Latter-day Saints and Historical Biblical Criticism," *Studies in the Bible and Antiquity* 8 (2016): 64–87. In Genesis 1 humanity is created together, male and female, while in Genesis 2 the male human is created first, followed by the female human.

16. Holland, "Because She Is a Mother," 36; emphasis in the original. The addition to 2 Nephi 2:25 is also in the original.

17. See Francis Brown, Samuel Driver, and Charles Briggs, *The Brown-Driver-Briggs Hebrew and English Lexicon* (1906; repr., Peabody, MA: Hendrickson, 2008), 781 (hereafter cited as *BDB*); Ludwig Koehler and Walter Baumgartner, *The Hebrew and Aramaic Lexicon of the Old Testament* (Leiden: Brill, 2001), 865 (hereafter cited as *HALOT*). There is a related noun deriving from the same root that appears another seven times, including in this verse; see *HALOT*, 865.

18. Claudia D. Bergmann, "Mothers of a Nation: How Motherhood and Religion Intermingle in the Hebrew Bible," *Open Theology* 6, no. 1 (2020): 135–36.

19. Meyers, *Discovering Eve*, 101–9.

20. In his letter to his son about baptizing infants, Mormon talks about how "the curse of Adam" is taken from little children through Jesus Christ (see Moroni 8:8). The reference seems to be to humanity's fallen nature (a major theme in the Book of Mormon). It is possible that Mormon's use of this phrase derives from his understanding of Genesis 3, but that is difficult to ascertain. Even if Mormon understands our fallen nature in connection with Genesis 3, it is still worth noting that the language "curse of Adam" or "curse of Eve" do not derive from the book of Genesis.

21. A good overview on this point appears in Deborah W. Rooke, "Feminist Criticism of the Old Testament: Why Bother?," *Feminist Theology* 15, no. 2 (2007): 160–74. The classic discussion of some of the problematic elements of this passage is in Phyllis Trible, *God and the Rhetoric of Sexuality* (Philadelphia: Fortress Press, 1978), 72–143.

22. Donald Parry reminds us that the pain of childbirth is life-giving. See Parry, "Eve Revisited," 211. In "The Family: A Proclamation to the

World," modern apostles and prophets remind us of the fundamentally equal role of men and women, even in things like the rearing of children: "In these sacred responsibilities, fathers and mothers are obligated to help one another as equal partners," ChurchofJesusChrist.org.

23. Parry argues in "Eve Revisited," 208–10, that the giving of life is central to the narrative in the Garden of Eden.

24. See *BDB*, 9; *HALOT*, 14. See also the discussion in Meyers, *Discovering Eve*, 81.

25. This is made clear by the presence of the definite article. Examples in which this is the case include Genesis 2:19, the first instance in 2:20, 2:21, 2:23, 3:8, 3:9, 3:20, 4:1. In some places, such as the second instance in 2:20, the definite article is not present, suggesting that it could be read as a name. But these instances in which th-e definite article is not present have a prefixed preposition, which can lose the marker of the definite article under certain phonological conditions. See Bruce Waltke and Michael O'Connor, *An Introduction to Biblical Hebrew Syntax* (Winona Lake, IN: Eisenbrauns, 1990), 26. In Genesis 5:1–2, *human* appears without the definite article, suggesting it could be understand as simply a personal name, but the usage of a plural suffix pronoun in 5:2 suggests that it is being understood in a collective sense, as in Genesis 1:27. The places in Genesis chapters 1 through 5 where *'ādām* seems to be functioning exclusively as a personal name are in Genesis 4:25 and Genesis 5:3–5. See *BDB*, 9.

26. See the discussion in Olson, *Women in the Old Testament*, 8.

27. Russell M. Nelson (citing Henry B. Eyring), "Sisters' Participation in the Gathering of Israel," *Ensign*, November 2018, 68–69.

28. Sheri Dew, "Are We Not All Mothers?," *Ensign*, November 2001, 96.

29. Parry, "Eve Revisited," 212.

30. Deborah means "bee" in Hebrew. There is some possible connection between her name and Near Eastern prophecy. See Daniel Vainstub, "Some Points of Contact between the Biblical War Traditions and Some Greek Mythologies," *Vetus Testamentum* 61 (2011): 324–34. Latter-day Saint authors have not commented much on Deborah. Camille Fronk Olson is a notable exception to this; see Olson, *Women in the Old Testament*, 107–27.

31. The others are Miriam (Exodus 15:20), Huldah (2 Kings 22:14), Noadiah (Nehemiah 6:14), and the unnamed prophetess who is the mother of Isaiah's son Maher-shalal-hash-baz (Isaiah 8:3). The New Testament adds Anna, who met the baby Jesus in the temple (Luke 2:36). See Lester Grabbe, *Priests, Prophets, Diviners, Sages: A Socio-Historical Study of Religious Specialists in Ancient Israel* (Valley Forge, PA: Trinity Press International, 1995), 115–16; Olson, *Women in the Old Testament*, 83–85.
32. The other individual is an unnamed woman who pleads for mercy from David's general Joab in 2 Samuel 20:16–22, with the specific reference in 20:19.
33. Guide to the Scriptures, "Prophetess," ChurchofJesusChrist.org.
34. An example of this would be the prophets who oppose Jeremiah or the rogue prophet Balaam in Numbers 22–24. On this point, it should be noted that the New Testament book of Revelation describes the spirit of prophecy as the testimony of Jesus (see Revelation 19:10). See the discussion in Avram R. Shannon, "Prophets and Prophecy in the Book of Mormon: The Case of Samuel the Lamanite," in *Samuel the Lamanite* (Provo, UT: Religious Studies Center, Brigham Young University, 2021), 3–24.
35. See Richard Neitzel Holzapfel, Dana M. Pike, and David Rolph Seely, *Jehovah and the World of the Old Testament* (Salt Lake City: Deseret Book, 2009), 172. They mention that Samuel is also a prophet, and he is portrayed in 1 Samuel as the last of the biblical judges.
36. See 2 Kings 2:12.
37. Holzapfel, Pike, and Seely, *Jehovah and the Old Testament*, 172.
38. Samuel acts in a juridical context in 1 Samuel 7:6.
39. Canaanite is a fairly obscure ethnonym here, usually referring in the Bible to a collection of various peoples. It is difficult to discern whom the biblical author intends here. See Susan Niditch, *Judges: A Commentary* (Louisville: Westminster John Knox, 2011), 64.
40. See Rannfrid Irene Thelle, "Matrices of Motherhood in Judges 5," *Journal for the Study of the Old Testament* 43 (2019): 437. See also J. Cheryl Exum, "Feminist Criticism: Whose Interests Are Being Served?," in *Judges and Method: New Approaches in Biblical Studies*, ed. Gale A. Yee (Minneapolis:

Fortress, 2007): 65–90. In particular, Exum characterizes Barak and Sisera as "little boys" alongside the mother figures of Deborah, Jael, and Sisera's mother in her discussion on pages 70–73.

41. Some biblical scholars have identified that linguistically both Exodus 15 and Judges 5 are some of the oldest parts of the Hebrew Bible (the Old Testament). Interestingly, both of these texts describe prophetesses and their songs. See Charles L. Echols, *"Tell Me, O Muse": The Song of Deborah (Judges 5) in the Light of Heroic Poetry* (New York: T&T Clark, 2008), 51–59. See also Angel Sáenz-Badillos, *A History of the Hebrew Language*, trans. John Elwolde (Cambridge: Cambridge University Press, 1993), 35.

42. Olson, *Women in the Old Testament*, 114–16.

43. See Meyers, *Discovering Eve*, 142–48. Meyers also notes that there is a public and private division between males and females. As an example of this, Proverbs 31:10–31 describes what the KJV calls a "virtuous woman," who is primarily praised for what she brings to the household economy. Significantly, the Hebrew for *virtuous woman* has nothing to do with how we ordinarily understand *virtue* in English, instead having a primarily economic meaning. The *virtuous woman* purchases flax and wool to make thread for cloth (31:14), she buys fields and plants vineyards (31:16), and she makes clothing not just for her family but also for sale outside the home (31:24).

44. Amy Easton-Flake also treats this story in "Recognizing Responsibility and Standing with Victims: Studying Women of the Old Testament," in the present volume, with intriguing insights. See also the discussion in Lauren Ellison, "Mothers: Heroes, Then and Now," *Religious Educator* 8, no. 3 (2007): 65–74.

45. Scott Langston notes that, as we saw with Deborah, this is a narrative in which "three women, all nameless, dominate the actions." Scott M. Langston, *Exodus through the Centuries* (Oxford: Blackwell, 2006), 21.

46. Mark S. Smith, *Exodus* (Collegeville, MN: Liturgical Press, 2011), 16–17.

47. Tracy Thompson, "A War Inside Your Head," *Washington Post Magazine* (February 15, 1998), W12, https://washingtonpost.com/wp-srv/national/longterm/mommywars/mommy.htm

48. Jacqueline E. Lapsley, *Whispering the Word: Hearing Women's Stories in the Old Testament* (Louisville: Westminster John Knox, 2005), 77.
49. Carol Meyers, *Exodus* (Cambridge: Cambridge University Press, 2005), 39.
50. This is likely not an example of the biblical focus on the male, since we are also not told Moses's father's name (Amram) at this point in the narrative. See the discussion in Meyers, *Exodus*, 42.
51. For a discussion of Shiphrah and Puah, see Olson, *Women of the Old Testament*, 167–81; see Easton-Flake, "Recognizing Responsibility and Standing with Victims," included in the present volume.
52. The famous Tannaitic sage R. Aqiva commented, "Through the merit of righteous women, Israel came out of Egypt." *Yalqut Shimoni*, 795:5. Text found on Sefaria.org; translation is the authors' own.
53. We cannot know what Amram did or did not do. We are once again limited by what the scriptures tell us.
54. Ellison, "Mothers," 67.
55. See the discussion in Olson, *Women of the Old Testament*, 91. In 1 Chronicles 4:17–18, a daughter of Pharaoh marries into the house of Judah, and some have connected this daughter of Pharaoh to the one who saves Moses. Since the identity of the pharaoh of the Exodus is still open to scholarly debate, we should not be surprised by our inability to identify Pharaoh's daughter here, though she is named Bithiah in 1 Chronicles 4:18.
56. The most famous exploration of this characteristic of Hebrew narrative is in Erich Auerbach, "Representations of Reality in Homer and the Old Testament," in *Modern Critical Views: The Bible*, ed. Harold Bloom (Philadelphia: Chelsea House Publishers, 1987), 45–58. This is a reprint of his chapter in *Mimesis: The Representation of Reality in Western Literature* (Princeton: Princeton University Press, 1953).
57. *BDB*, 328; *HALOT*, 328.
58. Indeed, Pharaoh's daughter becomes a potent symbol to many, including those in support of adoption and adoptees. See Langston, *Exodus*, 30–31.
59. Ellison, "Mothers," 67–68.
60. Meyers, *Exodus*, 40–42.
61. Ellison, "Mothers," 67.

62. Shawn W. Flynn, *Children in Ancient Israel: The Hebrew Bible and Mesopotamia in Comparative Perspective* (Oxford: Oxford University Press, 2018), 59–61.
63. Cynthia R. Chapman, *The House of the Mother: The Social Roles of Maternal Kin in Biblical Hebrew Narrative and Poetry* (New Haven: Yale University Press, 2016), 141.
64. Flynn, *Children in Ancient Israel*, 89.
65. Flynn, *Children in Ancient Israel*, 89.
66. For a discussion of the American ideology that presents nuclear families as an ideal, see Karen V. Hansen, *Not-So-Nuclear Families: Class, Gender, and Networks of Care* (New Brunswick, NJ: Rutgers University Press, 2005), 4–7.
67. We do not know from the text when or how Moses learned about his Israelite heritage. He certainly already knows it in Exodus 2:11–14 when he kills the Egyptian overseer. Since he was raised in the household of his Israelite mother and could have lived there until he was three, it is possible that he always knew of his Israelite heritage. In the New Testament, Hebrews 11:25 equates Moses's rejection of his Egyptian heritage with his rejecting "the pleasures of sin."

8

Naomi, Ruth, and Boaz
Borders, Relationships, Law, and Ḥesed

Gaye Strathearn and Angela Cothran

The book of Ruth presents a particularly fertile field for any exploration about issues of social justice. Its story deals with people crossing geographical, social, economic, and religious borders. Naomi and Ruth both experience the plight of being foreign refugees:[1] Naomi when she and her family fled to Moab to escape the famine in Bethlehem-judah, and Ruth when as a childless widow she chooses to follow Naomi back. For Ruth, in particular, the unspoken question is how will the people of Bethlehem-judah respond to her? Will she be valued as someone who adds to the Israelite culture, or will they fear her as someone who dilutes it?[2] As the women enter Bethlehem-judah, both are in need of the Mosaic stipulations that required the covenant Israelites to look after the marginalized in their community. The book of Ruth is also a story of relationships: wealth and poverty, Israelite and Gentile, landowner and laborer, and native and immigrant.[3] Moreover, it provides an important example of at least one group's application of the covenant responsibility in the Mosaic law to care for people who lived on the edges of Israelite society.

As discussed in other chapters in this volume, the Mosaic law emphasizes Israelite responsibility to look after the needy, who are often categorized into three groups: the widows, the orphans, and the *gērîm* (translated as "strangers" in the King James Version). This latter group consisted of Israelite and gentile people who lived within Israel's borders but had, for various reasons, been displaced. These *gērîm*, whether Israelites, resident aliens, or refugees, all enjoyed a protected status under the law of Moses.[4]

All three of these groups were particularly vulnerable, in part, because they usually did not inherit land, which was mostly passed down patriarchally and within an appointed tribe. Widows who had no husband were not provided for in the basic biblical law of inheritance (Numbers 27),[5] orphans had no father, and the *gērîm* did not have land appointed to them.[6] Since the Psalmist portrays God as a "helper of the fatherless" (Psalm 10:14), someone who "preserveth the strangers (*gērîm*)," and who "relieveth the fatherless and widow" (Psalm 146:9; compare 68:5), it is only natural that his laws would expect his covenant people to provide for the needy (Deuteronomy 26:11–13). When these people failed to live up to these standards, the prophets repeatedly denounced them and called them to repentance (e.g., Isaiah 1:16–18; Jeremiah 7:3, 5–7; Amos 2:6–7; 4:1; 5:11; 8:4–6), and God declared, "My wrath shall wax hot, and I will kill you with the sword" because they had broken their covenants (Exodus 22:24).[7]

The book of Ruth strongly connects with these covenantal obligations, not by debating legal statutes or condemning their violations but by being a rare biblical text that "provides us with evidence of how biblical law was actually followed in practice, [and] how it was negotiated and modified in accordance with the needs of the moment."[8] Both Naomi and Ruth were widows who experienced the pangs of poverty and knew what it was like to be a refugee in a foreign land. Even though these two women worked proactively to become self-sufficient in their pressing time of need, their story took place in a patriarchal society, and their efforts were fully realized only as they joined forces with Boaz. His actions are examples of how biblical laws could be interpreted in expanded ways and are a reminder that when dealing with social issues, it is often not enough to simply live the letter of the law. Many times, to truly help people in need, it is necessary for covenant people to extend themselves beyond the legal mandates.

Before delving into issues of social justice, it is important to first understand the book of Ruth in its larger context. The book's teachings on social justice are woven into a rich tapestry of biblical, historical, and theological themes. With that context setting the scene, we will then turn our attention to each of the three major players in the book of Ruth: Naomi, Ruth, and Boaz. Each provides an important window for modern readers to see how at least one ancient community applied the legal mandates of the law of Moses to provide for the disadvantaged in their community. While not everything in this book will resonate well with modern readers, it is important to recognize that they lived in a different time and culture than ours, making it unreasonable to try and impose our standards on them. Rather, we should look for the timeless principles that can also provide guidance for our efforts to reach out to those who are marginalized in our communities.

Dating the Book of Ruth

The book of Ruth refuses to reveal its origins easily. Its opening line says that the events took place during the time "when the judges ruled" (Ruth 1:1), meaning sometime between 1200 and 1000 BC. In the Septuagint, Latin, and English versions, the book of Ruth is found following the book of Judges. In the Hebrew version, however, the book is separated from Judges and found in the Writings section (the *Ketuvim*). One difficulty of dating Ruth to the time of Judges is that the two books present very different environments. In contrast to the book of Judges, which portrays "social upheaval, foreign invasions, lawlessness, and anarchy,"[9] the book of Ruth is set in a much more tranquil, pastoral setting. Scholars, therefore, generally argue for a later date. Two popular possibilities are that it was written either during the period of the United Monarchy (ca. 1000–930 BC) as a means to glorify the Davidic dynasty[10] or during the Persian period (ca. 537–332 BC) to oppose a certain interpretation of Deuteronomy opposing mixed marriages, as reflected in the writings of Ezra and Nehemiah (Ezra 9–10; Nehemiah 10:29–30).[11] From a linguistic perspective, there is also a third possibility, which takes into account the development of the Hebrew language from preexilic times, known as Standard Biblical Hebrew, to the language found in the postexilic period, known as Late Biblical Hebrew.[12] The book of Ruth contains elements from both Standard and Late Biblical Hebrew, which means that the text, *in its present form*, could not predate the late sixth century BC. However, the elements of Standard Biblical Hebrew may allow for the notion of an early version of the text that was later redacted into its present form. One theory is that the story may have started as a poem, and "after a period of oral transmission," it was written down and redacted into the form with which we are familiar.[13]

Setting the Stage: Ruth 1 in Context

The book of Ruth is deeply rooted in the Old Testament theme of covenantal fidelity and reminds readers that the goal of that covenant was always intended to bless *all* the families and nations of the earth (Genesis 12:3; 18:18; emphasis added). In particular, it focuses on the notion that blessings of the Abrahamic covenant could be extended to the Moabites, who had traditionally experienced strained relationships with the Israelites.[14] This strained relationship between Israel and Moab is highlighted by Deuteronomy's prohibition on Moabites participating in the Israelite community for up to ten generations (Deuteronomy 23:3–6).[15]

Ruth's ethnicity as a Moabite woman is a central focus throughout the story since readers are constantly reminded of her foreign identity. Nevertheless, the marriage of Ruth and Boaz ties the two nations together in two important ways. First, the marriage promotes the reunification of Terah's genealogical descendants through Abraham and his brother Haran (Abraham 2:1–4; Genesis 11:27–32). Second, it connects the Israelites and Moabites as the ancestors for both King David (Ruth 4:18–22) and the messianic Jesus (Matthew 1:1–17; Luke 3:32).[16] Thus the book of Ruth portrays "a social reality that is not envisioned in Deuteronomy."[17] There is no evidence that the author negatively viewed Elimelech's migration to Moab with his family. Rather, it seems that the people of Moab helped this refugee family for over a decade (Ruth 1:4).

The book of Ruth opens by describing a famine in Judea (1:1). Famines were a frequent reality in the biblical record.[18] They often resulted in the migration of nomadic families and tribes seeking food for themselves and pasture for their flocks.[19] The famine in Judea caused Elimelech and his family, like Abraham and Jacob before them, to migrate as refugees to the pastures of Moab, which had apparently escaped the famine.[20] The ensuing story revolves around three major characters: Naomi, Ruth, and Boaz. In the remainder of this chapter, we will examine issues of social justice such as gender, poverty, *ḥesed*, and the place of refugees through the lens of the intertwining lives of these three characters.

Naomi and Ruth

The book of Ruth and the book of Esther are the only books in the Old Testament that are "gynocentric," meaning they are named after women and focus on the stories of women, despite the facts that those women live in a male-dominated society and that the accounts eventually "return to a male story."[21] In fact, Ruth is one of the few places in scripture that gives us "a hint of a women's community and social life existing alongside yet distinct from male society."[22] Unfortunately, we do not know who wrote the book of Ruth. Traditionally, it has been assumed that it was written by a man, but scholars are increasingly entertaining the idea that it may have been written by a woman or, at least, may have come from women's storytelling traditions that were later blended with those of men.[23] The possibility that a male wrote the text always remains, but scholars have identified some elements within the story that support the gynocentric label for the book and at least the possibility of its female voice.[24]

First, in some important ways, the relationship between Naomi and Ruth starkly contrasts with that of other women in the Bible who are described as being in competition with each other: Sarah and Hagar, Leah and Rachel, Hannah and Peninah. As the story opens, Naomi, Ruth, and Orpah are all widows and childless in Moab—Naomi because her husband and two sons have died, and Ruth and Orpah because their husbands have died and (even after ten years of marriage) these two women had apparently not given birth to any children (Ruth 1:4). While childlessness is often a source of contention in other paired female stories in the Bible, after Orpah returns to her family, Naomi and Ruth instead tackle their needy circumstances together. Although that relationship should not be viewed as one of equals, the women of Bethlehem emphasize that Ruth loves Naomi and is "better to thee [Naomi] than seven sons" (4:15). Thus, the book of Ruth portrays these two women and their relationship with each other in a more favorable light than do other biblical stories of female pairs.[25]

Second, the story of the book of Ruth redefines "reality from a women's perspective."[26] For example, when Naomi makes the decision to return to Judah, she implores her daughters-in-law to each return to "her mother's house" so that they could each find rest in the "house of her husband" (Ruth 1:8–9). As many scholars have noted, this phrase "her mother's house" stands out because of its rarity in the Old Testament.[27] The story of Tamar in Genesis 38 indicates that widows normally returned to their "father's house," not their "mother's house."[28]

Likewise, in chapter 1 we find that Naomi's perspective on the bearing of sons is very different from the more usual emphasis on the "father's house" or lineage. In these latter instances, the birth of sons is stressed in the genealogies that promote the inheritances from father to son. In Ruth 4 this emphasis is found when the elders at the city gate invoke the Lord on Boaz's behalf: "the Lord make the woman that is come into thine house like Rachel and like Leah, which two did build the house of Israel" (Ruth 4:11–12). This blessing is fulfilled when the author (or a later redactor) added the genealogy from Boaz to King David at the close of the book (4:18–22). In contrast, chapter 1 focuses on Naomi's emphasis on bearing sons, which is not to ensure the longevity of the father's house but to ensure the ongoing support of their widowed mothers.[29]

While these details do not definitively point to female authorship, they suggest that the book was written from a women-centered perspective. They also show how the day-to-day living of the Mosaic law influenced the lives of the women in the covenantal community.

Naomi (and Ruth)

Although the book is named after Ruth, in some ways the story is focused more on Naomi. In the first chapter, Elimelech and his sons are gone by verse 5 and are referred to only obliquely after that (Ruth 1:8; 2:1, 3, 11, 20; 4:5, 9–10). As the chapter opens, Naomi and her family leave behind the famine in Bethlehem and emigrate to Moab. But while the pastures of Moab were initially a source of sustenance for her family, the story quickly shifts to Moab becoming a symbol of Naomi's barrenness since she loses her husband and both of her sons before they had produced any heirs. In ancient Israel, as in other ancient societies, marriage and children, particularly sons, were the major factors determining a woman's status in society.[30] With only rare exceptions, women were reliant on their fathers and later their husbands for economic support.[31] The first commandment God gave in the Bible was for Adam and Eve to "be fruitful and multiply" (Genesis 1:28). The anguish for a woman who was unable to bear children is highlighted in Rachel's cry to Jacob, "Give me children, or else I die" (Genesis 30:1). Children were not only a means of continuing the family lineage but were also an important source of labor on the family farms that provided the livelihood for most ancient Israelite families.[32]

The loss of her husband and sons threatened Naomi's status in Moabite society. Even after her husband died, her sons would have provided for their mother, but when they also died, Naomi was left without anyone to support her, and as a result she became vulnerable. The account does not indicate how long she remained in Moab after the death of her sons, but as soon as she heard that the famine had abated in Bethlehem, she decided to return, presumably because she had extended family connections there.

Both daughters-in-law began the journey with Naomi even though she repeatedly encouraged them to return to their homes, where she felt they would have opportunities to marry again. In encouraging them to return, she pronounced a blessing on them: "The Lord deal kindly with you, as ye have dealt with the dead, and with me. The Lord grant you that ye may find rest (Hebrew *mənûḥā*, "security"), each of you in the house of her husband" (Ruth 1:8–9). The Hebrew word translated here as "deal kindly" in verse 8 is *ḥesed*, a word that describes a divine characteristic but does not easily translate into English. Petitioners, like Naomi, can invoke God's *ḥesed* on others.[33] The King James Bible variously translates *ḥesed* with words like *kindness, grace, mercy, goodness*, and so forth, but none of these translations quite capture its covenantal aspect, which is emphasized in passages like Deuteronomy 7:12: "Wherefore it shall come to pass, if ye hearken to these judgments, and keep, and do them, that the Lord thy God shall keep unto thee the covenant and the mercy (Hebrew *ḥesed*) which he sware unto thy fathers."[34] On one level, we might therefore expect a petition for God's *ḥesed* to be extended to other covenant-making people, but Naomi is invoking it upon two non-covenant Moabite women who themselves had each exhibited *ḥesed* for their husbands and were then willing to sacrifice their own happiness to provide for Naomi.³⁵ While it is true that Ruth would later commit herself to Naomi and her God, Naomi also bestowed the blessing upon Orpah, and the text gives no indication that Naomi withdrew the petition when Orpah chose to return home to her family and, presumably, her Moabite god(s). In Naomi's mind, God's gift of ḥesed was not extended just to the Israelites but to all of his children, especially those who acted in divine ways. Naomi's blessing reminds us again that the Abrahamic covenant was intended to bless "all families of the earth" (Genesis 12:3).

When Naomi and Ruth arrived in Bethlehem, the personal, economic, and social weight of Naomi's experiences in Moab bubbled to the surface as she exclaimed to the Bethlehemites in Job-like anguish: "Call me not Naomi [Hebrew for 'pleasing'], call me Mara [Hebrew for 'bitterness']: for the Almighty hath dealt very bitterly with me. I went out full, and the Lord hath brought me home again empty: why then call ye me Naomi, seeing the Lord hath testified against me and the Almighty hath afflicted me?" (Ruth 1:20–21). In this cry we feel Naomi's very real pain and anguish as she struggled to understand why a God of ḥesed had caused this bitterness to come upon her. The contrast between famine and harvest that is woven throughout the narrative parallels Naomi's initial feelings of emptiness as she returns to Bethlehem with the fulness that she experiences when Ruth gives birth to Obed at the conclusion of the story and the women declare him to be "a son born to Naomi" (4:17). Thus, God's ḥesed was indeed poured out upon her.

When Naomi first returned to Bethlehem, she had two major objectives. First, there was the immediate need to obtain food. Apparently, Naomi still owned land in the region (Ruth 4:3), but she didn't have access to it, perhaps because Elimelech had "sold" it before fleeing to Moab, or "left it in the hands of a relative to look after in his absence," or the land had simply not been prepared and planted, although the author does not give any details.³⁶ Under Mosaic law, land belonged to God (Leviticus 25:23), who allocated parts of Canaan to Israelite families (that is, men) and tribes (Numbers 26:52–54;

33:54; Joshua 13–22). Under those circumstances the ancestral land was to remain within the family through inheritances.[37] If a person's economic situation necessitated its sale, then the law allowed for the land to be leased but mandated that it eventually be returned to the family either by a relative redeeming the land, as Boaz did in chapter 4, or by having it returned during the Year of Jubilee (Leviticus 25:8–13, 25–28). Without access to any harvest from Elimelech's (now Naomi's) land, the two women needed to take advantage of other provisions in the Mosaic law designed to provide for the poor, the widows, and the strangers in need.

Naomi's second objective, as detailed in Ruth 3, was to ensure long-term security for both her and Ruth. She asked Ruth, "My daughter, shall I not seek rest (Hebrew *mānôaḥ*) for thee, that it may be well with thee?" (3:1). Here the word *rest* can refer to absence of work, but it also denotes a freedom from the anxiety that comes from living in exile (Deuteronomy 28:65; Lamentations 1:3), or, as in Ruth and Naomi's case, someone who was a widow and had no family. In seeking to achieve both of these objectives, Naomi stepped back from the center of the story and worked in the wings, so to speak. Ruth then takes center stage, although Naomi will orchestrate meetings between Ruth and one of Elimelech's kinsmen by the name of Boaz.

Ruth (and Boaz and Naomi)

There is some ambiguity in the story over Ruth's status as she left Moab behind and entered into her new community in Bethlehem, ambiguity that raises important questions about identity and religious and ethnic affiliations. Up until Ruth 4:10, the author repeatedly emphasizes Ruth's Moabite identity (Ruth 1:4, 6, 22; 2:2, 6, 21; 4:5, 10). She is never considered to be an Israelite in the story, and Ruth is very aware of her marginal status. In her first dialogue with Boaz, she uses two telling words to describe herself. First, she refers to herself as a *nokrîyah* (2:10), which the King James Version translates as "stranger." But this translation masks an important nuance since the KJV translates both *gēr* (singular of *gērîm*) and *nokrîyah* as "stranger." We have noted earlier that *gēr* refers to both Israelite and gentile peoples who were displaced but enjoyed a protected status within a community. A *nokrîya*, however, emphasizes a foreigner without the legal protection of the *gērîm*. Thus, it emphasized "the person's otherness and separateness from the dominant culture."[38] At a later time in her conversation with Boaz, Ruth further emphasized her "otherness" and lack of social status by describing herself as a *šipḥa*—a slave girl, the lowest rank of servants[39]—who doesn't even have the same status as the other slaves (2:13).

This point begs the question of if, and when, as some have argued, Ruth converted to the Israelite religion (Targum of Ruth 1:16; 2:6, 11; 3:10).[40] The difficulty here is that it is probably anachronistic to talk about "conversion" in this context—at least conversion in the sense that we think about it today. This is because we have very little evidence of gentile conversion in the Hebrew Bible, so we are generally left in the dark about what a "conversion" would even look like in the setting of the book of Ruth. This is not to say that the religious boundaries between Israelites and Gentiles were impenetrable,[41] but only that the boundary was "not always clearly marked," especially for women.[42] While men were expected to be circumcised, we don't know of any set conversion rituals for women until much later. In the ancient world, it was presumed that a woman adopted the god(s) of her husband when she married. This may have been the case with Ruth when she married Mahlon,[43] but the Targum of Ruth describes Ruth as a proselyte (or convert) starting from when she declared her allegiance to Naomi and her God. "Intreat me not to leave thee, or to return from following after thee: for whither thou goest, I will go; and where thou lodgest, I will lodge: thy people shall be my people, and thy God my God: where thou diest, will I die, and there will I be buried" (Ruth 1:16–17; Targum of Ruth 1:16). This oath of commitment is formalized when Ruth concludes with "the Lord do so to me, and more also, if ought but death part thee and me" (1:17).[44] Even though Ruth was not Naomi's biological daughter with this oath Ruth assumed the role of a covenantal daughter with the inherent responsibility to not just worship Naomi's God but to also care for her as a daughter would care for her mother. Thus, the oath forged both an emotional and a legal attachment between the two women.[45]

Regardless of Ruth's religious status, Naomi and Ruth arrived in Bethlehem in a state of apparent poverty. Their situation was in stark contrast to the wealth of those who owned the Bethlehem fields at harvesttime. Naomi had originally journeyed to Moab because of a famine in Bethlehem. Now she returned in the midst of a bountiful harvest, but she still had no access to food. Naomi and Ruth, in many ways, were no different from people today who starve when the world enjoys a bounty of food. For the second time in the narrative, Ruth comes to the center stage of the story. The Mosaic law made provisions for the poor, the widows, and the *gērîm* by directing the Israelites to "not wholly reap the corners" of the field and to leave part of the produce for the needy to come and glean (Leviticus 19:9–10; 23:22; Deuteronomy 24:18–21). These commands implied that in Israel, people with means had an obligation to create opportunities for the poor. Of course, in an agrarian market, such an action would clearly have a negative impact on the economy of the harvest, and it is a reminder that this commandment was just as much a sacrifice for Israelites as was the offering of their animals on the altar.

Whether by design or provident luck—it is unclear in the text—Ruth ended up in one of the fields that belonged to Elimelech's relative, Boaz (Ruth 2:1, 3). Her decision to glean in the fields (2:2) highlights both her willingness to work and her commitment to support herself and Naomi, but it also reminds readers of her abject poverty and the economic divide between her status as a gleaner and that of Boaz as a landowner. The economic divide was yet another boundary for her to cross. As Jennifer L. Koosed has explained, "To glean one must transverse a border, step over a property line, enter into a field that is not one's own. Gleaners, almost by definition, are people who inhabit margins; they are also people who cross borders and live in Borderlands. More than racial or ethnic identity, more than nation of origin, the Borderlands in the book of Ruth are those of class difference."[46]

The narrator introduces Boaz as "a mighty man of wealth" (Ruth 2:1). The Hebrew word translated as "wealth" (*ḥayil*) indicates a landowner who, because of his landholdings, held a place of honor and responsibility in his community. In the narrative, Boaz's actions are an example of what the Mosaic laws of gleaning look like when they are lived. Because Boaz knew of Ruth's circumstances—how she had left behind her family and homeland to look after Naomi (2:11)—he was generous in his interpretation of the gleaning laws, extending "special protection and privileges"[47] to her, and he worked to break down some of the barriers that marginalized her from the community. In our reading, we have identified five major ways that he did this.

First, Boaz welcomed her to glean in his field and encouraged her not to seek to glean in other fields (Ruth 2:8). As a result, Ruth could devote all of her time to gathering food without wasting time moving from field to field. Second, he opened up all of his field to her. Not only was she allowed to glean in the "corners of the field" and collect the grain that remained after the initial harvest, but Boaz also gave her permission to remain close to his maidens and to harvest "even among the sheaves" (2:8, 14–15). Both of these invitations meant that she had access to the full field, not just to the leftovers, so she was able to gather more grain. Third, probably understanding the inherent dangers for a foreign Moabite woman to work alone in the fields, Boaz specifically instructed his young men to "not touch" her (2:9) nor to "reproach her" (2:15). The Hebrew words used in both of these warnings (*nāgaʿ* and *kālam*) carry connotations of violence, with *nāgaʿ* also indicating sexual assault. The fact that Boaz specifically commanded the young men against such actions strongly indicates that the danger of rape and abuse was a real possibility. Fourth, like Naomi before him, Boaz also invoked the God of Israel's blessing upon her. "The Lord recompense thy work, and a full reward be given thee of the Lord God of Israel, under whose wings thou art come to trust (Hebrew ḥāsâ, 'to seek refuge')" (2:12). The Hebrew word translated as "wings" in the KJV is kānāp, which is the same word used to describe the wings of the cherubim that covered the mercy seat on the ark of the covenant (Exodus 25:20) and is a symbol in Ezekiel for God's love of his covenant people (Ezekiel 16:8). Fifth, after a full day of work (2:7, 17), Boaz invited Ruth to join in a meal where she sat not in the shadows but beside the other workers (2:14). Boaz's actions in this chapter provide an important model for how refugees can and should be welcomed into a community. Not only did he treat Ruth with respect, but he also insisted that those who worked for him did likewise.

As a result of Ruth's hard work and Boaz's generous concessions that went beyond his legal responsibilities, Ruth took home to Naomi about an ephah of grain (Ruth 2:7–17), which is equivalent to anything between twenty-nine and fifty pounds of grain—more than enough to provide for the two women for an extended period.[48] That this amount greatly exceeded Naomi's expectations is made clear by her reaction to Ruth's bountiful return, "Blessed be he of the Lord, who hath not left off his kindness (Hebrew ḥesed) to the living and to the dead" (2:20). Naomi's use of the word ḥesed reminds readers of the recurring theme of God's lovingkindness to his children, which is often accomplished through the acts of other people. Robert L. Hubbard has noted that "whenever people of faith practice God-like ḥesed toward each other, God himself acts in them."[49] Naomi understood this bounteous harvest as a confirmation that God had not abandoned her in her time of loss and poverty, as she had charged him in 1:21. Naomi then recognized that Boaz was not just an answer to their immediate need for food, but someone who could also help with her and Ruth's long-term security.

Boaz as Gōʾēl for Ruth and Naomi

Throughout the story, the King James text frequently refers to Boaz as a "kinsman." The first reference in 2:1 is a translation of the Hebrew word modaʿ, which simply refers to a distant relative.

However, beginning in chapter 3, the rest of the citations are translations of the word *gōʾēl* (Ruth 3:9, 12, 13; 4:14), which has the more nuanced meaning of a "redeemer." In the Old Testament, *gōʾēl* had both physical and spiritual dimensions. On the spiritual level, God is frequently described as a *gōʾēl*.[50] On the more physical level, a *gōʾēl* was a close family member with a specific responsibility to "assist impoverished relatives during times of hardship," such as when they "lost their property, liberty, or lives by buying them out of bondage or avenging them."[51] In the book of Ruth, *gōʾēl* is always a reference to a human being, but readers would easily recognize the connection with the "familiar epithet for God," the Redeemer of Israel (*gōʾēl yiśrāēl*; Isaiah 49:7).[52] Thus Boaz acts as a mediator to assist Ruth and Naomi in their physical needs, but in doing so he again becomes the instrument of God's *ḥesed* for those in need.

As chapter 3 opens, Naomi identified Boaz as a *gōʾēl* and as the answer to her and Ruth's long-term needs for security. Since they were in the midst of a harvest, she directed Ruth to go to the threshing floor, where Boaz would work late into the night sorting the harvested barley. Using a stratagem, to be sure, Naomi instructed Ruth to not make herself known until Boaz had finished eating and drinking and had retired to sleep (Ruth 3:3–4). When he was asleep, Ruth lay down at his feet. The KJV says that at midnight he awoke and was "afraid" (3:8), but this could also mean that he had shivered because of the cold or was startled (Hebrew *ḥārad*) to find Ruth lying at his feet. While scholars debate what actually happened here,[53] it seems that the overall intent of verses 6–9 is to describe Ruth's belief that Boaz himself would be the fulfilment of the invocation he had bestowed upon her in the previous chapter. When Boaz asked her to identify herself, she answered, "I am Ruth, thine handmaid [Hebrew *ʾāmā*, 'servant'/'slave']."[54] She then invited Boaz to "spread therefore thy skirt over thy handmaid [servant/slave]; for thou art a near kinsman [*gōʾēl*]." The KJV uses the word *skirt*, but the Hebrew word is *kānāp*, the same word Boaz used in his earlier invocation, there translated as "wings." By using that same symbolic language, Ruth was asking

Boaz to be the human conduit of God's *ḥesed* that he had invoked upon her. She hoped that he would indeed look upon her with mercy and then act as her redeemer.

Boaz's response to Ruth shifts the emphasis from God's and Boaz's *ḥesed* to that of Ruth's, a reminder of Naomi's plea in chapter 1 that the Lord would bestow *ḥesed* upon her and Orpah (Ruth 1:8). He declared, "Blessed be thou of the Lord, my daughter: for thou hast shewed more kindness [*ḥesed*] in the latter end than at the beginning" (3:10). Her "beginning" *ḥesed* was a reference to her decision to leave home and family so that she could look after Naomi. The context suggests that Ruth's "latter" *ḥesed* refers to her actions at the threshing floor. Boaz linked them to her decision to seek Boaz rather than the "young men [Hebrew *bāḥûrîm*], whether poor or rich" (3:10). In every other case where the phrase "young men" is used in Ruth, the KJV translates the Hebrew word *nĕʿārîm*, which refers to young men or servants, but in this instance Boaz used the word *bāḥûrîm*, which is a little more specific than *nĕʿārîm*—*bāḥûrîm* refers to eligible, and particularly choice, young men. Boaz understood that Ruth could have had her pick of any of the young, eligible bachelors, and yet she (and Naomi) had chosen him. Why?

Some might think that it was simply because of his wealth and standing in the community, but since Boaz connected her choice with the divine attribution of *ḥesed*, we suggest that Boaz had in mind a more covenantal purpose. He responded to Ruth's plea for help by saying, "And now, my daughter, fear not; I will do to thee all that thou requirest: for all the city of my people doth know that thou art a virtuous woman" (Ruth 3:11). The word translated as "virtuous" (Hebrew *ḥayil*) here is the same word used by the narrator to describe Boaz in 2:1. The repetition of *ḥayil* to describe both Ruth and Boaz serves two purposes. First, since Ruth was not a wealthy woman, its use reinforces that Boaz was not just a man of wealth but also a man of strength or virtue. Second, it conveys to the reader that this couple would be equally yoked together. Although they came from different social, economic, political, and religious backgrounds, they were both strong in their desires to keep their covenantal obligations to look after those in need of their help. Ruth made an oath to look after Naomi, and Boaz understood his covenantal obligations to look after the poor, the widows, and the strangers in the land.

Boaz committed to help Ruth by redeeming Naomi's land (Leviticus 25:23–30) but acknowledged that there was a gōʾēl who was "nearer than I." He promised that if the latter did not step up to help, then Boaz would serve in that capacity (Ruth 3:12–13). After again providing grain for Ruth to take back to Naomi (3:15), he departed.

In chapter 4 Boaz moves to center stage in the narrative as he examines the best way to redeem Ruth (and Naomi). What is unique in this chapter is that Boaz acts as gōʾēl with a combination of legal customs that are usually discussed separately: redeeming Naomi's land and entering into a levirate marriage with Ruth.[55] Technically, neither of these actions were required of Boaz by law. On the one hand, Boaz knows of a gōʾēl who was "nearer than I" (Ruth 3:12). This gōʾēl apparently had the first right of refusal to redeem Naomi's land. Initially he showed interest in the land, but when Boaz tied the transaction to a levirate marriage with Ruth, the gōʾēl withdrew "lest I mar mine own inheritance" (4:3–6). The law of levirate marriage required a man to marry the widow of his deceased brother if there was no heir (Deuteronomy 25:5–10; Genesis 38:1–26). If the living brother refused the levirate marriage, then the widow was free to marry outside the family. The levirate marriage ensured that the deceased man's name "be not put out of Israel" (Deuteronomy 25:6; see Ruth 4:5, 10).[56] The firstborn child of the levirate marriage legally became the heir of the deceased brother. As a result, the property and lineage remained within the tribal family and the widow was provided for.[57] The biblical mandate invokes a levirate marriage only for brothers that "dwell together" (Deuteronomy 25:5–10), which may refer to the brothers "living on the same family estate" or simply "living in the same vicinity."[58] It appears that neither Boaz nor the "nearer gōʾēl" qualified as levirate candidates under these precise stipulations. When the "nearer gōʾēl" removed his shoe in front of the elders in the gate and gave it to Boaz (Ruth 4:7), he formally recused himself and passed on the responsibility to Boaz.[59] In fulfillment of his promise to Ruth, Boaz stepped up and took responsibility both to redeem Naomi's land and to enter into a levirate marriage with Ruth "to raise up the name of the dead upon his inheritance, that the name of the dead be not cut off from among his brethren" (4:10). Once again Boaz has generously interpreted any legal responsibilities he might have had in these cases. As a result of that generosity, the barrenness both of the land and of Naomi and Ruth that was introduced in chapter 1 has been replaced with fruitfulness, both for the land and for Ruth, for "the Lord gave her conception, and she bare a son" (4:13).

The Book of Ruth in the Modern World

Unfortunately, the struggles of Naomi and Ruth are still experienced by many people in the world today. We would like to suggest three principles that modern readers can take away from studying the book of Ruth.

First, both Naomi and Ruth knew what it was like to be a refugee, to be destitute, and to have to rely on legal statutes to enable them to put food on their family's table. Ruth was willing to work long hours to find food for herself and her mother-in-law. Even so, their lives were enriched by Boaz—someone who chose to use his surplus wealth to help the needy. He did not just live the letter of the law of looking after the poor, widows, and strangers; he was generous in how he interpreted the laws of gleaning, redeeming, and levirate marriage. All of us at times need someone like Boaz in our lives to help us navigate dark times, but we also need to *become* a Boaz so that we can be redeemers for those in our community circles who may be lost, hungry, or poor, or who may feel invisible or marginalized. In every society there are many like Naomi and Ruth and there are many like Boaz—but unfortunately, there are not enough like Boaz to feed *all* those like Naomi and Ruth. In a time and place where many of us enjoy prosperity and wealth, poverty and malnourishment continue even though food is simply being thrown away at an alarming rate.⁶⁰ War and famine continue to force people to flee from their homes and families. Amnesty International reports that globally there are 26 million refugees, half of which are children, who are seeking safe places for their families to both live and thrive.⁶¹ Ruth is a reminder that refugees can, and do, contribute in significant and meaningful ways in their adopted homes, but there is still much for us to do collectively and individually to welcome them and help them integrate into our society before all of God's children can feel safe, can be fed, and can feel loved in this mortal world. As covenant makers, it is *our* responsibility to reach out to those on the margins of our society. We cannot sit back and expect others to take care of them. Just as with the ancient Israelites, God expects each one of us to dedicate at least some of our personal "harvests" for the needy, even if all we have to give is a widow's mite.

Second, the law of Moses's obligations for the covenantal Israelites to look after the needy in their communities were not just in force during the Mosaic period but have been incumbent upon covenant-making people in *every* dispensation.⁶² As much as modern transportation, telecommunications, and the internet have united the world in unprecedented ways, there are still political, geographical, economic, ethnic, and religious borders that segregate God's children. Elder Jeffrey R. Holland has invited each member of the Church to be "committed to freeing the world from the virus of hunger, [and] freeing neighborhoods and nations from the virus of poverty." He continued to plead that we reach out to those who exist on the margins of our societies: "May we hope for . . . the gift of personal dignity for every child of God, unmarred by *any* form of racial, ethnic, or religious prejudice. Undergirding all of this is our relentless hope for greater devotion to the two greatest of all commandments: to love God by keeping His counsel and to love our neighbors by showing kindness and compassion, patience and forgiveness. These two divine directives are still—and forever will be—the only real hope we have for giving our children a better world than the one they now know."⁶³

Third, undergirding everything in the book of Ruth is the living reality that what brings people of different groups together in unity is God's ḥesed. In the book of Ruth, God is specifically mentioned in only two verses (Ruth 1:6; 4:13), yet if the reader looks closely, his ḥesed pervades the story. Naomi, Ruth, and Boaz are people who are covenantally committed and loyal to him and seek to show ḥesed in their interactions with others. Naomi and Ruth were destitute as they entered Bethlehem. Naomi thought that God had abandoned her. This story is a reminder that although God's ḥesed will not remove our trials and periods of darkness, it will always be available to us, not usually through divine epiphanies, but through the actions of his disciples who minister to one another. Ruth ministered to Naomi; Naomi ministered to Ruth; and Boaz ministered to both of them. As a result of each of these people choosing to minister, all of their lives were blessed both temporally and spiritually.

Scholar Alicia Ostriker reminds all who read it that the book of Ruth "is deeply optimistic, with an optimism generated . . . by looking at the possibilities of [ḥ]esed, or loving kindness—lovingly generous human behavior at the most intimate of levels."[64] The question for modern readers is how we can actively incorporate that same sense of covenantal ḥesed in our interactions with those on the periphery of our society.

Gaye Strathearn is a professor of ancient scripture at Brigham Young University.

Angela Cothran graduated with a BA in ancient Near Eastern studies and is a current student at the J. Reuben Clark Law School at Brigham Young University.

Notes

1. Athalya Brenner, "Ruth as a Foreign Worker and the Politics of Exogamy," in *A Feminist Companion to Ruth and Esther*, ed. Athalya Brenner, second series (Sheffield, UK: Sheffield Academic, 1999), 158–62; Agnethe

Siquans, "Foreignness and Poverty in the Book of Ruth: A Legal Way for a Poor Foreign Woman to Be Integrated into Israel," *Journal of Biblical Literature* 128, no. 3 (2009): 443–45. See also the chapter in this volume by Elizabeta Jevtic-Somlai and Robin Peterson, "Their Story Is Our Story Because We Were Strangers: The Relevance of Exodus 22:21 and of Leviticus 19:33–34 in Refugee Awareness Work."
2. Bonnie Honig, "Ruth, the Model Emigrée: Mourning and the Symbolic Politics of Immigration," in Brenner, *Feminist Companion to Ruth and Esther*, 54–56.
3. Gale A. Yee, "Ruth," in *Fortress Commentary on the Bible: The Old Testament and Apocrypha*, ed. Gale A. Yee, Hugh R. Page Jr., and Matthew J. M. Coomber (Minneapolis, MN: Fortress, 2014), 351.
4. Later interpretation of the strangers mentioned in the biblical injunctions developed into "righteous stranger" (*gēr ṣedek*), meaning a "converted Jew," but this is not the sense of the biblical text. Leon Sheleff, "The Stranger in Our Midst: The Other in Jewish Tradition—From Biblical Times to Modern Israel," *Israel Studies Bulletin* 14, no. 2 (1999): 6–8. We are grateful to Avram R. Shannon for pointing us to this source.
5. Hiers does argue, however, that "a widow could receive her husband's property by bequest" or other legal means. Richard H. Hiers, *Justice and Compassion in Biblical Law* (New York: Continuum, 2009), 35.
6. The daughters of Zelophehad successfully challenged the practice that only sons inherited land because their father had five daughters but no sons; as a result, the biblical laws were revised (Numbers 26:33; 27:1–11; 36:1–13; Joshua 17:3–6). Apparently, these revised laws were not always followed in practice. Tobit, rather than his wife, inherited his in-laws' wealth (Tobit 14:13–14). Hiers, *Justice and Compassion*, 33–35.
7. For a more detailed discussion, see David Rolph Seely and Jo Ann Seely, "The Cry of the Widow, the Fatherless, and the Stranger: The Covenantal Obligation to Help the Poor and Oppressed," in this volume.
8. Bernard S. Jackson, "Ruth, the Pentateuch and the Nature of Biblical Law: In Conversation with Jean Louis Ska," in *The Post-Priestly Pentateuch: New Perspectives on Its Redactional Development and Theological Profiles* (Tübingen, Germany: Mohr Siebeck, 2005), 78.

9. Julie Baretz, "Ruth the Moabitess at Bethlehem, Ruth 1–4," in *The Bible on Location: Off the Beaten Path in Ancient and Modern Israel* (Lincoln: University of Nebraska Press, 2015), 74.
10. The genealogical connection between Boaz and King David at the conclusion of the book suggests that the author/redactor is writing during the time of David and looking back to the time of Ruth as she or he connects David with his Moabite past (Yee, "Ruth," 351).
11. Roland E. Murphy, *Wisdom Literature: Job, Proverbs, Ruth, Canticles, Ecclesiastes, and Esther Canticles* (Grand Rapids, MI: Eerdmans, 1981), 86–87; Jeremy Schipper, *Ruth: A New Translation with Introduction and Commentary* (New Haven, CT: Yale University Press, 2016), 22. However, some have argued that "the whole tone of the work seems to argue that its original composition was not for polemical purposes." George S. Glanzman, "The Origin and Date of the Book of Ruth," *Catholic Biblical Quarterly* 21, no. 2 (1959): 204. Further evidence for dating Ruth to the Persian period also includes the thematic connections it has with the books of Esther and Jonah, all of which share a positive view of foreigners and show Jehovah reaching out to people other than the Israelites. Thus, they argue that Ruth's "universalist tone" of God loving all people fits well within a fourth-century context (Glanzman, "Origin and Date," 201).
12. For a discussion of the differences between Standard Biblical Hebrew and Late Biblical Hebrew in the book of Ruth, see Frederic William Bush, *Word Biblical Commentary: Ruth/Esther* (Waco, TX: Word Books, 1982), 25–29.
13. Glanzman, "Origin and Date," 202.
14. The biblical account traces the Moabite lineage to the illicit union between Lot with his daughter (Genesis 19:30–38). The JST of Genesis 19:37 specifically notes that Lot's firstborn daughter "dealt wickedly" when she planned the union.
15. When the Israelites traveled through the land of Moab on their way to the promised land, the Moabites refused to supply them with bread and water and hired Balaam to curse them (Deuteronomy 23:4). On another occasion, the Moabites are decried for enticing the Israelites to commit whoredoms with the daughters of Moab and to offer sacrifices to the

Moabite gods (Numbers 25:1–5). Lastly, during the reign of the Judges, Eglon, the king of Moab, organized a coalition with the Ammonites and Amalekites that invaded and oppressed Israel for eighteen years (Judges 3:14). Although there is no evidence to support their claim, some of our earliest interpreters of Ruth declared that she was a descendant from Eglon (Targum of Ruth 1:4). The later rabbis were aware of the tension between the Deuteronomic prohibition and the story of Ruth. They focus on the fact that the language of the commandment is masculine and so applies only to Moabite men and not women such as Ruth (m. Yevamot 8:3; b. Yevamot 77a:4). Jonathan Magonet, "Rabbinic Reading of Ruth," *European Judaism: A Journal for the New Europe* 40, no 2 (2007): 155.

16. Edward L. Greenstein, "Reading Strategies and the Story of Ruth," in *Women in the Hebrew Bible: A Reader*, ed. Alice Bach (New York: Routledge, 1999), 215–16. When David flees from Saul, he seeks refuge for his parents with the king of Moab (1 Samuel 22:3–4). The rabbis attribute David's struggle to be accepted as king because of his background, especially of Ruth's Moabite status" (Ruth Rabbah 4:8; 8:1). Magonet, "Rabbinic Reading of Ruth," 156.

17. Siquans, "Foreignness and Poverty," 443–44.

18. For example, Genesis 12:10; 26:1; 41:27; 2 Samuel 21:1; 1 Kings 18:2; 2 Kings 4:38; Haggai 1:11; Nehemiah 5:3. Where rainfall irrigation is utilized, requiring an annual precipitation of around nine inches a year for crops to grow, even a slight decrease in the rainfall can lead to a famine. L. de Blois and R. J. van der Spek, *An Introduction to the Ancient World*, 2nd ed. (New York: Routledge, 2008), 9–10.

19. Abraham left Ur and traveled to Haran, then to the land of Canaan, and then on to Egypt—all because of famine (Abraham 3:1, 4, 17, 21); Jacob sent his sons to Egypt because of a famine and eventually moved his family there (Genesis 42–47). These biblical migrations are consistent with other tribal migrations in the ancient Near East. In the twenty-first century BC, possibly also as the result of a drought, Semitic-speaking tribes known as the Amorites infiltrated southern Mesopotamia, establishing important city-states such as Mari and Babylon.

20. The KJV uses "country" to translate the Hebrew *sādeh*. We translate it as "pastures," which I think reinforces the fruitfulness of Moab that enticed Elimelech and his family to leave Bethlehem-judah. Later commentators attribute the deaths of Elimelech and his sons to a divine punishment either because they left Judah (*Bava Bathra*, 91a:8, 91b:3) or because they married foreign wives (Targum of Ruth 1:4).
21. Alicia Ostriker, "The Book of Ruth and the Love of the Land," *Biblical Interpretation* 10, no. 4 (2002): 344.
22. Ostriker, "Book of Ruth," 348.
23. Fokkelien van Dijk-Hemmes, "Ruth: A Product of Women's Culture?," in *A Feminist Companion to Ruth*, ed. Athalya Brenner, first series (Sheffield, UK: Sheffield Academic, 1993), 134–39; S. D. Goitein, "Women as Creators of Biblical Genres," *Prooftexts* 8, no. 1 (1988): 4; Ostriker, "Book of Ruth," 345–46; Irmtraud Fischer, "The Book of Ruth: A Feminist Commentary to the Torah," in Brenner, *Feminist Companion to Ruth and Esther*, 19.
24. Dijk-Hemmes, "Ruth: A Product of Women's Culture?," 136–37; Athalya Brenner, "Female Social Behaviour: Two Descriptive Patterns within the 'Birth of the Hero' Paradigm," *Vetus Testamentum* 36 (1986): 259, 66–67; George Savran, "The Time of Her Life: Ruth and Naomi," *A Journal of Jewish Women's Studies and Gender Issues* 30 (2016): 7.
25. The positive relationship between Naomi and Ruth does not mean that they considered themselves to be equal peers. Ruth uprooted her life to follow Naomi and appears to be her servant. Perhaps it is because of her age, but Naomi does not work in the fields alongside Ruth to put food on their table. Ultimately, the story concludes with Ruth's bearing a child that is identified as Naomi's son. For discussions on some of these issues, see Danna Nolan Fewell and David M. Gunn, "'A Son Is Born to Naomi!' Literary Allusions and Interpretation in the Book of Ruth," in Bach, *Women in the Hebrew Bible*, 233–39; and Yael Shemesh, "The Stories of Women in a Man's World: The Books Ruth, Esther, and Judith," in *Feminist Interpretation of the Hebrew Bible in Retrospect*, ed. Susanne Scholz (Sheffield, UK: Sheffield Phoenix, 2013), 1:248–58.
26. Dijk-Hemmes, "Ruth: A Product of Women's Culture?," 137.

27. The only other occasions are in the story of Rebekah (Genesis 24:28) and in the Song of Songs (3:4; 8:2).
28. Genesis 38:11; compare Leviticus 22:13. Robert L. Hubbard Jr., *The Book of Ruth* (Grand Rapids, MI: Eerdmans, 1988), 102. The phrase "mothers house" in the Song of Solomon (3:4; 8:2) seems to refer to the mother's bedroom, rather than a separate dwelling place. Hubbard, *Book of Ruth*, 102. In Genesis 24:28, the phrase seems to refer to the mother's family.
29. Dijk-Hemmes, "Ruth: A Product of Women's Culture?," 137.
30. For example, see Genesis 16:4, where Sarah's status is affected when her handmaid Hagar bears a son to Abraham.
31. The exceptions were generally servant women, who were provided for by their masters and mistresses, and prostitutes, who had their own source of income. Susan Ackerman, "Women in Ancient Israel and the Hebrew Bible," in *Oxford Research Encyclopedia, Religion*, https://oxfordre.com/religion.
32. Ackerman, "Women in Ancient Israel," 5.
33. *Ḥesed* was what God showed to Joseph when he was in prison (Genesis 39:21) and to the Israelites when God delivered them from Egypt (Exodus 15:13). For an example of someone petitioning that God would bestow *ḥesed* upon someone else, see Genesis 24:12.
34. Likewise, "Incline your ear, and come unto me: hear, and your soul shall live; and I will make an everlasting covenant with you, even the sure mercies [*ḥesed*] of David" (Isaiah 55:3; see also Psalm 25:10). Daniel L. Belnap, "'How Excellent Is Thy Lovingkindness': The Gospel Principle of Hesed," in *The Gospel of Jesus Christ in the Old Testament: The 38th Annual BYU Sidney B. Sperry Symposium* (Provo, UT: Religious Studies Center, Brigham Young University, 2009), 170–86.
35. Hubbard, *Book of Ruth*, 104.
36. Bernard S. Jackson, "Law and Narrative in the Book of Ruth: A Syntagmatic Reading," *Jewish Law Association Studies* 27 (2017): 102. It appears that Naomi's sons inherited their father's land, but since they had both died without heirs, Naomi inherited it from them; thus Boaz says that he bought "all that was Elimelech's, and all that was Chilion's and Mahlon's, of the hand of Naomi" (Ruth 4:9). See also Ruth 4:5, where Boaz tells the

near kinsman that he will buy the land from both Naomi and Ruth. Hiers, *Justice and Compassion*, 36–37.

37. Clearly, this principle of land ownership describes an ideal situation that was not always lived. Isaiah (5:8) and Micah (2:2) both condemn the aristocracy who take control of people's homes and lands.
38. Gale A. Yee, "'She Stood in Tears amid the Alien Corn': Ruth, the Perpetual Foreigner and Model Minority," in *They Were All Together in One Place: Toward Minority Biblical Criticism* (Atlanta: Society of Biblical Literature, 2009), 127.
39. *HALOT*, s.v. שִׁפְחָה.
40. The Targum of Ruth is one of a number of Aramaic translations and interpretations of the Hebrew Bible. For discussions on Ruth's possible conversion to the Israelite religion, see Bernard S. Jackson, "Ruth's Conversion: Then and Now," in *The Jewish Law Annual* 19, ed. Hanina Ben-Benahem and Berachyahu Lifshitz (London: Routledge, 2011), 53–61; Edward Campbell, *Ruth: New Translation with Introduction and Commentary* (New York: Doubleday, 1975), 80, 82; Kristen Nielsen, *Ruth: A Commentary*, trans. Edward Broadbridge (Louisville: Westminster John Knox, 1997), 49. For examples from members of the Church of Jesus Christ who assume that Ruth converted, see Aileen H. Clyde, "Confidence through Conversion," *Ensign*, November, 1992, 89; Thomas S. Monson, "Models to Follow" *Ensign*, November 2002, 61.
41. Initially, those outside the Abrahamic lineage seemed to have been absorbed in the covenant community. An example that hints at this assimilation is when Abram left Haran, he took in addition to his family "the souls that they had gotten in Haran" (Genesis 12:5; compare Abraham 2:15). Likewise, when Moses and the people of Israel left Egypt, "a mixed multitude went up also with them" (Exodus 12:38).
42. In the story *Joseph and Asenath*, Asenath became a proselyte to Judaism by destroying her idols, renouncing polytheism, and fasting and mourning for seven days (9.2; 10:13–17). The *Apocalypse of Baruch* describes a proselyte with language that is remarkably similar to Boaz's invocation for Ruth (2:12), "people who have left their vanities to take refuge under your wings" (41:4). Shaye J. D. Cohen, "Crossing the Boundary and Becoming a

Jew," *Harvard Theological Review* 82, no. 1 (1989): 13–33. Later rabbis indicated that a ritual bath (*mikvah*) and acceptance of the commandments was required for conversion. Jackson, "Ruth's Conversion," 54.

43. Jackson, "Ruth's Conversion," 53–61; Cohen, "Crossing the Boundary," 25.
44. Jack M. Sasson, *Ruth: A New Translation with a Philological Commentary and a Formalist-Folklorist Interpretation*, 2nd ed. (Sheffield, UK: JSOT, 1989), 30.
45. Brenner, "Ruth as a Foreign Worker," 159.
46. Jennifer L. Koosed, *Gleaning Ruth: A Biblical Heroine and Her Afterlives* (Columbia: University of South Carolina Press, 2011), 49.
47. Adele Berlin, "The Book of Ruth," in *The HarperCollins Study Bible: New Revised Standard Version with Apocryphal/Deuterocanonical Books, Student Edition*, ed. Harold W. Attridge and Wayne A. Meeks (San Francisco: HarperCollins, 2006), 385.
48. Sasson, *Ruth*, 57.
49. Hubbard, *Book of Ruth*, 72. See also Ostriker, "Book of Ruth," 352.
50. Job 19:25; Psalms 19:14; 78:35; Isaiah 41:14; 43:14; 44:6, 24; 47:4; 48:17; Jeremiah 50:34.
51. Yee, "Ruth," 354; Jennifer C. Lane, "The Lord Will Redeem His People: 'Adoptive' Covenant and Redemption in the Old Testament," in *Sperry Symposium Classics: The Old Testament*, ed. Paul Y. Hoskisson (Salt Lake City: Deseret Book, 1999), 49.
52. Ostriker, "Book of Ruth," 351–52.
53. Jackson, "Law and Narrative," 110, 112; Ostriker, "Book of Ruth," 346. Some understand the language to be a euphemistic description of a sexual encounter, but almost immediately Boaz described Ruth as a virtuous/worthy woman (3:11).
54. This is not the same word *šipḥah* that she used to describe herself in 2:13. Both words can be used synonymously to describe a slave status, but technically a *šipḥa* refers to "a girl who is not free but is yet untouched, whose duty was primarily to serve the woman of the house," while an *'āmā* refers to "a woman who is not free, and who could be a man's secondary wife." *HALOT*, s.v. שִׁפְחָה.
55. Brad Embry, "Legalities in the Book of Ruth: A Renewed Look," *Journal for the Study of the Old Testament* 41, no. 1 (2016): 34.

56. For a discussion on levirate marriage, see Jeffrey H. Tigay, "Excursus 23: Levirate Marriage," in *Deuteronomy: The Traditional Hebrew Text with the New JPS Translation* (Philadelphia: Jewish Publication Society, 1996), 482–83.
57. See Josephus, *Antiquities of the Jews* 4.8.254–56.
58. Tigay notes that "in Genesis 13:6 and 36:7 'dwelling together' means dwelling close enough to use the same pasture land." He continues, "in either case, this condition is perhaps related to the fact that the offspring of the levirate marriage will inherit the dead man's property. This may mean that in biblical times the marriage was obligatory only if the levir's home, where the widow and her future child would reside, was close to that property." Tigay, *Deuteronomy*, 231.
59. According to Deuteronomy 25, it was the widow's responsibility to take the sandal to the elders in the gate as a sign that the brother refused to participate in a levirate marriage (25:7–9), but in Ruth the nearer *gōʾēl* removes his sandal to "signal forfeiture of his rights as the rights of the kinsman-redeemer." Embrey, "Legalities in the Book of Ruth," 35.
60. It has been argued that the United States alone throws away 80 billion pounds of food each year; see https://www.rts.com/resources/guides/food-waste-america/.
61. See https://www.amnesty.org/en/what-we-do/refugees-asylum-seekers-and-migrants/global-refugee-crisis-statistics-and-facts/.
62. For examples, see Luke 3:7–14; James 1:27; Mosiah 4:26; Doctrine and Covenants 44:4–6; 72:10–12.
63. Jeffrey R. Holland, "A Perfect Brightness of Hope," *Ensign*, May 2020, 82–83.
64. Ostriker, "Book of Ruth," 346.

The Poor

9

The Poor and the Needy in the Book of Isaiah

Dana M. Pike

When we read Jesus's pronouncement in 3 Nephi that "great are the words of Isaiah" (3 Nephi 23:1), prophecies about the Messiah and the scattering and gathering of Israel are what may quickly come to mind. However, the book of Isaiah *also* contains important passages addressing the treatment of the poor and needy. These passages, which particularly focus on one of the many social ills in ancient Israelite society, range from condemning the unrighteous treatment of the poor to promising how the Lord will (eventually) deliver them.[1]

Stating the obvious, the Hebrew Bible (the Christian Old Testament) depicts the Lord's call to the ancient Israelites to live in a covenant relationship with him.[2] That covenant included not only devotion to Jehovah, but also the injunction to "love thy neighbour as thyself" (Leviticus 19:18).[3]

This paper reviews and analyzes the passages in the book of Isaiah dealing with "the poor" in order to present how the Israelites' Jehovah, the God who became our resurrected Lord, expected, and still expects, his covenant people to treat the poor and oppressed in their midst. Therefore, this is not a study of all biblical passages relating to "the poor."[4] Even with this limited focus on passages in the book of Isaiah, there are many important statements to assess that deal with Jehovah's view of peoples' covenant obligations to assist those in need. Following a brief summary of the context in which Isaiah lived, the Hebrew words that are translated as "poor" in the book of Isaiah will be overviewed, and then passages that mention the poor will be assessed.[5]

Isaiah in Context

For the purposes of this discussion, it is important to have a basic sense of the social environment in which Isaiah lived, since many of his statements about the poor are related to his setting (and are still applicable today). Isaiah was prophetically active in Jerusalem, the capital of the kingdom of Judah, from about the 730s to 690s BC.

Archaeological evidence and biblical texts combine to indicate that the first two-thirds of the eighth century were relatively stable politically and that there was real economic prosperity in both the northern kingdom of Israel and the southern kingdom of Judah.[6] Even so, rural living and subsistence farming and herding were still the norm for most Israelites.[7] During this time period, it appears that at least some of the newly rich estate owners and individuals in various leadership positions exploited many in the large subsistence class of people, causing economic hardships for them.[8] Plus, when a working family member became ill, injured, or died, or when rainfall was insufficient and crops were less productive, hunger and debt would have been real occurrences for many Israelites. Then, in the latter quarter of the eighth century, Assyrian invasions, warfare, death, deportations, destruction of crops and agricultural lands, and pressing tribute to Assyria brought additional challenges to vulnerable Israelites who lived in the land of Israel. Isaiah thus witnessed or was at least aware of all these developments.

Although it is difficult to determine the full extent of social abuses at that time, comments on social ills that affected the poor appear in the first chapter of the book of Isaiah, giving an instructive indicator of the general corruption in Judahite society. ("Judahites" designates those who lived in the southern Israelite kingdom, known as Judah. So, Judahites were Israelites who lived in the kingdom of Judah.) In Isaiah 1, which serves in many ways as a thematic introduction to the book, Jehovah pleads with his covenant people to turn in repentance from their collective sinfulness toward him: "And when ye spread forth your hands [in prayer], . . . your hands are full of blood. Wash you, make you clean; put away the evil of your doings from before mine eyes; cease to do evil; learn to do well; seek judgment [*mišpāṭ*, pronounced "mishpaht"], relieve the oppressed, judge the fatherless, plead for the widow. Come now, and let us reason together, saith the LORD" (Isaiah 1:15–18, see also v. 4). This condemnation of those who preyed on the weakest members of their society and the string of action verbs in this passage convey a sense of urgency and impending divine judgment, which is clearly announced throughout verses 2–20.

Note that the Hebrew word *mišpāṭ*, which is regularly translated as "judgment" in the KJV and which does mean "judgment," was often used with the sense of *just* judgment or "justice," the type of judgment Jehovah dispenses and desires among his people. The word *mišpāṭ* is translated as "justice" in modern English translations of Isaiah 1:17, and in most of the other passages cited below, and is often better understood in that way. Thus, in the context of passages such as Isaiah 1:17, seeking *mišpāṭ* "does not [solely] refer to aspects of the judicial process but rather to the concept of the administration of social justice: improving the condition of the impoverished, rescuing the oppressed from the oppressor, upholding the rights of the weak and needy."[9] Such expected *mišpāṭ*, which included the proper administration of justice for the poor and others in need, appears to have been seriously lacking among some, and probably many, of Jehovah's covenant people at the time of Isaiah. This general background provides a context to better understand the passages in the book of Isaiah that mention the poor.

Hebrew Words Meaning "Poor" in the Book of Isaiah

Several Hebrew words, occurring in singular and plural forms, are translated as "poor" and "needy" in the KJV and in most other English Bibles. Some of these are more common in one biblical genre than in others. They share a related semantic field, and various nuances are connoted by each of these terms, too many to fully explore here.[10]

However, in brief, the three Hebrew words in the book of Isaiah that are commonly translated as "poor" or "needy" are *'ebyôn* (plural *'ebyônîm*), which has been defined as meaning "economically or legally distressed; destitute; beggar"; *dal* (plural *dallîm*), which has been defined as meaning "poor; weak, inferior; lacking," often designating a "beleaguered peasant farmer"; and *'ānî* (plural, *'ăniyyîm*), which has been defined as meaning "economically poor; oppressed, exploited; suffering."[11] These meanings are based on the etymology of each word combined with their actual biblical usage.

Because the meanings and usage of these words sometimes overlap, some passages contain more than one of these terms, potentially providing nuance, emphasis, or poetic variety. Each of these three Hebrew words used in poetic passages in Isaiah, for example, occurs in parallel with one of the others. In such cases, Bible translators often render these words as "poor" and "needy" to avoid using "poor" twice in the same verse in English. Thus, in Isaiah 25:4, "Thou hast been a strength to the poor [*dal*], a strength to the needy [*'ebyôn*]" (see similarly, with plural forms, in Isaiah 14:30). Isaiah 26:6 reads, "Even the feet of the poor [*'ānî*], and the steps of the needy [*dallîm*]" (see those terms in reverse order in Isaiah 10:2). And in Isaiah 41:17, "The poor [*'ăniyyîm*] and needy [*'ebyônîm*] seek water." So, depending on the passage, there may be intended subtleties in the use of these different words, detectable or not by us; there may be examples of hendiadys (two nouns joined with a conjunction rather than one noun and a modifier; e.g., "the poor and needy" versus "the needy poor"); or there may just be examples of literary variety.[12] More specific discussion is beyond the scope of this paper, but this overview of Hebrew words used to designate the poor in the book of Isaiah helps in assessing what this major prophetic book teaches about the poor and about the Lord's expectations for their care. For those who are interested, the passages quoted below include in brackets the transliterated Hebrew words that were just reviewed.

Passages Specifically Mentioning the "Poor" in Isaiah

Condemnation of abuse

Passages in the book of Isaiah that specifically refer to the poor and needy (as well as in other prophetic literature in the Bible) generally fall into two broad categories. The first of these is condemnation of Israelites who mistreated and took advantage of other Israelites, thus generating or perpetuating poverty and want.

For example, in Isaiah 3 Jehovah pointedly says through Isaiah, "The LORD will enter into judgment [*mišpāṭ*] with the ancients [= leading elders] of his people, and the princes thereof: for ye have eaten up the vineyard; the spoil of the poor [*'ānî*] is in your houses. What mean ye that ye beat my people to pieces, and grind the faces of the poor [*'ăniyyîm*]? saith the Lord GOD of hosts" (Isaiah 3:14–15; compare Amos 2:6–7; 4:1).[13]

Isaiah 3:1–7 announces judgment against Judahite leaders, while verses 8–15 provide the explanation for this punishment, including the fact that corrupt leaders have inflicted abusive practices on the poor. Verse 14 collectively mentions the "spoil of the poor," with *'ānî* connoting those people who were not just economically poor but were also oppressed and exploited by more powerful and influential leaders. It was obvious who the guilty oppressors were since "the spoil of the poor [ʻānî]" they had acquired was in their own houses. The Hebrew noun translated as "spoil" in the KJV is from the lexical root *g-z-l*, which means "to seize, rob," which signified what was plundered or looted from the poor.[14]

Also, the recurrence of the noun ʻānî (ʻăniyyîm) in verse 15 reinforces the notion of intentional abuse against the oppressed poor. The Lord rhetorically asks the oppressing ones, "What mean ye that ye beat [or crush] my people to pieces, and grind the faces of the poor [ʻăniyyîm]?" Grinding their faces figuratively suggests the poor were walked on, with their faces pushed into the dust. This indictment of (some of) Judah's leaders condemns the arrogance and corruption of the rich and powerful who took unjust advantage of the powerless, hardly what Jehovah expected among this covenant people.

Similarly, Isaiah 5:7b–8 announces, "He [Jehovah] looked for judgment [*mišpāṭ*, "justice"], but behold oppression; for righteousness, but behold a cry. Woe unto them that join house to house, that lay field to field, till there be no place, that they may be placed alone in the midst of the earth!"

Isaiah 5:1–7 presents a reproving parable that communicates the lack of just judgment and the oppression of some Judahites, culminating in the poignant sentiment that Jehovah looked for justice and righteousness, but he found "oppression" and cries of distress instead. Even though words meaning "poor" are not included in Isaiah 5:8, the phrases in this verse—"that join house to house, that lay field to field"—are regularly interpreted as an indictment of rich estate owners who acquired property at the expense of the poor.[15]

These actions had theological as well as practical implications. Practically speaking, subsistence farming families needed their property to support themselves. Moreover, the Israelites believed the land of Canaan/Israel belonged to Jehovah. He was the divine land-Lord. As such, he had directed which tribes were to inherit which portions of the land (Numbers 36:2; Joshua 13:6; 18:6, 10). These allotments were subsequently divided up among the clans and extended families in each tribe. And by divine decree, a family's property was supposed to stay in that family.[16] The corrupt acquisition of other families' property, condemned in Isaiah 5:8, was against Jehovah's will, and it deprived poorer Israelites of a place to live, farm, provide for themselves, and, ultimately, have a sense of self-worth.

Sadly, exploitive and oppressive practices were not limited to estate owners and other wealthy Judahites. Despite Mosaic law to the contrary (e.g., Exodus 23:6–8; Deuteronomy 1:16–18), several passages in the book of Isaiah indicate the poor were also taken advantage of in legal proceedings involving conspiracy, bribery, false witnesses, and other forms of corruption. General critiques of these practices are found in the following two passages:

> Thy princes are rebellious, and companions of thieves: every one loveth gifts [i.e., bribes], and followeth after rewards: they judge not the fatherless, neither doth the cause of the widow come unto them. (Isaiah 1:23)

> Ah, you who are heroes in drinking wine and valiant at mixing drink, who acquit the guilty for a bribe, and deprive the innocent of their rights! (Isaiah 5:22–23 NRSV)

Again, some "princes" and other officials are here condemned for abusing the powerless and less fortunate in Judahite society, preferring bribes and drinking in excess over displaying compassion for widows, orphans, and other Israelites who were not part of their privileged circles. Elsewhere in Isaiah, corrupt Israelite leaders are metaphorically derided as "greedy dogs which can never have enough . . . : they all look to their own way, every one for his gain" (Isaiah 56:11).

While it may be assumed that at least some of the poor were the recipients of the unrighteous actions mentioned in the passages just quoted, the following passage makes this connection explicit: "Woe unto them that decree unrighteous decrees, and that write grievousness which they have prescribed; to turn aside the needy [*dallîm*] from judgment, and to take away the right [*mišpāṭ*] from the poor [*ăniyyēy*] of my people, that widows may be their prey, and that they may rob the fatherless!" (Isaiah 10:1–2).

The Hebrew word *dal* (here plural, *dallîm*) in Isaiah 10:2, translated as "needy" in the KJV, connotes the poor in general, especially those in the subsistence class. The accusation here is that the poor were turned aside or kept from just and fair consideration in legal matters—that there was respect of persons. The next phrase essentially reiterates this concept: the rights of "the poor [*ăniyyēy*] of my people" were being taken away (KJV) or robbed from them by corrupt leaders (the Hebrew verb is *g-z-l*; see above at Isaiah 3:14; 5:23). As previously noted in relation to Isaiah 3:14–15, the plural form of *'ānî* in 10:2 connotes people who were economically poor because of the exploitation they experienced at the hands of more powerful and less caring individuals. The accompanying accusations in 10:2 make this evident.[17] Finally, this verse suggests that "widows" and "the fatherless" were often among "the poor." People who had little were thus robbed by people who already had much. Therefore, some of Judah's officials and elders were pointedly condemned in the book of Isaiah, since payments and partiality appear to have often replaced the just dealings expected by Jehovah among his covenant people.[18]

Another important passage in this category of texts condemning the victimization of the poor is Jehovah's well-known rebuke of Judahites who were "going through the motions" of fasting but abusing the intent of the fast:

> Wherefore have we [Israelites] fasted, say they, and thou [Jehovah] seest not? wherefore have we afflicted our soul, and thou takest no knowledge? Behold [says Jehovah], in the day of your fast ye [Israelites] find pleasure, and exact all your labours. Behold, ye fast for strife and debate, and to smite with the fist of wickedness. . . . Is it such a fast that I have chosen? . . . Is not this the fast that I have chosen? to loose the bands of wickedness, to undo the heavy burdens, and to let

the oppressed go free, and that ye break every yoke? Is it not to deal thy bread to the hungry, and that thou bring the poor ['ăniyyîm] that are cast out [in]to thy house? when thou seest the naked, that thou cover him; and that thou hide not thyself from thine own flesh? (Isaiah 58:3–7)

Rather than smiting fellow Israelites "with the fist of wickedness," Jehovah expected ancient Israelites, as part of their fasting and covenant keeping, to reach out with compassion and generosity to the poor and needy among them. After condemning those who engaged in the religious act of fasting for their personal gain ("we have afflicted our soul"), Jehovah instructed what constituted an acceptable fast: one that was enjoined to compassionately assist "the poor ['ăniyyîm]"—those who had been exploited and oppressed—and others with related needs. There is no evidence that ancient Israelites gave a regular, formal "fast offering," as Latter-day Saints are encouraged to do in this dispensation. However, this passage emphasizes that "real" religion was more than just ritual action. Rather, it involved looking outward and included providing assistance to the poor and needy.

The conditions and the concerns expressed in Isaiah 58:3–7 and the other passages reviewed above demonstrate some Judahites' lack of covenant commitment to Jehovah. Social apathy, greed, exploitation of the powerless, and otherwise unjust social actions produced hardships and grief in the lives of many poor and needy Judahites. The poor thus experienced a serious lack of covenant compassion.

Some Israelites, no doubt, brought impoverished conditions upon themselves through regrettable choices, such as idleness or an excessive lifestyle.[19] However, this situation is *not* the focus in the book of Isaiah, which blames and denounces the unrighteous rich and powerful for the socioeconomic problems in Judah, including poverty. Thus, "like Amos, Isaiah viewed poverty as the creation of the wealthy."[20]

A final passage to review in this category of condemning the abuse of the poor is Isaiah 32:6–7: "For the vile person will speak villany, and his heart will work iniquity, to practise hypocrisy, and to utter error against the LORD, to make empty the soul of the hungry, and he will cause the drink of the thirsty to fail. The instruments also of the churl [= villain, scoundrel] are evil: he deviseth wicked devices to destroy the poor [*ănāwîm*] with lying words, even when the needy [*'ebyôn*] speaketh right" (Isaiah 32:6–7).

The Hebrew word *ănāwîm*, semantically related to *ănî*, is often connected with the lexical root *'-n-n*, with the sense of "bowed down," thus meaning in this passage those who are oppressed by others.[21] It occurs in parallel with the Hebrew word *'ebyôn*, here translated as "needy," which, as mentioned above, generally connotes "economically or legally distressed; destitute." Isaiah 32:6–7 does not specifically mention Judah's leaders and thus may be directed more broadly at people across Judahite society. However, the references to "vile" people who "speak villany, and . . . lying words" against the poor, even when they are in the "right," are reminiscent of the accusations against some Judahite officials in Isaiah 1:23; 5:22–23; and 10:1–2, all cited above.

Isaiah 32:6–7 actually occurs in a larger passage (32:1–8) that describes how a future ideal ruler will govern with justice, and would thus reverse and banish the contemptable behavior of individuals that is the focus of verses 6–7. These verses are included in this first category of passages that condemn the abuse of the poor in the book of Isaiah because these two verses focus on what were exploitive conditions in Judah contemporary with Isaiah. However, this larger passage provides a fitting segue to the second category of passages involving the poor in the book of Isaiah.

Jehovah will provide (future) help for the poor

The second major category of passages that mention the poor and needy in the book of Isaiah emphasizes how Jehovah would help deliver them from oppression and want by means of his own power *and* by sending just and compassionate rulers. These passages emphasize that "God is on the side of the powerless who trust in him."²² Depending on the context and content of each passage cited in this category, this divine aid can be understood to refer to Jehovah's support of the poor in antiquity, his still future deliverance when all poverty and oppression are eliminated, or his aid across an undefined span of time.

This principle of Jehovah caring for the poor is specifically stated in Isaiah 14:30, 32: "The firstborn of the poor [*dallîm*] shall feed, and the needy ['*ebyônîm*] shall lie down in safety. . . . The LORD hath founded Zion, and the poor [*ăniyê*] of his people shall trust in it."

These two verses are couched in a "burden" or judgment oracle against the Philistines (Isaiah 14:28–32; KJV reads "Palestina"), which contrasts the ominous consequences prophesied against them (14:29, 30b, 31) with the positive conditions to be experienced by Jehovah's people who trust in him (14:30a, 32). All three of the prominent words designating the "poor" in the book of Isaiah occur in this passage (all in the plural). Isaiah 14:30 announces that "the poor [*dallîm*]" and "the needy ['*ebyônîm*]" will be safely provided for, while there will be famine and destruction in Philistia. As indicated above, *dal* connotes those who were weak and poor, including subsistence farmers, and '*ebyôn* connotes those who were economically distressed and destitute. Although verse 30 does not explicitly indicate who will provide care for these needy ones, verse 32 presents the answer: "The LORD [Jehovah] hath founded Zion"; therefore, "the poor [*ăniyê*]" of his people shall trust [or, take refuge] in it." The word *ānî* connotes those who are economically poor and oppressed. This latter term seems to function here as a general designation for all the poor, oppressed, and beleaguered among the Lord's people, including those mentioned in verse 30.

The designation "Zion" often occurs in the Old Testament as an alternative name for Jerusalem, the "city of David" and David's dynasty. And, because of Jehovah's temple there, Zion also refers to the dwelling place of Israel's God. Thus, in Isaiah 14:32, "Zion" most likely conjured images in the mind of Isaiah's audience of a Zion ideal—a city of righteousness, justice, safety, and peace—Jehovah's ideal Jerusalem. As expressed in Isaiah 1:27, real characteristics of Zion include "judgment" (*mišpāṭ*, "justice") and "righteousness."[23]

Isaiah 25:1–5 is a future-looking passage emphasizing Jehovah's triumph over worldly powers. This chapter does not specify *when* Jehovah would or will destroy the proud and powerful of the world, other than saying he would do so "in that day" (most Latter-day Saints and many other Christians see the ultimate fulfillment in Jesus's Second Coming and the Millennium); however, this passage does indicate the righteous will praise Jehovah for his saving power, including this exclamation in verse 4: "For thou hast been a strength to the poor [*dāl*], a strength to the needy [*'ebyôn*] in his distress, a refuge from the storm, a shadow from the heat, when the blast of the terrible ones is as a storm against the wall" (Isaiah 25:4).

The verb *to be* at the beginning of verse 4—rendered in the past tense in the KJV—depicts the perspective of someone in the ideal future looking back at the "wonderful things" Jehovah has done (verse 1), including that his sustaining influence has been with the afflicted, including the poor. Since *dāl* and *'ebyôn* appear in poetic parallel, it is hard to know if they are used in a general, synonymous way, or if some nuance about the types of "poor" is intended. Either way, collectively, the poor are promised a future reversal of their ill fortunes if they trust in Jehovah.

In the book of Isaiah the theme of Jehovah's judgment against the proud and wicked is not limited to Israel's enemies. Based on his binding covenant relationship with them, Jehovah also promised to overthrow sinful Israelites but then to mercifully provide restoration and redemption for the faithful among them or their descendants (see, for example, Isaiah 1:24–27). Although such judgment can certainly be interpreted as having come upon the kingdom of Judah in Isaiah's lifetime, in 701 BC when the Assyrians caused great destruction throughout the kingdom (e.g., Isaiah 1:4–9), the language in most of these Isaiah passages alludes, for *complete* fulfillment, to a future time when *ideal* conditions would follow destruction.

With this understanding, some of the passages that mention the poor look to a righteous future ruler descended from David. Although commentators differ on when such passages have been or will be fulfilled, and by whom, as noted above, such passages are often interpreted by some Christians, including many Latter-day Saints, as prophecies of the Second Coming of Jesus Christ and his millennial reign on earth. So, for example, "And there shall come forth a rod out of the stem of Jesse, and a Branch shall grow out of his roots: and the spirit of the LORD shall rest upon him, the spirit of wisdom and understanding, the spirit of counsel and might; . . . with righteousness shall he judge the poor [*dallîm*], and reprove with equity for the meek of the earth: . . . and righteousness shall be the girdle of his loins, and faithfulness the girdle of his reins" (Isaiah 11:1–2, 4–5; compare 2 Nephi 30:9; Doctrine and Covenants 113:1–2; Jeremiah 23:5–6).

This messianic prophecy emphasizes that this "Branch" will, using the Lord's spirit (Isaiah 11:2) and in the fear of the Lord (11:3), judge the poor with "righteousness" (11:4). These attributes stand in contrast to the bribery, false witnesses, and other forms of corruption and exploitation at the expense of the poor evident among at least some of Judah's officials in the days of Isaiah. Even though it is presented as future assistance to future poor, it is likely that the word *dallîm* was originally intended here, as elsewhere, to indicate poor, weak, and distressed Israelites, often the impoverished subsistence farmers.[24] However, *in this passage* there is no indication that poverty will be fully eliminated by this righteous ruler (ultimately Jesus Christ, according to Latter-day Saints), at least initially, but the poor will be treated fairly and justly.

Other passages in this category that suggest future help for the poor, such as Isaiah 26:4–6, envision that deliverance will produce a reversal of fortunes for the poor *and* for the proud, with the result that the poor will have great cause to rejoice. "Trust ye in the LORD for ever: . . . for he bringeth down them that dwell on high; the lofty city, he layeth it low; . . . the foot shall tread it down, even the feet of the poor [*'ānî*], and the steps of the needy [*dallîm*]" (Isaiah 26:4–6; emphasis added).

These verses are part of a larger "song" of praise and thanksgiving (Isaiah 26:1–6). They specifically indicate that not only will the proud be brought low by Jehovah, but that "the feet of the poor [*'ānî*], and the steps of the needy [*dallîm*]" will "tread [or, trample] upon it"; that is, on the "lofty city" and all it represents (26:5). This is in contrast to the "strong city" of the righteous, presumably Jerusalem, mentioned in verse 1. The word *'ānî* usually connotes the oppressed and exploited who became economically poor. So the future reversal proclaimed in this passage seems to represent, conceptually, a contrast with the content of Isaiah 3:15, reviewed above, in which powerful Judahites were condemned because they "beat my people to pieces, and grind the faces of the poor [*'ăniyyîm*]."

A last passage in this category of deliverance of the poor is perhaps more familiar to Latter-day Saints because of the expanded commentary on Isaiah 29 found in 2 Nephi 27:[25] "And in that day shall the deaf hear the words of the book, and the eyes of the blind shall see out of obscurity, and out of darkness. The meek [*'ănāwîm*] also shall increase their joy in the L ORD, and the poor [*'ebyônê*] among men shall rejoice in the Holy One of Israel. For the terrible one [ruthless, tyrannical person] is brought to nought, . . . and all that watch for iniquity are cut off" (Isaiah 29:18–20; compare 14:30–32; 2 Nephi 27:29–31).

This passage is part of a larger text in chapter 29 that alternates pronouncements of woe and redemption (see "woe" in verses 1 and 15). Following judgments against Judahites who attempt to hide their doings from the Lord and others (verses 15–16; differently interpreted by different commentators), verses 17–21 prophesy an overturning of the proud and corrupt by Jehovah, who will (finally) reverse the exploitation of the oppressed and downtrodden, providing comfort and care and an opportunity for them to flourish. The meek and the poor, or the lowly and the destitute, will have good reason to rejoice in Jehovah, "the Holy One of Israel."[26]

Finally, one interesting subset of prophecies about the poor in the future, at least from the vantage point of Isaiah's more immediate future, is found in Isaiah 40–55 (these prophecies are "future" if one accepts that these chapters derive from Isaiah around 700 BC, but not if one accepts that these chapters are products of a "second" Isaiah in the 500s). As commonly interpreted, these chapters appear to be directed to Judahites deported to and eventually returning from Babylonia, and Jehovah's encouraging promises to restore them or their posterity to their own land (e.g., Isaiah 40:1–2; 48:20).[27]

Thus the "poor" in the following two passages were originally envisioned as upper-class Judahites themselves who went into Babylonian exile in 597, 586, and 582 BC (it was primarily upper-class individuals who were deported when the Babylonians conquered smaller kingdoms, not a broad cross-section of a society). They then figuratively became the poor and needy in their own deported circumstances. Jehovah promised to comfort and provide for them as they returned to Jerusalem and Judah.

> When the poor ['ăniyyîm] and needy ['ebyônîm] seek water, and there is none, and their tongue faileth for thirst, I the LORD will hear them, I the God of Israel will not forsake them. (Isaiah 41:17)

> Sing, O heavens; and be joyful, O earth; and break forth into singing, O mountains: for the LORD hath comforted his people, and will have mercy upon his afflicted ['ăniyāw]. (Isaiah 49:13)

Both of these verses contain a form of 'ānî, conceptually linking them to the passages about economically oppressed Israelites living in the kingdom of Judah, reviewed above, despite the fact that it is possible that most of these deported, upper-class Judahites were not as destitute in exile as their poor fellow Israelites had been back home in the days of Isaiah (see above for comments on the combination "the poor and needy").[28]

Summary and Conclusion

Based on the analysis of the passages reviewed above, one may indeed conclude that "great are the words of Isaiah" (3 Nephi 23:1).

By way of summary, the book of Isaiah squarely places the blame for poverty and suffering among Jehovah's covenant people in ancient Judah on those who had riches, power, and privilege, not on the poor themselves. Social injustices, including the mistreatment of the poor, were a form of covenant violation and brought the just judgments of Jehovah upon Israel in the north (via the Assyrians in the 730s–720s BC) and then later upon Judah in the south (via the Assyrians, 701; the Babylonians, 590s–580s). The covenantal dimension of these violations is evident in part in Jehovah's use of the designation "my people," which many times in the Old Testament refers to faithful Israelites. The phrase "my people" occurs in relation to the poor in Isaiah 3:15 and 10:2, and "his people" occurs in 3:14; 14:32; 49:13, all discussed above.

Additionally, in all these passages in the book of Isaiah, the words meaning "poor" designate a physical status and socioeconomic plight. The poor were economically impoverished and were seemingly powerless to alter their own circumstances.[29] Isaiah did "not portray the poor as people who are especially close to God because of their exploitation. The poor are victims."[30] In this light, the oppression and exploitation of the poor was decried by Jehovah, and by his prophet Isaiah, as violations of the covenant between Jehovah and his people Israel (of course, even the poor were expected to honor their covenant with Jehovah).

Finally, the book of Isaiah teaches that Jehovah strengthens the *faithful* poor during their afflictions (Isaiah 30:18; compare Psalm 22:24) and provides hope that in a future age, following divine judgment and the establishment of an ideal righteous ruler, all the wrongs that the poor have endured will be righted (Isaiah 11:1–5; 14:30, 29:18–20; 32; 32:6–7).

The cumulative effect of the Isaiah passages that mention the poor is that while awaiting the ideal ruler to arrive, upon whom "the spirit of the Lord shall rest . . . [and] with righteousness shall he judge the poor [*dallîm*]" (Isaiah 11:2, 4), Latter-day Saints, as latter-day covenant Israelites, share in the responsibility to do what is possible in a "covenant of compassion" to assist the poor and vulnerable in this time period. Jehovah still cares about the poor[31] and still condemns those who propagate poverty and exploit the needy.

What can Latter-day Saints do to help diminish the crushing reality of poverty for so many people around the world today? Although individuals may take somewhat different approaches to achieving the goal of aiding the poor, the passages from the book of Isaiah cited above provide a good starting point. Those who have entered into a covenant with Jehovah can

- ensure that "the spoil of the poor [*ʿānî*]" is not found in their houses (Isaiah 3:14),
- work to ensure that there is not a situation where "there be no place" for the poor to live (Isaiah 5:8),
- oppose those who devise "wicked devices to destroy the poor [*ʿănāwîm*] with lying words" (Isaiah 32:7),
- pray and fast to "undo the heavy burdens" of the poor (Isaiah 58:6),
- "deal thy bread to the hungry, and [see] that thou bring the poor [*ʿăniyyîm*] that are cast out [in]to thy house" (Isaiah 58:7), and
- work in harmony with the Lord and others to establish Zion, because "the Lord hath founded Zion, and the poor [*ʿăniyāy*] of his people shall trust in it" (Isaiah 14:32).

Thus, the concept expressed in the physicians' promise, "first do no harm," represents only part of the Lord's expectations regarding the poor. Positive actions are required to compassionately fulfill one's covenant with God and to help found Zion.

This last point about the poor trusting in Zion is, after all, the goal of every divinely initiated covenant community. Jehovah's people are called to (attempt to) live Zion-like ideals: to be of "one heart and one mind," to dwell in righteousness, to have "no poor among them," and to live according to "peace, justice, and truth" (Moses 7:18, 31; see also Alma 1:27; 4 Nephi 1:2–3). Most of these attributes are mentioned in the Isaiah passages discussed above. Thus, it is no surprise that Jehovah has instructed his covenant followers in this dispensation "to bring forth and establish the cause of Zion" (D&C 6:6; 11:6).

By pursuing Zion in their lives now, Latter-day Saints can compassionately fulfill an important dimension of their covenant with the Lord by caring for the poor and needy and those who are otherwise oppressed. Thus, for Latter-day Saints who are "trying to be like Jesus," the attributes of Jehovah, who is Jesus Christ, are worthy of emulation: "For you [Jehovah] have been a refuge to the poor [*dāl*], a refuge to the needy [*'ebyôn*] in their distress, a shelter from the rainstorm and a shade from the heat" (Isaiah 25:4 NRSV).

Dana M. Pike is a professor emeritus of ancient scripture at Brigham Young University.

Notes

I thank my wife, Jane Allis-Pike, and the anonymous reviewers who read and responded to previous drafts of this paper.

1. I am not aware of another review of passages focusing on the poor in the book of Isaiah by a Latter-day Saint author. Some Latter-day Saints have published books on the book of Isaiah as a whole, which are worth consulting, including Victor L. Ludlow, *Isaiah: Prophet, Seer, and Poet* (Salt Lake City: Deseret Book, 1982); and Donald W. Parry, Jay A. Parry, and

Tina M. Peterson, *Understanding Isaiah* (Salt Lake City: Deseret Book, 1998).

2. See, for example, Genesis 15; 17; Exodus 19. See also the comments of John Goldingay, "Covenant, OT and NT," in *The New Interpreter's Dictionary of the Bible*, vol. 1, ed. Katharine Doob Sakenfeld et al. (Nashville: Abingdon, 2006, Accordance edition 1.2), especially subparts D and E.

3. Unless otherwise noted, quotations from the Bible in this paper are taken from the King James Version of the Bible (KJV).

4. Since the issues highlighted in Isaiah often have parallels in other Old Testament prophetic passages, as well as in biblical legal, psalmic, and wisdom texts, occasional citations to some of them are also provided below. For additional information on poverty, as well as on other social challenges, in the Old Testament, see, for example, the other papers in this volume and these representative titles, some of which were expressly written to encourage Bible readers to do more to actively assist those in need: Daniel C. Juster, *Social Justice: The Bible and Applications for Our Times* (Clarksville, MD: Messianic Jewish Publishers, 2019); Cynthia Long Westfall and Bryan R. Dryer, eds., *The Bible and Social Justice, Old Testament and New Testament Foundations for the Church's Urgent Call* (Eugene, OR: Pickwick, 2015); Richard A. Horsley, *Covenant Economics: A Biblical Vision of Justice for All* (Louisville: Westminster/John Knox, 2009); Walter J. Houston, *Contending for Justice, Ideologies and Theologies of Social Justice in the Old Testament* (New York: T & T Clark, 2006); Leslie J. Hoppe, *There Shall Be No Poor among You: Poverty in the Bible* (Nashville: Abingdon, 2004); Christopher J. H. Wright, *Old Testament Ethics for the People of God* (Downers Grove, IL: InterVarsity Academic, 2004); Craig L. Blomberg, *Neither Poverty nor Riches: A Biblical Theology of Material Possessions* (Grand Rapids, MI: Eerdmans, 1999); Bruce V. Malchow, *Social Justice in the Hebrew Bible, What Is New and What Is Old* (Collegeville, MN: Liturgical Press, 1996); Moshe Weinfeld, *Social Justice in Ancient Israel and in the Ancient Near East* (Minneapolis: Fortress, 1995).

5. There is a long-running debate concerning when various portions of the book of Isaiah were initially written. The historical figure Isaiah prophesied primarily during the reigns of Ahaz and Hezekiah, kings of Judah (ca.

735–687 BC), and traditionally all 66 chapters of the book of Isaiah have been attributed to him. However, given that chapters 40–55 appear to presuppose the Judahite exile to and return from Babylonia in the 500s BC, and for other reasons, most scholars now posit that an anonymous "Second Isaiah" wrote chapters 40–66, and some posit that a different anonymous "Third Isaiah" wrote chapters 56–66. It is thus possible, depending on one's views, that some of the teachings of "Isaiah" about the "poor" are from more than one person and from more than one century. Since space does not permit further discussion here of the possible multiple authorship of the book of Isaiah, this paper deals with Isaianic passages as they occur in the canonical book of Isaiah. Furthermore, see the following for how some Latter-day Saints have recently dealt with this topic: Jeffrey R. Chadwick, "The Insight of Third Isaiah: Observations of a Traditionalist," in *The Unperceived Continuity of Isaiah*, ed. James H. Charlesworth (New York: T&T Clark, 2019), 76–93; and Kent P. Jackson, "Isaiah in the Book of Mormon," in *A Reason for Faith: Navigating LDS Doctrine and Church History*, ed. Laura Harris Hales (Provo, UT: Religious Studies Center, Brigham Young University; Salt Lake City: Deseret Book, 2016), 69–78.

6. For a summary of this time period, see, for example, Richard Neitzel Holzapfel, Dana M. Pike, and David Rolph Seely, *Jehovah and the World of the Old Testament* (Salt Lake City: Deseret Book, 2009), 276–83.

7. See, for example, William G. Dever, *The Lives of Ordinary People in Ancient Israel: Where Archaeology and the Bible Intersect* (Grand Rapids, MI: Eerdmans, 2012), 206, who states, "The bulk of the population of Israel and Judah in the 8th century B.C.E. lived in rural villages and towns."

8. The output of the robust Israelite economies in the first major portion of the eighth century was primarily enjoyed by wealthy estate owners and leaders comprising the small upper class. Merchants and artisans benefited, too, but there was never much of a middle class in ancient Israel. And Israelites who lived in cities could also fall victim to debt and poverty. For more on life in the two Israelite kingdoms in the eighth century BC, see, for example, Dever, *Lives of Ordinary People in Ancient Israel*, 142–205. See also, Hoppe, *No Poor among You*, 8–12; and Philip J. King and Lawrence E. Stager, *Life in Biblical Israel* (Louisville: Westminster John Knox, 2001),

192–94. The book of Ruth, depicting life in an earlier century, provides a representative account of one family's troubles (compare Exodus 23:11; Psalms 25:16; 70:5).

9. Barry L. Eichler, review of *Social Justice in Ancient Israel and in the Ancient Near East*, by Moshe Weinfeld, *Jewish Quarterly Review* 89, nos. 1–2 (July–October 1998): 187. See similar comments in Malchow, *Social Justice in the Hebrew Bible*, 16–17. See also Ludwig Koehler and Walter Baumgartner, *The Hebrew and Aramaic Lexicon of the Old Testament*, trans. and ed. M. E. J. Richardson (Leiden: Brill, 2000); hereafter abbreviated *HALOT*, s.v. *mišpāṭ*; and this statement from Anders Runesson, "Judgment," in *The New Interpreter's Dictionary of the Bible*, vol. 3, ed. Katharine Doob Sakenfeld et al. (Nashville: Abingdon, 2008, Accordance edition 1.2), subpart A: "The overwhelming majority of texts [in the Old Testament mentioning judgment], however, depict the God of Israel as representing the highest form of righteous rule and impartial judgment. God's judgment protects, in particular, the poor, the innocent, orphans, widows, day laborers, and immigrants. . . . Judgment means vindication and liberation for the oppressed and destitute."

10. For greater detail on all such words for "poor" in the Hebrew Bible, see the extensive discussion by J. David Pleins, "Poor, Poverty, Old Testament," in *Anchor Bible Dictionary*, ed. David Noel Freedman (New York: Doubleday, 1992), 402–14.

11. For these meanings, see Pleins, "Poor, Poverty, Old Testament," 403, 405, 408; and Malchow, *Social Justice in the Hebrew Bible*, 12–13, who references Pleins for the meanings he uses. See also the pertinent entries in *HALOT*. Regarding *'ānî*, the related Hebrew noun *'ŏnî* designates the condition of being oppressed and is variably translated as affliction, trouble, distress, misery. See, for example, Exodus 4:31; Isaiah 48:10.

12. Although not the focus of this paper, the combination the Hebrew words *'ānî* ("poor" in the KJV) and *'ebyôn* ("needy") in parallel phrases occurs multiple times in Psalms (e.g., 35:10; 72:4), as do occurrences in which they are juxtaposed in the same phrase as "the poor [*'ānî*] and needy [*'ebyôn*]" (Psalms 37:14; and e.g., 40:17; 70:5; 74:21). This may be a hendiadys and stock phrase to designate all the poor. Then, again, Psalm 72:13 reads, "He

shall spare the poor [*dal*] and needy [*'ebyôn*]," which the ESV renders as "the weak and the needy."
13. The phrase "the Lord" is the English substitution for the divine name *yhwh*, which in Hebrew is thought to have been pronounced Yahweh. "Jehovah" is a hybrid form of the consonants *yhwh* and the vowels of the Hebrew word translated "lord." See Dana M. Pike, "The Name and Titles of God in the Old Testament," *Religious Educator* 11, no. 1 (2010): 17–31, especially 19–21.
14. See *HALOT*, s.v. *gzlh*.
15. See, for example, NET Bible Notes, 2nd ed, n. 17, s.v. Isaiah 5:8. In Micah 2:1–2, Isaiah's contemporary Judahite prophet Micah had something even more explicit to say about this situation (compare Proverbs 30:14).
16. See Numbers 27:5–11; compare Numbers 36:1–13; Leviticus 25:25–28; and the reply of Naboth to King Ahab in 1 Kings 21:1–4.
17. The social setting for much of these corrupt activities was likely the gates of cities or towns, since gates and their surrounding areas were important locations for commerce, communication, and where local elders and other leaders would hear and render judgment on legal disputes (e.g., Deuteronomy 16:18–20). Ruth 4:1–12 recounts the story of Boaz at Bethlehem's gate with its elders.
18. The story of Naboth, Ahab, and Jezebel provides a classic illustration of this type of corruption in the northern kingdom a century or so before Isaiah (1 Kings 21:1–16). Other prophetic books contain similar sentiments to those expressed in Isaiah (see, for example, Amos 5:12; 8:4; Micah 2:1–2; 3:1–4, 9–12; Jeremiah 2:34; 5:26–29).
19. See statements to this effect in the book of Proverbs (e.g., Proverbs 6:6–11; 10:4; 21:17), which belongs to the genre designated "wisdom literature." For more on wisdom literature, see Holzapfel, Pike, and Seely, *Jehovah and the World of the Old Testament*, 238–45.
20. Hoppe, *No Poor among You*, 73. Similar sentiments are expressed elsewhere in the Old Testament and in the Book of Mormon. See, for example, 2 Nephi 9:30; Helaman 4:12.
21. See *HALOT*, s.v. "*'-n-n*." Malchow, *Social Justice in the Hebrew Bible*, 13, describes *'ănāwîm* as "a linguistic variant of *'ănî*. It has the same connotations of material want and oppression."

22. John N. Oswalt, *The Book of Isaiah, Chapters 1–39* (Grand Rapids, MI: Eerdmans, 1986), 537.
23. For a more complete description of the occurrences and use of "Zion" in the Old Testament, see, for example, J. J. M. Roberts, "Zion Tradition," and W. H. Bellinger Jr., "Zion," in *The New Interpreter's Dictionary of the Bible*, vol. 5, ed. Katharine Doob Sakenfeld et al. (Nashville: Abingdon, 2009, Accordance edition 1.2). And for further discussion of the issues of interpretation of this whole passage, Isaiah 14:28–32, see, for example, Oswalt, *Book of Isaiah, Chapters 1–39*, 605–6.
24. See, for example, the NET Bible rendition of 11:4: "He will treat the poor fairly, and make right decisions for the downtrodden of the earth."
25. Not surprisingly, people of other faiths do not understand the "book" in question to be the Book of Mormon, as is generally accepted by Latter-day Saints. See, for example, https://churchofjesuschrist.org/study/scriptures/gs/book-of-mormon.
26. The word ʿănāwîm, translated "meek" in this verse and rendered "poor" in Isaiah 32:7 (KJV; mentioned above), is sometimes translated "downtrodden" in 29:19 (e.g., NET Bible). Again, see *HALOT*, s.v. "'-n-n," which suggests the sense of "bowed, dejected," when people are in oppressed circumstances, and "humble, pious," when people are worshipping Jehovah.
27. See this generally accepted interpretive approach in, for example, Pleins, "Poor, Poverty, Old Testament," 408–9; Hoppe, *No Poor among You*, 96–97; and the *English Standard Version Study Bible* (ESV; 2008; Accordance version 2.0), s.v. Isaiah 40:1: "The assumed addressees in these chapters [Isaiah 40–55] are the exiles in Babylonian captivity; . . . Isaiah's perspective moves forward from his own eighth-century setting to the Jews' sixth-century exile predicted in 39:5–7."
28. Two different exceptions to what has been reviewed above are cited here:
    1. Isaiah 51:17–22 and 54:11 each contain a form of ʿānî, and each prophesy a rescue and renewal of Jerusalem/Zion. Often understood as applying to Jerusalem at the end of Babylonian sovereignty, these may be best understood as having multiple applications. Either way, since it is Jerusalem that is figuratively designated as ʿānî (translated in the KJV as "afflicted"), these two passages are not further discussed here.

2. The book of Isaiah contains one passage in which the word translated "poor" may be intended with a spiritual rather than a physical, economic sense. In Isaiah 66 the Lord reminds Israelites that he does not just want their external markers of worship, but their hearts as well, including this claim: "to this man will I look, even to him that is poor [ʿānî] and of a contrite spirit, and trembleth at my word" (Isaiah 66:2). The word ʿānî in this passage is often rendered in modern English translations as "humble" (e.g., ESV, NET), in order to better capture its connotation in combination with "contrite spirit" and trembling at the word of Jehovah. The sense of humility is possible, since ʿānî derives from a lexical root, the verb of which means "to be or become oppressed, wretched, bowed down, humiliated" (see *HALOT*, s.v. ʿ-n-h II). And there are some uses of the noun ʿānî elsewhere in the Hebrew Bible that suggest humility rather than economic poverty (e.g., Psalm 18:27 [28 in Hebrew; KJV, "afflicted"]; Zephaniah 3:12 [ʿānî and dāl; KJV, "afflicted and poor"; ESV, "humble and lowly"]; Zechariah 9:9 [KJV, "lowly"]; compare Matthew 5:3). In several such biblical passages there is disagreement on whether "poor" designates an economic poverty or a spiritual condition of humility. However, this use of ʿānî in Isaiah 66:2, in combination with "contrite spirit," is generally understood as an isolated example *in the book of Isaiah* of "poor" having a spiritual connotation, indicating humility.

29. See, for example, Hoppe, *No Poor among You*, 40.
30. Hoppe, *No Poor among You*, 102, speaks broadly about the presentation of the poor in the latter prophets, not just in Isaiah. See his similar assessment about passages in the Torah, p. 39.
31. This assertion is evident in, for example, the formal, institutional posture of The Church of Jesus Christ of Latter-day Saints, which now has "caring for those in need" as one of its four core missions. See the Church's 2020 *General Handbook*, §0.1. See also the remarks about this fourth mission already in 2010 by Elder Dallin H. Oaks, at https://www.churchofjesus christ.org/broadcasts/article/worldwide-leadership-training/2010/11/overview-of-the-new-handbooks.

10

"The Lord Hath Founded Zion, and the Poor of His People Shall Trust in It"
Covenant Economics, Atonement, and the Meaning of Zion

Matthew L. Bowen

When Latter-day Saints associate meanings with the name Zion, they usually think of two definitional statements from Restoration scripture. The first, part of a narrative description of Enoch's Zion, explains: "And the Lord called his people Zion, because they were of one heart and one mind, and dwelt in righteousness; and there was no poor among them" (Moses 7:18). Although this statement offers something of a brief etiology[1] for the Lord's naming of Enoch's Zion and the three requirements that Enoch's Zion met for the use of the name, it does not offer a linguistic etymology or a lexical meaning for *Zion*.

The second definition comes from a revelation given to the Prophet Joseph Smith on August 2, 1833, mere days after the members of the Church "had been forced to sign an agreement to leave Jackson County" (July 23, 1833).[2] In view of the immediate need to expand the Saints' view of Zion beyond a narrow geographical conception (compare Doctrine and Covenants 57:2–3; 58:37), the Lord described Zion in this revelation as a broader concept: "Therefore, verily, thus saith the Lord, let Zion rejoice, for this is Zion—the pure in heart; therefore, let Zion rejoice, while all the wicked shall mourn" (Doctrine and Covenants 97:21). This definition, like Moses 7:18, also does not offer an etymology or lexical meaning for *Zion*.

In this paper, I will explore possible meanings of the name *Zion* (Hebrew *ṣiyyôn*), especially in its Old Testament (OT) connotation as a people and as a place of protection for the Lord's afflicted poor (*ʿănāwîm*/ *ʿăniyyîm*), destitute (*ʾebyônîm*), and powerless (*dallîm*)[3] and how that conception fits with the Lord's naming of Zion in Moses 7:18. As a people and place of physical and spiritual protection, Zion requires the Lord's protective presence. I will accordingly explore the Zion protection concept in relation to texts in Isaiah 4:4–6; 14:32, the Psalms, 2 Nephi 26:24–33, and the Doctrine and Covenants. As a place of economic protection, Zion requires the observance of what Richard Horsley has described as "covenant economics."[4] I will examine Deuteronomy's program for achieving greater economic parity and at-*one*-ment among a covenant people living in the promised land (Deuteronomy 15:1–18) as a means of achieving the Zion ideal of Moses 7:18 ("no poor among them"). I will also analyze Nephi's paronomastic association[5] of Zion with commandments (*miṣwôt* < *ṣāwâ*) in 2 Nephi 26:24–33 and the relationship of covenant economics and economic equity to the Savior's Atonement, which makes oneness in righteousness possible among God's people. For a people to become of "one heart and one mind," to "dwell in righteousness" (or justice), eliminate economic and spiritual poverty, and become Zion (Moses 7:18) ultimately requires a mighty change of the heart and transformation through the Atonement of Jesus Christ and adherence to his covenant teachings. The societies of Enoch, Melchizedek, and the Lamanites and Nephites in 4 Nephi demonstrate that the ideal is possible.

The Etymology versus Paronomastic Meanings of Zion

The origin and etymology of the word Zion—*ṣiyyôn*—remains uncertain at best. Restoration scripture describes Zion as a name given by the Lord to his people and to a city during the time of Enoch (Moses 7:18)—Zion is used sixteen times in Moses 7.[6] In that chapter the name recurs in close connection with descriptions of the Lord's presence among his people, the righteousness or justice that provided economic and spiritual protection, and the subsequent protective measures the Lord took in bringing Zion to his own bosom (i.e., taking Zion to heaven by a divine embrace). It appears that Zion (*ṣiyyôn*) acquired similar connotations of economic, physical, and spiritual protection within the ancient Israelite and Judahite cultural context in which the name was used, whatever its etymological origin.

Biblical scholars generally agree that the term *ṣiyyôn* appears to stem from the Semitic root *ṣ-w/y-n*, which, as W. H. Bellinger Jr. notes, "contains a range of meanings from 'hill top' or 'mountain ridge' to 'fortress,' which comes to have the connotation of protection."[7] The Arabic verb *ṣāna*, which gives us a sense of how this verbal root might have been understood in other Semitic languages (including Hebrew), denotes "to preserve, conserve, keep, retain, maintain, sustain, uphold[,] . . . to protect, guard, safeguard, keep, save."[8] If Zion can be understood in terms of *ṣ-w/y-n*, "Zion would be 'the fortress'" that "would mean 'protect,'" states Thomas Römer.[9] Less likely is the suggestion that it denoted "barren place" from Hebrew *ṣiyyâ* ("dry") or "barren hill."[10] The idea that it derives from *ṣiyyûn*, "stone monument" or "gravestone,"[11] might also make some sense if viewed in the context of Zion being a rocky outcrop (compare the image of Zion and its king as "the Rock of Heaven" in Moses 7:53).

The weight of internal textual evidence in the Hebrew Bible suggests that *ṣiyyôn* connoted a place of protection—that is, a divine fortress. As biblical scholar Sheri L. Klouda puts it, "First and foremost, . . . Zion denotes the location of Yahweh's dwelling place and immediate presence, symbolizing **a place of security or safety** (Psalms 45:4–6; 76:2–3)" (boldface in scriptures is my emphasis).[12] Bellinger suggests that if Zion is understood in terms of *ṣ-w/y-n*, it "fits with the function of the place as a fortress at the time of David's capture of the city."[13] The Deuteronomistic History, preserving an earlier source, records that "David took **the strong hold of Zion** [*mĕṣudat ṣiyyôn*]: the same is the city of David" (2 Samuel 5:7; see also 1 Chronicles 11:5). Later, Zion acquired an "expansion of its geographical usage . . . often refer[ring] to the entire city of Jerusalem."[14] Klouda suggests that the association of the name with the old Jebusite fortress "probably reinforc[ed] the notion of a place of protection"[15]—that is, Zion acquired the meaning associated with the Hebrew noun *mĕṣûdâ*, "stronghold."

Isaiah's writings also associate the name Zion with protection and, in particular, refuge. Drawing on language and imagery of the Exodus and the Lord's protection of Israel in the wilderness, Isaiah foretells that after the purification of his people by "the spirit of judgment [justice], and by the spirit of burning" (Isaiah 4:4), the Lord will establish Zion as a place of protection: "And the Lord will create upon every dwelling place of **mount Zion**, and upon her assemblies, a cloud and smoke by day, and the shining of a flaming fire by night: for upon all the glory shall be **a defence**. And there shall be **a tabernacle for a shadow** in the daytime from the heat, and for **a place of refuge** [*maḥseh*], and for **a covert** from storm and from rain" (Isaiah 4:5–6). God's presence in Zion makes it a "defence," "a place of refuge" and a "covert," but only to the degree that the conditions of righteousness and justice (compare Moses 7:18) prevail there.

Isaiah 14:32 describes a similar conception of Zion: "**The Lord hath founded Zion**, and **the poor** [*ăniyyê*] of his people **shall trust** in it," which would be better rendered as "The Lord hath founded Zion, and the poor of his people **shall take refuge** [*yeḥĕsû*] in it" (Isaiah 14:32; see later in this chapter). Strictly speaking, the Hebrew verb *ḥāsâ* denotes "to take refuge in" rather than to "trust in"[16] and is cognate with the noun *maḥseh* from Isaiah 4:6, "place of refuge,"

"refuge."[17] The poor can trust or take refuge in Zion, as a people and a place, because Zion helps redress economic disparity through covenant economics.

Isaiah's use of *ḥāsâ* and *maḥseh* with reference to Zion "is rooted in the language of the Psalms," as the late Isaiah scholar Hans Wildberger noted.[18] Isaiah later uses this same terminology when he faults the Judahites for making foreign alliances rather than making the Lord and Zion their refuge: "Because ye have said, We have made a covenant with death, and with hell are we at agreement; when the overflowing scourge shall pass through, it shall not come unto us: for **we have made lies our refuge** [*maḥsēnû*], and **under falsehood have we hid ourselves**" (Isaiah 28:15). This collective sin becomes the basis for one of the most significant messianic/Zion promises[19] in scripture: "Therefore thus saith the Lord God, Behold, I lay **in Zion** for a foundation a stone, a tried stone, a precious corner stone, a sure foundation: **he that believeth shall not make haste**" (Isaiah 28:16). Zion is a place of protection for him or her "that believeth" precisely because the Lord and his covenant are the "stone" at its "foundation," its "tried stone," its "precious corner stone," and its "sure foundation" (Isaiah 28:16; compare Helaman 5:12). Without that stone and foundation, there is no Zion as a people or a place of protection, only as a variation on the "refuge of lies" (*maḥsēh kāzāb*, Isaiah 28:17).

Restoration scripture suggests that the idea of Zion as both a people and a place of protection extends back even further. The "people of God" who "dwelt in a land of promise" (Moses 6:17) came under Enoch's leadership (7:13–14) amid wars and bloodshed, and "the Lord came and dwelt with his people, and they dwelt in righteousness" (7:16). Moses 7:17 informs us that Enoch's people were subsequently "**blessed upon the mountains**, and **upon the high places**, and did flourish." In the very next verse, the Lord names his people Zion, but then makes clear that the people qualified for the name Zion, not because of the protective topography they occupied, but because they were a people "of one heart and one mind, . . . [who] dwelt in righteousness; and there was **no poor among them**" (Moses

7:18). In other words, they qualified for the name Zion and the Lord's protective presence because their righteous and just treatment of one another protected and elevated their most vulnerable.

The Book of Moses text goes on to describe Enoch's building of a "City of Holiness" that was also called Zion (Moses 7:19). Regarding this Zion city and the Zion people dwelling in it, Enoch stated to the Lord: "Surely Zion shall **dwell in safety** forever" (7:20). After it had been taken to heaven, the Lord characterized Zion above as something of a heavenly fortress and an antetype of the later earthly Zion rock-fortress: "And the Lord said: Blessed is he through whose seed Messiah shall come; for he saith—**I am Messiah, the King of Zion, the Rock of Heaven,** which is broad as eternity; **whoso cometh in at the gate and climbeth up by me shall never fall**" (7:53; compare Hebrews 12:22; John 10:1). *Rock* (Hebrew *ṣûr* or *selaʿ*) is a title for the Lord that is used in the Psalms, just as he uses it of himself here.

The theme of individuals being "caught up into Zion" and Zion's being taken up into heaven coincides with the recurring image of the divine embrace or being taken to God's bosom—the supreme measure of divine protection—that threads throughout Moses 7 (see Moses 7:24, 30–31, 47, 63, 69). Enoch witnessed the Lord receiving Zion to himself: "Lo, Zion . . . was taken up into heaven" (7:21, 23). The Enoch-Zion narrative describes this as both a process and an event: "And the Holy Ghost fell on many, and **they were caught up by the powers of heaven into Zion**" (7:27). Enoch sees the Lord weep over "the residue [remainder] of the people" (7:28) who were not caught up into Zion, who remained unprotected from the injustice and violence that prevailed in the world, and who were thus subject to the decreed judgments that would follow (7:28–40). Enoch, too—as he saw the wickedness and misery of those outside of the protection of Zion—wept (7:41–43).

Nevertheless, when Enoch saw Jesus Christ's advent in the flesh, he rejoiced that Christ's atoning sacrifice made the protective at-*one*-ment of him and Zion with the Lord possible: "Through faith **I am in the bosom of the Father,** and behold, **Zion is with me**" (Moses

7:47). Enoch further saw that latter-day Zion, like his own Zion, would be a people and a place of gathering and holiness. It would be a refuge from the "darkness" prevailing in the latter days and a protection from the "great tribulations" that would "come upon the wicked" (7:61, 66), with the Lord's presence signified by his tabernacle in its midst:

> And righteousness and truth will I cause to sweep the earth as with a flood, to gather out mine elect from the four quarters of the earth, unto a place which I shall prepare, **an Holy City,** that my people may gird up their loins, and be looking forth for the time of my coming; **for there shall be my tabernacle,** and **it shall be called Zion, a New Jerusalem.**
>
> And the Lord said unto Enoch: **Then shalt thou and all thy city meet them there, and we will receive them into our bosom, and they shall see us; and we will fall upon their necks, and they shall fall upon our necks, and we will kiss each other;**
>
> **And there shall be mine abode, and it shall be Zion,** ... and for the space of a thousand years the earth shall rest. (Moses 7:62–64)

Here the Lord avers that latter-day Zion, as a people and as a place with connotations of protection, would involve his people "gird[ing] up their loins and looking forth for the time of [his] coming."[20] Latter-day Zion, therefore, can only be a place of protection to the degree that its Protector can abide or dwell therein and its inhabitants walk with God, as in Enoch's Zion at the time the Lord took it up: "And Enoch and all **his people walked with God, and he dwelt in the midst of Zion;** and it came to pass that **Zion was not, for God received it up into his own bosom;** and from thence went forth the saying, Zion is Fled" (Moses 7:69). Enoch's Zion served to protect its inhabitants from economic and spiritual poverty, the contemporary sins of the world, the misery and wickedness that prevailed among humankind, and the divine judgments that would occur with the

Flood. Similarly, the Lord intends latter-day Zion to protect its inhabitants from economic and spiritual poverty, the sins of the current generation, and the divine judgments that will precede and attend the Second Coming of Jesus Christ.

A revelation given through the Prophet Joseph Smith on March 7, 1831, regarding the establishment of Latter-day Zion "with one heart and one mind" further reflects upon and enforces the foregoing concept of Zion as both a people and a place of protection:

> And **with one heart and with one mind, gather up your riches** that ye may purchase an inheritance which shall hereafter be appointed unto you.
>
> And it shall be called the New Jerusalem, **a land of peace, a city of refuge, a place of safety** for the saints of the Most High God.
>
> And **the glory of the Lord shall be there, and the terror of the Lord also shall be there,** insomuch that the wicked will not come unto it, **and it shall be called Zion.**
>
> And it shall come to pass among the wicked, **that every man that will not take his sword against his neighbor must needs flee unto Zion for safety.**
>
> And there shall be gathered unto it out of every nation under heaven; and it shall be **the only people that shall not be at war one with another.**
>
> And it shall be said among the wicked: Let us not go up to battle against Zion, for the inhabitants of Zion are terrible; wherefore we cannot stand. (Doctrine and Covenants 45:65–70)

In creating this striking picture of Zion, this revelation clearly reflects and extends the biblical connotations of Zion as a place of protection from physical danger and economic and spiritual poverty. It also draws on the images of Enoch's people as the power of the Lord rested on them and they became Zion, as recorded in Moses 7:13–20, becoming of one heart and mind and a terror to their enemies.

"No Poor among You": Zion, the Psalms, and the Covenant Economics of Deuteronomy 15

Since the Messiah is the anointed "King of Zion" (Moses 7:53), his atoning work is, in part, "to preach good tidings unto the meek [the poor, *ănāwîm*]" and "to appoint unto them that mourn in Zion, to give unto them beauty for ashes, the oil of joy for mourning, the garment of praise for the spirit of heaviness" (Isaiah 61:1, 3; Luke 4:18–19). The Psalms offer a picture of the Lord as the King of Zion who provides hope and protection to the poor (see, e.g., Psalms 9:10–11 [MT 11–12], 18 [MT 19]; 10:14; 12:5 [MT 6]; 34:6 [MT 7]; JST Psalm 14:5–7).

In conjunction with the Psalms, Moses's "Song of the Sea" provides a potential missing puzzle piece to the historical link between Enoch's Zion, Melchizedek's Salem, and the later Zion fortress attached to Jerusalem: "Thou shalt bring them [the Lord's people] in, and plant them in the mountain of thine inheritance, in the place, O Lord, which thou hast made for thee to dwell in, in the Sanctuary, O Lord, which thy hands have established. The Lord shall reign for ever and ever" (Exodus 15:17–18). Wildberger states that this passage from the Song of the Sea "makes clear that 'mountain,' 'abode,' and 'sanctuary' are alternate ways of saying the same thing. Yahweh [Jehovah] has established a residence on Zion (Ps. 74:2); Zion is the holy mountain precisely because that is where Yahweh's dwelling place is located (Ps. 43:3); his abode was established in Salem [later Jerusalem] and his dwellingplace in Zion (Ps. 76:3). Zion is God's seat of government and the cultic center,"[21] especially after Solomon's completion and dedication of the temple in 1 Kings 8, which supersedes the tabernacle as the resting place of the ark of the covenant, the Lord's stylized throne. We have previously noted the well-rooted connotation of Zion in the Hebrew Bible as a place of protection. Wildberger further notes that in the Psalms he quotes, "concepts about an impregnable mountain of God are used in a transferred sense and reapplied."[22] From the perspective of the Restoration, we can see Enoch's "high and lifted up" Zion whose king is "Messiah . . . the rock of Heaven" (a mountain image) being transferred and reapplied to Melchizedek's Salem-"heaven" (JST Genesis 14:26–36; Psalm 76:2 [MT 3]), which is later reapplied again to Zion-Jerusalem in the Psalms and in Isaiah.

Wildberger contrasts the Psalmists whose "refuge has been taken with Yahweh" (compare the abundant use of the verb *ḥāsâ* in the Psalms)[23]—rather than, strictly speaking, in Zion itself—with Isaiah who "highlights the inviolability of the city itself, even when threatened by mighty foes."[24] However, these concepts are not mutually exclusive: for Isaiah, Zion itself is the inviolable place of refuge *because* of its King—God himself is present within it.

Returning to the image of the Lord in Enoch's Zion as "Messiah" and "the King of Zion, the rock of heaven," the ancient Israelites' view of the Lord was deeply rooted in the cultic conception that he was the King of Zion. Klouda writes: "The psalmist describes Yahweh as a refuge for the oppressed who 'reigns in Zion,' avenging the blood of society's marginalized and executing righteousness for the weak and vulnerable."[25] Examples of the converging imagery of the Lord as both divine refuge and king in Zion include the following: "**The Lord also will be a refuge** [*miśgāb*] **for the oppressed**, **a refuge** [*miśgāb*] in times of trouble. And they that know thy name will put their trust in thee: for thou, Lord, hast not forsaken them that seek thee. Sing praises **to the Lord, which dwelleth in Zion** [*lyhwh yōšēb ṣiyyôn*; or, "to the Lord who sits enthroned in Zion"]: declare among the people his doings. When he maketh inquisition for blood, he remembereth them: he forgetteth not the cry of **the humble** [Qere: *ʿănāwîm*; Ketiv: *ʿnyym*]" (Psalm 9:9–12 [MT 10–13]). "Beautiful for **situation** [beautiful in height, *yĕpēh nôp*], the joy of the whole earth, is **mount Zion**, on the sides of **the north** [*ṣāpôn* = Mt. Zaphon], the city of the great King. God is known in her palaces [**citadels**, i.e., places of protection] **for a refuge** [*miśgāb*]" (Psalm 48:2–3 [MT 3–4]). These texts help us picture the type of protective Zion-abode and refuge in which the

Lord was believed to reign as its protective King—the King whose special concern is the poor and marginalized of his people.

More than *refuge*, *miśgāb* denotes "a high point for a refuge."[26] This noun derives from the verbal root *śāgab*, "to be too high, be too strong for"; "to be high, inaccessible"; "exalted"; "too high, unattainable."[27] Thus, *miśgāb* and the perceived meaning of Zion share some conceptual overlap. It seems to be in the sense of "a high point for refuge" that Moses 7:24 describes the situation to which Enoch and later Zion were eventually taken: "And Enoch was high and lifted up, even in the bosom of the Father, and of the Son of Man." In other words, having protected the most vulnerable among their people, Enoch and Zion were taken to heaven as a further protection from the sins of that age and the divine judgments that would inevitably follow. The metaphor of God as a high "cliff" for a "refuge"[28] is prevalent in the Psalms[29] and is the same one that we find in Moses 7:53: "I am Messiah, **the King of Zion, the Rock of Heaven**, which is broad as eternity; **whoso** cometh in at the gate and climbeth up by me shall never fall." Bellinger observes that "Yahweh's dwelling on Mount Zion is in line with the common ANE [ancient Near Eastern] mythical idea that gods lived on cosmic hills."[30] The various iterations of this ancient Near Eastern motif may reflect an earlier conception of sky-dwelling deities[31] similar to the one given us in Moses 7:21, 53 about the Lord dwelling in Zion and the city being elevated to "the Rock of Heaven" as "mine abode forever" (compare also Moses 7:64 and Genesis 28:12–13).

Later during the monarchic period, the Lord's enthronement as king in Zion was particularly symbolized by the ark of the covenant and its lid (*kappōret*), a stylized throne situated in the holy of holies of the tabernacle/temple where the Mosaic atonement rites (*kipper, kippurîm*) were performed. Psalm 9 metaphorically describes the Lord-enthroned-in-Zion as a "high point for a refuge [*miśgāb*]" (Psalm 9:10–11 [MT 11–12]). He himself, as an "oppressed and . . . afflicted"[32] servant,[33] would atone for the oppressed and would know their plight. Thus, the poor could take refuge in him and in Zion:

"The poor committeth himself unto thee; thou art the helper of the fatherless" (Psalm 10:14). Note how JST Psalm 14:5–7 ties together the concept of God being enthroned among the righteous, as he was among Enoch's people (Moses 7:16), with his role as protector of the poor and marginalized, and with the permanent establishment of Zion as the end goal in view:

> They *are* in great fear, for God *dwells* [sits enthroned in] in the generation [*bĕdôr*, literally, in the circle] of the righteous. **He is the counsel of the poor**, because they are ashamed of the wicked, and **flee unto the Lord, for their refuge.**
>
> *They are ashamed of* **the counsel of the poor** [*ʿăṣat-ʿānî*] because the Lord is **his refuge** [*maḥsēhû*].
>
> Oh that *Zion were established out of heaven*, the salvation of Israel. *O Lord, when wilt thou establish Zion?* When the Lord bringeth back the captivity of his people, Jacob shall rejoice, Israel shall be glad. (Italicized English words are those added in the JST.)

In order for Zion to be "established out of heaven" as envisioned in JST Psalm 14:5–7, the Lord's people must themselves become champions and protectors of the poor as shown in Moses 7:18. Few passages in ancient scripture give specific concrete legislative steps for how the Lord's people were to accomplish this. The "covenant economics" commandments of Deuteronomy 15:1–18 constitute a notable exception.

Although not directly tied to Enoch's Zion, Melchizedek's Salem, or Davidic concepts of Zion, the economic commandments of Deuteronomy 15 provided steps toward a more egalitarian covenant society. The first step in these covenant economics for protecting and elevating the poor in Israel/Zion was to institute a remission of debts during the Sabbatical year: "At the end of every seven years thou shalt make a release. And this is the manner of the release: Every creditor that lendeth ought unto his neighbour shall release it; he shall not exact it of his neighbour, or of his brother; because it is called the Lord's release" (Deuteronomy 15:1–2). As Horsley has observed, "The instruction given for the remission indicates explicitly that this was not a mere moratorium or postponement, but a cancellation of debts. Every creditor was to remit the claim held against the debtor, and not exact it against any member of the community (15:2)."[34] Bruce Birch describes the intent underlying the legislation thusly: "So that the poor would not remain permanently in debt, the law called for the remission of debts every seven years (Deut. 15:1–2; Lev. 25:1ff.), and if a poor man sold himself into servitude because of debts, he was to be given freedom in the seventh year (Lev. 25:39–55)."[35]

The telos (or end goal) of this Sabbatical remission and the legislation that follows is explicit. It is not as the KJV words it, "Save when there shall no poor among you" but rather "nevertheless [*ʾepes kî*][36] **there shall be no poor among you** [*lōʾ yihyeh-bĕkā ʾebyôn*]; for the Lord shall greatly bless thee in the land which the Lord thy God giveth thee for an inheritance to possess it: only if thou carefully hearken unto the voice of the Lord thy God, to observe to do all these **commandments** which I command thee this day" (Deuteronomy 15:4–5; alteration of the KJV translation is mine). The text and context of Moses 7:18 ("And the Lord called his people Zion, because they were of one heart and one mind, and dwelt in righteousness; **and there was no poor among them**") helps us appreciate that poverty need not be understood in purely economic terms, though it unquestionably includes that, but spiritual poverty can also include seeking relief from the oppression of sin or a lack of access to spiritual blessings (covenants, ordinances, doctrine, fellowship with the saints, and so forth). Just as a Zion without the Lord as its king is not Zion at all, a Zion that does not serve as a refuge and a place of protection and supply for its most vulnerable members—its economic and spiritually poor—is also not Zion.

When the Lord commanded members of the Church early in this dispensation to, "with one heart and one mind, gather up your riches" (Doctrine and Covenants 45:65) to establish Zion as a city, he made a direct lexical recollection of the account of Enoch's people in Moses

7. In this account, Enoch's people qualified for and received the name Zion because they were "of one heart and one mind, . . . dwel[ling] in righteousness" with "no poor among them" (Moses 7:18). The Lord was urging the saints to get serious about achieving the covenant utopian ideal of Deuteronomy 15:4 ("There shall be no poor among you"), which Enoch's Zion and the Nephites' and Lamanites' civilization after Christ's coming (see 4 Nephi 1:2–3, 15–18) had both achieved on similar principles (compare the oneness concept in Christ's intercessory prayers in John 17:11, 20–23 and 3 Nephi 19:23, 29).

Beginning in Deuteronomy 15:5 we see an emerging emphasis on the divinity and sanctity of the covenant economics in terms of its having been commanded (Hebrew *ṣāwâ*) by the Lord, an emphasis that Nephi will specifically make in connection with Zion/*ṣiyyôn* (2 Nephi 26), as we will see. There would be "no poor among" them, "only if thou carefully hearken unto the voice of the Lord thy God, to observe to do all these **commandments** [*hammiṣwâ*, singular, *commandment*] which I **command** [*mĕṣawwĕkā*] thee this day" (Deuteronomy 15:5).

Bruce Birch describes how the Deuteronomic legislation protected the poor: "The law codes also provide for protection of the dispossessed in other areas of the socioeconomic system. Persons were urged to lend money to the poor . . . but the law prohibited the taking of interest."[37] Deuteronomy 15:7–8 stipulated: "If there be among you a poor man of one of thy brethren within any of thy gates in thy land which the Lord thy God giveth thee, thou shalt not harden thine heart, nor shut thine hand from thy poor brother: But thou shalt open thine hand wide unto him, and shalt surely lend him sufficient for his need, in that which he wanteth." Also commenting on these verses, Horsley notes that "lenders had to reckon with the possibility that, since they themselves had little or no surplus as a cushion, they too might run out of food before the next harvest, or the next harvest might be poor. It was thus important to reinforce the custom of cooperation and mutual aid among villagers with covenantal exhortation such as Deuteronomy 15:7–8."[38] In other words, because the Israelites were part of a covenant community, they were reliant on one another. The Enochic Zion ideal with which Moses was familiar, as a place of economic and spiritual protection where there is "no poor among them" (Moses 7:18; Deuteronomy 15:4), could only be achieved to the degree that the community kept the covenant.

Jesus perfectly understood this, as reflected in his teaching in the Sermon on the Plain: "But love ye your enemies, and do good, and lend, hoping for nothing again; and your reward shall be great, and ye shall be the children of the Highest: for he is kind unto the unthankful and to the evil" (Luke 6:35). Writes Horsley, "The summary of the admonitions . . . 'love your enemies, and do good, and lend,' with its repetition of the covenantal insistence on liberal lending to one's needy neighbors (Exod. 22:25; Deut. 15:7–8), confirms . . . that we are listening to covenantal teaching."[39] The type of oneness for which Jesus prayed in his intercessory prayers (John 17:11, 20–23; 3 Nephi 19:23, 29) cannot be achieved without the inward transformation called for in Jesus's covenant sermons (Matthew 5–7; Luke 11:20–49; 3 Nephi 12–14). A Zion community is ultimately a covenant- and commandment-keeping community.

To achieve "one heart and one mind," to "dwell in righteousness," and to eliminate economic and spiritual poverty ultimately requires a mighty change of "heart."[40] Jesus emphasized in the Sermon on the Mount and in other teachings that the state of one's inner being matters most. The covenant economics laws of Deuteronomy 15 also reflect this:

> **Beware that there be not a thought in thy wicked heart**, saying, The seventh year, the year of release, is at hand; and thine eye be evil against thy poor brother, and thou givest him nought; and he cry unto the Lord against thee, and it be sin unto thee.
>
> Thou shalt surely give him, **and thine heart shall not be grieved** when thou givest unto him: because that for this

> thing the Lord thy God shall bless thee in all thy works, and in all that thou puttest thine hand unto.
>
> For **the poor shall never cease out of the land: therefore I command thee** [*mĕṣawwĕkā*], **saying, Thou shalt open thine hand wide unto thy brother, to thy poor, and to thy needy**, in thy land. (Deuteronomy 15:9–11)

The Lord emphasizes that heartfelt generosity to the liberated poor constitutes a commandment ("I command thee"). The intents of the hearts of the Lord's people—including their determination to be one—have always been the determining factors in the success or lack of success with their keeping of the commandments and instituting programs designed to help lift his people out of economic and spiritual poverty, because the inner being of individuals motivates outward actions. When Jesus said to his disciples, "Ye have the poor with you always, and whensoever ye will ye may do them good: but me ye have not always" (Mark 14:7), he referenced Deuteronomy 15:11. Matthew renders Jesus's words thus, "For ye have the poor always with you; but me ye have not always" (Matthew 26:11). Latter-day Saints should appreciate the elimination of poverty in Enoch's Zion (see Moses 7:18) as an achievement of the highest order in view of the preceding Deuteronomic statements and Jesus's own words regarding the seeming invincibility of human poverty.[41]

The covenant economics continue with an explicit command to give liberally to debt-slaves because they are among the community's most vulnerable. When poor Israelites were released from servitude as debt-slaves in the seventh year (as stipulated in Deuteronomy 15:12), they were not to "then be sent out empty-handed but given provisions from the flocks and harvest."[42] The Lord declared: "And when thou sendest him out free from thee, **thou shalt not let him go away empty: thou shalt furnish him liberally** out of thy flock, and out of thy floor, and out of thy winepress: of that wherewith the Lord thy God hath blessed thee thou shalt give unto him. And **thou shalt remember that thou wast a bondman in the land of Egypt,** and the Lord thy God redeemed thee: therefore **I command thee** [*mĕṣawwĕkā*] this thing to day" (Deuteronomy 15:13–15). Jeremiah describes Judah's destruction and exile by the Babylonians as a consequence of a longstanding failure to keep this commandment, despite Zedekiah's "liberty" proclamation (see Jeremiah 34:8–22). After freeing their slaves in obedience to this royal decree, some of the princes and wealthier Judahites had reclaimed their fellow Judahites as slaves—that is, they forced their return into the most vulnerable economic circumstances possible. These constituted decidedly *anti-*Zion actions. As Sharon Ringe notes, "The language with which Jeremiah reports God's indictment when they renege on their agreement parallels that of Deut. 15:12."[43] Jeremiah describes this as a covenant failure, and it constituted a reversal of the work of the Messiah as detailed in Isaiah 61:1–3 ("to proclaim liberty to the captives, . . . to proclaim the acceptable year of the Lord, . . . to appoint unto them that mourn in Zion").

There is no wiggle room in this commandment. Jaime L. Waters observes that in keeping it, ancient Israelites became more like the Lord: "Generosity is mandated because Yahweh has been generous to Israel. While the Priestly law in Num. 15:17–21 mandates a reciprocal offering given to Yahweh because of the gifts he provides, the law in Deut. 15:14–15 is a law to imitate Yahweh. The importance of sharing Yahweh's blessings is especially highlighted."[44]

Notably, the Lord calls to his people's remembrance Israel's recent experience as poor slaves in Egypt, an experience from which the Lord had redeemed them. As Birch puts it, "It is the constant remembrance of [the] Exodus in recital and praise that keeps the Exodus experience available as a source of hope, but such remembrance is also to be a source of *humility*."[45] The Exodus offered ancient Israel and Judah all the evidence that they should have needed to convince them that the Lord wanted a better life for even the poorest of his people and that he was ever to remain the source of that hope. As Jennifer C. Lane points out, the book of Deuteronomy reiterated to the ancient Israelites that their (then) newly formed relationship with the Lord "extended from the covenants that he made with Abraham, Isaac, and Jacob/Israel."[46] As Isaiah reminded them, he was their *gōʾēl*,[47] their *kinsman-redeemer*—the term itself implying kinship with the redeemed.[48] Thus, "they knew that [Jehovah's] redemption grew out of the family relationship formed through the covenants they had made."[49] Such remembrance helped them understand the true nature of their relationship to the Lord and to each other (as equals). Remembering the Lord's actions in their behalf in times past reflected their faith that "when the Lord shall build up Zion, he shall appear in his glory" and that "he will regard the prayer of the destitute, and not despise their prayer" (Psalm 102:16–17).

The collective ancient Israelite and Judahite failure to righteously build Zion over time ("they build up Zion with blood," Micah 3:10) and their eventual expulsion from the land of promise find their parallel in the Saints' failure to build Zion in Missouri and in their expulsion from that land. Elder D. Todd Christofferson explains:

> Under the direction of the Prophet Joseph Smith, early members of the Church attempted to establish the center place of Zion in Missouri, but they did not qualify to build the holy city. The Lord explained one of the reasons for their failure:
>
> "**They have not learned to be obedient to the things which I required at their hands,** but are full of all manner of evil, **and do not impart of their substance, as becometh saints, to the poor and afflicted among them**; and are not united according to the union required by the law of the celestial kingdom" (D&C 105:3–4).
>
> "There were jarrings, and contentions, and envyings, and strifes, and lustful and covetous desires among them; therefore by these things they polluted their inheritances" (D&C 101:6).[50]

From the hindsight of a twenty-first century perspective, we can see how the ancient Israelites and Judahites and the early Saints of this dispensation failed to establish Zion. Elder Christofferson further recommends, "Rather than judge these early Saints too harshly, however, we should look to ourselves to see if we are doing any better."[51]

The essentiality of all of the foregoing commandments and obedience thereto for the establishment of Zion could not have been articulated more clearly than when the Lord declared his "will" to the early saints "concerning the redemption of [his] afflicted people" (Doctrine and Covenants 105:1). He further stated: "And **Zion cannot be built up unless it is by the principles of the law of the celestial kingdom**; otherwise **I cannot receive her unto myself**. And my people must needs be chastened until they learn obedience, if it must needs be, by the things which they suffer" (105:5–6).

"God received" Enoch's Zion "up into his own bosom" because of its "righteousness"—its justice—and elimination of poverty (Moses 7:18). Similarly, Melchizedek's Salem "did repent" and "wrought righteousness [or justice], and obtained heaven" (JST Genesis 14:34) by also caring for "the poor" through tithes (JST Genesis 14:37–38). So, too, the Lamanites and Nephites show that the ideal can be attained (4 Nephi 1:2–3, 13–18). Nevertheless, the Lord's people remain without the divine protection intended for Zion to the degree that they disregard the Lord's commandments, not least his Zion commandments upon which Zion's economic, physical, and spiritual protections are predicated. In other words, though "children of Zion, . . . many . . . were found transgressors, therefore they must needs be chastened" (Doctrine and Covenants 101:41; compare also 101:1–5). Regarding these Zion commandments, another prophet, Nephi (whose writings strongly reflect the influence of Deuteronomy and Isaiah), had much to offer his people and us.

"And He Hath Commanded His People": The Zion Commandments of 2 Nephi 26:24–33

Nephi gives the Lord's people in the latter days a useful roadmap for "doing better." Although Enoch's Zion deservedly gets ample attention from Latter-day Saints for its success, Nephi also had a specific vision for achieving Zion. Unsurprisingly, that vision is deeply rooted in the writings of Isaiah, who mentions Zion no less than forty times. Most of the references to Zion in the Book of Mormon are quotations from the writings of Isaiah.[52] Nephi cites the Lord's love for the world, evident in his atoning sacrifice, as the motivating factor for doing all he does and commanding all he commands. A Zion people must be willing to love, sacrifice, consecrate themselves, and eliminate poverty in order to assist in the work of "draw[ing] all . . . unto him":

> **He doeth not anything save it be for the benefit of the world; for he loveth the world, even that he layeth down his own life that he may draw all men unto him.** Wherefore, **he commandeth none** that they shall not partake of his salvation.
>
> Behold, doth he cry unto any, saying: Depart from me? Behold, I say unto you, Nay; but he saith: **Come unto me all ye ends of the earth, buy milk and honey, without money and without price.**
>
> Behold, **hath he commanded** any that they should depart out of the synagogues, or out of the houses of worship? Behold, I say unto you, Nay.
>
> **Hath he commanded** any that they should not partake of his salvation? Behold I say unto you, Nay; but he hath given it free for all men; **and he hath commanded** his people that they should persuade all men to repentance.
>
> Behold, **hath the Lord commanded** any that they should not partake of his goodness? Behold I say unto you, Nay; but all men are privileged the one like unto the other, and none are forbidden.
>
> **He commandeth** that there shall be no priestcrafts; for, behold, priestcrafts are that men preach and set themselves

up for a light unto the world, that they may get gain and praise of the world; **but they seek not the welfare of <u>Zion</u>.**

Behold, the Lord hath forbidden this thing; wherefore, **the Lord God hath given <u>a commandment</u> that all men should have charity, which charity is love.** And except they should have charity they were nothing. Wherefore, **if they should have charity they would not suffer the laborer in <u>Zion</u> to perish.**

But **the laborer in <u>Zion</u> shall labor for <u>Zion</u>**; for if they labor for money they shall perish.

And again, **the Lord God <u>hath commanded</u>** that men should not murder; that they should not lie; that they should not steal; that they should not take the name of the Lord their God in vain; that they should not envy; that they should not have malice; that they should not contend one with another; that they should not commit whoredoms; **and that they should do none of these things; for whoso doeth them shall perish.**

For none of these iniquities come of the Lord; for he doeth that which is good among the children of men; and he doeth nothing save it be plain unto the children of men; and he inviteth them all to come unto him and partake of his goodness; and he denieth none that come unto him, black and white, bond and free, male and female; and he remembereth the heathen; and all are alike unto God, both Jew and Gentile. (2 Nephi 26:24–33; economics- and commandment-related terminology has been bolded, and paronomastic terminology has been underlined)

Nephi's Zion instruction here is remarkable for, among many reasons, his dramatic emphasis on what the Lord has—and has not—commanded. The repetition of a verb translated as "command" (compare Hebrew *ṣwy/ṣwh*; Egyptian *wḏ*, "command")[53] and a noun translated as "commandment" (compare Hebrew *miṣwâ*; Egyptian *wd*, "command, decree")[54] intersects with the name Zion (*ṣiyyôn*) and has the paronomastic effect[55] of emphasizing Zion as the practical result or realized effect of obedience to divine commandments. The most important of the Zion-commandments that Nephi lists is "charity, which charity is love"—or, as Nephi describes it later, "a love of God and of all men" (2 Nephi 31:20). Charity is the love with which the Savior showed perfect obedience to the Father in performing his atoning sacrifice. Following the Savior's ministry among the Lamanites and Nephites at the temple in Bountiful, Mormon records that the Lamanites' and Nephites' collective keeping of this commandment allowed them to achieve Zion among Lehi's descendants: "And it came to pass that there was no contention in the land, because of the love of God which did dwell in the hearts of the people" (4 Nephi 1:15). They became *at-one*.

Nevertheless, as Nephi makes clear, one cannot keep the commandment to "have charity" and at the same time "suffer the laborer in Zion to perish" (2 Nephi 26:30). The commandments in Deuteronomy 15 have this same intent: to eliminate the economic barriers that inhibit spiritual growth, to enable the laborer in Zion to labor for Zion and to thus prevent the laborer in Zion from perishing, since we are, in a very real sense, "all beggars" (Mosiah 4:19). Hence also the Lord's commandments against priestcrafts, which Nephi defines as self-serving actions that "seek not the welfare of Zion" (2 Nephi 26:29). Nephi's Zion is, in the language of Isaiah, a refuge for "the poor" and "he [or she] that hath no money" (Isaiah 55:1). Nephi quotes the latter verse when Jesus invites, "Come unto me all ye ends of the earth, buy milk and honey, without money and without price" (2 Nephi 26:25; compare also 2 Nephi 9:50, where Jacob quotes this verse). Nephi indisputably draws this invitation from Isaiah 55:1, a text especially addressed to the poor: "Ho, every one that thirsteth, come ye to the waters, and he that hath no money; come ye, buy, and eat; yea, come, buy wine and milk without money and without price" (compare Matthew 5:3, 6; 3 Nephi 12:3, 6). Everyone in Zion has wealth or gifts from Christ (1 Corinthians 7:7; 12:7)—spiritual and otherwise—that can help to elevate the economic and spiritually poor in Zion (which on some level includes everyone); thus these types of poverty in Zion would eventually be eliminated.

Among the commandments necessary for achieving Zion, Nephi recites a list of commandments related to the Decalogue (the Ten Commandments in Exodus 20). These commandments are expressed as negative prohibitions against murder ("thou shalt not kill"), lying ("thou shalt not bear false witness"), taking the name of the Lord in vain ("thou shalt not take the name of the Lord thy God in vain"), stealing ("thou shalt not steal"), envying ("thou shalt not covet"), creating strife or contention, and committing whoredoms ("thou shalt not commit adultery") (2 Nephi 26:32). All of these sins damage lives and relationships. They inhibit spiritual progress and at-*one*-ment among God's children. Those who persist in such sins cannot love the world and their fellow human beings in the way that the Lord does and thus cannot perfectly keep the commandment to have charity. They cannot take on his nature and character. They cannot build Zion on earth or belong to that divine Zion sociality of which the celestial kingdom consists (compare Doctrine and Covenants 130:2). To attempt to "build up Zion [ṣiyyôn] with blood, and Jerusalem with iniquity" (Micah 3:10) is not to build them at all.

Conclusion

Although the ultimate etymological origin of the name Zion remains uncertain, in Restoration scripture it is initially bestowed as the name of a people and a place (Moses 7:18–19) and is associated with the divine protection that accompanies God's presence among his covenant-keeping people (Moses 7:16–20). Similarly, in the Hebrew Bible it appears to have been understood in terms of the Semitic root *ṣ-w/y-n*, associated with hilltops, mountain ranges, and fortresses, thus suggesting the meaning of a "place of protection." The image of Zion as a mountaintop, rock fortress, or place of protection is reflected in

Zion's elevation to God by divine embrace as the supreme measure of protection in Moses 7:21, 23–24, 27, 30–31, 62–63, 69 and especially in Moses 7:53, where the Lord describes himself as "Messiah, the King of Zion, the Rock of Heaven." Zion's connotation as a place of protection for the poor, reflected in Moses 7:18, was reinforced by its association with the *měṣûdâ* ("fortress") near Jerusalem and with the Psalms' descriptions of the Lord, the king of Zion, as a *miśgāb* ("high point of refuge") and a *maḥseh* ("place of refuge"). For Isaiah, Zion was thus the "place of refuge" (Isaiah 4:5–6) in which the poor could "take refuge" (Isaiah 14:30, 32).

Physical and spiritual poverty constitute a barrier to relational at-*one*-ment and spiritual progress. The Lord instituted covenant economics (Deuteronomy 15:1–18) in the form of commandments for the protection of the poor, making possible the ideal of "no poor among you" (compare Moses 7:18). In 2 Nephi 26, Nephi makes a paronomastic link between Zion (*ṣiyyôn*) and Zion-commandments (compare Hebrew *ṣāwâ, miṣwâ*), the greatest of which is charity—the love that motivated the Savior's giving of himself in his Atonement. Full, Christ-like obedience to these Zion-commandments enables his people to assist in the messianic work of "drawing all . . . unto him" (2 Nephi 26:24–33; compare Isaiah 61:1–4).

Matthew L. Bowen is an associate professor of religious education at Brigham Young University–Hawaii.

Notes

1. That is, an account of origin. Etiology derives from the Greek word *aitia* meaning "cause." For a brief discussion of the phenomenon of biblical etiology, see Michael H. Floyd, "Etiology" in *The New Interpreter's Bible Dictionary of the Bible* (Nashville: Abingdon 2007), 2:352. Floyd explains, "As a critical term applied to narrative, etiology refers to stories that tell how something came to be or came to have its definitive characteristics.

In Scripture such stories are typically told about names of persons and places, rites and customs, ethnic identities and other natural phenomena" (p. 352).

2. See preface to section 97 in the 2013 edition of the Doctrine and Covenants published by The Church of Jesus Christ of Latter-day Saints.
3. For a helpful discussion of Hebrew terms describing the poor, see Nathan Bills, *A Theology of Justice in Exodus* (University Park, PA: Eisenbrauns, 2020), 50.
4. Richard A. Horsley, *Covenant Economics: A Biblical Vision of Justice for All* (Louisville: Westminster/John Knox Press, 2009), passim.
5. Paronomasia is a form of wordplay involving the juxtaposition or repetition of words with similar sounds.
6. See Moses 7:18–21 [5x], 23, 27, 31, 47, 53, 62, 64, 68–69 [4x].
7. William H. Bellinger Jr., "Zion," in *The New Interpreter's Dictionary of the Bible* (Nashville: Abingdon Press, 2009), 5:985.
8. Hans Wehr, *A Dictionary of Modern Written Arabic*, ed. J. Milton Cowan, 4th ed. (Urbana, IL: Spoken Language Services, 1994), 621.
9. Thomas Römer, *The Invention of God*, trans. Raymond Geuss (Cambridge, MA: Harvard University Press, 2015), 130. "Some scholars have claimed that [ṣiyyôn] is derived from a Hurrite word meaning 'water,' but others have suggested that it is related to the root s-y-y which would make Zion 'the dry place.' However, a more plausible root would be ṣ-w/y-n; a comparison with the identical root in Arabic suggests that this would mean 'protect,' so Zion would be the fortress" (p. 130).
10. Ludwig Koehler and Walter Baumgartner, *The Hebrew and Aramaic Lexicon of the Old Testament* (Leiden, NL: Brill, 2001), 1022; hereafter cited as *HALOT*.
11. *HALOT*, 1022–23.
12. Sheri L. Klouda, "Zion," in *Dictionary of the Old Testament: Wisdom, Poetry, and Writings: A Compendium*, ed. Tremper Longman III and Peter Enns (Downers Grove, IL: InterVarsity, 2008), 936.
13. Bellinger, "Zion," 985.
14. Bellinger, "Zion," 986.
15. Klouda, "Zion," 939.

16. *HALOT*, 337. Compare Akkadian *ḫesû*, "to cover up, shroud." Jeremy Black, Andrew George, Nicholas Postgate, eds., *Concise Dictionary of Akkadian* (Wiesbaden: Harrassowitz, 2000), 114.
17. *HALOT*, 571.
18. Hans Wildberger, *Isaiah 13–27: A Continental Commentary*, trans. Thomas H. Trapp (Minneapolis: Fortress Press, 1997), 101.
19. Peter quotes Isaiah 28:16 with reference to Jesus in 1 Peter 2:4–8 (in connection with Isaiah 8:14–15 and Psalm 118:22). Paul similarly quotes Isaiah 28:16 in Romans 9:33 (in conjunction with Isaiah 8:14–15) and in Romans 10:11. In the Book of Mormon, Jacob plausibly quotes or paraphrases it in reference to Jesus in Jacob 4:15–17 (in connection with Psalm 118:22 and Isaiah 8:14–15). Helaman directly alludes to it in Helaman 5:12 (compare "sure foundation").
20. The concept in Moses 7:62 is similar to the Exodus when the Israelites ate the Passover with their "loins girded, [their] shoes on [their] feet, and [with their staffs] in . . . hand" (Exodus 12:11).
21. Wildberger, *Isaiah 13–27*, 100.
22. Wildberger, *Isaiah 13–27*, 100.
23. For example, Psalms 2:12 [MT 11]; 5:11 [MT 12]; 7:1 [MT 2]; 11:1; 16:1; 17:7; 18:2, 30 [MT 3, 31]; 34:8, 22 [MT 9, 23]; 36:7 [MT 8]; 37:40; 57:1 [MT 2]; 61:4 [MT 5]; 64:10 [MT 11]; 71:1; 118:8–9; 144:2.
24. Wildberger, *Isaiah 13–27*, 101.
25. Klouda, "Zion," 937.
26. *HALOT*, 640.
27. *HALOT*, 1305–6.
28. *HALOT*, 640.
29. Psalms 9:9 [MT 10]; 18:2 [MT 3] (2 Samuel 22:3); 46:7, 11 [MT 8, 12]; 48:3 [MT 4]; 59:9, 16–17 [MT 10, 17–18]; 62:2, 6 [MT 3, 7]; 94:22; 144:2.
30. Bellinger, "Zion," 986.
31. Compare Latin *deus/dea* ("god/goddess"; cognate with Greek *Zeus*; Latin *Jupiter*) as deriving from Indo-European **dyeu*, the daytime sky.
32. Isaiah 53:7 (Mosiah 14:7). Abinadi quotes this verse with reference to Christ in Mosiah 13:35. Compare also Isaiah 53:4 (Mosiah 14:4).
33. Isaiah 53:11 (Mosiah 14:11).

34. Horsley, *Covenant Economics*, 45.
35. Bruce C. Birch, *Let Justice Roll Down: The Old Testament, Ethics, and Christian Life* (Louisville, KY: Westminster/John Knox Press, 1991), 181–82.
36. On the syntactical function and meaning of ʾepes kî, see Bruce M. Waltke and M. O'Connor, *An Introduction to Biblical Hebrew Syntax* (Winona Lake, IN: Eisenbrauns, 1990), 672 (§39.3.5e.).
37. Birch, *Let Justice Roll Down*, 181.
38. Horsley, *Covenant Economics*, 42.
39. Horsley, *Covenant Economics*, 106.
40. Compare Mosiah 5:2; Alma 5:12–14; 19:33.
41. A key verb in Mark 14:7, *will*, is also a key term in our sacrament prayers and a key concept in the law of consecration. The concept is designed to eliminate physical and spiritual poverty among the Lord's people.
42. Birch, *Let Justice Roll Down*, 182.
43. Sharon H. Ringe, *Jesus, Liberation, and the Biblical Jubilee* (Eugene, OR: Wipf and Stock, 2004), 23.
44. Jaime L. Waters, *Threshing Floors in Ancient Israel: Their Ritual and Symbolic Significance* (Minneapolis: Fortress Press, 2015), 65.
45. Birch, *Let Justice Roll Down*, 130. Birch elsewhere (p. 165) notes, "The slave formula appears primarily as a separate and distinct command: 'Remember that you were a slave in the land of Egypt' (Deut. 5:15; 5:15; 16:12; 24:18, 22)."
46. Jennifer C. Lane, *Finding Christ in the Covenant Path: Ancient Insights for Modern Life* (Provo, UT: Religious Studies Center, Brigham Young University; Salt Lake City: Deseret Book, 2020), 22.
47. Isaiah 41:14; 43:1, 14; 44:6, 22–24; 27:4; 48:17, 20; 49:7, 26; 52:9; 54:5, 8; 59:20; 60:16; 63:9, 16. See further Isaiah 35:9; 51:10; 52:3; 62:12; 63:4.
48. Numbers 5:8; Ruth 3:9, 12–13; 4:1, 3, 6, 8, and 14.
49. Lane, *Finding Christ*, 21.
50. D. Todd Christofferson, "Come to Zion," *Ensign*, November 2008, 37–38; emphasis added.
51. Christofferson, "Come to Zion," 38.

52. 1 Nephi 21:14; 22:14, 19; 2 Nephi 6:12–13; 8:3, 11, 16, 24–25; 10:13, 16; 12:3; 13:16–17; 14:3–5; 18:18; 20:12, 24, 32; 22:6; 24:32; 27:3; Mosiah 12:21–22; 15:14, 29; 3 Nephi 16:18; 20:36–37, 40; Moroni 10:31; compare 1 Nephi 13:37.
53. Raymond O. Faulkner, *A Concise Dictionary of Middle Egyptian* (Oxford: Griffith Institute, 1999), 73.
54. Faulkner, *Concise Dictionary*, 74.
55. This putative paronomasia (a play on words with similar sounds) involving Zion assumes that, although we only have the text in English, Nephi used Hebrew ṣwy/ṣwḥ-terms or the Egyptian term wḏ (compare 1 Nephi 1:2)—terms that would have created this literary effect.

11

Remembering Redemption, Avoiding Idolatry
A Covenant Perspective on Caring for the Poor

Jennifer C. Lane

In our day, as latter-day Israel, a covenant perspective on abundance can help us overcome barriers to caring for the poor. Like the Israelites of old, it is when a prideful and idolatrous relationship with what we think is ours replaces a humble relationship with God that we limit our willingness to impart "our" substance. The Old Testament teaches us that remembering our redemption, our dependence on God, and his greatness allows us to avoid the idolatry of trusting in riches.

The connection between remembering redemption and avoiding idolatry is embedded in the first of the Ten Commandments found in Exodus 20: "I am the Lord thy God, which have brought thee out of the land of Egypt, out of the house of bondage. Thou shalt have no other gods before me" (Exodus 20:2–3). I am using the term *idolatry* in the broader sense of having another god before God (20:3) rather than in the narrower sense of making and worshipping graven images

(20:4).[1] Remembering their redemption keeps Israel in a spirit of worship and dependence on God for all they have. Forgetting their redemption leads Israel to glorify themselves and set their hearts on their riches. These changed feelings about "their" wealth changes their feelings about caring for those in need.

While ancient Israel also occasionally succumbed to the temptation to worship literal graven images as idols, I argue that the more metaphorical sense of idolatry in which we worship our own success, wealth, and accomplishment was also a temptation for the ancient Israelites. I claim that the texts examined herein, particularly those from Deuteronomy, show that the commandments the Israelites were given, such as those regarding the Sabbatical year, were also designed to help them remember that the Lord had redeemed them and was the source of all they had. In remembering their redemption, they avoid the idolatry of thinking of themselves as the source of their success. I also argue that the command to have no other gods before God focused the Israelites on the need to remember the Lord rather than solely warning them against worshipping others gods or idols. By giving this command to remember the Lord and his goodness in redeeming them, the Lord was giving the Israelites a way to avoid the pride and idolatry of trusting in their own resources.[2]

The foundational connection between remembering redemption and avoiding idolatry is shown in the Ten Commandments in Exodus but is also reinforced in Deuteronomy. The house of Israel is warned that even in the abundance they have received, they should not "forget the Lord, which brought [them] forth out of the land of Egypt, from the house of bondage" nor should they "go after other gods" (Deuteronomy 6:12, 14). We can see the more metaphorical sense of idolatry in Deuteronomy 8 where the danger is explicated for the Israelites and that in forgetting their redemption, they will say *"my power and the might of mine hand hath gotten me this wealth"* (8:17; emphasis added). They are warned that in forgetting the Lord they will "walk after other gods, and serve them, and worship them," a warning that certainly became literal at times but one that can also be understood more metaphorically as putting their trust in their material resources and their own power (8:19).

The Lord's redemption of the children of Israel from their bondage in Egypt came in fulfillment of his covenant with the patriarchs and also served as the foundation of his covenant relationship with all Israel as established in the law of Moses.[3] The warnings to remember this redemption can be found throughout the Pentateuch—the five books of Moses—and in this paper I will seek to show how remembering redemption is consistently connected to framing how the Israelites are to think about their own wealth and how they are to relate to those in need. Remembering that they were redeemed from Egypt would help them remember that all that they have should be understood as a stewardship and a gift and thus should help them be more willing to share these resources.[4]

While seeking to closely examine these Old Testament texts to more fully understand their doctrinal connections, I primarily focus not on the historical experience of the children of Israel but on what we as latter-day Israel can learn from these biblical teachings. Studying the Lord Jehovah's covenant and commandments and the passages about his goodness in redeeming the Israelites from their bondage helps the children of Israel to always remember him and foster a strong relationship with him. As we study biblical Israel's experiences with Jehovah, the premortal Christ, we can gain deeper insights into our own covenant relationship with the Lord as we remember all that we have is because of the price he paid for our redemption.

I have developed five subsections in order to clearly delineate my argument. First, I argue that the house of Israel is repeatedly taught that covenant blessings are the foundation of their abundance, and I explore how the Israelites were warned, particularly in Deuteronomy, not to think that they personally are the source of their wealth and prosperity. I then show how covenant requirements, especially those described in Deuteronomy 15 regarding the Sabbatical year, were set to remind the Israelites that the land they owned and the wealth they had built ultimately belonged to God, and thus they needed to share their resources. Next, I explore biblical insights into the greatness of God and posit that these Old Testament texts show us how pride and idolatry can come from forgetting God's greatness and that all things come from him. Finally, I conclude by considering that when we remember God's greatness and our dependence on him, we are blessed with wealth—both temporal and spiritual—and can then use it to bless others.

Covenant Blessings as the Foundation of Abundance

The first of the Ten Commandments, to have no other gods before God, is so familiar to us that we may not think it needs much comment. But by recognizing the role of covenant and redemption in the way the Lord frames this command, we can see how closely tied this is to his expectations regarding care for the poor. The first commandment begins with a statement of God's relationship to the children of Israel: "I am the Lord thy God" (Exodus 20:2). This "may be taken as a summary of the 'covenant formula' ('I will be your God, and you shall be my people')."[5] David L. Baker, a biblical scholar, notes that "this short phrase is particularly characteristic of the Holiness Code (Lev. 18–26) and is used in several laws on wealth and poverty. It often concludes laws on matters that cannot be judged or punished by human courts, because they are not objectively measurable, such as generosity or oppression."[6]

After Exodus 20:2 presents the Lord's role as Israel's God, the rest of the verse acts as a preamble to the command to have no other gods before Jehovah and is likewise foundational in establishing the true relationship of Israel to all that it has and is. The Lord explains, "I am the Lord thy God, which have brought thee out of the land of Egypt, out of the house of bondage" before commanding, "Thou shalt have no other gods before me" (Exodus 20:2–3). The connection between remembering redemption and avoiding idolatry in this passage is not an idle saying but is rather the explanation for how the covenant people are to see their lives and all that they have.[7] Every other commandment, including those in the Ten Commandments and throughout the law of Moses, is grounded in this relationship. Particularly regarding commands that involve how to care for vulnerable people, the Israelites are reminded of their redemption, their true condition as stewards, and how they had been given all they needed to succeed and find wealth.

Striking restatements of this connection between remembering redemption and avoiding idolatry are found in Deuteronomy where the theological ground for the commandments is more fully developed. In these passages, the Israelites are given explanation for the command that there be a regular pattern of resetting economic relations. These commands for the seventh year are first found in Exodus 23, where the initial focus is caring for the poor: "And six years thou shalt sow thy land, and shalt gather in the fruits thereof: but the seventh year thou shalt let it rest and lie still; that the poor of thy people may eat" (23:10–11). Requirements for observing the Sabbatical year include forgiving debt and releasing those who had been serving in temporary debt servitude—an economic restructuring that would have been painful for those who had to give up what they felt was owed them and what they felt they owned. However, these commands had the potential to reverse systemic injustice and the perpetuation of a wealth divide that could never be closed.

Framing these covenant obligations to be generous and care for the poor is a stark reminder for the children of Israel that what they have is not their own. They are warned not to think that they are the source of their wealth and prosperity. In Deuteronomy 6 we find the Shema, *the* command that is to be ever present for the covenant people:

> Hear, O Israel: The Lord our God is one Lord:
>   And thou shalt love the Lord thy God with all thine heart, and with all thy soul, and with all thy might.

> And these words, which I command thee this day, shall be in thine heart:
>
> And thou shalt teach them diligently unto thy children, and shalt talk of them when thou sittest in thine house, and when thou walkest by the way, and when thou liest down, and when thou risest up.
>
> And thou shalt bind them for a sign upon thine hand, and they shall be as frontlets between thine eyes.
>
> And thou shalt write them upon the posts of thy house, and on thy gates. (Deuteronomy 6:4–9)

And then, directly following the great commandment of the covenant, the command to "love the Lord thy God with all thine heart, and with all thy soul, and with all thy might" (Deuteronomy 6:5), the Israelites are then warned about the danger of a metaphorical idolatry. They are warned not to think that all God has given them is theirs, not to love their possessions, and not to forget God.

In this warning about potentially setting their confidence in their wealth, they are told to remember their redemption: "When the Lord your God has brought you into the land that he swore to your ancestors, to Abraham, to Isaac, and to Jacob, to give you—a land with fine, large cities that you did not build, houses filled with all sorts of goods that you did not fill, hewn cisterns that you did not hew, vineyards and olive groves that you did not plant—and when you have eaten your fill, *take care that you do not forget the Lord, who brought you out of the land of Egypt, out of the house of slavery*" (Deuteronomy 6:10–12 NRSV; emphasis added).[8] The abundance that they will experience in the promised land carries with it a tremendous danger of pride and forgetfulness. Forgetting God is a kind of idolatry that is seen in the false worship of their "own" accomplishments. It is a feeling that all they have received comes from their own strength and wisdom, forgetting that it is an unearned gift.

Directly after this warning, the first commandment in the Ten Commandments is essentially repeated again: "Thou shalt fear the

Lord thy God, and serve him, and shalt swear by his name. Ye shall not go after other gods, of the gods of the people which are round about you" (Deuteronomy 6:13–14 KJV). Since we know about the history of the Israelites' practice of worshipping the gods of the Canaanites, we may neglect to see the implicit metaphorical idolatry in their attitude toward material possessions and abundance as their "own" rather than as their stewardship and gift. They were being taught that how they treat and use what they have been given is how to show their love for the Lord.

As the covenant people today we must also remember and be able to explain that our obedience to commands, including the command to care for the poor, is rooted in our redemption: "And when thy son asketh thee in time to come, saying, What mean the testimonies, and the statutes, and the judgments, which the Lord our God hath commanded you? Then thou shalt say unto thy son, We were Pharaoh's bondmen in Egypt; and the Lord brought us out of Egypt with a mighty hand: . . . and he brought us out from thence, that he might bring us in, *to give us* the land which he sware unto our fathers" (Deuteronomy 6:20–21, 23 KJV; emphasis added). Everything that we are asked to do and everything that we are given must be understood in terms of the gift of Christ's spiritual redemption, of which the redemption of the Israelites from Egypt was a type.[9]

In Deuteronomy 8 this reminder to remember redemption as a way to have a right relationship with wealth is restated but with a subtle nuance. Rather than emphasizing everything that Israel was given whole cloth without their own effort, as explained in chapter 6, chapter 8 includes a warning that even when their efforts are part of their success, they must not forget the One who provided all the conditions needed for that success.[10]

The language of this warning again connects remembering redemption with avoiding idolatry. The Israelites are told to remember that the Lord brought them out of Egypt so that they "do not exalt [themselves]" and metaphorically worship their own wealth.

> When you have eaten your fill and have built fine houses and live[d] in them,
>
> and when your herds and flocks have multiplied, and your silver and gold is multiplied, and all that you have is multiplied,
>
> then do not exalt yourself, *forgetting the Lord your God, who brought you out of the land of Egypt*, out of the house of slavery. . . .
>
> Do not say to yourself, "My power and the might of my own hand have gotten me this wealth."
>
> But *remember the Lord your God, for it is he who gives you power to get wealth*, so that he may confirm his covenant that he swore to your ancestors, as he is doing today. (Deuteronomy 8:12–14, 17–18 NRSV; emphasis added)[11]

Directly after this reminder that the power to get wealth comes from God, we find a reminder of the first commandment: "And it shall be, if thou do at all forget the Lord thy God, and walk after other gods, and serve them, and worship them, I testify against you this day that ye shall surely perish" (Deuteronomy 8:19 KJV). Again, I believe that this commandment against idolatry should be understood directly in relationship to how the covenant people see their wealth, as was discussed previously. While the Old Testament writers might not write about this commandment in explicit terms of idolatry, I think that is what we are implicitly seeing in these texts: remembering redemption allows one to have a right relationship with God and to not move into metaphorical (or literal) idolatry—putting anything in the place of God. This is reinforced in some manuscripts that link Deuteronomy 8:19–20 with verses 1–18, implying that "turning to other gods is an inevitable result of forgetting ones' dependence on God."[12] These texts emphasize that the covenant blessings the children of Israel have received, including redemption, should bring a recognition of complete dependence on God for all good things that they have received and all that they have accomplished.

This clear Deuteronomic theology regarding Israel's complete dependence on God is part of the concept of the greatness of God in the Old Testament that I will explore in a later section. The biblical demand that the covenant people remember God's greatness was a way for the children of Israel to avoid the idolatry of boasting of and worshipping their own achievements, which could lead them to ignore the needs of others. This insight could be restated as the need to remember the greatness of God and one's own nothingness. The exact expression of human nothingness in contrast to God's greatness is not found in the Old Testament but is in a Book of Mormon quote from King Benjamin (Mosiah 4:5, 11). I believe that King Benjamin's speech perfectly captures the biblical concept of the complete dependence that the covenant people should have on God.

Covenant Requirements for "No Poor among Them"

In Deuteronomy 15, the covenant requirements to care for the poor are directly connected with recognizing one's dependence on God's mercy and his covenant faithfulness. The regulations for the seventh-year remission of debts and the release of Israelites serving in temporary enslavement in Deuteronomy 15 had the potential to function as a structural reminder that what the wealthy perceived as their resources was not actually theirs. In this chapter, the recognition that it is not their land or their wealth is tied to there being "no poor among them" (15:4). This phrase should be particularly evocative for Latter-day Saints because this condition of having "no poor among them" is specified as a condition for establishing Zion: "And the Lord called his people Zion, because they were of one heart and one mind, and dwelt in righteousness; and there was no poor among them" (Moses 7:18).

Of course, there clearly were poor people among the Israelites, but Deuteronomy 15 provides a connection between recognizing that

Israel's land was given by God and how the Israelites should treat those in need. The phrase "no poor among them" can give us important insights into the kind of society that we are to build. In the King James translation, however, having "no poor among them" is merely a theoretical possibility: "Save when there shall be no poor among you" (15:4). Other translations of Deuteronomy 15:4–5 provide much more helpful insights about having "no poor among them." The phrase could be seen as a moral imperative: "However, there *should not be any poor among you*, for the LORD will surely bless you in the land that he is giving you as an inheritance, if you carefully obey him by keeping all these commandments that I am giving you today" (NET Bible; emphasis added). The phrase can also be seen as a covenant promise: "There *shall be no needy among you*—since the Lord your God will bless you in the land that the Lord your God is giving you as a hereditary portion—if only you heed the Lord your God and take care to keep all this Instruction that I enjoin upon you this day" (JSB; emphasis added).

When we trust that this is the kind of society the Lord wants us to establish as his covenant people, then we can seek to learn from the mechanisms of wealth redistribution that the Lord established in the law of Moses, and we can also learn about the internal attitude that he commanded his people to have regarding material abundance. The goal here is to understand the theological underpinnings for these commands concerning the Sabbatical year instead of exploring what we can say about their practical effects in the history of Israel. We do not live under the law of Moses, but our latter-day covenant relationship with the Lord also has expectations about how we should use and feel about the material resources at our disposal.

The first command about the Sabbatical year in Deuteronomy 15 was debt release: "This is the manner of the remission: every creditor shall remit his claim, on whatever he has lent to his neighbor; he shall not exact it from his neighbor or his brother, for a remission to the Lord has been proclaimed" (15:2 Baker translation).[13] We might think that debt release is a lateral rather than a vertical action—meaning that it is about the relationship between people and not between people and God. But there is an important clue in the phrase "a remission to the Lord." This translation by Baker brings out the literal sense of "a remission to the Lord" and shows "its correspondence with 'sabbath to the Lord'" (Exodus 20:10 Baker translation). In the Ten Commandments, the explanation that the "seventh day is a sabbath to the Lord" (Exodus 20:10 NIV) shows that the emphasis for Sabbath day observance is to show the Lord how we remember him.[14]

Thus, saying that debt release in the Sabbatical year is a "remission to the Lord" would emphasize that we are showing the Lord how we remember him by forgiving the debts others owe us. This concept reemphasizes that Old Testament law is not primarily economic or political but that "its underlying goal is maintenance of the covenant relationship between the people and their God."[15] Forgiving any outstanding debts during the seventh year was a way of showing the Lord that they remembered his mercy and generosity toward them.[16] This Old Testament vision is captured in King Benjamin's explanation that "when ye are in the service of your fellow beings ye are only in the service of your God" (Mosiah 2:17).

The text also reemphasizes the need to be generous and lend to those in need, even if this loan might come shortly before the Sabbatical year when the debt would be canceled (see Deuteronomy 15:9). Not worrying about repayment goes against normal human reasoning, but this passage asks for behavior that goes against a limited view of self-interest: "If a fellow Israelite from one of your villages in the land that the Lord your God is giving you should be poor, you must not harden your heart or be insensitive to his impoverished condition. Instead, you must be sure to open your hand to him and generously lend him whatever he needs" (Deuteronomy 15:7–8 NET). Remembering that the land has been given by God should change the way we see the needs of the poor, and remembering God's generosity to us can help us be willing to be generous to others.

In addition to the normal human hesitancy to share, the text helps us understand that the timing of the Sabbatical can potentially make it harder to offer a loan to those in need. The lender is told to check a fearful hesitation to help those in need by having the right heart: "Beware that there be not a thought in thy wicked heart, saying, The seventh year, the year of release, is at hand; and thine eye be evil against thy poor brother, and thou givest him nought; and he cry unto the Lord against thee, and it be sin unto thee. Thou shalt surely give him, and thine heart shall not be grieved when thou givest unto him: because that for this thing the Lord thy God shall bless thee in all thy works, and in all that thou puttest thine hand unto" (Deuteronomy 15:9–10 KJV). The Lord promises that when we are willing to sacrifice for others, our generosity will be met with blessings in everything we do, and we also avoid our stinginess being counted against us as sin.[17] Here again, financial generosity given "without a grudging heart" expresses trust in God as the source of abundance, and "because of this the Lord your God will bless you in all your work and in everything you attempt" (15:10 NIV).

The next wealth distribution provision tied to the Sabbatical year is the command to release the Hebrews who were enslaved. Those who had been enriched by the free labor of these enslaved laborers were not just to release them without compensation: "Thou shalt not let him go away empty," rather "thou shalt furnish him liberally out of thy flock, and out of thy floor, and out of thy winepress: *of that wherewith the Lord thy God hath blessed thee* thou shalt give unto him" (Deuteronomy 15:13–14 KJV; emphasis added). Note the reminder here that it is with the abundance with which they have been blessed by God that they, in turn, were to bless others.

In the next verse this action to free those who were enslaved is tied to their remembering that "you were slaves in Egypt and the Lord your God redeemed you. That is why I give you this command today" (Deuteronomy 15:15 NIV). The covenant expectation that we remember our captivity and our redemption helps us transcend our selfishness by pushing us to always remember our dependence on God's mercy and generosity. This expectation also helps us to act with similar mercy to others, even when helping to improve others' lives comes at the cost of an immediate sacrifice to our own way of life. As with the command to loan even when it would not be repaid, the Lord promises that he will make up the difference when he asks the Israelites to release people who were temporarily enslaved. He reminds his people that blessings will come from the sacrifice involved: "It shall not seem hard to you when you let him go free from you, for at half the cost of a hired worker he has served you six years. So the Lord your God will bless you in all that you do" (15:18 ESV). The loss in capital need not "seem hard" when the children of Israel remember their abundance and trust that they will be further blessed for acting to free their fellow Israelites.

In summary, with the commands in Deuteronomy 15 for the seventh-year remission of debts and freeing of the Israelites who were enslaved, the covenant people are asked to remember that what they have been given is from God and that they need to trust that their abundance comes from God. This command invites a perspective of humility toward and a trust in God concerning our financial relationships with others. This perspective is both an expression of gratitude for the redemption that allowed us to be in this covenant relationship, and it is also an expression of trust in the blessings promised to us because of our covenant relationship with the Lord. We remember our redemption as we choose to obey the Lord's will in how we use our resources.

This perspective of humility and trust is essential because each of the commands in Deuteronomy 15 that are associated with the Sabbatical year were ways to redistribute wealth and prevent a perpetually widening gap between the rich and the poor. While we do not have these specific commands today, the Lord has shown his intention for there to be a covenant society in which there are no poor or needy among us. In our day the application of the command to "open your hand wide" (Deuteronomy 15:8 NKJV) may come through personal spiritual impressions, but as we remember our redemption we will be increasingly willing to follow impressions to give up that which we might naturally see as ours.

As we also seek to remember our redemption and that what we have is not our own, we can find our own ways to follow the Old Testament model of giving up repayment of a loan or labor to which one has become accustomed. This deepening of conversion, a change of heart about our possessions, allows us to more fully live out our covenant of consecration. By asking people to regularly and voluntarily renounce claims to their wealth, the Lord provides the opportunity for people to remember their redemption and that everything they have comes from him. Using King Benjamin's words that so beautifully summarize this Old Testament theology, we must remember "the greatness of God, and [our] own nothingness" (Mosiah 4:11). Therefore, remembering God's greatness is, by definition, remembering one's own nothingness and the dependence on God for all that one has and is able to do.

Greatness of God

The Old Testament theology of the greatness of God shows how we should see ourselves in relation to God. Having this right relationship with God is needed to overcome barriers to caring for the poor and needy. The Hebrew root *g-d-l* communicates the idea of greatness, prominence, and importance. This can have both positive and negative connotations. This verb is used when God's greatness is praised, but it is also used in the verbal form hithpael, meaning "to become arrogant or magnify oneself," which could imply that one is magnifying oneself over God.[18] The noun form *gedûllâ* "denotes the great acts of God," and the verb *gōdel*, in seven of its thirteen biblical uses, "refer[s] to the greatness of God, especially the greatness of God in redeeming his people from bondage in Egypt."[19] "In reference to humankind," however, "*gōdel* is used negatively to denote human arrogance."[20]

In Deuteronomy we see several passages explaining that God wants to show his people his greatness. "O Lord God, thou hast begun to shew thy servant thy greatness, and thy mighty hand: for what God is there in heaven or in earth, that can do according to thy works, and according to thy might?" (Deuteronomy 3:24 KJV). The Lord is without comparison for his works and his might, and he reveals his glory and greatness through the prophets and the temple. "And ye said, Behold, the Lord our God hath shewed us his glory and his greatness, and we have heard his voice out of the midst of the fire: we have seen this day that God doth talk with man, and he liveth" (5:24).

God's "greatness, his mighty hand, and his stretched out arm" are particularly seen in "his miracles, and his acts, which he did in the midst of Egypt unto Pharaoh the king of Egypt, and unto all his land; And what he did unto the army of Egypt, unto their horses, and to their chariots; how he made the water of the Red sea to overflow them as they pursued after you, and how the Lord hath destroyed them unto this day; And what he did unto you in the wilderness, until ye came into this place" (Deuteronomy 11:2–5). Remembering their redemption would be critical to remembering the greatness of God and their own nothingness—that is, their own dependence on God for all that they have and are and, after remembering this, to then give of what they have to those in need (see Mosiah 2:20–22; 4:21–23).

God's greatness in giving not only obliges us to give, since what we have is his and not our own, but also models how we should give. A striking passage in Psalm 145 shows how God gives in a way that he asks us to follow. First we read of God's greatness: "Great is the Lord, and greatly to be praised; and his greatness is unsearchable" (Psalm 145:3). The psalmist reminds us that God is not only great but also good and merciful: "The Lord is good to all: and his tender mercies are over all his works" (145:9). Note the language with which the psalmist praises God's generosity: "Thou openest thine hand, and satisfiest the desire of every living thing" (145:16). This is exactly how the covenant people are asked to give: "If there be among you a poor man of one of thy brethren within any of thy gates in thy land which the Lord thy God giveth thee, thou shalt not harden thine heart, nor shut thine hand from thy poor brother: But *thou shalt open thine hand wide unto him*, and shalt surely lend him sufficient for his need, in that which he wanteth" (Deuteronomy 15:7–8; emphasis added). As we choose to not harden our hearts or shut our hand from our poor sisters and brothers, we develop hearts like the Lord's.

Fully appreciating the greatness of God and our own nothingness allows us to recognize that everything we have is really God's and not our own. Knowing the greatness of God opens us up to see ourselves and others in a truer light, realize that riches come from God, and understand that we are instruments in God's hand to use his resources to bless others and further his work. As we remember the greatness of God and act accordingly, we move toward living out the principle that there should be "no poor among them" in Zion. If, however, we forget that our abundance is a gift from God, the very attitude of arrogantly thinking that our greatness is the source of our wealth is idolatry.

Danger of Forgetting God's Greatness

The psalmist speaks very directly about the danger of pride and idolatry: "If riches increase, set not your heart upon them" (Psalm 62:10).[21] An illustration of how prosperity can lead to turning against God and betraying Israel's covenant relationship can be found in the experience of the Israelites as recounted in Deuteronomy 32.[22] In this poetic text, the Israelites are asked to "remember the days of old" when they had been led and fed in the wilderness (32:7). "For the Lord's portion is his people; Jacob is the lot of his inheritance. He found him in a desert land, and in the waste howling wilderness; he led him about, he instructed him, he kept him as the apple of his eye. As an eagle stirreth up her nest, fluttereth over her young, spreadeth abroad her wings, taketh them, beareth them on her wings: So the Lord alone did lead him, and there was no strange god with him" (32:9–12).

So far, we see the Israelites' dependence on God highlighted because they were found "in a desert land, and in the waste howling wilderness" (Deuteronomy 32:10). Thus, as a child is nurtured by and dependent on parents, the children of Israel were borne on eagle wings, fed, and led by Jehovah, their covenant father. But rather than recognizing their dependence on God as the covenant parent, we see that when Israel prospered (growing "fat") it rejected God: "Jeshurun [here meaning Israel] waxed fat, and kicked: thou art waxen fat, thou art grown thick, thou art covered with fatness; then he forsook God which made him, and lightly esteemed the Rock of his salvation," turning away to other gods (32:15). This was a betrayal of the divine source of all they had received: "Of the Rock that begat thee thou art unmindful, and hast forgotten God that formed thee" (32:18).

Just as literal idolatry is a betrayal of God, setting our hearts upon other "gods"—like riches, especially in times of prosperity—is also a betrayal. As Psalm 62:10 warns, "If riches increase, set not your heart upon them." Growing "fat" in prosperity can lead to transferring our heart away from "lov[ing] the Lord [our] God" as we should, "with all [our] heart, and with all [our] soul, and with all [our] might," thus leading us to become idolatrous and betray the Lord (Deuteronomy 6:5).

Modern-day prophets have also warned that setting our hearts upon riches is idolatry. President Spencer W. Kimball clearly taught that our god is whatever we put our trust in. His teachings directly follow the Old Testament connection between setting our heart on riches and betraying our covenant responsibilities to the Lord and his children. President Kimball explained,

> Few [people] have ever knowingly and deliberately chosen to reject God and his blessings. Rather, we learn from the scriptures that because the exercise of faith has always appeared to be more difficult than relying on things more immediately at

hand, carnal [people have] tended to transfer [their] trust in God to material things. Therefore, in all ages when [people] have fallen under the power of Satan and lost the faith, they have put in its place a hope in the "arm of flesh" and in "gods of silver, and gold, of brass, iron, wood, and stone, which see not, nor hear, nor know" (Dan. 5:23)—that is, in idols. This I find to be a dominant theme in the Old Testament. Whatever thing [people set their] heart and [their] trust in most is [their] god; and if [their] god doesn't also happen to be the true and living God of Israel, [those people are] laboring in idolatry.[23]

This misplacement of our hearts and our trust is identical to the problem laid out in Psalm 10: "The wicked in his pride doth persecute the poor: let them be taken in the devices that they have imagined. For the wicked boasteth of his heart's desire, and blesseth the covetous, whom the Lord abhorreth. The wicked, through the pride of his countenance, will not seek after God: God is not in all his thoughts" (Psalm 10:2–4). By focusing on what we have and putting our trust in that, our relationship with God is corrupted and we can "persecute the poor" by withholding our hand from helping them in their need. By not really knowing the greatness of God, we boast of our "heart's desire, and [bless] the covetous" rather than those in need.

Remembering God's Greatness and Blessing Others

The Old Testament shows us the dangers of loving and trusting our wealth more than we love and trust God, but it also shows us a way out, a way to remember God by using what we have to bless others. Over and over again the children of Israel are told to remember their captivity and the gift of redemption provided by the Lord. Remembering their redemption and that the promised land and all its abundance were their gifts and their stewardship could provide his people with the spiritual grounding to have wealth and to use it the right way. Similarly, remembering God's greatness and our dependence on him can allow us to use our wealth to bless others.

The Lord knew how dangerous comfort and abundance would be for his covenant people, so he put the first commandment first. Old Testament scholar Robin Wakely insightfully observes that "for Israelites, the antidote to the complacency induced by careless amnesia, which is tantamount to disobedience, is faithful remembrance. . . . They must always remember that it is Yahweh who empowers them to gain wealth, and they must never arrogantly boast that they have acquired their own riches . . . entirely through their own efforts (Deut. 8:17–18)."[24] Always remembering our spiritual captivity and our redemption can help us keep both the first and the second commandments. Our love for the Lord, which grows out of our recognition of our complete dependence on his mercy and grace, helps us remember that our riches come from God and that it is our covenant responsibility to "open [our] hand wide" as God opens his hand to us (see Psalm 145:16). When we remember our nothingness and God's greatness, we will use our abundance to bless others and establish Zion with "no poor among us."

We catch a glimpse of this right heart when riches are used to build the kingdom of God. Consider the sublime words of a repentant King David dedicating land and supplies for the building of the temple at the end of his life: "Thine, O Lord, is the greatness, and the power, and the glory, and the victory, and the majesty; for all that is in the heaven and in the earth is thine; thine is the kingdom, O Lord, and thou art exalted as head above all. Both riches and honour come of thee, and thou reignest over all; and in thine hand is power and might; and in thine hand it is to make great, and to give strength unto all. Now therefore, our God, we thank thee, and praise thy glorious name" (1 Chronicles 29:11–13). Remembering God's greatness is recognizing that all we have comes from him. He is the one who can "make great" and give "power and might" to get abundance.

Along with recognizing God's greatness, in Chronicles we also see what it looks like to remember our own nothingness: "But who am I, and what is my people, that we should be able to offer so willingly after this sort? for all things come of thee, and of thine own have we given thee. For we are strangers before thee, and sojourners, as were all our fathers: our days on the earth are as a shadow, and there is none abiding. O Lord our God, all this store that we have prepared to build thee an house for thine holy name cometh of thine hand, and is all thine own" (1 Chronicles 29:14–16). We must remember we are strangers and sojourners before God, as were all our ancestors—all of our wealth comes from God's hand. Remembering our redemption means remembering that all we have comes from God and that it really is his, not ours. This keeps us in the right relationship with God—as his humble servants and stewards, seeking to know his will about how he would have us use the gifts and abundance that we have been given to bless others.

Like David, we likewise raise our voices: "We give thee but thine own / Whate'er the gift may be / For all we have is thine alone, / A trust, O Lord, from thee."[25] But to be willing to consecrate our lives and use our resources to bless others as God would have us do, we have to not just sing the words. We must feel this dependence and gratitude both deeply and daily, but it is so easy to forget. In the words of this hymn: "May we thy bounties thus / As stewards true receive, / And gladly, as thou blessest us, / To thee our first-fruits give / To comfort and to bless, / To find a balm for woe, / To tend the lone and fatherless / Is angels' work below." The Old Testament theology of abundance asks us as the Lord's servants to recognize that we are stewards of what we have and that we are required to use what we have been entrusted with "to comfort and to bless, to find a balm for woe, [and] to tend the lone and fatherless."

Conclusion

The prophetic voice that echoes through the Old Testament to see ourselves and our resources in the proper light is not absent in our day. We are reminded that "the Lord has blessed us as a people with a prosperity unequaled in times past. The resources that have been placed in our power are good, and necessary to our work here on the earth." Continuing, President Kimball said that he was "afraid that many of us have been surfeited with flocks and herds and acres and barns and wealth and have begun to worship them as false gods, and they have [begun to have] power over us."[26] This idolatry comes when we set our hearts on our riches.

By loving our riches more than God, we give them power over us that leads us to hesitate to open our hand wide to those who are poor. We hesitate when our generosity might impinge on our own personal comfort. We hesitate when we feel we are entitled to more than others because of our hard work and diligence. We hesitate when we fear that we will lose our security. President Kimball wondered, "Do we have more of these good things than our faith can stand? Many people spend most of their time working in the service of a self-image that includes sufficient money, stocks, bonds, investment portfolios, property, credit cards, furnishings, automobiles, and the like to *guarantee* carnal security throughout, it is hoped, a long and happy life."[27] Like the command in Deuteronomy 15 to reduce financial security by lending even when it would not be repaid or limiting the benefits that we can get from other people's labor, there are times when God asks us to give to others and trust that he will be the source of our abundance and security. The need to trust in God rather than in our riches may be asked of us in sacrifices like a formal call to serve, but often the sacrifices we are asked to make come through quiet promptings to our heart.

President Kimball specifies that as the covenant people, "our assignment is to use these many resources in our families and quorums to build up the kingdom of God—to further the missionary effort and the genealogical and temple work; to raise our children up as fruitful servants unto the Lord; to bless others in every way, that they may also be fruitful."[28] Living to help others find both spiritual and temporal well-being is living to "bless others in every way, that they may also be fruitful." A covenant perspective on wealth is a virtuous cycle in which all consecrated efforts are compounded as those we bless become more fruitful in blessing others.

Our covenant obedience to the first commandment—to love God first and not have wealth become an idol—prepares us to more fully live out the second commandment to love our neighbor. Seeking to "bless others in every way, that they may also be fruitful" is our stewardship. We are asked to care for the poor and needy in such a way that we do it "unto the Lord" so that we have nothing to boast of ourselves. If done as an expression of stewardship and gratitude for our own redemption, our service becomes a way of always remembering the greatness of God in our redemption.

By asking us to use our material blessings to focus on the needs of other people and to prioritize helping them over our own sense of what we own and what we are owed, we are kept safe from the danger that President Kimball explicitly warned about: "Expend[ing] these blessings on our own desires, and as Moroni said, '[adorning] yourselves with that which hath no life, and yet suffer[ing] the hungry, and the needy, and the naked, and the sick and the afflicted to pass by you, [but noticing] them not' (Morm. 8:39)."[29] Making the needs of others more important to us than "that which hath no life" is the means by which we avoid making our possessions our gods. Choosing to notice the hungry, needy, naked, sick, and afflicted and then not letting them pass by us keeps us from forgetting our redemption.

Blessing others through positive action keeps us alive to an embodied memory of God's blessings to us. President Russell M. Nelson explained that "*living* that second great commandment is the *key* to becoming a true disciple of Jesus Christ."[30] We always remember God when we *live out* the right relationship with the abundance he has given us (see Doctrine and Covenants 104:18). We always remember him when we do not turn away from the face of the poor but instead share what we have been given. All that we have and all that we are is a gift, but it is in how we *use* what we have been given that we always remember him.

We can avoid the danger of "walk[ing] in [our] own way, and after the image of [our] own God, whose image is in the likeness of the world, and *whose substance is that of an idol*" (Doctrine and Covenants 1:16; emphasis added). We can avoid the pride of focusing on our own strength or the idolatry of trusting in our "own" resources by remembering our redemption and our Redeemer. Our remembering will be shown, as President Nelson said, in "a conscientious effort to care about others as much as or more than we care about ourselves . . . especially when it is not convenient and when it takes us out of our comfort zone."[31] The building of Zion and our own spiritual safety demand that we learn from the Old Testament that the Lord is the source of all that we have. As we remember his mercy and power in redeeming us, we will have a spirit of consecration with all that we have been given. We will truly remember our redemption as we "open our hand wide" to those in need and work toward there being "no poor among us."

Jennifer C. Lane currently serves as Neal A. Maxwell Research Associate at the Maxwell Institute for Religious Scholarship at Brigham Young University.

Notes

1. While we consistently use the term *idolatry* in a more general or metaphorical sense in the modern world, in an ancient setting, worship of physical idols also took place. In ancient Israel and in the surrounding cultures, representations of other gods existed as physical idols, and the Israelites were commanded to not worship them nor to bow down and serve them. Rather, they were commanded to worship Jehovah, the God with whom they had covenanted to serve and remember.
2. Many Book of Mormon prophets teach of the biblical connections between pride and idolatry, and their teachings exhibit their deep reflection on these biblical messages. For example, Jacob warns against "pride; and those of you which have afflicted your neighbor, and persecuted him because ye were proud in your hearts, of the things which God hath given

you" (Jacob 2:20); King Benjamin exhorts us to "remember, and always retain in remembrance, the greatness of God," which will lead to a desire to "impart of the substance ye have one to another" (Mosiah 4:11, 21); and Abinadi reminds us that "if ye teach the law of Moses why do ye not keep it? Why do ye set your hearts upon riches?" (Mosiah 12:29).

3. Deuteronomy 7:7–8; 1 Nephi 17:40; see Jennifer C. Lane, "The Lord Will Redeem His People: Adoptive Covenant and Redemption in the Old Testament," in *Sperry Symposium Classics: The Old Testament*, ed. Paul Y. Hoskisson (Provo, UT: Religious Studies Center, Brigham Young University; Salt Lake City: Deseret Book, 2005), 298–310.

4. While they are given their freedom and the land as part of redemption, both the land and the people of Israel belong to the Lord. See Leviticus 25:23, 42; 1 Corinthians 6:19–20.

5. David L. Baker, "Why Care for the Poor? Theological Foundations of Old Testament Laws of Wealth and Poverty," *Proceedings of the Irish Biblical Association* 29 (2006): 9.

6. Baker, "Why Care for the Poor?," 9. Examples of these laws include: generosity at harvest time (Leviticus 19:9–10), "legal equality between resident aliens and native-born Israelites" (24:22), "honesty in buying and selling" (25:13–17), "granting freedom to bonded labourers in the jubilee year (Lev. 25:54–55)." Baker, "Why Care for the Poor?," 10.

7. In the Old Testament, covenant Israel was told to look back to the redemption from Egypt to remember their relationship with the Lord. We see in the Book of Mormon, New Testament, and modern-day revelations that those who understand the spiritual redemption made by the Lord Jesus Christ, of which the redemption from Egypt was a type, have even more reason to be eternally grateful and to worship God alone and have no other gods before him.

8. Jeffrey H. Tigay notes: "This reminder that the Israelites did not create the material wealth they are about to possess is an implicit warning against the attitude of self-sufficiency that prosperity can induce." Further, "The idea that material wealth and satiety can lead to pride and arrogance and forgetting one's dependence on God is a persistent concern in the Bible. It is repeated several times in Deuteronomy (8:12–14; 11:14–16; 31:20; 32:15) and elsewhere. Proverbs 30:8–9 sums up this concern as follows: 'Give

me neither poverty nor riches, but provide me with my daily bread, lest, being sated, I renounce, saying, 'Who is the Lord?' The Talmud quotes a popular proverb to similar effect: 'Filled stomachs are a type of evil.'" Jeffrey H. Tigay, *The JPS Torah Commentary: Deuteronomy* (Philadelphia: The Jewish Publication Society, 1989), 80.

9. In Deuteronomy 7:7–8, lest the people become boastful in their being redeemed, they are reminded of the covenant basis for redemption: "The Lord did not set his love upon you, nor choose you, because ye were more in number than any people; for ye were the fewest of all people: But because the Lord loved you, and because he would keep the oath which he had sworn unto your fathers, hath the Lord brought you out with a mighty hand, and redeemed you out of the house of bondmen, from the hand of Pharaoh king of Egypt."

10. "The idea as expressed here is reflected in Hos. 8:14 'Israel has forgotten his maker and built temples and Judah multiplied fortified cities.'" Moshe Weinfeld, *Deuteronomy 1–11*, Anchor Bible Series 5 (New York: Doubleday, 1991), 394.

11. In Deuteronomy 8:13, "the same Hebrew verb, *r-b-h*, is used in all three cases [to describe Israel's possessions growing: *multiplied, increased, prospered*]. It is the leitmotif of chapters 7–8. . . . Although the increase of Israel's cattle and wealth, like the building of houses (v. 12), will naturally require effort on its part, Moses does not say 'and you have multiplied your herds and flocks,' but rather 'your herds and flocks have multiplied.' In this way he avoids giving the impression that this increase will be due to Israel's own activity." Tigay, *Deuteronomy*, 95. Joel S. Kaminsky observes, "Once Israel was secure in the land, God's daily activities of sustenance were in the background and less easily noticed than in the wilderness period. As Deuteronomy 8 notes, God's gift of strength to the Israelites to enable them to build wealth can create the mistaken impression that they are a self-made people." Joel S. Kaminsky, "'The Might of Mine Own Hand Has Gotten Me This Wealth': Reflections on Wealth and Poverty in the Hebrew Bible and Today," *Interpretation: A Journal of Bible and Theology* 73, no. 1 (2019): 9.

12. Tigay, *Deuteronomy*, 96.
13. Baker, "Why Care for the Poor?," 12.
14. Baker, "Why Care for the Poor?," 12.

15. Baker, "Why Care for the Poor?," 12.
16. In the parable of the unforgiving servant in Matthew 18:21–35, we see the Savior's message that forgiving others, including sacrificing getting back what we feel is owed us, is required to always remember the infinite forgiveness of debt that we have been given because of Christ.
17. See a beautiful discussion of this in Kaminsky, "The Might of Mine Own Hand," 11. He comments, "In one sense, blessing begets blessing, and curse begets curse."
18. Martin G. Abbeg, "*gdl*," in *New International Dictionary of Old Testament Theology and Exegesis*, ed. Willem A. VanGemeren (Grand Rapids, MI: Zondervan, 1997), 1:824.
19. Numbers 14:19; Deuteronomy 3:24[21]; 5:24; 9:26; 11:2; 32:3. Abegg, "*gdl*," 826.
20. Abegg, "*gdl*," 827. "The northern kingdom of Israel rejected God's word, claiming that they could rebuild and be stronger than before (Isa 9:9[8]). Assyria (10:12; Ezek 31:7), as well as Egypt are accountable for their own (Ezek 31:2) 'greatness' before God." Abegg, "*gdl*," 827.
21. "Wealth is a gift of God (Deuteronomy 8:17–18; cf. Num 31:9; Isaiah 61:6). However, the Israelites are warned of its potential dangers. It is wrong to set one's heart on riches, for true security is provided by God alone (Ps 62:10[11])." Robin Wakely, "*ḥayil*," in *New International Dictionary*, 2:123.
22. Tigay notes that in this summary of blessings, "Israel should consider its history in order to be reminded of all that God did for it." Tigay, *Deuteronomy*, 302.
23. Spencer W. Kimball, "The False Gods We Worship," *Ensign*, June 1976, 4.
24. Wakely, "*ḥayil*," 123–24.
25. William Walsham How, "We Give Thee but Thine Own," in *Hymns* (Salt Lake City: The Church of Jesus Christ of Latter-day Saints, 1985), no. 218.
26. Kimball, "False Gods We Worship," 4.
27. Kimball, "False Gods We Worship," 4; emphasis in original.
28. Kimball, "False Gods We Worship," 4.
29. Kimball, "False Gods We Worship," 4–5.
30. Russell M. Nelson, "The Second Great Commandment," *Ensign*, November 2019, 100; emphasis in original.
31. Nelson, "Second Great Commandment," 100.

Refugees

12

Their Story Is Our Story Because We Were Strangers
The Relevance of Exodus 22:21 and Leviticus 19:33–34 in Refugee Awareness Work

Elizabeta Jevtic-Somlai and Robin Peterson

The marginalized and disadvantaged reside in the shadows of societies' comforts. In the bustle of our daily routine, these strangers remain unseen, hidden from our view, and are oftentimes forgotten. But not to God. He establishes early on in his dealings with the children of Israel that those whom society shuns are ever present in his view. God often chooses personalized imagery and narrative through his prophets to vividly teach his people how these strangers, in actuality, are a reflection of his very own people and need to be treated as such. Introducing the laws that will govern the children of Israel following their exodus from Egypt, God cautions his people on multiple occasions to "neither vex a stranger, nor oppress him" because, as he consistently instills in his people, they too "were strangers in the land of Egypt" (Exodus 22:21). With this short statement, he reiterates Israel's own story of slavery in order to stress the need for his people to empathize with the stranger. The power of weaving their own story into an eternal principle of charity lies in an endeavor to engage their "mind, emotions, spirit, [and] body"[1] to effect a change of attitude[2] and with it, potentially, a course of action favorable to God. In other words, he nudges them not only to remember their own story but to use it to embrace the stranger since the story of a stranger they may encounter tomorrow was their own story yesterday. In Leviticus, this weaving is even more prominent as God elaborates that "the stranger that dwelleth with you shall be unto you as one born among you, and thou shalt love him as thyself; for ye were strangers in the land of Egypt: I am the Lord your God" (Leviticus 19:34). In his attempt to curb human propensities, God provides both the children of Israel and Latter-day Saints today with several important messages.

His first vital message is a type of preemptive deconstruction of the notion of an "us" versus "them," thereby providing an opportunity for creating interconnectedness based on the simple understanding of what it feels like to have been there. God suggests that while wounds—enslavement in a foreign land and the accompanying brutality—do heal, the scars that they leave are there to remind us to empathize with those who are fighting battles of their own. Second, God asks Israel to love the stranger as they would love themselves. The notion of loving "as thyself" evokes the idea of looking into a mirror, seeing a reflection—full of blemishes, imperfections, and insecurities—and embracing it with wholehearted appreciation. As a result, allowing oneself to be loved despite one's imperfections also grants one the right and opportunity to embrace and love other human beings, while fully realizing that they are just as imperfect. This imagery invites one to mirror God's love for an individual by providing respite from duress and haven from sociopolitical and juridical insecurities because, in God's eyes, the reflections both of oneself and of a stranger are equal.[3] Third, this reflection is meant not purely for self-justification and self-preservation but as a precursor to the exercise of kindness,[4] an eternal principle with eternal consequence, which ultimately leads to holiness. As such, God's final point to the children of Israel is that embracing one's own imperfections and granting other human beings the right to be imperfect opens a gate toward greater understanding, appreciation, love, and acceptance of the people around us, no matter their race, nationality, religion, skin color, or any other determinators that tend to divide us as people. The decree to love strangers is about seeing the divine potential within others and within ourselves, viewing them and us as children of God, and perceiving all of us as offspring from eternal parents. The act of loving the stranger is about removing the blindfolds of mortality and remembering one another as God does so that our actions are driven by kindness, restraint, and greater tolerance.

The images evoked in the Leviticus verses, which are messages and meanings repeated throughout scripture, are both beautiful and complex. The fact that God uses that particular story of slavery and exodus to impress upon the minds of the children of Israel the gravity of the code attached to the story makes it particularly powerful. Daniel Taylor suggests that the use of a particular story is a vital characteristic of conveying a message or teaching a lesson because "propositions depend on the stories out of which they arise for their power and meaning and practical application. The story provides the existential foundation on which the proposition rests. If no story, then [there is] no significance for the proposition."[5]

In other words, stories imprint propositions on our mind in a memorable way. While first presented in the Old Testament as a code to the children of Israel,[6] the decree to take care of the stranger is still acutely applicable today. It has found its echo across many cultures and religions, including in the early Church and during the restoration of the gospel. And while the code mentions those who are enslaved, homeless, poor, or marginalized based on physical, mental, emotional, racial, ideological, geographical, educational, or other less obvious denominators, we will focus specifically on the code's objective to protect one of the most sidelined groups in our society today—the refugees. We elaborate on the relationship between the stranger in the Old Testament and the refugee, thereby making the case that the laws presented in the Old Testament's Pentateuch are also applicable today and would benefit the modern-day refugee.

The Refugee

Based on the definition of the United Nations (UN) High Commissioner for Refugees at the Geneva Convention of 1951 and its subsequent modification in the Protocol of 1967, a refugee is someone who,

> as a result of events [that have occurred] . . . and owing to well-founded fear of being persecuted for reasons of race, religion, nationality, membership of a particular social group or political opinion, is outside the country of his [or her] nationality and is unable or, owing to such fear, is unwilling to avail himself [or herself] of the protection of that country; or who, not having a nationality and being outside the country of his [or her] former habitual residence as a result of such events, is unable or, owing to such fear, is unwilling to return to it.[7]

One of two elements must be present to classify people as refugees—namely, (1) for reasons beyond their control, the individuals were forced (or made) to leave their homes and livelihoods to survive or (2) the individuals fear returning home because they do not enjoy the protection of their own countries or peoples. In summary then, these people leave everything behind not only out of necessity but also out of a well-founded fear for their lives and the lives of their loved ones; by default, they find themselves in a particularly vulnerable state. In Myrto Theocharous's essay "Refugee Asylum: Deuteronomy's 'Disobedient' Law," he compares the characteristics found in Deuteronomy 23 to those in the definition of a refugee. In this chapter, Moses lays out specifications as to who may enter the congregation in the Israelite camp in order to keep it clean and holy before the Lord. While the chapter as a whole is strictly clear as to who is considered clean and worthy of being in the congregation, the tone differs in verses 15 and 16 because they forbid a Moabite from entering (an aspect discussed later in this paper). Having admonished the Israelites only a verse earlier that they should ensure that the "camp be holy: that he see no unclean thing in thee, and turn away from thee," Moses goes on to establish the rule that they "shalt not deliver unto his master the servant which is escaped from his master unto thee." Rather, the servant seeking the refuge "shall dwell with thee, even among you, in that place which he shall choose in one of thy gates, where it liketh him best: thou shalt not oppress him" (Deuteronomy 23:14–16). Theocharous suggests that the "characteristics of the refugee . . . are also present in the law of Deut. 23:16–17 [15–16]: (a) the fact that it most probably concerns foreigners who seek refuge in another land, (b) the element of fear that is clearly discernible and (c) the obvious urgent need for asylum protection."[8]

Theocharous goes on to explain that while the original verses and the law discuss the specific treatment of a slave, it should be noted that in antiquity, the term *slave* was not "restricted to [actual] slaves, but it generally characterizes [any person] under authority."[9] This idea suggests that the person defined as the slave in the passage has experienced fear, flight from dangerous circumstances, and asylum seeking, which denotes that the slave is also a refugee as defined by the UN. Concluding, Theocharous explains that "understanding the slave as [a] 'refugee' allows the reader to examine what the law says, not only with respect to slavery, but also with respect to refugee asylum."[10]

Refugee scholars Christopher Wright and Marcel Macelaru explore the fact that migration itself is such a common thread throughout the Bible that readers "hardly notice it as a major feature." This migratory theme shows that while not all movements had the same purposes, many were similar in that they were made out of necessity for the migrants' survival and their own protection, as well as that of their posterity.[11] Looking further into the migration patterns, Jonathan Burnside suggests that the term *stranger* was readily used to define someone migrating "from another tribe, city, district or country" who had left his or her homeland out "of necessity."[12] We can easily conclude that while migration was a typical occurrence in antiquity, the Lord himself did want Israelites to pay attention to the migrants, especially to those who were leaving their homelands out of necessity. He alluded to that idea by using Israel's own Exodus story to clearly remind the Israelites that not only were they strangers in a land but there was also a certain parallel in their own movement to freedom, a parallel comparable to the movement characterizing the refugee: movement driven by fear, persecution, and oppression. The Lord states to Moses, "Behold, the cry of the children of Israel is come unto me: and I have also seen the oppression wherewith the Egyptians oppress them" (Exodus 3:9). The Lord later affirms that he "will bring [them] up out of the affliction" (3:17) and that he remembers the covenant he has made "to give them the land of Canaan, the land of their pilgrimage, wherein they were strangers" (6:4). The necessity for migrating out of Egypt, the actual Exodus with all its challenges and trials, and the longing for the promised land evoke imagery easily comparable to modern images of thousands of people walking across deserts and crossing large bodies of water in hopes of arriving in a place that will provide safety—a type of a promised land. God did not define the term *stranger* to denote specifically a refugee or a fugitive, yet he was quick to remind the children of Israel what it was like to be a stranger on multiple occasions. We therefore suggest that the refugee is included in God's request to extend kind and protective treatment to the stranger, a treatment that would fit the needs of today's refugee.

In his talk "Refuge from a Storm," given at general conference in April 2016, Elder Patrick Kearon reminded us that "there are an estimated 60 million refugees in the world today, which means that '1 in every 122 humans . . . has been forced to flee their homes,' and half of these are children."[13] Elder Kearon echoes the Lord's reminder that the children of Israel were strangers in their land, and he reinforces the notion that we—as an extension of the children of Israel through our baptismal covenants and as children of God—need to reconsider the provisions of care and protection extended to refugees. Just like God reminded the children of Israel that they were once strangers, Elder Kearon exhorts us today to remember that as members of the Church, we "don't have to look back far . . . to reflect on times when we were refugees, violently driven from homes and farms over and over again."[14] He then asks, "What if *their* story were *my* story?,"[15] a question first asked by Sister Linda K. Burton in her April 2016 general conference talk, and answers that question for members of the Church by stating, "Their story *is* our story, not that many years ago."[16] His caution to the membership to "be careful that news of the refugees' plight does not somehow become commonplace when the initial shock wears off" is strikingly similar to the Lord's warning issued in Leviticus 19:33–34 to not let the children of Israel forget that they were once strangers. Like the children of Israel, we need to remember the "millions of refugees worldwide, whose stories no longer make the news."[17]

It is no wonder that Elder Kearon's plea encouraged many Latter-day Saint individuals and groups to spare no effort in reaching out and providing necessary help. One such effort was the founding of a refugee awareness nonprofit organization in 2015 named Their Story Is Our Story (TSOS). With the goal to ensure that the stories that "no longer make the news" and the people behind them are still remembered, TSOS documents first-person stories and accounts of refugees' journeys from homes lost to homes found. Established by a handful of writers, artists, and humanitarians who wanted to put their talents to work on behalf of refugees entering Europe, TSOS headed to Greece in the spring of 2016 to film, photograph, interview, paint, and ultimately befriend refugees for the first time.[18] Hoping to capture a couple dozen stories, the team returned with over seventy interviews involving nearly two hundred people. Since then, TSOS has grown to include dozens of team members—including refugees and former refugees—from several countries and continents. Having traveled the world documenting stories of refugees, refugee volunteers, and refugee-supporting organizations and, more recently, by conducting interviews via the internet and in the communities where refugee programs are already established, TSOS has gathered hundreds of stories and produced dozens of videos, all of which can be found on the TSOS website and in the Global Refugee Archive housed at Brigham Young University's Harold B. Lee Library. TSOS believes that raising awareness and allowing the viewer to be educated through these stories can help further the Lord's law to not oppress the stranger to but remember him or her. Since the stories collected have helped strengthen the discussion at hand, they will be used as case studies in the discussions herein of the verses from Exodus and Leviticus.

Deconstructing the "Us" versus "Them"

It is often supposed that the function of the Old Testament is to tell the story of God's chosen people, the children of Israel.[19] However, upon closer examination, we can see that the story begins before that, with the creation of humankind as a whole. Only in Genesis 12 are we introduced to Abraham and thus to the eventual birth of Israel. While this might seem a trivial point, Old Testament scholar Hans-Georg Wünch postulates that this sequence of events bears an important message about Israel's self-perception and their perception of strangers:

> What does it say about Israel that its Holy Scriptures start with the fact that God created Adam and Eve in his image and therefore humankind as a whole, not [as] Israel's predecessors only? What does it say about Israel that the first covenant between Yahweh and humans is one with the whole of humanity, not one with Israel? All of this makes [it] clear that Israel does not understand itself as the centre of humanity or as the most important nation amongst all others. As a latecomer in history, Israel understands its own identity as directly coming from Yahweh, who picked up this

small and almost meaningless people and made it his people. Therefore, its identity rests in Yahweh, not in its own strength or relevancy.[20]

His postulate leads to the conclusion that the children of Israel perceived themselves as a peculiar people among all of God's creations. This led Israel to clearly delineate between those who belonged in the "us" inner circle of the covenant and those who belonged in the "them" circle partly because the patriarchs Abraham, Isaac, and Jacob were strangers in Canaan themselves, and as a people, the Israelites were surrounded by the worship of gods other than Yahweh. In reality, when God told Abraham that he will "bless them that bless thee, and curse him that curseth thee: and in thee shall all families of the earth be blessed" (Genesis 12:3), he created the contradiction in which Abraham was given the foreknowledge that through his seed the blessings would be bestowed upon humankind, while at the same time alluding to the fact that Abraham's seed would "be a stranger in a land that is not theirs, and shall serve them; and they shall afflict them four hundred years" (Genesis 15:13).

Let us remember that the "Egyptians made the children of Israel to serve with rigour: and they made their lives bitter with hard bondage. . . . Every son that is born ye shall cast into the river, and every daughter ye shall save alive" (Exodus 1:13–14, 22). Nonetheless, God reassured Jacob in a vision and said, "I am God, the God of thy father: fear not to go down into Egypt; for I will there make of thee a great nation. I will go down with thee into Egypt; and I will also surely bring thee up again" (Genesis 46:3–4).

The suffering the Israelites endured was central to their development of empathy and understanding for the plight of others.[21] Therefore we can see that God helped the Israelites learn from their painful experiences how to be a blessing unto the nations. In essence, it could be concluded that God's hope for Israel was that their story of migration and estrangement would create a holy and a just society where "religious and social duties and responsibilities are inseparable."[22] And since God is long-suffering, he created very specific rules and instituted rituals to remind the children of Israel of their heritage and to provide a code for them to learn how to remember the other without abandoning their covenantal duties. In fact, God created the code as part of that covenant to ensure that the children of Israel would be aware of the other as a stranger. However, by allowing strangers to dwell among the children of Israel, the Israelites eventually learned a way to be "in the world, but not of the world."[23] This covenantal duty was as important to the Lord as it was to the children of God. As a result, they distinguished themselves from different types of strangers and used three different words to describe the level of potential danger to the covenant—whether the strangers might lead the children of Israel astray, show some sympathy to the covenant, or even desire conversion—and the associated course of action and interaction toward a stranger: namely, *gēr* (resident alien, sojourner, guest), *nēkār* (foreigner), and *zār* (outsider).[24] Of the three, scholars agree that *gēr* is the most neutral in connotation and is the term most often used in the Old Testament verses.[25] The term *gēr* is used ninety-two times throughout the Pentateuch,[26] and it is used to describe the patriarchs and the children of Israel while in other lands,[27] and, as Burnside explains, also a

> person from another tribe, city, district or country who has left his [or her] homeland and who is no longer directly related to his original setting. He is someone who lacks the customary social protection of privilege and who has, of necessity, placed himself under the jurisdiction of someone else. . . . This being so, it is sensible to suggest that the noun *ger* should be translated as "immigrant." The phrase "resident alien" is awkward and the term 'sojourner' is archaic. "Immigrant" . . . adds the motif of "social conflict." It does this in three main ways. First it highlights the original circumstances of social conflict that are inevitably responsible for causing people to become immigrants in the first place. People usually become

gerim as a result of social and political upheaval. This could be caused by war, famine, oppression, plague and other social misfortunes. Second it is consistent with the conflicts that can result when immigrants try to settle in a new environment.... Third, it highlights the immigrant's "outsider" status in the adopted social setting.[28]

By choosing to use the word *gēr* to describe both the children of Israel while in their migratory state and a stranger as mentioned in the Leviticus verses, God creates an interconnectedness between the two different groups of people and deconstructs the separation of "us" and "them" at an emotional level. At this point, it should be highlighted that all through their existence as the covenant people, the children of Israel struggled to remain a peculiar people. While their identity rested in the Lord, as Wünch pointed out, the children of Israel often adopted the belief structures of others around them, sometimes to the point that they walked away from the covenant and perverted the ways of the Lord. Even during their exodus journey there are instances of such behavior. This is not what the Lord means, however, when he seeks for them to deconstruct the "us" versus "them." What the Lord is asking the children of Israel is to not forget, to develop empathy based on that memory for the plight of others, and to be a blessing unto others. In other words, the Lord reminds the children of Israel that while they are his covenant people and he wants them to remain as such, the stranger is also the Lord's creation. The stranger is a child of God, a *gēr* deserving of protection because, as Burnside points out, his or her migration is based on social or political upheaval and is therefore not optional. One might suggest that at this point in time, Israel had a shared story of oppression to connect them with the other, but this might not be the case for them as well as for us today. By default, this may lead to our inability to deconstruct our own "us" versus "them" fences. In this paper, we argue that the inability to deconstruct the "us" versus "them" does not lie in a lack of a shared story but rather in the *perception* of such. Elder

Kearon reminded us that we do have a shared story of oppression through the stories of our own beginnings as God's chosen people. This is why the images from the Grecian shore of the lifeless body of Alan, a drowned three-year-old refugee, along with his older brother, Galib, five, and their mother, Rehanna, thirty-five, provide connection—we remember our own struggle during the early years of the Restoration, and this helps us to build empathy for the other.[29] God himself shows us that this interconnectedness is present in more ways than we imagine and that it can easily be reinforced through the powerful imagery of remembering and acknowledging the other, as Lisa Campbell's story shows:

> Like most people in the US, I hadn't been aware of the scale of the refugee disaster until . . . I saw for myself the piles of life jackets and the boats stacked on the beach. . . . It was hard to wrap my head around what I was seeing. I was horrified at the stories that I heard.
>
> There is probably not an emotion that I didn't experience, standing there day after day on the shore, watching the boats come in. . . . I had no refugee experience, but I'm a do-er. . . . I ended up running the camp for 18 months, until the Greek government shut it down. . . . From my perspective, this work is like being a mother. . . . I've learned that love is a choice. When they [the refugees] were informed that the camp[30] was closing, these people came to me and said things like: "You've been like a mother to me, I don't know what I'm going to do without you." And I realized that I had met my goal—which was to take care of them and show them they are loved. . . .
>
> The residents of our camp felt like "refugee" had become a dirty word. But they're refugees because they want the same things in life that you and I want. We had engineers, lawyers, teachers, musicians, artists, police officers—people from all walks of life. They were just like you and me.[31]

Figure 1. *Lisa Campbell. Photography by Christophe Mortier. Courtesy of TSOS, 2016.*

As we learn about the stories of refugees, we quickly realize that their stories are reflections of our own. While we might not be able to specifically relate to stories of persecution and maltreatment, we can identify instances in our lives that have been challenging, meaningful, and important and connect them with the stories of others. Campbell's experience shows not only dedication to Christlike love but also a realization that human-to-human interaction reveals more similarities than differences; as she learned, *they* are just like *us*. Remembering that something relatable is within every person's narrative helps us to deconstruct the reservations we may hold toward others. As a peculiar people and as a covenant people, the Lord asks us to allow emotional connection to occur, just as he asked of the children of Israel. This allowance opens us up for the next level of spiritual transformation—that of loving the other as we love ourselves. But what does it mean to love another as oneself? God provides the answer in the Pentateuch.

Love a Stranger as Thyself

Luma Khudher suggests that an important aspect of the commandment given in Leviticus 19:33–34 is the belief that the *"ger is under God's special protection."*[32] This could be the case because of their vulnerable state or because of God's ability to perceive the Israelites' apprehension in dealing with anyone outside of the covenant. To curb potential human propensities that would result from either their vulnerability or apprehension, God instituted a wise system that provided specific obligations about what it meant for the children of Israel to implement the commandment of loving a stranger. Being observers of the letter of the law, the Israelites were made aware that this was not a mere "sentimental generalization" but rather an actionable commandment.[33] Wright and Macelaru summarize the laws God gave:

- comprehensive protection for foreigners from any and all forms of abuse and oppression (Exodus 22:21; Leviticus 19:33)
- protection from unfair treatment in court (Exodus 23:9; Deuteronomy 1:16–17; 24:17–18)
- inclusion in Sabbath rest (Deuteronomy 5:12–15; compare Exodus 20:9–11)
- inclusion in worship and covenant—*gērîm* were to be included in the whole life of the community, especially if they were assimilated through circumcision (Exodus 12:48–49; Leviticus 16:29–30; 17:12, 15; 18:26; 24:16; Numbers 15:14; Deuteronomy 14:28–29; 16:10–14; 26:12–13; 29:10–13; 31:12)
- provision of fair employment practices (Exodus 21:2–11; Deuteronomy 15:12–18; 21:14–15)
- access to agricultural produce, or "gleaning rights" (Leviticus 19:9–10; 23:22; 25:23; Deuteronomy 24:19–22)
- equality before the law with native inhabitants (Numbers 15:15–16).

These protection provisions constitute some of the best practices for transitional societies and the successful integration of refugees and asylum seekers into modern-day societies.[34] For the purposes of this paper, let it suffice that we underline once again the notion of the Lord ensuring that "loving as thyself" comes with a provision of specific protections that the state and people of Israel were to grant to the refugee. To this day, these protections aid newcomers in feeling accepted in and becoming valuable, contributing members of their new societies.

The story of Ruth beautifully portrays the fact that these protections were applicable even after the time of Moses. In this book we are introduced to a family who leaves Bethlehem and moves to Moab because of a famine in the land. In other words, we are introduced to a refugee family who would today fall under the category of a climate refugee. We learn from the first few verses that life for this family is not easy. When the husband and sons of the family pass on, the widow, Naomi, desires to return to her native land, knowing that she will find enough mercy back home to sustain her. However, Naomi has acquired two daughters-in-law (Ruth and Orpah), who have different nationalities and worship different gods from the people in Bethlehem. As a result, neither of her daughters would qualify as *gērût*, and their worship of gods other than Yahweh would be looked down upon by the people in Bethlehem. Naomi may have feared that her daughters-in-law would not be extended financial mercy upon their return to her native land and that the likelihood of them securing good marriages would be limited. Consequently, Naomi implores them to remain in their own country where they might have other prospects for financial security and protection through new marriages. Ruth must have been aware of the conditions she would possibly endure by going back to Israel with Naomi. But Ruth tells Naomi, "Entreat me not to leave thee, or to return from following after thee: for whither thou goest, I will go; and where thou lodgest, I will lodge: thy people shall be my people, and thy God my God: Where thou diest, will I die, and there will I be buried: the Lord do so to me, and more also, if ought but death part thee and me" (Ruth 1:16–17). In her famous statement, Ruth, a Moabite woman, steps away from everything that endangers her from being seen as *gēr* or equal in the covenant, an action that makes her words even more poignant. She renounces her old way and willingly takes on Naomi's God to be hers too, dismantling any notion of fear or rejection that her presence in Israel could cause. Her unfailing love and devotion to Naomi is stronger than that fear, and the years of living under the same roof have likely made a true convert out of her, one who identifies with Naomi's people. That this could very likely be the case is not only supported by her poignant statement but also by the fact that none of the terms for *stranger* are found in the text of the story when Ruth is described. Because her heart was pure, she was given God's special protection. As the book progresses, we see that this purity of heart led to Ruth's marriage with Boaz and a lineage that produced a king of Israel—ultimate clues that she had been accepted into the covenant.

The introduction to the book of Ruth in the Old Testament seminary manual explains that the book of Ruth "addresses the belief held by some . . . [that the children of Israel] should separate themselves entirely from those who were not of Israelite descent . . . [and provides] valuable balance by reminding its readers that the great-grandmother of the revered King David was a faithful woman from Moab who converted to Israel's religion and married within the covenant. Ruth demonstrated kindness to others and loyalty to the Lord. One of the main messages of the book of Ruth is that such faithfulness is more important than ethnicity."[35]

Ruth's story shows us that when we encounter a stranger, even one who has a different ethnicity or worships a different god, it is more important to look into the heart and to embrace the person as a child of God because we never know who stands before us. Ruth not only becomes the great-grandmother of David but is also "an ancestor of our Savior Jesus Christ."[36]

The message is clear. The treatment we provide to today's refugees will have a lasting effect and can help them (re)discover God, change society for better, and be benefactors to our own posterity. Alternatively, our neglectful treatment toward the refugees (or rather the protection we hesitate to provide) can make their lives more difficult, as shown in Naomi's story, and can contribute to their struggle to secure their future and peace. TSOS has documented many stories on both sides of the spectrum. Faroosh's desperate plea personifies the plight of thousands of refugees that have been forced to flee their homes in search of safety and security but have found only a lack of protection upon arrival in foreign lands:

> In the name of God, my name is Faroosh. We are from Afghanistan. I used to work in the media in Afghanistan. We didn't have economic problems there. We left our country because of security problems. I worked as a cameraman in a private television program where we made a documentary movie about the Taliban and the war. I was threatened by the Taliban several times. We went to dangerous places like the Kandahar Province to report and film. When they realized what we were doing the Taliban attacked us.
>
> Due to the dangerous situation, we fled from Afghanistan into Iran. After that we spent about 12 hours walking through the mountains until we arrived in Turkey. At first, I had planned to stay in Turkey but the police arrested us. They were not nice with us and they were not helpful. Also, Turkey was not a safe country to live in. There were two or three suicide bombings while we were there.
>
> Because of all these problems we came here to Greece but we don't see any progress in our situation. We have no freedom to move on to other European countries. We don't have enough money to go forward and we don't know about our future.

Figure 2. *Faroosh and his family. Photography by Lindsay Silsby. Courtesy of TSOS, 2016.*

If peace returns to Afghanistan one day, we will definitely go back. I had a peaceful and good life there. I had a house and a job. The only problem was the war and the lack of life security. I think there is no solution for my country unless our leaders solve the problems.[37]

Stuck in a limbo, Faroosh and his family have struggled to move on and establish their lives because they are seen as strangers and are treated as such by their country of reception. Despite their abilities, they cannot progress any further because they are not seen as equal contributors to the society in which they find themselves. That is, the love they are afforded does not match the love one would give to oneself. Rather, it is the bare minimum care that the reception country's citizens feel obligated to provide.

On the other hand, part of Leonard's story shows the great potential for refugees and their long-term outcomes when they are provided protection and assistance:

In 1997, I was coming [home] from school with a bunch of kids. We saw 2 men come and they took us. We were forced to join the military. I was 17 at the time. After 6 months, they decided to take us back, to go fight. And, when I went to the other side of the water, to the dock, I heard a strong voice telling me, "Run, Leonard, run!" . . . The closest refugee camp was in Malawi, a different country. In the refugee camp, life wasn't easy. I call it the hell on this earth. . . . In 2004 I came to the United States.

I ended up being homeless. . . . After a week, I heard a strong voice saying "Leonard, this is not what brought you to America. You can be better than this. You need to ask for help. If you don't ask, no one will help you. You need to ask for help." I thought, "Who can I ask for help?" One Saturday morning, I saw somebody pull a car into the back of the library [parking lot]. A couple got out of the car, old people. I followed them, and I kept yelling, "I need help, I need help." The wife heard me yell, and then she yelled to her husband, "Doug, can't we help this young man?" I said, "I am a refugee from Congo, and I'm homeless."

He answered, "Oh we have met a lot of people from Congo. We served a mission in South Africa. Here's my business card." So, they left me with a business card and told me to call them. On Monday I called them, and they said, "We were thinking about you. Can you come live with us?" I was like, "Yes, I will come live with you." So, I went to live with them in South Jordan [Utah]. And over there, they were farmers, so I learned how to milk cows and a lot of other things. They paid all my tuition for 5 years and now I have a Bachelor's degree. Imagine, I never finished high school, I don't have a high school diploma. But I have a bachelor's degree today.

I got a job with a small company called Health Access Project. We partner with the Department of Workforce Services to provide health care to refugees. Doing case management for refugees in medical settings, I found out that the problems I had when I came to this country are still the same problems refugees are having now. I decided to use my personal experience to help other people. So, I took $3,000 from [my] bank account, I took an office, and I started putting all the legal papers together and today we have an organization called Utah Valley Refugees. We bring refugees from Salt Lake County and all over the United States to come here. What we do with them is just simple. We help them with medical needs. We help them with housing. We teach English classes at the office and we also have classes on employment. We partner with Utah Valley University, so we have students who are going there. So far, in 3 years now, we have been able to help more than 100 families. And among those 100 families, 5 families have already bought a home. They are homeowners. We have a few people who are in the military, we have 2 Utah Valley University graduate students. We actually hired a case manager who was among the first refugees we helped here.

I feel blessed today. I feel blessed and I feel successful. I call myself one of the most successful refugees in this country. I came here 15 or 16 years ago. Now, I own a home. I have a good job. I have a family. I have

Figure 3. *Leonard Bagalwa. Photography by Kristi Burton. Courtesy of TSOS, 2019.*

a degree. If you compare me to a person my age who was born here, I think we are on the same level. And they have been here more than almost 40 years! I always thank our Heavenly Father for that help from above.[38]

The elderly couple mentioned by Leonard occupies only a small space in his personal narrative, and yet their act of selfless love made an incredible difference in the life of the young man they saw standing before them and eventually in the lives of many others who were blessed through him. Does this not sound like the fulfillment of the promise given to Abraham, "and in thee shall all families of the earth be blessed?" These two stories show that loving others as we love ourselves means that we should provide others with the same opportunities we have been given and be the instrument God uses to fulfill his promise of blessing all families of the earth. What effect would such fulfillment have on the giver? Because all of God's laws served a higher purpose for the children of Israel and because his final goal is to accomplish the immortality and eternal life of humankind (Moses 1:39), we can conclude that God implemented the law of loving others as ourselves to aid in the exaltation of the entire human family.

The Path to Holiness

God himself prefaces Leviticus 19 with a call for Israel to "speak unto all the congregation of the children of Israel, and say unto them, Ye shall be holy: for I the Lord your God am holy" (Leviticus 19:2). This is why scholars of the Old Testament have suggested that the laws found in Leviticus constitute the Holiness Code, or the Laws of Holiness, because they call for the "ethic of imitating God (*imitatio Dei*)," or, rather, they "[imitate] the acts of God" toward another human being.[39]

The idea of imitating God received much attention in antiquity, where Plato himself asserted that the doctrine of *imitatio Dei* meant "becoming like God" by mimicking his higher ways for the betterment of the world.[40] Maimonides, a medieval Jewish philosopher, suggests that "the perfection in which [people] can truly glory is attained by [them] when [they have] acquired—as far as this is possible for [them]—the knowledge of God, the knowledge of his providence, and of the manner in which it influences his creatures in their production and continued existence. Having acquired this knowledge, [people] will then be determined always to seek lovingkindness, justice, and righteousness and thus to imitate the ways of God."[41]

But how do we imitate God? Since one of his attributes that is often repeated throughout the scriptures is his ability to remember and act upon that memory,[42] a plausible way to imitate God could be seen in our ability to preserve memory. As we do this, we can offer strangers relief and encourage kindness and mercy toward them as we act upon that remembrance for the benefit of others. In the story of Ruth, both Ruth and Naomi are imitating the acts of God toward another human being as they care for each other. However, while we often speak of Ruth's unfailing devotion to Naomi, we sometimes neglect to realize that Naomi's remembrance of her own plight and its utilization to benefit Ruth is what creates the spiral of imitating acts. Naomi loves this young woman even before we enter the story, and through her kind and wise continual direction, Naomi eventually secures Ruth's future. However, because Naomi shows kindness, she is granted financial stability, blessings, and, finally, holiness from God. After her son's death, Naomi could easily have dismissed Ruth. But just like Lisa Campbell in TSOS's first story, Naomi loved Ruth as if she were her own flesh and blood. The memory of that love is what makes Ruth stay with her, and the resulting dance of reciprocity in caring for each other elevates them both. Naomi, the refugee of yesterday—like Leonard in TSOS's third story—becomes the deliverer to Ruth, the refugee of today, because of Naomi's ability to remember. Let us not forget that both Ruth and Naomi are actual ancestors of King David and of Christ. The same promises and blessings that we often attribute to Ruth for her faithfulness in her story are also promised to Naomi because of her own refugee story that has made her strong, resilient, loving, and charitable. Nonetheless, it is ultimately in the act of remembering, loving, protecting, and accepting a Moabite woman (as if she were her own child) that Naomi finds holiness and is rewarded with incredible posterity, holiness, and a closeness to God.

One should take note of August Klostermann's definition of love as "an event where even the highest degree of self-reference dissolves into an even higher self-giving."[43] Loving one's neighbor and the stranger involves special kinds of creative acts that open up new and transformative spaces and relations in all regions of social life, usually divided by race, economic class, gender orientation, and religion. Holiness is thus achieved not through exclusion or separation but by an inclusive attitude, thereby including those who are different from you.[44]

Refugees today differ from those in the local communities in which they find themselves. Elder Kearon expounds on this, reminding us that "being a refugee may be a defining moment in the lives of those who are refugees, but being a refugee does not define them. Like countless thousands before them, this will be a period—we hope a short period—in their lives. Some of them will go on to be Nobel laureates, public servants, physicians, scientists, musicians, artists, religious leaders, and contributors in other fields. Indeed, many of them were these things before they lost everything. This moment does not define them, *but our response will help define us.*"[45]

The act of remembering is important to the Lord. It is his way to remind us of the covenant and to demonstrate that this covenant is still in effect, as long as we fulfill our part (see Isaiah 49:14–16). It is therefore in the act of remembering the stranger that we demonstrate that we are doing our part to keep our covenant with him or her. Elder Kearon's words remind us that whether or not we, as covenant people, follow the Holiness Code has an impact on our own opportunity (not on the refugees' opportunities) to imitate God and become more like him. As modern-day covenant children of God, we need refugees to attain exaltation just as much as they need us in order to achieve that goal. God gives us an open invitation to be saviors on the mount, and if we accept that call, not only will our acts of kindness define us, but they will also refine us[46] until we receive the image of God in our countenances (Alma 5:14).

Conclusion: Stories Are a Way to Remember

God besought the children of Israel not to forget their own story of marginalization. This concept constitutes the greater commandment of remembrance given to the covenant people and is deeply ingrained in the Old Testament as well as in modern-day scripture. In the illustrated reference work for Latter-day Saints, *Jehovah and the World of the Old Testament*, Richard Holzapfel, Dana Pike, and David Seely describe the importance of what they term as the "Eleventh Commandment": "The Hebrew verb *zakar*, 'to remember,' is used no fewer than 169 times in the Old Testament in one form or another. Often called the Deuteronomic imperative, the call to remember could be appropriately identified as the 'Eleventh Commandment.' Recollection or remembrance thus becomes the vehicle through which the faith of the ancestors is maintained and passed to the next generation."[47]

Through the covenant of remembrance, we receive holiness and exaltation, not only because it strengthens our faith but also because it calls upon us to act as God would. In covenanting to remember him, we covenant to keep his commandments and observe his laws. Ultimately, the goal is to lead us to covenant that we will remember his children as he remembers us, but even more importantly, it will lead to us remembering them as *he* does and acknowledging our divine kinship to others as our siblings and as his children (Mosiah 18:9–10, 27–29). In antiquity, this commandment was fulfilled by passing on stories orally and recording them for future posterity in journals and books. By this passage of stories, the human family is linked and connected through the generations of time, and bonds are created that would not exist otherwise. In essence, remembrance through story gathering and story sharing becomes the act through which human families are bound to each other until they are all linked back to God. With its vast library of stories, media assets, and contributions from other like-minded organizations, TSOS's digital and scholarly archive encompasses all aspects of the refugee experience. This open access and digitally searchable archive will be the first of its kind in the world and serves as a nexus of "all things refugee," from firsthand stories curated by both refugees and nonrefugees, to film, photography, scholarly research, artwork, theater, music, maps and charts, conference proceedings, podcasts, and other information resources yet to arise on the rapidly expanding and constantly changing landscape of refugee experiences. By so doing, TSOS aims to live up to preserving the memory of the strangers who are children of God and who need us to keep a record of and remember their sufferings (Doctrine and Covenants 123:1–6). At this hinge point in our world's progress where there are more forcibly displaced people (70.8 million+) and bona fide refugees (30 million+)[48] than at any other time in recorded history, creating the archive is one important way to honor the law in Leviticus 19:33–34. The principal hope is that this deep well of knowledge will become a resource to help change perceptions about and the reception of refugees, assist leaders and citizens as they seek to understand and respond intelligently to refugee crises, and facilitate the knowledge that there is no "us" versus "them." Indeed, as we take care of the refugee, we will realize "that the neighbor here is the one who, as made by God, shares our *imago Dei*," and that as such, we will recognize that we "are variations on a theme, the theme of finite yet strikingly beautiful and varied images of God who need each other."[49]

Elizabeta Jevtic-Somlai is director of public relations and strategy at Their Story is Our Story (TSOS).

Robin Peterson is director of archives at Their Story is Our Story (TSOS).

Notes

1. Daniel Taylor, "Story-Shaped Faith," in *The Power of Words and the Wonder of God*, ed. John Piper and Justin Taylor (Wheaton, IL: Crossway Books, 2009), 109.
2. In her book, *Telling the Gospel through Story*, Christine Dillon discusses the impact using stories has in the conversion process of each individual listener. She emphasizes that the retelling of biblical stories can change people from hostile to sympathetic and help them develop new ways to understand God, life, the world, and their space in it as faith-oriented beings. For a more detailed discussion, see Christine Dillon, *Telling the Gospel through Story* (Downers Grove, IL: InterVarsity Press, 2002), 23–30.
3. See 2 Nephi 26:33; Acts 10:34–35; 17:26; Romans 2:11; Galatians 3:28.
4. Dan Belnap, "'How Excellent Is Thy Lovingkindness': The Gospel Principle of *Hesed*," in *The Gospel of Jesus Christ in the Old Testament* (Provo, UT: Religious Studies Center, Brigham Young University; Salt Lake City: Deseret Book, 2009), 170–86.
5. Taylor further elaborates, "Imagine having all the propositions of the Bible but none of the stories. No Genesis or Exodus, none of the historical books of the Old Testament, no Gospels, no Acts—only Romans, parts of the Epistles, and scattered assertions and commands from here and there. Those assertions and commands would still be true, but we would have very little idea of what to do with them." Taylor, "Story-Shaped Faith," 108–9.
6. In his paper, Robert E. Lund suggests that God provided the rules for the children of Israel to "improve the condition of the people" and strengthen their spirituality. For a detailed discussion, see Lund, "Teaching Old Testament Laws," *Religious Educator* 8, no. 3 (2007): 52; W. Cleon Skousen suggests a similar theme, stating that despite all the efforts made by Moses to create another Enoch society, "he lacked a people worthy of it." See W. Cleon Skousen, *The Third Thousand Years* (Salt Lake City: Ensign Publishing, 1964), 255.
7. "Handbook on Procedures and Criteria for Determining Refugee Status and Guidelines on International Protection," UNHCR: The UN Refugee

Agency; USA, reissued 2019, p. 18, https://unhcr.org/en-us/publications/legal/5ddfcdc47/handbook-procedures-criteria-determining-refugee-status-under-1951-convention.html, unfortunately, not at my fingertips.
8. Myrto Theocharous, "Refugee Asylum: Deuteronomy's 'Disobedient' Law," *Studies in Christian Ethics* 30, no. 4 (2017): 465.
9. Theocharous, "Refugee Asylum," 465.
10. Theocharous, "Refugee Asylum," 465.
11. Christopher J. H. Wright and Marcel V. Macelaru, "The Refugee Crisis—A Shared Human Condition: An Old Testament Perspective," *Transformation* 35, no. 2 (2018): 93.
12. Jonathan P. Burnside, *The Status and Welfare of Immigrants: The Place of the Foreigner in Biblical Law and Its Relevance to Contemporary Society* (Cambridge: Jubilee Centre, 2001), 13–14.
13. Patrick Kearon, "Refuge from the Storm," *Ensign*, May 2016, 111.
14. Kearon, "Refuge from the Storm," 111.
15. Linda Burton, "I Was a Stranger," *Ensign*, May 2016, 14.
16. Kearon, "Refuge from the Storm," 111.
17. Kearon, "Refuge from the Storm," 113.
18. "About Us," Their Story Is Our Story, https://tsosrefugees.org/about.
19. Hans-Georg Wünch, "The Stranger in God's Land—Foreigner, Stranger, Guest: What Can We Learn from Israel's Attitude towards Strangers?," *Old Testament Essays* 27, no. 3 (2014): 1135.
20. Wünch, "Stranger in God's Land," 1135.
21. Leon Sheleff suggests that true awareness of the purpose of Israel's experience should have "provided a conceptual framework that would make Israeli leaders more sensitive to the pleas and plight" of the strangers in their midst. For more information, see Sheleff, "The Stranger in Our Midst: The Other in Jewish Tradition—From Biblical Times to Modern Israel," *Israel Studies Bulletin* 14, no. 2 (1999): 6–8. Ultimately, their suffering was a similitude of Christ's suffering. As Alma suggests, Christ needed to experience the pain and anguish in his physical form to be able to reach into the depths and gather all his creations to him, and the children of Israel experienced a small portion of this when they waded through their

bondage in Egypt and became better able to understand the far-reaching nature of the Atonement (see Alma 7:11–12).

22. Stephen J. McKinney, Robert J. Hill, and Honor Hania, "Old Testament Perspectives on Migration and Responsibility for the Refugee," *Pastoral Review* 11, no. 5 (2015): 59.
23. James A. Cullimore, "To Be in the World but Not of the World," *Ensign*, January 1974, 119–21. See John 15:19; 17:14–15.
24. Wünch, "Stranger in God's Land," 1140.
25. See Luma A. Khudher, "'You Were Once Foreigners': Biblical Law on Care for the Stranger in Our Midst," *Bible Today* 56 (2018): 9–12; Wright and Macelaru, "Refugee Crisis," 94–95.
26. Burnside, *Status and Welfare of Immigrants*, 13.
27. Genesis 15:13; 23:4; Exodus 22:21–23; 23:9; Leviticus 19:34. See also Khudher, "'You Were Once Foreigners,'" 9; Wright and Macelaru, "Refugee Crisis," 94.
28. Burnside, *Status and Welfare of Immigrants*, 13–14.
29. Adnan R. Khan, Jonathon Gatehouse, and Nancy Macdonald, "The Tragedy That Woke Up the World," *Maclean's* (2015): 14–19.
30. The more appropriate terminology would be a *refugee center*, or a *transit center*; however, many non-governmental organizations name their establishments "refugee camps."
31. Global Refugee Archive, Story 409; Lisa Campbell, interview by TSOS team, spring 2016, https://scholarsarchive.byu.edu/tsos_interviews/9/.
32. Khudher, "'You Were Once Foreigners,'" 9.
33. Wright and Macelaru, "Refugee Crisis," 95.
34. Integration is most often described as a process that enables a newcomer to achieve an "equal footing with the native population in terms of functioning in society, . . . particularly through meaningful socioeconomic inclusion." The process itself takes years and is very complex. From learning the language and customs of the land, to establishing home and livelihood, the most successful integration is a two-way street requiring "adaptation on the part of the newcomer but also by the host society." For a more detailed discussion, see Dirk Jacobs and Andrea Rea, "The End of National Models? Integration Courses and Citizenship Trajectories

in Europe," *International Journal on Multicultural Societies* 9, no. 2 (2007): 264–83.
35. "Introduction to the Book of Ruth," in *Old Testament Seminary Teacher Manual* (2015), 286.
36. Thomas S. Monson, "Models to Follow," *Ensign*, November 2002, 61.
37. Global Refugee Archive, Story 005; Faroosh, interview by TSOS team, spring 2016, https://scholarsarchive.byu.edu/tsos_interviews/1/.
38. Global Refugee Archive, Story 640; Leonard Bagalwa, interview by TSOS team, summer 2019, https://scholarsarchive.byu.edu/tsos_interviews/12/.
39. August Klostermann, "Beiträge zur Entstehungsgeschichte des Pentateuchs," *Zeitschrift für die gesammte Lutherische Theologie und Kirche* 38, no. 3 (1877): 416. See also Hendrik L. Bosman, "Ethical Redefinition of Holiness," *Old Testament Essays* 31, no. 3 (2018): 572, 579.
40. David N. Sedley, "The Ideal of Godlikeness," in *Oxford Readings in Philosophy: Plato*, ed. G. Fine, vol. 2 (New York: Oxford University Press, 1999), 309–28. See also Harry A. Wolfson, *Philo: Foundations of Religious Philosophy in Judaism, Christianity, and Islam, Volume 1: Structure and Growth of Philosophical Systems from Plato to Spinoza* (Cambridge, MA: Harvard University Press, 1962), 194–96; Charles Duke Yonge, trans., *The Works of Philo, Complete and Unabridged* (Peabody, MA: Hendrickson, 1995), 62.
41. Maimonides, *Guide of the Perplexed*, 3:54. See also Sefer ha-Mitzvot, Rabbinic teaching, Positive Commandment 8, https://chabad.org/library/article_cdo/aid/940233/jewish/Positive-Commandment-8.htm. Howard Kreisel, "'Imitatio Dei' in Maimonides' Guide of the Perplexed," *AJS Review* 19, no. 2 (1994): 169–211.
42. Genesis 9:15–16; Leviticus 26:42, 45; Jeremiah 31:34.
43. Klostermann, "Beiträge zur Entstehungsgeschichte des Pentateuchs," 416.
44. Bosman, "Ethical Redefinition of Holiness," 587–88.
45. Kearon, "Refuge from the Storm," 114; emphasis added.
46. Elizabeta Jevtic-Somlai, "Reshaping Refugee Rhetoric," *Bridges Magazine* 1 (2019), https://kennedy.byu.edu/reshaping-refugee-rhetoric.
47. Richard Neitzel Holzapfel, Dana M. Pike, David Rolph Seely, *Jehovah and the World of the Old Testament* (Salt Lake City: Deseret Book, 2009), 140.

48. "Refugees," United Nations, Global Issues, 2019, https://www.un.org/en/sections/issues-depth/refugees.
49. Cecilia González-Andrieu, *Bridge to Wonder: Art as a Gospel of Beauty* (Waco, TX: Baylor University Press, 2012), 10.

13

The Experience of Israelite Refugees
Lessons Gleaned from the Archaeology of Eighth-Century-BC Judah

George A. Pierce

Statistics from the United Nations Refugee Agency show that at the end of 2019, "79.5 million individuals have been forcibly displaced worldwide as a result of persecution, conflict, violence or human rights violations."[1] Thus, while public attention often shifts to other concerns such as pandemics, politics, or economics, the refugee situation is persistent, requiring attention. Refugees have a prominent, although sometimes overlooked, place in biblical and Restoration scripture and in the history of The Church of Jesus Christ of Latter-day Saints from its nascent years in Ohio, Missouri, and Illinois to the present. Notably, this includes Elder Dieter F. Uchtdorf, who was a refugee early in life and has shared lessons learned from that experience.[2] Church authorities have alerted and instructed members about the plight of modern refugees and encouraged activities that would provide aid and comfort to such displaced persons.[3] Further, the Church has provided supplies to refugees in fifty-six countries, volunteered time and efforts to help integrate displaced persons into new communities, and dedicated a website to increase refugee awareness and to suggest ways members can be of assistance.[4]

The ancient kingdom of Judah faced similar migrations of displaced persons from the northern kingdom of Israel. While the eighth century BC started as a period of great prosperity for both

Figure 1. *Map of Israel and Judah in the eighth century BC. Map by the author.*

kingdoms, that century witnessed the conquest, exile, and devastation of the kingdom of Israel and an Assyrian campaign that greatly affected Judah. Starting with the Syro-Ephraimite War (2 Kings 16:5–7; Isaiah 7), the Assyrian empire, ruled by Tiglath-pileser III, conquered and annexed the Galilee in 732 BC.[5] Later, the Assyrian king Sargon II laid siege to Samaria, fully conquering the northern kingdom in 721 BC (2 Kings 17:6–23). While some of Israel's population was left in the land, nearly forty-one thousand citizens of the northern kingdom of Israel were deported and sent into exile.[6] Thousands more escaped the ruin and desolation of the Assyrian onslaught by migrating south to Judah as displaced refugees.

This paper examines the textual and archaeological evidence for Israelite refugees in the kingdom of Judah in the eighth century BC and what we, as modern believers, can learn from the material culture, experience, and treatment of refugees in Judah. This paper attempts to show the relevant practical applications that may arise from supplementing scripture with archaeology and what lessons for interacting with and assisting the disenfranchised and marginalized within society may be gleaned from both the archaeological and biblical records. Lessons from the prophetic oracles about Judah and its relationship with both the Lord and the displaced persons from the northern kingdom, while initially intended for the ancient Judahites, continue to have relevance and practical application for modern believers.

Refugees in the Biblical Text

In the Old Testament, the status and experience of characters as settled or migrant/nomadic persons, temporary sojourner, or refugee is often described in the text and, in some cases, is foundational to the narrative. The refugee status of Israel's patriarchs and matriarchs include instances such as the flight to Egypt by Abraham during a drought (Genesis 12:10) and the migration by Jacob and his family during an extensive famine (Genesis 46). The Exodus from Egypt and subsequent festivals honoring that foundational event focus on the Israelites being refugees. The book of Ruth relates the story of Elimelech, Naomi, and their sons relocating to Moab, and the return of Naomi, accompanied by her daughter-in-law Ruth, to her ancestral home of Bethlehem (Ruth 1:1–2, 22). Other examples include the flights of David and other disenfranchised men to the wilderness (1 Samuel 19–20), Hadad the Edomite (1 Kings 11:14), Jeroboam (1 Kings 11:40), and Elijah (1 Kings 17:2–5). Jeremiah refers to the presence of Judahite refugees in Ammon, Moab, and Edom (Jeremiah 40:11), as well as to Judahites who fled to Egypt (Jeremiah 42–44; 2 Kings 25:26). Places of refuge in the Old Testament include the hills, the wilderness, caves, and neighboring polities such as Moab or Egypt. Notably, the family of Lehi fleeing as refugees from the destruction of Jerusalem by divine command is central to the Book of Mormon (1 Nephi 2:2–4), and their sojourn in the wilderness appears typical of the refugee experience in the Old Testament. In the New Testament, Joseph, Mary, and Jesus are depicted as refugees fleeing a political threat and returning to their homeland only after divine instruction (Matthew 2:13–15).

Despite the recurring motif of refugees elsewhere across biblical genres, the Old Testament historical narratives of 2 Kings and 2 Chronicles are curiously silent about the migration of refugees from the kingdom of Israel to the kingdom of Judah as a result of Assyrian campaigns. Because of this gap in biblical history, the presence and experience of these expatriates and lessons for the modern believer can best be gleaned from the archaeological record. The experience of the Judahites and the prophetic critique to trust in the Lord also provide an additional lesson for the modern believer.

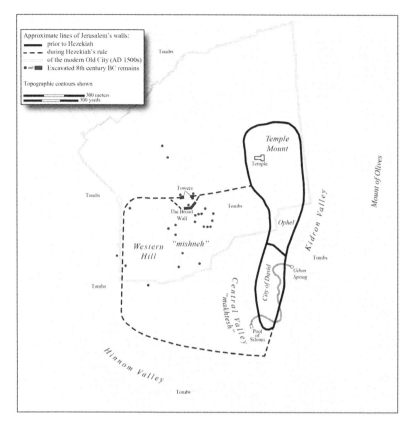

Figure 2. *Map of Jerusalem in the eighth century BC. Map by the author.*

Refugees and the Archaeology of Judah and Jerusalem

Ancient Jerusalem was situated on two hills framed and divided by three main valleys. The Eastern Hill comprises the spur called the City of David, the Temple Mount, and a saddle between the two known as Ophel. The Kidron Valley to the east and the Tyropoeon (or Central) Valley to the west define the Eastern Hill. The Western Hill is topographically higher than the Eastern Hill and is demarcated by the Tyropoeon Valley to its east and the Hinnom Valley to the west and south. In the later biblical periods, the Western Hill was known as the *mishneh* ("the second district"; 2 Chronicles 34:22 Christian Standard Bible) and the Tyropoeon Valley was likely the *maktēš* ("hollow" in Christian Standard Bible) mentioned in Zephaniah 1:11. The Gihon Spring, near the base of the City of David's eastern slope, was the primary source of water throughout the Old Testament period.

Because of Jerusalem's role as the royal city of the Davidic monarchy and its centrality for worship, biblical scholars and archaeologists in the Holy Land have sought to determine the location and extent of Jerusalem's boundaries during the biblical period prior to the Babylonian conquest. Archaeological excavations in the nineteenth and twentieth centuries indicate that the earliest traces of settlement were on the Eastern Hill, specifically the spur called the City of David. The date of settlement of the Western Hill and the extent of Jerusalem have also been debated. Did biblical Jerusalem encompass both hills, or was it limited to the City of David and the Temple Mount until the Second Temple period?

Archaeological fieldwork conducted in Jerusalem by Israelis after the Six-Day War provides some answers to these questions. Throughout much of its history, Jerusalem has occupied two hills: the Eastern Hill (City of David, Ophel, and the Temple Mount) and the Western Hill. However, only the Eastern Hill was occupied from Jerusalem's beginnings in the Neolithic period until sometime in the eighth century BC. Tombs on the western side of the Eastern Hill that date to the ninth century BC provide a boundary for expansion of the city at least until sometime after that date.[7] The Western Hill has shown few signs of any activity until at least the late ninth–early eighth centuries BC in the form of small, scattered agricultural installations with little to no architecture related to habitation. Excavations in the present-day Jewish Quarter of the Old City, located on the Western Hill, revealed increased, extensive construction efforts dated to the last quarter of the eighth century BC.[8] The excavators dated four phases of construction using pottery associated with the

Figure 3. Eighth-century-BC architecture excavated in the Jewish Quarter of the Old City of Jerusalem. Photograph by Zev Radovan.

floors and walls. The structures were made of undressed field stones with plastered walls. Floors that survived consisted of crushed and tamped chalk or beaten earth. The ceramic assemblage dated from the mid-eighth century through the early seventh century BC based on parallels to other Judahite sites such as Lachish, Beersheba, Arad, and Beth Shemesh. Other excavation areas in the Jewish Quarter exposed mostly fragmentary walls and floors with some indication of an agricultural installation for pressing olives or grapes. Additional building remains were found in excavations at the Jerusalem Citadel near Jaffa Gate, the Armenian Garden, and on Mount Zion. Because of the position of houses beyond fortified areas, excavators were confident that this portion of Jerusalem was unwalled and outside the defensive walls of Jerusalem.[9]

Finds in this area included ceramic figurines depicting women that may be connected to fertility (termed Judahite Pillar Figurines), animal figurines, and storage jars bearing royal seal impressions.[10] Two seals, used to sign documents and verify identity, were found. One bears the name "Sapan (son of) Abimaʿas," and the other reads "Menahem (son of) Yobanah." An ink inscription on a storage jar fragment (an ostracon) contained the name Mikhayahu and the phrase *[ʾĒl] qōnēh ʾāreṣ*, meaning "God creator of earth."[11] Writing discovered on an additional ostracon possibly refers to an examination or investigation about taxes and an individual named *Bqy* (biblical Bukki), a name connected to the tribe of Dan (Numbers 34:22).[12] These finds, though not overwhelming in their character, may indicate an affiliation of these individuals with the northern kingdom of Israel, as discussed below.

The seemingly sudden flourish of building activity on the Western Hill during the eighth century BC observed in the archaeological record precipitated questions about the demography of Jerusalem in the centuries prior to the Babylonian destruction and what may have caused such growth. Archaeologists estimate that the population of Jerusalem prior to the eighth century BC was around six to eight thousand people and then swelled to approximately twenty to thirty thousand people in the second half of the eighth century.¹³ This rapid development cannot be explained by natural population growth or economic expansion.¹⁴ Magen Broshi suggests "two waves of mass migration" of refugees: the first from the fall of the northern kingdom of Israel from 732 to 721 BC and the second from Sennacherib's campaign against Judah and Philistia in 701 BC. This theory, with some modification and nuance, has been generally accepted.¹⁵ Assessing the archaeological, anthropological, and historical evidence, the presence of refugees from the northern kingdom of Israel settling in Judah and Jerusalem is difficult to dispute.

The city of Jerusalem was not the sole city to experience a population increase during the late eighth century BC. Other Judahite cities—including Beersheba, Tell Beit Mirsim, and Lachish—also experienced growth. The number of settlements in the hills south of Jerusalem and in the region of lower hills to the west of Judah bordering the coastal plain called the Shephelah similarly increased. Archaeological surveys have documented eighty sites in the hill country south of Jerusalem and only twenty-one in the Judean Shephelah dated to the tenth and ninth centuries BC. In the mid to late eighth century BC, the number of settlements increased to 100 in the southern hill country and 250 in the Shephelah.¹⁶ Archaeologist Israel Finkelstein suggests that the sites in the Shephelah were established after 734 BC when Judah became a vassal to Assyria and integrated into the Assyrian economy, and these sites were olive oil production centers attracting "Israelite experts in olive culture and olive oil industry."¹⁷ Throughout the kingdom of Judah, as much as half of the population may have consisted of displaced refugees from the northern kingdom of Israel.¹⁸

The death of Sargon II in 705 BC afforded an opportunity for the Judahite king Hezekiah to rebel against his vassal status to Assyria. As part of his rebellion, and in preparation for an expected Assyrian retaliation by the new king, Sennacherib, Hezekiah implemented administrative and public works projects reflected in the archaeology of biblical Jerusalem. Commodities such as wine, oil, and grain were gathered from farms and royal estates and collected in storage jars with stamped handles bearing royal seal impressions. These jars and their contents were redistributed to fortified centers, likely to serve as food reserves for those centers in case of Assyrian siege.[19] Areas of Jerusalem that developed in the eighth century BC as a result of refugees from the northern kingdom of Israel, such as the Western Hill with its residential buildings, agricultural installations, and other extramural architecture, represented a sizable area of the city. The residents of this newly developed area of Jerusalem, likely displaced persons and families from the northern kingdom of Israel, were left vulnerable because of their location outside the established city walls, and this exposed population necessitated the construction of a fortification wall to protect this part of Jerusalem.

While excavating the Jewish Quarter of Jerusalem, Nahman Avigad and his team uncovered a massive fortification wall dated to the late eighth century BC and the period of King Hezekiah (2 Chronicles 32:5).[20] Archaeological excavations of this so-called "Broad Wall" revealed a 65-meter (213 feet) stretch of wall 7 meters (23 feet) wide that was preserved up to 3.3 meters (11 feet) high in places. This served as the foundation for a much taller superstructure of stone or mud bricks that did not survive.[21] In places, the wall was constructed on bedrock, but Avigad's team found that some building foundations were intentionally filled to provide a foundation for this massive fortification wall. Because of building activities of later periods, the course of the wall cannot be accurately determined, but Avigad posited that the wall was part of a fortification system that encompassed nearly all of the Western Hill and joined with the fortification around the City of David and the Temple Mount.[22]

Another element of Hezekiah's preparation for revolt against the Assyrians was the digging of the Siloam Tunnel (2 Kings 20:20; 2 Chronicles 32:3–4). This project stemmed from the need to provide water to the growing population of the Western Hill as well as the necessity of protecting Jerusalem's water supply from Assyrian forces should Jerusalem be besieged. This engineering feat diverted

THE EXPERIENCE OF ISRAELITE REFUGEES   333

Figure 4. *A portion of the "Broad Wall" built in the eighth century BC. Note the houses in the upper portion of the picture over which the wall is built. Photograph by Zev Radovan.*

the waters of the Gihon Spring from the eastern side of the City of David underground to a pool in the Tyropoeon Valley between the Eastern and Western hills within the city walls. The tunnel runs for 643 meters (2,100 feet) and was accomplished by two teams cutting through the bedrock from opposite ends, following natural fissures in the limestone.[23] Given the tools and geology, it is estimated that the tunneling took at least four years to complete. After the tunnel was completed, an account was inscribed on the walls of the tunnel:

> [The day of] the breach. This is the record of how the tunnel was breached. While [the excavators were wielding] their pick-axes, each man toward his co-worker, and while there were yet three cubits for the brea[ch,] a voice [was hear]d each man calling to his co-worker; because there was a cavity

in the rock from the south to [the north]. So on the day of the breach, the excavators struck, each man to meet his coworker, pick-axe against pick-[a]xe. Then the water flowed from the spring to the pool, a distance of one thousand and two hundred cubits. One hundred cubits was the height of the rock above the heads of the excavat[ors].[24]

Both the Broad Wall and the Siloam Tunnel required a massive effort from large crews of laborers who constructed the fortifications and hewed out the watercourse, and we can infer the identities of those who carried out such projects, as discussed below.

Arguments against Refugees

While the validity of the hypothesis that Jerusalem's growth was the result of northern refugees has been widely recognized since the 1970s, some scholars have recently questioned the influx of refugees into Jerusalem and Judah and their influence on population and society, arguing against any Israelite presence in the southern kingdom after the fall of Samaria.[25] Certain archaeologists suggest that the areas of the Western Hill in Jerusalem experienced a gradual development during the eighth century BC rather than a raid growth accompanying a flood of refugees.[26] Biblical scholar Nadav Na'aman makes four claims against an influx of refugees from the northern kingdom of Israel into Judah and Jerusalem. First, he states that an "unbroken settlement in Jerusalem for hundreds of years makes it impossible to test the theory of enormous population growth in the city as a result of mass migration from Israel after its annexation by the Assyrians in 720 BCE."[27] Second, Na'aman asserts that the Assyrians would not permit a large population of refugees to move from Israel to Judah. He claims that Hezekiah would not have interacted with the inhabitants of Samaria, painting a picture of Assyrian troops guarding the borders and sweeping the countryside for captives and people to exile.[28] Third, Na'aman argues that the absence of Israelite names with the theophoric element *-yau*, a shortened form of Yahweh (the Hebrew version of the name Jehovah), in surviving inscriptions, seals, or sealings indicates the absence of northern Israelite refugees in Jerusalem in the last quarter of the eighth century BC.[29] Finally, Na'aman bolsters his argument against the rapid growth of Judah and Jerusalem by noting the apparent dearth of artifacts that are distinctly Israelite, rather than Judahite, that would signal the presence of refugees.[30] He does concede that if there were "immigrants from Israel [who] arrived in Judah after Sargon's campaign, they were not very numerous, [and] that many of them soon returned to their ancestral lands"; however, he does not draw upon any biblical or extrabiblical texts or any archaeological evidence to substantiate his claim.[31]

Textual and Archaeological Indications of Refugees

While some of these critiques warrant attention and nuance regarding the archaeology of biblical Jerusalem, Finkelstein and others have published more recent rebuttals and reappraisals based on more current archaeological evidence, anthropological observations, and textual studies of the Bible and Assyrian sources. Excavations have shown that some areas of the Western Hill and its slopes were already gradually being developed in the ninth–eighth centuries BC.[32] However, these are not the same areas excavated by Avigad. While one area may have had some evidence of settlement, most of the Western Hill buildings are later than the mid-eighth century BC based on parallel ceramic assemblages dated by radiocarbon to 766–745 BC at Beth Shemesh, a Judahite site in the Shephelah.[33]

Concerning the pace of the refugee arrival and construction of buildings on the Western Hill, it is helpful to recognize two anthropologically observed types of refugee movement. *Anticipatory movement* ahead of a crisis is typically accomplished by those whose social standing allows them the option to flee. In contrast, *acute movement* occurs in a crisis when individuals have little time to prepare to leave; this movement is usually a last resort by those who are less wealthy.[34] Acknowledging the potential for refugees from the Galilee to migrate to southern Samaria as early as 732 BC, and other refugees from Samaria to Judah up to and after 720 BC, we must realize that the influx of refugees was a process that lasted for more than a decade and that there was likely a second wave with the 701 BC campaign of the Assyrian king Sennacherib in Judah. This runs counter to Na'aman's biggest assumption—that refugees moved from Israel to Judah after the conquest of Samaria by Sargon II and the annexation of the northern kingdom into the Assyrian empire.[35]

Scholarly claims about Hezekiah's reluctance to upset Assyria, assertions of Assyria's strict policies for refugees, and examples of refugee extradition have little relevance bearing on the plight of Israelite refugees moving to Jerusalem and Judah in the eighth century.[36] Attestations of vassal treaties detailing the responsibilities of a vassal king within the Assyrian empire have been translated and studied for their details. Often called loyalty oaths or loyalty treaties by scholars (Akkadian *adê sakānu*), these documents formally bound a subject to the Assyrian empire through a series of oaths, along with curses if the oaths were not upheld. Assyrian kings imposed these loyalty oaths on kings, provincial governors, and peoples throughout the empire—"the people of Assyria, great and small."[37] Examples of Assyrian loyalty or vassal treaties for the land of Israel mention payment of tribute by the Israelite kings Jehu, Joash, and Menahem, as well as oaths for the Philistine cities of Ashkelon and Ekron in the Assyrian annals of Tiglath-pileser III and Sennacherib.[38] No example of treaties is currently known for the kingdom of Judah, although Ahaz the Judahite king is mentioned as a vassal paying tribute to the Assyrian king Tiglath-pileser III (2 Kings 16:7–8; 2 Chronicles 28:16–21).[39] Interaction between the kingdoms of Israel and Judah in the eighth century BC, including diplomatic contact and reports from northern refugees, would have informed Judahites, including the prophet Isaiah, about the Assyrian vassal policies and the royal ideology against which King Hezekiah and Isaiah would contend in their own ways.[40]

Regarding the lack of Israelite theophoric elements in names, the meager number of personal names attested in eighth century BC Judah prevents any strong case being made either way. Na'aman states that the "assumption that Israelite refugees joined the leadership of the kingdom of Judah in a matter of a few years, and that Hezekiah chose to integrate them into his senior administration, above the main clans of Judah, seems most unlikely."[41] However, recent excavations have recovered a sealing (the impression of a stamp seal) bearing the name "Ahiav ben Menahem" that may indicate the presence of Israelite refugees in the City of David.[42] Both of these names are attested in the Bible as names of northern kings. "Ahiav" is a textual variant of the name Ahab, attested only as an infamous king of Israel in 1 Kings 16:29–22:40 and as a false prophet at the time of Jeremiah in the seventh century BC. Menahem appears in the Bible only as the name of a king of the northern kingdom.[43] Avigad also found the name Menahemon on a seal impression in the Jewish Quarter excavations and also recovered an ostracon with the name *Bqy* that may be connected to the tribe of Dan. Additionally, Shebna, an official of King Hezekiah who received chastisement in Isaiah 22:15–19, may have a shortened name that was northern Israelite in origin.[44]

If these individuals were from the kingdom of Israel, it is likely that Hezekiah sought to integrate these northerners into the kingdom of Judah to unify the people. The prophecy of Isaiah 9:1–7 may have been seen as "commentary and political policy."[45] Individuals and families hailing from elite backgrounds would probably have fled Israel in an anticipatory movement years ahead of the actual Assyrian siege. As biblical scholar William M. Schniedewind posits, the refugees from the north were likely not farmers or pastoralists or unskilled labor.[46] Rather, it is more likely that the northern Israelites who initially fled to Judah in anticipation of Israel's destruction were skilled craftsmen or social and cultural elites such as priests, scribes, or government officials, many of whom would have been literate.[47] The critique of Micah 3:9–10 against the "heads of the house of Jacob, and princes of the house of Israel" who were perverting justice may allude to the integration of northern Israelite elites integrated into the administration of Judah.[48] Archaeologist Aaron A. Burke suggests that the Israelites from the northern kingdom who migrated to Judah were "merchants and emissaries who were abroad at the time of the invasion, but also more substantial groups of individuals living near borders."[49] The ancestors of Lehi may likely have emigrated from their tribal territory of Manasseh in Israel to Jerusalem at this time.

Although names may not provide strong evidence of an Israelite presence, unnamed or unattributed compositions such as the Siloam Tunnel inscription suggest an Israelite element to the workforce that dug the tunnel. A reading of the Siloam Tunnel inscription indicates that it was not a royal dedicatory inscription to commemorate the completion of the waterway under Hezekiah's auspices. The text does not mention the king or a deity, and it was located six meters (twenty feet) inside the tunnel from its outlet at the Pool of Siloam. Gary A. Rendsburg and Schniedewind suggest that the inscription is the product of "engineers, craftsmen, and labourers whose aim was to commemorate their accomplishment."[50] Within the inscription, some elements (the form *reʿô* for "friend," the use of *hāyat* rather than *hāyâ* for "there is," *mōṣaʾ* for "spring," and *nqbh* rather than *teʿālâ* for "tunnel or conduit") appear to be connected to an Israelian dialect of Hebrew prevalent in Ephraim and Benjamin, rather than to Jerusalemite Hebrew. These elements led Rendsburg and Schniedewind to suggest that the author of the inscription and those responsible for the construction of Hezekiah's Tunnel were Israelite refugees from southern Samaria, "somewhere along the Ephraim-Benjamin border."[51] While Rendsberg and Schniedewind's proposal has been met with some skepticism, their efforts to show that the labor force likely included northern Israelite refugees acknowledge the reality of integrating displaced persons into society as part of a royally commissioned project.

Regarding distinctly Israelite artifacts in Judahite contexts, no clear distinction can be made between common pottery of Israel and Judah in the eighth century BC, given the similarities in vessel type, form, and decoration. This lack of distinguishing features is not surprising given the close contacts between the kingdoms, which shared a cultural heritage, a language, and social customs. Differences in tomb construction and layout between the tombs in the Kidron Valley and present-day Silwan near the City of David and tombs in the Hinnom Valley west of Jerusalem and to the north of Jerusalem at the Basilica of St. Etienne may indicate the presence of northern Israelites, but the dearth of Iron Age burials from Samaria hinders any detailed comparison.[52] Finklestein lists several Israelite influences and cultural elements present in the material culture and architecture of Judah in the late eighth century BC.[53] These include olive oil production facilities in Judah showing technology from the northern kingdom; northern elements of pottery forms present in the ceramic assemblage at late eighth-century Beersheba; limestone cosmetic bowls and square bone seals that abound in Israel and later appear in Judah; ashlar masonry (stones that are dressed into rectangles) that appears at northern sites such as Megiddo and Samaria and appear later in the eighth century at Beersheba and Ramat Rahel; longitudinal pillared buildings likely used as storehouses or stables at Megiddo in the late ninth and early eighth century that are later seen in the eighth and early seventh century BC at Beersheba; voluted palmette capitals found at Megiddo, Hazor, and Samaria that appear in later architecture at Ramat Rahel, the City of David, and other locations peripheral to biblical Jerusalem;[54] and, according to Finkelstein, the incorporation of northern texts and traditions into the Judahite literature that would become the Bible.

Lessons from Biblical Archaeology and the Plight of Refugees

Although some scholars have debated "the validity of the notion of refugees" in ancient Israel and Judah,[55] the evidence of a rapid settlement in Jerusalem, an increase of settlements in the hill country and Shephelah, names with Israelite affiliation on seal impressions,

Israelite Hebrew in the Siloam Channel, and numerous cultural elements and influences indicate that Israelite refugees were present in late-eighth-century-BC Judah. Using a framework designed to identify risks faced by refugees being resettled in a new area, Burke relates the perils encountered by modern refugees to those of the ancient world, highlighting efforts employed to mitigate those risks. Such jeopardies include landlessness, joblessness, homelessness, marginalization, food insecurity, increased morbidity and mortality, loss of access to common property assets, and community disarticulation.[56] Burke demonstrates that each of these risks were lessened by the efforts of the Judahite administration led by Hezekiah. He suggests that the Israelite refugees either (1) became dependent on the king to provide until they were integrated into the local economy by finding labor wherever possible, or (2) were employed on royal work projects, accomplishing needful objectives for the state.[57]

Burke states that "the construction of the Siloam Tunnel, as well as the dismantling of houses, quarrying of stone, and the construction of the Broad Wall, as well as the work required for water systems attributed to Hezekiah were, therefore, much more than strategic planning by Judah for a future Assyrian attack. They must also be regarded as elements of a shrewd approach to the gainful employment of Jerusalem's landless and unemployed Israelite refugee population in an effort to secure their allegiance."[58] This would have been crucial because scholars estimate that 53 percent of the population of Jerusalem and nearly half of the overall population of Judah consisted of Israelite refugees.[59] By using Israelite labor to accomplish these projects, Hezekiah and the administration provide a lesson in mitigating marginalization of refugees by providing an avenue of integration and unity with their new community.

Schniedewind and Finkelstein both suggest that Judah benefited from the influx of cultural elite Israelite refugees. These elites brought an increased literacy that helped to bolster the literacy of Judah and also influenced the development of the Hebrew Bible. The northern Israelite refugees that were integrated into the Judahite government probably helped the Judahite state to become more organized. As Finkelstein states, "A fully organized and well-administered state in Judah is the outcome of the [refugee] processes that took place in the late 8th century B.C."[60] Including refugees and their descendants into local administration at any level, not only for representation of these peoples but also to use their learned skills, is an important lesson for any group trying to integrate a refugee population.

It is worth noting that instructions on the treatment of "strangers" (Hebrew gēr), those vulnerable persons who are outsiders in relation to a core family, are found in various biblical law codes, including the Covenant Code (Exodus 22:20–23:9, 12), the Holiness Code (Leviticus 17–26), and throughout Deuteronomy.[61] While answers to the risks of landlessness, homelessness, joblessness, and morbidity may be seen in archaeological correlates, the biblical gēr laws focused on inclusion of displaced and vulnerable people to mitigate food insecurity and loss of access to common property while providing food and access to community resources such as gleaning (Deuteronomy 14:21, 24:19–22).[62] Lessons about inclusion are apparent from the participation of gēr in feasts, festivals (16:1–17), and covenantal renewal (29:9–14), among other rituals and ceremonies that address the perils of community disarticulation and separation from kinship groups by reinforcing the kinship experienced as a community and people of Jehovah. The Lord's same compassionate encouragement for favorable treatment of marginalized strangers and their inclusion into society, meant to be echoed by Israel and Judah, is reflected in the messages of Isaiah (Isaiah 56:1–7), Jeremiah (Jeremiah 7:6–7; 22:1–3), Ezekiel (Ezekiel 22:7, 29; 47:22–23), and Zechariah (Zechariah 7:9–10).

Both the Bible and archaeology illustrate efforts by Hezekiah to promote unity between Israelites and Judahites by centralizing religion and commemorating the Passover, a foundational event in the history of the house of Israel. Second Chronicles 30 relates the invitation made by Hezekiah to Israelites from the Galilee and tribal territories of Manasseh and Ephraim to celebrate Passover in Jerusalem. Although only some from Asher, Manasseh, and Zebulun attended (2 Chronicles 30:11), northern Israelites, Judahites, and resident aliens (displaced persons) from both kingdoms were united in observance of Passover. Hezekiah ordered the ruin of locations used for fertility rituals; closed and desecrated shrines/altars at Lachish, Beersheba, and Arad; destroyed items that had become objects of veneration; and established a singular worship center in Jerusalem (2 Kings 18:3–5; 2 Chronicles 31:1). Furthermore, Schniedewind suggests that Hezekiah named his son Manasseh in an additional attempt to unify the people by evoking the name of an ancestor, tribe, and territory connected to the house of Joseph and the northern kingdom of Israel.[63] Manasseh married Meshullemeth, the daughter of Haruz of Jotbah (2 Kings 21:19), and it is possible that Jotbah is Yodfat in the Galilee. This marriage would have also strengthened ties between Judah and Galilean Israelites.

While Hezekiah, the Judahite administration, and probably Jerusalem's populace attempted to lessen the risks and dangers felt by the Israelite refugee population as they integrated into Judahite society, a lesson can be learned from the construction of the Broad Wall on the Western Hill. As a royal project aimed at enclosing the Western Hill and protecting the vulnerable population living outside the fortification walls of the Eastern Hill, the construction of the Broad Wall, which would have provided employment and subsistence through redistributed foodstuffs, appears to be a noble endeavor. The same can be said for the cutting of the Siloam Tunnel and the diversion of the Gihon Spring runoff to a collecting pool within the city walls. However, both the wall and the tunnel resulted in the marginalization of those whom the projects benefited. The Broad Wall bisects several eighth-century-BC dwellings, with some houses intentionally in-filled to provide a foundation for the wall. The need to build this fortification "with sufficient urgency to sacrifice the houses in its way"[64] is reflected in Isaiah 22:9–11, in which the prophet chastises the leadership and people of Jerusalem: "Ye have seen also the breaches of the city of David, that they are many: and ye gathered together the waters of the lower pool. And ye have numbered the houses of Jerusalem, and the houses have ye broken down to fortify the wall. Ye made also a ditch between the two walls for the water of the old pool: but ye have not looked unto the Maker thereof, neither had respect unto him that fashioned it long ago."

Isaiah clearly identified the primary problem with the Judahite leadership and people—namely, their preoccupation with physical preparations rather than trusting in the Lord and focusing on their covenant relationship by looking to and having respect for the One who made the water and the stone.[65] Biblical scholar John N. Oswalt notes, "[The Judahites] congratulate themselves that they are not corrupt as the northern kingdom of Israel had been, and so they believed they have survived because of their merits when Israel fell. But Isaiah and the other prophets see clearly that all the same trends are at work in Judah that so tragically affected Israel."[66] Those trends include pride, neglect of the marginalized such as the widow, orphan, and displaced persons, and lack of faith in the Lord to provide and protect the covenantal people. Additionally, we can see the concern of the prophet and the danger in neglecting or ignoring the considerations of those living on the Western Hill whose houses were "broken down to fortify the wall" and who cut the water conduit—in both cases, likely Israelite refugees. Thus, while the Broad Wall and the Siloam Tunnel were beneficial to the populace of Jerusalem, concern for those displaced by building the wall should have been exercised together with a faith in the Lord.

An additional lesson can be garnered from the experience of King Ahaz of Judah and his willingness to initiate a vassal treaty with the Assyrian Tiglath-pileser III, with its accompanying loyalty oath. Loyalty to Assyria came with a temporal price of a yearly tribute but also a spiritual price of trusting Assyria to fight their battles rather than relying on faith in Jehovah. Frequent journeys to Assyria to pay tribute by Israelite and Judahite emissaries who saw, experienced, and communicated the Assyrian royal ideology and propaganda to their home countries may have precipitated the prophetic counsel to not place political trust in Assyria or other temporal kings and kingdoms.[67] The prophets Hosea and Isaiah cautioned against and condemned Israel and Judah for making alliances with Assyria. Hosea warned that Assyria would not cure their wounds or provide for them (Hosea 5:13; 14:2–3), and Isaiah prophesied that Assyria would overwhelm Judah (Isaiah 8:6–8, 11–13) and would eventually be judged for its own arrogance (Isaiah 10:5–19).

Conclusion

Exploring the fall of the northern kingdom of Israel, the migration of refugees to Judah, and the efforts of the Judahite administration to integrate the two populations provides lessons from the past for our present. The study of the Israelite refugee migration as a result of the fall of Israel to the Assyrian empire originated in biblical studies as a means of explaining northern Israelite views in the Hebrew Bible, which was primarily written, compiled, and redacted by southern Judahites. Later, archaeologists looked to Israelite refugees to explain the growth of Judah and Jerusalem toward the end of the eighth century BC. The archaeology of Iron Age refugees in Jerusalem complements the witness and message of the Bible and the instruction of Church authorities regarding the treatment of dispossessed and vulnerable children of God.

In addition to the message for the population of Judah and its leadership to trust in the Lord rather than on their labor-intensive preparations (which overlooked the needs of the poor) in the face of overwhelming odds, the main lesson that the experience of the Israelite refugees teaches is the importance of unity to avoid marginalization and community disarticulation. As part of the family of God, we should strive to include those who have lost their connections to a homeland, employment, or family. Talents should be recognized and encouraged to better the community of God and further the work of the kingdom. Most importantly, respect and inclusion may rebuild familial bonds that are weakened or severed. In the October 2018 general women's session, President Dallin H. Oaks related a story about a bullied refugee and noted that such "meanness" was "a tragic experience and expense to one of the children of God."[68] His counsel to reach out in kindness and be loving and considerate is timely for all who interact with vulnerable persons.

Efforts by the Judahites to foster a unity between "strangers" living among them may not be explicitly evident in the archaeological record of Judah or in the biblical text, but the use of Israelite labor to create the Siloam Tunnel and the Broad Wall, seal impressions and ostraca with Israelite names, and Hezekiah naming his son Manasseh all strongly suggest ways that the Judahites incorporated refugees from the northern kingdom of Israel into the administration, labor force, and society of Judah. Likewise, efforts to care for refugees and integrate them into the community can be part of the legacy for modern believers and fellow children of God. President Russell M. Nelson taught, "Making a conscientious effort to care about others as much as or *more* than we care about ourselves" is a source of joy. By following the teachings of the Old Testament to open our hands to the poor and needy, including refugees (Deuteronomy 15:11), believers can actively live out their commitment to the two great commandments (Matthew 22:37–39).[69]

George A. Pierce is an assistant professor of ancient scripture at Brigham Young University.

Notes

1. This number includes 26 million refugees, 45.7 million internally displaced people, and 4.2 million asylum-seekers; see https://unrefugees.org/refugee-facts/statistics/. For the purposes of this paper, "refugee(s)" and "displaced person(s)" refer to those who have been forced to flee their country because of persecution, war, or violence according to the

UN Refugee Agency definition (https://unrefugees.org/refugee-facts/what-is-a-refugee/).

2. See Dieter F. Uchtdorf, "Two Principles for Any Economy," *Ensign*, November 2009, 55–58; Uchtdorf, "The Gift of Grace," *Ensign*, May 2015, 107–10.

3. Linda K. Burton, "I Was a Stranger," *Ensign*, May 2016, 13–15; Patrick Kearon, "Refuge from the Storm," *Ensign*, May 2016, 111–14.

4. Russell M. Nelson, "The Second Great Commandment," *Ensign*, November 2019, 99; see https://churchofjesuschrist.org/refugees.

5. Tiglath-pileser III (Akkadian *Tukultī-apil-Ešarra*, meaning "my trust is in the son of the Ešarra") was the throne name of an Assyrian general originally named Pulu who carried out a successful coup to become the Assyrian king. The biblical narrative states that Menahem, the king of Israel, paid tribute as a vassal to the Assyrian king, named Pul in Lo. This same Assyrian king, later called Tiglath-pileser in the Bible, campaigned against the Israelite king Pekah, conquering the region of the Galilee and "carr[ying] them captive to Assyria" (2 Kings 15:29).

6. K. Lawson Younger Jr., "The Deportations of the Israelites," *Journal of Biblical Literature* 117 (1998): 211, 218.

7. Magen Broshi, "The Expansion of Jerusalem in the Reigns of Hezekiah and Manasseh," *Israel Exploration Journal* 24 (1974): 21n2; burials in the Iron Age were located outside city boundaries because of the smell and other practicalities of burials; besides, the presence of tombs within the city would render the area ritually unclean.

8. Nahman Avigad, *Discovering Jerusalem* (Nashville: Thomas Nelson, 1983), 31–45.

9. Nahman Avigad, "Excavations in the Jewish Quarter of the Old City, 1969–1971," in *Jerusalem Revealed: Archaeology in the Holy City, 1968–1974*, ed. Yigael Yadin (Jerusalem: Israel Exploration Society, 1975), 44.

10. The impressions of the royal seals contain the Hebrew word *lmlk*, "belonging to the king," with either a four- or two-winged solar disk or scarab, and the town names of either Hebron, Ziph, Socoh, or a center not found in the Bible called *Mmst*.

11. Vocalization by the author. The phrase as written on the ostracon is *[-l] qn 'rṣ*; see Avigad, *Discovering Jerusalem*, 41. The reconstruction of 'Ēl at the beginning is based on this same epithet for God being used by Melchizedek (Genesis 14:19) and associated with Jehovah by Abraham (Genesis 14:22).
12. Avigad, *Discovering Jerusalem*, 41–44.
13. Broshi, "Expansion of Jerusalem," 23–24. Some population estimates are as high as 40,000–120,000 people for all of Judah at this time; see J. Edward Wright and Mark Elliott, "Israel and Judah under Assyria's Thumb," in *The Old Testament in Archaeology and History*, ed. Jennie Ebeling, J. Edward Wright, Mark Elliott, and Paul V. M. Flesher (Waco: Baylor University Press, 2017), 448. In terms of settled area, archaeologist Israel Finkelstein estimates that the city grew from ten hectares to sixty hectares in the mid to late eighth century BC; see Israel Finkelstein, "Migration of Israelites into Judah after 720 BCE: An Answer and an Update," *Zeitschrift für die Alttestamentliche Wissenschaft* 126 (2015): 197.
14. Broshi, "Expansion of Jerusalem," 23. This view is supported by later publications; see Magen Broshi and Israel Finkelstein, "The Population of Palestine in Iron Age II," *Bulletin of the American Schools of Oriental Research* 287 (1992): 51–52; and Israel Finkelstein and Neil Asher Silberman, *The Bible Unearthed: Archaeology's New Vision of Ancient Israel and the Origin of Its Sacred Texts* (New York: Touchstone, 2002), 243.
15. Some scholars have argued for a more gradual growth in the eighth century BC, either supplemented by a limited number of refugees from the northern kingdom of Israel or totally devoid of refugees entirely.
16. Finkelstein, "Migration of Israelites," 200–201.
17. Finkelstein, "Migration of Israelites," 196. This would correspond with the rise in olive pollen in the eighth century BC present in the palynological record; see George A. Pierce, "Environmental Features," in *The T&T Clark Handbook of Food in the Hebrew Bible and Ancient Israel*, ed. Janling Fu, Cynthia Shafer-Elliott, and Carol Meyers (London: Bloomsbury, 2021), 1–31.
18. Wright and Elliott, "Israel and Judah," 449. Later, as a result of the campaign of the Assyrian king Sennacherib against Judah in 701 BC that destroyed forty-six walled cities and villages and devastated the

countryside, the number of rural villages and farmsteads in the Shephelah decreased from 250 to 85, and the rural population of Judah shifted as these internal refugees moved within the kingdom of Judah to sites in the Judean wilderness and Negev. See Israel Finkelstein, "The Archaeology of the Days of Manasseh," in *Scripture and Other Artifacts: Essay on the Bible and Archaeology in Honor of Philip J. King*, ed. Michael D. Coogan, J. Cheryl Exum, and Lawrence E. Stager (Louisville: Westminster John Knox, 1994), 173. See also Israel Finkelstein, "The Settlement History of Jerusalem in the Eighth and Seventh Centuries BC," *Revue Biblique* 115 (2008): 512–13.

19. Amihai Mazar, *Archaeology of the Land of the Bible* (New York: Doubleday, 1992), 457–58.
20. Avigad, *Discovering Jerusalem*, 46–49.
21. Avigad, "Excavations in the Jewish Quarter," 43–44.
22. Avigad, *Discovering Jerusalem*, 57–59.
23. Mazar, *Archaeology of the Land of the Bible*, 484.
24. K. Lawson Younger Jr., "The Siloam Tunnel Inscription," in *The Context of Scripture*, vol. 2, *Monumental Inscriptions from the Biblical World*, ed. William W. Hallo and K. Lawson Younger Jr. (Leiden: Brill, 2003), 145–46 (COS 2.28).
25. In examining possible reasons for the growth of Jerusalem in the eighth century BC, archaeologist Aren Maeir summarizes the arguments used against an influx of refugees from the northern kingdom of Israel; see Aren M. Maeir, "The Southern Kingdom of Judah: Surrounded by Enemies," in *Old Testament in Archaeology*, 399.
26. Nadav Na'aman, "When and How Did Jerusalem Become a Great City? The Rise of Jerusalem as Judah's Premier City in the Eighth–Seventh Centuries B.C.E.," *Bulletin of the American Schools of Oriental Research* 347 (2007): 24–27; see also Na'aman, "The Growth and Development of Judah and Jerusalem in the Eighth Century BCE: A Rejoinder," *Revue Biblique* 116 (2009): 321–35; and Avraham Faust, "The Settlement of Jerusalem's Western Hill and the City's Status in Iron Age II Revisited," *Zeitschrift des Deutschen Palästina-Vereins* 121 (2005): 97–118.

27. Na'aman, "Growth and Development of Judah and Jerusalem," 324. Na'aman also claims that the same ceramic forms and styles were used from ca. 800 BC to 586 BC; see Nadav Na'aman, "Dismissing the Myth of a Flood of Israelite Refugees in the Late Eighth Century BCE," *Zeitschrift für die Alttestamentliche Wissenschaft* 126 (2014): 9. However, this stance clashes with the detailed pottery study in Joe Uziel, Salome Dan-Goor, and Nahshon Szanton, "The Development of Pottery in Iron Age Jerusalem," in *The Iron Age Pottery of Jerusalem: A Typological and Technological Study*, ed. D. Ben-Shlomo (Ariel: Ariel University Press, 2019), 59–102.
28. Na'aman, "Rise of Jerusalem," 29. He bases his argument on the actions of the king of Cush (a kingdom south of Egypt in modern Sudan); this king extradited the king of Ashdod, who had rebelled against the Assyrian king Sargon II. However, Na'aman fails to distinguish between migrant refugees and a rebellious king seeking exile during a revolt.
29. Na'aman, "Rise of Jerusalem," 37.
30. Na'aman, "Growth and Development of Judah and Jerusalem," 325.
31. Na'aman, "Growth and Development of Judah and Jerusalem," 323.
32. Joe Uziel and Nahshon Szanton, "New Evidence of Jerusalem's Urban Development in the 9th Century BCE," in *Rethinking Israel: Studies in the History and Archaeology of Ancient Israel in Honor of Israel Finkelstein*, ed. O. Lipschits, Y. Gadot, and M. J. Adams (Winona Lake, IN: Eisenbrauns, 2017), 429–39.
33. Finkelstein, "Settlement History of Jerusalem," 502.
34. Egon F. Kunz, "The Refugee in Flight: Kinetic Models and Forms of Displacement," *International Migration Review* 7 (1973): 131–32.
35. Na'aman, "Growth and Development of Judah and Jerusalem," 323; see also Na'aman, "Dismissing the Myth," 5.
36. Na'aman's examples date from either long before the period (e.g., Hittite treaties from the fifteenth to the fourteenth century BC) or from the reign of the Assyrian kings Esarhaddon and Ashurbanipal in the seventh–sixth centuries BC. See Na'aman, "Rise of Jerusalem," 31–35.
37. The Vassal Treaty of Esarhaddon does have injunctions against treason, open rebellion, and supporting those involved with such activities, but the descriptions of treason (secretly plotting an overthrow of the crown) or

rebellion and insurrection (openly fighting against Assyria) do not suggest any connection to a migrant refugee population fleeing from an Assyrian campaign. See Simo Parpola and Kazuko Watanabe, "Esarhaddon's Succession Treaty," in *Neo-Assyrian Treaties and Loyalty Oaths*, State Archives of Assyria 2 (University Park: Penn State University Press, 1988), http://oracc.org/saao/Q009186/. Na'aman also admits that sources mention the flight of refugees from the Assyrian empire to "Shubira and Urartu, two kingdoms to the north of Assyria"; see Na'aman, "Rise of Jerusalem," 34. To date, no evidence of Assyrian policy regarding such refugees fleeing from one kingdom to another is extant in Assyrian sources.

38. Shawn Z. Aster, "An Assyrian Loyalty-Oath Imposed on Ashdod in the Reign of Tiglath-Pileser III," *Orientalia* 87 (2018): 275–76.

39. See COS 2.117C for the Assyrian account of Israelite tribute. The process of an emissary delivering tribute and accepting vassal status is detailed in Shawn Z. Aster, "Israelite Embassies to Assyria in the First Half of the Eighth Century," *Biblica* 97 (2016): 175–98.

40. Aster, "Israelite Embassies to Assyria," 197. The Assyrian royal ideology consisted of the religious legitimacy of the king as leader of the worship of Ashur, the king as the military leader who would expand the empire, the universal nature of the empire, and the doctrine of Assyrian invincibility. These ideas were communicated by the Assyrians in wall reliefs, stelae, rock art carved into cliffs, sculptures, and seals.

41. Na'aman, "Rise of Jerusalem," 37.

42. Anat Mendel-Geberovich, Ortal Chalaf, and Joe Uziel, "The People behind the Stamps: A Newly Founded Group of Bullae and a Seal from the City of David, Jerusalem," *Bulletin of ASOR* 384 (2021): 159–82.

43. Joan Comay, *Who's Who in the Old Testament* (New York: Bonanza Books, 1980), 40–43, 260.

44. The full Israelite name would have been "Shebnayau"; see Christopher B. Hays, "Re-Excavating Shebna's Tomb: A New Reading of Isa 22, 15–19 in Its Ancient Near Eastern Context," *Zeitschrift für die Alttestamentliche Wissenschaft* 122 (2010): 558–75.

45. William M. Schniedewind, *How the Bible Became a Book: The Textualization of Ancient Israel* (Cambridge: Cambridge University Press, 2004), 69.

46. Schniedewind, *How the Bible Became a Book*, 95.
47. Subsequent migrations of northern Israelites may have consisted of an acute movement of people who were non-elite and less literate.
48. Schniedewind, *How the Bible Became a Book*, 94.
49. Aaron A. Burke, "An Anthropological Model for the Investigation of the Archaeology of Refugees in Iron Age Judah and Its Environs," in *Interpreting Exile: Displacement and Deportation in Biblical and Modern Contexts*, ed. Brad E. Kelle, Frank R. Ames, and Jacob L. Wright (Atlanta: Society of Biblical Literature, 2011), 46.
50. Gary A. Rendsburg and William M. Schniedewind, "The Siloam Tunnel Inscription: Historical and Linguistic Perspectives," *Israel Exploration Journal* 60 (2010): 191.
51. Rendsburg and Schniedewind, "Siloam Tunnel Inscription," 198–99.
52. Aaron A. Burke, "Coping with the Effects of War: The Archaeology of Refugees in the Ancient Near East," in *Disaster and Relief Management*, ed. Angelika Berlejung (Tübingen: Mohr Siebeck, 2012), 277.
53. Finkelstein, "Settlement History of Jerusalem," 509; see also Finkelstein, "Migration of Israelites," 202–3.
54. Three examples were recently found near the Armon Hanatziv Promenade in Jerusalem in what was likely a royal or elite building; see Tzvi Joffre, "Davidic Dynasty Symbol Found in Jerusalem: Once in a Lifetime Discovery," *Jerusalem Post*, September 3, 2020.
55. Philippe Guillaume, "Jerusalem 720–705 BCE: No Flood of Israelite Refugees," *Scandinavian Journal of the Old Testament* 22 (2011): 197.
56. Burke, "Anthropological Model," 43.
57. Burke, "Anthropological Model," 50.
58. Burke, "Coping with the Effects of War," 281.
59. Burke, "Anthropological Model," 49.
60. Finkelstein, "Settlement History of Jerusalem," 507.
61. The laws regarding strangers appear in Deuteronomy 1, 5, 10, 14, 16, 23–24, and 26–29; for a treatment of the *gēr* and their inclusion as part of the family of Israel and Jehovah, see Mark R. Glanville, *Adopting the Stranger as Kindred in Deuteronomy* (Atlanta: Society of Biblical Literature, 2018).

62. The prime example of a *gēr* gleaning is found in the story of Ruth gleaning in the field of Boaz during the cereal harvest (Ruth 2:1–17). Additionally, although they are not displaced persons, the actions of Jesus's disciples eating grain from a field is justified under the same Deuteronomic provision (Matthew 12:1).
63. Schniedewind, *How the Bible Became a Book*, 94.
64. Dan P. Cole, "Archaeology and the Messiah Oracles of Isaiah 9 and 11," in *Scripture and Other Artifacts*, 64.
65. The use of second person plural verbs throughout Isaiah 22:9–11 indicates that the prophet is not addressing a particular person but a group of people, which likely included the population of Jerusalem as a whole and their leadership, such as the royal steward Shebna, who received condemnation later in the same chapter (Isaiah 22:15–19). See Joseph Blenkinsopp, *Isaiah 1–39: A New Translation with Introduction and Commentary* (New York: Doubleday, 2000), 333–34.
66. John N. Oswalt, *The NIV Application Commentary: Isaiah* (Grand Rapids: Zondervan, 2003), 269.
67. Aster, "Israelite Embassies to Assyria," 194–97.
68. Dallin H. Oaks, "Parents and Children," *Ensign*, November 2018, 67.
69. Nelson, "Second Great Commandment," 100.

14

The *Gēr* in the Pentateuch and the Book of Mormon
Refugee Treatment under the Mosaic Law

Krystal V. L. Pierce

The Hebrew word *gēr* (גר) in the Old Testament has been translated as "stranger," "alien," "foreigner," and, most recently, "refugee."[1] Passages within the Pentateuch explicitly stipulated the treatment of the *gēr* under the Mosaic law, especially within the Covenant (Exodus 21–23), Deuteronomic (Deuteronomy 1–34), and Holiness Codes (Leviticus 17–26). The use of the term *gēr* typically referred to a displaced person, either a refugee of the northern kingdom of Israel displaced by the Assyrian invasion, an internally displaced Judahite, or a displaced foreigner from another kingdom. Simply put, *gēr* were those who had left their settlement land and kinship ties to live in a new place, which left them landless and dependent. These refugees were no longer protected under personal citizenship or inheritance laws and were therefore vulnerable to exploitation and abuse.

This description of displaced persons can also apply to certain groups of people in the Book of Mormon, including the Anti-Nephi-Lehies and their children, Zoramites, Lamanite royal servants, and Lamanite soldiers, all of whom were discussed in the book of Alma. The treatment of these refugee groups might have been influenced by the stipulations outlined in the Mosaic law, which was included in the brass plates. In this paper, the social, judicial, and religious laws concerning the *gēr* in the Pentateuch will be discussed in relation to the narratives surrounding the above-mentioned groups of refugees found in the book of Alma. The treatment of the *gēr* in the Book of Mormon will be analyzed according to these laws, demonstrating that the people of the Book of Mormon not only followed the Mosaic law regarding the *gēr* but went even further to provide protection, inclusion, and compassion toward these displaced and vulnerable groups.

Sources of the Mosaic Law

In order to establish if the *gēr* laws of the Pentateuch were followed in the Book of Mormon, we must first assess the sources of the Mosaic law for the people of the Book of Mormon. One of the reasons the Lehites brought the brass plates with them to the promised land was so they could "keep the commandments of the Lord according to the law of Moses," because "the law was engraven upon the plates of brass" (1 Nephi 4:15–16; see 5:11). The brass plates are mentioned numerous times throughout the rest of the Book of Mormon, including in the book of Alma, where Alma gave the plates to his son Helaman (37:3).[2]

Early in the Book of Mormon, the Nephites followed the judgments, statutes, and commandments of the Lord according to the law of Moses (2 Nephi 5:10). Observance of the Mosaic law continued throughout the Book of Mormon until the appearance of Jesus Christ to the Nephites, when the law was fulfilled and reinterpreted (3 Nephi 9:17; 12:17–19; 15:1–10; 25:4; 4 Nephi 1:12; Ether 12:11).[3] In the book of Alma, the Nephites were "strict in observing the ordinances of God, according to the law of Moses" (Alma 30:3). The Mosaic law was also mentioned in association with two refugee groups found in the Book of Mormon. In Alma 25:15–16, the Anti-Nephi-Lehies were described as keeping the law of Moses, and in Alma 34:13–14, the missionary Amulek taught the law to the Zoramites, who had not been observing it (31:9).[4]

It is clear that the brass plates contained the law of Moses and that the Nephites, and sometimes other groups, tried to follow the law in the Book of Mormon. However, the exact relationship between the five books of Moses in the brass plates and the current canonical form of the Pentateuch in the Old Testament is less clear. The Mosaic laws concerning the *gēr* are found in Exodus, Leviticus, Numbers, and Deuteronomy. According to the Documentary Hypothesis, sections of these four books were written, collated, and edited during different periods in the history of Israel.[5] Only the *gēr* laws found in Exodus and certain sections of Deuteronomy can be securely dated by scholars to time periods prior to the departure of the Lehites from Jerusalem, thus making it possible for the *gēr* laws to have been part of the law in the brass plates.[6]

Definitions of *Gēr* in the Pentateuch

The nominative form of the Hebrew word *gēr* in the Pentateuch has been translated as "stranger," "alien," "foreigner," "immigrant," and "refugee."[7] These designations are typically based on a specific social and historical context that is also tangentially related to the composition and redaction history of the text. Three main sociohistorical theories are used to define the provenance of the *gēr* in Exodus and in the Deuteronomic Core. The most widely accepted theory posits that the *gēr* represents a person who comes from a non-Israelite and non-Judahite kingdom. These foreigners immigrated to Judah and Israel because of the Assyrian deportations that affected Philistia, Egypt, Assyria, and the Transjordan in the seventh century BC.[8]

A second sociohistorical theory defining the *gēr* is also related to the Assyrian conquest but focuses on the invasion of the northern kingdom circa 721 BC. In this theory, the *gēr* represents an individual from Samaria who fled south into the kingdom of Judah in the wake of the Assyrian destruction of the north.[9] The third and final theory about the provenance of the *gēr* advocates that the term refers to Judahites who have been internally displaced from their own home because of invasion or indebtedness. This could be related to Sennacherib's campaign around 701 BC, when massive domestic displacement in Judah gave rise to a large class of poor and landless people, or even earlier in the eighth century BC, when Judah's movement toward more extensive structures of statehood led to increased social stratification and more permanent indebtedness.[10]

Recently, several scholars have demonstrated that not one of the three sociohistorical theories defining the *gēr* adequately covers all the contexts in which the term is used in the Pentateuch. As for the first theory (when *gēr* refers to "foreigners"), migration patterns and archaeological excavations have shown that only a small number of non-Israelites were living in Judah and Israel during the seventh century BC.[11] The second and third theories (when *gēr* refers to northern Israelites fleeing south or displaced Judahites, respectively) pose problems as well because the Deuteronomic conception of kinship between Israel and Judah would not lead to a designation of every Israelite or Judahite as "other" in Judah.[12]

Biblical scholar Mark Glanville has recently argued that the definition of *gēr* in the Hebrew Bible should include varying numbers of individuals representing each of the three sociohistorical theories. Since there is not an exclusive provenance for the *gēr*, Glanville provides a more comprehensive definition of the *gēr* as "people who have been displaced from their former kinship group and patrimony and from the protection that kinship and land affords and who seek sustenance in a new context."[13] Furthermore, these displaced individuals have left their homes because of life- or freedom-threatening events yet are still susceptible to oppression, exploitation, or forced bondage in their new land. Today, the official term for a person falling under these definitions is *refugee*.[14]

Definitions of Gēr in the Book of Mormon

There are at least five groups in the book of Alma that could be designated as *gēr* according to the definitions discussed above. These groups include the Anti-Nephi-Lehies (Alma 35; 43; 47; 53–58; 62; Helaman 3) and their children (53–58), the Zoramites (31–35; 43), the Lamanite royal servants (46–47), and the Lamanite soldiers (62). Persons from each of these groups were displaced from their original homes and kinship groups because of life-threatening violence or bondage and sought sustenance, inheritance, and safety in a new location.

In the first year of the reign of the judges, the sons of Mosiah began a mission in the land of Nephi that led to the conversion of thousands of Lamanites (Alma 17:4–6). The converts chose to be called by a new name, "Anti-Nephi-Lehies," and entered into a covenant to no longer shed blood (23:16–17; 24:15–18). As a result of this covenant, many were killed by other Lamanites who hoped to "destroy the people of Anti-Nephi-Lehi" (24:20–22; 25:5–7; 27:2–3). The Anti-Nephi-Lehies escaped out of the land of Nephi and were allowed to enter Nephite territory, where they were given the land of Jershon (27:14; 28:26). Although the Anti-Nephi-Lehies were "among the people of Nephi" for at least thirty-one years, they always retained their unique refugee identity—for example, they never referred to themselves as Nephites and were never called Nephites by others (27:27). The Nephites typically gave them the designation of "the people of Ammon" or "the Ammonites"[15] and repeatedly mentioned their Lamanite history and ancestry (53:10; 56:3; Helaman 3:12).

The Anti-Nephi-Lehies were also refugees in the sense of being vulnerable in their new home. Although there is no evidence of Nephite abuse against them, the refugees worried that the Nephites would "destroy" them because of the violent history between the

Nephites and Lamanites and even offered to become slaves to the Nephites (Alma 27:6–8). It must have been difficult for some Nephites to accept the arrival of the Lamanite refugees, especially those who had previously suggested to Ammon that the Nephites should "take up arms against [the Lamanites], that we destroy them and their iniquity out of the land" (26:25).

The next group from the book of Alma that could fall under the definition of *gēr* was from the Zoramites, a group of Nephite dissenters who had left the land of Zarahemla (Alma 30:59; 31:8). In the seventeenth year of the reign of the judges, Alma, Amulek, and five other Nephites began a mission among the Zoramites (30:6). They were successful among the poorer Zoramites (32:2), but the "more popular part of the Zoramites" became angry because many of the teachings focused on an egalitarian system of worship that removed power and control from the current civil and religious leaders (35:3). These Zoramite rulers, priests, and teachers searched through the people to discover who believed the teachings of the missionaries, and "those who were in favor of the words which had been spoken by Alma and his brethren were cast out of the land; and they were many" (35:3–6). The Zoramite refugees then joined the Anti-Nephi-Lehies in the land of Jershon (35:6).

The Zoramite refugees continued to be vulnerable in their new home because the Zoramite leaders demanded that the Anti-Nephi-Lehies cast the recent refugees out of Jershon and because the Zoramite rulers then joined with the Lamanites for war (Alma 35:8–9, 11). The Lamanites appointed the Zoramite leaders to become chief captains in the army to "preserve their hatred" (43:6–7). Eventually the Zoramite refugees, along with the Anti-Nephi-Lehi refugees, had to leave their new home in Jershon because of life- and freedom-threatening danger (35:13). Additionally, the Zoramite refugees remained at risk because they were not likely welcomed by every Nephite, especially since the Zoramites from which they had fled believed that they had been elected by God and would therefore be saved, while the Nephites would be cast "down to hell" because of their "foolish traditions" (31:16–17).

In the following year, another group of possible *gēr* emerged among the Lamanites in the land of Nephi. Amalickiah, a Nephite dissenter, had joined the Lamanites and had become one of their military commanders (Alma 46:7; 47:1, 3). Amalickiah desired the Lamanite throne, so he had one of his followers assassinate the Lamanite king (47:22–24). The Lamanite royal servants, however, were blamed for the king's death, and Amalickiah told the Lamanites to "go forth, and pursue his servants that they may be slain" (47:26–27). The servants escaped into the wilderness and eventually traveled to the land of Zarahemla, where they "joined the people of Ammon" and the Zoramite refugees (47:29). A decade later, one of the Lamanite royal servants, who was named Laman, was mentioned as a solider in the army of Moroni. Moroni had appointed the refugee Laman to help liberate Nephite prisoners from the Lamanites in the land of Nephi (55:5–23).

The war between the Lamanites and the Nephites continued for thirteen years, and many Nephites died protecting the Anti-Nephi-Lehi refugees, who would not defend themselves because of their covenant to not shed blood. However, two thousand of their sons, who had not entered into that covenant, joined together to "fight for the liberty of the Nephites" under the command of Helaman (Alma 53:16–19). Although these refugee sons "called themselves Nephites" and considered Nephite territory to be "their country," they seem to have retained some of their refugee identity among the Nephites (53:16, 18). In Helaman's letter to Moroni, he referred to the sons as "stripling Ammonites" or "those sons of the people of Ammon," identified them as "descendants of Laman," and mentioned their Lamanite history of "unbelief" (56:3–4, 57; 57:6; 58:39).[16] Although the Anti-Nephi-Lehi refugees had escaped life- and freedom-threatening events over a decade earlier, their vulnerability was still present because they had to rely on their sons to "protect the Nephites and themselves from bondage" (53:17).

One more large group of possible *gēr* in the book of Alma consists of over four thousand Lamanite soldiers and prisoners (Alma 62:17, 29). In the thirty-first year of the reign of the judges, Moroni and Pahoran marched their army toward the city of Nephihah, which was controlled by the Lamanites. On the way, they came across a large group of Lamanite soldiers, many of whom "were caused . . . [by the Nephites] to enter into a covenant that they would no more take up their weapons of war against the Nephites" (62:15–16). About four thousand of these Lamanite refugees were sent to live with "the people of Ammon," who had already been joined by the Zoramite refugees and the Lamanite royal servant refugees (62:17). After Moroni and Pahoran conquered Nephihah, many of the Lamanite prisoners from the city were also allowed to "join the people of Ammon and become a free people" (62:27–28). For the Nephites to accept these Lamanite soldiers into their territory and trust them in the middle of war must have been challenging.

All five of the aforementioned groups in the Book of Mormon fit under the general definition of *gēr* from the Pentateuch. Mosaic laws concerning the *gēr* found in Exodus and the Deuteronomic Core cover social, judicial, and religious issues. Because the Book of Mormon does not contain large sections of law code like the Pentateuch, establishing whether the Nephites followed the Mosaic law in their treatment of the *gēr* must instead be discovered by examining the narratives of the Anti-Nephi-Lehies and their sons, the Zoramites, the Lamanite royal servants, and the Lamanite soldier refugees.

The *Gēr* in Social Law

The social law grouping of the Mosaic law in Exodus 22:20 through 23:9 and in the Deuteronomic Core (Deuteronomy 14:22–29; 15:1–18; 24:17; 26:12–15) focused on the ethics of protecting the most vulnerable in the community from exploitation surrounding labor and production. Social laws concerning the *gēr* can be separated into four categories: oppression, employment, participation, and motivation.

The most common social stipulation concerning the *gēr* simply stated that they must not be oppressed. The Hebrew verbs translated as "oppress" in these verses, *lāḥaṣ* (Exodus 22:21; 23:9), *yānāh* (Exodus 22:21), and *ʿāšaq* (Deuteronomy 24:14), also meant "vex," "maltreat," or "extort," and typically referred to the exploitation of a weaker party for economic gain.[17]

In the Deuteronomic Core, prohibiting the oppression of the *gēr* specifically referred to protecting a refugee who had been hired for employment "in thy land within thy gates," which could denote an individual's own settlement, village, or city or somewhere nearby (Deuteronomy 24:14–15).[18] The law stipulated that hirelings should be paid for their labor before the sun went down on the day they worked, due to an ongoing dependence on a daily wage for survival or the need to pay off outstanding debts. The law required that the hired *gēr* be treated the same as hired "brethren," which incorporated the refugee into the Deuteronomic brother-sister ethic of justice and compassion for kindred.[19] The *gēr* had been uprooted from their own land and kindred and should therefore be treated as part of the local kin grouping, upon which they were dependent for their livelihood.

The Deuteronomic brother-sister ethic was also related to the inclusion of the *gēr* as an active participant in the community. The social laws concerning the *gēr* in the Deuteronomic Core stipulated that the harvest residue should be given to the refugee, orphan, and widow (Deuteronomy 24:19–21). According to the law, the landowner should not return to the field, orchard, or vineyard to gather the leftover grain, olives, or grapes after the initial harvest, but the landowner should instead allow vulnerable individuals to glean produce for themselves. The "triad of the vulnerable," which includes the refugee, orphan, and widow, represented those who are without kindred, land, or sustenance.[20] The Mosaic law attempted to alter the status of these impoverished people, including the *gēr*, by fostering their inclusion as kindred and participants in the community.

The gleaning law was not only just a matter of charity but also an example of case law with "governing primary rights and duties," in which it was the right of the *gēr* to possess the residue and it was the duty of the landowner to allow possession.[21] Allowing the *gēr* to harvest and "own" the residual produce provided some means of self-sustainability and provisioning of valuable resources. A further social food law stipulated that any unclean meat should be given to the *gēr*, because "holy people unto the Lord" should not consume it.[22] While some scholars have grappled with the "deliberate tension in this text between dynamics of inclusion . . . and the otherness of the *gēr* that is signified in the eating of the [unclean meat]," this tension disappears in the Joseph Smith Translation of the verse, which clarified that the unclean meat should "not" be given to the *gēr*.[23] Therefore, this refugee food law not only included the *gēr* as part of the Lord's holy people but also commanded that they should receive a portion of the divine supply of clean meat.

Each set of social, judicial, and religious *gēr* laws was accompanied by one or more motivation clauses to inspire obedience to the law. These clauses typically related the purpose of the law and outlined associated blessings or punishments. The overarching motivation clause for the social laws concerning the *gēr* was related to the Egypt-Exodus motif. In the Covenant Code, the readers of the Mosaic law were reminded that they were once "strangers in the land of Egypt" (Exodus 22:21; 23:9), and according to the Deuteronomic Core, they were "bondm[e]n in the land of Egypt" (Deuteronomy 24:22). Because the Israelites experienced the hardships surrounding oppression and slavery while foreigners in Egypt, they should not permit foreigners in their own land to be treated in the same way. If the Israelites do, the Lord will hear the cries of the oppressed and punish the oppressors, just as he punished the Egyptians (Deuteronomy 24:15). In this way, the Lord fulfills the role of the divine judge in the legal system of the Mosaic law.

The social stipulations concerning the *gēr* in the Mosaic law focused on the freedom, subsistence, employment, and protection of the refugee. Social laws concerning the freedom of the *gēr* are found in relation to the Anti-Nephi-Lehies, the Lamanite soldiers, and the

Zoramites. When the Anti-Nephi-Lehies offered to become the slaves of the Nephites so that they could live among the Nephites, Ammon stated that his father, King Mosiah, had established an antislavery law among the Nephites (Alma 27:8–9). This law was referenced in Mosiah 29, where the king declared that "this land [should] be a land of liberty, and every man may enjoy his rights and privileges alike" (Mosiah 29:32). A similar law was referenced in the book of Alma, stating that "all men were on equal grounds" (Alma 30:11; see 30:7). The Lamanite soldier refugees were also described as "a free people" (62:27). Although the Anti-Nephi-Lehi and Zoramite refugees were initially settled in Jershon, the refugees had the freedom to leave the city and move elsewhere (35:13; Helaman 3:12).

The Egypt-Exodus motif used as motivation for the *gēr* social laws in the Pentateuch is also found in the Book of Mormon. Not only did Nephi and Abinadi mention the "bondage" of Egypt (1 Nephi 19:10; Mosiah 12:34), but Alma also referenced the "bondage and captivity" of Egypt to his son Helaman (Alma 36:28).[24] However, the book of Alma introduced a novel motivation for establishing and maintaining freedom among the Nephites. After Alma mentioned the "bondage and captivity" of Egypt to Helaman, he supplemented it with the idea of the Lehites escaping the "bondage and captivity" of Jerusalem to come to a free land. After speaking about the Anti-Nephi-Lehi refugees, Ammon possibly referenced the *gēr* social laws of the Covenant Code; however, instead of citing that they were "strangers in the land of Egypt," he mentioned that they were still "wanderers in a strange land" (Alma 26:36). The motivation for keeping the *gēr* (and the Nephites) free not only came from the reminder that their ancestors were once strangers and slaves in Egypt but also came from the knowledge that they were in bondage in Jerusalem and were still strangers even in their day.

An important aspect of the social laws concerning the *gēr* in the Deuteronomic Core was caring for the impoverished, which included the refugee, orphan, and widow. A similar essence of social law charity was also found in the treatment of the most destitute group of refugees in the Book of Mormon, the Zoramites, who were persecuted in their own land because of their "exceeding poverty" (Alma 32:5). After the Zoramites were cast out of their land and became refugees in the land of Zarahemla, not only did the Nephites "minister unto them" but the Anti-Nephi-Lehies also nourished and clothed them and administered to them (35:7, 9). Amulek taught the Zoramites that caring for the needy, the naked, the sick, and the afflicted was an important part of religious worship (34:28–28).

The Mosaic law surrounding refugees not only focused on charity for the impoverished but also sought to help them with the means for self-sufficiency and protection from exploitation in employment. When the Anti-Nephi-Lehies left their land for Zarahemla, Ammon and the other sons of Mosiah helped them gather their flocks and herds to take with them, which allowed for some pastoral means of support for the refugees (Alma 27:14). Once the Anti-Nephi-Lehies reached Zarahemla, the Nephites gave the land of Jershon "for an inheritance" to the refugees, who later also gave some of that land to the Zoramite gēr "for their inheritance" (27:22, 26; 35:9, 14; 43:12). Under the Mosaic law, the inheritance land gift was a legally binding contract that gave a man and his descendants the right to occupy and possess the land in perpetuity.[25] Owning these lands meant that the Anti-Nephi-Lehies and Zoramites could provide for their own subsistence.

As was commonly described in the social laws of the Covenant Code and Deuteronomic Core, refugees in the Book of Mormon also worked for the local inhabitants in their new land and therefore required protection from exploitation and oppression. The Anti-Nephi-Lehies gave the Nephites a "large portion of their substance," and the Lamanite soldier refugees also worked for the Nephites by tilling the ground, raising grain, and herding flocks so that the Nephites were "relieved from a great burden" (Alma 27:24; 43:13; 62:29). Although these arrangements could appear imbalanced and oppressive, the Nephites used these payments to help maintain their armies, who continually offered protection, suffered "afflictions and tribulations," and even gave their lives for the refugees (27:24; 53:12–13).[26] Some of the *gēr* in the Book of Mormon were also employed in the Nephite army, including the Zoramites, the sons of the Anti-Nephi-Lehies, and the Lamanite royal servants (35:14; 53:17–18; 55:4–5).

The *Gēr* in Judicial Law

The judicial laws in the Deuteronomic Core provided further provision for the *gēr* in the sphere of procedural law, granting them full recourse in the legal system. Previous to the Mosaic law, a displaced and impoverished individual was not provided with legal rights and was therefore vulnerable to abuse in the courts.[27] The legal vulnerability and perilous relationship with judiciary proceedings in the Old Testament were evidenced in the stories of Lot and the men of Sodom (Genesis 19:9), the wife-sister narratives of the ancestors in Egypt (Genesis 12:10–20; 26:6–11), Naboth's vineyard (1 Kings 21:1–29), and the prophet Amos (Amos 5:10–13). The function of the judicial law was to use a relative egalitarianism to fortify the legal process against the influence of those with power.

The judicial law found in Deuteronomy 24:17 provided protection for refugees in legal procedure, instructing that "thou shalt not pervert the judgment of the [*gēr*]," nor the orphan nor the widow. The law was addressed to the whole community, including judges, litigants, and witnesses, while the verb *nāṭā* ("pervert," or also meaning "stretch out" or "bend") was associated with misguiding justice and parity in judicial process.[28] Individuals in the triad of the vulnerable, especially refugees, were to receive equal and fair treatment under the law, which may be "the clearest requirement of [the *gēr*'s] inclusion in the public life of Israel."[29]

As with social laws concerning the *gēr*, judicial laws of the Deuteronomic Core were also accompanied by a motivation clause connected with the Egypt-Exodus motif (Deuteronomy 24:18). However, the motivation clause referenced in judicial law moved a step beyond an aide-mémoire of the bondage in Egypt to a new focus concerning the Lord's deliverance and redemption from that slavery. Because God had liberated their ancestors (the Israelites) from captivity in a foreign land, refugees must also be saved and protected from bondage while in their new land. The defenselessness of the *gēr* was emphasized, along with the associated blessings that were promised to those who work to keep refugees free from bondage. If the *gēr* can successfully and continually be delivered from freedom- and life-threatening events, the Lord will also continue to save and redeem the liberators from oppression.

Aspects regarding refugees in the Deuteronomic judicial law can be found in the Book of Mormon, especially among the Anti-Nephi-Lehies and their children. In Alma 30, the anti-Christ Korihor traveled among the Nephites prevaricating, falsely accusing civil and religious leaders, reviling priests and teachers, and blaspheming against God, all of which were punishable crimes under Nephite (and Mosaic) law (Alma 30:12–60).[30] When Korihor arrived in Jershon and continued to break the law, the Anti-Nephi-Lehies arrested him and took him to the local high priest, who banished Korihor from their land (30:19–21). The refugees must have had enough legal rights and recourse to have been able to arrest Korihor—who may have been a Nephite[31]—and bring him to be judged by their high priest.[32] Under the law of Moses, witnesses who falsely accused an individual of a crime could suffer the same punishments as the guilty party for the accused crime (Deuteronomy 19:15–19). Thus it is remarkable that the vulnerable Anti-Nephi-Lehi *gēr* were the first not only to arrest Korihor but also to follow through with his judgment and punishment, leading Alma to state that "they were more wise than many of the Nephites" (Alma 30:20).

The Egypt-Exodus motivation clause that was integral to the judicial law concerning the *gēr* in the Pentateuch was also present in the Book of Mormon. Nephi mentioned and used the concept of ancestral deliverance from Egyptian bondage as motivation several times, as did Limhi and Abinadi.[33] The same motif continued throughout the book of Alma, where both Alma and Moroni reminded the Nephites of the Lord's deliverance of their ancestors from bondage and captivity in Egypt (Alma 29:11–12; 36:28; 60:20). Because their ancestors were redeemed from slavery while foreigners, the Nephites must also liberate and protect the foreign refugees from events that would threaten their freedom or lives.

The most extreme parallel example of deliverance and protection of refugees were Ammon and the Anti-Nephi-Lehies, who, because of their covenant not to shed blood, were completely defenseless against the other Lamanites in their homeland. When these Lamanites began to oppress the Anti-Nephi-Lehies, the Lord commanded Ammon to "get this people out of this land, that they perish not" (Alma 27:12). Ammon became a Moses-like figure, not only in physically leading the people out of danger and through the wilderness but also in spiritually mediating between the people and the Lord through Ammon's supplication. Ammon and Alma also facilitated the "reception and safety" of the refugees among the Nephites, who voted to allow the admittance of the refugees and to give them land because they "would not suffer that they should be destroyed" (28:8; 43:12). The Nephites placed their armies between the land of the Anti-Nephi-Lehi *gēr* and the Lamanites and protected them for decades (53:10–12).

Eventually, the refugee sons themselves engaged in the fight to "protect the Nephites and themselves from bondage," which was an ever-present threat from the Lamanites (Alma 53:17). However, as in the Egypt-Exodus motivation clause, the sons and their Nephite leaders fully acknowledged the role of the Lord in the refugees' original and continued deliverance. The sons were taught by their Anti-Nephi-Lehi mothers that God would deliver them, and the sons stood "fast in that liberty wherewith God ha[d] made them free" (56:47; 57:21; 58:40). In his letter to Moroni, Helaman repeatedly stated that it was God who had "delivered" and would continue to "deliver" the refugee sons from their enemies (57:35–36; 58:11, 37). Even after the wars with the Lamanites had ceased and there was peace among the Nephites, Mormon recalled that it was the Lord who had "delivered them from death, and from bonds," again referencing the divine role in their deliverance from freedom- and life-threatening situations—as found in the motivation clause for judicial law concerning the *gēr* (62:50).

The *Gēr* in Religious Law

In the Pentateuch, religious law concerning the *gēr* focused on transforming the relationship between refugees and their new community in terms of worship and kinship. An ethic of inclusion for the *gēr* in relation to religious and household concerns was embedded in the Egypt-Exodus motivation clause associated with preservation. Religious laws embracing the *gēr* included the third-year provision of the tithe, two harvest celebrations, and the Festival of the Firstfruits. Instructions regarding the *gēr* and the third-year tithe notably frame the Deuteronomic Core (Deuteronomy 14:28–29; 26:12–15). The Mosaic law stipulated that a tithe of one tenth of production should be paid annually to the temple; however, every third and sixth year, the tithe should be stored in the community for the ongoing sustenance of vulnerable or landless people, including the refugee, the orphan, the widow, and the Levite.[34]

The law of the third-year tithe also required that the *gēr* should "eat [within thy gates] and be satisfied," demonstrating that the allotment of the tithe to the *gēr* was not just about charity but was also about inclusive household feasting and community kinship (Deuteronomy 14:29; 26:12). In the ancient Near East, communal feasting broke down social stratification and forged powerful brother-sister-type relationships.[35] The *gēr* became part of the localized family structure in partaking of household produce, and they also became part of the religious community through the consumption of the "hallowed things" of the temple (26:13). The holiness of the sacred portion was transferred to the refugee so that "the fact that [*gēr*] are allowed to consume the sacred portion . . . is explained on the grounds that they are regarded as members of the covenant community."³⁶ This theology of "corporate holiness" demonstrated that the *gēr* were part of the fellowship of the Lord.³⁷

The *gēr* were also included in the Mosaic law instructions regarding the Deuteronomic festival calendar (Deuteronomy 16:1–17). Refugees were incorporated as participants in the Feast of Weeks (16:9–12) and the Feast of Tabernacles (16:13–15), which were harvest festivals for the community to celebrate the Lord's provision and blessings of agricultural abundance. These pilgrimage festivals forged a communal identity for those who belonged to the people of the Lord. The law specified that the guest list should include children, servants, Levites, *gēr*, orphans, and widows (16:11, 14). The inclusion of refugees as participants enfolded the *gēr* into the nuclear family as brother or sister, thus overcoming differences in origin, culture, social status, and wealth.³⁸ Refugees not only became part of the family but were also "grafted" into the nation and people of the Lord, so that "fictive kinship became kinship of the flesh or blood."³⁹

The *gēr* were also listed among the religious laws surrounding the Deuteronomic Festival of the Firstfruits (Deuteronomy 26:1–11). During this festival, the participants returned the firstfruits of the harvest to the Lord in a ritual of thanksgiving that focused on the gifts of abundance and life. Unlike the harvest festivals, the list of participants only included the household and landless Levites and refugees, demonstrating that refugees played a special role in the celebration (26:11). The *gēr* were incorporated as coheirs of the divine blessings of the land and its produce, which were a significant part of the brother-sister ethic embedded in the theology of the land gift, especially for landless refugees.⁴⁰

During the Festival of the Firstfruits, participants carried the basket of firstfruits on a pilgrimage journey from the farm to the sanctuary, where the food was given to the priest to set on the altar of the Lord (Deuteronomy 26:1–4). The participants would then recite aspects of the Exodus narrative, including the Israelites' wandering, sojourning, enslavement, deliverance, preservation, and finding of the promised land, most of which had been symbolically reenacted through the pilgrimage (26: 5–9). The motivation clause of the Egypt-Exodus motif associated the displaced *gēr* with Israel's own displacement in Egypt. Because the Lord emancipated and preserved vulnerable Israel through the wanderings in the wilderness, the lives of vulnerable refugees should also be preserved through Israel, who "always remains a redeemed community, a receiving community."[41] As part of the Firstfruits Festival and the Exodus narrative, the Lord stood as divine king, judge, liberator, and protector of displaced peoples, continually hearing their cries and preserving their lives (26:7–8).

Although none of the festivals of the Pentateuch were specifically mentioned by name in the Book of Mormon and although the tithe was only referenced twice, the treatment of the *gēr* in the Book of Mormon followed the Mosaic law in transforming relationships of kinship and worship.[42] The motivation clause of the Egypt-Exodus preservation motif associated with the Festival of the Firstfruits was also referenced several times in the Book of Mormon, in which the Lord was credited with preserving the lives of the children of Israel against the Egyptian armies and while wandering in the wilderness.[43] The *gēr* of the Book of Mormon were perfectly aligned with this motif in the book of Alma, in which Ammon referred to himself and the Anti-Nephi-Lehies as "wanderers in a strange land" but that God "has been mindful of us" (Alma 26:36). Like Moses, the Lord also spoke to Ammon about facilitating the preservation of oppressed people: Ammon was told to "get this people [the Anti-Nephi-Lehies] out of this land, that they perish not; . . . for I will preserve them" (27:12).

After the refugees reached their new land, the preservation motif of the Festival of the Firstfruits continued with Helaman and the sons of the Anti-Nephi-Lehies, who, like Joshua and the Israelites,[44] believed that "God would deliver them" and that "he will not suffer that we should fall" in their fight against the enemy (Alma 56:46–47; see 58:37). The Lord not only delivered the refugee sons frequently from the Lamanites, but also preserved the sons' lives throughout many battles; indeed, "not one soul of them . . . did perish" (57:25; 58:39). Because many Nephites were killed in these same battles, the sons' "preservation was astonishing to [the] whole army," who "justly ascribe[d] it to the miraculous power of God" (57:26). The Egypt-Exodus motivation clause from the religious category of the Mosaic laws was clearly present among the *gēr* in the Book of Mormon, as were the themes of kinship and worship reflected in the third-year tithe and harvest festivals of the Pentateuch.

The religious laws concerning the *gēr* in the Deuteronomic Core focused on enfolding the *gēr* into the nation and family of the Lord. These themes of inclusion and the brother-sister ethic were also present throughout the treatment of the refugees in the Book of Mormon. The Nephites not only allowed the Anti-Nephi-Lehies, the Zoramites, the Lamanite royal servants, and the Lamanite soldier refugees to enter their territory, but also gave some of them land "for their inheritance" (Alma 27:22; 35:9, 14). In this way, the Nephites went beyond the mere stipulation that the *gēr* partake of the produce from the Lord's land gift (as found in the Festival of the Firstfruits) and actually provided an inheritance land gift for the refugees, thus allowing them to literally become coheirs to the Lord's blessing of the land gift. While the Anti-Nephi-Lehies never referred to themselves as Nephites, their sons considered themselves to be Nephites and Nephite land to be "their country" (53:16, 18; 56:5). Helaman also included the sons in his reference to the "people of Nephi," showing that the refugees had been grafted into the nation (56:54).

The *gēr* of the Book of Mormon became kindred of the Nephites, not only through the land gift and incorporation into the nation, but also through more personal and familial associations. Ammon, Alma, and Amulek all spoke of their love for the refugees, calling them "dearly beloved" and "beloved brethren" numerous times.[45] The legacy of this affection was even mentioned over four centuries later, when Mormon described the "exceeding love which Ammon and his brethren had" for the refugees (Alma 53:11). Many more examples of how the Nephites demonstrated their love for the refugees have already been discussed, but nothing was more powerful than the Nephites giving up their own lives to protect the refugees, treating them as though they belonged to the Nephites' own nuclear families. Helaman formed a special kinship with the sons of the Anti-Nephi-Lehies, continually referring to them as "my . . . sons, (for they are worthy to be called sons)," and the sons in turn called Helaman "father" (56:10, 17, 27, 30, 39, 44, 46; 57:22). The display of familial kinship toward the refugees of the Book of Mormon reflects the theology of inclusivism that the religious laws outlined in the Pentateuch.

In the Book of Mormon, the integration of the *gēr* into Nephite religious life would have been imperative since many of the refugees had been "converted unto the Lord" (Alma 23:6), as were some of the *gēr* in the Pentateuch.[46] Ammon rejoiced in the missionary work that brought the Anti-Nephi-Lehies to the Lord, commenting that they were no longer "strangers to God" (26:9). It is possible that a double entendre was meant in this statement about the refugees, since the Hebrew word *gēr* was translated as "stranger" in the KJV, as was the Late Egyptian loan-word *qar*, and so, the translation of "stranger" may also have been used in the Book of Mormon.[47] In this way, the refugees were no longer "strangers" to the Nephites or the Lord. As in the religious law stipulating that the *gēr* consume the holy third-year tithe, the refugees of the Book of Mormon became members of the covenant community and "people of the Lord" (27:5, 14).

According to the Mosaic code, the *gēr* in the Pentateuch were integrated into the worship and celebration of the Lord through participation in the harvest festivals held in the households and sanctuary of Israel. After the Anti-Nephi-Lehies reached their new land, the Nephites supported the refugees' worship of the Lord through establishing a church in Jershon and numbering the *gēr* "among the people who were of the church of God" (Alma 27:27; 28:1). The Nephites also continually sustained the Anti-Nephi-Lehi refugees in keeping their unique covenant with the Lord to not shed blood, "lest they should commit sin" (27:23). When the refugees desired to take up weapons and fight in the war, they were "overpowered by the persuasions" of Helaman, so that they would not break their covenant with the Lord (53:14–15).

Conclusion

It appears that the Nephites attempted to follow the Mosaic law concerning the *gēr* in the appropriate treatment of the Anti-Nephi-Lehies, the Zoramites, the Lamanite royal servants, the children of the Anti-Nephi-Lehies, and the displaced Lamanite soldiers, which were groups of refugees discussed in the book of Alma. Under the social category of the law of Moses, the Nephites protected the *gēr* from oppression and exploitation in employment, while also promoting the refugees' self-sustainability and allowing their full participation in the community. Judicially, the refugees were permitted full recourse in the legal system, which also prohibited abuse of the vulnerable. The Nephites especially followed the Mosaic law's religious stipulations concerning the *gēr* and fully transformed the relationship of the refugees with the Nephite community in terms of inclusion into the nation, family, and covenant people of the Lord.

The Nephites also seemed to be aware of the Egypt-Exodus motivation clauses attached to the social, judicial, and religious laws of the *gēr* in the law of Moses. In the Book of Mormon, this motif was continually referenced in relation to the Israelites' enslavement and oppression in Egypt, divine deliverance and redemption, wanderings and preservation in the wilderness, and arrival in the promised land. The Nephites possibly understood these motivation clauses and their association with the correct treatment of refugees in liberating and protecting them from internal or external enslavement and oppression, as well as relying on and thanking the Lord for assistance. The motivation clauses inspired obedience not only through a shared cultural history but also through the many temporal and spiritual blessings that the Nephites received from their compassionate treatment of refugees. Some of these blessings included the Nephites receiving a "great support" with provisions, warfare, labor, and sustenance, as well as becoming a "highly favored people of the Lord" (Alma 27:30; 53:19; 56:8, 19).

The social, judicial, and religious *gēr* laws in the Covenant Code and Deuteronomic Core were meant to promote social reform in Israel's community. The purpose of the stipulations was "not to reproduce a book of statutory law but [to] radically reorder society according to its sister-brother ethic."[48] The treatment of refugees in the book of Alma demonstrated a successful result of this theology of inclusion from the early Covenant and Deuteronomic Codes. The Nephites even went a step further than the stipulations of the early Mosaic law when they provided an inheritance land gift for the refugees that matched the more progressive *gēr* reforms of the later Holiness Code.[49] However, the ultimate validation for the Nephite kinship-inclusion of the *gēr* under the Mosaic law occurred when the Savior visited the Nephites and reconfirmed the charitable treatment of refugees, demonstrating the perpetual importance for followers of Jesus Christ to treat vulnerable people with the utmost compassion (3 Nephi 24:5).

Krystal V. L. Pierce is an assistant professor of ancient scripture at Brigham Young University.

Notes

1. In the legal codes of the Pentateuch, *gēr* always appears in the singular, which is the fixed form of the noun within legal texts. The word was used as a group collective that could refer to one or more persons. The plural *gērīm* appears only five times in the Pentateuch, where it is always used to refer to the Israelites in the Egypt-Exodus motif and never to the *gēr* of the Mosaic Law (Exodus 22:21; 23:9; Leviticus 19:34; 25:23; Deuteronomy 10:19).
2. For the brass plates, see 1 Nephi 3–5, 13, 19, 22; 2 Nephi 4–5; Omni 1; Mosiah 1, 10, 28; Alma 37; 3 Nephi 1, 10.

3. The Mosaic law is mentioned in 1 Nephi 4, 17; 2 Nephi 5, 11, 25; Jacob 1, 11; Mosiah 2–3, 12–13, 16, 24; Alma 25, 30–31, 34; Helaman 13, 15; 3 Nephi 1, 9, 12, 15, 25; 4 Nephi 1.
4. Besides the Anti-Nephi-Lehies, other Lamanites are also described as following the law of Moses (see Helaman 13:1; 15:5).
5. The Documentary Hypothesis proposes that the current version of the Pentateuch was formed through a long process of writers and editors producing documents referred to as the J, E, D, and P sources (see also note 6). For treatments of the Documentary Hypothesis, see Richard Friedman, *The Bible with Sources Revealed* (New York: HarperOne, 2003); Richard Friedman, *Who Wrote the Bible?* (New York: HarperOne, 1997); Joel S. Baden, *The Composition of the Pentateuch: Renewing the Documentary Hypothesis* (New Haven, CT: Yale University Press, 2012).
6. All of the *gēr* laws in Exodus are part of the Covenant Code (see chapters 21–23), which is believed to have been compiled by a priest living in the northern kingdom of Israel around 922–722 BC as part of the E source; see Frank Crüsemann, *The Torah: Theology and Social History of Old Testament Law* (Minneapolis: Fortress, 1996), 215. The *gēr* laws in the Holiness Code (Leviticus 17–26) and in Numbers are integrally related to the controversial P source, which many scholars date to the sixth or fifth centuries BC; see Jeffery Stackert, *Rewriting the Torah: Literary Revision in Deuteronomy and the Holiness Legislation* (Tübingen: Mohr Siebeck, 2007). The *gēr* laws in Deuteronomy are found in both the framework (chapters 1–11, 27–34) and the law core (chapters 12–26). Because most scholars date the collation of the Deuteronomic framework to the sixth century BC and the law core to the seventh century BC, only *gēr* laws from the latter will be included in this study. Eckhart Otto, "The History of the Legal-Religious Hermeneutics of the Book of Deuteronomy from the Assyrian to the Hellenistic Period," in *Law and Religion in the Eastern Mediterranean*, ed. Anselm C. Hagedorn and Reinhard G. Kratz (Oxford: Oxford University Press, 2013), 213–14.
7. For a synthesis on the use and translation of these terms, see Mark R. Glanville, *Adopting the Stranger as Kindred in Deuteronomy* (Atlanta: SBL Press, 2018), 7–11. "Stranger" is used in the King James Version (KJV) of

the Bible, "alien" or "resident alien" is used in the New Revised Standard Version (NRSV), and "foreigner" is used in the New International Version (NIV).

8. See Reinhard Achenbach, "Der Eintritt der Schutzbürger in den Bund: Distinktion und Integration von Fremden im Deuteronomium," in *"Gerechtigkeit und Recht zu üben" (Gen 18,19)*, ed. Reinhard Achenbach and Martin Arneth (Wiesbaden: Harrassowitz, 2009), 242; Rainer Albertz, "From Aliens to Proselytes: Non-Priestly and Priestly Legislation concerning Strangers," in *The Foreigner and the Law*, ed. Reinhard Achenbach, Rainer Albertz, and Jacob Wöhrle (Wiesbaden: Harrassowitz, 2011), 55, 61.

9. See Moshe Weinfeld, *Deuteronomy and the Deuteronomic School* (Oxford: Clarendon, 1972), 90–91.

10. Nadav Na'aman, "Sojourners and Levites in the Kingdom of Judah in the Seventh Century BCE," *Zeitschrift für altorientalische und biblische Rechtsgeschichte* 14 (2008): 237–79.

11. Nadav Na'aman, "Population Changes in Palestine following Assyrian Deportation," in *Ancient Israel and Its Neighbors: Interaction and Counteraction*, ed. Nadav Na'aman (Winona Lake, IN: Eisenbrauns, 2005), 212–15.

12. Glanville, *Adopting the Stranger*, 138–42. The concept of cultural identity is so complex that the designation of "other" can be applied to someone from outside the nuclear family, household, city, or nation. For a complete discussion of cultural identity theory, see Krystal V. L. Pierce, "Living and Dying Abroad: Aspects of Egyptian Cultural Identity in Late Bronze Age and Early Iron Age Canaan" (PhD diss., University of California, Los Angeles, 2013), 48–77.

13. Glanville, *Adopting the Stranger*, 267.

14. The office of the United Nations High Commissioner for Refugees (UNHCR) defines refugees as "persons who are outside their country of nationality or habitual residence and unable to return there owing to serious and indiscriminate threats to life, physical integrity or freedom resulting from generalized violence or events seriously disturbing public order." *UNHCR Resettlement Handbook*, 2011, 19.

15. See Alma 27–28, 30, 35, 43, 53, 56–58, 62 and Helaman 3.

16. It is possible that the Anti-Nephi-Lehies and their sons' Lamanite identity was also referenced when Helaman repeatedly mentioned that the sons were taught religious truths by their mothers, which seemed to be a unique concept among the Nephites (56:47–49; 57:21).
17. See James Strong, *New Strong's Exhaustive Concordance* (Nashville: Thomas Nelson, 2003), 3238, 3905, and 6231; J. Gordon McConville, *Deuteronomy* (Leicester: InterVarsity Press, 2002), 362.
18. See Glanville, *Adopting the Stranger*, 203–5.
19. For the Deuteronomic brother-sister (or brotherhood) ethic, see Otto, "History," 219–20; Kenton Sparks, *Ethnicity and Identity in Ancient Israel* (Winona Lake, IN: Eisenbrauns, 1998), 237.
20. Although the combination of the orphan and the widow can be a metonymy for all impoverished people, the addendum of the *gēr* marked a separate and additional social problem of displacement (Glanville, *Adopting the Stranger*, 67).
21. Dale Patrick, "Casuistic Law Governing Primary Rights and Duties," *Journal of Biblical Literature* 92 (1973): 181.
22. The unclean meat, or "anything that dieth of itself," probably denoted an animal carcass that had not been properly slaughtered; see Kenton Sparks, "A Comparative Study of the Biblical Laws," *Zeitschrift für die alttestamentliche Wissenschaft* 110 (1998): 596.
23. Glanville, *Adopting the Stranger*, 96; Albertz, "From Aliens to Proselytes," 55.
24. The events surrounding the Zoramites in the Book of Mormon have also been compared to other pericopes of the Old Testament, including the Eden narrative and Isaian prophecies; see Adam S. Miller, ed., *An Experiment on the Word: Reading Alma 32* (Provo, UT: Neal A. Maxwell Institute for Religious Scholarship, 2014).
25. Moshe Weinfeld, *The Promise of the Land: The Inheritance of the Land of Canaan by the Israelites* (Berkeley: University of California Press, 1993), 184–85, 258–59.
26. It has also been suggested that the support provided to the Nephite army by the Anti-Nephi-Lehies was in exchange for their exemption from military service as stipulated under the law of Moses. John W. Welch, "Law

and War in the Book of Mormon," in *Warfare in the Book of Mormon*, ed. Stephen D. Ricks and William J. Hamblin (Provo, UT: Foundation for Ancient Research and Mormon Studies; Salt Lake City: Deseret Book, 1990), 63–65.

27. Raymond Westbrook, "Slave and Master in Ancient Near Eastern Law," in *Law from the Tigris to the Tiber*, ed. Bruce Wells and Rachel Magdalene (Winona Lake, IN: Eisenbrauns, 2009), 171.

28. Strong's Concordance, 5186. Achenbach, "Der Eintritt der Schutzbürger," 243.

29. McConville, *Deuteronomy*, 363.

30. John W. Welch, *The Legal Cases in the Book of Mormon* (Provo, UT: BYU Press, 2008), 299.

31. On the origins of Korihor, see Welch, *Legal Cases*, 274–76.

32. It has also been suggested that the Anti-Nephi-Lehies were allowed to live under their own legal system that was independent from Nephite laws (Welch, *Legal Cases*, 280–81).

33. 1 Nephi 4:3; 17:23, 27, 40; 19:10; 2 Nephi 25:20; Mosiah 7:19, 12:34.

34. Peter Altmann, *Festive Meals in Ancient Israel* (Berlin: de Gruyter, 2011), 220.

35. Victor Turner, *Dramas, Fields, and Metaphors: Symbolic Action in Human Society* (Ithaca, NY: Cornell University Press, 1974), 196–201.

36. Yan Yu, "Tithes and Firstlings in Deuteronomy" (PhD diss., Union Theological Seminary, 1997), 68.

37. Glanville, *Adopting the Stranger*, 197–98.

38. Georg Braulik, "The Joy of the Feast," in *Theology of Deuteronomy* (Richland Hills, TX: Bibal, 1994), 58.

39. Frank Moore Cross, *From Epic to Canon: History and Literature in Ancient Israel* (Baltimore: John Hopkins University Press, 1998), 7.

40. McConville, *Deuteronomy*, 380.

41. Glanville, *Adopting the Stranger*, 206.

42. It is possible that the Feast of Tabernacles was celebrated in the Book of Mormon; see Stephen D. Ricks and John W. Welch, *King Benjamin's Speech: "That Ye May Learn Wisdom"* (Provo, UT: Foundation for Ancient Research and Mormon Studies, 1998). The tithe was mentioned by Alma

in reference to Abraham and Melchizedek (Alma 13:15) and was again mentioned by the Savior when he shared Malachi's teachings (3 Nephi 24:8–10).

43. See 1 Nephi 4:2; 17:27; 19:10; Mosiah 7:19; Alma 29:12; 26:28; Helaman 8:11.
44. See Joshua 2:23–24; 10:8–12; 11:6.
45. See Alma 26:9; 27:4; 31:35; 32:24, 43; 33:14, 17; 21, 23; 34:17, 28, 30, 37, 39–40.
46. See Alma 19:16–17, 31; 22:23; 23:3, 6, 8, 13–16; 24:6; 25:6; 53:10. Sparks, *Ethnicity*, 264. On the comparative righteousness of the converted refugees in the Book of Mormon, see Todd M. Compton, "The Spirituality of the Outcast in the Book of Mormon," *Journal of Book of Mormon Studies* 2/1 (1993): 139–60.
47. For the Egyptian borrowing of *gēr* as *qar*, see James E. Hoch, *Semitic Words in Egyptian Texts of the New Kingdom and Third Intermediate Period* (Princeton: Princeton University Press, 1994), 295–96.
48. Glanville, *Adopting the Stranger*, 49–50.
49. See note 6 above; Albertz, "From Aliens to Proselytes," 57–58. On the other hand, the reflection of the Holiness Code in the actions of the Nephites might demonstrate that this section of the Mosaic law was actually a part of the brass plates. Further research into the *gēr* laws of the Holiness Code and Deuteronomic Framework relating to the treatment of refugees in the Book of Mormon is warranted and has been planned for a future study.

Persons with Disabilities

15

Disability and Social Justice in Ancient Israelite Culture

David M. Calabro

The ideal of compassion toward those with disabilities runs like a binding thread through the texts of the Old Testament, including the law of Moses, the sacred poetry of the Psalms, the wisdom literature of Job and Proverbs, and the recorded visions of Israel's prophets. These texts belong to a different cultural world from modern Western society; thus the conceptualization of disabilities that they embody may appear unfamiliar. Yet they also reveal a response to disabilities that resonates with modern Judeo-Christian values, including those of the restored gospel of Jesus Christ.

Some passages, however, may initially appear to stand in counterpoint to the compassionate ideal. Among these texts are the Lord's commandment regarding the priestly service at the altar, which restricts this activity to those without certain "defects" (Leviticus 21:17–23), and the account of David's conquest of Jerusalem, which mentions "the lame and the blind" in a way that is usually interpreted as negative (2 Samuel 5:8). However, in each case, a careful contextual analysis supports an interpretation in line with the compassionate ideal.

In what follows, I will discuss some aspects of the ancient Israelite cultural context that are important for an accurate understanding of the compassionate ideal enjoined in the Old Testament. Then I will briefly review some of the biblical texts that provide evidence of this ideal. Finally, I will discuss the two potentially problematic biblical passages mentioned above: Leviticus 21:17–23 and 2 Samuel 5:8. I will show that these two passages, contrary to what might appear from a casual reading, actually fit with the overall biblical ideal of social justice for those who have disabilities. I will conclude with some remarks suggesting how an accurate understanding of the Old Testament's consistent response to disabilities may contribute to our knowledge of ancient Israelite society.

Cultural and Social Context

People with disabilities made up a large component of ancient Israelite society, and the concept of disability was salient in the culture. The frequency of invasion, together with the lack of modern medical care, would mean that disabilities were common. Some biblical texts describe practices of ritual mutilation of enemies, including the gouging out of the right eye (1 Samuel 11:2) and the gouging out of both eyes (Judges 16:21; 2 Kings 25:7); the shaving of half of the beard (2 Samuel 10:4) is analogous, though not as permanent.[1] Punitive mutilation—including the cutting off of the hand (Deuteronomy 25:12), the removal of eyes or teeth (Leviticus 24:19–20), and the cutting out of the tongue (Proverbs 10:31)—was also practiced.[2]

The Hebrew language itself embodies a cultural view of disability as a set-apart category significant enough to warrant its own linguistic markers. The *qittil* noun pattern in Biblical Hebrew—that is, the class of nouns originally having two short *i*-vowels and a doubled middle root letter—is often described as a linguistic pattern for "bodily defects."³ In reality, the pattern applies to many nouns that are not strictly associated with disabilities, such as *gēʾē*, "proud"; *gibbēaḥ* and *qērēaḥ*, both meaning "bald"; *ʿiqqēš*, "twisted, perverted" (only in a moral sense); *piqqēaḥ*, "clear-sighted"; and *ṣiḥē*, "parched with thirst" (see table 1). The linguistic pattern could thus be more accurately described as a pattern for conditions that diverge from a stereotypical norm. Nevertheless, the prominence of disabilities in this category underscores the frequency and salience of disability in ancient Israelite society. The fact that thirst belongs to this category is especially illuminating since it suggests that such divergences were conceived of as temporary states rather than as eternal or defining characteristics of the self. In later Hebrew, more nouns are added to this category, and there is a trend toward narrowing the category to disabilities in a strict sense, a trend also seen in Arabic.⁴

Table 1. Examples of Biblical Hebrew *qittil* pattern in nouns denoting divergent conditions

Word	Translation	Biblical references
ʾiṭṭēr	undexterous (in the right hand; i.e. left-handed)	Judges 3:15; 20:16
ʾillēm	mute	Exodus 4:11; Psalm 38:14; Proverbs 31:8; Isaiah 35:6; 56:10; Habakkuk 2:18
gēʾē	proud	Job 40:11–12; Psalms 94:2; 123:4; 140:6; Proverbs 15:25; 16:19; Isaiah 2:12; Jeremiah 48:29
gibbēaḥ	bald	Leviticus 13:41
gibbēn	hunchbacked	Leviticus 21:20

ḥērēš	deaf	Exodus 4:11; Leviticus 19:14; Psalms 38:14; 58:5; Isaiah 29:18; 35:5; 42:18–19; 43:8
kēhē	dim (of eyesight)	Leviticus 13:6, 21, 26, 28, 39, 56; 1 Samuel 3:2; Isaiah 42:3; 61:3
ʿiwwēr	blind	Exodus 4:11; Leviticus 19:14; 21:18; Deuteronomy 15:21; 27:18; 28:29; 2 Samuel 5:6, 8; Job 29:15; Psalm 146:8; Isaiah 29:18; 35:5; 42:7, 16, 18–19; 43:8; 56:10; 59:10; Jeremiah 31:8; Lamentations 4:14; Zephaniah 1:17; Malachi 1:8
ʿiqqēš	twisted, perverted	Deuteronomy 32:5; 2 Samuel 22:27; Psalms 18:27; 101:4; Proverbs 2:15; 8:8; 11:20; 17:20; 19:1; 22:5; 28:6
pissēaḥ	lame	Leviticus 21:18; Deuteronomy 15:21; 2 Samuel 5:6, 8; 9:13; 19:27; Job 29:15; Proverbs 26:7; Isaiah 33:23; 35:6; Jeremiah 31:8; Lamentations 4:14; Malachi 1:8, 13
piqqēaḥ	clear-sighted	Exodus 4:11; 23:8
ṣiḥē	parched with thirst	Isaiah 5:13
qērēaḥ	bald	Leviticus 13:40; 2 Kings 2:23

Despite the prevalence of physical disabilities in ancient Israel, archaeological evidence suggests that technological or architectural adaptations for those with disabilities were few. Modern aids that we may take for granted, such as motorized mobility devices, automatic doors, corrective lenses, and hearing aids were, of course, absent from ancient Israelite life. Even aids that do not require modern technology—such as wheelchairs, wheeled carts, handrails, and permanent ramps—are not attested as aids used for people with disabilities in ancient Israel or its environs. The Bible mentions the use of a staff or crutch as an aid for mobility (2 Samuel 3:29 and Zechariah 8:4), but there is as yet no evidence for prosthetic limbs in ancient Israel; the concept, though, is attested in Egypt.[5] Indeed, accessibility must have been a significant challenge for people with disabilities living in urban environments, given the uneven stairways and flagstones typical of excavated sites. This set of observations is important in contextualizing the biblical injunctions to care for those who were disabled because it implies that such care was not taken up as an institutional responsibility, at least not in the architectural sphere, while technological adaptations were insufficient to minimize the need for such care. Therefore, if individual members of the community (including family members and others) neglected to extend aid, those with disabilities would have been subject to terrible hardship.[6]

Evidence of the Compassionate Ideal

The ideal of compassion toward those with disabilities runs consistently through diverse books and genres in the Old Testament, which suggests that this ideal was an important part of ancient Israelite culture. Representative passages include the following:[7]

> You shall not revile the deaf, nor put a stumbling block in front of the blind, but you shall fear your God. I am the Lord. (Leviticus 19:14)

> Cursed be the one who misleads a blind person on the road. (Deuteronomy 27:18)

> The king said, "Is there no one remaining of the house of Saul, to whom I may show God's kindness?" Ziba said to the king, "There remains a son of Jonathan; he is crippled in his feet." The king said to him, "Where is he?" Ziba said to the king, "He is in the house of Machir son of Ammiel, in Lo-debar." Then king David sent and brought him from the house of Machir son of Ammiel, from Lo-debar. So Mephibosheth son

of Jonathan son of Saul entered the presence of David and fell on his face, prostrating himself. David said, "Mephibosheth!" He answered, "Here I am, as your servant." David said to him, "Do not be afraid, for I will surely show you kindness for the sake of your father Jonathan. I will restore to you all the land of your grandfather Saul, and you shall eat bread at my table always." (2 Samuel 9:3–7)

I put on righteousness, and it clothed me. My justice was like a robe and a turban. I was eyes to the blind and feet to the lame. (Job 29:14–15)

He who does justice to the oppressed, who gives bread to the hungry. The Lord sets the prisoners free. The Lord opens (the eyes of) the blind. The Lord lifts up those who are bowed down; the Lord loves the righteous. (Psalm 146:7–8)

Open your mouth for the dumb, for the rights of all the destitute. Open your mouth, judge righteously, defend the rights of the poor and needy. (Proverbs 31:8–9)

These passages represent a great diversity of contexts. Leviticus 19 sets forth laws for ritual and moral holiness. Deuteronomy 27:18 gives one of a series of curses the Levites are to utter as the people pass over the Jordan River to possess the promised land (Deuteronomy 27:14–26). Second Samuel 9 narrates a righteous deed David performed for the son of his deceased best friend. In Job 29, Job is recounting his righteous acts of social justice in poetic form. Psalm 146 praises the Lord for his righteous deeds. And Proverbs 31 consists of "the sayings of king Lemuel," taught to him by his mother, recommending advocacy for those who cannot speak for themselves as a general principle. Thus the compassionate ideal is not just a literary motif associated with a particular genre. Instead, it is situated in the religious culture that lies behind all these texts.

In these passages, there is an implied connection between the Lord's compassion and that expected of his people. The laws, including Leviticus 19:14, begin with the injunction, "You shall be holy: for I, the Lord your God, am holy" (Leviticus 19:2). Psalm 146:7–8 describes the Lord as the model of goodwill toward the disadvantaged, including those with disabilities (here specifically toward people who are blind). Many prophetic texts describe a culmination of the Lord's mercy in healing disabilities during a paradisiacal future time. Perhaps the clearest of these prophetic texts is in the book of Isaiah:

> Strengthen the weak hands, steady the feeble knees. Say to the fainthearted, "Be strong! Do not fear! Your God will come with vengeance, God (will come) with a recompence. He will come and save you." Then the eyes of the blind will be opened and the ears of the deaf unstopped. Then the lame will leap like a deer, and the tongue of the dumb will sing. For water will gush forth in the desert, and torrents in the desolate land. (Isaiah 35:3–6)

Texts in a similar vein include Isaiah 29:17–19; Jeremiah 31:7–9; Micah 4:6–7; Zephaniah 3:18–20.[8]

Leviticus 21:17–23: Restricted Work

In Leviticus 21, the Lord restricts some classes of priests with "defects" from approaching the altar to perform the priestly service:

> Speak to Aaron and say: No one of your descendants, for all generations, if he has a defect, shall approach to offer the food of his God. For any man who has a defect shall not approach: a man blind, lame, pierced, or deformed; a man having a broken foot or a broken hand; hunchbacked, a dwarf, one having an eye defect, having a rash, having running sores, or having crushed testicles. No man who has a defect from the descendants of Aaron the priest shall draw near to offer the Lord's sacrifices made by fire. As he has a defect, he shall not draw

near to offer the food of his God. Of the food of his God, both of the most holy and of the holy, he shall eat. But he shall not enter to the veil, nor approach the altar, for he has a defect, that he may not profane my sanctuaries; for I am the Lord who sanctifies them. (Leviticus 21:17–23)

Some interpreters understand this passage as a stigmatization of people with disabilities. According to Saul Olyan, "the priest or potential high priest of Leviticus 21 who has a 'defect' is stigmatized in the sense that his potential to profane the sanctuary's holiness is greater than that of his fellows who lack 'defects,' and an ever-present threat; he is both stigmatized and marginalized in that he is cut off from the most highly esteemed ritual activity normally open to him."[9] Olyan treats this passage as one of a range of biblical texts exhibiting a "marginalizing and stigmatizing discourse" with regard to disabled people. At one extreme is the saying in 2 Samuel 5:8b, which appears to exclude people that are blind or lame from the temple altogether (see further below), while at the more positive extreme is the promise of temple participation to eunuchs in Isaiah 56:3–5 (which Olyan interprets as a critical response to the exclusion of people with genital injuries in Deuteronomy 23:1).[10] Leviticus 21:17–23, according to Olyan, lies between these two extremes, since it permits priests with "defects" to eat the food from sacrifices on sacred space,[11] yet it excludes them from the honor of priestly service.

However, the interpretation of Leviticus 21:17–23 as a stigmatizing text seems at odds with the concept of the Lord as a champion of those with disabilities (as found, for example, in Psalm 146:7–8). The text is not merely a statement of policy, but scripture communicating the word of the Lord; the passage concludes with the declaration, "for I am the Lord who sanctifies them."[12] Of course, it is possible for biblical texts to present different theological viewpoints. Yet even elsewhere within the priestly laws of Leviticus, a compassionate attitude toward those with disabilities is attributed to God. Indeed, the injunction not to revile the deaf or place a stumbling block in front of the blind (Leviticus 19:14) concludes with a declaration similar to that in Leviticus 21:23: "I am the Lord."

An important issue in Leviticus 21:17–23 is that of deciding what the law was intended to guard against. Olyan's interpretation assumes that a priest would want to participate in the offering of sacrifice because this was "the most highly esteemed ritual activity normally open to him." Even with the law in place, a priest with disabilities might "flout the restrictions imposed on his service" and perform the service at the altar anyway, presumably because of the esteem associated with this role. Should he do so, "his actions would result in profanation of the sanctuary."[13] Thus, according to Olyan, the law restricted priests with disabilities from endangering the sanctuary, which their desire to perform the altar service might otherwise lead them to do.

I would suggest an alternative interpretation of the regulation in Leviticus 21:17–23. In this interpretation, what the law guarded against was the coercion of priests with disabilities to perform the service at the altar in order to earn the sacrificial food, or even while being denied the food. The purpose of the commandment in Leviticus 21:17–23 could have been to guarantee that priests with disabilities were exempt from the altar service and were entitled to sustenance from the sacrifices. This interpretation assumes that it was the privilege of eating the sacrificial food and not the service at the altar that was the more highly esteemed prerogative of priests. This interpretation would be in keeping with the compassionate portrayal of the Lord here in the priestly laws and in other biblical passages.

Neither of the interpretations of this passage can be proven with certainty. However, I will endeavor to show that this latter interpretation is as much a possibility as the other. Five considerations help to establish that this is the case. First, one may question the assumption that the altar service was the most highly esteemed priestly activity. It is doubtful that this service was more highly esteemed than participation in the ritual meal in which the priests would share the Lord's food, an activity that is explicitly permitted for priests with disabilities in Leviticus 21:22.[14] The terms used to describe the food in this verse, "most holy" and "holy," underscore the sacred significance of the meal. Other passages indicate that eating this food would occur beside the altar "in the holy place" (Leviticus 6:16, 26; 7:6; 10:12–13; 24:9) or, in the case of priestly initiation, at the door of the tabernacle (Exodus 29:32; Leviticus 8:31). The priests with disabilities mentioned in Leviticus 21 would therefore be in the same sacred spaces as the priests serving at the altar.

The narrative of Hannah, Samuel, and Eli in 1 Samuel 1–2 repeatedly shows that the sacrificial food was associated with prestige. According to this narrative, Elkanah honored his wife Hannah by giving her a double portion of the sacrificial meat (1 Samuel 1:5).[15] The greed of Eli's sons Hophni and Phinehas in taking the meat from others led to a divine accusation that Eli and his sons were fattening themselves with the chief parts of the offerings (1 Samuel 2:29). Eli was also told that his descendants would beg Samuel to appoint them to a priestly office so that they might "eat a piece of bread" (1 Samuel 2:36), implying that at least some people viewed priestly service as the work required for the privilege of eating the sacrificial food. Indeed, the service at the altar was hard and messy work, as I will explain below, not the kind of work that would normally be desirable.

Second, not all types of disabilities disqualified a priest from the service at the altar, which casts doubt on the idea that stigmatization is a primary purpose here. For instance, while those who are blind are excluded, those who are deaf and mute are not. A great deal of discussion has centered on the interpretation of the terms for the types of "defects" (*mûm*) in this and other related passages and on the rationale governing what does and does not count as a "defect." A number of these terms are rare and have been subject to different translations. The category of "defect" has also been characterized in a number of ways, such as having to do with visible damage, asymmetry, ugliness, or impurity.[16]

Despite the uncertain meaning of some of the terms, most of these "defects" would likely present practical problems with performing the priestly service. From the description of sacrificial procedures in Leviticus 1–7, it is evident that the service at the altar was labor-intensive, involving the slaughtering of animals, cutting and preparing of the parts, executing complicated food preparations, tending the fire of the altar, moving frequently between the altar and the laver to wash hands and feet, and doing other tasks around the temple court. Some of the "defects," including blindness, lameness, deformation, and having a broken foot or hand, would render the service physically difficult or even impossible.[17] Other "defects," such as being pierced or having crushed testicles, may be associated with ritual mutilation that would occur with captives, which would incur social stigma independent of the exclusion from temple service.[18] Under these circumstances, being required to perform the highly visible role of attendance at the altar would put the person with the disability in a difficult position physically or socially. Thus one can read the directive in Leviticus 21:17–23 as a provision for those whose condition would make temple service especially problematic. In the case of those mutilated as captives, the directive would be comparable to David temporarily relieving from service the men whose beards were partially shaved and whose garments were cut halfway by the king of the Ammonites (2 Samuel 10:4–5).

Third, Olyan compares Leviticus 21:17–23 with Leviticus 22:18–25, which gives a list of defects that render an animal unfit for a sacrificial offering.[19] The word for *defect* (*mûm*) in both texts is the same, and some of the specific "defects" are also the same. This comparison initially seems to support the idea that Leviticus 21:17–23 is based on stigma associated with bodily "defects," but the comparison ultimately fails to support this idea. According to Leviticus 22:23, one can give a bull or a sheep that is deformed or stunted as a freewill offering but not in fulfillment of a vow. The word for *deformed* here is also found in the list of "defects" excluding priests from altar service in Leviticus 21:18. Since freewill offerings were offered by fire on the altar like other offerings (Leviticus 22:18; Numbers 15:3), this exception challenges the notion that stigma is the core issue. Did deformity somehow incur less stigma than other "defects," and if so, why would a similar exception not apply in the case of a priest with a deformity or in the case of the fulfillment of a vow? A more suitable explanation is that the regulation is meant to "ensure that families did not donate animals (for sacrifice) . . . that they could not use for themselves"[20] and that the exception (perhaps an arbitrary one) is granted in order to make the regulation more feasible or to lessen its impact.

Fourth, an interpretive crux in this passage is the purpose clause in verse 23, "that he may not profane my sanctuaries" (wĕ-lōʾ yĕḥallēl ʾet-miqdāšay). According to Olyan, this clause shows the perceived threat posed by priests with disabilities, whose "actions would result in profanation of the sanctuary, meaning the loss of its holiness, the divine quality par excellence and essential to the sanctuary's continued operation."[21] However, the clause can be interpreted differently. One uncertain aspect of this clause is its grammatical relationship to the preceding clauses. It could legitimately be translated as "and he shall not profane my sanctuaries," meaning that in addition to not performing the altar service, these priests are not to engage in any of the activities that would profane the sanctuary, as described elsewhere in the priestly code. Thus, in this interpretation, the exemption from the altar service is not to be construed as a release from other priestly obligations.

Another uncertain aspect of the passage is the meaning of the phrase "profane my sanctuaries." It is important to note that the issue here is not one of impurity. The priestly laws in Leviticus distinguish carefully between the opposition of holy and profane on the one hand and the opposition of clean and unclean on the other.[22] Uncleanness or pollution was transmitted through contact. Leviticus 7:21 indicates that in cases of personal uncleanness, eating of the sacrificial food was forbidden on penalty of death; such a situation does not seem to be at issue in Leviticus 21:17–23, which permits the consumption of the holy food and mentions no penalty. Further, contact itself does not seem to be at issue. If it were, permitting the priests to eat the sacrificial food in the holy places would jeopardize the sanctuary.[23] What is at issue is specifically the work of serving at the altar (Leviticus 21:17, 18, 21, 23).

An instructive comparison may be made between the purpose clause in verse 23 and the warning against profaning the Sabbath by performing work on that day, as expressed, for example, in Exodus 31:

> You shall keep my Sabbaths, for it is a sign between me and you, for all generations, that you may know that I am the Lord who sanctifies you. You shall keep the Sabbath, because it is holy to you. The one who profanes it must be put to death, for any one who performs work on it, that soul shall be cut off from among his people. (Exodus 31:13–14)

Here the phrase "the one who profanes it" is used to translate the Hebrew word *měḥalĕlêhā*, a participle of the same verb used in Leviticus 21:23 (where the verb appears in the imperfect: *yĕḥallēl*).[24] Just as performing work on the Sabbath would profane the Sabbath, performing the priestly service while in a state of disability would profane the sanctuary. Also note here that the prohibition is accompanied by the declaration "I am the Lord who sanctifies you," similar to "I am the Lord who sanctifies them" in Leviticus 21:23.[25]

The root meaning of the verb *ḥillēl*, "to profane," is "to untie, loosen."[26] To profane something holy is to loosen something that God has bound. This root meaning is appropriate both in Exodus 31:14 and in Leviticus 21:23. The verb *to profane* in the case of Leviticus 21:23 may have to do not with rendering the sanctuary itself unholy (just as one cannot render the Sabbath unholy by transgressing it) but rather with the loosening of a divinely ordained social order. The social order in both cases is one in which people are mercifully exempted from labor—during sacred time (the Sabbath) in the case of Exodus 31 and on sacred space (the sanctuary) in the case of Leviticus 21.[27] Since God's sanctuary is a house of order (Doctrine and Covenants 88:119), he can justifiably refer to the order he has established as identical to his "sanctuaries."

Fifth and finally, although the fact that the law in Leviticus 21:17–23 is framed as a commandment may support the idea that the text has a stigmatizing purpose, this fact could also make sense if the text is interpreted as an exemption from labor. We see elsewhere that God mandates mercy, as shown in the law of the Sabbath (Exodus 31:13–14), the commandments regarding the collection of manna during the wanderings of the children of Israel in the wilderness (Exodus 16:15–30), and the injunction to help an enemy (Exodus 23:4–5). Once again, a comparison with the law of the Sabbath is particularly instructive. Like the law in Leviticus 21:17–23, the law of the Sabbath grants exemption from labor.[28] Yet the law of the Sabbath is framed as a commandment with the severest possible penalty, death (Exodus 31:14). We may not fully understand the reasons for this strict formulation. However, from the standpoint of social dynamics, it is worth noting that exemptions from labor are fragile. If one person chooses to labor, it becomes harder for others to continue to enjoy the exemption.[29] Thus one purpose of the commandments in Exodus 31 and Leviticus 21 may be to safeguard the divinely established social order of mercy.

2 Samuel 5:8: David's Attitude toward People Who Are Lame and Blind

As it is rendered in most translations, 2 Samuel 5:8 seems to report an instruction given by David to his soldiers to slay people who are lame or blind in the Israelites' conquest of the city of Jerusalem. Here, according to these translations, David says that his soul hates those who are lame and those who are blind. The verse is also significant because of what appears to be a popular saying, preserved at the end of the verse, that those who are blind or lame may not enter "the house"—usually interpreted as the temple.

This verse presents a number of interpretive difficulties, which arise from both the apparent textual corruption of the verse and its convoluted grammar. The following sampling of a few prominent English Bible translations illustrates the variation arising from different attempts to reconcile the difficulties in this verse:

> And David said on that day, Whosoever getteth up to the gutter, and smiteth the Jebusites, and the lame and the blind, *that are* hated of David's soul, *he shall be chief and captain.* Wherefore they said, The blind and the lame shall not come into the house. (KJV; italicized words in original)

> David had said on that day, "Whoever would strike down the Jebusites, let him get up the water shaft to attack the lame and the blind, those whom David hates." Therefore it is said, "The blind and the lame shall not come into the house." (NRSV, similar to NIV)

> That day, David said, "Whoever gets up the tunnel and kills a Jebusite . . ." As for the blind and the lame, David hated them with his whole being. (Hence the saying: the blind and the lame may not enter the Temple.) (New Jerusalem Bible)

The principal difficulty here is that the verse seems to contain one or more incomplete sentences.[30] Rendered woodenly, David's speech in the vocalized Masoretic Hebrew text reads as follows: "Whoever slays a Jebusite, and he will reach (or *that he might reach*) the water shaft, and the lame and the blind, those hated by David's soul." The King James Version inserts a whole clause to resolve the incomplete grammar: *"he shall be chief and captain"* (the italics indicate that the words are supplied by the King James translators; the clause is added based on the parallel verse in 1 Chronicles 11:6—which is, however, different enough that the insertion is unjustified). The New Jerusalem Bible similarly assumes an unexpressed predicate, signaled by an ellipsis. The NRSV tries to resolve the difficulty by inserting an extra verb, *attack*, to go with the direct object *the lame and the blind*.

From an exegetical standpoint, all of these interpretations are problematic because they conflict with the portrayal of David elsewhere in 2 Samuel. No other passages portray David as bearing any particular hatred toward either people with disabilities or Jebusites. On the contrary, he provides generously for his friend's lame son Mephibosheth (2 Samuel 9:3–7), and David engages in a friendly transaction with Araunah the Jebusite (2 Samuel 24:20–25).

The difficulties with this verse may be resolved by taking David's speech as a single sentence, with the final phrase governing what precedes. This final phrase presents its own complexities because of textual variation. The received consonantal text can be translated as either "they hate David's soul" or "David hates him with (his) whole being."[31] This was changed in the vocalized Masoretic text to "those hated by David's soul." Another reading is found in the Dead Sea Scrolls manuscript 4QSam^a: "David's soul hates." Adopting the reading of 4QSam^a, David's entire speech can be rendered without difficulty as follows:

> David's soul hates anyone who slays a Jebusite that he might reach the water shaft, or (who slays) the lame or the blind.

In terms of the overall syntax, the speech would then be very similar to Psalm 11:5 and Isaiah 1:14, both of which also refer to the Lord's soul hating something, with the complex direct object coming first in the sentence, followed by the verb and the subject. In this interpretation, the direct objects *the lame* and *the blind* go with the participle *who slays*.

A similar interpretation could be applied to the Masoretic Hebrew text (with a slight change to the vowels of the last verb), although this interpretation is somewhat messier:

> Whoever slays a Jebusite that he might reach the water shaft, or (who slays) the lame or the blind, David hates him with (his) whole being.

This interpretation of David's speech makes it consistent with other indications of David's attitude toward his enemies and toward those with disabilities. David repeatedly becomes angry at those who slay his enemies unrighteously (2 Samuel 3:27–39; 4:5–12). And we have already discussed David's compassion toward Mephibosheth, the lame son of David's friend Jonathan (2 Samuel 9:3–7).[32]

The last part of the verse seems, at first glance, to report a general saying that excludes those who are lame or blind from entering sacred space. The NRSV, for instance, translates this last part of the verse thus: "Therefore it is said, 'The blind and the lame shall not come into the house.'" Most translations are similar, including the ancient Greek version known as the Septuagint, which even specifies that it is "the house of the Lord" (*oikon kyriou*) that those who are lame or blind are not to enter.

Yet the interpretation of this last part of the verse is also ambiguous. In fact, rather than construing the complex subject *the lame and the blind* to relate to the singular verb *he shall enter* (*yābôʾ*), it makes better grammatical sense to construe the complex subject with the plural speech verb:[33]

> Therefore the blind and the lame kept saying, "He shall not enter the house."

In this interpretation, 2 Samuel 5:8 aligns with the statement by the Jebusites just two verses earlier that David "shall not enter here" and that the blind and the lame could repel him (2 Samuel 5:6).

That "the house" here refers to the temple is not certain. When David conquered Jerusalem, the temple on Mount Moriah had not yet been constructed. The NIV renders this word as "the palace," an interpretation explicitly argued by biblical scholars such as Vargon, Schipper, and others.[34] This last part of the verse could thus be understood as reporting that those who were lame or blind among the Jebusite defenders, when they heard of David's resolve not to kill any of them, decided to use this to their advantage in order to protect the palace area from David's men.

In summary, the entirety of 2 Samuel 5:8 could be translated as follows:

> David's soul hates anyone who slays a Jebusite that he might reach the water shaft, or (who slays) the lame or the blind. Therefore the blind and the lame kept saying, "He shall not enter the house."

This translation is in accordance with the earliest attested reading, namely that of 4QSam^a, which I believe to be closest to the original.

The interpretation argued above for 2 Samuel 5:8 resolves the grammatical and exegetical difficulties inherent in most other interpretations. It is therefore appropriate to read this verse in a way that is consistent with the ideal of compassion toward those with disabilities, as attested elsewhere in David's career. With this interpretation, we can see that the two passages, 2 Samuel 5:8 and 2 Samuel 9:3–7, present the cultural hero David as a role model of the compassionate ideal.

Conclusion: Compassion as a Cultural Value

This study has not reviewed all the biblical texts that have to do with disabilities and attitudes toward those with disabilities. The analysis shows, however, that the ideal of compassion toward those with disabilities is a strong theme that runs throughout the Old Testament. Some passages which may initially seem to support a contrary, purposely stigmatizing attitude can be shown to align with the charitable ideal or at least to permit such an interpretation. The picture that emerges from this investigation is one of consistency, with biblical passages showing a single cultural value of compassion toward those with disabilities during all periods of ancient Israelite history. This differs from the picture offered by some modern studies, such as that of Olyan, which portray an ancient Israelite world having diverse cultural values.

It is interesting that the only institutional response to disability evident in the various passages discussed above is to legislate protection of those with disabilities from physical harm or denigration by other people. The laws in Leviticus 19:14 and Deuteronomy 27:18 are framed as negative commandments, forbidding one to hinder or curse the disabled. Likewise, Leviticus 21:17–23 mandates that people with "defects," including some classes of people with disabilities, shall not serve at the altar (thus protecting them from physical and social straits). One modern scholar claims that this passage in Leviticus 21 provides "a sort of social security in the case of later acquired impairment."[35] However, this provision does not extend beyond the allotment available to priests in general. No proactive legislation on an institutional level, such as a mandate for inclusive employment or for buildings to be accessible, is evident in the Bible. Instead, the biblical text promotes the responsibility to care for those with disabilities as a personal religious expectation—not legislated, but inculcated as a cultural value. This teaching includes the frequent portrayal of God as the model champion of the rights of those who have disabilities, as we see in Leviticus 21:17–23, among other passages. It also includes the association of the popular hero David with compassion toward those with disabilities, as we see in 2 Samuel 5:8 and 2 Samuel 9:3–7.

On the basis of these conclusions, it is possible to suggest some thoughts concerning the wider implications of the cultural ideal that prevailed in ancient Israel. First, from the standpoint of those with disabilities, the emphasis on personal responsibility to provide care no doubt required grace in accepting help from others, as well as some degree of physical hardship and even risk of not having basic needs met. Those with disabilities could not expect institutional aid as a right, other than priests receiving their portion of the sacrificial food to eat in the sacred precincts. Many biblical texts classify those with disabilities along with other people who are disadvantaged, especially those who are poor. Those with disabilities, like those who are poor, would likely have to beg for assistance from their peers, unless they had close friends or family who would give them consistent help (Leviticus 19:14–15; Isaiah 29:17–29; Proverbs 31:8–9).

Second, these findings in the Old Testament may permit a reinterpretation of the overall history of attitudes toward disabilities in the Jewish and early Christian traditions. The compassionate ideal found in the Old Testament reverberates in other ancient scripture, such as the story of the individual with paralysis who was carried by his friends in Mark 2:3–12, the numerous New Testament stories of Jesus healing people with infirmities, and the healing of the multitudes in 3 Nephi 17:6–10. We can therefore discern hints of a *longue durée* history of this ideal beyond ancient Israel. We see this ideal also surviving in modern communities of faith, including in The Church of Jesus Christ of Latter-day Saints.[36] As with so many other religious values, ancient and modern covenant Israel share a common heritage.

David M. Calabro is the curator of Eastern Christian manuscripts at the Hill Museum and Manuscript Library at Saint John's University.

Notes

1. The treatment of slain enemies is similar, including the removal of the foreskin (1 Samuel 18:25, 27), decapitation (1 Samuel 17:51, 54; 31:8–13; 2 Kings 10:7), and the severing of the hands and feet (2 Samuel 4:12).
2. Saul M. Olyan, *Disability in the Hebrew Bible: Interpreting Mental and Physical Disabilities* (Cambridge: Cambridge University Press, 2008), 38–45.
3. Joshua Fox, *Semitic Noun Patterns* (Winona Lake, IN: Eisenbrauns, 2003), 264–65. Fox derives the pattern ultimately from *qattil.
4. Postbiblical Hebrew nouns belonging to this category include *qiṭṭēaʿ*, "missing a hand or foot"; *giddēm*, "missing a hand"; *ṣimmēm*, "with misshapen ears"; *ṣimmēaʿ*, "with misshapen ears"; *ʿiqqēl*, "clubfooted"; and *ḥiggēr*, "limping." Also significant in this connection is the Hebrew *qattal-t pattern for diseases and blemishes, showing that there was a semantic separation made between bodily divergences/disabilities and diseases/blemishes: *qaddaḥat*, "fever"; *yallepet*, "scab"; *sappaḥat*, "scab"; *baheret*, "white patch of skin"; and *ṣāraʿat*, "skin disease." See Fox, *Semitic Noun Patterns*, 234. In Arabic, the pattern for bodily divergences is *ʾaqtal (fem.

*qatlāʾ, pl. *qutl), the same pattern used for colors. As in Hebrew, a distinction is made between these divergences and diseases, which use a different pattern (*qutāl).

5. For the evidence of the use of prosthetics in ancient Egypt, see Jacqueline Finch, "The Ancient Origins of Prosthetic Medicine," *Lancet* 377 (2011): 548–49.
6. By way of comparison, a moral obligation to care for people with disabilities in one's own family is evident in ancient Egypt, but there we also find evidence of palace-supported care for workers with disabilities. See Rosalie David, "Egyptian Medicine and Disabilities: From Pharaonic to Greco-Roman Egypt," in *Disability in Antiquity*, ed. Christian Laes (New York: Routledge, 2017), 82–83.
7. In order to represent my understanding of the terms for disabilities as accurately as possible, I use my own translations of biblical passages except where otherwise indicated.
8. Olyan, *Disability in the Hebrew Bible*, 78–92, sees all of these texts as reinforcing the stigmatization of disabled people in various ways. Many of his claims in this regard are unwarranted. For instance, the promise of a future in which disabilities will be healed is a message of hope and does not necessarily imply that disabled people "have no place in a model world," nor do I see any implication that "disabled persons require Yhwh's special intervention to mitigate the marginalizing effects of their disabilities, thus allowing their inclusion." It is true that disabled people in these prophetic passages "function, to a large degree, as vehicles for the display of Yhwh's agency," but this is only because the texts are not primarily about disabilities, but about the Lord's future works.
9. Olyan, *Disability in the Hebrew Bible*, 31.
10. Olyan, *Disability in the Hebrew Bible*, 27–36.
11. In the context of priestly initiation, the priest would eat the food "at the door of the tabernacle of the congregation" (Exodus 29:32; Leviticus 8:31); in other cases, the appropriate location was in the court of the tabernacle, where the altar was located (Leviticus 6:16, 26).
12. The pre-1978 policy restricting Black members of The Church of Jesus Christ of Latter-day Saints from ordination to the priesthood may be cited

as an example of the significant distinction between policy and scripture. The only scripture directly related to this policy is Official Declaration 2 at the end of the Doctrine and Covenants, which revokes the policy and explicitly permits ordination to the priesthood "without regard for race or color."

13. Olyan, *Disability in the Hebrew Bible*, 31.
14. On the ritual meal, see David Calabro, "The Lord of Hosts and His Guests: Hospitality on Sacred Space in Exodus 29 and 1 Samuel 1," *Proceedings of the Eastern Great Lakes and Midwest Biblical Societies* 27 (2007): 19–29.
15. The King James Version states that Elkanah gave Hannah "a worthy portion," but the Hebrew here means "a double portion" (as rendered in the NIV and the NRSV).
16. Olyan, *Disability in the Hebrew Bible*, 29–31; Rebecca Raphael, *Biblical Corpora: Representations of Disability in Hebrew Biblical Literature* (New York: T&T Clark, 2008), 34–39.
17. Being deaf or mute would not have presented a major problem for most aspects of temple service. This perhaps coincided with an avoidance of loud voices by humans on sacred space. Zacharias's performance of the duties of high priest was therefore permissible, even after he was rendered mute by an angel (Luke 1:8–22).
18. The idea that some of these "defects" are associated with captivity is supported by a text from the Dead Sea Scrolls, 4Q266, which mentions "captivity among the Gentiles" as a factor that disqualifies a descendant of Aaron from priestly service. See Jacob Milgrom, *Leviticus 17–22: A New Translation with Introduction and Commentary* (New York: Doubleday, 2000), 1829.
19. Olyan, *Disability in the Hebrew Bible*, 30–31. Milgrom, *Leviticus 17–22*, 1821–22, 1825–28, 1836–40, pursues the connection between these two passages in depth.
20. Edgar Kellenberger, "Mesopotamia and Israel," in Laes, *Disability in Antiquity*, 49.
21. Olyan, *Disability in the Hebrew Bible*, 31.
22. For a thorough treatment of this distinction in Leviticus 21, see Milgrom, *Leviticus 17–22*, 1831–32.

23. See the similar statement by Milgrom, *Leviticus 17–22*, 1825.
24. Other passages referring to "profaning" the Sabbath using this same Hebrew verb include Ezekiel 22:8; 23:38; Nehemiah 13:17.
25. This declaration is common in passages having to do with the law of the Sabbath. See also Leviticus 19:3; 30; 26:2; Ezekiel 20:12, 20.
26. Francis Brown, S. R. Driver, and Charles A. Briggs, *A Hebrew and English Lexicon of the Old Testament* (Oxford: Clarendon Press, 1939), 320.
27. Other passages also draw a parallel between the Sabbath and the sanctuary, including Leviticus 19:30; 26:2; Ezekiel 23:38.
28. The Sabbath day, like other sabbatical periods of time such as the release of debts on the sabbatical year and the release of Israelite slaves on the Jubilee year, is a sign of the Lord's mercy to his people in freeing them from oppression—it is a day on which nobody can be forced to labor. Thus Deuteronomy 5:12–15 enjoins Sabbath observance in memory of the deliverance from Egypt: "And remember that you were a servant in the land of Egypt, and that the Lord your God brought you out from there with a mighty hand and an outstretched arm."
29. A personal anecdote may help to illustrate this principle. When my daughter Esther was born, I became eligible for several weeks of paternity leave. Although I was tempted to forego some of the leave, my supervisor insisted that I take all the leave for which I was eligible; to do otherwise, he said, would be to jeopardize the benefit that others had fought to obtain.
30. Jeremy Schipper, "Reconsidering the Imagery of Disability in 2 Samuel 5:8b," *Catholic Biblical Quarterly* 67 (2005): 426–27n13, ably describes the grammatical difficulties in this verse, but he does not consider the solution proposed here (see below).
31. Compare Isaiah 26:9: "With my whole being (lit. 'my soul') I have desired you in the night." In both cases, the noun *soul*, without a preposition, is understood in an adverbial sense.
32. S. R. Driver reports an interpretation by Budde along the same lines, resulting in the following translation: "Whoso smiteth a Jebusite, toucheth his own neck (i.e. brings his own life into danger); the lame and the blind David's soul hateth not." However, this interpretation involves extensive conjectural emendation of the Hebrew text. Driver concludes

that "[Budde's] conjecture is clever . . . and it attributes to David a fine and chivalrous thought; but it is too bold to command acceptance." See S. R. Driver, *Notes on the Hebrew Text and the Topography of the Books of Samuel*, rev. 2nd ed. (Oxford: Clarendon Press, 1913), 261.

33. See E. Kautzsch, ed., *Gesenius's Hebrew Grammar*, trans. A. E. Cowley (New York: Dover, 2006), 468, §146d–f.
34. Shmuel Vargon, "The Blind and the Lame," *Vetus Testamentum* 46 (1996): 499–500; Schipper, "Reconsidering the Imagery of Disability," 422–23n2.
35. Kellenberger, "Mesopotamia and Israel," 49.
36. "Disabilities," Gospel Topics, https://churchofjesuschrist.org/study/manual/gospel-topics/disability.

16

"Open Thou Mine Eyes"
Blindness and the Blind in the Old Testament

Richard O. Cowan

Participating in this fiftieth anniversary Sperry Symposium is a definite privilege for me. Perhaps I am the only presenter during this jubilee year who actually had the privilege to be a faculty colleague of Dr. Sidney B. Sperry. I first met him when as a youth I attended a series of lectures he gave in Southern California on "Our Book of Mormon." He impressed me with his organized scholarship, his in-depth but easy-to-understand presentation, and his faith in the restored gospel of Jesus Christ. Then, when I joined the BYU faculty at age twenty-seven, Brother Sperry became a valued mentor who treated me, a very junior colleague, with genuine interest and kindness. He always seemed to have time to answer my questions and provide direction.

I remember the first Sperry Symposium that took place on a single evening with only three presenters. A few years later, this event moved to Saturday mornings in the old Joseph Smith Building auditorium. I first presented in 1977 and have been honored to participate numerous times since then. This year's focus on Old Testament teachings about compassion for marginalized and disadvantaged groups has special interest in today's society and to me personally, because I am blind.

An awareness of how our modern society views groups with disabilities can bring the Old Testament's teachings on the subject into sharper focus. While earlier generations were comfortable using terms such as *blind*, today they may seem too blunt or harsh, so softer terms such as *visually impaired* have become more popular. Similarly, *handicapped* has more commonly been replaced with the more euphemistic terms *disabled*, *persons with disability*, or *persons with special needs*. The Old Testament, however, does not employ euphemisms but rather is direct and even blunt. *Blind* is consistently used to refer to those without physical sight. Meghan Henning, an associate professor at the University of Dayton, points out that "there is no term for disability among the cultures that produced the biblical text." "Rather," she insists, "there were standards of bodily normativity." Persons whose bodies were considered "nonnormative" were regarded not only as different but as deficient and defective, so they "were excluded religiously and socially."[1]

In the Old Testament the term *blind* may refer to the literal loss of sight or to a more metaphorical inability or unwillingness to see spiritually. This presentation focuses on the Old Testament's teachings concerning the blind—including the causes of physical or spiritual blindness, the image of those who are blind, how they should be treated, and the hope for overcoming blindness.

Causes of Physical and Spiritual Blindness

Physical blindness was a widespread challenge in the ancient Near East, and the Old Testament suggests some possible causes—natural, human, and divine. Three examples of people with poor eyesight are familiar. Isaac, Jacob or Israel, and Eli readily come to mind. In all three of these cases, their blindness was described as resulting from natural causes, their sight being "dim" as a consequence of advancing age (see Genesis 27:1; 48:10; and 1 Samuel 3:2; 4:15). Disease was another widespread natural cause of blindness in the ancient world, but it is not specifically reflected in Old Testament teachings. One might ask, though—wasn't the ban on eating pork instituted to eliminate a potential cause of blindness? Writing in the *Encyclopaedia Judaica*, Rabbi Jeffrey Howard Tigay rejected this hypothesis: "There is no evidence that the biblical injunction against eating pork was intended or understood to prevent trichinosis or other diseases which cause blindness."[2]

There were also examples, fortunately few, of individuals who were blinded by their enemies—a not uncommon practice in the ancient Near East. After Delilah caused Sampson to have his hair cut, which resulted in him losing his power, the Philistines "put out his eyes" and bound him (Judges 16:15–21). After the army of Nebuchadnezzar, king of Babylonia, had conquered the kingdom of Judah, they "put out the eyes of Zedekiah" (2 Kings 25:7). The law of Moses itself seems to have condoned even the Lord's people inflicting this harsh punishment: "eye for eye" (Exodus 21:24; Leviticus 24:20; Deuteronomy 19:21). Although this penalty is found in the Torah, Rabbi Tigay questions whether this extreme penalty "was ever carried out literally in Israel."[3]

Divine power is the most common cause of blindness mentioned in the scriptures. The Old Testament acknowledges God as the creator of all things, including people in widely different circumstances. The Lord taught Moses: "Who hath made man's mouth? Or who maketh the dumb, or deaf, or the seeing, or the blind? have not I the Lord?" (Exodus 4:11). One can only speculate about why Jehovah would create certain individuals to be blind, for the Old Testament does not give any definitive answers. Two events in the Old Testament underscored God's power over vision. The record in Genesis includes an interesting account of blindness being inflicted by divine power on a specific occasion to achieve a specific end. When an angry mob from

Sodom surrounded Lot's house and demanded that he surrender two "angels" who were inside, these angelic visitors "smote [members of the mob] with blindness" in such a way that "they wearied themselves to find the door" (see Genesis 19:1–11). The record does not state whether this blindness was permanent or was subsequently removed. Much later, at the time of the prophet Elisha, divine power over sight was again demonstrated in an unusual way. When the Syrians had surrounded the city of Dothan, Elisha asked the Lord to spiritually open the eyes of his servant, enabling him to behold supernatural "horses and chariots of fire" and to realize that "they that be with us are more than they that be with them." Then, at Elisha's request, the Lord blinded and later opened the eyes of the Syrians so that Elisha could lead them away to another place (see 2 Kings 6:8–23).

Two experiences in the New Testament possibly exhibited a similar phenomenon. When a mob seized Jesus and threatened to throw him over a precipice, he was protected, "passing through the midst of them, [and] went his way" (Luke 4:29–30). Here Jesus's safety is described as "miraculous,"[4] since the mob is apparently unable to see Jesus even though they may have been able to see everything else. Similarly, when Jesus later joined the two disciples on the road to Emmaus, they did not recognize him because their eyes were "holden." Even though they discussed prophecies about the Savior as they walked along with him, they were not able to recognize him until "their eyes were opened" (see Luke 24:13–32). A writer in *The Interpreter's Bible* insists that "Luke intends us to understand that their senses were supernaturally dulled, not that they were blinded by intense preoccupation," and that they later knew him when "the miraculous inhibition that had prevented the disciples from recognizing their traveling companion" was removed.[5]

Passages in the Old Testament frequently link blindness with wickedness. Through Moses, the Lord enumerated blessings that would follow righteousness and warned of cursings that would be the consequence of disobedience. Deuteronomy chapters 27 and 28 contain such a list. Blindness was among the negative outcomes of wickedness: "The Lord shall smite thee with madness, and blindness, and astonishment of heart: and thou shalt grope at noonday, as the blind gropeth in darkness" (Deuteronomy 28:28–29). Although the wording seems quite graphic, the threatened blindness perhaps referred more to spiritual darkness rather than to literal blindness. As a teaching meant to instill the consequences of obedience or disobedience, the Lord directed Moses and the children of Israel to set up large stones on which the law would be written and to have representatives of specified tribes shout out promised blessings from Mount Gerizim and representatives of the other tribes shout out the curses resulting from disobedience—including blindness—from Mount Ebal, two prominent hills in the center of the promised land (see Deuteronomy 11:26–29; 27:1–4). The array of cursings could have been presented more briefly, one commentator noted, "yet the purpose of the repetition is not primarily intellectual analysis. It is rather the homiletical aim of building up the total impression by picture after picture, each viewed repeatedly from different angles, so that the reader or hearer may see it all, feel it deeply, and never forget it."[6]

While the notion of large groups becoming spiritually blind as a result of wickedness is readily acknowledged, the idea of certain individuals becoming physically blind as a consequence of personal sin is not as obviously recognized. One possible example might be the verse in Proverbs that warns that birds of prey would pluck out the eye of one who is disrespectful of his or her parents (see Proverbs 30:17). Also, there is evidence that in biblical times physical blindness might be linked with sin. This is illustrated by a New Testament incident that may have reflected attitudes carried over from Old Testament times. John describes the occasion when Jesus met an individual who was congenitally sightless. The Lord's disciples inquired, "Master, who did sin, this man, or his parents, that he was born blind?" The Savior did not refute the concept that sin might cause literal blindness, but rather he suggested another purpose: "Neither hath this man sinned, nor his parents: but that the works of God should be made manifest in him" (John 9:1–3). Even though we may not always fully understand how an individual's blindness, for example, fits into God's grand scheme of things, it nevertheless is comforting to know that he is aware of our condition and will bless us according to our needs and for our ultimate good.

Description and Status of the Blind

The Old Testament typically describes individuals who are physically blind as helpless, such as groping at noonday in darkness (see Deuteronomy 28:29). The prophet Zephaniah likened the spiritual fate of the wicked to the physical condition of people who are blind: "I will bring distress upon men, that they shall walk like blind men, because they have sinned against the Lord" (Zephaniah 1:17).

Isaac, with his diminished eyesight, is portrayed as not being fully in charge. This was in marked contrast to the usual pattern in this highly patriarchal era. One commentator described the family as a "little kingdom that was ruled by the father," who specifically "ruled over the wife, children," and "everyone in the household."[7] In this instance, Rebekah (rather than Isaac) received divine guidance concerning which of their sons should be given the birthright. Isaac's dimmed vision enabled her to disguise Jacob to feel and smell like Esau (see Genesis 27:1–29). Rebecca's and Jacob's behavior may seem inappropriate, especially in light of Isaac's disability. But, as Dr. Sidney B. Sperry pointed out, the Hebrews came out of "an Oriental culture . . . whose language, manners, and customs were much different from our own."[8]

Similarly, the biblical record suggests that Jacob or Israel's diminished eyesight was a factor when he blessed Joseph's two sons, Manasseh and Ephraim (see Genesis 48:10–19). Joseph positioned the two boys in such a way that Jacob's right hand would rest on the head of Manasseh, the older brother, assuming that he would receive the birthright blessing. The scriptural record does not state whether or not Israel could see which son was being placed under his right hand, but "as he embraced the boys, a discerning impulse moved him, and he followed this inward moving as against what Joseph had supposed he would do."[9] He therefore crossed his arms so his right hand would rest on the head of Ephraim, the younger brother.

Then, centuries later, it is clear that King Jeroboam's wife planned to take advantage of the prophet Ahijah's visual impairment in order to get a blessing; the Lord, however, revealed the plot to the elderly prophet (see 1 Kings 14:4–6). Thus these Old Testament examples point out that the Lord's inspiration and power were available to overcome disabilities such as visual impairment and ensure the right outcome.

Still, offerings to the Lord were to be perfect in every detail. The law of Moses prohibited a man with "blemishes" from officiating at the altar or approaching the veil lest he "profane" the sanctuary; among the several specifically mentioned disqualifying blemishes were blindness and "a blemish in his eye" (see Leviticus 21:17–23). Sacrificial animals likewise needed to be free from any blemishes; here again, blindness was specifically mentioned as a disqualifier (Leviticus 22:22; Deuteronomy 15:21). Therefore, the prophet Malachi later queried rhetorically: "If ye offer the blind for sacrifice, is it not evil? And if ye offer the lame and sick, is it not evil? (Malachi 1:8). These provisions undoubtedly contributed to the generally unfavorable image of those who were blind.

Blindness as a Metaphor

The rather discouraging image of those who are blind made blindness a fit metaphor for unfavorable spiritual attributes and conditions. This usage is prevalent in the Old Testament. Blindness is sometimes used to represent a lack of intellectual capacity or understanding. Even in today's English, the absence of blindness is reflected in such positive terms as in*sight* or en*light*enment. Blindness being used as a metaphor "for ignorance or lack of comprehension," insisted Professor Henning, "reflects ancient cultural attitudes towards disabilities."

She further noted, "The reason that these metaphors worked in their ancient context and still play well in the contemporary world is because of the negative value that is placed upon bodies that are in some way different from what is considered the norm."[10]

Sometimes blindness was not so much the inability to see, but the unwillingness to see. Jeremiah, who ministered at a time of crisis in faith when the kingdom of Judah faced great perils,[11] demanded: "Hear now this, O foolish people, and without understanding; which have eyes [and presumably the capacity to see], and see not [apparently because they chose not to]; which have ears, and hear not: Fear ye not me? saith the Lord" (Jeremiah 5:21–22). In similar language, Ezekiel, who ministered after the people had been taken into captivity,[12] warned: "Son of man, thou dwellest in the midst of a rebellious house, which have eyes to see, and see not; they have ears to hear, and hear not: for they are a rebellious house" (Ezekiel 12:2). Notice how the Psalmist described useless human-made idols in almost identical discouraging terms: "They have mouths, but they speak not: eyes have they, but they see not" (Psalms 115:5, 135:16). Isaiah also used blindness to describe negligence of duty: "His watchmen are blind: they are all ignorant, they are all dumb dogs, they cannot bark; sleeping, lying down, loving to slumber" (Isaiah 56:10).

More seriously, blindness described the loss of moral direction. For example, judges were warned that bribes or gifts may "blind the eyes of the wise, and pervert the words of the righteous" (Deuteronomy 16:19; compare Exodus 23:8). Again, in conjunction with his instructions for the ceremony at Mount Ebal, Jehovah lamented that blindness would be the condition of those who would not "hearken unto the voice of the Lord [their] God, to observe to do all his commandments and his statutes" and that "these curses shall come upon [them] and overtake [them]" (see Deuteronomy 28:15–29). Speaking of the wicked people of his day, Isaiah declared: "We wait for light, but behold obscurity; for brightness, but we walk in darkness. We grope for the wall like the blind, and we grope as if we had no eyes: we stumble at noonday as in the night; we are in desolate places as dead men" (Isaiah 59:9–10). Jeremiah likewise lamented that the wicked people in Jerusalem had "wandered as blind men in the streets, they have polluted themselves with blood, so that men could not touch their garments" (Lamentations 4:14). In sum, it appears that these prophets were condemning the refusal to see rather than the inability to see. The writer of Proverbs cautioned, "Where there is no vision [particularly spiritual], the people perish" (Proverbs 29:18).

Treatment of People Who Are Blind

The people of Israel were expected to help those in need, including those who were blind. The prophet Isaiah admonished, "Strengthen ye the weak hands, and confirm the feeble knees" (Isaiah 35:3). Job apparently fulfilled this responsibility. As he recounted his benevolent acts, he specifically affirmed that he had aided those who were sightless: "I was eyes to the blind, and feet was I to the lame. I was a father to the poor" (Job 29:15–16).

Through Moses, the Lord reviewed a series of commandments related to loving one's neighbor and treating others justly and graciously. He enjoined, "Thou shalt not curse the deaf, nor put a stumblingblock before the blind, but shalt fear thy God: I am the Lord" (Leviticus 19:14) Then, in like spirit, as Moses listed behaviors to shout from Mount Ebal and which should be condemned, he declared, "Cursed be he who maketh the blind to wander out of the way. And all the people shall say, Amen" (Deuteronomy 27:18). This suggests that there was widespread agreement with the concept of being helpful to people who were blind or had other disabilities.

Overcoming Blindness

Although the Old Testament presents a rather dismal image of physical and spiritual blindness, it also affirms that there is hope to overcome them. The Psalmist petitioned, "Open thou mine eyes" (Psalm 119:18). Several passages in the Old Testament specifically affirm that

God has power to restore sight to the blind. "The Lord openeth the eyes of the blind: the Lord raiseth them that are bowed down: the Lord loveth the righteous" (Psalm 146:8). The prophet Isaiah perhaps more than anyone else spoke of blindness being overcome: "I the Lord have called thee in righteousness . . . to open the blind eyes, to bring out the prisoners from the prison, and them that sit in darkness out of the prison house" (Isaiah 42:6–7). "And I will bring the blind by a way that they knew not; I will lead them in paths that they have not known: I will make darkness light before them, and crooked things straight" (Isaiah 42:16).

The divine power to restore sight was highlighted especially as Isaiah looked forward to the conditions that would prevail when the Lord would come to earth. Notice how these familiar and oft-quoted prophecies are linked with the promise that blindness would be overcome: "The desert shall rejoice, and blossom as the rose. . . . Then the eyes of the blind shall be opened, and the ears of the deaf shall be unstopped. Then shall the lame man leap as an hart, and the tongue of the dumb sing: for in the wilderness shall waters break out, and [there shall be] streams in the desert" (Isaiah 35:1, 5–6). Concerning the eyes of those who are blind being opened, Donald W. Parry's commentary on Isaiah explains: "This statement has a literal, physical application, but it also refers to those who are spiritually blind, deaf, and dumb, who will be made whole through their conversion to the restored gospel."[13]

Isaiah specifically prophesied that in the latter days the Lord would "proceed to do a marvellous work among this people, even a marvellous work and a wonder" (Isaiah 29:14). Latter-day Saints frequently cite this passage as a prophecy of the Restoration of the gospel and of the publication of the Book of Mormon.[14] "And thou shalt be brought down, and shalt speak out of the ground, and thy speech shall be low out of the dust" (Isaiah 29:4). Professor Parry insists that "this chapter provides many details about the book of scripture that is the keystone of our religion."[15] Then Isaiah added, "And in that day shall the deaf hear the words of the book, and the eyes of the blind shall see out of obscurity, and out of darkness" (Isaiah 29:18).

Even though the context of these prophecies suggests that they referred primarily to overcoming spiritual blindness, they could well refer to restoring physical sight as well. In many instances, they could well apply to both. Certainly God has the power to restore physical sight as well as to end spiritual blindness. Still, the Old Testament presents few, if any, examples of healing physical blindness. On the other hand, these would be a frequent part of the Lord's earthly ministry.

The New Testament Picture

The New Testament continues both the Old Testament's description of people who are physically blind as not being able to find their way and the metaphoric use of blindness to represent the lack of a moral compass. On one occasion, for example, the Savior condemned the Pharisees as "blind leaders of the blind," observing that "if the blind lead the blind, both shall fall into the ditch" (Matthew 15:14).

The New Testament also presents a theme absent from the Old Testament. The Gospels contain numerous accounts of the Lord healing those who are blind, both physically and spiritually. While the New Testament echoes the image of blind people being helpless, it also emphasizes an additional and positive facet in their character. Many of them had a deep and yearning faith in the Savior. Bartimaeus, a man who was blind, was sitting at the side of the road near Jericho as Jesus passed by and cried out: "Jesus, thou Son of David, have mercy on me." Many tried to quiet him, "but he cried the more a great deal," and Jesus called for him to come and asked: "What wilt thou that I should do unto thee?" The blind man then said unto him, "Lord, that I might receive my sight." Jesus answered, "Go thy way; thy faith hath made thee whole," after which the blind man "immediately . . . received his sight, and followed Jesus in the way" (Mark 10:46–52; compare Matthew 20:30–34). Others full of faith brought a man who was blind to the Lord and asked him to touch the man. The Lord took him by the hand, placed saliva in his eyes, "put his hands upon him," and asked him what he saw. His sight was still distorted, so the Lord placed his hands upon him again, and this time the man saw clearly (see Mark 8:22–26). Perhaps the piecemeal nature of this miracle heightened its impact. John gave some interesting details as he related the Master's healing of the man who was born blind. The Lord declared: "I am the light of the world." Then Jesus "spat on the ground, and made clay of the spittle, and he anointed the eyes of the man who was blind with the clay, and said unto him, Go wash in the pool of Siloam." He did so "and came seeing" (John 9:1–7). Notice how Jesus involved more senses than one and allowed the blind recipients to participate in their healing. Later, the man born blind was challenged, "Give God the praise: we know that this man [who healed you] is a sinner. He answered and said, Whether he be a sinner or no, I know not: one thing I know, that, whereas I was blind, now I see" (John 9:24–25). Thus the faith of these blind individuals certainly was rewarded. Other accounts of Jesus healing the blind include, for example, Matthew 11:5, Luke 7:22, and Matthew 12:22. When multitudes of people saw Jesus healing the blind, "they glorified the God of Israel" (Matthew 15:31).

Blindness in the Latter Days

Physical blindness continues to exist in the modern world, but because of advances in medical science, there are fewer blind people. The perception of blindness is also more enlightened than in Old Testament times. The image of people who are blind has also improved, exemplified by popular admiration for the accomplishments of individuals such as Helen Keller.

Latter-day scriptures decry spiritual blindness as did the Old Testament. The Book of Mormon prophet Jacob warned, "Wo unto the blind that *will* not see (2 Nephi 9:32; emphasis added). In the days of wicked King Noah, "the eyes of the people were blinded; therefore they hardened their hearts against the words of Abinadi" (Mosiah 11:29). A well-known latter-day revelation describes heirs of the terrestrial kingdom as "honorable" people "who were blinded by the craftiness of men" (Doctrine and Covenants 76:75).

Modern revelation reaffirms the Old Testament's assurance that blindness can be healed. The faithful will "cause the blind to receive their sight, and the deaf to hear, and the dumb to speak, and the lame to walk" (Doctrine and Covenants 35:9). Various "signs shall follow them that believe," including this promise: "In [Jesus's] name they shall open the eyes of the blind, and unstop the ears of the deaf" (84:65, 69). These promises seem to include the restoration of physical sight as well as overcoming spiritual blindness.

Still, the promised restoration of physical sight may not come immediately. Therefore individuals are left to cope with attendant challenges. Teachings of Latter-day prophets can provide helpful perspectives. After Joseph Smith had languished in Liberty Jail for over three months, he pleaded with the Lord for understanding. In response, the Master gave this assurance: "Thine adversity and thine afflictions shall be but a small moment; and then, if thou endure it well, God shall exalt thee on high" (Doctrine and Covenants 121:7–8). Later, the Lord reviewed many of the trials Joseph and his family had experienced and then affirmed, "Know thou, my son, that all these things shall give thee experience, and shall be for thy good" (122:7). "There is a divine purpose in the adversities we encounter every day," testified Elder James E. Faust. "They prepare, they purge, they purify, and thus they bless."[16]

Of course, how we deal with these challenges can affect their influence on our lives. As Ella Wheeler Wilcox expressed it, "One ship sails East, / And another West, / By the self-same winds that blow, / 'Tis the set of the sails / And not the gales, / That tells the way we go."[17] The Lord counseled, "Search diligently, pray always, and be believing, and all things shall work together for your good" (Doctrine and Covenants 90:24).

An oft-quoted passage from the Book of Mormon provides perspective concerning the importance of how we respond to disabilities, including blindness. Through Moroni, the Lord declared, "I give unto men weakness that they may be humble; and my grace is sufficient for all men that humble themselves before me; for if they humble themselves before me, and have faith in me, then will I make weak things become strong unto them" (Ether 12:27). The Savior has assured, "Be thou humble; and the Lord thy God shall lead thee by the hand, and give thee answer to thy prayers" (Doctrine and Covenants 112:10). Humbling oneself is not an acknowledgment of inferiority but rather a recognition of one's true relationship to others. In this case an acknowledgment of our dependence on the Savior. In his Atonement, Jesus suffered for more than just the sins of humankind. Decades before the Savior's mortal ministry, Alma, another Book of Mormon prophet, taught, "He will take upon him death, that he may loose the bands of death which bind his people; and he will take upon him their infirmities, that his bowels may be filled with mercy, according to the flesh, that he may know according to the flesh how to succor his people according to their infirmities" (Alma 7:12, see Doctrine and Covenants 62:1). Hence, as we face our disabilities (such as blindness), we can certainly rejoice in the assurance expressed by the angel Gabriel to Mary, "For with God nothing shall be impossible" (Luke 1:37).

Echoing the injunction given through Isaiah, a latter-day revelation also admonishes reaching out to help others: "Succor the weak, lift up the hands which hang down, and strengthen the feeble knees" (Doctrine and Covenants 81:5; compare Isaiah 35:3; Job 4:4). Heeding this counsel, The Church of Jesus Christ of Latter-day Saints as an organization has been active in assisting groups with disabilities. The Church's website affirms: "All of God's children are on earth to be given the opportunity to learn and live the gospel of Jesus Christ. Members of the Church with differences or disabilities that affect their activities or interactions also [should] have meaningful opportunities to minister, teach, serve, and lead. Every person's contribution is needed in the Lord's kingdom. . . . Our Father in Heaven knows and loves all of His children, and He is aware of the challenges we face."[18]

Thus Church programs not only avoid placing "stumbling blocks before the blind" as the Old Testament admonishes, but the Church actually seeks to remove them. One of the greatest needs of Latter-day Saints who are blind is having direct access to the scriptures and other literature. For over a century, the Church has sought to bridge this gap. In 1904 Church President Joseph F. Smith directed the organization of the Society for the Aid of the Sightless with the stated mission to publish literature for the blind, aid in their education, improve their condition, and cooperate with others to work for these ends through education and legislation. The society's work was carried out primarily by Albert M. Talmage (the blind brother of Elder James E. Talmage) and his wife, Sara. Beginning in 1912 they published a monthly braille magazine, *The Messenger to the Sightless*, that included materials of religious and general interest.[19] This put the Church in the vanguard of religious organizations disseminating literature to the blind throughout the world. Publishing the Book of Mormon piecemeal in braille on their hand-operated press was an important and challenging project for the Talmages. Since those beginnings, all of the standard works and a few other Church books appear in braille. In 1958 audio recordings began to be used. Now the Church's magazines, the *Come, Follow Me* study outlines, and other materials are distributed in digital form. An advisory committee, composed of approximately ten blind members (including the present author), meets regularly to assure that the Church's programs and materials are removing "stumbling blocks before the blind" as effectively as possible.

Summary and Conclusion

Although the Old Testament described people who are blind as helpless and used this affliction as a metaphor for the lack of spiritual understanding and direction, it nevertheless affirmed that with God's help such blindness can be overcome. Healing those who were physically blind was a repeated event in the Savior's mortal ministry, and surely his gospel provides the means to overcome spiritual blindness. The teachings of modern prophets shed light on the role of challenges (such as blindness) in our personal growth. The restored Church has sought to follow the Old Testament's encouraging, benevolent treatment of those who are blind. It has made the scriptures and other materials available in formats accessible to blind people; it also promotes other programs enabling those who are blind to participate fully in gospel activities and, as the Old Testament promised, to be able to overcome the limitations of their disability. Truly The Church of Jesus Christ of Latter-day Saints is helping those who are blind to realize the fulfillment of the Psalmist's petition to "open thou mine eyes" (Psalm 119:18).

Richard O. Cowan is a professor emeritus of Church History and Doctrine at Brigham Young University.

Notes

1. Meghan Henning, "Disabilities in the Bible," *Biblical Odyssey* (SBL Online forum), June 2020.
2. Rabbi Jeffrey Howard Tigay, "Blindness," in *Encyclopaedia Judaica*, 2nd ed. (Jerusalem: Keter Publishing House, 1982), 3:753.
3. Tigay, "Blindness," 753.
4. George Arthur Buttrick et al., eds., *The Interpreter's Bible* (New York: Abingdon Press, 1982), 8:95.
5. Buttrick, *Interpreter's Bible*, 8:421, 427.
6. Buttrick, *Interpreter's Bible*, 2:497–98.
7. Ralph Gower, *The New Manners and Customs of Bible Times* (Chicago: Moody Press, 1987), 57.

8. Sidney B. Sperry, *The Spirit of the Old Testament* (Salt Lake City: Deseret Book, 1980), 6, 30.
9. Buttrick, *Interpreter's Bible*, 1:815
10. Henning, "Disabilities in the Bible."
11. S. Kent Brown, "History and Jeremiah's Crisis of Faith," in *Isaiah and the Prophets*, ed. Monte S. Nyman (Provo, UT: Religious Studies Center, Brigham Young University, 1984), 105–18.
12. Gerald N. Lund, "Ezekiel: Prophet of Judgment, Prophet of Promise," in Nyman, *Isaiah and the Prophets*, 75–88.
13. Donald W. Parry, et al., *Understanding Isaiah* (Salt Lake City: Deseret Book, 1998), 318.
14. See, for example, LeGrand Richards, *A Marvelous Work and a Wonder* (Salt Lake City: Deseret Book, 1988), 67; and Mark E. Petersen, *Isaiah for Today* (Salt Lake City: Deseret Book, 1981), 77.
15. Parry, *Understanding Isaiah*, 259.
16. James E. Faust, "The Refiner's Fire," *Ensign*, May 1979, 53.
17. Ella Wheeler Wilcox, "'Tis the Set of the Sail," thoughtco.com.
18. "Disabilities," Gospel Topics, https://www.churchofjesuschrist.org/study/manual/gospel-topics/disability.
19. Society for the Aid of the Sightless minutes, manuscript, Church History Library, Salt Lake City, Utah.

Prophetic Critiques

17

Covenants, Kinship, and Caring for the Destitute in the Book of Amos

Joshua M. Matson

At the outset of the book of Amos, the Old Testament prophet captures the attention of the ancient Israelites when he condemns the inhabitants of Tyre, a port city north of Israel often used synonymously to reference the Phoenicians, for not remembering "the brotherly covenant" (Amos 1:9), or as it appears in a different translation, "the covenant of kinship" (1:9 NRSV).[1] The Israelites easily recognized and eagerly accepted this condemnation because they were the victims of the covenantal breach from one of their neighboring regional powers.[2] Amos, however, did not travel from the southern kingdom of Judah to speak comfort to the ears of the Israelites. Instead, the prophet uses the condemnation of Tyre, as well as the condemnations of other surrounding nations cited in Amos 1–2, as a subtle and persuasive introduction to the condemnation he was about to pronounce upon Israel's social elite for their own forgetfulness of the covenant of kinship toward their fellow Israelites.

An understanding of the relationship between covenants and kinship in the world of the Old Testament has powerful implications when discussing the need to care for the disadvantaged and marginalized, especially when focusing on a society built on covenants that aimed to forge kinship relationships. Biblical scholar Frank Moore Cross observes that one of the central purposes of all covenant making in the ancient Near East was the creation of kinship.[3] Thus, at the heart of covenant making is "the obligation of the kinsman to uphold the welfare of his fellow kinsman."[4] Put another way, the Israelites were under covenant to "open [their] hand wide unto [their] brother" (Deuteronomy 15:11). Amos leverages this understanding of kinship through covenants and utilizes kinship language throughout his writings when he refers to the family of Israel (Amos 3:1) and their interrelated positions as daughters, sons, brothers, children, wives, and fathers.[5] Amos employs these terms to remind his audiences of their covenantal kinship to one another, regardless of social, religious, or economic status.

Kinship created by covenants plays a central role in the law given to the Israelites through Moses (Leviticus 25). Additionally, Israel and the surrounding nations had entered formal covenants of kinship through treaties during the days of David and Solomon (2 Samuel 5:11; 1 Kings 5:26; 9:13; and 16:31). In the days of Amos's ministry (760–750 BC), it appears these covenants had been disregarded not only by Israel's neighbors, but by the Israelites themselves, prompting "roars from Zion" intent on bringing destruction to the covenant breakers (Amos 1:2 NRSV).[6] The consequences of forgetting the covenant of kinship, however, had not yet arrived, and Israelite society bore no marks of such destruction. Instead, the Israelites were enjoying an era of peace and prosperity (2 Kings 14:23–29). In this golden age of the divided monarchy, Amos reprimands the elite of Israelite society for their exploitation of the destitute for personal gain and prophesies concerning the consequences that loom on the horizon because they will not remember their kinship covenants.

Although scholars overwhelmingly recognize the prophet's call for social justice as the central theme of his work,[7] they cite Amos 5:21–24 to bring into question the unity of Amos's writings with Jewish law, arguing that there is a dichotomy between orthodoxy (correct worship/belief) and orthopraxy (correct action) in the prophet's writings.[8] The message of Amos, however, reconciles both orthodoxy and orthopraxy in ancient Israel when studied through covenants of kinship. To demonstrate this coherency, I will first explore how covenants in the ancient world created kinship and discuss how such covenants included mechanisms to care for the destitute in ancient society. This will provide needed context to Amos's oracles against the nations (Amos 1–2) and his indictments and visions against Israel (Amos 3–9). Additionally, this context will show how the elite in Israel, and to a lesser extent her neighboring nations, were guilty of breaking the covenants by not only neglecting the poor, needy, and destitute but taking advantage of them for their own personal gain, prompting the condemnation and destruction foretold by Amos. In conclusion, I will reflect on how covenants in the Restoration, particularly those associated with baptism, the law of consecration, and temple sealings, comprise modern-day covenants of kinship among members of The Church of Jesus Christ of Latter-day Saints. Contemporizing the message of Amos reminds us that we are also under covenant to aid the poor and needy, especially in times of peace and prosperity, and warns of the stark consequences that await us if we do not.

The Covenants of Kinship in the World of the Old Testament

While the phrase *covenant of kinship* appears only in Amos 1:9, covenants and kinship were at the heart of ancient Near Eastern society. As noted biblical scholar Jonathan Klawans has observed, "Hard-and-fast distinction between ritual[9] and ethics has prevented scholars from appreciating the degree to which ritual and ethics are inherently connected—and virtually inseparable."[10] To illustrate the inseparable nature of the concept of covenants and kinship in the world of the Old Testament, it is necessary to first outline the linguistic and cultural context for the words *kinship* and *covenant* as they appear in Amos 1:9. The Hebrew term translated as "brotherly" or "kinship" in this verse is 'aḥîm (אחים). When joined with *covenant* (bĕrît ברית), the term is a specific reference to one's "duty towards tribal kinsmen."[11] Anthropologist Meyer Fortes refers to the kinship suggested by this context as an "ethic of generosity" in which "kinsfolk are expected to be loving, just, and generous to one another and not to demand strictly equivalent returns of one another."[12]

In the world of the Old Testament, covenants that create kinship can be categorized in three forms: familial, temporal, and divine. Familial covenants of kinship are the result of a shared parentage or lineage. Temporal covenants of kinship are the result of oaths and treaties made between nation-states or societal leaders with the intent to strengthen political alliances and dissuade against conflict. Divine covenants of kinship are the result of the acceptance of a religious law through formal rites that emphasize one's shared equality with others of the covenant in the eyes of deity. Kinship obtained through a shared lineage is the result of the familial units created by covenants made between husbands and wives that transfer to their posterity. Kinship through temporal and divine means, however, is associated with the Hebrew term *bĕrît*, usually translated as "covenant," "contract," or "agreement."[13] Cross argues that *bĕrît* is related to various words in Akkadian, Arabic, Aramaic, and Hebrew that are translated as "covenant, treaty, or oath."[14] However, such translations fail to portray the full range of meaning for the term within an ancient context. Johannes Pedersen states that these words go beyond the mere action or ceremony of a covenant in the ancient world and instead portray "the relationship between those who belong together with all the rights and obligations which spring from this relationship. It encompasses consequently both the relationship between those related by kinship and those united by covenant."[15] Amos alludes to each of these forms of covenants of kinship in his writings. A brief historical background of each form of the covenants of kinship is helpful to understand the underlying covenants that were breached by the Israelites and their neighbors and led to Amos's pronouncement of condemnations.

Covenantal kinship through lineage

Sharing lineage presupposes a covenant of kinship and is readily evident from the beginning of the Old Testament. The Lord's commandment to Adam and Eve to "become one flesh" (Genesis 2:24) was not merely a reference to their marriage relationship, but a reference to "the offspring they produce, who share their 'flesh.' The birth of every child illustrates the biological and social connectedness of humankind."[16] In other words, because of the covenants made by Adam and Eve with one another regarding their marital relationship, their offspring were covenantal kin. This type of covenantal kinship through lineage is emphasized in the biblical text with references describing the kinship between the descendants of Jacob and the descendants of Esau, known as the Edomites (Numbers 20:14; Deuteronomy 2:4; and Obadiah 10; 12). Commenting on the kinship context of these verses, Peter C. Craigie observes that the children of Israel viewed the descendants of Esau with "relative equanimity."[17]

This view of the Edomites is preserved in the writings of Amos as he refers to the actions of the descendants of Esau involving pursuing "his *brother* with the sword" and casting "off all pity" (Amos 1:11; emphasis added). The phrase translated as "cast off all pity" in the King James Version of the Bible is difficult to decipher in the original Hebrew. While on the surface it does not appear to make direct reference to the kinship between Jacob and Esau, the Greek translation of the Old Testament (known as the Septuagint) reads "and violated his (own) womb" (1:11 New English Translation of the Septuagint), which has led one translator to take liberties in translating the Hebrew as "violated his obligations of kinship."[18] By directly referencing the shared national lineage of the people of Edom and

Israel, the authors of the Old Testament emphasize the covenant of kinship that was inherent by birth.[19]

Covenantal kinship through temporal treaties

Covenantal kinship is also formed by temporal oaths and treaties agreed to by nation-states and societal leaders. Examples of these covenants of kinship are found throughout the Old Testament as the nation-state of Israel navigated its relationship with neighboring nations.[20] It is beyond the scope of this chapter to provide a lengthy recitation of the history of temporal covenantal kinships created by Israel, but some are of specific interest to our discussion of the book of Amos. Amos mentions six nation-states that entered one (or more) of the temporal covenants of kinship with Israel: Aram (Syria), Philistia, Phoenicia, Edom, Ammon, and Moab (Amos 1:3–2:1). While Edom's relationship to Israel is primarily based on shared national lineage (Amos 1:11),[21] Israel made covenants with Phoenicia (1 Kings 5:12), Ammon (2 Samuel 10:2), Aram (2 Samuel 8:6), and Moab (2 Samuel 8:2) during the reigns of David and Solomon. The Philistines' relationship with the Israelites is tenuous at best in the Old Testament narrative, but as biblical scholar Hanna Kassis observes, "Gath (a city ruled by the Philistines) . . . is tied to Israel in some kind of treaty relationship, as can be gathered from 1 Kings 2:39–40."[22] As with entering any other covenant in antiquity, the Israelites and their neighbors covenanted to change their view of one another from competing nation-states to fellow kin. While these covenants of kinship all predate the time of Amos by nearly two hundred years, recognition and awareness of these covenants and their impact on sociopolitical relationships in ancient Israel would likely have been known, though no mention of them is made in the Hebrew Bible; such covenants, however, were often memorialized by the erecting of monuments.[23]

Covenantal kinship through the acceptance of divine law

Covenantal kinship can also be produced through the acceptance of a shared divine law. Temporal covenants of kinship in antiquity often outline the consequences that would follow should the treaty be violated, leading to the dissolution of the political alliance or the return to hostile relationships.[24] Covenants of kinship associated with divine law, however, carried with them an even greater societal responsibility to care for all those who had entered the covenant, as well as increased consequences for disregarding the obligation of kinship. In Leviticus 17–26, the Lord outlines numerous laws that can be viewed as part of the divine covenants of kinship.

Among the obligations outlined as part of this divine law were laws that directly address the way in which kin were to be treated with the explicit use of the term *brother* (*'ah*). Included among these obligations are prohibitions against "[hating] your brother in thine heart" (Leviticus 19:17), "[bearing] a grudge against the children of thy people" (19:18), "cheating one another" (25:14 NRSV), and "[taking] interest in advance or otherwise make a profit from [your brother]" (25:36 NRSV). In addition to these prohibitions, the laws include mandates for how one is to care for one's kin (including those from neighboring nations) when they have come upon hard times. This can be succinctly summarized as "love thy neighbor as thyself" (19:18). If "thy brother be waxen poor, and fallen in decay with thee" (25:35), those of the covenant "shall support them; they shall live with you as though resident aliens" (25:35 NRSV). Included in this command is an allusion to laws to care for "resident aliens" or foreign refugees that appear in earlier texts of the Old Testament (Exodus 22:21; 23:9; Leviticus 19:33–34). If "thy brother that dwelleth by thee be waxen poor, and be sold unto thee" the law prohibited that individual from being enslaved (Leviticus 25:39) and from being treated harshly (25:46). If those who fell upon these destitute circumstances were purchased by a foreigner (non-Israelite), there was a built-in guarantee of redemption if one of their kin had sufficient means to do so (25:47–49). Such redemption laws were perpetual and applied to the offspring of the destitute as well.

As just outlined, those who accepted the covenant given by God to Moses were obligated, among other things, to care for their kin. After outlining the blessings that should come upon the Israelites for adhering to their covenant obligations (Leviticus 26:3–13), God himself provides an assurance declaring, "I will maintain my covenant with you" (26:9 NRSV). These promises extended to all Israelites, but especially to those who found themselves marginalized and disadvantaged. They could stand before God as recipients of a divine commitment, a commitment that this covenant would be honored, creating a societal safety net should any of the people of the covenant come upon hard times. But what happens when the elite of society choose to disregard the covenants of kinship and forget those who are disadvantaged and marginalized? Such a scenario is exactly the focus of the prophet Amos.

Breaking the Covenants of Kinship in the Days of Amos

As referenced in the introduction, Amos pronounces judgments upon the neighboring nations of the ancient Israelites as a subtle and persuasive preface to the indictment God has called him to pronounce upon the Israelite elites. The repetitive use of the noun *transgressions* to explain the actions of Israel's neighbors (Amos 1:3, 6, 9, 11, 13; 2:1, 6) serves as a preamble to his more direct message. The Hebrew term translated here as "transgression" is *pšʿ* (פשע), which is defined as "an offence concerning persons and property."[25] Amos employs this same noun when he speaks for the Lord in declaring "that in the day . . . I shall visit the *transgressions* of Israel upon him" (3:14; emphasis added). This declaration is linked to a similarly pointed accusation of Israel by Amos earlier in chapter 3: "The Lord has spoken against you, O people of Israel, against the whole *family* that I brought up out of the land of Egypt: You only have I *known* of all the *families* of the earth; therefore, I will punish you for all your iniquities" (3:1–2 NRSV; emphasis added). While Amos surprisingly uses *'āwon* (עָוֹן) to describe the misdeeds of the Israelites, Francis Andersen and David Noel Freedman observe that the noun employed in verse 2 is to be read with the *pš'* used in Amos 3:14 as a "firm link to unify the whole chapter."[26] Amos employs covenantal and familial language in this indictment to emphasize the divine covenant that has been breached.

Breaking familial and temporal covenants of kinship— the oracles against the nations (Amos 1–2)

Amos's indictment against the nations neighboring Israel was prompted by both ethical and covenantal transgressions that predate the prophet,[27] but those actions nevertheless shaped his current society. While a breach of ethics is a serious enough crime to warrant the prophet's attention, the fact that these transgressions were against individuals in nation-states that were considered kin through temporal covenants exacerbates the situation. Amos's indictments against Israel's neighbors centers around the repeated employment of the verb *pš'*, demonstrating that the misdeeds of the surrounding nations are primarily linked to offenses against persons and property. Amos argues that even when nation-states are at war with one other, an ethical standard should be maintained for the dignity of humankind. When the misdeeds of these nations are outlined, they can be separated into two types: martial brutality or human slavery, both aimed at increasing the wealth or luxury of the elite.

Amos declares punishments upon three nations for acts of inhumane martial brutality. The prophet begins by indicting Damascus, the capital of Aram (Syria), because "they have threshed Gilead with threshing instruments of iron" (Amos 1:3 ASV). The threshing mentioned here is not a reference to an annihilation of territorial land but instead is a symbolic reference to martial brutality. The symbolic use of threshing in reference to martial brutality is used elsewhere in the writings of Old Testament prophets (Isaiah 41:15–16 and Micah 4:13). This likely is a reference to the breaching of the covenant of kinship by the expansion of Aram's territory into the region by Hazael in 814 BC (2 Kings 10:32–33). Similarly, Amos indicts Ammon for having "ripped open pregnant women in Gilead in order to enlarge their territory" (Amos 1:13 NRSV). The image of a woman who is with child being harmed reminds the reader of the injunction given at Sinai that "if men strive, and hurt a woman with child, so that her fruit depart from her, and yet no mischief follow: he shall be surely punished" (Exodus 21:22). Amos's final reference to martial brutality relates the atrocities of Moab. In their attempt to expand their territory farther to the south in Edom, the Moabites "burned the bones of the king of Edom into lime" (Amos 2:1). Such desecration of human remains is not only an act of violence but a disregard for the individual's life, an act that is not even permitted for criminals in Israelite law (Deuteronomy 21:22–23). In an ancient context, each of these acts of martial brutality was enacted upon victims viewed by the aggressive party as "non-human" and "prey"[28] since they were foreigners or in a lower social position than the aggressors. These views were in stark opposition to the covenants of kinship shared between Israel and each of these nations previously. Such acts of martial brutality, unfortunately, were also prevalent among the Israelite elites throughout the history of ancient Israel (2 Kings 23:16).

Further declarations against inhumane actions are at the center of Amos's indictments against nations participating in the trading of enslaved peoples, namely Gaza, one of the port cities of Philistia, and the city of Tyre. Both cities are accused of carrying "away captive the whole captivity, to deliver them to Edom" (Amos 1:6; see 1:9). These references underscore the involvement of the Philistines and the Phoenicians in the trade of enslaved peoples to Edom, including those who were Israelites,[29] and therefore had claim on the heavenly covenants that ensured their protection from enslavement by their kin and foreigners (Leviticus 25:39, 49). The result of breaking this covenant of kinship was "the dissolution of a covenant treaty. . . . The unilateral violation of such relationships constituted a grievous error, worthy of the approaching divine retribution."[30] As mentioned earlier,

Tyre's transgression is directly tied to not remembering "the covenant of kinship" (1:9 NRSV), but when contextualized with their central role in the triangular trade of enslaved peoples, it becomes even more evident that the Edomites had a disregard for kinship of any who were not within a privileged position.

The punishments pronounced by Amos for disregarding covenants of kinship in Israel's neighboring nations are aimed at the elite class and the symbols of their power and wealth. In almost every pronounced consequence, Amos references the sending of fire to devour the nation-states' "palaces" (Amos 1:4, 7, 10, 12, 14; and 2:1). The word translated as "palaces" shares the Hebrew root *r-w-m* (רום), which means "high/lifted up" or, as one dictionary defines it, a "dwelling tower with several stories,"[31] suggesting that an appropriate English translation could be "high-rise." The focus of Amos's prophecy is that these high-rises, the residences of the social and economic elite in the major cities of these nation-states, would be devoured by fire. In addition to prophesying about the loss of property exclusively associated with the elite, Amos also prophesies that the Lord will disrupt the current political structures that continue to allow such individuals to maintain power. For Aram, Amos decrees that the Lord will "send a fire into the house of Hazael, which shall devour the palaces of Benhadad" (1:4). The destruction outlined here is not directed merely to physical structures but also against two of the dominating dynasties in Syrian politics. Similarly, Amos continues by prophesying against the Ammonites that "their king shall go into captivity, he and his princes together" (1:15). In Moab, the Lord will "cut off the judge from the midst thereof, and will slay all the princes thereof with him" (2:3). Taken together, Amos's pronouncements of punishment are directly pointed at the elite, those who have acquired success by exploiting the disadvantaged, actions that were especially egregious since they were against those who were once kin through temporal covenants. This focus on the elite is not reserved for the foreign nations condemned by the prophet, but is also the focus of Amos's pronouncements against Israel.

Breaking the divine covenants of kinship—indictment and prophecies against Israel's elite (Amos 3–9)

While Amos's indictments against the nations surrounding Israel are direct and carry dire consequences, they merely serve as a preface to the reprimand given to the divine covenantal inhabitants of Israel who commit similar atrocities against their own kin. Unlike many other Old Testament prophets whose messages are aimed at the collective of society, Amos's message carefully singles out the social elites in Israel. Like the implied audience in the Oracle against the Nations, Amos concentrates his message on the privileged of Israelite society. Amos declares, "They know not to do right, saith the Lord, who store up *violence* and *robbery* in their *palaces*" (Amos 3:10; emphasis added). The Hebrew word for *palace* here is the same one Amos used when prophesying destruction upon the elite of other nations. This connection is further emphasized in the pronounced judgment upon Israel connected with Amos 3:14. After Amos declares that the Lord will visit the Israelites on account of their transgressions, the punishment that is pronounced is that the Lord will destroy the "winter house with the summer house; and the houses of ivory shall perish, and the great houses shall have an end" (3:15). As Shalom Paul observes, "The luxurious way of life of pomp, pleasure, and prosperity of the elite, along with their crimes of exploitation, oppression, and perversion of justice, are cardinal causes for the prophet's categorical threats of the impending catastrophe of destruction and deportation."[32]

A careful reading of the consequences outlined by Amos shows that, in addition to the common themes of destruction, death, and exile, the elite in Israel were to receive a punishment like that of the elite in the neighboring nations, punishments that would leave their possessions in shambles and lead to changes in the political power structure of the society. Throughout Amos's indictment and visions, he references consequences that would have meant little to the marginalized but would have been threatening to the elite. He begins by referencing that only the "corner of a couch" and "part of a bed"

(Amos 3:12 NRSV) would remain after the judgments of God came upon them. Unlike today, couches and beds were luxury items in the world of the Old Testament and were accessible only to the affluent. These references can best be understood through the lens of Amos's profession as a pastoralist (7:14). In ancient Israelite pastoral customs, a hired shepherd was responsible for the well-being of each animal in the flock. Should an animal die while under the shepherd's watch, the shepherd would be held personally responsible by his or her superiors. However, the shepherd could be absolved of personal blame provided there was physical evidence that the livestock was killed by a beast of prey. The presentation of the remains of the corner of a couch and a part of a bed to the Lord symbolically absolves Amos and the lower classes of society of responsibility for the destruction of the elite. Other items that were to be destroyed that would enrage the elite include their own high-rises (6:8), winter and summer homes (3:15), ivory homes (3:15), great houses (3:15), beds of ivory (6:4), and excessive livestock and produce (6:4, 6). The wealth and prestige the elite Israelites acquired through exploitation would be the focus of the Lord's destruction.

Scholars observe that Amos begins his indictment of the children of Israel with the direct reference to their covenantal relationship with God quoted earlier (Amos 3:2) and uses it to strengthen scholarly argument for the polemic between orthodoxy and orthopraxy.[33] In doing this, scholars suggest that Amos's primary message is that such a covenant did not absolve them from an ethical standard. This view, however, minimizes the correlation between covenants and kinship. Instead, reading Amos's indictment against the children of Israel while recognizing the inseparable connection between kinship and covenant emphasized that Israel's covenants with God, both from a familial and a divine perspective, required an even higher awareness and practice of the ethical standard, one that exceeded that of the temporal covenants of kinship entered into by other nations.

While the divine obligations of kinship accepted at Mount Sinai (Leviticus 25:35) are alluded to in the writings of Amos (Amos 2:4), the prophet explicitly reaffirms the kinship of his Israelite audience by making frequent references to the familial kinship of the house of Israel (5:1, 4, 25; 6:1, 14; 7:10; and 9:9), reference to the patriarch Judah (2:4–5), and three references to the patriarch Joseph (5:6, 15; and 6:6). The three references to Joseph are particularly instructive because they establish a familial kinship among the prophet's audience. First, Amos warns that if the Israelites will not "seek the Lord," he "will break out like fire in the house of Joseph" (5:6). This reference to the house of Joseph is intended to draw upon the familial language and underscore the kinship of Amos's audience. Additionally, this reference echoes the destruction that was pronounced by Amos upon the Aramaean house of Hazael (1:4), suggesting that the prophet was pronouncing that the house of Joseph (a possible allusion to Bethel, the national center of the northern kingdom and the seat of governance)[34] would also be disposed of and lose their elite status. Amos's second reference to Joseph appears to again highlight the kinship nature of the Israelites as the "remnant of Joseph" (5:15), or the remaining posterity of a shared ancestor. The last statement appears as a direct statement to the social elites in connection with their lavish lifestyle. After listing their many luxurious items, Amos acknowledges that they "are not grieved for the affliction of Joseph" (6:6). While scholarly consensus supports this as a reference to the impending destruction of the northern kingdom, read within the context of Amos's condemnation of the elite, this reference may be a rebuke upon the elite for not noticing the economic inequality and dire situation of the destitute and poor among them who were also of the lineage of Joseph. Similar statements of kinship appear in the writings of Amos's contemporary, Hosea (Hosea 1:10–2:1), and, the Psalms (Psalm 22:22–23).

Amos airs a plethora of grievances against the elite of the Israelites that go against the covenants of kinship. Such grievances include oppressing the poor (Amos 4:1), crushing the needy (4:1), trampling the poor (5:11), pushing aside the needy in the gate (5:12), and trampling the needy (8:4). Each of these transgressions constitutes an omission of deeds that would be explicitly expected in the kinship covenant discussed above. In addition to disregarding kinship, Amos also condemns actions that took advantage of the destitute, including unethically raising the price on food and purchasing individuals as enslaved persons. Amos condemns deceptions in the selling of wheat—the elite made "the ephah small, and the shekel great, and falsif[ied] the balances" (8:5)—and taking from the poor levies (taxes) of grain (5:11). In each of these cases, the elite took advantage of the poor to increase their own profits, actions forbidden by the law (Leviticus 19:35–36; 25:14). When the disadvantaged could no longer operate under these circumstances, the elite in Israel would "buy the poor for silver, and the needy for a pair of shoes" (Amos 8:6), actions that stand in opposition to the covenant of kinship outlined in Leviticus 25:39–43 and lead to the enslavement of fellow Israelites. As Old Testament scholar Gregory Chirichigno points out, "excessive taxation is one of the possible causes for debt-slavery and the alienation of land, it is also most likely that the control of resources and lending by the ruling elite, which included both state officials and private landowners, caused many small farmers to sell their dependents and themselves into debt-slavery, and eventually to sell their land."[35] In all these ways, the elite and privileged of Israelite society were failing to take care of their kin. Even worse, they were exploiting them for their personal gain. When viewed against the divine covenants of kinship, it becomes clear that the Israelites had violated their obligation to care for the disadvantaged and marginalized.

Understanding these transgressions against the poor and needy in the context of the covenants of kinship not only illuminates the historical context of the crimes but also provides a clearer picture of why the consequences outlined by Amos are directed so pointedly at the elite. Amos's message is equally applicable to individuals throughout time who seek to uphold the covenants of kinship. Today, those who are not careful may find themselves feeling the same "ease" (Amos 6:1) experienced by the Israelite elite that disconnected them from the afflictions of their own kin (6:6).

Modern Covenants of Kinship

Understanding the centrality of caring for the disadvantaged within ancient covenants of kinship is instructive for readers of Amos in any dispensation. This function of covenants in the creation of kinship is equally apparent in the restored gospel of Jesus Christ. Today members of The Church of Jesus Christ of Latter-day Saints make divine covenants of kinship that include an explicit directive to "bear one another's burdens, that they may be light" (Mosiah 18:8). Additionally, members of the faith community are encouraged to utilize familial language to refer to one another as "sister" or "brother." This view of kinship is further emphasized since each Church member is to "esteem his brother [or sister] as himself" (Doctrine and Covenants 38:24–25). But who is the "brother" spoken of in this revelation? According to President Marion G. Romney, the covenant of baptism extends beyond membership in the Church and "the scriptures clearly establish the fact that caring for the poor is a covenantal obligation" (Mosiah 4:26)[36] regardless of social, religious, or economic status. Commenting on this covenant to care for others, President Henry B. Eyring has said, "Every member has made a covenant to do works of kindness as the Savior would do. So, any call to bear witness and to care for others is not a request for extra service. . . . Each is a chance to prove what blessings flow from being a covenant people, and each is an opportunity for which you agreed to be accountable."[37] Like the Israelites of old, Latter-day Saints have made covenants of kinship that are rooted in "lov[ing] thy neighbour as thyself" (Leviticus 19:18). In addition to the covenant made at baptism, endowed members of the Church covenant within the walls of holy temples to receive and honor the law of consecration.[38] This covenant ensures that all who enter it will "voluntarily dedicate their time, talents, and material wealth to the establishment and building up of God's Kingdom"[39] so that all can have "all things common among them; therefore there [are] not rich and poor" (4 Nephi 1:3).[40] Like the Israelites of old, Latter-day Saints have made these heavenly covenants of kinship with God and are not immune from the consequences should they neglect the poor and the needy.

According to a 2009 Pew Research survey, a majority of Latter-day Saints (54 percent) are in the middle- or high-income bracket in the United States,[41] which situates them well within the wealthiest people in the world.[42] In almost every respect, Latter-day Saints in the United States can be considered among the elite and privileged. Such a fact serves as a warning for us to be aware of our own desires and purposes. Members of the Church who have made covenants of kinship should regularly reflect on where their desires are and course correct if they find that their hearts are set upon the things of this world (Doctrine and Covenants 121:35) more than upon the well-being of their kin. When the prophet Moroni sees our day, he similarly laments, "Why do ye adorn yourselves with that which hath no life, and yet suffer the hungry, and the needy, and the naked, and the sick and the afflicted to pass by you, and notice them not?" (Mormon 8:39). President N. Eldon Tanner gets to the heart of the issue for both the ancient Israelites and modern readers. He declares, "The most difficult thing for us seems to be to give of ourselves, to do away with selfishness. If we really love someone, nothing is a hardship. Nothing is hard for us to do for that individual. There is no real happiness in having or getting, but only in giving. Half the world seems to be following the wrong scent in the pursuit of happiness. They think it consists of having and getting, and in having others serve them, but really it consists of giving and serving others."[43] The stark warning from the text of Amos and the history that follows reveal that those who disregard their covenants of kinship and focus on having, getting, and being served will eventually lose it all.

Conclusion

This detailed study of the connection between covenants and kinship helps illuminate the prophetic writings of Amos and make them applicable in our own day. By understanding the way in which covenants and kinship were inseparable in the world of the Old Testament, we better understand the obligations that were associated with covenant making among peoples of the ancient Near East and the consequences that were the result of obedience or disobedience to them. This understanding is instructive on multiple levels. Recognizing covenant kinship is helpful in contextualizing the prophecies of Amos, especially in reconciling the themes of orthodoxy and orthopraxy within the book. Amos's reprimand of those of elite status among the Israelites and the surrounding nations is understood as the articulation of direct consequences for breaking familial, temporal, and divine covenants of kinship. These consequences, while including general elements of death, destruction, and exile, were unique because they included direct reference to material possessions that were more highly valued by the elite than by their fellow kin. Such an understanding increases awareness for us as Latter-day Saints of the kinship that is inherent in the covenants we have made and reminds us to take those covenants seriously by caring for the disadvantaged and marginalized among us and other nations, especially in times of our own ease and security.

Joshua M. Matson is a religious educator with Seminaries and Institutes who is teaching at Bingham High School.

Notes

1. John Priest, "The Covenant of Brothers," *Journal of Biblical Literature* 84 (1965): 400–406. The King James Version of the Bible is the primary English translation of the Bible that will be cited throughout this chapter. If the KJV is used, a citation to a biblical verse is cited without specifying the translation. Other translations will sometimes be referenced, especially when kinship language is more faithfully preserved, and will be cited appropriately.

2. Francis I. Andersen and David Noel Freedman, *Amos: A New Translation with Introduction and Commentary* (New Haven, CT: Yale University Press, 2008), 261.
3. Frank Moore Cross, *From Epic to Canon: History and Literature in Ancient Israel* (Baltimore: Johns Hopkins University Press, 1998), 11–13.
4. Cross, *From Epic to Canon*, 4.
5. According to Cross, "The language of 'brotherhood' and 'fatherhood,' 'love,' and 'loyalty,' is 'covenant terminology.' This is to turn things upside down. The language of covenant, kinship-in-law, is taken from the language of kinship, kinship-in-flesh." See *From Epic to Canon*, 11. Examples of Amos's use of kinship terminology are found throughout Amos. The term *love* (אהב, *'āhav*) is used in Amos 4:5 and 5:15; *brother* (אח, *'aḥ*) in 1:9 and 1:11; *son/child* (בן, *bēn*) in 2:11; 3:1, 12; 4:5; 7:17; and 9:7; *daughter* (בת, *bat*) in 7:17; *wife* (אשה, *'iššā*) in 4:3 and 7:17; and *father* (אב, *'āv*) in 2:4 and 2:7.
6. Andersen and Freedman, *Amos*, 226–27.
7. See John Barton, *The Theology of the Book of Amos* (Cambridge: Cambridge University Press, 2012); Ferry Yefta Mamahit, "Establishing Justice in the Land: Rhetoric and Theology of Social Justice in the Book of Amos" (PhD diss., University of Pretoria, 2010); and Walter Houston, *Contending for Justice: Ideologies and Theologies of Social Justice in the Old Testament* (London: T&T Clark, 2006), esp. 58–71.
8. Scholars identify tension in the text of Amos between social justice and religious law as an important theme of the book; see Nili Wazana, "Amos against Amaziah (Amos 7:10–17): A Case of Mutual Exclusion," *Vetus Testamentum* 70 (2020): 209–28; and John W. Hilber, "Liturgy and Cult," in *Dictionary of the Old Testament Prophets: A Compendium of Contemporary Biblical Scholarship*, ed. Mark J. Broda and J. Gordon McConville (Downers Grove, IL: IVP Academic, 2012), 513–24.
9. According to George E. Mendenhall, the enactment of a covenant "almost always [included] some kind of ritual act that is regarded as essential to the ratification of the binding promise." See Mendenhall, "Covenant," in *Anchor Bible Dictionary*, ed. David Noel Freedman (New York: Doubleday, 1997), 1179.

10. Jonathan Klawans, *Purity, Sacrifice, and the Temple: Symbolism and Supersessionism in the Study of Ancient Judaism* (Oxford: Oxford University Press, 2006), 249.
11. Ludwig Koehler, Walter Baumgartner, and Johann J. Stamm, *The Hebrew and Aramaic Lexicon of the Old Testament*, trans. and ed. Mervyn E. J. Richardson, 4 vols. (Leiden: Brill, 1994–1999), s.v. אח; hereafter *HALOT*.
12. Meyer Fortes, *Kinship and the Social Order: The Legacy of Lewis Henry Morgan* (London: Routledge, 1969; repr., 2004), 237.
13. *HALOT*, s.v. ברית.
14. Cross identifies these terms as follows: Arabic *ʻahd*, Aramaic *ʻâdayyāʼ*, Akkadian *rikšātum*, and Hebrew *ʻēdōt* (עדות); see Cross, *From Epic to Canon*, 16–17.
15. Johannes Pedersen, *Der Eid bei den Semiten in seinem Verhältnis zu verwandten Erscheinungen sowie die Stellung des Eides im Islam* (Strasbourg: Karl J. Trübner, 1914), 8; trans. Frank Moore Cross in *From Epic to Canon*, 16.
16. J. Andrew Dearman, "The Family in the Old Testament," *Interpretation* 52 (1998): 117–29.
17. Peter C. Craigie, *The Book of Deuteronomy* (Grand Rapids, MI: Eerdmans, 1976), 108.
18. James L. Mays, *Amos: A Commentary* (Philadelphia: Westminster Press, 1969), 35.
19. It should be noted that the posterity of Jacob and Esau are not the only descendants in the Old Testament who receive the benefits of a covenant of kinship; see the covenant made between David and Jonathan in 1 Samuel 18:1–3 and reaffirmed in 2 Samuel 1:26. Cross comments that "the covenant is binding on the offspring of David and Jonathan. David is to protect Jonathan's name (lineage) in the event of his death. In life and death, loyalty appropriate to kinsmen is to be kept unbroken." See Cross, *From Epic to Canon*, 9.
20. Scott W. Hahn, *Kinship by Covenant: A Canonical Approach to the Fulfillment of God's Saving Promises* (New Haven, CT: Yale University Press, 2009), 28–31.

21. While Edom is primarily discussed in the Old Testament in kinship with Israel based on their shared ancestry, 2 Samuel 8:13 and 1 Kings 11:15 describe events in which David and Solomon subjugate Edom through a treaty that forges a covenant of kinship primarily based on political alliances.
22. Hanna E. Kassis, "Gath and the Structure of 'Philistine' Society," *Journal of Biblical Literature* 84 (1965): 259–71.
23. See Samuel Greengus, "Covenant and Treaty in the Hebrew Bible and in the Ancient Near East," in *Ancient Israel's History: An Introduction to Issues and Sources*, ed. Bill T. Arnold and Richard S. Hess (Grand Rapids, MI: Baker, 2014), 126. The inscriptions of Bar-Ga'yah and Mati'el from Sefire are an example of such monumental inscriptions memorializing a treaty between nation-states contemporaneous to the time of Amos; see Joseph A. Fitzmyer, "The Inscriptions of Bar-Ga'yah and Mati'el from Sefire," in *The Context of Scripture: Canonical Compositions, Monumental Inscriptions, and Archival Documents from the Biblical World*, vol. 2 of Monumental Inscriptions from the Biblical World, ed. William Hallo (Leiden: Brill, 2000), 213–17.
24. Noel Weeks, *Admonition and Curse: The Ancient Near Eastern Treaty/Covenant Form as a Problem in Inter-Cultural Relationships* (London: T&T Clark International, 2004).
25. *HALOT*, s.v. פשע.
26. Andersen and Freedman, *Amos*, 383.
27. Jason Radine, *The Book of Amos in Emergent Judah* (Tübingen, Germany: Mohr Siebeck, 2010), 72.
28. Ilona Zsolnay, review of *Violence and Personhood in Ancient Israel and Comparative Contexts*, by T. M. Lemos, *Journal of the American Oriental Society* 140 (2020): 251–53.
29. Tchavdar S. Hadjiev, *The Composition and Redaction of the Book of Amos* (Berlin: De Gruyter, 2009), 45–46.
30. Keith N. Schoville, "A Note on the Oracles of Amos against Gaza, Tyre, and Edom," in *Studies on Prophecy: A Collection of Twelve Papers*, ed. G. W. Anderson et al. (Leiden: Brill, 1974), 58.
31. *HALOT*, s.v. ארמון.

32. Shalom M. Paul, "Amos III 15—Winter and Summer Mansions," *Vetus Testamentum* 28 (1978): 358–60.
33. Andersen and Freedman, *Amos*, 383.
34. Andersen and Freedman, *Amos*, 46.
35. Gregory Chirichigno, *Debt-Slavery in Israel and the Ancient Near East* (Sheffield: Sheffield Academic Press, 1993), 127.
36. Marion G. Romney, "Caring for the Poor—A Covenantal Obligation," *Ensign*, November 1978, 89.
37. Henry B. Eyring, "Witnesses for God," *Ensign*, November 1996, 31.
38. David A. Bednar, "Prepared to Obtain Every Needful Thing," *Ensign*, May 2019, 103.
39. Guide to the Scriptures, "Consecrate, Law of Consecration," https://churchofjesuschrist.org/study/scriptures/gs/consecrate-law-of-consecration.
40. The context of 4 Nephi 1:3 is instructive in this manner. Mormon, in his recitation of the history of the Nephites, emphasizes that there were no poor among both the Nephites and the Lamanites, suggesting that the benefits of consecration extended beyond covenantal boundaries.
41. Pew Research Center, "A Portrait of Mormons in the U.S.," https://pewforum.org/2009/07/24/a-portrait-of-mormons-in-the-us.
42. Pew Research Center, "How Americans Compare with the Global Middle Class," https://pewresearch.org/fact-tank/2015/07/09/how-americans-compare-with-the-global-middle-class.
43. N. Eldon Tanner, "The Great Commandment," in Conference Report, April 1967, 104.

18

Justice and Righteousness
Jeremiah against King and People

David A. LeFevre

Jeremiah was a prophet, which in Hebrew is *nābî'*, a term that refers to people who were messengers and spokespeople for Israel's God.[1] They were to speak the words of Yahweh to the people that were needed for that time and place. Jeremiah was one of many who came at this time in history to the southern kingdom of Judah.[2] He was called by the Lord to "speak whatever I [the Lord] command you" (Jeremiah 1:7 NRSV), which included words intended

> to pluck up and to pull down,
> to destroy and to overthrow,
> to build and to plant.[3]

Some of Jeremiah's words—such as *plucked up, pulled down, destroyed,* and *overthrew*—included his pronouncements against kings, leaders, and the people, condemning them for covenantal violations manifest in their treatment of those in greatest need in their society.

As explained in this paper, violating God's teachings about social justice—teachings that Jeremiah and other prophets defined as caring for the orphan, the widow, and the stranger (those on the margins of Jewish culture and economics)—led directly to the destruction about which he and other prophets forewarned. The key phrases in the charge against the people are presented early in Jeremiah's book:

> If you return, O Israel, says the Lord,
>   if you return to me,
> if you remove your abominations from my presence,
>   and do not waver,
> and if you swear, "As the Lord lives!"
>   in truth, in *justice*, and in *uprightness*,
> then nations shall be blessed by him,
>   and by him they shall boast.
> (Jeremiah 4:1–2; emphasis added)

Though the total charges of wickedness include worshipping false gods and turning away from Yahweh, the Lord,[4] this paper focuses on the social justice issues raised in Jeremiah's condemnation that the people did not live with "justice" and "uprightness," both of which refer to how orphans, widows, and strangers (refugees) were treated by the king, his leaders, and his subjects.

A Brief History

Jeremiah 1:2 records that the word of the Lord came to Jeremiah in the days of Josiah, king of Judah (640–609 BC). But little, if any, of Jeremiah's recorded teachings take place in that period. The added note in 1:3 that the word of the Lord "came also in the days of King Jehoiakim son of Josiah of Judah, and until the end of the eleventh year of King Zedekiah son of Josiah of Judah" accurately reflects the bulk of the material in Jeremiah's book. The writings of Jeremiah are not presented to us in chronological order—indeed, much of the book cannot be dated to any specific time, and what is tied to identifiable events skips around through Jeremiah's life as the reader progresses through the chapters. There is a discernible thematic structure to the book, but even within its subsections the intent of the editor(s) is not always clear to us today.[5] However, since Jeremiah's oracles are often directed at monarchs, having a basic understanding of the kings of his lifetime helps establish the context of individual pronouncements.

Josiah was eight years of age in 640 BC when he became king after his father, Amon, was killed in an apparent palace coup (2 Kings 21:23–24; 22:1). It is recorded that Josiah "did what was right in the sight of the Lord" (22:2). In 609 BC he led an army against Egypt and was killed in battle. His son Jehoahaz was put on the throne by the people in about June 609 BC (23:29–30). Jehoahaz's reign lasted only three months because the Egyptian pharaoh Necho summoned Jehoahaz to Riblah and sent him in captivity to Egypt, where he died (23:33–34; see also Jeremiah 22:10–11, where Shallum is another name for Jehoahaz).[6] Necho placed another son of Josiah, Jehoiakim (rendered Eliakim in 2 Kings 23:34), on the throne in his brother's place about September 609 BC and exacted a heavy tribute from the new vassal. Jehoiakim held his position on the throne for eleven years (23:33–36).

Jehoiakim did not follow the religious practices of his father but built himself a lavish palace at the expense of others (Jeremiah 22:13–19), allowed pagan practices to dominate religious life (7:17–18; 11:9–13), and put to death prophets who spoke against him (26:20–23). During his reign, the Babylonian army defeated Egypt and marched through Syria and Palestine. To avoid destruction, Jehoiakim pledged his allegiance to Nebuchadnezzar and Babylon, but a short time later when Babylon suffered a defeat at the hands of Egypt, Jehoiakim determined to shift his allegiance back to Egypt (2 Kings 24:1). Accordingly, in December 598 BC, the Babylonians came to punish Jerusalem. As they approached, it appears that Jehoiakim was killed in an internal coup, likely in the hope that Nebuchadnezzar might not destroy the city, and Jehoiakim's eighteen-year-old-son, Jehoiachin, was put on the throne (Jeremiah 22:18–19; 36:30–31; 2

Kings 24:6, 8). When Nebuchadnezzer arrived, however, he deposed Jehoiachin and carried him away to Babylon to spend the rest of his life in captivity. Nebuchadnezzer then put another son of Josiah, Mattaniah, on the throne and changed his name to Zedekiah. The Babylonians ransacked the palace and temple and took many captive who were essential to the functioning of the city (2 Kings 24:11–18; 1 Nephi 1:4). Zedekiah's reign came to an end when he, too, rebelled against Babylon. The Babylonian army returned to Jerusalem in July 587 BC, this time to destroy the city. Zedekiah was forced to watch the slaying of his sons, after which he was blinded and taken captive to Babylon. The Babylonians then deported even more people (2 Kings 25:1–21).[7]

During these tumultuous times Jeremiah preached and taught the critical need to care for the poor and the helpless and, at the same time, sought to save the city from destruction; however, he was consistently met with opposition from kings, city leaders, and many of the people. In this chapter, I will examine two events in Jeremiah's ministry that best demonstrate his effort to preach and save—his call to action for the new king and his sermon at the temple, both of which occurred during Jehoiakim's early reign.

Call to Action for the New King (Jeremiah 22:1–19)

Though the date is not certain, the events in these verses appear to have occurred early in the reign of Jehoiakim, likely in the late summer of 609 BC, shortly after he replaced his brother Jehoahaz as king. Several references in these verses seem to correspond to that time. For example, Jeremiah declares that "Shallum" will never return to Jerusalem but will die "in the place where they have carried him" (Jeremiah 22:12). As explained above, Shallum is Jehoahaz, the king just prior to Jehoiakim "who went away from this place" (22:11). The verses also mention "him who is dead" (22:10), a clear reference to Josiah's death that had occurred just a few months earlier that year.

These verses in Jeremiah 22 divide readily into three sections: 1–9 are a call for the king and royal officials to do right; 10–12, a lamentation for Josiah and Jehoahaz; and 13–19, a declaration of woe directed at the king, Jehoiakim. Verse 1 begins as Jeremiah is commanded by Yahweh, "Go down to the house of the king of Judah, and speak there this word" (Jeremiah 22:1). The command to "go down" implies that Jeremiah was likely at the temple when the Lord spoke to him, since the temple was the highest place in Jerusalem.[8] The first words from the Lord through Jeremiah to the king, his officials, and the other people going in and out of the king's palace are *ăśû mišpāṭ ûṣĕdāqâ*, "act with justice and righteousness" (22:3). The two nouns in this phrase are the focal point of Jeremiah's message to the king and court and are worth a close examination.

The first, *mišpāṭ*, is a rich term with many meanings related to litigation ("act," "place," "process," "legal case," and "legal decision"), laws and ordinances, and rights under the law.[9] In the more than four hundred occurrences of this term in the KJV, this masculine noun is most often translated as "judgment," but that word choice doesn't reflect the depth of the word in our current vocabulary. No single term expresses it perfectly, but *justice* is probably the best fit.[10] God can demand *mišpāṭ* of us because he is a God of *mišpāṭ* (Isaiah 30:18), he judges the whole earth with *mišpāṭ* (Genesis 18:25),[11] and he reflects in his own actions his just claims and expectations for our treatment one toward another. *Mišpāṭ* is the foundation of the Mosaic law (Deuteronomy 33:10), including its offerings (see Leviticus 5:10, where *mišpāṭ* is translated as "the manner" in the KJV). Even the breastplate worn by the high priest is called the breastplate of *mišpāṭ* (Exodus 28:15), signifying the need for the high priest to consider what is in his heart when rendering judgment.[12]

The second noun, *ṣĕdāqâ*, is so linked to *mišpāṭ* that they lie together "at the very heart of a true understanding of the Biblical world-and-life view."[13] This feminine noun is often translated as "righteousness," but like *mišpāṭ*, *ṣĕdāqâ* can have several nuanced meanings, including "justice," "being made right," "deliverance," and "blameless behavior."[14] It represents "deeds not obligatory upon the doer."[15] The term ṣĕdāqâ is tightly linked to the covenant: ṣĕdāqâ is "the execution of covenant faithfulness and the covenant promises. God's righteousness as His judicial reign means that in covenant faithfulness to His people He vindicates and saves them."[16]

When Jeremiah challenges the people at the royal house to act with mišpāṭ and ṣĕdāqâ, as detailed below, he is declaring that because of the Sinaitic covenant the Israelites made with God, they are to treat those around them according to what is right and just. In Jeremiah 22:9, envisioning the city's future destruction, some ask why Yahweh would do this, and others answer, "Because they abandoned the covenant of the Lord their God." To further associate this condemnation with Israel's covenant, in verse 3 Jeremiah calls out four specific groups that need just and righteous attention from the leaders.

"*Deliver from the hand of the oppressor anyone who has been robbed*" (Jeremiah 22:3). The last verb, translated as "robbed," is gāzal, meaning to "tear away," "seize," or "steal," including with violence or force.[17] Verses 13–19 explain that King Jehoiakim (specifically named in verse 17) is the oppressor alluded to in verse 3. He used conscripted labor early in his reign to build himself a fine palace, with cut windows and cedar paneling, and to paint it vermillion, a bright red. In fact, Jeremiah accuses the king of completing this lavish building effort by using negative forms of the same verbs: Jeremiah puts the negative particle lō' in front of both mišpāṭ and ṣĕdāqâ, literally saying that Jehoiakim built the house with *not righteousness* and built his upper rooms with *not justice* (22:13–14). Jeremiah declares that just because Jehoiakim can force people to build his palace doesn't make him a king: "Did not your father [Josiah] eat and drink and do justice (mišpāṭ) and righteousness (ṣĕdāqâ)? Then it was well with him" (22:15). In other words, Josiah as king was supplied with needed daily sustenance, and at the same time he was just and fair toward the people. Jeremiah declares that Jehoiakim should be as Josiah was, rather than oppressing the people for personal benefit and comfort, which is a violation of Mosaic law.

"*Do no wrong or violence to the alien*" (Jeremiah 22:3). The two verbs are *yānâ*, meaning to "oppress," "mistreat," or "be violent,"[18] and *ḥāmas*, to "treat violently" or to "wrong."[19] The term for "alien" is *gēr*, meaning a "sojourner," "foreigner," or "new arrival."[20] Today we might say "refugee" because a *gēr* was someone who was driven from home by war, famine, or pestilence, one who sought shelter in another village or with a different tribe where his or her rights were likely curtailed.[21] The Mosaic covenant requires fair treatment of people coming in from outside the Israelite culture (Leviticus 19:33), but Jeremiah proclaims that those in the palace (his audience as shown in verse 1) were treating people from outside their kingdom with oppression and violence.

"*Do no wrong or violence to . . . the orphan, and the widow*" (Jeremiah 22:3). Orphans and widows were also being treated with oppression and violence. Because wives with no husband and children with no father[22] had few legal rights in their society, caring for widows and orphans required extra effort on the part of the people. Scripture made clear that caring for these individuals was an important part of the covenant and was expected of the people,[23] and Jeremiah continued to teach that consistently, whether directing his comments at palace officials or making other pronouncements throughout his ministry, as mentioned below.

Caring for the three groups mentioned—the stranger, the fatherless child, and the widow—is a critical part of the law and the Sinaitic covenant that had been in place since the days of Moses (Exodus 22:21–22). The concept of assuring justice for these marginalized individuals is especially strong in Deuteronomy,[24] the likely text that was brought to the attention of both king and subjects in the days of Josiah and that triggered his reform efforts (2 Kings 22:8–11).[25] Jeremiah strongly condemns their failure to care for the marginalized and calls upon the king and leaders to repent and live up to the Sinaitic and Deuteronomic covenants.

Jeremiah promises that acting in *mišpāṭ* and *ṣĕdāqâ*—justice and righteousness—toward these marginalized members of society will result in kings being able to enter in safety through the open gates of the royal palace (representing an extended time of peace and safety), while riding on horses and in splendid chariots, alongside their servants and the people (representing the continuation of Davidic rule over the people of Judah). However, Jeremiah warns that failing to act in justice and righteousness will result in "this house" becoming "a desolation" (Jeremiah 22:4–5). The Hebrew word for "house" is *bayit*, which refers both to the physical palace-under-construction from which Jeremiah is delivering this message and to the posterity of the king, the house of David.[26] Both palace and posterity are threatened by the lack of justice and righteousness.

Jeremiah next declares Yahweh's words against this lavish palace-building project that Jehoiakim had undertaken, which Jeremiah compared to Gilead and Lebanon (both beautiful and prosperous places). He revealed that without repentance, Yahweh would make it an uninhabited desert by bringing destroyers against it who would cut up the fine cedar beams and burn them (22:6–7).

Jeremiah reveals the ultimate result of doing justice and righteousness and caring for the poor and the needy by asking a question: "Is not this to know me? says the Lord" (22:16). To "know" God is more than knowing about him or being acquainted with him. The term used, *daʿat*, refers to knowledge gained through personal experience.[27] This kind of knowledge is possessed by God himself (Psalm 139:1–18), but he shares it with humans (Psalm 94:10; Proverbs 2:6). It also appears in the name of the tree in the Garden of Eden (the tree of knowledge; Genesis 2:9, 17), by whose fruit Adam and Eve could know good and evil (3:5). The prophet Hosea (roughly 150 years before Jeremiah) spoke of this knowledge thematically in his book because the knowledge of God was missing in Israel, and its absence was destroying the people (Hosea 4:1, 6).[28] Indeed, God prefers this knowledge of him among the people far more than burnt offerings in the temple (6:6). Jeremiah's point is that this intimate, personal knowledge of Yahweh comes through living in justice and righteousness and in how we perform acts of social justice—especially toward those on the edges of society and with the fewest privileges, such as refugees, widows, and orphans. To care for the dispossessed is to know God.

However, Jeremiah prophesies that Jehoiakim will not know God in this way because he is focused on "dishonest gain," "shedding innocent blood," and "practicing oppression and violence" (Jeremiah 22:17). Therefore, no one shall lament Jehoiakim, but he shall be buried like a donkey—dragged out of the city and tossed out like trash outside the city gates (22:18–19). Unfortunately, the king did not humbly receive this call to repent but was angry at this and other pronouncements from Jeremiah. This discord was the beginning of great animosity between the two men. Later, when a scroll with Jeremiah's words was read to him, Jehoiakim listened, but as each section was finished, he cut it from the scroll with a knife and burned it in the fire. At the end of the reading, he called for Jeremiah's arrest, along with that of his scribe, Baruch (36:20–26).

The message of these verses in Jeremiah 22, then, is that the king especially, but also the other leaders, were not following the example of Josiah, Jehoiakim's father. Rather, they were abusing their positions of power and privilege by putting burdens on the people for the leaders' benefit and ignoring the care of those who were in greatest need. Such a violation of God's law and covenant obligations will bring these leaders to destruction.

Sermon at the Temple (Jeremiah 7:1–15; 26:1–24)

Two chapters, Jeremiah 7 and 26, relate an account of Jeremiah preaching at the temple. Scholars generally agree that these chapters transmit two versions of the same event, with chapter 7 giving the longer version of the sermon and chapter 26 giving a fuller report of its aftermath.[29] The sermon occurs in "the beginning of the reign of King Jehoiakim" (Jeremiah 26:1), meaning the period of time that began after his installment by Egypt's pharaoh but before his first full regnal year, which started with the new year in the spring.[30] For maximum effect, this sermon may have been delivered in the fall of 609 BC in conjunction with the Feast of Tabernacles (or Booths), which was held at the temple in late September or early October,[31] when large crowds would be in attendance. Unlike the call to action to the king and his court in 22:1–19, this sermon is directed to "all you people of Judah" (7:1) gathered at the temple.

Jeremiah begins by announcing, "Thus says the Lord of hosts, the God of Israel: Amend your ways and your doings, and let me dwell with you in this place" (Jeremiah 7:3). Since Jeremiah is standing in the gate of the temple (7:2), "this place" in verse 3 refers to the temple, emphasized by the repeated use of the word in verse 4. Verse 7 has a nearly identical phrase: "then I will let you dwell in this place" (NASB), though in verse 7 "this place" refers to the land, not the temple. This repetition of the verb "to dwell" serves to bracket and tie together the pronouncements in verses 4–7 but adds an important twist. Ancient Hebrew was written only with consonants, not vowels, with the vocalizations being added in written form hundreds of years later by Masorete scribes.[32] Scholars have noted that the early Latin translation (predating the oldest Hebrew text with vowel markings) of verse 3 conjugated the verb as "I will dwell," essentially quoting the promise of Exodus 25:8, "I will dwell among them" (NIV).[33] If correct, this emended reading reveals wordplay on Jeremiah's part: the same verb *to dwell* is vocalized slightly differently in the two verses, offering a twofold promise to the people: If they repent and change, Yahweh will dwell with them in the temple *and* Yahweh will let them dwell in the land.

Jeremiah outlines the changes Yahweh expects from the people in verses 7:4–6. They are not to trust in the words of the false prophets, who say, "the temple of the Lord," which Jeremiah repeats three times in emphasis (or perhaps in mockery of their misplaced confidence). This saying that Jeremiah denounces refers to the people's traditional belief that having the temple of Yahweh in the city would protect them from their enemies, a belief perhaps based on Isaiah 37:33–35.[34] But Jeremiah declares these thrice repeated words are actually *šeqer*, which can mean "deception," "falsehood," or even "disappointment."[35] The Lord had indeed promised preservation and other great blessings (e.g., Deuteronomy 7:12–15), but only if the people were obedient to the ordinances and covenants he had given them. Later, perhaps unknowingly confirming Jeremiah's words, Ezekiel symbolically described the departure of the Lord from his house: "Then the glory of the Lord went out from the threshold of the house and stopped above the cherubim. The cherubim lifted up their wings and rose up from the earth in my sight as they went out with the wheels beside them. They stopped at the entrance of the east gate[36] of the house of the Lord; and the glory of the God of Israel was above them. . . . And the glory of the Lord ascended from the middle of city" (Ezekiel 10:18–19; 11:23).

Jeremiah then describes the specific behaviors the Lord requires of the people of Judah for the city to be saved, and the prophet accomplishes this by going back to the language of verse 3 with increased emphasis to teach the people to amend their ways and doings (verses 5–6).

"*Truly act justly one with another*" (Jeremiah 7:5). Here again he uses the word *mišpāṭ*, demanding that the people act with justice toward each other. As reflected in the translation to "truly act justly," the Hebrew is emphatic with a doubling of the verb *ʿāśô taʿăśû mišpāṭ*, literally "to make make justice." This verb repetition in Hebrew is an intensification of the action, employed often in the Old Testament and twice in this verse alone.[37]

"*Do not oppress the alien, the orphan, and the widow, or shed innocent blood in this place*" (Jeremiah 7:6). While the word *ṣĕdāqâ* does not appear in this verse, this is a near quote from 22:3, which defines justice and righteousness in Jeremiah's writings. As explained above, the social acts of caring for the refugee, the fatherless child, and the widow (representative of oppressed people in their society) are a critical part of the covenant between the Israelites and Yahweh. The reference to "innocent blood" is what is known as judicial murder—where someone is killed through abuse of the legal system[38]—which is a consistent charge of Jeremiah against the king, his leaders, and, now, the people in general.

"*Do not go after other gods to your own hurt*" (Jeremiah 7:6). Rejecting Israel's God means rejecting the commandments and covenants that are core to that relationship. After the people rejected the second half of the Ten Commandments (Exodus 20:12–17) by mistreating others, Jeremiah implores them not to also reject the first half (Exodus 20:1–11), which relates to their relationship with Yahweh. To the crowd at the temple, Jeremiah exclaims that denying the covenant relationship they have with the Lord will truly result in their own ruin and destruction.

Jeremiah asks them how they could do all manner of evil and then come to worship Yahweh in his house and declare, "We are safe!" (Jeremiah 7:9–10). Their activities mimic robbers who commit their crimes, then flee to their cave ("den") for safety (7:11).[39] To refute their false sense of safety, Jeremiah evokes the image of the house of the Lord at Shiloh, which was destroyed by Israel's enemies (1 Samuel 4).[40] Evidently the destruction was still visible in some way in their day ("see what I did to it," invites Yahweh in verse 12). Because they have not listened to him and his prophets, Yahweh will destroy the temple in Jerusalem and carry away the people, which is what had happened to the northern kingdom (7:13–15).

The result of Jeremiah's sermon that called for justice and righteousness among the people was his arrest, leading to perhaps the best documented trial in the Old Testament. With the priests, (false) prophets, and people all against him, he was taken to the city gate for judgment and sat before the princes (Jeremiah 26:8–10). The priests and prophets acted as prosecutors, ironically declaring that Jeremiah "deserves the sentence of death" (26:11), which phrase uses the word *mišpāṭ*, meaning that, in their opinion, justice for Jeremiah was death. Jeremiah acknowledges speaking the words that they accused him of saying—words that were his call of repentance to the people—then declares, "I am in your hands" (26:14). He warns, however, that if they put him to death, they would be killing an innocent man and would bring divine judgment upon themselves (26:15).[41] Others next cited the conflicting precedents of Micah and Urijah. Micah prophesied against Jerusalem but was listened to by the king (26:17–19) and was thereby able to save the city, but Urijah, Jeremiah's contemporary who declared a message similar to Micah's, was killed by Jehoiakim in an act of judicial murder—a perfect example of what Jeremiah had previously condemned (26:20–23). Fortunately, Jeremiah had support from some people in the government (26:24), and in the end the princes said they would not find Jeremiah at fault and reversed the charge of the priests and prophets by saying, "This man does *not* deserve the sentence (*mišpāṭ*) of death, for he has spoken to us in the name of the Lord our God" (26:16).

Additional Examples of Cries for Social Justice

Jeremiah continued to teach and call for the people to act with justice and righteousness throughout his ministry, and he recorded other instances in which the Lord affirmed the importance of such actions. At one time, Yahweh had a conversation with Jeremiah, expressed poetically, and invited him to find anyone acting correctly:

> Run to and fro through the streets of Jerusalem,
>   look around and take note!
> Search its squares and see if you can find one person
>   who acts justly [*mišpāṭ*]
>   and seeks truth—
> so that I may pardon Jerusalem.
> (Jeremiah 5:1)

Jeremiah counters that the poor people don't know the law (*mišpāṭ*) but hopes that if he can preach to the rich who do know the law (*mišpāṭ*), things will be better (Jeremiah 5:4–5). But the Lord calls the rich "lusty stallions, each neighing for his neighbor's wife," and asks, "Shall I not punish them for these things?" (5:8–9), referring to the wealthy's complete rejection of justice. On another occasion the Lord told Jeremiah that humans should not glory in their own wisdom, might, or riches, but should boast in their knowledge of the Lord. "I act," he declares, "with steadfast love, justice [mišpāṭ], and righteousness [ṣĕdāqâ] in the earth, for in these things I delight, says the Lord" (9:23–24).

Jeremiah also hoped for a better future in which the principles of justice and righteousness would be fully observed under the direction of the Messiah of the house of David. "The days are surely coming, says the Lord, when I will raise for David a righteous [ṣaddîq, "rightful," a term related to ṣĕdāqâ] Branch, and he shall reign as king and deal wisely, and shall execute justice [mišpāṭ] and righteousness [ṣĕdāqâ] in the land" (Jeremiah 23:5). And again, "In those days and at that time I will cause a righteous [ṣĕdāqâ] Branch to spring up for David; and he shall execute judgment [mišpāṭ] and righteousness [ṣĕdāqâ] in the land" (33:15). Later in his ministry, Jeremiah counseled those carried away to Babylon to have hope as well:

> We tried to heal Babylon,
>   but she could not be healed.
> Forsake her, and let each of us go
>   to our own country;
> for her judgment [mišpāṭ] has reached up to heaven
>   and has been lifted up even to the skies.
> The Lord has brought forth our vindication [ṣĕdāqâ];
>   come, let us declare in Zion
>   the work of the Lord our God.
> (Jeremiah 51:9–10)

In Jeremiah's teachings, establishing justice and righteousness meant caring for those in need (particularly refugees, widows, and orphans), being fair and just in dealing with others, and not abusing any positions of power or authority. This meaning is the essence of the law given through Moses and other prophets to the Israelites, the application of its best principles, and the pattern (of how we should interact with others) established for us by God himself. Today, we can only hope that our response to Jeremiah's call for people who are marginalized to be treated with justice and righteousness is radically different from how the residents of Jerusalem in Jeremiah's day treated them. We cannot do as those in Jerusalem did and ignore Jeremiah's voice without likewise suffering a tragic fate.

David A. LeFevre is an independent scholar in the Seattle, Washington, area.

Notes

1. Francis Brown, S. R. Driver, and Charles A. Briggs, *The Brown-Driver-Briggs Hebrew and English Lexicon* (Peabody, MA: Hendrickson, 2001), 611–12 (hereafter *BDB*); William L. Holladay, ed., *A Concise Hebrew and Aramaic Lexicon of the Old Testament* (Grand Rapids, MI: Eerdmans, 1971), 225 (hereafter *CHALOT*).
2. The prophet Lehi was a contemporary of Jeremiah (1 Nephi 1:4–6), as were Huldah the prophetess (2 Kings 22:14–20; 2 Chronicles 34:22–28) and Zephaniah (Zephaniah 1:1). Other contemporary prophets likely included Habakkuk, whose book has no date though his message about the Babylonians (Habakkuk 1:6) ties him to this period; Nahum, who writes about the fall of Assyria (Nahum 1:1), which happened in 612 BC; and Ezekiel and Daniel, who were contemporaries but received their calls after being carried away into or near Babylon (Ezekiel 1:1–2; Daniel 1:1–6), so they did not minister in Jerusalem as Jeremiah and the others did.
3. Jeremiah 1:10 NRSV. Quotes from scripture in this chapter will be from the New Revised Standard Version unless otherwise specified. Many of these six verbs are repeated in prose format in other sections of Jeremiah (including 12:14–17; 18:7–9; 24:6; 31:28, 40; 33:4; 42:10; 45:4) and indicate how Jeremiah and the Lord incorporated Jeremiah's personal mission statement into his teachings to the people.
4. References to "the Lord" in the KJV and other translations generally refer to the Hebrew word *yhwh*, which is typically transliterated as *Yahweh* by most scholars today but previously had been transliterated as *Jehovah*. The

exact pronunciation is not known, but *yhwh* is the most common name for the Hebrew God of the Old Testament.

5. Scholars generally agree that the book of Jeremiah as we have it today was prepared by the hand of one or more editors, whether by Baruch, his scribe, or by other unnamed people. Notably large differences exist between the Hebrew version and the Greek version in the Septuagint. See J. A. Thompson, *The Book of Jeremiah* (Grand Rapids, MI: Eerdmans, 1980), 27–50. See also David Rolph Seely, "The Ministry of Jeremiah," in *Studies in Scripture, Volume 4: First Kings to Malachi*, ed. Kent P. Jackson (Salt Lake City: Deseret Book, 1993), 196–98.

6. See 1 Chronicles 3:15; 2 Chronicles 21:17; Thompson, *Book of Jeremiah*, 476; Tremper Longman III and David E. Garland, eds., *The Expositor's Bible Commentary: Jeremiah–Ezekiel* (Grand Rapids, MI: Zondervan, 2010), 7:45. It was a common practice for kings to take a new name when they ascended to the throne; in Jeremiah's lifetime, Shallum became Jehoahaz, Eliakim became Jehoiakim, and Mattaniah became Zedekiah. Jack R. Lundbom, *Jeremiah 21–36* (New Haven, CT: Yale University Press, 2004), 130.

7. For more details about the history of Judah during Jeremiah's time, see Thompson, *Book of Jeremiah*, 9–27; Longman and Garland, *Jeremiah–Ezekiel*, 7:40–46; Christopher J. H. Wright, *The Message of Jeremiah* (Downers Grove, IL: InterVarsity Press, 2014), 17–22; Jack R. Lundbom, *Jeremiah 1–20* (New Haven, CT: Yale University Press, 1999), 102–20; William L. Holladay, *Jeremiah 1: Commentary on the Book of the Prophet Jeremiah* (Minneapolis: Fortress Press, 1986), 1–10; Michael Grant, *The History of Ancient Israel* (New York: Charles Scribner's Sons, 1984), 140–42, 152–57.

8. Longman and Garland, *Jeremiah–Ezekiel*, 7:299. Another time, when the civil leaders at the palace heard Jeremiah was causing an uproar at the temple, they "came up from the king's house" to the temple gate to hold court and pass judgment (Jeremiah 26:10).

9. R. Laird Harris, Gleason L. Archer Jr., and Bruce K. Waltke, *Theological Wordbook of the Old Testament* (Chicago: Moody, 1980), 948–49 (hereafter *TWOT*); *BDB*, 1048–49; *CHALOT*, 221.

10. *TWOT*, 948, comments that the best English rendering "ought by all means to be the word 'justice.'"
11. Isaiah 42:4 says that the Lord will not "faint or be crushed until he has established justice (*mišpāṭ*) in the earth."
12. *TWOT*, 949.
13. *TWOT*, 949.
14. *TWOT*, 752–55; *CHALOT*, 303. One easily thinks of the king of Salem, *malkî-ṣedeq*, "Melchizedek," whose name means "my king is righteousness," likely in reference not to himself but to the King of Kings, the Most High God (*ēl ʿelyôn*), whom he worshipped (Genesis 14:18–19).
15. Jack R. Lundbom, *Jeremiah 21–36* (New York: Doubleday, 2004), 119.
16. *TWOT*, 755.
17. *BDB*, 159–160; *CHALOT*, 58.
18. *BDB*, 413; *CHALOT*, 136; Holladay, *Jeremiah 1*, 580.
19. *BDB*, 329; *CHALOT*, 109.
20. *BDB*, 158; *CHALOT*, 63–64.
21. *CHALOT*, 64.
22. The Hebrew term *yātôm* means specifically a child with no father and does not require that both parents be deceased, which is the typical definition of *orphan* today. See *BDB*, 450; *TWOT*, 419; *CHALOT*, 148.
23. For example, see Exodus 22:22; Psalm 68:5; Isaiah 1:17, 23; 10:2.
24. See Deuteronomy 10:18; 14:29; 16:11, 14; 24:17, 19–21; 26:12–13; 27:19.
25. Many believe Deuteronomy was the book that was found in the temple during the time of Josiah and Jeremiah, a book that strongly influenced Jeremiah's writings; see Thompson, *Book of Jeremiah*, 44–50; Longman and Garland, *Jeremiah–Ezekiel*, 7:37–39.
26. In a parallel passage in chapter 21, the prophetic message is delivered to the "house of David," the only time that phrase appears in Jeremiah and uses similar language to "execute justice" and deliver the oppressed and robbed or suffer the wrath of God "like fire" (21:12).
27. *TWOT*, 366–67; *CHALOT*, 73.
28. Isaiah similarly declared that the people would go into captivity because of a lack of such knowledge (Isaiah 5:13) but that one day this knowledge would fill the earth (11:9).

29. Lundbom, *Jeremiah 1–20*, 454; Holladay, *Jeremiah 1*, 239–40.
30. Longman and Garland, *Jeremiah–Ezekiel*, 7:338; William L. Holladay, *Jeremiah 2* (Minneapolis: Fortress Press, 1989), 103.
31. William L. Holladay, *Jeremiah: A Fresh Reading* (Eugene, OR: Wipf and Stock Publishers, 2012), 27.
32. Walter C. Kaiser Jr., *The Old Testament Documents: Are They Reliable and Relevant?* (Downers Grove, IL: InterVarsity Press, 2001), 43. The text the Masoretes created is called the Masoretic Text or MT.
33. The vocalization for the proposed qal verb in verse 3 is šākantî, "I will dwell," rather than that presented in the current Masoretic text's piʿel verb, šakkĕnâ: "I will cause [you] to dwell." See Holladay, *Jeremiah 1*, 236–37; Longman and Garland, *Jeremiah–Ezekiel*, 7:159; Holladay, *Jeremiah: A Fresh Reading*, 27–28. Compare Exodus 29:45; 1 Kings 6:13; Ezekiel 43:9; Zechariah 2:14–15; 8:3, which all use the "I will dwell" verb form, and Deuteronomy 12:11 and 14:23, where the Lord causes his name to dwell in the temple.
34. Lundbom, *Jeremiah 1–20*, 461.
35. *BDB*, 1055; *CHALOT*, 383.
36. Perhaps this was the very gate from which Jeremiah delivered this message. See Longman and Garland, *Jeremiah–Ezekiel*, 7:159; Lundbom, *Jeremiah 1–20*, 460.
37. The other occurrence is the phrase at the beginning of the verse: "truly amend" is *yatab* doubled, literally "do good, do good." On repetition of verbs, see Holladay, *Jeremiah 1*, 242–43.
38. Thompson, *Book of Jeremiah*, 278.
39. Jesus, of course, will quote this verse when he cleanses the temple in Jerusalem in his day (see Matthew 21:12; Mark 11:17; Luke 19:46).
40. Though the destruction of the city is not documented in the Old Testament, except for a somewhat indirect reference in Psalm 78:59–64, Jeremiah's hometown was the location of the house of priests that descended from Eli, the priest presiding over the tabernacle at Shiloh at the time of its destruction. The priestly family of Abiathar was sent to Anathoth by Solomon (1 Kings 2:26–27), making it likely that Jeremiah knew at least orally the story of the city's fiery destruction, which has been well

documented by archaeology. Lundbom, *Jeremiah 1–20*, 468–69; Holladay, *Jeremiah 1*, 247–48.

41. Compare Mosiah 17:10, where Abinadi declares, "And if ye slay me ye will shed innocent blood, and this shall also stand as a testimony against you at the last day," and Alma 60:13, where Moroni writes to Pahoran, "For the Lord suffereth the righteous to be slain that his justice and judgment may come upon the wicked." Though we don't know the words behind the translation in Alma, the phrase "justice and judgment" in Moroni's letter aligns nicely with the meanings of *mišpāṭ* and *ṣĕdāqâ*.

19

"Go Ye and Learn What That Meaneth"
Mercy and the Law in the Old Testament's Prophetic Literature and in the Gospels

Daniel O. McClellan

One day, as the Savior sat at dinner in Capernaum with tax collectors and sinners, a group of Pharisees approached his disciples and asked, "Why does your teacher eat with tax collectors and sinners?" (Matthew 9:11).[1] In his response, Jesus described his mission in therapeutic terms and appealed to the Old Testament prophet Hosea: "The healthy do not need a doctor, but the sick do. Go learn what this means: 'I want mercy and not sacrifice'; because I have not come to call the righteous, but sinners" (Matthew 9:12–13; compare 12:7).[2] The main point of the response is that Jesus sits with the morally and socially "sick" because his mortal mission is to them, and they are in greater need of the healing power of his presence and message. This explanation, however, bookends a rather peculiar quotation of a passage from Hosea that seems to denigrate temple sacrifices. The quotation appears again in Matthew 12:7. After the Pharisees have condemned Jesus's disciples for plucking and eating grain on the Sabbath, the Savior recalls that David ostensibly violated the law when he entered the temple and ate the Bread of the Presence (1 Samuel 21:1–6) and that priestly work also seems to violate the Sabbath, yet this work is required.[3] Jesus continues, "But if you had understood this—'I want mercy and not sacrifice'—you would not have condemned the innocent."[4]

In each of Christ's first two disputes with the Pharisees, Matthew (and Matthew alone) then has the Savior using this prophetic critique to frame his rejection of their complaints. At first blush, the quotation seems to be a passing rhetorical jab at the harsh legalism of the Pharisees,[5] and Church scholars and curricula have largely treated it as such,[6] but the rhetoric fits into a much broader pattern of prophetic critiques of power that seemingly subordinate the temple and its ordinances to the interests of justice. This pattern has largely gone overlooked within the Church. Matthew has the Savior twice insisting that the Pharisees misunderstand the meaning of a specific scripture, but as modern students of the scriptures, are we exempt from Jesus's charge to "go learn what this means"?

This paper will tug at the loose thread of this rebuke in search of a clearer picture of the particular prophetic critique that rebuke deploys, the role of the law according to that critique, and its adaptation to the Gospels' circumstances, rhetorical exigencies, and understanding of the law. The paper begins with a discussion of ancient Near Eastern conceptualizations of cosmic order, justice, and the law. These concepts operated quite distinctively in the ancient Near East, and properly situating the prophetic critique of power will necessitate orienting our perspective to their conceptual frameworks. At that point, we will move on to the socioeconomic circumstances of the eighth century BC—the time when that prophetic critique emerged—to the content and rhetorical goals of that critique, and, finally, to its deployment by Gospel authors. Many generalities in this interrogation will be inescapable, just as many contexts, exigencies, and perspectives will be irretrievable. Nevertheless, we can still approximate a clearer understanding of "what this means."

Cosmic Order, Justice, and the Law in the Ancient Near East

The term *justice* is common in the Latter-day Saint lexicon today, and in that context, it is most saliently framed as an outcome of judgment, whether to the blessing or punishment of the individual. According to this usage, the semantic focus is not on the actions of the individual or on the circumstances they bring about but rather on the consequences brought about by God's system of reward or punishment.[7] Anciently, however, justice was understood differently, and it fit within a quite distinctive conceptual framework related to social roles and their connection to maintaining cosmic order. Ancient understandings of righteousness and mercy also grew out of this conceptual framework.

The foundation of that framework was the cyclical nature of time. In the ancient Near East, each new year was not simply a new point along a linear timeline, but each year marked the resetting of the previous year's cycle of seasons and the restarting of that cycle for a new year.[8] The continuation of the cycle was not necessarily a given and was dependent on several factors. In a successful yearly cycle, order had to triumph over chaos, which allowed the seasons to transition normally, floods and rains to occur where they were supposed to occur, crops to grow, and families, villages, and nations to meet their needs and be at peace. Order was associated with functionality, and in the broader ancient Near Eastern world, it was thought to have been initially established through a primordial patron deity's victory over a chaotic deity who was usually linked with symbols associated with uninhabitable spaces, such as serpents, monsters, and the sea.[9] While the leading deities and their divine council were understood to most directly influence the subsequent maintenance of that order through the continual suppression of the forces of chaos, the behavior of humans—particularly their performance of rituals and their maintenance of a social equilibrium—was an additional means of helping that order to be maintained.[10] According to this worldview, if deities grew unhappy with the people of their nations, either because of failure to perform the proper ritual acts or because of disorder in their communities, the maintenance of order could be withdrawn as a means of punishment or instruction.[11]

The king was the main point of contact between the human world and the divine and thus was the human with the most influence over the maintenance of both the social and cosmic order. The king's two primary responsibilities to his divine patrons were the facilitation of the rituals and festivals of the temple cult (what we might call the vertical relationship) and the establishment and maintenance of social order (the horizontal relationship) most commonly symbolized by justice (*mišpāṭ* in Hebrew). Kings in the ancient Near East rhetorically emphasized the proliferation of justice in their kingdoms as a means of asserting the divine approbation of their administration, legitimizing their rule, and mitigating discontent and rebellion.[12] An example of this proliferation is the epilogue of the famous law code of Hammurabi (ca. 1792–1750 BC), which states that the gods Anu and Enlil established Hammurabi's rule "to make justice prevail in the land, to abolish the wicked and the evil, to prevent the strong from oppressing the weak."[13]

Justice, according to this understanding, constituted "the privileges owed to each citizen as member of a family unit with a certain recognized socioeconomic status."[14] While we tend to speak of an individual's *rights* in contemporary jurisprudence, the ancient model viewed an individual's *duties* to others as more salient, likely because of the significance of everyone's actions to the broader social order, at least in reflective reasoning about the law. It was not necessarily the suffering of the victims and the violation of their rights that were the main concerns, but it was the broader prosocial implications of the actions of the offender. In the case of violations, justice required the restoration of the social balance. In this sense, the same kind of order that was obtained within the cosmos and among the roles that comprise it must also be obtained among the different social roles within society. The latter could be understood as a reflection of the former.

Because kings could not directly oversee all activity in their kingdoms, two mechanisms were developed for ensuring the maintenance of both types of relationships. Rituals (more directly overseen by priestly classes) maintained the vertical relationship, while law codes (more directly overseen by councils or by individuals who had been designated as judges) were the primary mechanism for maintaining the horizontal relationship and ensuring the maintenance of justice.[15] To the degree that the kings upheld justice within their purviews and facilitated the proper performance of the requisite ritual acts, the gods ensured cosmic order within their own jurisdictions. Scholars have identified multiple discrete collections of laws in the Old Testament, including Exodus's Covenant Code, the Holiness Code in Leviticus, the Deuteronomic Code, and others.[16] The most common types of laws were casuistic, or "case law," which identified a specific kind of situation or case and then prescribed a specific resolution.[17] The Ten Commandments found in Exodus 20:2–17 and Deuteronomy 5:6–21 are what are known as apodictic laws, or laws that absolutely require or prohibit certain actions, independent of the circumstances. Apodictic laws are far less common among ancient laws.

The law collections of the Old Testament are distinct in several other ways from the other legal collections of the ancient Near East. Because the Old Testament is concerned with presenting Jehovah as Israel's ultimate king, the laws do not originate with the human king but with Jehovah. As a result, there is no boasting about the king's own establishment of justice. Instead, Jehovah is presented as the pinnacle and the ultimate source of justice and righteousness. Additionally, in the way they have been preserved, the laws do not exist as independent collections but are embedded within historical narratives that assert their divine origins.[18] They also employ conventions associated with vassal treaties, with Jehovah in the role of suzerain (or dominant party).[19] Thus the laws are accepted by covenant and demand faithfulness.[20] Ritual and festival requirements are also included alongside the more secular laws. Because Jehovah is the originator of the laws, violation of those laws represents not only a threat to the social equilibrium but an offence directly against Jehovah.[21]

The socially marginalized were the focus of the majority of the legal concerns for justice but not because they were the most common day-to-day victims or complainants. Morris Silver explains, "The Ancient Near East designated victims by terms more or less conventionally translated as 'orphan,' 'widow,' 'poor person,' and 'peasant.' The referents are much less real-world social groupings than intellectual constructs. That is, the terms refer to the *ideal victim*."[22] These groups functioned rhetorically as a diagnostic indicator of the presence or absence of justice, and the most acutely marginalized—widows, orphans, and the poor—became the proverbial canaries in the coal mine of justice. Vulnerable groups already experienced greater hardships, but the laws drew a rhetorical line in the sand regarding the exploitation of the groups past which there would be trouble.

Jehovah's law obligated each member of the community to care for and actively seek the well-being of others in the community, particularly the most vulnerable. Under the conceptual umbrella of this obligation, the terms *righteousness* (*ṣĕdāqâ*) and *mercy* (*ḥesed*) in the Old Testament referred to different dimensions of fidelity to the community and to the maintenance of justice within it.[23] Righteous people were those who were loyal to God, to the community, and to the preservation of justice, and—if they had the authority—corrected or removed violations of or threats to that justice. Today we tend to think of righteousness as a strict fidelity to the law, but anciently the scope of righteousness did not stop at the law—it extended beyond the law to the outcomes it was intended to produce. Proverbs 29:7 explains, "A righteous person knows the legal claim of the poor; a wicked person does not understand such knowledge." The law was not an end unto itself, it was a means to an end, and righteousness was concerned with the latter.

Operating within this same conceptual framework, mercy (*ḥesed*) referred to actions that averted danger from members of the society who were not in a position to avert it themselves.[24] Mercy was to be a regular aspect of righteous individuals' engagement with their community—particularly with vulnerable members of the community, to whom the righteous individuals were expected to extend refuge and aid and over whom they should not exploit a harmful advantage. Like righteousness, mercy also widened its gaze beyond the law to the prosocial outcomes at which the law was aimed.[25] The story of Ruth is a wonderful illustration of this. Boaz, himself a righteous man, was happy to marry Ruth because of her multiple acts of ḥesed. She not only offered to remain with Naomi despite having no obligation to do so, but in seeking out a gô'ēl, or "redeemer," for marriage instead of marrying whomever she pleased, she could carry on her deceased husband's line, thus perpetuating Naomi's lineage and bringing glory to her.[26] In each case, Ruth (herself a marginalized member of society) did for others what they could not do for themselves, overturning their unfortunate circumstances not because the law required it—it didn't—but because she loved Naomi.[27]

Israel and Judah in the Eighth Century BC

With this rough understanding of the broad orientation of justice, mercy, and law in early Israel, we can focus on the circumstances to which Hosea and the other prophets were responding. Early in the eighth century BC, imperial pressure on the northern kingdom of Israel and the southern kingdom of Judah from larger regional powers like Assyria and Aram briefly withdrew, allowing the kings who reigned throughout the second quarter of that century—Jeroboam II in Israel (ca. 781–745 BC) and Uzziah in Judah (ca. 781–747 BC)—to exploit their especially lengthy reigns to undertake significant reforms that increased their economic power and their military ambitions. Prior to the eighth century, and with some few exceptions, urban and rural settlements were mostly small and scattered, and much of the agricultural production was limited to subsistence farming and some surplus for mostly local trade.[28] To expand their kingdoms, both kings needed to intensify agricultural production to increase their surplus supplies—particularly olive oil, wine, and wheat—for international trade, primarily with Phoenicia. The northern kingdom had a larger and more organized administration and was also better suited for agricultural production, so it would have taken the lead in this process and would likely have mediated trade for the southern kingdom.[29]

As their administrations grew larger and more complex, both kingdoms increased in urbanization and in number of cities.[30] These changes would have fundamentally restructured life for those working the land. Subsistence farmers would have grown whatever was needed to provide for their households and would have spread out risk among a diversified number of agricultural products. The failure of one crop could be compensated by the success of another that was less affected by whatever went wrong. In this way, farmers prioritized the security that a diverse range of crops provided rather than the efficiency of a single crop. On the other hand, the "command economy" that was being implemented by the monarchy would have involved leveraging taxation, debt, or military protection to compel farmers to grow increasing volumes of whatever was most efficient for the region's soil and climate, as well as whatever was most profitable to the administration.[31] While this would increase the flow of wealth and luxury goods to the urban elite, the tax burden and the restructuring of the farmers' livelihoods would dramatically increase the risk to those living precariously off an unpredictable land. In a more subsistence-based society, a low yield resulting from drought, accident, or some other circumstances could be mitigated through no-interest "survival loans" offered by other members of the village, who were well aware that they themselves could be on the business end of such circumstances before too long. In the command economy of the eighth century BC, however, funds for loans were frequently available only through the wealthy landlords from the urban centers, who usually loaned silver bullion at interest, often required the property as collateral, and usually required payment during the harvest, when the value of grain was at its lowest. In these circumstances, defaults would be common. The result would be an increase in debt slavery, foreclosures, and the prevalence of land consolidation on the part of the elite,[32] all of which would have increased insecurity and instability among the lower classes.

The Prophets Respond

The elite of Israel and Judah found many ways to exploit the poor, and they were fiercely condemned by prophets of the eighth century BC. Amos's rhetoric is perhaps the most thorough and condemns such exploitation as oppressive taxes (Amos 5:11), abuses of loan securities (2:8), debt slavery (2:6), and manipulations of the mechanisms of trade (8:5–6).[33] Amos presents those engaged in these practices as those "who trample the needy, and bring to ruin the poor of the land" (8:4). Similarly, Isaiah condemns those who "make widows your prey, and orphans your spoil" (Isaiah 10:2), and rhetorically asks, "What do you mean by crushing my people, and grinding the faces of the poor" (Isaiah 3:15)?

The prophets particularly excoriated the wealthy and the privileged who exploited the vulnerable in order to enrich themselves. Isaiah 5:8, for instance, pronounces woes upon those engaged in some corrupt manner of land consolidation: "Woe to those who join house to house,[34] / who attach field to field, / until there is no space left, / and you are left to dwell alone / in the midst of the land."[35] Micah 2:2 addresses the same practice: "They desire fields, so they snatch up— / houses, so they take away; / they oppress a man and his house— / a person and his inheritance." The reference here to "inheritance" draws attention to the Mosaic law's concern for keeping land within the family line. While not always consistent, the various laws related to the transfer of land in the Old Testament prioritize a patrimonial system in which the land is inherited based on lineage.[36] The importance of keeping land within the family line is punctuated by both Leviticus's law of land redemption (Leviticus 25:25–31) and Deuteronomy's law of levirate marriage (Deuteronomy 25:5–10), both of which require the redemption of property for the original owner or their progeny. Land consolidation severed these ancestral ties, violating a foundational principle of the nation of Israel and throwing the integrity of the community into disarray.[37]

Corruption was found not only among those who were directly cheating the poor of their property and their goods. The court system, which was supposed to be a means of redress for the marginalized, was also rife with corruption, according to the prophets. Isaiah condemns a long list of wicked people who have "ignored the word of the Holy One of Israel" (Isaiah 5:24), including those who "acquit the guilty because of a bribe, and deprive the innocent of their rights" (5:23). Isaiah 10:1–2 warns such corrupt leaders: "Woe to those who enact iniquitous statutes, / and who write oppressive decrees, / to shove aside the poor from judgment, / and to rob the afflicted of my people of justice; / to make widows your prey, / and orphans your spoil."

Here the broader undermining of justice comes into greater focus. Amos 5:7 accuses Israel's rulers of turning "justice into wormwood" and of bringing "righteousness to the ground." Verses 10–12 of this chapter embed a critique of oppressive taxation ("you trample the poor, / and exact taxes of grain from them") within a denunciation of corrupt elders who facilitate that oppression by ignoring the pleas of victims inside the city gate ("you takers of bribes, / while the needy in the gate / you shove aside"), the traditional site of legal proceedings. Micah 3:11 expands on this criticism, again highlighting the hypocrisy of exploiting the poor and obstructing justice while relying on the protection of the Lord, whose continued presence in Israel was not unconditional: "Her [Israel's] rulers give judgment for a bribe, / her priests instruct for a price, / her prophets divine for silver; / still they lean upon Jehovah, saying, / 'Is Jehovah not in our midst? / Can any harm come upon us?'"

For the prophets, the willingness on the part of the privileged to participate in the requisite sacrifices, offerings, festivals, and feasts (despite their oppression of the marginalized) and their willingness to make offerings from illicitly gotten gains represented a gross perversion of the law and an abdication of the responsibility to facilitate justice.[38] In this regard, the rituals and festivals associated with the temple had devolved into self-serving, credibility-enhancing displays—ways for the wealthy to signal to others their commitment to important Israelite values and ideals so that they could continue to benefit from membership and prominence within the social in-group, even as they knowingly violated the law's requirements associated with the maintenance of justice. The performance of ritual acts based on such selfish motivations and the use of exploited goods was considered by the prophets to be an affront to Jehovah, not only because it neglected parts of the law associated with justice but also because that neglect represented an existential threat to the cosmic order. For the prophets, the law had a broader purpose beyond just the imposition of certain fines and punishments and the realization of certain sacrifices and festivals. For the wealthy to pick and choose aspects of the law whose fulfillment served their own sociocultural exigencies, while abdicating the broader responsibility to effect justice and to maintain the cosmic order, was a violation of the law as a whole.[39]

This conceptual and rhetorical framework contributed to Hosea's statement about mercy and sacrifice, a statement that occurs within the broader context of the prophet's condemnation of the Israelites for their hypocrisy and their failure to maintain fidelity to Jehovah and his covenant. Hosea 6:5–7 describes the woeful state of both Israel and Judah: "Therefore I have hewn them by the prophets, / I have killed them by the words of my mouth, / and my judgment goes forth as light.[40] / For I want mercy, and not sacrifice, / and the knowledge of God more than burnt offerings. / And they, like Adam, transgressed the covenant. / See, they have acted treacherously against me!"[41] Here Jehovah suggests that offering sacrifices and burnt offerings to him is not the ultimate fulfillment of the law and that to offer those sacrifices while violating his covenant and his principles of justice is precisely sin. Hosea 8:13 explains the following regarding Israel's sacrifices: "Jehovah does not accept them."

Other eighth-century prophets engage in similar rhetorical flourishes.[42] The opening chapter of Isaiah is perhaps the most vociferous:[43]

11 "What does the multitude of your sacrifices matter to me?"
        Jehovah says,
    "I have had my fill of burnt offerings of rams and of the
        fat of steers.
    I do not delight in the blood of bulls and lambs and
        goats.
12 When you come to see my face,[44]
    who required it of your hand
    to trample my court?
13 You will bring no more vain offerings;
    incense is an abomination to me.
    New moons and sabbaths, the convocation call—
    I cannot tolerate a sinful assembly.
14 My soul hates your new moons and your festivals.
        They have become a burden upon me
    I am weary of bearing.
15 And when you spread out your hands,
        I will hide my eyes from you;
    even though you multiply prayers,
        I will not hear.
    Your hands are full of blood."

The verse following has a famous pair of imperatives that frequently appear in Church lessons independent of the context of justice: "Wash you, make you clean" (KJV). This passage and verse 18 ("Come now, and let us reason together" [KJV]) most commonly appear in Church messaging about repentance and the Atonement, but in Isaiah these passages bracket serial imperatives in verse 17 that make clear that the intention in the context is to reorient Israel to caring for the disadvantaged: "Learn to do good, / seek justice, / guide the oppressed, / give justice to the orphan, / plead the cause of the widow!"

It is not only the vertical relationship with God that was being neglected but also—and just as importantly—the horizontal relationship with the underprivileged and the marginalized. Here is the heart of the concern with the prophetic critique: the law does not only require Israelites to appropriately worship God; they are also equally responsible to act righteously, to aid the poor and the needy, and to contribute to the maintenance of a just society. Indeed, a healthy vertical relationship is precluded by neglect of horizontal relationships. In verse 20 Isaiah holds the threat of social disintegration over the heads of the privileged if they fail to obey Jehovah's call to justice: "But if you refuse, and you rebel, / by the sword you will be devoured, / for the mouth of Jehovah has spoken." Ultimately, according to the prophets, Israel and Judah failed to heed their warning, and after the larger northern kingdom attempted to throw off Assyrian vassalage, it was destroyed in 722 BC following a lengthy and destructive siege, as prophesied by Isaiah.[45]

While the precise circumstances of the eighth century would not be realized again for the nation of Judah, the economic centralization of the nation in Jerusalem embedded a stark social stratification that would offer other opportunities for the socially privileged and the powerful to further exploit the poor and the marginalized and thus threaten the cosmic order that sustained Jehovah's people. Space does not allow for a thorough interrogation of each set of circumstances and the specific framing of the critique, but some brief comments will be included that illustrate the deployment of the same critique by prophets outside the eighth century BC.[46]

Jeremiah, for instance, warns that Judah's negligence regarding the law will result in Jerusalem's destruction. In Jeremiah 6:19, Jehovah warns of impending doom for neglecting his instruction.[47] Jeremiah 7:4–7 offers the possibility of deliverance, again highlighting the folly of trusting in the protection of the temple while neglecting justice: "Do not trust in these lying words, saying, 'The temple of Jehovah, the temple of Jehovah, the temple of Jehovah is here!' For if you truly improve your ways and your deeds, if you act justly, one with another, if you do not oppress the refugee, the orphan, the widow, or shed innocent blood in this place, and if you do not follow after other gods, to your own harm, then I will dwell with you in this place, in the land that I gave to your ancestors from eternity until eternity." The sacrificial rites are also subordinated to obedience to all of Jehovah's commandments in Jeremiah 7:22–23: "For I did not speak to your ancestors and did not command them in the day that I brought them out from the land of Egypt concerning burnt offerings and sacrifices. But this thing I did command them, saying, 'Heed my voice, and I will be your God, and you will be my people, and you shall walk in every way that I command you, so that it will be well for you.'" These texts drive home the point that it is not the temple or its offerings that facilitate God's protective presence but the presence of justice.

In the latest canonical setting in which the critique appears within the Old Testament, the prophet Malachi condemns the postexilic Jewish community as well as their priests for profaning the ordinances of the temple, stating in Malachi 1:7–8, "You are offering defiled food upon my altar, then you say, 'How have we defiled it?' By insisting the table of Jehovah be despised. And when you offer the blind in sacrifice, is that not evil? And when you offer the lame and the sick, is that not evil? Try offering that to your governor. Will he be pleased with you, or show you favor? says Jehovah of Hosts." In verse 10, Jehovah insists he will not accept offerings from the hands of the priests, and Malachi 2:3 warns, "I will rebuke your offspring and spread entrails on your faces—the entrails of your festivals—and you will be carried off with it."

The most sustained, emphatic, and significant use of this prophetic critique, however, occurs immediately before or during catastrophic social disintegration. As we saw above, among the eighth-century prophets who initiated this critique, it preceded Assyria's destruction of the northern kingdom. Jeremiah's warnings precede Jerusalem's destruction at the end of the seventh century and Judah's exile to Babylon. The people cannot expect to long neglect their duty to care for those in need and remain free and independent. Similarly, the Savior's own deployment of this prophetic critique against Judaism's ruling classes is set only a few decades prior to Rome's destruction of Jerusalem. The next segment will discuss the circumstances and rhetorical purposes of that deployment.

Justice and the Prophetic Critique in the Gospels

This paper began with Jesus's references in Matthew to Hosea's succinct employment of the prophetic critique, but it is taken up in other places in the Gospels. To better understand the rhetorical goals of the Gospel authors' appeals to this particular critique, a brief discussion of the socioeconomic circumstances of the region in the first century AD is necessary. After the death of Herod the Great in 4 BC, his kingdom was divided up among his sister and three of his sons, with his son Herod Archelaus ruling as ethnarch over Samaria, Judea, and Idumea. Archelaus's cruelty and rank incompetence compelled the Jewish community to appeal to Rome for the empire to take over direct rule, which the emperor Augustus did in AD 6, creating the Roman province of Judea. The area had been subject to client rulers for some time before that, which had spurred tension between the more conservative elements of the Jewish community and those who were willing to compromise in the interest of gaining influence and power, and this tension included a class dimension.[48] Under Roman rule and as clients of the empire, local aristocrats were trusted to oversee urban centers, while rural populations were largely left alone since they were thought to be too disorganized to cause any significant or lasting trouble.[49] These aristocrats had to defer to Roman authorities, who frequently abused and oppressed the masses, leading to significant social unrest, particularly in Jerusalem.[50]

The central economic force of Judea was the Jerusalem temple, which attracted money and goods, mostly from pilgrimages to the temple and from economic activity taking place beyond Judea (though Jerusalem also produced some of its own goods).[51] This disconnected the agricultural populations from the wealthy in Jerusalem, but as in the eighth century BC, it also made the former highly reliant on loans from the latter when times were tough, which they frequently were. While interest was evidently charged at times,[52] lenders appear to have been predominantly motivated, as in earlier periods, by the potential for foreclosure and land consolidation. They could further benefit if they could convince the borrower to stay on as a tenant instead of selling the land to pay off the loan. This proliferated tenant farming and its attendant poverty. There is even evidence that first-century borrowers could be required to publicly declare that they would repay the loan even after the Sabbatical year canceled the debt (in direct violation of Deuteronomy 15:7–10).[53] These and many other practices contributed to significant insecurity and intense class divisiveness in Judea up through the conquest of Jerusalem by the Romans in AD 70.

The Gospels present Jesus as directly addressing many of these dynamics during his ministry, though the rhetoric is slightly different from that of the prophets, as the target audience of the Gospels was not the social elite as it frequently was for the prophets. Rather, the message was often addressed directly to the poor and so offers them encouragement and consolation as frequently as it condemns their oppressors. The most prominent example of this message is the first beatitude from the Sermon on the Mount (Matthew 5:3) and the Sermon on the Plain (Luke 6:20), which announces that the kingdom of heaven belongs to the poor. Here Luke refers directly to a socioeconomic circumstance, but Matthew refers to the "poor in spirit," which is a rhetorical contrast to the proud and haughty.[54] Matthew is referring primarily to the humble, but the socioeconomic dimension cannot be ignored, particularly in light of the rhetorical impact of the contrast being drawn between those who are expected to possess the kingdom of heaven and those whom Jesus announces as the possessors.[55]

The socioeconomic dimension is also relevant in light of Jesus's emphasis on the obstacles the wealthy have to humility—obstacles that are not faced by the poor.[56] Gaining and maintaining wealth too often crowds out concern for the "weightier aspects of the law." In Matthew 19:24, Jesus declares that "it is easier for a camel to pass through the eye of a needle than for a rich person to enter the kingdom of heaven." Mark shares the same warning via the parable of the rich young man. After telling the rich young man to sell all he has and give the money to the poor—only to have the young man depart in sorrow—Jesus looks around and proclaims, "How difficult it will be for those having wealth to enter the kingdom of heaven!" (Mark 10:23). Luke 12's parable of the rich fool criticizes the tendency of the wealthy to prioritize maintaining their wealth over and against serving the broader needs of their community and condemns the proverbial rich person to death, declaring, "So it is with people who store up treasures for themselves but are not rich toward God" (Luke 12:21). The classic expression of this difficulty is Jesus's discourse on wealth in the Sermon on the Mount, which begins by declaring, "Where your treasure is, there your heart will also be" (Matthew 6:21), and ends with the franker warning in verse 24, "You cannot serve God and money."[57]

Matthew also criticizes the wealthy for their oppression of the poor. Jesus most explicitly takes up the prophetic critique in condemning the scribes and Pharisees for their prioritization of the wrong commandments: "Woe to you, scribes and Pharisees, for you tithe mint, dill, and cumin but neglect the weightier aspects of the law: justice and mercy and faith. But these you should have done, without neglecting the others" (Matthew 23:23). In other words, they meticulously and conspicuously observed select minutiae of the law but neglected its more important prescriptions. Here the author of Matthew—who seems concerned that the importance of the law of Moses would not be emphasized—avoids the rhetorical excesses of the prophets regarding those aspects of the law that the societal elite were fulfilling. The Gospel of Mark is not as concerned with exalting the law and makes explicit the prioritization of the broader goals of the law over and against ritual requirements, although those broader goals are put into the mouth of a scribe, who comments in response to Jesus's identification of the two great commandments, "And to love him with all the heart and with all the understanding and with all the might, and to love the neighbor as oneself is more than all the burnt offerings and sacrifices" (Mark 12:33). The narrator comments that Jesus saw this as a wise answer. If we return to Matthew, the telling of the same story there is careful to remove that marginalizing rhetoric about burnt offerings and sacrifices (Matthew 22:35–39). Jesus makes the generalization from the particular laws, not the scribe, and quotes Deuteronomy 6:5 ("Love Jehovah your God") and Leviticus 19:18 ("Love your neighbor"), summarizing, "On these two commandments hang the whole law and the prophets" (Matthew 22:40).[58] The reference to "the whole law and the prophets" makes it clear that he is referring not just to the discrete law of Moses found in the Pentateuch but to all Jewish scripture;[59] it is all subsumed within the author's care for both the vertical relationship with God and the horizontal relationship with humanity.

Conclusion

This interrogation of the prophetic critique has shown deep and abiding prophetic concern for the law's facilitation of justice, particularly in regard to caring for the marginalized and the oppressed. Social stability could not be maintained with the escalating insecurity and unrest that comes from the widespread exploitation of the poor on the part of the elite. According to the prophets, engaging in this exploitation while performing the public requirements of the law in order to be seen of others and to advance one's own personal interests is a profoundly hypocritical subversion of the purposes of that law. The law did not exist as an end unto itself, but as a means to a more elevated end: a heart changed by God and filled with love and mercy that would help unify and perfect the people of God. A temporary realization of this goal in the Book of Mormon is found in Mosiah 5:2: "And they all cried with one voice, saying: Yea, we believe all the words which thou hast spoken unto us; and also, we know of their surety and truth, because of the Spirit of the Lord Omnipotent, which has wrought a mighty change in us, or in our hearts, that we have no more disposition to do evil, but to do good continually."

Jesus's deployment of this critique is similarly aimed at those who would make the law an end unto itself in order to serve their own interests, but the circumstances and audience in Matthew are different. Both of Jesus's quotations of Hosea 6:6 come in response to criticism of Jesus's ostensible indifference to the then contemporary standards regarding table fellowship with sinners and detailed parsings of Sabbath restrictions, but in neither case was Jesus directly defending the poor or the oppressed. He was instead criticizing the scribes and Pharisees for leveraging rather marginal legal considerations in order to condemn the going about and doing good of him and his disciples. In the earlier instance (Matthew 9:13), Jesus was fellowshipping with sinners who were in greater need of his ministrations than were the righteous. In the latter (Matthew 12:7), Jesus rejected the notion that Sabbath restrictions are an end unto themselves and highlighted the priority taken by temple sacrifices over those restrictions. In the verses that follow, Jesus heals a man on the Sabbath and declares, "It is lawful on the Sabbath to do good" (Matthew 12:9–13). With these quotations of Hosea 6:6, Jesus deploys a generalization of the prophetic critique of temple sacrifice and applies it to other situations where the priority of the law might undermine or obstruct more important duties toward God and neighbor.

This is not to say the Savior was not concerned with the kinds of circumstances that catalyzed the original critique in the eighth century BC. On the contrary, the Gospels demonstrate that Christ was overwhelmingly concerned with the treatment of society's most vulnerable and repeatedly championed their needs, excoriating those who marginalized and oppressed them. These matters of the law were "weightier" than the ritual minutiae that facilitated the credibility-enhancing displays of the leaders and prominent members of the Jewish community. The law for these leaders was not a path to creating a more godly and more just society. It was a tool they used for their own personal interests, and as the Savior clearly stated, when the law exists to facilitate being seen of others, "they have their reward" (Matthew 6:2, 5).

This is an easily overlooked and frequently dismissed aspect of Christ's gospel, and perhaps it is this rhetorical point from the Savior that offers us the greatest opportunity for self-reflection following this discussion. Does our love for God compel us to help justice "flow like waters, and righteousness like a constant stream" (Amos 5:24)? Do we strive to love our neighbor as ourselves? Do we maintain that love is one of the weightier matters of the law, or do we exploit the law as an excuse to prioritize our own interests? In a period of such extreme instability and of continued injustices committed against marginalized groups, where are our hearts? Has the Spirit "wrought a mighty change ... in our hearts," so that we, like the Savior, seek "to do good continually" (Mosiah 5:2)? Do we see God's commandments as a means of being seen of others and of exercising influence and control, or do we see them as a means to turn our society into Zion and generate hearts full of mercy?

Daniel O. McClellan is a scripture translation supervisor for The Church of Jesus Christ of Latter-day Saints.

Notes

1. All translations are my own (unless otherwise noted) and are rendered to prioritize clarity and accessibility.
2. The quotation of Hosea 6:6 comes from the ancient Greek translation of the Bible (Septuagint), which renders the Hebrew *ḥesed ḥāpaṣtî* ("I delight in mercy") with the Greek *éleos thélō* ("I want mercy").
3. Scholars suggest that the responsibilities to prepare the Sabbath offering as outlined in Numbers 28:9–10 represent the clearest violation of the Sabbath that is required of the priestly office. For example, see Craig A.

Evans, *Matthew* (Cambridge: Cambridge University Press, 2012), 250. Rabbinic commentary, such as the Talmudic tractate *Shabbat* 132b, states that temple service "overrides" (*dôḥâ*) the requirements of the Sabbath.

4. In Mark's telling of this story (Mark 2:23–28), the Savior's response does not echo the prophetic critique of the cult, but rather is limited to the assertion that "the Sabbath was made for man, and not man for the Sabbath. Thus, the Son of Man is lord even of the Sabbath" (2:27–28).

5. For a discussion of the interpretive difficulties with Matthew's quotations of Hosea 6:6, see David Hill, "On the Use and Meaning of Hosea VI. 6 in Matthew's Gospel," *New Testament Studies* 24, no. 1 (1977): 107–19.

6. For example, the Old Testament teacher's manual for the Gospel Doctrine class has said the following for years about the passage in Hosea, "Christ twice referred to this verse to answer criticism from the Pharisees." *Old Testament: Gospel Doctrine Teacher's Manual* (Salt Lake City: The Church of Jesus Christ of Latter-day Saints, 2001), 169. The manual instructs teachers to review the passages in the New Testament and discuss what they mean. According to the New Testament manual, Jesus "wanted the people to focus on loving others, not merely on performing public religious ceremonies." *New Testament: Gospel Doctrine Teacher's Manual* (Salt Lake City: The Church of Jesus Christ of Latter-day Saints, 1997), 41. Jennifer Lane comments that Jesus "is challenging their fundamental conception of holiness and the law by questioning their focus on their own ritual purity while ignoring the spiritually sick among the covenant people." Jennifer C. Lane, "Hostility toward Jesus: Prelude to the Passion," in *Celebrating Easter*, ed. Thomas A. Wayment and Keith J. Wilson (Provo, UT: Religious Studies Center, Brigham Young University, 2007), 145.

7. The Church's Guide to the Scriptures, for instance, describes justice as follows: "The unfailing consequence of blessings for righteous thoughts and acts, and punishment for unrepented sin. Justice is an eternal law that requires a penalty each time a law of God is broken (Alma 42:13–24). The sinner must pay the penalty if he [or she] does not repent (Mosiah 2:38–39; Doctrine and Covenants 19:17). If he [or she] does repent, the Savior pays the penalty through the Atonement, invoking mercy (Alma 34:16)." The only two Old Testament passages cited in the entry are Ezekiel 18:4

(paraphrased as "The soul that sinneth shall die") and Micah 6:8 ("What doth the Lord require of thee, but to do justly?").

8. For a discussion of how this changed over time, see Zev I. Farber, "Israelite Festivals: From Cyclical Time Celebrations to Linear Time Celebrations," *Religions* 10, no. 5 (2019): 1–19.

9. Sometimes this battle is associated with creation, as in *Enuma Eliš*, and other times it is not, as in the Baal cycle. See Rebecca S. Watson, *Chaos Uncreated: A Reassessment of the Theme of "Chaos" in the Hebrew Bible* (Berlin: de Gruyter, 2005); David Tsumura, *Creation and Destruction: A Reappraisal of the Chaoskampf Theory in the Old Testament* (Winona Lake, IN: Eisenbrauns, 2005), 143–46; John H. Walton, *Ancient Near Eastern Thought and the Old Testament: Introducing the Conceptual World of the Hebrew Bible* (Grand Rapids, MI: Baker Academic, 2006), 184–95. One of the biblical relics of these early mythological stories is the Leviathan (Isaiah 27:1; Psalm 74:14; Job 3:8). See also John Day, *God's Conflict with the Dragon and the Sea: Echoes of a Canaanite Myth in the Old Testament* (Cambridge: Cambridge University Press, 1985).

10. "The temple was the control center for order in the cosmos and that order had to be maintained. The deity needed to be cared for so that he/she could focus his/her energies on the important work of holding forces of chaos at bay. The rituals, therefore, served not simply as gifts to the deity or mechanical liturgical words and actions. The rituals provided a means by which humans could play a role in maintaining order in the cosmos." Walton, *Ancient Near Eastern Thought*, 130.

11. Regarding Egypt, Rolf Gundlach explains: "The royal performance of the cult, generally speaking, invoked the sacred power for the preservation of *maat*, the order of the world." Rolf Gundlach, "Temples," in *The Oxford Encyclopedia of Ancient Egypt*, ed. Donald B. Redford (Oxford: Oxford University Press, 2001), 3:365.

12. For a discussion of this rhetoric in the ancient Near East and its alteration in the Hebrew Bible to subordinate the king to God, see Bernard M. Levinson, "The Reconceptualization of Kingship in Deuteronomy and the Deuteronomistic History's Transformation of Torah," *Vetus Testamentum* 51, no. 4 (2001): 511–34.

13. Martha Roth, trans., "The Laws of Hammurabi," in *Context of Scripture*, 3 vols., ed. William W. Hallo and K. Lawson Younger (Leiden: Brill, 2003), 2.131:336 (hereafter COS). Hammurabi goes on to assert, "I established truth and justice as the declaration of the land. . . . I enhanced the well-being of the people" (p. 337). Similarly, the Neo-Assyrian king Esarhaddon (681–669 BC) was extolled in one text as having "revived the one who was guilty and condemned to death; you have released the one who was imprisoned for many [ye]ars. Those who were sick for many days have got well, the hungry have been sated, the *parched* have been anointed with oil, the needy have been covered with garments." "226. The King's Reign Is Good: Petition for Urad-Gula," in *Letters from Assyrian and Babylonian Scholars*, ed. Simo Parpola (Helsinki: Helsinki University Press, 1993), 178; emphasis in original.

14. Raymond Westbrook, "Social Justice in the Ancient Near East," in *Social Justice in the Ancient World*, ed. K. D. Irani and Morris Silver (Westport, CT: Greenwood, 1995), 161.

15. On the oversight of law codes, see Raymond Westbrook, "Introduction: The Character of Ancient Near Eastern Law," in *A History of Ancient Near Eastern Law* (Leiden: Brill, 2003), 1:29. The Laws of Ur-Namma, the earliest surviving of ancient Near Eastern law collections, dates to around 2100 BC. These collections flourished in the second millennium BC with the publication of the Laws of Lipit-Ishtar, the Laws of Eshnunna, the Laws of Hammurabi, Hittite Laws, and the Middle Assyrian Laws. English translations can be found in the second volume of *The Context of Scripture*: Martha Roth, trans., "The Laws of Ur-Namma (Ur-Nammu)" (COS 2.153); Roth, trans., "The Laws of Lipit-Ishtar" (COS 2.154); Roth, trans., "The Laws of Eshnunna" (COS 2.130); Roth, trans., "The Laws of Hammurabi" (COS 2.131); Harry A. Hoffner Jr., trans., "Hittite Laws" (COS 2.19); Roth, trans., "The Middle Assyrian Laws" (COS 2.132).

16. On these codes, see Ze'ev Falk, *Hebrew Law in Biblical Times: An Introduction* (Jerusalem: Wahrmann Books, 1964); Michael Walzer, "The Legal Codes of Ancient Israel," *Yale Journal of Law and the Humanities* 4, no. 2 (1992): 335–49; Tikva Frymer-Kenski, "Israel," in Westbook, *History of Ancient Near Eastern Law*, 1:975–1046; Bernard M. Levinson, *Legal*

Revision and Religious Renewal in Ancient Israel (Cambridge: Cambridge University Press, 2008); David P. Wright, *Inventing God's Law: How the Covenant Code of the Bible Used and Revised the Laws of Hammurabi* (Oxford: Oxford University Press, 2009).

17. Perhaps the most famous example of ancient Near Eastern case law is the law concerning the "goring ox," which comes from the Laws of Hammurabi but is found also in the Laws of Eshnunna and in Exodus 21:28–31. According to this law, if someone's ox should escape from the enclosure and gore someone to death, the owner is not liable. If the ox is a "habitual gorer," however, and the owner has been warned but fails to keep the ox restrained, the owner is liable for the value of the lost life, which differs according to the deceased's social role. For a brief discussion of the similarities and differences between the two laws, see Wright, *Inventing God's Law*, 7–8.

18. See Richard H. Hiers, *Justice and Compassion in Biblical Law* (New York: Continuum, 2009); Assnat Bartor, *Reading Law as Narrative: A Study in the Casuistic Laws of the Pentateuch* (Atlanta: Society of Biblical Literature, 2010); Gershon Hepner, *Legal Friction: Law, Narrative, and Identity Politics in Biblical Israel* (New York: Peter Lang, 2010).

19. See Bernard M. Levinson, "The Neo-Assyrian origins of the canon formula in Deuteronomy 13:1," in *Scriptural Exegesis: The Shapes of Culture and the Religious Imagination, Essays in Honour of Michael Fishbane*, ed. Deborah A. Green and Laura S. Lieber (Oxford: Oxford University Press, 2009), 25–45; Bernard M. Levinson and Jeffrey Stackert, "Between the Covenant Code and Esarhaddon's Succession Treaty: Deuteronomy 13 and the Composition of Deuteronomy," *Journal of Ancient Judaism* 3 (2012): 123–40.

20. Deuteronomy adds the demand that the people love their suzerain with all their hearts, which corresponds to similar demands from the vassal treaties of the Neo-Assyrian Esarhaddon (681–669 BC). On this, see Nathan MacDonald, *Deuteronomy and the Meaning of "Monotheism"* (Tübingen, Germany: Mohr Siebeck, 2003).

21. Proverbs 14:31 warns, "He that oppresses the poor insults his Maker."

22. Morris Silver, "Prophets and Markets Revisited," in Irani and Morris, *Social Justice in the Ancient World*, 182–83; compare Charles Fensham, "Widow, Orphan, and the Poor in Ancient Near Eastern Legal and Wisdom Literature," *Journal of Near Eastern Studies* 21, no. 2 (1962): 129–39.
23. The Egyptian term *mꜣꜥ.t*, usually translated "truth," conveys a similar sense. "Maat is right order in nature and society, as established by the act of creation, and hence means, according to the context, what is right, what is correct, law, order, justice and truth." Siegfried Morenz, *Egyptian Religion*, trans. Ann E. Keep (Ithaca, NY: Cornell University Press, 1973), 113.
24. This description draws in part from Carsten Ziegert, "What Is חֶסֶד? A Frame-Semantic Approach," *Journal for the Study of the Old Testament* 44, no. 4 (2020): 711–32. "Mercy" is just a convenient gloss for the term *ḥesed*, but the English word does not capture the full semantic depth and range of the concept as presented in the Old Testament. Additionally, other Hebrew terms can be glossed the same way but refer to different concepts.
25. In the postexilic book of Zechariah, Jehovah commands Israel in the second person plural: "Render true justice, and show mercy and compassion one to another" (Zechariah 7:9).
26. See André LaCocque, *Ruth: A Continental Commentary*, trans. K. C. Hanson (Minneapolis: Fortress Press, 2004), 28–32, who understands Ruth to be "characterized by *ḥesed*" (p. 32), which he describes as "the virtue of excess" that helps people "accomplish commandments beyond the letter" (p. 28). Edward F. Campbell Jr. similarly describes Ruth as "basically about extraordinary caring and concern, kindness that is above and beyond the call of duty." Campbell, *Ruth: A New Translation with Introduction, Notes, and Commentary* (Garden City, NY: Doubleday, 1975), 110. For another treatment that situates Ruth and *ḥesed* within Jewish halakhah, see Yossi Prager, "*Megillat Ruth*: A Unique Story of *Torat Hesed*," *Traditions* 35, no. 4 (2001): 15–22.
27. See Kerry Muhlestein, "Ruth, Redemption, Covenant, and Christ," in *The Gospel of Jesus Christ in the Old Testament*, ed. D. Kelly Ogden, Jared W. Ludlow, and Kerry Muhlestein (Provo, UT: Religious Studies Center, Brigham Young University, 2009), 187–206.

28. Leviticus's law of land redemption does draw a clear distinction between "houses in villages that do not have walls around them" (batê haḥăṣêrîm 'ăšer 'ên-lāhem ḥōmâ sābîb), which may be redeemed at any time or must be released at the Jubilee, and a "dwelling-house within a walled city" (bēt-mōšab 'ir ḥōmâ), which has a window of redemption of one year and is not required to be released at the Jubilee (Leviticus 25:29–34). For a discussion of urbanization in ancient Israel, see Lester L. Grabbe, "Supurbs or only Hyp-urbs? Prophets and Populations in Ancient Israel and Socio-Historical Method," in 'Every City Shall Be Forsaken': Urbanism and Prophecy in Ancient Israel and the Near East, ed. Lester L. Grabbe and Robert D. Haak (Sheffield: Sheffield Academic Press, 2001), 95–123.

29. For more on the status of the north during the eighth century BC, see Gilad Itach, "The Kingdom of Israel in the Eighth Century: From Regional Power to Assyrian Provinces," in Archaeology and History of Eighth-Century Judah, ed. Zev I. Farber and Jacob L. Wright (Atlanta: SBL Press, 2018), 57–77; Israel Finkelstein, "Jeroboam II in Transjordan," Journal for the Study of the Old Testament 34, no. 1 (2020): 19–29. For the status of Judah, see Avraham Faust, "Society and Culture in the Kingdom of Judah during the Eighth Century," in Farber and Wright, Archaeology and History of Eighth-Century Judah, 179–203.

30. The northern kingdom is estimated to have had a population of around 350,000 people prior to Assyria's invasion, with the southern kingdom about a third that size. Magen Broshi and Israel Finkelstein, "The Population of Palestine in Iron Age II," Bulletin of the American Schools of Oriental Research 287 (1992): 47–60. See also Faust, "Society and Culture in the Kingdom of Judah," 180–84.

31. Marvin L. Chaney, "3. The Political Economy of Peasant Poverty: What the Eighth-Century Prophets Presumed but Did Not State," Journal of Religion and Society 10 (2014): 39–40.

32. For more detailed discussions, see Andrew J. Dearman, Property Rights in the Eighth-Century Prophets: The Conflict and Its Background (Atlanta: Scholars Press, 1988), 18–57; D. N. Premnath, "Latifundialization and Isaiah 5.8–10," Journal for the Study of the Old Testament 40, no. 1 (1988): 49–60; Stuart Love, "Failing to Do Justice: The Quandary of the Poor in

Eighth Century Israel and Judah," *Leaven* 1, no. 2 (1990): 11–17; Gregory C. Chirichigno, *Debt-Slavery in Israel and the Ancient Near East* (Sheffield: Sheffield Academic Press, 1993), 125–29; Chaney, "Political Economy of Peasant Poverty," 39–42. See also Silver, "Prophets and Markets Revisited," 179–98.

33. A discussion of these different practices is found in Love, "Failing to Do Justice," 11–17.

34. The generic Hebrew term *bayit* usually means "house," but it can also be used to refer to a house and its associated property, the property by itself, or metonymically to the members of the household. Here the most likely sense is that reference is being made to the dwelling place and the property.

35. For this reading, see Dearman, *Property Rights*; Brevard S. Childs, *Isaiah: A Commentary* (Louisville: Westminster John Knox Press, 2001), 47; H. G. M. Williamson, *A Critical and Exegetical Commentary on Isaiah 1–27 in Three Volumes. Volume 1: Commentary on Isaiah 1–5* (London: T&T Clark, 2006), 351–54; Ivan D. Friesen, *Isaiah* (Scottdale, PA: Herald Press, 2009), 55; J. J. M. Roberts, *First Isaiah: A Commentary* (Minneapolis: Fortress Press, 2015), 78–79.

36. For discussions on the laws of land inheritance, see Richard H. Hiers, "Transfer of Property by Inheritance and Bequest in Biblical Law and Tradition," *Journal of Law and Religion* 10 (1993): 121–55.

37. This is an ideal that descends from the broader role of ancestral property rights in the constitution of the nation of Israel. Francesca Stavrakopoulou, *The Land of Our Fathers: The Roles of Ancestor Veneration in Biblical Land Claims* (New York: T&T Clark, 2010), 135–48. Genesis 23 presents Abraham as refusing to accept property as a gift from the Hittites so that he could bury Sarah. Instead, he insists on paying full price as a means of securing rightful ownership and ensuring that the property remains in his line, with the burial sites functioning as an additional witness to ownership for future generations (Genesis 23:13–20; 50:13).

38. Jonathan Klawans summarizes, "The prophetic critique of contemporary cultic practice stemmed from the fact that many sacrifices were being offered by those whose property was unduly earned, being proceeds from the exploitation of the poor. Because proper sacrifice presupposes due

ownership, a thieving society cannot render due offerings, at least not in the prophetic understanding of these matters." Jonathan Klawans, *Purity, Sacrifice, and the Temple: Symbolism and Supersessionism in the Study of Ancient Judaism* (Oxford: Oxford University Press, 2006), 249.

39. This concern for the law's broader purpose is not found in the Old Testament outside the prophetic literature, which may stem from the monarchy's patronage and oversight of both scribal and priestly classes, who would have been responsible for the Old Testament's legal and historical literature. Many Old Testament prophets operated independent of that monarchy and were frequently critical of it. Note that Jeremiah echoes the prophetic critique (Jeremiah 7:22) and also criticizes the king (Jeremiah 21:1–7) and the "lying pen of the scribe" (Jeremiah 8:8).

40. The Masoretic Text reads "your judgment," but this is widely understood as a corrupted reading. My translation follows the Septuagint's use of the first person singular suffix.

41. "See" renders the adverb *šam* (meaning "there"), which usually has a locative function, but the usage here suggests a more deictic function similar to *hinneh* ("look") that signals the reader to what follows.

42. In Amos 5:21–24, Jehovah announces, "I hate, I despise your festivals, / and I will not smell the aroma of your solemn assemblies. Even though you offer burnt offerings to me, and grain offerings, / I will not accept them; / and your peace offerings of your fatted animals / I will not look upon favorably. Turn away from me your noisy songs, / and the melody of your harps I will not hear. But let justice flow like waters, / and righteousness like a constant stream."

43. See Bohdan Hrobon, *Ethical Dimension of Cult in the Book of Isaiah* (Berlin: de Gruyter, 2010), 75–115; Theresa V. Lafferty, *The Prophetic Critique of the Priority of the Cult: A Study of Amos 5:21–24 and Isaiah 1:10–17* (Eugene, OR: Pickwick Publications, 2012).

44. This refers to the commandment found in Exodus 34:24 and Deuteronomy 16:16. Almost all translations render "when you come to appear before me," but this phrase is based on the Masoretic Text's manipulation of the vocalization of the consonantal text. The root *r-'-h*, "to see," appears unambiguously in the infinitive qal stem, which is the active stem. At some point

anciently, however, discomfort with that reading catalyzed a substitute reading of the active infinitive as a passive niphal, which would require the addition of a preformative *he* that is absent from the text (*lr'wt* appears in the text, but the niphal would be *lhr'wt*). The Masoretic scribes imposed (most of) the vowels of the passive stem upon the consonants, giving us the reading *lera'ōt*. The direct object of that seeing, *panāy*, "my face," also lacks a preposition necessary to make sense of a passive reading of the verb (compare 1 Samuel 1:22; 1 Kings 11:9).

45. There has been significant debate on the circumstances surrounding the fall of Samaria. On this debate, see John H. Hayes and Jeffrey K. Kuan, "The Final Years of Samaria (730–720 BC)," *Biblica* 72, no. 2 (1991): 153–81; Bob Becking, *The Fall of Samaria: An Historical and Archaeological Study* (Leiden: Brill, 1992); K. Lawson Younger Jr., "The Fall of Samaria in Light of Recent Research," *Catholic Biblical Quarterly* 61, no. 3 (1999): 461–82; compare Itach, "Kingdom of Israel," 66–69.

46. In the earliest canonical setting in which this prophetic critique is found—prior to the eighth century, but likely composed after—the central concern is actually not for justice but is extended to obedience to all of Jehovah's commands. In 1 Samuel 15:22–23, the prophet Samuel condemns King Saul for taking animals from the possessions of the Amalekites to offer as sacrifice, despite the explicit command that they were to devote those animals to destruction. The prophet rhetorically asks, "Does Jehovah delight as much in burnt offerings and sacrifices, / as in heeding the voice of Jehovah? / Look, heeding is better than sacrifice, / and listening is better than the fat of rams."

47. The KJV reads "law" here, but the Hebrew *tōrâ* means "instruction," not "law." It derives from the root *y-r-h*, which means "to instruct, teach."

48. The books of the Maccabees, found in the Apocrypha, focus on these conflicts in the second century BC. Perhaps the most extreme example of this tension is represented by the Essene community that separated itself from other Jewish communities and, along the shores of the Dead Sea, set up a community that opposed the control of the temple by what it considered a corrupt and impure administration. See Eyal Regev, "Abominated Temple and a Holy Community: The Formation of the Notion of Purity

and Impurity in Qumran," *Dead Sea Discoveries* 10, no. 2 (2003): 243–78; Lawrence H. Schiffman, *Qumran and Jerusalem: Studies in the Dead Sea Scrolls and the History of Judaism* (Grand Rapids, MI: Eerdmans, 2010), 81–97.

49. For a discussion of the dozen or so different Jewish messiah figures from the first century who gathered followings that challenged Roman hegemony, see Trevan G. Hatch, *A Stranger in Jerusalem: Seeing Jesus as a Jew* (Eugene, OR: Wipf and Stock, 2019), 107–09.

50. Josephus documents several such abuses in book 18 of his *Antiquities of the Jews*.

51. A great source for the socioeconomic circumstances of this period is Martin Goodman, *The Ruling Class of Judaea: The Origins of the Jewish Revolt against Rome A.D. 66–70* (Cambridge: Cambridge University Press, 1987). See also Martin Goodman, *Judaism in the Roman World: Collected Essays* (Leiden: Brill, 2007), 59–67.

52. Some rabbinic criticisms indicate this. See, for instance, *Bava Metzia* 5:11 and *Mishnah Sanhedrin* 3:3.

53. This was called the "prosbul." For a discussion on the topic, see Goodman, *Ruling Class of Judaea*, 57–58.

54. The phrase "poor in spirit" occurs in the War Scroll, from the Dead Sea Scrolls (1QM 14:7), where it stands in contrast to the hard of heart. Isaiah 61:1–2, which is the text read by the Savior in the Nazareth synagogue (Luke 4:18), also sits in the background of this beatitude.

55. One of the central rhetorical frameworks of the Sermon on the Mount is the stark contrast between what was commonly expected regarding the kingdom of heaven and what Jesus announces. His vision of that kingdom turns the most predominant expectations of the day on their heads.

56. Alma 32 also discusses the relationship between poverty and humility at some length.

57. The KJV's *mammon* is a transliteration of the Greek word *mamōnas*, which itself is a Greek transliteration of the Aramaic word *mamon*, "money, profit." The Aramaic word doesn't occur in the Old Testament but appears in the Dead Sea Scrolls (1QS 6:2; CD 14:20) and in the Targum and is also attested in Mishnaic Hebrew.

58. For a brief discussion of Rabbi Hillel's hermeneutical rule regarding generalizing from the particular and particularizing from the general, see Matthew L. Bowen, "Jewish Hermeneutics in the New Testament Period," in *New Testament History, Culture, and Society: A Background to the Texts of the New Testament*, ed. Lincoln H. Blumell (Provo, UT: Religious Studies Center, Brigham Young University; Salt Lake City: Deseret Book, 2019), 97–98.

59. While the New Testament does refer to a tripartite division of scripture (Luke 24:44), it is more commonly reduced to a binary (Matthew 5:17; 7:12; Luke 16:29–31; Acts 13:15; 24:14; Romans 3:21). As many scholars have noted, the tripartite division does not seem to have been important in the first century. See, for instance, Timothy H. Lim, "The Alleged Reference to the Tripartite Division of the Hebrew Bible," *Revue de Qumrân* 20, no. 1 (2001): 23–37; John J. Collins, *The Scepter and the Star: Messianism in Light of the Dead Sea Scrolls*, 2nd ed. (Grand Rapids, MI: Eerdmans, 2010), 22–23.

Index

A

Aaron, 32–33
Abrahamic covenant, 56–57, 73–74, 76–77, 186
Absalom, 142, 143–44, 154n37
abundance, covenant blessings as foundation of, 268–73
abuse
    cycle of, 134
    of poor condemned in Isaiah, 217–22
    silence of victims of, 144–45, 146
    of Tamar, 141–46, 155n43, 155n45
Adam, 159–63, 177n25
    sons of, 103, 117n9
agency, 36, 137
Ahaz, King, 343
Ahiav, 337
Allen, T. George, 10
'āmā, 209n54
Amalickiah, 359
Ammon, 367, 370, 372
Amnon, 142–43, 144, 154n37

Amos, book of, 427–29, 443–44
    and breaking covenants of kinship, 434–41
    condemnation of exploitation of poor in, 63, 477
    and covenants of kinship, 429–34
'ănāwim, 222, 235n26
ancient Near East
    conceptualizations of law, justice, and cosmic order in, 471–75
    covenants of kinship in, 429–34
    cry of oppressed in, 50–51
    furniture in, 438–39
    ideal of just society in, 48–50
    kings in, 472–73
Andersen, Francis, 435
'āni / 'ăniyyim, 216–17, 218, 220, 223, 226, 227, 233n12, 236n28
Anti-Nephi-Lehies, 357–58, 363, 364, 366, 367–68, 370–71, 372–73
Archelaus, 483
Ashur, 350n40
Assyria, 325, 331–33, 334, 336, 343–44, 350n40, 355–56

Atonement
  looking to, 114–15
  and relationship of covenant economics and economic equity, 237
Avigad, Nahman, 332, 337

B

Babylon, 451–52
Baker, David L., 268, 275
Barak, 165, 166
Bar Hebraeus, 20
Barhebraeus' Scholia on the Old Testament: Part I: Genesis—II Samuel (Sprengling and Graham), 21
barrenness, 133, 151–52n16, 189–90, 200
Bartimaeus, 417
bayit, 456, 495n34
beds, in Old Testament world, 438–39
Bellinger, W. H. Jr., 239, 240
Bellis, Alice Ogden, 130–31, 144–45, 247
belonging, 113–14, 121n29, 122n40. *See also* inclusion
Bennion, Adam S., 3, 4
bĕrit, 430
Birch, Bruce, 249, 250, 253, 263n45
blackness, 104, 117–18n9, 118–19n13
blind / blindness, 407–8, 421–22. *See also* eyes, putting out
  causes of physical and spiritual, 408–12
  David's attitude toward, 396–400, 405n32
  description and status of, 412–13
  in latter days, 418–21
  as metaphor, 413–15
  in New Testament, 417–18
  responding to, 420
  treatment of, 415
Boaz, 82, 185, 187, 194, 195–201, 202, 475
Book of Mormon
  definitions of *gēr* in, 357–60
  gēr in judicial law in, 366–68
  gēr in religious law in, 370–73
  gēr in social law in, 362–63
  need for seminary course on, 3–4
  sources of Mosaic law for people of, 354–55
  Sperry's writings on, 13–16
  treatment of *gēr* in, 354, 373–74
Bradshaw, Jeffrey, 105
Braithwaite, Robert Jr., 7
brass plates, 354, 355
Brigham Young University, Sperry invited to teach at, 18–19
Broad Wall, 332, 340, 342–43
Brooks, David, 101–2, 115
Broshi, Magen, 331
Brueggemann, Walter, 135
brutality, martial, 435–36
Burke, Aaron A., 338, 340
Burnside, Jonathan, 297–98, 302–3
Burton, Linda K., 299
BYU sports fan, service rendered by, 42–43

C

Calvin, John, 153n23
Campbell, Edward F. Jr., 493n26
Campbell, Lisa, 304
Canaan, 108–9, 118n12, 118–19n13
Canaanites, 165, 178n39
"caught up into Zion," 242
change of heart, 251–52
charity, and building Zion, 257, 258
childbearing, 133, 136, 161
children
  in ancient Israelite families, 190
  raising, 176n22
Chirichigno, Gregory, 441
choice, 36, 137
Christensen, Ross T., 21–22
Christofferson, D. Todd, 254–55
Church of Jesus Christ of Latter-day Saints, The
  belonging and unity in, 113–14, 121n29, 122n40
  challenge of seeing others deeply in, 112–13, 122n32
  covenants of kinship in, 442–43
city of Enoch, 33, 35, 103, 237, 242, 243–44, 247, 249–50
communal feasting, 368–69
contrite spirit, 236n28
conversion, to Israelite religion, 193, 208n42

cosmic order
  ancient Near Eastern conceptualizations of, 471–75
  temple as control center for, 490n10
couches, in Old Testament world, 438–39
court system, corruption in, 478
covenant blessings, as foundation of abundance, 268–73
Covenant Code, 79–80, 88–90, 96n29, 302
covenant economics, 237, 248–54
covenants. *See also* Abrahamic covenant
  and building Zion, 35
  as forming new relationship, 74–76
covenants of kinship, 427–29, 443–44
  breaking, in days of Amos, 434–41
  in modern day, 442–43
  in Old Testament world, 429–34
Craigie, Peter C., 431
cries, of poor and oppressed, 50–51
Cross, Frank Moore, 428, 430, 445n5

D

dal / dallîm, 216–17, 220, 223
Damascene cookies, 40–42
David, attitude toward lame and blind, 396–400, 405n32
Deborah, 164–67, 177n30
Deborah's Song, 166
debt, 61–62, 79, 84–87, 98n54, 274–75. *See also* Jubilee; Sabbatical year
debt-slaves, 252–53
deformity / deformed, 393–94. *See also* disabilities
Deuteronomy 15, 248–54, 276–77
Dew, Sheri, 163
dignity, and meaningful work in building Zion, 36–37
Dillon, Christine, 318n2
disabilities, 383–84, 400–402. *See also* blind / blindness
  assistance for those with, 386–87, 401, 403n6, 420–21
  and David's attitude toward lame and blind, 396–400
  evidence of Israelite ideal concerning compassion for, 387–89

Israelite cultural and social context of, 384–87
  responding to, 420
  and restrictions in priestly service, 389–96, 401, 404n17, 413
divine covenants of kinship, 430, 433–34
  breaking, 438–41
Documentary Hypothesis, 355, 375n5
Driver, S. R., 405n32

E

'ebyôn / 'ebyônîm, 216–17, 222, 223, 233n12
economics, covenant, 237, 248–54
Edom and Edomites, 431–32, 436–37, 446n21
Egypt, care for poor and oppressed in, 48–49
Eli, 392
Elisha, 410
elite
  Amos's indictment of, 437, 438–41
  exploitation of poor by, 477
Elkanah, 392
empathy
  of Israelites, 303
  for refugees, 293–94, 304
Enoch
  as example of seeing others, 111–15
  first attempt to make, see residue, 106–10
  God's rebuke of, 102–4
  narrowing audience of, 104–6
  second attempt to make, see residue, 110
  vision of Zion as refuge, 242–43
Enoch, city of, 33, 35, 103, 237, 242, 243–44, 247, 249–50
Ephraim, 412–13
Esarhaddon, 491n13
  Vassal Treaty of, 349n37
Esau, 431
ethics, in war, 435–36
etiology, 260n1
Eve, 159–63
Exodus, 32–33, 253, 362–63, 365–68, 369–71, 373

Exodus, women in book of, 146–50
eyes, putting out, 384, 409. *See also* blind / blindness
Eyring, Henry B., 442

F

Fall of Adam, 159, 160–63, 176n20
familial covenants of kinship, 430, 431–32
  breaking, 435–37
famines, 187, 205n19
fasting, 220–21
fatherless. *See* orphans
Faust, James E., 419
feasting communal, 368–69
Feast of Tabernacles, 83–84, 369
Feast of Weeks, 83–84, 369
feminism, 128–29
feminist hermeneutic, 128–32, 150–51n4
Fensham, F. Charles, 50
Festival of the Firstfruits, 369–70
festivals
  offerings at, 83–84
  refugees included in, 369–70
Finkelstein, Israel, 331, 339, 340, 341, 347n13
Floyd, Michael H., 260n1
Flynn, Shawn W., 171
food, sacrificial, 391–93, 394, 413, 469–70, 482, 495n38, 497n46
Fortes Meyer, 430
Freedman, David Noel, 435
Frymer-Kensky, Tikva, 138, 143, 155n45

G

Gafney, Wilda C., 144, 149
Gaza, 436
g-d-l, 278
gedûllâ, 278
Gench, Frances Taylor, 127
generalizations, 101–2
generosity, 59–60, 61, 82, 195, 200, 252–53, 275–76, 285
gēr / gērim. *See also* refugees; strangers
  biblical laws concerning, 341
  care for, 54, 455
  children of Israel described as, 302–3
  defined, 70n18, 192–93, 353
  definitions in Book of Mormon, 357–60
  definitions in Pentateuch, 355–57
  in judicial law, 365–68
  under Mosaic law, 184
  in religious law, 368–73
  Ruth as, 183, 192–93, 196, 200–201, 307–8
  in social law, 360–65
  and sources of Mosaic law for Book of Mormon people, 354–55
  treatment of, in Book of Mormon, 354, 373–74
Ghafouri, Nemam, 39–40
Givens, Fiona, 111
Givens, Terryl, 111
Glanville, Mark, 356
gleaning, 52, 59–60, 81–82, 194–96, 351–52n62, 361–62
God
  barrenness as punishment from, 133
  becoming like, 90
  blindness inflicted by, 409–10
  covenants and our relationship with, 75–76
  first attempt to make Enoch see residue, 106–10
  forgetting, as idolatry, 270
  greatness of, 278–84
  imitating, 313–16
  justice and righteousness as attributes of, 56, 453–54
  knowing, 456–57
  mercy of, 78
  rebukes Enoch, 102–4
  recognizing, in trials, 139–40
  recognizing dependence on, 272–73
  rejection of, 460
  remembering, 275, 282–84, 286
  and restoration of sight, 415–16
  second attempt to make Enoch see residue, 110
  trust in, 223, 276, 277, 285, 344
  weeps over residue, 107–8, 120n24
gōdel, 278
gōʾēl, 196–200, 254

Gong, Gerrit W., 114
goring ox, 492n17
Graham, William Creighton, 21
Gundlach, Rolf, 490n10

H

Hagar, 132–41, 151–52n16, 153n23
Hammurabi, 49, 50, 151–52n16, 472, 490–91n13
Hannah, 392
ḥāsa, 240–41
healing
    and restoration of sight, 415–18
    on Sabbath, 487
    of those with disabilities, 389, 403n8
heart
    change of, 251–52
    set upon wealth, 281–82, 285, 485
Hebrew
    and context of compassion for disabled in Israel, 384–86
    importance of study of, 13, 26n52
    Sperry's study of, 10
    and Sperry's writings on Book of Mormon, 13–16
    words meaning "poor" in Isaiah, 216–17
Helaman, 372
Henning, Meghan, 408, 413–14
Herod the Great, 483
ḥesed, 76, 78, 190–91, 196, 197–98, 202, 207n33. *See also* mercy
Hezekiah, 331–33, 334, 336, 337, 340, 341–42
hillēl, 395
Hinckley, Gordon B., 149–50
Holiness Code, 80, 268, 313–16, 379n49
Holland, Jeffrey R., 140, 160, 201
Holt, Edward H., 19
Holy Land, Sperry visits, 21–22
Holzapfel, Richard, 165, 316
Hophni, 392
Horsley, Richard, 237, 249, 250, 251
Hubbard, Robert L., 196
humility, 236n28, 253, 277, 283–84, 288–89n8, 420
Huntsman, Eric D., 122n40

I

idolatry
    in ancient world, 287n1
    connection between pride and, 287–88n2
idolatry, avoiding, 265–68, 284–87
    and covenant blessings as foundation of abundance, 268–73
    and covenant requirements to care for poor, 273–78
    and danger of forgetting God's greatness, 280–82
    and greatness of God, 278–80
    and remembering God's greatness and blessing others, 282–84, 286
ignorance, blindness as metaphor for, 413–14
imperfection, 294–95
impurity, 394
inclusion, 114, 121n29, 122n40
    of refugees, 310–13, 340–41, 344–45, 361, 362, 368–70, 371–72
individual agency, 137
infertility, 133, 151–52n16, 189–90, 200
inhumane martial brutality, 435–36
Innominates club, 24n30
Iraq, 39–40
Isaac, 412
'iṣābun, 161
Isaiah
    and care for poor, 63, 477
    on eyes of blind being opened, 416–17
    "The Text of Isaiah in the Book of Mormon," 13–16
Isaiah, poor in book of, 213–14, 228–30
    context of, 214–16
    and dating of book of Isaiah, 231–32n5
    Hebrew words meaning "poor," 216–17
    passages mentioning "poor," 217–28
Ishmael, 138–39, 154n29
Israel (Jacob), 412–13

Israel and Israelites. *See also* Mosaic law
    Amos's indictment of elite, 437, 438–41
    blessed with prosperity, 289n11
    corruption in court system of, 478
    dependence on God, 272–73
    disabled in cultural and social context of, 384–87
    in eighth century BC, 475–77
    exploitation of poor by elite, 477
    gathering of, 35
    history of social justice in, 56
    learning from historical experience of, 267
    migration of, 298
    "mother in," 166
    population prior to Assyrian invasion, 494n30
    redemption of, 267, 278, 288n7
    refugees and deliverance of, 293–94, 295, 362–63, 365–68, 369–71, 373
    relationship with God, 75–76
    strained relationship between Moabites and, 186, 204–5n15
    suffering of, 319n21
    temporal covenants of kinship made by, 432
    and "us" versus "them" mentality, 300–305
    vulnerable and helpless people in, 52–54
    wealth disparities in, 232n8
Israelite judges, 164–65

J

Jacob, 412–13
Jael, 165
Japinga, Lynn, 140, 147
Jehoahaz, 451, 452
Jehoiachin, 451–52
Jehoiakim, 451, 452–57
Jehovah. *See also* Jesus Christ
    blindness inflicted by, 409–10
    as King of Zion, 246–47
    as kinsman-redeemer, 253–54
    and Old Testament law collections, 473–74
    to provide for poor, 222–28
    understanding covenant relationship with, 267
    Zion as dwelling place of, 245–46, 247
Jeremiah
    additional cries for social justice, 461–63
    calls Jehoiakim to action, 452–57
    and care for poor, 63
    condemns people for social justice violations, 449–50
    contemporaries of, 463n2
    context of, 450–52
    preaches at temple concerning social justice, 457–61
    warns of Jerusalem's destruction, 481–82
Jeroboam II, 475–76
Jerusalem
    destruction of, 481–82
    growth of, 330–31, 347n13
    refugees in archaeology of, 327–39
    rescue and renewal of, 235n28
Jerusalem temple, 483–84
Jesse, Branch of, 225
Jesus Christ. *See also* Jehovah
    condemns misuse of law and exploitation of poor, 483–86, 487–88, 489n6
    disputes with Pharisees, 469–70
    as embodiment of compassion and mercy, 67–68
    heals blind, 417–18
    inability to see, 410
    looking to coming of, 114–15
    mortal mission to morally and socially sick, 469
    remembering, 287
    social justice and, 69
    suffering of, 319n21
Jethro, 30–31
Job, 65–66
Jochebed, 30, 146–47, 168–72
Jonadab, 144
Joseph, 412–13, 440
Josiah, 451
Jubilee, 61–62, 86–87, 89–90, 98n54

Judah
    alliances between Assyria and, 336, 343–44
    and definitions of *gēr* in Pentateuch, 355–56
    in eighth century BC, 475–77
    Jeremiah's counsel to, 459–60
    population prior to Assyrian invasion, 494n30
    refugees in, 324–25, 340–41, 345
    refugees in archaeology of, 327–39
    rural population shift in, 347–48n18
Judea, 483–84
judges, Israelite, 164–65
judgment
    and Abrahamic covenant, 56–57
    for abuse of poor, 224–26, 228, 233n9
    as attribute of God, 56
    and Mosaic law, 57–58
justice. See also *mišpāṭ*; social justice
    and Abrahamic covenant, 56–57
    ancient Near Eastern conceptualizations of, 471–75
    as attribute of God, 56
    in caring for vulnerable, 55
    defined, 489n7
    and individual, 64–65
    and Israel and Judah in eighth century BC, 475–77
    Job as model of, 65–66
    and Messiah, 69
    mišpāṭ as, 215–16
    and misuse of law and condemnation of exploitation of poor in New Testament, 483–86, 487–88, 489n6
    and monarchy, 62
    and Mosaic law, 57–58
    and prophets, 62–63, 477–83
just society, ideal of, 48–50

K

Kaminsky, Joel S., 289n11
Kassis, Hanna, 432
Kearon, Patrick, 298–99, 315
Khudher, Luma, 306
Kimball, Spencer W., 281–82, 285, 286
kingdom of God, 283

kings
    in ancient Near East, 472–73
    during Jeremiah's time, 450–52
kinship. See covenants of kinship
Kirtland Temple, 34
Klawans, Jonathan, 429, 495n38
Klostermann, August, 315
Klouda, Sheri L., 239–40, 246
Koosed, Jennifer L., 194–95
Korihor, 366

L

laborers, release of enslaved, 276–77
LaCocque, André, 493n26
Lamanite royal servants, 359, 371
Lamanite soldiers and prisoners, 360, 364–65, 371
lame, David's attitude toward, 396–400. See also disabilities
land, allocation of, under Mosaic law, 191–92, 218–19
land of inheritance, 76, 90, 298, 364, 477–78
land redemption, 477–78, 493–94n28
Lane, Jennifer, 74, 253–54, 489n6
Lapsley, Jacqueline E., 147–48
Larsen, David, 105
Latter-day Saint Charities, 39–40
law. See also Mosaic law
    ancient Near Eastern conceptualizations of, 471–75
    and condemnation of exploitation of poor in New Testament, 483–86, 487–88, 489n6
    and Israel and Judah in eighth century BC, 475–77
    and prophets' condemnation of exploitation of poor, 477–83
Laws of Holiness. See Holiness Code
legal proceedings, taking advantage of poor, 219
lending laws, 84–85
levirate marriage, 80–81, 199–200, 210n58, 477–78
Leviticus 21:17–23, 389–96, 401
Lewis, C. S., 175n11
Liahona, 113

lineage
    covenantal kinship through, 430, 431–32
    and land inheritance, 477–78
Lipit-Ishtar, 50–51
Lohfink, Norbert, 59
Lot, 409–10
love, for others and of oneself, 294–95. See also neighbor, commandment to love
loyalty oaths / loyalty treaties, 336, 343–44, 349n37
Lund, Robert E., 318n6
Lunn, Arthur Constant, 9, 24n30, 24–25n31
Lyon, T. Edgar, 18

M

maat, 490n11, 493n23
Macelaru, Marcel, 297, 306
MacLean, Norman, 20
Madsen, Truman G., 22
Maeir, Aren, 348n25
maḥseh, 240–41
Maimonides, 314
Manasseh, 342, 412–13
marriage, levirate, 80–81, 199–200, 210n58, 477–78
Marriott, Neill F., 158, 159, 166
martial brutality, 435–36
McKay, David O., 19
měhalĕlehā, 395
memory, preserving, 314–17
Menahem, 337
Mendenhall, George E., 445n9
mercy. See also *ḥesed*
    and Israel and Judah in eighth century BC, 475–77
    land of inheritance and covenantal, 90
    and legal concerns for justice, 474–75
    Messiah as embodiment of, 67–68
    and misuse of law and condemnation of exploitation of poor in New Testament, 483–86, 487–88, 489n6
    and prophets' condemnation of exploitation of poor, 477–83
Messiah, as embodiment of compassion and mercy, 67–68. See also Jehovah; Jesus Christ

Meyers, Carol, 137, 179n43
Micah, 461
migration, 297–98, 335–36. See also refugees; strangers
minority, respect for, 38
miśgāb, 246–47
mišpā, 55, 215–16, 453, 455–56, 459, 461–62. See also justice
Missouri, failure to build Zion in, 254
Moab and Moabites, 186, 189, 204–5n15
mobility aids, 386–87
moral direction, blindness as metaphor for lack of, 414
Mosaic law
    commandments regarding care for poor in, 48, 52, 59–62, 183–84
    and covenants of kinship, 428
    establishment of, 31–32
    gēr in judicial law under, 365–68
    gēr in religious law under, 368–73
    gēr in social law under, 360–65
    justice and judgment and, 57–58
    land allocation under, 191–92, 218–19
    mišpāṭ as foundation of, 453
    and redemption of Israel, 267
    sources of, for Book of Mormon people, 354–55
    treatment of refugees under, 302, 373–74
Moses
    and building Zion, 30–34
    deliverance of, 146–48, 149, 168–72
    knowledge of Israelite heritage, 181n67
    and Song of the Sea, 245
Mosul, liberated from ISIS forces, 37
motherhood and mothering, 157, 172–73
    changing understandings of, 167
    Deborah as example of, 164–67, 177n30
    defined, 158
    Eve as example of, 159–63
    Pharaoh's daughter and Jochebed as examples of, 168–72
"mother in Israel," 166

N

Naʿaman, Nadav, 334–35, 336, 337, 349n28
Naomi
    Boaz's relation to, 196–99
    emphasis on bearing sons, 189
    poverty of, 194–95
    pronounces blessing on daughters-in-law, 190–91
    as refugee, 183
    returns to Bethlehem, 191–92
    Ruth's relationship with, 188, 193–94, 206n25, 307–8, 314–15, 475
    shows *ḥesed* in interactions with others, 202
    social context of, 184–85
Nauvoo Relief Society, organization of, 34–35
Nebuchadnezzar, 451–52
Necho, 451
neighbor, commandment to love, 73–74, 91–92. *See also* poor and oppressed, obligation to help
    and care for vulnerable demographics, 78–87, 201
    and covenants and relationship formation, 74–76
    discipleship and, 286
    and divine covenants of kinship, 432–33
    and failure to keep covenant, 88–90
    as focus of Abrahamic covenant, 76–77
    principles underlying, 90–91
    refugees and, 306–13, 315
    and seeing divine potential in ourselves and others, 294–95
Nelson, Russell M.
    on abandoning prejudice, 136, 153n22
    on Abrahamic covenant, 73
    on caring about others, 345
    on cooperation, 148
    on Fall, 163
    on gathering of Israel, 35
    on loving neighbor, 286
    on remembering our redemption and Redeemer, 287
Nephites, 33–34. *See also* Anti-Nephi-Lehies

New Testament
    blindness in, 417–18
    condemnation of misuse of law and exploitation of poor in, 483–86, 487–88, 489n6
nokriyah, 192–93
nursemaids, 170–71

O

Oaks, Dallin H., 132, 345
Old Testament, law collections of, 473–74. *See also* motherhood and mothering; women of Old Testament, studying
Olson, Camille Fronk, 151n4
Olyan, Saul, 390, 391, 394, 403n8
oppression, resistance to, 146–48
orphans
    care for, 48, 52, 53–54, 88, 184, 455, 459–60
    and commandment to love neighbor, 78–79
    and festival offerings, 83–84
    as focus of legal concerns for justice, 474
    justice and righteousness in caring for, 55–58
Ostriker, Alicia, 202
Oswalt, John N., 343
others, seeing. *See* seeing others
ox, goring, 492n17

P

Parry, Donald W., 416
Passover, 83–84, 341–42
Paul, Shalom, 438
Pedersen, Johannes, 430
Pentateuch
    definitions of *gēr* in, 355–57
    gēr in judicial law in, 365–66
    gēr in religious law in, 368–69, 371
    gēr in social law in, 360–62
Peshitto, 20–21
Pett, Peter, 153n23
Pharaoh
    resistance to, 146–48
    Sarah taken as wife of, 134, 152n17

Pharaoh's daughter, 30, 147, 168–72, 180n55
Pharisees, 469–70, 485
Philistines
    Israelites' relationship with, 432
    judgment oracle against, 223
Phinehas, 392
Pike, Dana, 165, 316
Plato, 313–14
poor and oppressed, obligation to help, 47–48. *See also* covenants of kinship; Isaiah, poor in book of; neighbor, commandment to love
    in ancient Israel, 52–54
    and commandment to love neighbor, 78–87
    covenant requirements concerning, 273–78
    and cry of oppressed in ancient Near East and Bible, 50–51
    and establishment of Zion, 248–49, 250, 251–52
    and failure to keep covenant, 88–90
    and greatness of God, 278–80
    and ideal of just society, 48–50
    and individual, 64–65
    Job as model of justice and righteousness, 65–66
    and justice and righteousness in caring for vulnerable, 55
    in law of Moses, 59–62
    and legal concerns for justice, 474
    and Messiah, 67–69
    and misuse of law and condemnation of exploitation of poor in New Testament, 483–86, 487–88, 489n6
    in modern day, 201, 229
    and monarchy, 62
    Nephi's instruction on Zion and, 258–59
    and prophets, 62–63, 477–83
    and remembering God's greatness and blessing others, 284–87
    and remembering redemption and avoiding idolatry, 265–68
    Ruth and, 183–84, 194–96, 200–201
pork, injunction against, 409
pregnancy, 161
prejudice, 136, 153n22
pride, 270, 280, 287–88n2, 288–89n8
priesthood keys, and building Zion, 34–36
priestly service, disabilities and restrictions concerning, 389–96, 401, 404n17, 413
privilege, recognizing and dealing with, 140
"profaning of sanctuaries," 394–95
promised land, 76, 90, 298
prophetess, 164. *See also* Deborah
prosperity. *See also* wealth
    and forgetting God's greatness, 280, 281–82
    Israel blessed with, 289n11
protection, Zion as place of, 237, 240–44, 246–48, 259–60
Provo East Stake, 40
Psalms, Zion in, 245–48
Puah, 146

Q

$^*qittil$ noun patter, 385–86

R

rape, of Tamar, 141–46, 155n43, 155n45
Rebecca, 412
redeemer
    Boaz as, 197–200
    debt relief through, 85
    Jehovah as, 253–54
redemption, remembering, 265–68, 284–87
    and covenant basis for redemption, 289n9
    and covenant blessings as foundation of abundance, 268–73
    and covenant requirements to care for poor, 273–78
    and danger of forgetting God's greatness, 280–82
    and greatness of God, 278–80
    Israel and, 288n7
    and remembering God's greatness and blessing others, 282–84, 286

refuge, Zion as place of, 237, 240–44, 246–48, 259–60
refugees. See also *gēr / gērîm*; strangers
  in archaeology of Judah and Jerusalem, 327–39, 344
  Bible archaeology and plight of, 339–44
  care for, 310–13, 455, 459–60
  characteristics of, in Deuteronomy, 296–97
  and commandment to love others, 306–13, 315
  defined, 296, 376n14
  empathy for, 293–94, 304
  and imitating God, 313–16
  inclusion of, 310–13, 340–41, 344–45, 361, 362, 368–70, 371–72
  integration of, 320n34
  in Judah, 324–25, 340–41, 345
  marginalization of Israelite, 340
  in modern day, 200–201, 298–300, 304–5, 309–13, 323–24
  in Old Testament, 325–26, 344
  remembrance through stories of, 316–17
  Ruth as, 183, 196, 200–201, 307–8
  study of Israelite, 344
  treatment of, 308–9
  types of movement of, 335–36
  and "us" versus "them" mentality, 294–95, 300–305
relationship, covenant making as forming new, 74–76
Relief Society, organization of, 34–35
remembrance, 314–17
Rendsburg, Gary A., 338
repentance, 32–33
residue
  defined, 103
  first attempt to make Enoch see, 106–10
  God weeps over, 107–8, 120n24
  second attempt to make Enoch see, 110
Restoration, 111–12, 121n29
Resurrection, looking to, 114–15
rich fool, parable of, 485

rich young man, parable of, 485
righteousness. See also *ṣedeq / ṣĕdāqa*
  as attribute of God, 56, 453–54
  in caring for vulnerable, 55
  Jeremiah's sermon calling for, 457–61
  Job as model of, 65–66
  and legal concerns for justice, 474
  and Mosaic law, 57–58
Ringe, Sharon, 253
Römer, Thomas, 239
Romney, Marion G., 442
Ruth
  Boaz's relation to, 196–99
  ethnicity of, 187
  gleans in Boaz's fields, 82, 195–96
  identity and religious and ethnic affiliations of, 192–93
  Naomi pronounces blessing on, 190–91
  Naomi's relationship with, 188, 193–94, 206n25, 307–8, 314–15, 475
  poverty of, 194–95
  as refugee, 183, 307–8
  shows *ḥesed* in interactions with others, 202, 475
  social context of, 184–85
Ruth, book of, 183–88
  author of, 187–88
  context of, 185, 186–87
  dating, 185–86, 204n11
  lessons learned from, 200–202
  as told from women's perspective, 188–89

S

Sabbath day, 275, 395, 396, 405n28, 487, 488n3, 489n4
Sabbatical year, 61, 85–86, 248–49, 269, 274–76
sacrifice, 83–84, 275–76, 277, 479, 495n38
sacrificial food, 391–93, 394, 413, 469–70, 482, 495n38, 497n46
Sakenfeld, Katharine Doob, 128–29, 139
ṣāna, 239
"sanctuaries, profaning of," 394–95
Sarah, 132–41, 151–52n16, 152n17, 153n23

Satan, 32, 107
Schniedewind, William M., 337, 338, 340, 342
"Scholia of Bar Hebraeus to the Book of Kings, The" (Sperry), 20–21
2 Nephi, Zion commandments in, 255–59, 260
2 Samuel 5:8, 396–400
ṣedeq / ṣĕdāqa, 55, 453–54, 455–56, 462. *See also* righteousness
seeing others, 101–2
    Enoch as example of, 111–15
    and Enoch's narrowing audience, 104–6
    first attempt to make Enoch see residue, 106–10
    and God's rebuke of Enoch, 102–4
    second attempt to make Enoch see residue, 110
Seely, David, 165, 316
selfishness, 443
sexual assault, 141–46, 155n43, 155n45
Shebna, 337
Sheleff, Leon, 319n21
Shema, 269–70
Shephelah, 331, 347–48n18
shepherds, hired, in Old Testament world, 439
Shiphrah, 146
silence, of abuse victims, 144–45, 146
Siloam Tunnel, 332–34, 338, 340, 342–43
Silver, Morris, 474
sin, blindness linked to, 411–12
šipḥa, 193, 209n54
Sisera, 165
ṣiyyon, 239–40, 261n9. *See also* Zion
Skousen, W. Cleon, 318n6
slaves and slavery, 276–77, 297, 363, 436–37, 454
Smith, Joseph, 34–36, 38, 419
Smith, Joseph Fielding, 13, 26n52
social justice, 449–50. *See also* poor and oppressed, obligation to help
    and individual, 64–65
    Jeremiah calls Jehoiakim to action concerning, 452–57
    Jeremiah's cries for, 461–63
    Jeremiah's sermon calling for, 457–61
    and kings of Jeremiah's time, 450–52
    and Messiah, 69
    and monarchy, 62
    and prophets, 62–63
Sodom and Gomorrah, 56–57
Song of the Sea, 245
sons of Adam, 103, 117n9
Sperry, Eva Braithwaite, 7–9, 10, 11
Sperry, Harrison Sr., 17, 27n69
Sperry, Sidney B.
    attends University of Chicago Divinity School, 5–12, 16–18
    doctoral dissertation of, 20–21
    enters seminary system, 3–4
    graduate work of, 4–13, 16
    on Hebrew culture, 412
    missionary service of, 3
    patriarchal blessing of, 1–2
    PhD coursework of, 16–18
    "The Scholia of Bar Hebraeus to the Book of Kings," 20–21
    teaches at BYU, 18–19
    "The Text of Isaiah in the Book of Mormon," 13–16
    visits Holy Land, 21–22
spirit, contrite, 236n28
Sprengling, Martin, 7, 12–13, 21
stereotypes, 101–2
strangers. *See also* gēr / gērim; refugees
    care for, 53, 54, 184, 341
    and commandment to love neighbor, 78–79, 306–8, 315
    and divine covenants of kinship, 432–33
    empathy for, 293–94
    and festival offerings, 83–84
    and Jubilee, 98n54
    justice and righteousness in caring for, 55–58
    love for, 294–95
    and migration in Bible, 297–98
    modern-day application of decree on caring for, 295–96
    Ruth as, 183, 192–93, 196, 200–201, 307–8
stripling warriors, 359, 367, 376–77n16

suffering
    of Christ and Israel, 319n21
    and cycle of abuse, 134
surrogacy, 151–52n16
Syrian refugees, 40–42

T

Talmage, Albert M, 421
Talmage, James E., 5
Talmage, Sara, 421
Tamar, 141–46, 155n43, 155n45
Tamar Campaign, 145
Tanner, N. Eldon, 443
Taylor, Daniel, 295, 318n5
Taylor, John, 62
temple
    as central economic force of Judea, 483–84
    and cosmic order, 490n10
    Jeremiah on protection of, 481–82
    Jeremiah's sermon at, 457–61
temple covenants, and building Zion, 35
temporal covenants of kinship, 430, 432
    breaking, 435–37
Ten Commandments, 259, 265, 460
"Text of Isaiah in the Book of Mormon, The" (Sperry), 13–16
Their Story Is Our Story (TSOS), 299–300, 309, 317
Theocharous, Myrto, 296, 297
third-year tithe, 60–61, 82–83, 91, 368
Tigay, Jeffrey H., 288–89n8, 289n11, 409
Tiglath-pileser III, 325, 336, 343, 346n5
time, cyclical nature of, 471
tithe, third-year, 60–61, 82–83, 91, 368
toil, 160–61
transgressions, and breaking covenants of kinship, 434–35
tree of knowledge of good and evil, 159–60
trials
    purpose of, 419–20
    recognizing God's help in, 139–40
Trible, Phyllis, 130, 132, 135–36, 142, 155n43
trust
    in God, 223, 276, 277, 285, 344
    in material things, 281–82, 285
    in Zion, 223, 230, 240–41
Tyre, condemned by Amos, 427, 436–37

U

Uchtdorf, Dieter F., 323
uncleanness, 394
unity
    in building Zion, 37–38
    through inclusion, 114, 121n29, 122n40
University of Chicago Divinity School, 5–12, 16–18
University of Idaho, 19
Urijah, 461
Ur-Namma / Ur-Nammu, 49, 50, 491n15
Urukagina, 49
"us" versus "them" mentality, 294–95, 300–305
Utah Valley Refugees, 312
Uzziah, 475–76

V

vassal treaties, 336, 343–44, 349n37
Vassal Treaty of Esarhaddon, 349n37
victimization of women, 134–37
virtuous woman, 179n43

W

Wakely, Robin, 283
wartime ethics, 435–36
Waters, Jaime L., 253
Watson, Lynn, 37
Watson, Sandy, 37
wealth
    covenant perspective on, 285–86
    and forgetting God's greatness, 280
    heart set upon, 281–82, 285, 485
    humility and, 288–89n8
    Israel blessed with, 289n11
    of Latter-day Saints, 443
    proper use of, 285
    and remembering redemption and avoiding idolatry, 271–72
    used to build kingdom of God, 283
Weems, Renita, 141

West, Gerald, 145
wetnurses, 170–71
wickedness, blindness linked to, 410–12
widows. *See also* Naomi; Ruth
    care for, 48, 52, 53, 88, 184, 455, 459–60
    and commandment to love neighbor, 78–79
    and festival offerings, 83–84
    as focus of legal concerns for justice, 474
    and gleaning, 82
    justice and righteousness in caring for, 55–58
    and levirate marriage, 80–81, 199–200, 210n58, 477–78
Wilcox, Ella Wheeler, 419
Wildberger, Hans, 241, 245, 246
Williams, Delores, 139
Wilson, Guy C., 19
woman, virtuous, 179n43
women of Old Testament, studying, 127–28, 150. *See also* motherhood and mothering
    and feminist hermeneutic, 128–32, 150–51n4
    Sarah and Hagar, 132–41, 151–52n16, 152n17, 153n23
    Tamar, 141–46, 155n43, 155n45
    women of Exodus, 146–50
work, 36–37, 160–61
Wright, Christopher, 297, 306
Wünch, Hans-Georg, 300–301

Y

Yahweh. *See* Jehovah
yātom, 53–54

Z

Zechariah, 65
Zedekiah, 452
Zion
    "caught up into," 242
    city of Enoch as, 103, 237, 242, 243–44, 247, 249–50
    commandments regarding, in 2 Nephi, 255–59, 260
    definitions of, 237–38
    in Deuteronomy, 248–54
    etymology versus paronomastic meanings of, 239–44, 259, 261n9
    Jehovah as King of, 246–47
    as Jehovah's dwelling place, 245–46, 247
    as place of protection, 237, 240–44, 246–48, 259–60
    poor trusting in, 223–24, 230
    in Psalms, 245–48
    rescue and renewal of, 235n28
    trust in, 223, 230, 240–41
Zion, building, 29, 43–44
    everyday actions for, 36–38
    examples of those living principles for, 39–43
    failure in, 254–55
    latter-day, 244
    Moses and, 30–34
    Nephi's instruction on, 255–59, 260
    and priesthood keys given to Joseph Smith, 34–36
    and protection of poor, 248–49
Zondi-Mabizela, Phumzile, 145
Zoramites, 358–59, 363–64, 371